THE HETERODOX HEGEL

Suny Series in Hegelian Studies

William Desmond, Editor

THE HETERODOX HEGEL

Cyril O'Regan

With a Foreword by Louis Dupré

STATE UNIVERSITY OF NEW YORK PRESS

Published by
State University of New York Press, Albany

Printed in the United States of America

For information, address State University of New York Press,
State University Plaza, Albany, N.Y., 12246

Production by Marilyn P. Semerad
Marketing by Dana E. Yanulavich

Library of Congress Cataloging-in-Publication Data

O'Regan, Cyril, date.
The Heterodox Hegel / Cyril O'Regan ; with a foreword by Louis Dupré.
p. cm.—(SUNY series in Hegelian studies)
Includes bibliographical references and index.
ISBN 0-7914-2005-1 (hc : alk. paper).—ISBN 0-7914-2006-X (pb : alk. paper)
1. Hegel, Georg Wilhelm Friedrich, 1770–1831—Religion.
2. Lutheran Church—Influence. 3. Mysticism—History—19th century.
I. Title. II. Series.
B2949.R3073 1994
193—dc20 93-36365
CIP

10 9 8 7 6 5 4 3 2 1

This book is dedicated to the memory
of my mother and father

Phyllis O'Regan (1927–1985)
Thomas O'Regan (1922–1984)

CONTENTS

Foreword by Louis Dupré ix

Acknowledgments xiii

List of Abbreviations xv

Introduction 1

Part 1. Ontotheological Foundations **27**

Chapter 1. Hegelian Rendition of the *Deus Revelatus* of Christianity 29

Section 1.1 Against Negative Theology 31
Section 1.2 Narrative and the *Deus Revelatus* 44
Section 1.3 Trinity as Adequate Theological Articulation 63

Part 2. The Trinitarian Structuration of the Epochal Divine **81**

Chapter 2. The First Narrative Epoch: The "Immanent Trinity" 85

Section 2.1 Hegelian Logic as *Logica Divina* 86
Section 2.2 The "Immanent Trinity" as Speculatively Informed *Vorstellung: LPR* and Other Hegelian Texts 107
Section 2.3 Trinitarian Swerve: Dynamic, Narrative Modalism 126

Chapter 3. The Second Narrative Epoch: Creation and The Epoch of the Son 141

Section 3.1 Hegelian Legitimation of the Representation of Creation 144

Section 3.2 Creation as Fall and Evil 151
Section 3.3 Hegelian Swerve from the Normative Christian Tradition 169

Chapter 4. Epochal Overlap: Incarnation and the Passion Narrative 189

Section 4.1 Hegel's Mature Christological Position: Trinitarian Contextualization of *Theologia Crucis* 190
Section 4.2 *Deus Patibilis:* Hegel and Luther: Agreement and Swerve 209

Chapter 5. The Third Narrative Epoch: The Moment or Kingdom of the Spirit 235

Section 5.1 Spiritual Community (*Gemeinde): Corpus Mysticum* 238
Section 5.2 Complex Mystical Determination: Complex Mystical Inflection 249

Chapter 6. The Third Narrative Epoch: The Inclusive Trinity 287

Section 6.1 Holy Spirit—Spirit: Spirit—"Immanent Trinity" 288
Section 6.2 The Genre of Hegelian Apocalypse 298
Section 6.3 The Genre of Hegelian Theodicy 310

Part 3. Narrative and Logico-Conceptual Articulation 327

Chapter 7. Representation and Concept: Speculative Rewriting 331

Section 7.1 Representation and Concept in Hegel's Mature Works 333
Section 7.2 Agents of Speculative Rewriting 339
Section 7.3 Hegel and the Perdurance of Narrative 363

Notes 371

Bibliography 465

Indexes 489

Foreword

The history of Hegel's succession has been as dialectical as his own philosophy. Almost immediately after the master's death, his disciples divided into two sharply opposed camps and what Marx ironically referred to as the battle of the Diadochi began. The right wing having been charged with publishing Hegel's writings considered itself the legitimate heir. The leftist rebels, though irreverent of the letter, revitalized the dynamic movement of Hegel's dialectic, using its principles to stir up a revolt against the entire social and religious system in which Hegel's philosophy had been born. Yet, when they ended up rewriting the dialectic in the language of philosophical and historical materialism, it became manifest that they could no longer lay claim to the prophet's mantle. With the camps thus emptied of the original combatants, the battles did not cease. As other generations emerged, new "wings" developed. A new right codified Hegel's religious thought for theology courses, created textbooks of his logic, and enshrined his political philosophy in conservative doctrines. A new leftism originated after the war with the French existentialists and the "negative dialectic" of the Frankfurt School. Even now that Hegel studies are moving toward a nonpartisan, historical and textual analysis, the old divisions have not subsided altogether! Philosophy of religion in particular remains hotly disputed territory—especially in these United States. Studies tend to result in all-or-nothing conclusions. Either Hegel was an orthodox, though occasionally somewhat original, Christian—or he was thoroughly secular.

Precisely at this point Cyril O'Regan's work differs—not so much by not belonging to either of the warring factions as by changing the perspective. Concern with Christian dogma stands at the heart of Hegel's thinking, he argues, and the fact that he considered the Trinity the central mystery of the Christian revelation shows his theological seriousness. But that theological concern in no way restricts Hegel to the main tradition. The present study uncovers a number of hidden, unquestionably religious, but highly unorthodox sources at the root of Hegelian speculation. Boehme and some Gnostic writings feature prominently. His repeated profession of allegiance to the Lutheran faith ought not to be taken as a brief of trinitarian orthodoxy. Professor O'Regan draws attention to Hegel's unconventional understanding of the dogma of the Trinity as articulating at once God's intimate, self-enclosed life *and* the essential incompleteness of that divine life if detached from its expression in creation and redemption. The Trinity does not remain enclosed within itself. Its divine mystery is also, and foremost, inclusive of all worldly reality. Indeed, already God's inner life possesses a 'narrative' quality, insofar as it constitutes the 'prolepsis' to the story of creation and redemption.

Some may regard Hegel's innovating conceptions forays into theosophical territory, straying too far from the base of orthodoxy still to qualify for the name of Christian thinking. They may detect a transfer of the Christian mystery to dubious Neoplatonic (specifically, Proclean) grounds. Others, however, are likely to recognize the presence of an older, mystical tradition that, though never exactly coinciding with the terms of the established doctrine, was allowed to develop alongside it. Remaining in intimate sympathy with a theological orthodoxy that continued to feed it, it again and again ended up renewing and revitalizing the meaning of orthodox doctrine. Is such a religious, though unorthodox, reading yet another expression of the old 'right'? I believe not, because the conception here presented allows so much room even for the secular religiosity of our time that the categories of the earlier division no longer apply. Hegel's theory, as interpreted by Cyril O'Regan, presents us with something new—unquestionably religious, even faithful to the basis of the Christian tradition, but so thoroughly transforming its interpretation that it may well point the way toward a different, as yet unexplored, understanding of religion. This study paradoxically shows Hegel as a revolutionary (the leftist battle cry!) *precisely* in being a Christian religious thinker. The conservative reading of Hegel as the theologian of Lutheran orthodoxy has been decisively abandoned, yet the new interpretation, however comprehensive of the secular, stands at the opposite end of the 'secularist' spectrum of the left.

Any innovative vision of the classical system demands a recapturing of the innocence of that original readership to which the text still appeared in its own light, uncluttered by libraries of subsequent commentary. But innocence itself turns into naïveté if one treats an old script as if it were a new writing. This produces the kind of original reading well known to correctors of undergraduate papers. Each decade produces a harvest of such fresh readings. If hermeneutics has taught us one thing, it is that commentary opens different perspectives we cannot afford to ignore. This book, with its Protean comprehensiveness and its staggering erudition, is not original by ignoring the past. Cyril O'Regan has assimilated all that preceded—not only the wise and the well-expressed, but also the merely well-intentioned. He has allowed each voice to be heard and generously to be judged. Still, a self-contained vision that accommodates everything without yielding to anything enables his study to carry this eruditional burden without collapsing under the weight of its knowledge. Only poets are wont to be, at once, so comprehensive and so single-minded. In fact, what in the end stands out in this study may well be its poetic quality—an intellectual vision totally incarnated in language. Poetic here means more than well-written. Indeed, some readers may object to the author's involuted expression and often disconcertingly original wording. But his work displays that rarer quality in the learned writer: the ability to think in and through language. Language here functions as the vehicle that carries thought forward, rather than merely expressing it. Readers of philosophical texts seldom enjoy the presence of a fully worded conception. Cyril O'Regan has granted it in his book.

LOUIS DUPRÉ

Acknowledgments

To teachers such as Louis Dupré, the late Hans Frei, and John Smith I am conscious of owing much. I strongly suspect that this "much" is a mere fraction of what is really owed. Yale's benevolence has continued in the shape of my now colleagues, George Lindbeck, Gene Outka, and Kathyrn Tanner, all of whom, at important stages of the composition of this work were gentle in their criticism and generous in their praise. I owe a particular debt of gratitude to George Seidel of St. Martin's Abbey, Lacey, Washington. He served as my ideal reader in the writing, and he encouraged Celtic wildness rather than caution. Rebecca Gilbert, John Jones, and Mieke Holkeboer played the role of three graces in reading the manuscript in order to somehow translate it into American. Apart from standardizing my schizophrenic spelling—neither American nor Irish at this stage—they offered helpful stylistic comments, served as grammatical juries, and sometimes quietly prodded me to rein in a rhetoric that was in danger of being overblown. I add a note of gratitude to the editor of the SUNY Hegel Series, William Desmond. His enthusiasm for this work helped in no small way to bring this work to completion. Yet again, I would like to foreground Louis Dupré. I am delighted that he could honor my request to write the Foreword. It is more elegant than anything that follows. This book is not Ger's, my partner's, tale. She has more important tales of her own. Since she is even more conscious than John Fowles that the story is not in the world but the world in the story, I cannot but be mindful of the distance to be travelled to that somewhere in the subjunctive past and the impossible future.

Abbreviations

Hegel:

DE	*Difference Essay*
Enc	*Encyclopedia of Philosophical Sciences*
ETW	*Early Theological Writings*
FK	*Faith and Knowledge*
GL	Glockner (specifically Glockner's *Jubiliäumsäusgabe* edition of Hegel's work)
LHP	*Lectures on the History of Philosophy*
LHP1	*Lectures on the History of Philosophy,* vol. 1
LHP3	*Lectures on the History of Philosophy,* vol. 3
LPH	*Lectures on the Philosophy of History*
LPR	*Lectures on the Philosophy of Religion*
LPR1	*Lectures on the Philosophy of Religion,* vol. 1
LPR3	*Lectures on the Philosophy of Religion,* vol. 3
PR	*Philosophy of Right*
PS	*Phenomenology of Spirit*
SL	*Science of Logic*

Others:

Anw	*Die Anweisung zum seeligen Leben* - Fichte
DW	*Deutsche Werke* - Meister Eckhart
EG	*De Electione Gratiae* - Jacob Boehme
MM	*Mysterium Magnum* - Jacob Boehme
SR	*De Signatura Rerum* - Jacob Boehme
S.TH	*Summa Theologica* - Aquinas
TP	*Theosophic Points* - Jacob Boehme
TT	*Tripartite Tractate* - Nag Hammadi Library
WA	*Ausgewahlte Werke* - Luther

Note: E is abbreviation for English translation
E is usually followed by page number of a standard English translation of a Hegel text
G is abbreviation for German text
G is usually followed by a page number of a standard German edition of a Hegel text.

Introduction

If anything has the status of a given in the scene of interpretation, at present, it is interpretation's own avowal of its lost innocence. From the paradise of transparent naming, interpreters have awoken to find themselves in a fallen state that presents itself as structural, that appears under the sign of 'always'. Nostalgia may still continue to maintain a kind of awkward, tentative presence, but suspicion and culpability bear their adult insignia so well that the precritical, premodern mode of interpretation can only be viewed as the age of childhood or the age of myth. The truth that could only be gained in a struggle with an innocence that was presumed rather than real is that no object, conceptual or otherwise, is out there. All objects as such are constructed or invented. This view, for which its supporters are anxious to claim Hegelian pedigree, has its apotheosis in a new myth, the myth of the strong invention. Jorge Luis Borges's allusive story, "The Circular Ruins,"[1] in which a mendicant solitary finally succeeds in dreaming a creature into existence, is an *Urtext* of the power of imagination, the hegemony of invention, which, however, is always exposed to failure, to lesser orders of realization, and, at a limit, abortion. Strong invention is the regulative ideal, not the always successfully completed fact. The self-disintegrating artifact is a possibility,[2] as is the hybrid creature,[3] which is a thing put together, bonded externally without any unifying economy. The Borges text defines the scene of hermeneutic option: the either/or of strong and weak invention, where the strong delivers an internally coherent entity, and where the weak issues a purely partial realization or no realization at all. For those who see all human and cultural activity in this way, subjectivity is exalted. Yet subjectivity is not reduced to arbitrariness: it is regulated by its success or failure in achieving wholeness and coherence in the artifact.

The above hermeneutic view is tantalizing. Yet, while the epistemological critique of naïve realism, in interpretation as elsewhere, should be accepted as a gain, the larger claims of the criticizers of the previous hermeneutic regime cannot be similarly sustained. Sometimes lurking beneath the skepticism for the given is a florid romanticism of originality, beneath diagnosis, a prescription, an incitement to dismantle the barrier between production or *poiesis* and the decidedly secondary scene of interpretation. However, even within this skeptical manifold, not all criteria of critical judgment are thrown out. While correspondence is rejected, coherence clearly is not. Another, relative value of the skeptical view, now almost an ethos, is that it prepares one for the real world of interpretation whose embattled landscape gives lie to any actual consensus. Perspectival variation, massive volatility appear to characterize assertions concerning all but the least important conceptual objects. One not unimportant such object is the thought of George Wilhelm Friedrich Hegel. Wilhelm Raimund Beyer's *Hegel-Bilder* by no means intentionally supports the ethos of hermeneutic skepticism.[4] Nevertheless, his parade of pictures of Hegel, from revolutionary Hegel to fascist Hegel, from a catholic Hegel to an Protestant evangelical Hegel, has the effect, not only of honestly admitting the lack of actual consensus, but of bringing into question its very possibility. Of course, Beyer deliberately selects the least complex and most assertoric of these pictures in order to highlight the variety of interpretation. In doing so, however, he, in effect, deconstructs them, for most, if not all, of the competing interpretations appear to be based upon a tendentious logic of exclusion, rather than on a more Hegelian logic responsive to nuance, tension, and web of relation. Whatever else one can expect of the conceptual object that is Hegelian thought, it is not likely to be available to simple, one-sided description.

Beyond the humility of skepticism and the arrogance of self-assured reading lies a modality of interpretation which attempts, and has attempted, to *approximate* to the internal complexity of Hegelian thought. Mindful with Hans George Gadamer that 'absolute truth' is merely a construct within Hegelianism and neither a reality for the interpreter nor the reality of the interpretive act,[5] such an interpretation is prepared to posit truth without assuming, thereby, that the final word has been said. The act of interpretation on this view is an attempt to correspond to an object that sets definite constraints on invention and promotes critical approximation. If final definition is not given, if adequation is never fully realized, this says more about the inexhaustibility of the object than the subjectivity of interpretation. It would betray a lack of fidelity to truly genuine achievement not to point out that, in addition to those who generate the noise of agon, there has been a core of interpreters, both responsive and responsible, who have realized partial consensus and constructed a complex, if not fully complete, picture. It is within this ambit that the present interpretation circles, or circulates, hoping to add detail, at least give the picture a sharper outline. The only thing that cannot be promised is that the picture consists of a few clear, bold lines.

Within this ambit there is no warrant not to take seriously the questions of the theological predilection of Hegel's thought and the intimacy of theology and philosophy. Where the intimacy between theology and philosophy is such as to point to an intrinsic unity, modern philosophers and philosophically minded theologians have not been shy in speaking of 'ontotheology'. While the term is ugly, it can be justified on the pragmatic grounds that it is current in the modern critical assessment of Hegel.[6] Though not all commentators and critics would agree with respect to the connotation and extension of the term,[7] broadly speaking, the assertion of the ontotheological nature of Hegelianism responds to three explicit and oft-repeated avowals on the very surface of Hegel's texts: (1) the content-identity of religion and philosophy; (2) the specification that the content religion and philosophy share is 'truth' or 'God'; and (3) the further specification that the normative representation of God is provided by Christianity,[8] in which God is not pure being, or goodness, but spirit as movement, life, and reconciliation. It is not only right-wing and middle ground readings of Hegel that are prepared to argue for a theological or ontotheological typification. Left-wing reading also implies it. The Feuerbachian agenda of a 'transformational criticism' is premised upon a theological reading of Hegel, who is seen as the apogee of the Christian theological tradition.[9] Kojève in his rescue of the humanist and atheistic Hegel confesses, if somewhat reluctantly, the theological essence of the thought of the historical Hegel.[10] Adorno's negative dialectic is parasitic upon a positive dialectic of a theological type that is the foundation of what he regards as utopian and tyrannical in Hegelian thought.[11] And deconstruction, even if it displays some attempt at claiming Hegel,[12] itself gives testimony that Hegel represents the critical threshold of the ontotheological tradition that fatefully allies meaning, truth, and God.

Granted this confirmation by the left-wing hermeneutic of Hegelianism's ontotheological accent, it would be dishonest to suggest absolute consensus. Richard Solomon and Alan White provide two of the more noticeable recent instances of demurring.[13] Solomon's *In the Spirit of Hegel* provides a particularly truculent example of an antitheological reading of Hegel. Hegel is not rendered, à la left-wing revisionism, as a humanist not quite able to free himself from the theological horizon of western metaphysics and Christianity but rather is accused of "subterfuge" (p. 582), his philosophy nothing more than a pretense of Christian apologetics (p. 614). Similarly, White, aware that he is rowing a boat not only against the current of the general critical recognition but also Hegel's own explicit avowal, thinks himself justified in denying any transcendent-theological center in Hegel.[14] Hegel is best interpreted as involved in the extension and correction of Immanuel Kant's *transcendental* enterprise. Both Solomon and White concur in presuming that the theological or ontotheological element is mere surface not to be taken seriously. One may reply to this that, while it is hermeneutically reputable to suggest that there is a split between surface and depth, specifically, that there exists a depth grammar at odds with the surface-theological grammar, those who promote such a position have the responsibility of explaining the how and why of the theological surface. This responsibility is taken extremely lightly, the theological surface not so much explained as shunted aside, or, to use Roland Barthes's felicitous locution, "exdenominated."[15] In Barthes, "exdenomination" connotes the refusal of admittance into discourse of a relevant phenomenon. The process, Barthes claims, is most often unconscious, and commonly nonindividual. Here, however, in the case of Hegel interpretation, exdenomination is neither unconscious nor nonindividual, but consciously rhetorical and eccentric.

Though the present work will argue for the theological reading of Hegel and marshal evidence in its support, such argument and presentation of evidence will be quite limited. The work speaks *from* the consensus it diagnoses as uniting left-wing, right-wing, and middle ground interpretation. Speaking from this consensus, it promotes the view that the really imperative task is to attempt a more precise identification of the theological species or variety (speculative) of Christianity appealed to by Hegel. Only on this basis will it move to a more formal discussion of the relation between theology and philosophy. In essential respects this task is not new and is represented in earlier nineteenth-century reflection on Hegel (Franz von Baader, Ferdinand Christian Baur, Franz Anton Staudenmaier),[16] as it is in the twentieth century by such Hegel scholars as Albert Chapelle, Emil Fackenheim, and Iwan Iljin.[17] The version of the task undertaken here is one of the most complex to date, and I should, at the outset, own up to what likely will be a display of inordinate ambition. It is possible, even probable, that the enterprise may finally look more Icarus-like than Promethean. My only excuse, other than tempermental constitution, is that Hegel excites risk, if not recklessness, and at least the rewards are high. Clarification of Hegel's position has, I believe, important lessons for those who attempt to forge an alliance between theology and philosophy, between any determinate religious system and conceptual thought.

The present text distinguishes itself from previous similar attempts in three ways. (1) It proposes (and answers) an integrated series of questions, nothing short of which is sufficient to clarify the religious or theological species Hegel thinks can be brought into rapprochement with philosophy, indeed, which Hegel thinks admits of full assimilation by philosophy.[18] (2) It unites a number of different approaches to Hegel that have proved fruitful, if incomplete: (a) the approach via the theologoumenon of the Trinity, an approach opened up in the 1920s by Johannes Hessen but brought to completion in the more recent studies of Jörg Splett, Piero Coda, and Dale M. Schlitt,[19] and (b) the narrative or epochal approach presented by Iwan Iljin in his *Die Philosophie Hegels as kontemplative Gotteslehre* (1946).[20] and (3) It attempts within the bounds of a *systematic* approach to address questions of a religio-theological type that have exercised Hegelian commentators and critics—questions that have as yet not found definitive answer or truly been seen in relation to each other. Four questions strike me as being especially worthy of address: (1) Hegel's relationship to the theology of Luther; (2) Hegel's relationship to the speculative mysticism of Jacob Boehme; (3) Hegel's relationship to the mystical tradition in general; and (4) Hegel's relationship to Gnosticism.

Conceived, then, as the integral of aims 1, 2, and 3, the present enterprise may be seen to be more flattered by the giantesque than driven by the conceptual need for coherence. But the view taken here is that it is precisely the demand for coherence that dictates the comprehensiveness of the present work. For coherence is ultimately conferred, and preserved, not by a single question and answer, but by a network of questions and answers seen in their interrelations among one another. Whereas a single question and answer may, indeed, prove illuminating, typically it adds another simple picture to the available stockpile and is unable to adjudicate between its own claims and the claims of other simple pictures or provide criteria of adjudication. The multiquestion approach has a far greater chance of success, for this procedure involves weighing pictures against each other, mutual critique and adjustment, and the selection of features to form the composite and complex final picture. Here, the criteria of adjudication become generated in the series of adjustments forced on one by the differing pictures. Put another way, the criteria are internal rather than external. By weaving together this complex set of hermeneutic operations, the present work holds *systematicity* as a genuine value,[21] however challenged this value is in the modern and postmodern milieu. As a virtue of a formal kind, systematicity cannot be, or at least ought not to be, replaced by *aperçu*. I should like at this juncture to comment in somewhat more detail on what I have suggested to be the three differentials of the present work.

1. A network of questions of greater and greater specificity is generated by and from the basic question of the theological or nontheological essence of Hegel's thought. If Hegel's use of God-language is taken seriously and not explained away, then, on a purely formal level, the religio-theological essence of Hegelian thought can be affirmed. A second question follows from the first. This question concerns the identity of the specific kind of God-talk affirmed by Hegel, which, it turns out, is the God-talk countenanced by Christianity or the Christian community. A third question, following upon the second, hinges upon being able to isolate in a more particular way the model or models of Christianity to which, explicitly or implicity, Hegel displays most affinity. A condition of the possibility of the raising of this question is the exposé and critique of two assumptions often at play in Hegelian interpretation when the relation of Christianity to the philosophy of concept is broached: (1) the assumption that there exists a publicly available Christianity, shared and agreed upon by Hegel and Hegelian commentators and critics alike; and (2) the assumption that Christianity is some kind of Platonic form unchangeably present in every historical manifestation. Failure to critique such assumptions leads to the hermeneutic dead end complained of by Walter Jaeschke:

> His [Hegel's] claim that his philosophy simply comprehends the idea of Christianity is by and large judged against the standard of an almost atemporally understood, originally pure Christianity. Depending on the intentions of the interpreter, Hegel's views in the philosophy of religion are consequently either reinterpreted until they fit this standard or they are rejected for not conforming to it—which might have been foreseen from the outset, given such an interpretation.[22]

The third question leads to a fourth. Hegelian allegiance to a specific model or specific models of Christianity, as well as his position in general, is rendered more determinate by raising the question (4) whether, with respect to particular theologoumena, e.g., Trinity, creation, etc., Hegel diverges or swerves from the standard Christian accounts.[23] Needless to say, the object here is not heresy-hunting, but swerve serves as a symptom of the model or models of Christianity that are effective in the Hegelian selection of species. The fourth question naturally devolves into the questions of whether divergences from the standard Christian position are systematically interconnected. Put another way, the question can be raised whether, in addition to express allegiance to a standard Christian position, e.g., Lutheran and local symptoms of a variety of Christian models, the Hegelian rendition points to a depth grammar only fully capable of purview when all and every swerve is taken into account. It is only on the basis of the elucidation of questions (1)–(5) that the question (6) of the relation of religion to philosophy, representation to concept, or, in Hegel's terms, *Vorstellung* to *Begriff,* can be raised with full concreteness. For it cannot be decided beforehand that the *nature* of Christianity, or rather, Hegel's selection of its species, is incidental to determining the essence of Hegelianism or incidental to the mechanism of translation from *Vorstellung* to *Begriff.* Too often interpreters of Hegel have tended to treat the question on a purely abstract level and have not moved beyond the first or second level of interrogation.

Thus, it is the position adopted here that the ground-question of the alliance of theology and philosophy involves a self-generating series of questions forming a circuit. Anything short of this sixfold series is likely to fail to take all the evidence into account and generate a misleading picture, since sufficient attention has not been paid to a host of Hegelian decisions that are unusual if not unique. Obviously, the more general questions such as (1) and (2) can be handled with relative ease and should be capable of quick dispatch. But the more differentiated questions, i.e., (3)–(6), admit of no such dispatch, given the volume of Hegel's work, the variety of his sources, the ambiguity of his expression, and the massive range of disagreement among Hegelian commentators and critics. In pursuit of answers to these questions, the approaches of (2) and the interests of (3) are not segregated elements. The questions of our sixfold set are answered by appeal to the narrative and trinitarian predilections of Hegel, as well as elaboration of the systemic liaisons (3) whose constitutive power must be adjudicated.

2. While the intrinsic relation between Hegelianism and Christianity has long been recognized, being confessed in left-wing Hegelianism's denunciation of the historical Hegel and right-wing Hegelianism's baptism of orthodoxy,[24] the affirmation of the constitutive power of the theologoumenon of the Trinity has taken a good deal longer to proclaim, and even now is a position that must be argued for. Feuerbach was certainly prepared to posit the Trinity as a key theologoumenon assimilated by the Hegelian system,[25] but the Incarnation and the notion of spirit and community were also diagnosed as pivotal. Perhaps Ferdinand Christian Baur in his history of the doctrine of the Trinity, *Die christliche Lehre von der Dreieinigkeit,* was the only thinker of the nineteenth century who truly recognized the importance of the theologoumenon in Hegel, but his work was relatively ignored. The break with nineteenth-century democracy was initiated by Johannes Hessen's monograph, *Hegels Trinitätslehre, Zugleich eine Einführung in sein System* (1922), furthered by Jörg Splett's *Die Trinitätslehre G. W. F. Hegels* (1965), and consummated in Piero Coda's *Il negativo e la trinita* (1987) and Dale M. Schlitt's *Hegel's Trinitarian Claim* (1984). The last-named text offers a fully comprehensive treatment of the topic and, with the possible exception of Coda's work, surpasses previous work in insight and knowledge of the primary and secondary sources. Schlitt's thesis,[26] which, in large part, is agreed on in Coda's less philosophically inclined text, is that all other theologoumena recapitulated in Hegel, either on the level of philosophy of religion or philosophy proper—and Schlitt has particularly in mind incarnation, redemption, and the spiritual community—are subservient to, indeed, are subsumed under, the Trinity, which is conceived in the most expansive way possible to include the *operationes ad extra* of the divine.

Schlitt's methodical exegesis of Hegel's trinitarian commitment touches upon an aspect of Hegel's thought that many would assert as an identifying feature of Hegelianism, i.e., process and becoming. The individual and cultural becoming hallowed by the *Phenomenology of Spirit* (*PS*) as the condition of the possibility of personhood has been found by critics to be reinforced by the emphasis on time and history that is a mark of all Hegel's nature texts. Moreover, literary critics and philosophers alike have been struck by the correspondence between Hegelian thought and narrative, especially between Hegelian thought and that genre of narrative called the *Bildungsroman* that has the story of the genesis of personhood as its subject.[27] Hegel may have broadened its expanse and projected the model of individual becoming onto the historical network as a whole, yet the model remains determinative throughout all of its applications. As Mark Taylor has pointed out,[28] the model was not only capable of capturing the becoming of the individual and the entire ambit of the historical becoming of human culture, it was, in addition, open to theological framing in which global becoming could be considered the process that was limited by the alpha of creation and the omega of eschaton and apocalypse. It seems, however, that Taylor sets stricter limits to the theological extension than is necessary and, in doing so, implies that narrative only touches upon divine operations and not on the divine itself. Narrative, narrative becoming, Hegel suggests on numerous occasions, can be predicated of the divine in a truly radical way. This is clearly recognized by Iwan Iljin and is axial in his *Die Philosophie Hegels als kontemplative Gotteslehre* (1946). For Iljin, the narrative thrust of Hegel's texts extends beyond the economic order. Indeed, read in one way Iljin suggests that the immanent-economic distinction no longer applies, since all elements of the divine are touched by becoming. On the basis of this insight, Iljin elaborates his epochal view of the divine. An epoch is a narrative phase of becoming. Iljin is persuaded that, even before the creation of nature and finite spirit, the divine undergoes a species of narrative development, i.e., development of an atemporal kind.[29]

It, indeed, would be wonderfully convenient if Iljin provided a definitive statement concerning the narrativity of the divine. Certainly, a major debt is owed to him for having reminded us that with Hegel the narrativity of the divine is radical and not merely economic. But Iljin's work is not methodologically self-conscious. He neither addresses the question of what precisely are those narrative elements responsible for narrative coherence in the elaboration of the epochal divine, nor the question of the applicability of the trinitarian scheme to the complex ontotheological elaboration of the divine, and the relation of both to the Christian narrative that is constantly evoked. His agenda was the general philosophical one of indicating the ontotheological and narrative essence of Hegelianism. In this he succeeds admirably, and it is the theologian who is in need of deeper examination of narrative structure as this structure impinges upon the divine and in need of a more focal awareness of narrative level. Attendance to these needs permits a more perspicuous rendering of Hegel's divine than has been possible up to now.

Narrative theory, especially in the form provided by Gerard Genette, greatly assists in the first of these two tasks. In particular I wish to borrow from Genette the analytic pair 'prolepsis' and 'analepsis'.

Speaking of them in *Narrative Discourse* Genette writes: "here begin the problems (and disgraces) of terminology."[30] Not merely am I perpetuating this disgrace in my borrowing, but shortly I am going to exacerbate it by adding an ugly polysyllabic pair of my own. Before perpetrating such offense, it is apposite to present Genette's general understanding of these terms. Prolepsis is defined as "any narrative maneuver that consists in narrating or evoking in advance an event that will take place" (p. 40). Analepsis is defined as "evocation after the fact of an event that took place earlier in the point of the story" (ibid.). Rendered thus, prolepsis and analepsis are not especially helpful with respect to the topic at hand, i.e., the elucidation of the narrative of the divine. As used by Genette, the categories belong to the order of the signifier rather than the signified or, to avail of a standard narrative theory distinction, the order of narrative rather than story.[31] It is recommended here that prolepsis and analepsis be understood not merely as figures of discourse but as touching upon the ontological or ontotheological stratum. In short, what is recommended is a shift of accent from narrative to story. This adjustment is perfectly in the spirit of Hegel, who nowhere sanctions any absolute split between discourse and its object, and everywhere sees discourse as disclosive of the real.[32] Keeping the Hegelian view of language clearly in mind, though at the risk of ambiguity, the term *narrative* will be retained even when the focus is primarily on the level of what in narrative theory would be designated as *story*. A second emendation closely relates to the first. In Genette, while events or episodes of a narrative may relate to the development of a subject or subjects in a story, properly speaking narrative (as discourse) relates to the presenter (writer) and re-presenter (reader). The ontological turn found necessary if Genette's categories are to have more than limited use for an interpretation of Hegel suggests placing the constitution of subject through event and episode at the center without, however, excluding the prerogatives of discourse or its economy. The displacement of discourse does not mean its excision, and prolepsis and analepsis continue to have discursive as well as ontological and/or ontotheological function. Yet narrative as discourse is dependent upon narrative as ontotheological elaboration as the very condition of its possibility.

Together these emendations allow us to redefine prolepsis and analepsis in a way that makes them more useful for our analysis of Hegel. In general and formal terms, that is, terms that apply equally to the level of reality and discourse, prolepsis can be redefined as the anticipation of as yet unrealized episodes or events. When it touches upon the ontological or ontotheological stratum, prolepsis focally concerns unrealized episodes or events that are constitutive of subjectivity. In this second and more specific sense, prolepsis corresponds closely to Herbert Huber's description of *Geist* or *Spirit* in *Idealismus und Trinität* as *'potentielle-antizipative Totalität'*.[33] Continuing this line of redefinition, analepsis in general and formal terms refers to the recollection of completed episodes or events. When the horizon is that of developing subjectivity, analepsis concerns the preservative gathering not merely of episodes and/or events but also of states of self constituted by previous episodes and/or events. And to say this is to do more than point to a psychological phenomenon. On the level of reality, analepsis in no way corresponds to memory as normally understood. Analepsis points not to a massive data base but to the effective history of self-constitution, not all of which is transparent or readily available, but all of which is layered in the last or final constitution of self.[34]

At this juncture it might plausibly be objected that modification vitiates the rationale for introducing such terminology in the first case. And certainly it is true that, through emendation, prolepsis and analepsis begin more and more to approximate to Hegel's own language of *an-sich* and *implicit* on the one hand and *an-und-für-sich* and *Erinnerung* on the other. Yet approximation is not identity, and an alien and technical terminology has determinate advantages over the coins pressed in Hegel's linguistic mint. Three are conspicuous. First, there is the general advantage of not being ruled by Hegel's own linguistic habits which tend in interpretation to prove imperialistic. Second, there is an advantage of having a vocabulary more transparently flexible than Hegel's own in operating on the double level of discourse and reality. And third, the admittedly meagre appropriation of a single analytic pair has the advantage of suggesting at least the possibility of a much larger scale rapprochement of narrative theory and a theological hermeneutics of Hegel than has thus far been attempted. This rapprochement, in the opinion of the present author, would be to the mutual benefit of both.

To the narrative pair of Genette I wish to add a pair of my own invention. This pair, 'synclasis' and 'anaclasis', can for practical purposes be translated as 'narrative closure' and 'narrative openness', respectively. It is incumbent on me to offer reasons for resorting to the ugliness of neologism. The fundamental reason is that the hermeneutic-theological horizon within which Hegel is alive and discussed is presently occupied by three highly influential perspectives on narrative closure and openness. Of these three perspectives, two might be said to be generated in definite hermeneutic postures with respect to Hegel—though one more clearly than the other—and the third gets elaborated in the context of a trinitarian theology that bears more than a family resemblance to the Hegelian position. The first hermeneutic perspective fastens the categories of closure and openness in a decisive way to the narrative of history. This perspective on Hegelianism has long been a fashion in left-wing revisionist readings from the Polish philosopher August Cieszkowski to Adorno,[35] but also informs Gadamer's far from left-wing critical disposition and Eric Voegelin's perceived right-wing stance.[36] Whether left-wing or not, the hermeneutic perspective which more or less exclusively focuses upon Hegel's view of history seriously restricts the ontological value of the categories of closure and openness, just as the focus upon the presence of the divine in history restricts their possible theological value. In the latter case the vision, which is a kind of mis-vision, reaches merely the *economic* activity of the divine, and thus the categories of closure and openness fail of fully fledged ontotheological employment.

The second modality of interpretation is the hermeneutic position of deconstruction. Though in principle a practice, not a theory, a reflection on discourse, not on reality,[37] deconstruction takes a quite definite stand with respect to the Western conceptual and intellectual tradition which it nominates after Heidegger as the ontotheological tradition. Whatever the internal differences within this tradition, and the different forms of its expression, primarily philosophy and theology but also art, the tradition is ineluctably committed to meaning and truth, where meaning and truth are either immediate or mediate. In either case the presence of meaning and truth constitutes a milieu of transparence that is, in principle, infinite but closed. The closure may be as distinct as the closure of a circle (Parmenides) or the closure of circle and line (Hegel),[38] yet, in any event, closure is operating at an absolutely fundamental and unrestricted level. For Derrida in particular, it is Hegel who represents the apotheosis of the ontotheological tradition as well as deconstruction's creative foil. In *Positions* Derrida expresses himself well on this point: "We have never finished with a reading or rereading of Hegel, and, in a certain way, I do nothing other than attempt to explain myself on this point."[39] The note of admiration is unmistakable and perhaps for Nietzschean reasons: Hegel as the connoisseur of logocentricism, Hegel, for whom concept, word, and narrative are the media in which the ineffable is challenged and excised,[40] and nonsense banished, is the lone enemy worthy of respect. Derrida sees Hegelian logocentricism as more powerful than other forms because it is more seductive. The confession of history and temporality, the admittance into discourse of becoming, invites us to think that closure is ruptured, whereas, in reality, everything is restrained within the economy of meaning and truth and its final and complete appearance, its parousia.[41] Not only is this parousia loudly proclaimed, but in the boldest possible way in modernity it is identified with God, the God of the Judeo-Christian tradition. Thus, for Derrida, closure is the principle and end, the arché and telos of Hegel's system; not only do history and temporality not break the hegemony of the circle, but, in their cessation-completion, as elucidators and gatherers of meaning, they confirm it. What is especially interesting about deconstruction's hermeneutic attitude, particularly of Derrida's, is that the real issue with Hegel lies at a more basic level than the level of history. After Heidegger and Levinas,[42] Derrida's interpretation of Hegel deepens the issue of closure. Like them, he seems to view the closure of history as an expression of a closure at once more systemic and radical. The implied contrary of openness is, thus, also invested with credentials that go beyond the merely historical. The art of deconstruction, while play, is yet a serious play. This serious play shows, unveils, uncovers the hubris of a discourse that would be complete. Taken at its word deconstruction cannot indulge in statement, in metadescription, and, least of all, in prescription. That despite itself it manifests a tendency to do so is evident in Mark Taylor's *Erring* which clearly indulges in an evaluative language of prescription and proscription.[43] Openness is a prescription, a metaphysical or quasi-metaphysical recommendation; closure, a proscription, a quasi-metaphysical no-no. While convinced that deconstructionists, and Derrida in particular, see Hegel in a fuller and more penetrating light than the interpretive regime that has Hegel's view of history and temporality as its focus, nonetheless, deconstructionist use of the antithetical pair *closure* and *openness* has to be seen as thoroughly evaluative. This evaluative component in deconstruction cuts squarely against the grain of my intention, which is to provide a descriptive, taxonomic account of Hegel, by means of descriptive, nonevaluative categories. The fact remains, however, that deconstruction is a highly influential hermeneutic discourse, and, if it does not have full occupancy of the linguistic territory within which closure and openness are important discursive items, it is in good standing. While different in fundamental respects, the two hermeneutic positions discussed thus far do tend to be mutually reinforcing. The evaluative use of the categorical pair in deconstruction is also present in the first hermeneutic regime, even if the focus is more narrow. All of this provides motive for linguistic escape, a motive that begins to seem compelling when one reminds oneself that, in deconstruction, narrative openness very well may be a contradiction in terms, not merely nonsense that somehow is entertained, but an actual utterance for which one can offer no protocol. For it seems to be the view of deconstruction that narrative always implies closure, what Frank Kermode has called "the sense of an ending."[44]

A third and final motive for suspicion of, and steering away from, common usage is the fact that in Jürgen Moltmann's *The Trinity and the Kingdom* a use of 'closed' and 'open' is authorized with respect to the Trinity in a theological elaboration that clearly, maybe even self-consciously, resembles Hegel's own.[45] In that text, for instance, open, as a term used to characterize the Trinity, refers to the interpenetration, or *perichoresis,* of the divine persons with each other,[46] and the reciprocity between Trinity and creation in which the Trinity is not immured from being affected by creation's multiplicity, differentiation, and, above all, pathos. The very affinity of Moltmann's position with Hegel's constitutes the greatest danger of conflation. Precisely because of this, it is vital to keep the distinctiveness of the Hegelian view in mind. In Hegel the Trinity is not merely relational through and through and open to the finite in a way unparalleled before him in the mainline Western theological and philosophical tradition(s), but, as Iljin and Schlitt have both noted,[47] the eternal Trinity is characterized by process as much as relation. In short, it itself appears to have a story-character. Finite reality, or its appearance, does not introduce story or narrative; it continues it. Certainly without such continuation the narrative would be truncated. But the point is, the Trinity would itself unfold its own self-referential—some theologians might say narcissistic—narrative.[48] Thus, openness in Hegel and Moltmann have different contexts and, gaining meaning from these contexts, are not interchangeable. The same holds for Moltmann's and Hegel's use of closed.

If present occupation of the hermeneutic field provides a motive for sharp terminological distinction, unless one is thoroughly convinced by William Blake's motto that "I must create a system or be enslav'd by another's" (*Jerusalem,* chap. 1. 10.20) it cannot be regarded as providing sufficient warrant for the actual linguistic pair adopted. The choice of a Greek pair was influenced by: (1) the general virtues of a technical metalanguage I espoused when dealing with Genette's pair of prolepsis and analepsis; and (2) the aesthetic consideration of symmetry, i.e., to a technical Greek pair it seems appropriate to add another technical Greek pair. Again there is nothing here that could be thought to provide sufficient warrant. Justification lies ultimately in the sphere of use, though I am convinced that the chilling effect of uncouth vocabulary will wear off in the execution of the work. Enough, perhaps, has been said about the raison d'être of the major narrative concepts and terms that will be put to work in the interpretation of Hegelian ontotheology. But before we turn to (3), it should be pointed out that trinitarian and narrative analysis both have as their regulative object Spirit (*Geist*) as active, manifesting, and reconciling divine. Accordingly, it should be expected that these approaches can overlap, intersect, and amplify each other. The present text stands firmly behind the integration of these particular modes of analysis.

3. Neither the developing series of questions, nor the combination of trinitarian and narrative analysis, is extrinsic to our treatment of the four areas of relation (Hegel's relation to Luther, mysticism in general, Boehme, and Gnosticism). Correlatively, the treatment of the four areas of relation is not incidental to answering the more determinate questions of the interrogative series, i.e., Q (3)–(6), above all Q (3)–(5), which are decisive for identifying the version of Christianity Hegel offers as the quintessence. Again, treatment of relation is not incidental to determining the specific kind of narrative and trinitarian commitment authorized by Hegel. The point could be put more trenchantly: the treatment of relation might be considered as important, if not crucial, to the execution of the first two mentioned tasks. Still, while it is intuitively obvious that the study of important relations Hegel had with other individual thinkers and distinct varieties of thought would help to illuminate his ontotheological position, it is not immediately self-evident that precisely the four relations we propose as worthy of examination enjoy privileged status. Other relations appear to have genuine claims of priority. Hegel's relation to Aristotle, Kant, Spinoza, for instance, cut deeply and arguably influence his thought in a more immediate way than Luther, the Christian mystical tradition, the theosopher Jacob Boehme, or Gnosticism. Any supercedence these four relations might enjoy, therefore, is best regarded as a function of the fact that these religious, mystic, and mythological representations are better situated than philosophy qua conceptual articulation to offer ontotheological renditions that might plausibly be accepted as renditions of Christianity. Precedence, while infrastructural, would not necessarily be absolute. Concretely speaking, this could mean that on the level of concept, where Christianity is rid of the deficits of representation, the influence or impact of Spinoza would come into its own.[49]

Spinoza's influence, however, would not be responsible for Hegel's basic vision but would help to prune Christian thought of any deformation that was simply a function of the symbolic mode in operation.

In the case of the thought of Luther, Christian mysticism, Jacob Boehme, and Gnosticism, there is evidence of Hegelian familiarity, though the extent and depth of Hegel's knowledge varies. It is also the case that all four varieties of thought were commended by Hegel as offering braver and more perspicuous renditions of Christianity than were current in his own day. Of the four varieties of thought, it is the first to which Hegel most consistently defers. Hegel's testimony of his Lutheranism, "I am and always was a Lutheran," is well known and should be taken seriously,[50] though, for obvious reasons, it cannot be regarded as conclusive. Hegel, after all, could be lying. At a very minimum he might be self-deceived. The plethora of passages extolling the pneumaticism of Lutheran Protestantism are not easy to ignore, even if it is admitted that Hegel makes claims of knowledge of the divine that go far beyond what Luther thinks possible within the ordinance of Christian faith and places the doctrine of the Trinity at the center of an explication of Christianity in a way Luther's own texts do not countenance. Two recent authors who take the Hegel-Luther liaison quite seriously are Ulrich Asendorf and James Yerkes. Asendorf's *Luther und Hegel* is, by far, the most comprehensive text on the topic, and Asendorf treats of the problematic of relation in minute detail.[51] Compared with Asendorf's text, Yerkes' *The Christology of Hegel* is both more impressionistic and more general. Yet Yerkes throughout his text constantly calls attention to the relation between Luther and Hegel.[52] For both authors, but especially Asendorf, the emphasis tends to fall on continuity. While in itself there is nothing problematic with this, to avoid the danger of collapsing the one in the other, it should be remembered that continuity does not exclude discontinuity, or understanding, misunderstanding, even willful misunderstanding. To say this is to leave open the possibility that, on crucial theological issues such as creation, the nature of evil, and incarnation, Hegel might depart from Luther's own position. To say this is, also, to leave open the possibility that the underlying narrative commitments might differ dramatically. Given the number and variety of other non-Lutheran influences, it would be no more than sensible to entertain the antecedent probability that Hegel and Luther will not be the same in every respect. Accordingly, accepting in broad terms Asendorf's and Yerkes' thesis of continuity, the present work will attempt to remain sensitive to Hegelian departures from Luther.

The second area of liaison is the nonobvious one of Hegel's relationship to mysticism. Liaison is nonobvious since Hegel, with his embargo against the hidden, the unknowable, the unspeakable, might be regarded as the most antimystical of philosophers. Yet the reflections of Ernst Benz, H. S. Harris, and to a lesser extent Frederick Copleston should give us pause. Benz, in his *Les sources mystiques de la philosophie romantique allemande,* and Harris in his two works of Hegelian biography, *Towards the Sunlight* and *Night Thoughts,*[53] provide considerable evidence that Hegel was both an avid and appreciative reader of mystical texts. Copleston in his essay, "Hegel: the Rationalization of Mysticism," makes the quite general claim that, at bedrock level, Hegel evidences a commitment to a mystical view of God, work, and self.[54] This mystical view is translated, however, into a vocabulary that disguises this fact. Copleston's essay is as powerful in evocation as it is thin in argument and demonstration. Nonetheless, his essay does orient one in the direction of looking to see whether Hegel's reading and approval of Christian mystics, for example, Meister Eckhart, has any effect upon his understanding of the nature of Christianity and his construal of the divine. Here no genus of mysticism, specifically Christian mysticism, is presupposed, and the general task of charting relation becomes the sum of specific tasks of charting relation between Hegelian theology and theologies of different mystical sources with distinct ideas, symbols, and emphases.

The assertion of relation between Hegel and Jacob Boehme is not new. In the nineteenth century, liaison was loudly asserted by Schelling in the form of an accusation and clearly implied in Ferdinand Christian Baur's great dogmatic works.[55] Exegesis of this putative relation has not been a major preoccupation of twentieth-century Hegel commentary and criticism. But then neither has exegesis of Hegel's relation to mysticism, of which, in a sense, Hegel's relation to Boehme is a specification. There have been notable exceptions. Fine scholars such as Malcolm Clark and Jean Hyppolite have suggested this particular area of relation to be a lacuna in the scholarship and have called for further investigation,[56] the latter opining that Jacob Boehme might be of singular importance in the attempt to comprehend the theological dimension of *PS.* Malcolm Clark in his important *Logic and System* puts the point even more strongly: explication of the relation between Hegel and the speculative mysticism of Jacob Boehme would be revelatory of the Hegelian system as a whole, which gives every evidence of being essentially theological in nature.[57] What is demand and *aperçu* in Clark and Hyppolite is fully comprehensive execution in

David Walsh. Walsh's dissertation, "The Esoteric Origins of Modern Ideological Thought: Boehme and Hegel" (University of Virginia, 1978), represents the first and, as yet, the only book-length account of the influence of Boehme upon Hegel. Basing his argument on the verified fact of Hegel's ownership of Boehme's collected works and the knowledge of Boehme illustrated not only in the *Lectures on the History of Philosophy* (*LHP*), where Hegel devotes as much space to Boehme as he does to Spinoza, but also both explicit reference and allusion in other texts such as the Berlin *Lectures on Philosophy of Religion* (*LPR*) and the *Encyclopedia of Philosophical Sciences* (*Enc*), Walsh proposes the bold thesis that the influence of the theosophy of Jacob Boehme is nothing less than constitutive of Hegelian ontotheology.[58] Yet, while it is the case that Walsh is able to show the presence of Boehmian elements in a large number of Hegel's texts, it is far from certain that he sustains his thesis that Hegelian ontotheology is constituted by Boehmian borrowing. Conversely, though the borrowings noted by Walsh are by no means trivial, if and only if Walsh demonstrated that Boehmian borrowings had impact in all of the pivotal areas of the Hegelian system could his thesis be regarded as proved. It is not evident that Walsh has provided such a demonstration. Moreover, Walsh's methodology, which appears to be of a straightforward causal kind, is not sufficient to the task. In the fact of Hegel's knowledge of Boehme's texts, and the presence of Boehmian symbols and ideas in Hegel's major and minor texts, Walsh seems to find warrant for the suggestion that, in the final analysis, Boehmian theosophy is the primogenitor of the Hegelian system. That this is not sound methodologically can be easily illustrated by considering the case of Plato or Aristotle, both of whom are acknowledged presences in Hegel's texts. A rehearsal of borrowings on a scale equal to Walsh's would hardly fail to evince a quite different thesis of constitution than the one advanced in his monograph. The genetic-causal model of explanation fails to do justice to the complexity of the hermeneutic situation in which complexes of ideas compete with each other in transmission, in which complexes rarely maintain their integrity, and in which complexes of ideas enter ideational contexts so different that their meaning is fundamentally altered. The problematic nature of Walsh's methodology and the somewhat generous estimate of the evidential grounds warranting the claim of Boehmian determination of Hegelian ontotheology tends to undermine his program. Yet this does not mean that Walsh's vision is eccentric or even that his thesis is incorrect. Massive structural correspondences can be shown to exist between Boehmian theosophy and

Hegelian ontotheology. These correspondences at the level of central theologoumena such as the Trinity, creation, evil, etc., as well as the depth-narrative level, are of such a unique kind that Boehme stands out as the singlemost important modern precedent of the type of religio-philosophical scheme articulated by Hegel.

The relation of Hegelian ontotheology to Gnosticism is, perhaps, the least obvious of our complex of four. Not that Hegelian ontotheology has not been, from time to time, labelled with the epithet *gnostic.* Both Eric Voegelin in the twentieth and Ferdinand Christian Baur in the nineteenth century think the label fits. Yet Voegelin's and Baur's actual employment of the term, and the bases upon which they warrant employment, are by no means the same. In texts such as *Science, Politics, and Gnosticism* and *From Enlightenment to Revolution,*[59] where Voegelin accuses Hegel of being gnostic, the term seems to denote knowledge, knowledge of the reality of God, world, and human being and history and their relation, where knowledge is absolute and divine rather than relative and human. Employed in this way the term does not evoke, in any tangible way, Gnosticism as a discernible historical phenomenon of the early centuries of the common era. More of a relationship is implied when Voegelin suggests that gnosis as a superlative form of knowledge carries soteriological freight, for it is clearly a characteristic of Gnosticism that it is knowledge rather than faith, or knowledge rather than ethical behavior, that accounts for salvation. But, of course, this characteristic is, in itself, insufficient to distinguish Gnosticism from other religious systems such as Hinduism, Buddhism, and Neoplatonism. In addition to the soteriological role played by knowledge, Gnosticism is characterized by quite determinate ideas and symbols of God, creation, evil, etc., and these determinate views are nowhere explicitly evoked by Voegelin as part of the content denoted by 'gnostic' or their presence as warranting use of the term. Voegelin's use of the term *gnostic* is general and content-thin and not likely to be of great assistance if the aim is a specific and content-rich use of the term.

The case is different in Baur's magisterial *Die christliche Gnosis* (1835).[60] Employment of 'gnostic' in that text is tied firmly to the various esoteric systems of the first centuries which all evidenced a profound speculative impulse, and which articulated views concerning a host of theologoumena that increasingly came into conflict with emerging orthodoxy typified by such figures as Irenaeus. When Baur speaks, therefore, of Hegelian ontotheology being gnostic, he is using the term in a much more determinate way and setting more definite criteria of employment than that offered by Voegelin. Moreover, greater determination in meaning and greater specificity with respect to use make the assertion of the gnostic character of Hegelian ontotheology testable in a way not possible in Voegelin's hermeneutic scheme. Wishing to subscribe to the values of determinacy in meaning, specificity in use, and testability, the present work takes Baur and not Voegelin to set the basic coordinates of meaning and use of the term. By way of recognizing this, it is recommended that the epithet be capitalized. Capitalization implies that the term functions descriptively denoting a complex set of theologoumena, but it does not necessarily imply agreement with Baur as to what these theologoumena are[61] or agreement with regard to the methodology best suited to isolate the theologoumena that define Gnosticism as a system or individual Gnostic systems. What the definite criteria of Gnostic systems are can only be determined on the basis of modern technical scholarship which now has at its disposal primary texts of Gnosticism as well as the reports of the heresiologists.[62] Considering the available sources, Baur's understanding of Gnosticism is staggeringly insightful, but only exposure to primary texts would be sufficient to guard against the tendency to de-emphasize those features that separate Philo from Valentinian Gnosticism and Valentinian Gnosticism from what Baur calls the Pseudo-Clementine literature. Methodological amendment of Baur's use of gnostic with respect to Hegelian ontotheology and other modern religious philosophies, including Boehmian theosophy, would take the form of a selection of a quite specific Gnostic system, in this case the Valentinian-Gnostic system, and testing whether Hegelian theologoumena provoke comparison with Valentinian depictions of the divine realm, creation, evil, etc. The working hypothesis, which corroborates and further specifies a thesis advanced as early as 1835, is that Hegelian ontotheology does, in fact, repeat or recapitulate depictions that are uniquely Valentinian.

There are three parts to the present work. Part 1, consisting of chapter 1, rehearses the foundational Hegelian determination of Christianity as a religion of revelation, a view of Christianity which, if it finds its consummate expression in Lutheranism, suffers a monumental forgetfulness in modernity. Theologies in modernity, according to Hegel, offer by and large quite counterfeit renditions of Christianity based on presumptions of the unknowability of God and the lack of intrinsic relation between God and world, God and human being. Diagnosing a number of influential modern theological species, therefore, as negative theologies of a degenerate type, Hegel interestingly opposes to them the epistemic and ontological courage of Christian mysticism. At the center of Hegel's espousal of Christianity as the religion of revelation is his vision of the *Deus Revelatus* or the self-revelatory God. For Hegel, the *Deus Revelatus* is narratively enacted and, as such, is constrained by properties endemic to all narratives. In our text we speak of four, or two pairs, prolepsis-analepsis, anaclasis-synclasis. However, Hegel not only argues for a narrative interpretation of the *Deus Revelatus*. He also suggests that the *Deus Revelatus* submits to a trinitarian construal. In doing so, Hegel brings the theologoumenon of the Trinity to the center of theology in a way unparalleled in modern Protestant thought. Indeed, it could be asserted that Hegel heals the split between natural theology and a theology of revelation or, more specifically, between natural theology and trinitarian theology,[63] by suggesting that an adequate revelation theology or, what amounts to the same thing, an adequate trinitarian theology, is inclusive of the theology of divine attributes and proofs of God's existence, both of which ordinarily would be subsumed under the natural theology rubric. For Hegel, of course, it is a point of crucial importance that narrative and trinitarian articulation of the *Deus Revelatus* not be presumed to offer fundamentally different descriptions. These descriptions are at once complementary and overlapping. Narrative articulation is made subject to trinitarian form, and trinitarian articulation is narrative articulation. It is precisely because of the narrative constitution of the Hegelian Trinity that, appearances of similitude notwithstanding, it differs crucially from the classical view.

Part 2 represents the center of the present interpretive work, for here is exegeted the various episodes and/or theologoumena, i.e., creation, incarnation, etc., of Hegel's trinitarianly interpreted narrative scheme. With the trinitarian elaboration *LPR 3* and *PS* favored over the *Enc* as the principle of organization, this part of the work is divided into five chapters, with chapter 2 focusing on the intradivine milieu, chapter 3 on creation, chapter 4 on incarnation and the christological passion-narrative, and chapters 5 and 6 on spiritual community and the achieved realization of narrative and trinitarian process.

More specifically, it is argued in chapter 2 that Hegelian depiction of the intradivine milieu, which is at once the first narrative phase and first trinitarian modulation of the *Deus Revelatus,* while it corresponds in some approximate way to traditional Christian depictions of the intradivine, nonetheless cannot be asserted to be identical with them. The Hegelian rendition does not correspond to the Nicean view, or any facsimile thereof, and could not be expected to so correspond, given Hegel's fundamental critique of the language of person and his strange evocation of heterodox Christian thinkers such as Valentinus and Jacob Boehme. It is suggested that it is Jacob Boehme who provides the precedent within the Lutheran field for a view of the intradivine Trinity which, after the manner of traditional trinitarian categories, is best described as narrative modalism. Such nomination is not intended to obviate but reinforce and complement discussion concerning other crucial points of demarcation between the Hegelian and classical envisagement of the intradivine trinitarian sphere; specifically, Hegelian understanding that (1) the intradivine trinitarian sphere is proleptic of further narrative adventure and must be so, since subjectivity or personhood is there only a partial realization, and (2) the intradivine trinitarian sphere, which, in one sense, forms a narrative whole with narrative closure (synclasis), is at a depth-level narratively open (anaclasis), and, again, has to be, since narrative closure on the level of the intradivine would issue in the mutilated or truncated divine.

Chapter 3 acknowledges Hegel's general support of the Christian theologoumenon of creation as an approximate symbol of the first movement of the divine *ad extra.* Creation itself, however, is assigned a trinitarian localization, and Hegel thinks that, as the intra-divine Trinity is interpretable by the symbol of the Father, the sphere of creation is interpretable by the symbol of the Son. Hegel's support of the theologoumenon of creation, it is noted, is not undifferentiated, and his criticisms of a host of construals envisioning divine manifestation as a series of discrete, externally related, acts are laid bare. It is argued that despite surface commitment to the standard Christian model of *creatio ex nihilo,* Hegelian commitment is ultimately to a *Creatio ex Deo* model of creation. Essay at further determination of the species of the *creatio ex Deo* model involved suggests that neither Spinozism nor Neoplatonism are appropriate *taxa,* but that Boehme and Valentinian Gnosticism are definite possibilities, since the articulation of creation under the auspices of the symbols of fall and evil there finds its most conspicuous presentation in the ontotheological tradition before Hegel and Schelling.

Chapter 4 examines the Hegelian rendering of the incarnation and passion narrative, which, within the framework of *LPR 3* and *PS* but not in the *Enc,* is assigned to the second moment of the trinitarian sphere of the Son. Acknowledging that Hegel shows little interest in classical Christology of an ontological type and seems implicitly to accept Lutheran reservations with respect to its value, Hegelian texts are combed with a view to discerning whether evocation of Luther's theology of the cross points to a real or merely verbal commitment. It is argued that while the commitment is certainly not merely verbal Hegel's narrative-trinitarian articulation of the *Deus Revelatus* issues in fundamental alternations of Luther's *theology of the cross.* These alterations, it is suggested, are of such a unique kind that it is all the more remarkable that they do have a precedent within modernity, indeed, within the Lutheran tradition, i.e., Jacob Boehme.

Chapters 5 and 6 examine the role of spiritual community and the closure of the trinitarian narrative of the divine. In chapter 5 is reviewed Hegelian elaboration of spiritual community and its identification with the mystical body. Hegel's assumption that his elaboration of spiritual community corresponds to that of Lutheran orthodoxy is challenged, and it is argued that the Lutheran model he recapitulates is informed by, or, as I put it, is inflected by, distinct varieties of mysticism, three of which are discussed, i.e, the Eckhartian, the Joachimite, and the Boehmian. Chapter 6 thematizes the relation of spiritual community to the closure of narrative trinitarian process (Holy Spirit) and reflects on the elevation of the spiritually informed human being into the intradivine, now conceived in its analeptic mode rather than its proleptic mode. Moreover, some attempt is made to characterize trinitarian articulation as a whole in terms of its apocalypse and theodicy commitment.

Part 3 consists of chapter 7 and centers on the move from representation to the concept Hegel finds necessary if philosophy is to play the kind of protective and rehabilitative role vis-à-vis religious discourse that Hegel thinks it can, and ought to, play in modernity. The central issues investigated are whether the change of symbolic form involves (1) transcending the narrative commitment in evidence at the level of even the highest order representation, and involves (2) determining conceptual discourse as nonautonomous in the event that concept cannot be said to liberate itself of the narrative commitment suggested in his texts. Despite some of the textural evidence going in the opposite direction, it is argued that the specific genius of the Hegelian position lies in the fact that conceptual discourse does not surrender all trace of the narrative commitment constitutive of representation, while at the same time remaining autonomous in the specific sense of being able to account for its own presuppositions and thus, by implication, determinative of them.

Despite the suggestion here of something like overweening ambition, it is important to point to the extrinsic and intrinsic modesty of the present text. The extrinsic modesty of the text is largely a function of the fact that *The Heterodox Hegel* is but a fragment of a much larger whole. In the context of the whole, the present text serves as a foundation for more narrowly, yet more deeply, focused claims that crucially involve a comprehensive treatment of the infrastructural narrative relation between Hegelian ontotheology, Boehmian theosophy, and Valentinian Gnosticism. For it well may be the case that it is narrative relation that subtends and contextualizes affinities respecting the construal of important Christian theologoumena. What makes the treatment of narrative relation so important is that, in the absence of sustaining the case for narrative relation, it is not clear how taxonomically justified one is identifying Hegelian ontotheology either as Boehmian or Valentinian or Boehmian-Valentinian. For practical reasons, such a discussion will have to be postponed until another time: the level of detail required successfully to prosecute the thesis of infrastructural narrative relation is such that it would make the monograph too long.

The hermeneutic program to be enacted here is also modest on intrinsic grounds. One obvious ground is the manifest selectivity regarding texts; another is the more or less thematic mode of treatment which almost invariably tends to have the effect of flattening development and defocusing nuance; and another again is the partial epoché at least of topical areas whose treatment would definitely throw light on the nature of the Hegelian enterprise. Nevertheless, even if it were not the case that Goethe's injunction "dare to be finite" functioned as something like an imperious command, a minimal sense of hermeneutic responsibility forces selection of texts, permits thematic treatment when the interest is decidedly on the identity and, thus, identifying characteristics of Hegelian ontotheology as a whole, and sanctions something like bracketing of topical areas such as German Idealism and, to a lesser extent, Kant. Concretely, the text selection is sufficiently standard so as not to be intrinsically problematic, though some Hegel commentators and critics will likely cavil with the prominent role awarded *LPR* on the grounds that no text not published in Hegel's lifetime should be granted hermeneutic priority over Hegel's published opera. Most definitely this objection has merit and clearly preempts any commentator or critic basing a case exclusively on this text. Fortunately, the present work has no such ambition. Though *LPR* indeed serves a more important hermeneutic role than some commentators would be prepared to sanction, the fact is that *LPR* is called on because it can transparently be seen to reinforce positions of an ontotheological orientation explicitly taken in Hegel's published works and to amplify and contextualize the more compact ontotheological renditions of texts like *PS* and *Enc.* Perhaps, an equally challengeable hermeneutic decision is my partial *epoché* of discussion of post-Kantian thought-systems that were obviously so important in the genesis of Hegelian thought and thereafter critical conversation partners. The first thing to emphasize is that the *epoché* is partial; Fichte and Schelling (and even Kant) do come in for some discussion. However, what will not be found in this text is any attempt to contextualize Hegel in terms of the post-Kantian problematic he undoubtedly shared with the other major Idealists, nor any attempt to preoccupy myself with the vicissitudes of a highly complex set of relations. This ought not to be read as implying that this discussion is unimportant or redundant. Indeed, in a certain sense the present text is understood as a first attempt to generate categories of analysis which might be useful in examining the other Idealists and their various systems along with their complicated trajectories.

It is hoped that neither the extrinsic nor intrinsic modesty of the text, nor their sum, will issue in a work devoid of hermeneutic nerve. In its profiling of Hegel, in its conjuration of *eidos* to be added to the museum of interpretive shapes that is showing signs of overcrowding, this text is, in its own way, remarkably thetic. Among other things, it wishes to assert both the radical narrative character and trinitarian essence of Hegelian ontotheology, while suggesting that systematic oddness of Hegel's renditions vis-à-vis the mainline theological and philosophical traditions put him in strange company; at the same time, it wishes to focus Hegel's mystical affinities by discussing the way in which Hegelianly rendered theologoumena point to quite specific mystical constellations; it wishes to insist upon the sincerity of Hegel's Christian and Lutheran disposition, while acknowledging divergence; and lastly, it wishes to configure a Hegel who belongs to the heterodox margins of the ontotheological tradition, but whose marginality is not such as to traject him extratextually outside the tradition into a kind of hermeneutic free fall.

PART 1

Ontotheological Foundations

The attempt to delineate the foundations of Hegel's ontotheological rendition of Christianity should be accompanied by the cautionary note that Hegel's debts are many, his influences varied, his allegiances multiverse. But, having said this, despair at determining the broad pattern of Hegelian circumscription and the major lines of demarcation between his view and others in the theological or ontotheological tradition does not logically follow. If such patterns and lines are not on the surface, excavation does not need to reach impossibly deep levels to discern them. Chapter 1 represents my attempt to elucidate Hegel's infrastructural commitments and the basic principles in and through which Hegel circumscribes the essence of Christianity, the core of the Christian vision of the divine and the divine-human relation. Such an elucidation is vital if Hegel's articulation in its complex detail is to be understood, for Hegelian rendition of the Christian vision is decisive for what he has to say with regard to specific theologoumena such as the intradivine Trinity, creation, incarnation, redemption, church, salvation, mystical union, etc. Moreover, such elucidation allows us not only to see the correspondence or lack of correspondence between Hegelian rendition of Christian theologoumena and more standard accounts, but makes possible an account of relation that goes beyond the purely descriptive.

1

HEGELIAN RENDITION OF THE *DEUS REVELATUS* OF CHRISTIANITY

Hegel, rarely ahistorical and never an advocate of the 'innocent' phenomenon, recognizes that the question of the essence of Christianity is a matter of interpretive decision in a hermeneutical field where one's selection competes with other possible choices. The hermeneutical field has both historical depth and contemporary spread. Indeed, the Enlightenment and immediate Post-Enlightenment situation is one of interpretive metastasis, and the resulting conflict of interpretation urgently demands adjudication. Hegel's specific act of adjudication constitutes an interpretation of extraordinary complexity, appealing on different occasions to distinct aspects of the Christian tradition for support, at one time St. Paul, another Luther, another the varieties of mysticism represented by Eckhart, Joachim de Fiore and Jacob Boehme.[1] While Hegel's appeal is historically dense, it is also discriminating. In particular, detailed differentiation of the object 'Christianity' presupposes a primary circumscription constituted by the exclusion of any ontotheological orientation that does not take revelation to be absolutely crucial to the definition of Christianity. Hegel finds much of post-Reformation theology and almost all post-Kantian ontotheology lacking for this reason. If revelation means anything, he argues, it means that the divine bridges the gap between infinite and finite and makes itself known. Unfortunately the basic tendency of modern theology is just the contrary: the stress falls heavily upon the absolute transcendence and radical unknowability of the divine.

Hegelian determination of the object Christianity is further specified when Hegel rules that the revelatory essence of Christianity implies that at its center is a God who reveals, makes known. If Christianity, as with other religions, is defined by its object,[2] this object is defined by transparence and knowability. The self-revealing God of Christianity finds its adequate discursive expression in the term *Spirit* (*Geist*). For Hegel, Spirit does not denote a particular aspect of the divine, either a particular person of the Trinity as theological orthodoxy would have it[3] or a specific set of acts, but rather the divine considered in its entirety and exhaustive compass of its acts. More succinctly and more positively expressed, Spirit is the title Hegel gives to the divine considered as an encompassing act or process of revelation. Quite obviously this view is not standard: if it does not subvert, it certainly torques the ontotheological tradition or its Judeo-Christian mainstream. Positing process of the divine does not in principle, however, reduce the divine to time and history, even if it is, in fact, crucial to Hegel's ontotheological proposal that the divine be seen in a much closer relationship to time and history than traditionally conceived. What the positing of process does imply is that, at an infrastructural level, the divine is plot, story, or narrative with a beginning, middle, and end.[4] Thus, whatever Hegelian criticisms of narrative varieties of thought in the ontotheological tradition in general and the Judeo-Christian theological tradition in particular—and these criticisms are perspicacious and eloquent[5]—with appropriate reserve Hegel can be said to read Spirit as designating a narrative elaboration in which the divine moves from an initial state of indetermination to a state of full determination by means of a process understood more as a drama than quiescent evolution.

Confessing himself a Christian philosopher, Hegel opines that the Christian story of creation, incarnation, redemption, and sanctification is at the core of the drama of divine elaboration, is central to any theological account of Christianity, and is inexpungible from any philosophical redescription, what I would prefer to call "speculative rewriting." But Hegel rows against the then contemporary current of hostility to dogma in insisting not only that the doctrine of the Trinity—albeit subject to emendation—is a useful symbol of the self-revealing God confessed in Christianity, but that it should, in fact, be construed as both its key symbol or representation (Vorstellung), and the pivot for Christianity's positive, rehabilitating relationship with philosophy. For Hegel, then, the narrative process of the revelation of the divine, inclusive of, but not exhausted by, the revelatory matrix of the Christian story, is best understood in trinitarian terms, or best understood as a trinitarian unfolding.

The three elements of circumscription touched on above will occupy us in this chapter. Section 1 focuses upon Hegel's basic circumscription of Christianity as the religion of revelation and his drawing a decisive line of demarcation between his own understanding and modern interpretations that champion the unknowability of the divine and absolutize the distinction between the infinite and finite. Section 2 thematizes the narrative, process character of the *Deus Revelatus* Hegel espies at the center of Christian faith and confession. Section 3 touches in a preliminary way on Hegel's appeal to the Trinity as the lens through which the narrative unfolding of the divine must be seen.

Section 1.1 Against Negative Theology

For Hegel, the Romantic Intuitionists define a modern thought-current that is, at the very least, latently anti-intellectual and, he would argue, ultimately antitheological in inspiration and commitment. His debate with Romantic Intuitionism, or with key intellectual figures which he will later see as a group sharing common assumptions, gets an airing as early as *Faith and Knowledge* (*FK*) (1802). By the time of *PS* (1807), Hegel has determined both the full compass of inclusion and his primary targets. The *Enc* (#61–78), *LPR* (1 & 3), and to a lesser extent, *LHP 3* do no more than to bring to full explicitness arguments that found a more rhetorical and tendentious expression in the Jena text. Regarding thinkers as apparently distinct as Jacobi, Schelling, and Schleiermacher as each offering at a fundamental level the same rendition of Christianity, theology, and philosophy, he feels called upon to demur. He objects on both subjective and objective grounds to what he regards as Romantic Intuitionism's basic axiom: no knowledge, that is, no discursive knowledge, of God is either actual or possible. Hegel retorts: "That one can know nothing at all of God is an empty standpoint" (*LPR 1* 1824 E 266, G 173); it is empty because it ignores, or, at the minimum, fails to take adequate account of, the full stretch of reason. To the degree to which Romantic Intuitionism understands itself as confirming and translating Christianity for and into the modern cultural milieu, Hegel diagnoses Romantic Intuitionism to be in complete contradiction to the central thrust of the Christian message it is philosophy's task to safeguard. Hegel loudly insists that the thesis of the noncognizability of God to have no foundation in Christianity:

> I declare such a point of view and such a result to be directly opposed to the whole nature of the Christian religion, according to which we should know God cognitively, God's nature and essence, and should esteem this cognition above all else. (Ibid. 1821 MS E 88, G7)

From the section on revealed Religion in the *Enc* comes a collateral asseveration:

> These assertions (and more than assertions they are not) are the more illogical, because made within a religion which is expressly called the revealed; for according to them it would rather be the religion in which nothing of God was revealed, in which he had not revealed himself, and those belonging to it would be the heathen 'who know not God'. (#564, Miller p. 298)

Not only is Romantic Intuitionism in contradiction to scriptural injunction (Matthew 5:48) (*LPR 1* 1821 MS E 87–88, G 6–7), but also to classical theology which, whatever its other failings, wholeheartedly endorses scriptural affirmation of the potential for knowledge of God (ibid. 1824 E 299–300, G 203–204; E 309, G 213). No such *sacrificium intellectus* can be condoned (ibid. 1821 E 107, G 26). If the passage cited above from the *Enc* (#564) in large measure connotes a structural contrast between a positive theology faithful to Christianity and its revelation center and a negative theology unfaithful to it, Hegel also places romantic Intuitionism within the historic field of Christianity and its emergence and diagnoses Romantic Intuitionism as constituting a deformation, indeed a regression. Romantic Intuitionism attempts to avoid the consequences of the revolution of Christianity (*LPR 1* 1824 E 300, G 204). In essence, the theology or ontotheology of Romantic Intuitionism is nothing more than a form of idolatry rendered passé by the emergence of the confession of Christianity. The *Enc* is clear on this point:

> If it were needful to win back and secure the bare belief that there is a God, or even to create it, we might well wonder at the poverty of the age which can see again in the merest pittance of religious consciousness, and which in its church has sunk so low as to worship at the altar long ago that stood in Athens dedicated to the 'Unknown God' (*dem Unbekannten Gotte*). (*Enc* #73, Wallace p. 107, *GL8*:179)

Almost invariably Hegel is at his most sarcastic and vituperative when Jacobi is under discussion. For Hegel, Jacobi is a bête noire who symbolizes all the excesses of Romantic Intuitionism. The attack is relentless and unsparing. Jacobi assumes the status of victim in *FK*,[6] and is still a victim in much later texts such as the *Enc* (#61–78) and *LPR 1* (1821 MS E 254, G 162). In *PR* and *LPR* Jacobi is less exposed to the raw chill of Hegel's polemics as he appears to function as one example among others of what Hegel presumes to be the consensus negative theology view. All of Hegel's most significant objections to Jacobi are elaborated in the early text. Hegel finds Jacobi's aphoristic esprit thoroughly uncongenial (E 117) and agrees with Kant respecting proper philosophical style and method. More importantly, he disagrees with the content of Jacobi's work. Already setting the stage for his later criticism of Schleiermacher, Hegel deplores Jacobi's substitution of feeling and instinct for reason (E 118). The consequences of this substitution from Hegel's point of view are disastrous. We are asked to make a sacrifice of intellect, forbidden any knowledge of the infinite or God. Hegel is anything but urbane in making these fundamental criticisms. In what appears to be a homologization of the relation of Hölderlin's *Empedocles* to fire as the *prima materia* and Jacobi's suggested relation of subjectivity and the divine infinite,[7] Hegel snidely refers to the burning of the midges of subjectivity in the fire of the Absolute (E 141). Hegel has no taste for such Empedoclean-like annihilation on the level of cognition and thinks it betrays the real purpose and necessity of philosophy. The real purpose and necessity of philosophy—and here Hegel is already forging an alliance between philosophy and theology—is, as Epictetus declared, to praise God, and knowledge of God is the highest form of praise (E 118). Hegel will make essentially the same point later in the *Enc* (#62, 63) and in *LPR 1* (1821 MS E 84, G 4; 1827 E 153, G 63–64) when he twins worship (*Gottesdienst*) and knowledge. Knowledge, i.e., discursive knowledge, is assigned by Jacobi exclusively to the finite horizon, with a kind of nonrational cognition going into emergency operation with respect to the transcendent beyond. Even here, however, no genuine contact between finite and infinite is achieved, just the bare conviction of existence. The *what* of the divine infinite is not and cannot be disclosed (*Enc* #73). To be persuaded otherwise is to ignore, according to Jacobi, the definitive restrictions to the limits of knowledge established by Kant. In general for Hegel, then, Jacobi's irrationalist proposal sunders epistemological continuity and vitiates ontological coherence. Jacobi's position is, in principle, an ontotheology of *Jenseits* in which the divine infinite is unreachable and unknown. When Hegel in the *Enc* denominates Romantic Intuitionism as negative theology, or theology of the Unknown God, it is probably the case that Jacobi is foremost in his mind, for it is Jacobi who sets Romantic Intuitionism's reductionist baseline, and Hegel is increasingly unwilling to grant that other, more subtle, more creative, Romantic Intuitionists escape this baseline's inertial pull.

The critique of the Romantic Intuitionists extends further than Jacobi. In the scintillating preface to *PS,* in addition to Jacobi,

Schelling is a central object of attack. Hegel is not unaware that distinctions could plausibly be made within Intuitionist thought, for instance, that Schelling's *intellectual intuition* is not equivalent to Jacobi's *empirical intuition,* and, indeed, appears to controvert Jacobi's premise of metaphysical incommensurability. A distinction Hegel would have been prepared to grant in the period of *FK* and *DE* is rescinded in *PS*.[8] With the discovery of his own philosophical voice, difference, for Hegel, is much less significant then similarity. In the context of Schelling's transcendental Idealism, the controversion of the premise of incommensu-rability is, in any event, more apparent than real. Intellectual intuition does not issue in knowledge. Moreover, the postulated identity of the reflective self and the Absolute rules out the possibility of both distinction *from* and *within* the Absolute. It is the latter debit of intellectual intuition that spawns the unforgettable one-liner: the Schellingian Absolute, or more generally the A = A of Identity Philosophy, is the night in which all cows are black (*PS* #16). If the estimate of Schelling's philosophy is here arguably unfair, as Werner Marx has contended,[9] it is, nonetheless, interesting to note Hegelian identification of Identity Philosophy's theological tendency. As Hegel sees it, Identity-Philosophy definitely belongs within the negative theology manifold. The divine infinite is hidden; knowledge is ignorance. Consequently, there is no meaningful transcending of the finite-infinite gap of separation. The theological or ontotheological situation is, from a Hegelian point of view, ultimately no different than in Jacobi for whom faith at once authors and authorizes the transition from one self-enclosed sphere to another. The leap into the beyond under the aegis of intellectual intuition establishes no intrinsic connection between orders of reality hermetically sealed from each other. Schelling, then, it is implied, leaves the basic parameters of Jacobi's negative theology intact. And such a theology has no warrant as an interpretation of Christianity which discloses the truth of reality, even if the modality or form of disclosure is capable of being surpassed. Though the tone is more respectful in later works, especially in *LHP 3,*[10] nothing written there suggests that Hegel has withdrawn his basic criticisms of Schelling's ontotheological position. Ignoring the later post-Identity-Philosophy work of Schelling, Hegel in *LHP 3* simply focuses on the earlier Schelling much indebted to Fichte's *Science of Knowledge*. If from the vantage point of his later ontotheological production Schelling christens his earlier work negative philosophy, Hegel at first implicitly, then explicitly, names it the worship of the Unknown God.

Schleiermacher, too, is increasingly identified as remaining within the negative theology parameters of Romantic Intuitionism, and over a period he replaces Jacobi and Schelling as Hegel's main debating partner with respect to the definition of Christianity, theology, and the relation of philosophy to both. Already in *PS* in the section on the Unhappy Consciousness (*das unglückliche Bewusstsein*) Hegel takes a swipe at the nondiscursive archeology proposed by Schleiermacher in *On Religion: Speeches to its Cultured Despisers* (1800).[11] He turns Schleiermacher against himself in suggesting a negative connotation to religiosity construed under the aegis of music as both its basic metaphor and key modality of expression. If Schleiermacher is understood, and to some extent understands himself,[12] to be forging an alliance between a kind of mysticism and a dogmatically thin Christianity, Hegel sanctions neither the kind of mysticism, the brand of Christianity, nor their relation. The section on Revelatory Religion (sect. 7) in *PS* could be construed as Hegel's constructive counterproposal.

Hegelian criticisms both broaden and deepen in the Berlin lectures on religion (*LPR*). The broad ideological drift of these lectures is responsive to Schleiermacher's stature in the academy, with the 1824 lectures responding directly to the publication of Schleiermacher's *magnum opus,* the *Glaubenslehre.*[13] It is Hegel's general opinion that, whatever its intention, Schleiermacher's theology of feeling (*Gefühl*) effectively displaces thought from the center of Christianity. And paralleling his tactic of refusing to clearly distinguish between Schelling and Jacobi, Hegel refuses to differentiate Jacobi and Schleiermacher. Given Hegel's clearly elaborated distinction between feeling (*Gefül*) and intuition (*Empfindung*), as Hodgson reminds us,[14] this strategy of homologization, perhaps most clearly in evidence in the 1824 Lectures (*LPR 1* 1824 E 266 ff), must be construed as rhetorical. Having assimilated *Gefühl* to *Empfindung,* Hegel then accuses Schleiermacher's position of the debits of Jacobi's, i.e., empiricism, passivity. Hegel is here deliberately ignoring the radical level of apprehension claimed for *Gefühl* by Schleiermacher. In neither *On Religion* nor the *Glaubenslehre* is 'feeling' construed as an 'ontic' act or passion.[15] If feeling is characterized by receptivity, nevertheless, its proper domain is the depth rather than the surface level, the ontological rather than the purely ontic—to invoke an influential Heideggerian distinction. Feeling may, perhaps, be symptomed by and deciphered from passions (and actions) on the ordinary level of experience and response, but feeling, specifically the feeling of absolute dependence upon a divine whence, cannot as such be identified with a specific discrete passion. In the

Hegelian misreading of Schleiermacher's axial principle, the dogmatic theologian is in the business of countenancing passivity as both an intellectual and ethical value. Hegel believes it self-evident that, posited as an intellectual value, passivity reneges on the autonomy of thought that is definingly human and religious, just as its positing as an ethical value represents a betrayal of modern culture with its emphasis upon activity.

Schleiermacher is also under attack in the Introduction to *LHP*. But perhaps the most sustained attack of all is to be found in Hegel's foreword to the rationalist apologist H. Fr. W. Hinrichs's *Die Religion in inneren Verhältnisse zur Wissenschaft* (1822).[16] The fundamentals of Hegelian disagreement do not differ in substance from those advanced in *LPR 1,* and the opposition of perspectives is again drawn in quite broad strokes. The flaw in Schleiermacher's position is that it does not and cannot extend beyond the self (pp. 231–232) and can offer no real description of the object or objective correlative (i.e., God) intuited or felt. Feeling, in any event, effectively excludes reason whose traditional status in philosophy and theology as the differentiating and truly specifying characteristic of human being cannot, Hegel thinks, be challenged (ibid. p. 229). Indeed, if Schleiermacher is correct, Hegel concludes then "a dog would be the best Christian for it possesses the feeling of its dependence in the highest degree and lives merely in feeling" (ibid. p. 238). For Hegel then, the Schleiermachian theological scheme, if indeed it can be called theology in the full and proper sense (ibid. p. 242), is purely negative. Within such a scheme God as such is the unknowable (ibid. p. 232).

Hegel's misreading of Schleiermacher occludes but, nonetheless, cannot fully hide issues of profound and direct importance to theology, philosophy, and their relation. Hegelian declaration notwithstanding, Schleiermacher is not in the strictest sense an antirationalist. Reason is affirmed and accorded a role. Though instrumental in character, reason can, and in fact does, express and translate the feeling of dependence and its privileged expressions into rational technical-discourse.[17] Therefore, the issue between Hegel and Schleiermacher ultimately concerns, not so much excising reason, as setting limits to its legitimate deployment. Hegel presumes Schleiermacher to be much too restrictive in assigning to discursive thought merely an instrumental role, and the fear that guides Schleiermacher's restriction he regards as unfounded. Thought is only dangerous to Christianity when its species is that of *Verstand,* the freezing, hypostatizing, analytic understanding. Thought, considered under its most capacious, flexible, and synthetic aspect of *Vernunft,* constitutes no threat to either Christianity or theology, and its functioning, therefore, does not have to be rigorously controlled. Thought, considered under this second aspect, Hegel suggests, is innocent of the charge of insensitivity to Christian confession and its relatively first-order reflection; indeed, it is intrinsically theological in essence. The disagreement between Schleiermacher and Hegel is here systemic. Yet, on a purely formal level, it can be said that both Schleiermacher and Hegel belong to the Anselmian tradition in theology.[18] Both posit continuity between faith and conceptual articulation, their disagreement being focused in the latitude accorded, or not accorded, to the functioning of conceptual articulation. This disagreement, in turn, can be regarded as a function of two other decisions: (1) a decision concerning whether the perspective from which the relation between faith and conceptual articulation is most adequately viewed is archeological or teleological; (2) a decision concerning whether the presence of conceptual articulation signifies necessity on the level of thought (*Denkennotwendigkeit*) or possibility (*Denkenmöglichkeit*).[19] Both of these decisions will be briefly analyzed, though the emphasis will fall heavily on the former.

The perspective from which Schleiermacher views the relationship of faith (in his case, feeling) and conceptual articulation is unequivocally archeological. While conceptual articulation is not unimportant, it is a decidedly secondary affair depending upon, and referring back to, a primitive religiosity that exists at the bedrock level of human being, Christianly formed and constituted human being in particular. The case is otherwise with Hegel. Hegel announces the Anselmian style of his theological-philosophical enterprise in *LPR 1* (1821 MS E 211, G 119; 1827 E 154, G 65–66) by playing upon the etymological connections between 'devotion' (*Andacht*) and 'thought' (*Denken*). Yet the emphasis falls not upon the archeological deposit of feeling but rather religiosity's or faith's teleological completion, first of all in the representations, i.e., *Vorstellungen,* of dogmatic theology and, ultimately, in philosophy which, Hegel suggests, is self-founding, self-constituting discourse (ibid. 1821 MS E 217–219, G 126–128). Teleologically required, the representations of dogmatic theology are, for Hegel, anything but secondary. Representations are an absolutely indispensable means of and for the expression of truth. In fact, according to Hegel, truth is not fully articulate in modes of expression more basic than dogmatic representation[20] and certainly is not fully articulate in Schleiermacher's archeological deposit. The distinct emphasis and thrust Hegel provides his elaboration of the relation between the less articulate and more articulate modes of expression is rendered with particular clarity in the following passage from *LHP:*

> Devotion is a feeling of the unity of God and man but it is a thoughtful feeling. Thinking is implied in the word 'devotion'; devotion is a drive towards thought, a thinking, reaching out to unity; a frame of mind adapting itself to the unity.[21] (*LHP 1* E 124)

Of course, Hegel and Schleiermacher also depart concerning the question of whether the discursive articulation can assume the modality of necessity. Contra Schleiermacher, Hegel suggests that it is precisely the goal of discursive formation to achieve autonomous self-grounding, and thus constitute itself as a discourse of necessity.[22] Whatever the possibility of such a discourse, Schleiermacher is convinced that such a discourse could not be hospitable to Christianity, given its claim of revelation and irreducible historicity.[23] For Schleiermacher, Lessing's broad, ugly ditch between accidental truths of history and necessary truths of reason[24] is not crossed, and cannot be crossed, under the banner of Hegelian concept and the promise of preservation contained in Hegelian *Aufhebung.*[25]

There is one further point of dispute between Hegel and Schleiermacher I would like to rehearse here. (The conversation between these thinkers will be renewed in section 3). From Hegel's point of view, Schleiermacher's theology of feeling does not reach the divine as such. While Schleiermacher does posit relationality, the circuit of feeling is so narcissistically self-referential that relationship in any meaningful sense is ruled out. To insist that religion or theology be defined by the genitive (*LPR 1* 1821 MS E 188, G 55) is, in Hegel's view, to take a decisive step beyond Schleiermacher. Again Hegel is hardly being fair to his opposition. If nothing else, however, Schleiermacher serves as a foil by which Hegel's own views gain clarity and definition. Specifically, it is in and through his conversation with Schleiermacher that Hegel comes to see, not only in a sharper way than before the relational nature of religion signaled in the very word,[26] but the constitutive nature of relationality.

For Hegel, then, Romantic Intuitionism's theology of the Unknown God is a modern decadent phenomenon trespassing against the essence of Christianity which, he insists, is revelation. Jacobi, Schelling, and Schleiermacher, each in his own way, is guilty of this trespass. In large part, Hegel's point is descriptive: it is the case that Christianity speaks of a God disclosed to us in the finite and perceived and received in the spirit. Pneumaticism is, for him, not separable from revelation but, taking his stance from within Lutheran confession, is seen to be a crucial aspect of the overall dynamic of revelation. The point is repeated again and again in Hegel's mature works, especially in *LPR 1*.[27] Yet, it is also the case that in combating the Romantic Intuitionists there are times when Hegel clearly moves beyond the descriptive. Talk of the revelation essence of Christianity shifts to talk of the metaphysical or ontological implausibility (read impossibility) of God *not* revealing Himself. Put more concretely, in the post-Enlightenment agon of definition, Hegel avails of the Platonic construct that God is not envious (*LPR 1* 1821 MS E 103, G 23; *Enc* #564) and cannot fail to disclose himself. Of course, in an obvious sense, Hegel's availing of the construct is purely tactical. In another, nonobvious sense, Hegel has transformed the level of discourse. Hegel is no longer merely arguing that, as a matter of fact, the divine reveals itself; he is engaged in offering ontotheological reasons respecting the *why*. This shift in the level of discourse will be exegeted further in section 2. Here, it is sufficient to make some note of it. What cannot be postponed is a somewhat fuller account of the genealogy of negative theology and its complete ambit.

From Hegel's perspective any account of the genealogy of negative theology's modern style must necessarily take account of Kant. The picture of Kant as the great iconoclast, *der Allzermalende,* is perhaps nothing more than an influential caricature, but there was nothing inconsistent in both accepting the sincerity of Kant's profession that he had limited the claims of knowledge to make room for faith and in seeing that the *First Critique* thoroughly undermined theology's truth claims, which no renovation of the scope and function of reason could correct. Practical reason could certainly function transregulatively, to use James Collins' term,[28] but for Hegel this provides no substitute for the loss of the transregulative use of *theoria.* Theologically, the consequences are disastrous. More serious (because more basic) than the undermining of the integrity of the proofs for God's existence is the skeptical consequence that in the strict sense nothing can be known about God.[29] God can still be affirmed, though now affirmation has the status of a postulate rendered by practical reason. The postulate character of the affirmation dictates among other things that the Kantian *Summum Bonum* cannot legitimately be considered the transcendental equivalent of God as Truth. And correlative to the unknowability of God on the level of *theoria* is the gap which opens up between the infinite and finite, the divine and the human. Hegel, at least from *PS* on (the case is different in *FK*),[30] offered a critical reading of Kant that diagnosed him a worshipper of the Unknown God and unchristian, not because of the overestimation of thought (of which Kant was commonly accused), but because of his undervaluing of it. Nevertheless, Hegel remained more equivocal with respect to Kant than with the Romantic Intuitionists. He continued to have a sense long after *FK*'s paean of Kant that the synthetic a priori and synthetic unity of apperception were Hegelian intuitions in disguise and that Kant simply failed to accept fully the radicality of his discovery.[31] Nonetheless, in the mature Hegel, the critical stance is the dominant one. A theology of *Verstand* can only be a theology of the Unknown God. Moreover, it is right and proper to construe Kant as an essential link in the causal chain that has its term in the excess that is Romantic Intuitionism. This judgment is to the fore in *LHP 3,* as it is in Hegel's important foreward to Hinrichs's rationalist apologist text.[32] According to the latter text, the part played by Kant in the emergence of modern negative theology is considerable. At one point, Hegel is even tempted to make Kant the primogenitor (p. 235). Yet this does not represent Hegel's final view. Looked at more comprehensively, Kant himself is as much product as producer, a product whose seeds can be traced back to Enlightenment rationalism and Pietism. And, as Hegel argued first in *PS,* from a theological point of view, Enlightenment rationalism and fidelistic Pietism are very much two sides of the same coin. The happy consciousness of the Enlightenment, its claim of cognitive mastery, its vocation of complete discursive control, are spurious (#573). Seeing himself very much as a pathologist, Hegel diagnoses, not merely that rationalism is an insidious disease inherently unfriendly to Christianity, but that rationalism is the site of modernity's debacle of nonrecognition and misidentification. Nowhere in the modern cultured world is the gap between claim and realization, aim and achievement, larger. No less than for pietistic faith does the substance it so complacently presents as a possession lie beyond it. The Enlightenment differs from Pietism only in its pretense. Pietism honestly confesses what, at a depth level, is the essence of the Enlightenment, i.e., the despair of knowledge to reach reality and truth.

The genealogy of Romantic Intuitionism has the effect of displaying the full compass of modern deformation. Hegel's critical standard is Reformation, specifically Lutheran, Christianity. Yet, if modern theology is disadvantaged with respect to Reformation Christianity, it is also disadvantaged when compared with classical theology, both patristic and medieval. Medieval theology comes in for special praise on a number of occasions (*LHP* E 125, 141; Hinrichs E 242). But here one should be careful not to read Hegel in a flatfooted way. As clearly shown in *LPR*, *LHP*, and *LPH*, Hegel endorses in large measure Lutheran criticisms of medieval scholastic theology. His support of medieval theology, therefore, should be regarded as rhetorical and strategic. Hegel must be read as saying: even medieval theology is superior to theology's modern counterfeit to the degree to which there is confidence in the power of reason really to know God. Comparatively speaking, medieval theology, especially in its refusal to countenance the doctrine of double truth (*LPR 1* 1827 E 154, G 65; 1824 E 134, G 49–50), is profoundly confident of the ability of discourse to name the divine. Accordingly, medieval theology is to be found on the kataphatic side of the great theological divide, i.e., the divide between kataphatic or positive and apophatic or negative theology. Hegel, however, does not leave matters resting here. On a more fundamental level kataphatic designation—and thus approval—can be withdrawn from medieval-scholastic, as well as other theological, modalities that stress the power of cognition. In a move of some subtlety, Hegel extends the ambit of negative theology to cover precisely that kind (or those kinds) of metaphysical theology commonly thought to be the precise contrary. Hegel reasons:

> When the notion of God is apprehended as that of the abstract and most real being, God is, as it were, relegated to another world beyond: and to speak of knowledge of him would be meaningless. Where there is no definite quality, knowledge is impossible. (*Wo keine Bestimmtheit ist, da ist auch keine Erkenntnis möglich*). Mere light is mere darkness (*Das reine Licht ist die reine Finsterniss.*) (*Enc* #36 *zu,* Wallace p. 58, *GL8:*114)

Wolffian Rational Theology is an obvious referent here. Perhaps Spinoza's articulation of God as Substance also lays itself open to the same charge. But the medieval-scholastic elaboration of the *Summum Esse* seems also to lie within the zone of criticizability. What Hegel appears to be suggesting is that, kataphatic appearance notwithstanding, ontotheologies other than Romantic Intuitionism and its immediate ancestors, when examined more carefully, disclose a degenerate negativity of content. And this insight, expressed in symbolic terms in the equation of light and darkness, could be regarded as receiving its nonsymbolic codification in the transition of Being to Nothing which opens the self-constituting movement of Hegelian logic. Being, Hegel writes in the *Logic,* is the ineffable or unsayable (*ein Unsagbares*) (*Enc* #87, *GL8:*208), and Nothing represents the apotheosis of the unsayable. But, as Jean Hyppolite has persuasively argued, Hegelian logic, and Hegelian ontotheological discourse in general, is pitted against the hegemony of the ineffable in all and every manifestation.[33] Chapelle renders Hyppolite's insight specific to the theological field. For Chapelle, Hegel's theological enterprise is characterized by the attempt to banish assumptions of divine ineffability and unknowability that are deeply embedded within the ontotheological tradition.[34] At the very least, the obviousness of assumption must be banished, at the maximum—and here I play upon a figure of Wittgenstein—the spell of assumption must be broken. Hegelian theology, then, is nothing short of an apotropaic or spell-breaking activity. A token, even if a pretty formal one, of spell-breaking activity is the unmasking of the facade of the ontotheology of abstract being. If Hegel's deconstruction is correct, an ontotheology of Being cannot avoid hallowing Nothing, the most extreme of apophatic designations within the ontotheological tradition. Given the asserted intimacy between metaphysics and theology, the spelling-out of the Nothing implied in Being also spells-out the theology of the Unknown God lurking in the shadow of the apparent kataphaticism of a theology of the *Summum Esse.*

Confidence in the ability of thought to reach the divine infinite is therefore, for Hegel, a necessary but not sufficient condition for avoiding negative theology. Thought must be fully disclosive of divine reality; otherwise, haunted by the unsayable,[35] and limited by the ungraspable other, it is trajected beyond Christianity's horizon of full subjective and objective transparence. In Hegelian texts Christianity is considered under a number of different rubrics. It is spoken of as the absolute religion (*die absolut Religion*), the consummate religion (*die vollendete Religion*), the revealed religion (*die geoffenbarte Religion*), and the revelatory religion (*die offenbare Religion*). These rubrics dominate in certain texts, the last mentioned in *PS,* the second-last in the *Enc,* the first two in *LPR 1.* But whatever the rubric, it is Christianity's keynote that the very nature of divine reality is disclosed, and disclosed to a being capable of both comprehension and appreciation. Comprehension and appreciation demand an openness that is only present in a mode of cognition, both holistic and noninstrumental. To this modality of cognition Hegel sometimes gives the name of reason (*Vernunft*), but equally often he names it Spirit (*Geist*) and self-consciously places it within the Lutheran manifold.

By way of concluding the opening section of this chapter, it might be worth commenting briefly on a feature of the Hegelian treatment of the Christian theological tradition that may seem especially puzzling, namely, Hegel's quite affirmative appraisal of the mystical and, by implication, mysticism as a specification of Christianity. At the beginning of this section we noted Hegel's avowal of the normativity of the Pauline view of Christianity. This, however, is interesting not only because of Paul's emphasis upon revelation but also because of the latter's revision of the meaning of mystery. In St. Paul's hands, mystery is read antithetically to mean revealed. As Chapelle has hinted, the Hegelian reprise of Paul extends to this revision.[36] The mysterious, or the mystical (*Enc* #82 *zu*), is not the undisclosed but rather the disclosed. The reprise of the Pauline revision makes Hegel at one with the attitude characteristic of the early Church Fathers who associated *to mysterion* with the definitive soteriological revelation of God in Jesus Christ.[37] The reprise has the effect that, notwithstanding all the evidence against the mystics, Hegel does not apply the label of negative theology to them. Nowhere does he suppose they are the worshippers of the *Deus Occultus* as Luther claimed.[38] Here Hegel clearly departs from Luther and, perhaps, the dominant attitude in the Lutheran tradition. Though Hegel parallels Luther's attack on, and impatience with, negative theology, he does not unearth the same targets. Neither Pseudo-Dionysius himself or the Dionysian tradition in theology come in for attack; Meister Eckhart, who cannot but be understood as an exemplar, even if original translator, of this tradition comes in for high praise. This praise is such that one hardly suspects that Eckhart is the initiator of apophatic vocabulary in the German ontotheological tradition,[39] prepared to go to the very extreme apophatic reaches and call God "nothing." Hegel ignores the apophatic vocabulary of Eckhart, as he also tends to ignore its presence in other mystics. Given the evidence of excision of such vocabulary from his own discourse,[40] there is reason to suggest he ignores it deliberately. Reflective of an operation that he seems to perform on his own discourse, Hegel exercises on the discourse of the mystics what might be called *apophatic erasure*.[41] For Hegel, it appears, what is truly significant is the epistemological and ontological brazenness of mysticism (*Enc* #82), which, Lutheran orthodoxy's criticisms notwithstanding, remains thoroughly faithful to the revelatory essence of Christianity. Hegel is neither disingenuous nor strategic when he writes:

> For the mystical (*das Mystische*) is not concealment of a secret (*ist nicht Vorborgenheit eines Geheimnisses*), or ignorance (*oder Unwissenheit*), but consists in the self knowing itself to be one with the divine being or that this therefore is revealed (*dieses also geoffenbart ist*). (*PS* #722, Miller p. 437, *GL2*:550)

There can be little doubt that in his typification Hegel has highlighted a much neglected aspect of mysticism—what might be characterized, following Joseph Maréchal, the realization of *presence*.[42] For Hegel, however, the presence of the divine to the human does not constitute merely *a* core feature of mysticism but *the* core. Mysticism in the full and proper sense, therefore, is not merely different to any and all varieties of negative theology; it represents negative theology's antitype.

Section 1.2 Narrative and the Deus Revelatus

In the previous section we saw Hegel's reprise of the Pauline reading of Christianity. Nevertheless, revelation ascription does more than situate Christianity as one example among others of a species of religion called "revealed religion." For Hegel, Christianity does not stand on the same footing as Judaism or Islam, which given certain understandings of revelation (e.g., Enlightenment, Fichte) could be paired with Christianity.[43] Accepting and, or course, exegeting the Pauline definition of Christianity implies, for Hegel, the claim of Christianity's incommensurability, since what is characteristic of revelation is not that it is a truth spoken from beyond about the beyond to an immanent other devoid of its own power or authority, but rather a genuine act of 'nearing' in which the divine becomes fully rendered, fully present in the nondivine. Yet, as hinted already, ascription in Hegelian texts is ambiguous between two different understandings: (1) a descriptive, first-level understanding; (2) an interpretive, second-level understanding. Appeal to Paul or Luther does not always guarantee that a merely descriptive understanding is being supported. General shifts in the level of discourse, specifically from focus upon the event of revelation to definition of the divine, undermine the descriptive, first-level understanding of revelation. Hegel's use of the platonic construct "God is not envious" provides a token of just such undermining. But the discursive shift specifies itself, announces itself even more loudly, in the shift of understanding with regard to revelation. It is the view of the *Enc,* for instance, that God defines himself as an act of revelation or manifestation (#381 *zu*). Here Hegel clearly moves from understanding (1) to understanding (2). In doing so, Hegel places himself in a tensional relationship with Luther and Lutheran orthodoxy. Yet, Hegel cannot be assimilated without further ado to his patristic and medieval predecessors who comfortably shift from the descriptive to the interpretive, ontotheological level of reflection and discourse. For Hegel, the secret of Christianity is the god of Christianity, or simply God. But God is not adequately rendered in such constructs as divine grace, divine freedom, or divine love, though Hegel neither denies that these constructs are theologically useful—particularly the last two[44]—nor neglects to make use of them. Rather, he takes it as evident that the fact that God is disclosed is not accidental to God's definition, indeed, is central to it. To point to the distinctiveness of the Hegelian move is not to suggest absolute originality. Ernst Benz, who has if not singlehandedly, at least most ably, painted the mystical backdrop of German Idealism, could point to Oetinger's construal of God as *Ens manifestativum sui* as a precursor of the Hegelian *Deus Revelatus,*[45] though he would, perhaps, agree with Alexandre Koyré that in his construal Oetinger is simply annotating, maybe even anointing, the vision of the divine held by the earlier German speculative mystic, Jacob Boehme.[46]

To delineate the divine as an act of revelation is, for Hegel, to insist that God is Spirit (*Geist*). To elaborate the one is to elaborate the other. As an act of revelation or manifestation, Spirit involves movement, process (*Enc* #378 *zu*), and differentiation which is at once let be, yet overcome and assimilated (ibid.; *LPR 1* 1824 E 119, G 36; E 142–143, G 56–57). A text from the 1827 Lectures on religion offers a fairly comprehensive description:

> Spirit, if it is thought immediately, simply, and at rest, is not spirit; for spirit's essential character is to be altogether active. More exactly, it is the activity of self-manifesting. Spirit that does not manifest or reveal itself is something dead. "Manifesting" signifies "becoming for an other." As "becoming for an other" it enters into antithesis, into distinction in general, and thus is it a finitizing of spirit. (*LPR 1* 1827 E 176, G 85)

On the level of description the *Enc* adds little to the above. Hegel again joins together differentiation and manifestation (#383–384). But one can sense the addition of a criteriological note: without differentiation or manifestation, Spirit does not achieve full actuality (*Wirklichkeit*), or otherwise stated, full personhood or subjectivity. Even the divine, or perhaps especially the divine, is a result, not a given, not an 'immediate' in Hegel's own technical terminology. It is *PS* which introduces the image complex that subsequently accompanies much of Hegel's discourse about God, i.e., images of journey, exile, and homecoming, though the ideas of which these images are the compact, symbolic expression are present in his earliest thought. While the main concern of *PS* is human becoming in its individual and social-historic aspect, its epistemic and culture-forming aspect, the text as a whole, especially in the Preface and sections 6–8, suggests a larger horizon of becoming than the anthropological sphere. Spirit and divine subjectivity are equated in #23 of the *PS,* just as the identity is implied elsewhere, e.g., #20. Thus, when Hegel subsumes the process or, to use Mark Taylor's word, the "wayfaring,"[47] character of Spirit under the meta-image of the circle (*der Kreis*), he cannot be thought to have merely human subjectivity as his referent. Spirit, or Subject, Hegel writes:

> is the process of its own becoming, the circle that presupposes its end as its goal *(als seinen Zweck),* having its end also as its beginning; and only by being worked out to its end, is it actual. (Miller p. 10, *GL2:*23)

While Hegel is clearly at pains to emphasize the connection between beginning and end, process and result, aim and destination, he is not to be thought in his advocacy of the circle to be promoting a figure of self-cancelling movement. 'Return' is an intrinsic element of circularity, but Hegel does not say that in every material respect the end is the same as the beginning. The true (*das Wahre*), Hegel is anxious to announce in the same paragraph, is not the simple unity of beginning but the complex, differentiated unity of an end constituted by doubling, opposition, and negation. In Hegel's circle the line (process) is not destroyed. Both the *Enc* and *LPR* substantiate and amplify the ontotheological insight of *PS*. Beginning and end are locutions which are understood to apply to the divine (*Enc* #379 *zu*, #381 *zu*; *LPR 1* 1821 MS E 84, G 4; E 221, G 130; E 225–7, G 134–136), and the fact that they apply signals a significant ontotheological departure. Whereas in the classical ontotheological tradition God is alpha and omega as the still point of reference for the restless, troubled world of becoming, in Hegel, alpha and omega specify the *terminus a quo* and the *terminus ad quem* of a divine process of self-constitution. Revision, however, has a much broader scope than this.

Hegel wishes to situate himself within the mainstream ontotheological tradition, and to facilitate doing so he is prepared, at least for the purposes of protocol, to accept the identification of Being and God. But this acceptance, perhaps most to the fore in Hegel's two major logical works, is, as most students of Hegel are willing to confess, quite preliminary.[48] Identification will turn out not merely to be inadequate but false, unless immediate, abstract Being gives way to Being as process, and issues in Being enriched, deepened, and fully comprehensive. Hegel is eloquent in *SL:*

> The richest is therefore the most concrete and subjective, and that which returns (*Zurücknehmende*) into the simplest depth (*die einfachste Tiefe*) is the most-powerful and all-embracing (*Ubergreifendste*). The highest, most concentrated point is the pure personhood (*ist die reine Persönlichkeit*). . . . (*SL* 841, *GL5*:349)

Hegel is here speaking of the divine Idea. He might have been speaking of Spirit which represents the optimum of subjectivity and personhood. If the Idea or Spirit still can be meaningfully included within the discourse of Being, as Gerhard Schmidt after Heidegger claims,[49] nevertheless, Being in Hegel cannot be understood after the traditional manner. In Hegel, the last thing God is is simple, immediate, static Being (*Enc* #87–88). For Hegel, Being is the emptiest of all categories and thus in itself insufficient as a characterization of the divine. But what is denied to abstract Being is not denied to Being considered in the most concrete sense. In the spirit of reconciliation, Hegel redefines Being in such a way that it fits his description of the divine as realized end, achievement, and, of course, process.[50] In both the *Enc* and *LPR* passages can be found where God is called Being, but not Being *tout court*. Being is qualified by adjectives such as active, restless (*Enc* #378 *zu*).

While Hegel attempts to remain within the received coordinates of the ontotheological tradition, it is clear that he is engaged in an act of subversion in which the hegemony of Being is effectively challenged and overcome by Act. Undoubtedly the move is overdetermined and reflects no one influence. If we are to take Hegel at his word, his revision is called for by Christian optics regarding the nature of God. To cite Fichte's intuition concerning the primacy of Act (*Tathandlung*) over Being as a proximate precedent is not to say that Hegel is grossly mistaken with regard to the cause of revision,[51] but simply to suggest that this foundational move of the *Wissenschaftslehre* provides warrant, credibility, and reinforcement for a move Hegel feels justified in making on other grounds. The radicality of Hegel's move is not lessened by recalling that the classical ontotheological tradition, particularly the medieval scholastic tradition which claimed Aristotle as a philosophical support, was able to conceive the divine as pure act (*actus purus*). Just as Hegel can speak the language of Being, he can speak the language of pure act (*LPR 3* 1821 MS E 78, G 16). But as with the meaning of Being the meaning of *actus purus* has shifted dramatically. In the classical ontotheology of Aquinas,[52] for instance, *actus purus* points to the nullity of potentiality in God and, thus, the nullity of becoming. For Hegel, by contrast, God is only as the movement from potential to actual, that is, God is only as the process of actualization.

There are two ontotheological views in particular against which Hegel posits his dynamic process view of the *Deus Revelatus,* i.e., Schelling and Spinoza. We have already commented upon Hegel's pastiche of Schelling's Identity Philosophy in *PS*. While *PS* represents the definitive public rupture between Schelling and Hegel, *DE,* in its modest rehabilitation of the status of Fichte vis-à-vis Schelling, represents a portent of such a rupture. On the reading of *PS,* Identity Philosophy is a rigid monism which rules out movement, activity, and becoming in the divine precisely because difference and negativity are ruled out. Hegel's reading is not flattering: Schelling's vision of God amounts to viewing God as a tautology (#23). Caricature or not, Hegel is vehement in combating any vision of the divine which does not include moments of exile and return. The deficiency of Identity Philosophy can also be considered from a more specifically gnoseological point of view. Hegel diagnoses that not only does Identity Philosophy exclude the possibility of infinite knowledge of the divine, it also excludes divine knowledge of itself. If manifestation is possible only through differentiation, such also is the case with regard to knowledge.[53] Thus, despite Schelling's assertion of the coincidence of thought and being[54] and the actuality of knowledge, Hegel denies coincidence and denies knowledge as prerogatives of the initial state of the divine. Coincidence is a terminal reality, as is knowledge. Yet it is not improper to speak of the divine from the point of view of the realized state.[55] *PS* certainly does. So also does the *Enc* (#564).

Spinoza is the other foil against whom Hegel defines his own Christian allegiance to God as Spirit. In a certain sense Spinoza is *the* foil, for at least in the view of *PS* (Preface) Schelling's Identity Philosophy is reducible in the last instance to Spinoza's philosophy of Substance. Conciliatory gestures such as the declaration that Spirit is not merely Substance but Subject as well (#28, 29) do little to disguise the fact that Hegel is speaking much more of an either/or than a both/and. Given the affiliation, if not filiation from Hegel's critical point of view, between the thought of Spinoza and Schelling, it should not be surprising that Spinoza's Substance is subjected to essentially the same criticisms as Schelling's Absolute. And this, indeed, is the case: in Spinoza the divine is perceived as static, lifeless, rendered once and for all. Again the fairness of Hegel's judgment might be questioned, with some Spinoza scholars ready to argue for the dynamism of Substance, particularly under its aspects of *Natura Naturans.*[56] Fair or not, Hegel's judgment of the ontotheology of Substance is both consistent and persistent. In continuity with *PS,* the *Enc* concludes that the Christian avowal of God as Spirit is the direct contrary of Spinoza's support of an abstract, ultimately impersonal divine. The judgment of *LHP 3* is similar. Here Hegel covers the entire range of objections against Spinoza, but at the center again is his claim that Spinozist Substance is a rigid identity (E 252; *GL19:*368) that is the direct contrary of Spirit as active and living divine (E 258; *GL19:*378). Of especial concern to Hegel is the issue whether the positing of an ontotheology of Substance implies the positing of an impersonal divine. Hegel rules that it does, but it is interesting to note his grounds, since he shares with Spinoza many of the same objections against the dominant Judeo-Christian 'personal' depiction of the divine. A number of these objections will be unfolded in later chapters (see chapter 3 below) and need not detain us here. In assessing whether a view of the divine is personal or impersonal, Hegel has some definite criteria in mind. One of these criteria is the gnoseological one of self-consciousness. If self-consciousness can be predicated, it almost automatically follows that one can predicate personhood or subjectivity. Hegel is thoroughly unpersuaded, however, that Spinoza has accounted for 'the moment of self-consciousness' in Being (E 288; *GL19:*410). Aware that *thought* is posited by Spinoza as one of the two attributes fully expressive of Substance, Hegel thinks that its place has been mis-assigned. Spinoza posits thought as a fully realized given. For Hegel, thought as a given is not thought. Thought is only possible as result.

Bildundsroman and Beyond

It is not unusual in Hegelian commentary to remark on the similarity between *PS* and the *Bildungsroman* genre of literature typical of early German Romanticism, the central focus of which is the becoming or formation of selfhood.[57] The 'how' of this formation may differ from one author to the next, though usually the emphasis falls upon the situation of alienation as the indispensable condition for the achievement of the desired result. The literary genre testifies again and again that the self is only by negation of what it is as given, by loss or surrender of attitude, emotion, perspective, and way of being it takes for granted. *Bildungsroman* is founded upon the paradoxical estimate of human being or the estimate of the paradox that is the human situation: the self which is, is not, the self which is not, is. Or, to use the hermeneutical language of Paul Ricoeur, the cultured self is only 'by detour'. Among exponents of the genre, perhaps Goethe most clearly sees the basic lineaments and can separate the essential from the inessential features.[58] Werther might possibly be regarded as an instance of self-formation, yet from the maturer point of view of *Wilhelm Meisters Lehrjahre,* neither Werther nor his death exhaust the possibilities of the genre, nor provide its paradigm. *Bildungsroman* can be separated in principle from its attendant thanatology, and Goethe does so separate it when he masterfully adopts alchemical language to announce the genre's generic disposition.[59] The self is the alchemical opus par excellence, the task of forging an identity from the crude *prima materia* from which it starts by submitting to the crucible in which gold is separated out from the dross. As task, the self is all act and encounter, its encounter initially taking the form of a cultural world that it suffers because it is not owned, an experience of alienation and loss, it having surrendered its former home and its comforting pieties. As result, the self is all mastery, depth, and comprehensiveness. Fully constituted and realized, it lives on a deeper and more expansive level of existence, experience, passion, and self-awareness.[60] One might say that the self lives a different order of reality than the initial crudity from which it necessarily must be forged. Fully constituted and realized, the self has expunged the eccentric, the merely idiosyncratic. The eccentric is the dross of the accidental, the *caput mortuum* to be laid aside.[61] The obverse side is the elevation of properties of selfhood that are truly universal and nonaccidental. 'Journeying' declares, moreover, that these properties are not in the least bit abstract: they are deliverances of experience and are concretized and valorized by being personally appropriated. Not a natural possession of all and each, universal properties exist only as a narrative, elective, taking possession.

Given Goethian appraisal of education (*Bildung*), it is not implausible to construe *PS* as providing a discursive equivalent to, or even generalizing translation of, *Bildungsroman.* The discursive language of becoming, process, alienation, exile, rupture of natural consciousness, fully realized subjectivity, the metaphorical language of journey, road, homecoming, circle, as well as the actual sketch of the genesis of self-consciousness and reason in part 1, all warrant the claim that *PS* is engaged, at the very least, in a collateral enterprise. But there are grounds for saying more. While admittedly the emphasis in the first part of *PS* is dominantly epistemological, that text could be regarded as unfolding, in a manner trimmed of adventitious detail, the basic pattern of self-realization rendered by *Bildungsroman*. That is to say, Hegel's account of the movement toward full self-recognition, and appropriation by detour through ever richer and more adequate perspectives and comportments toward reality, is nothing less than a metalevel discursive translation of *Bildungsroman*.[62]

Though the hypothesis of relation between *Bildungsroman* and *PS* represents a genuine insight, care must be exercised so as not to proceed to more extravagant claims. Such temptations include: (1) the temptation to claim that the observed relation between *Bildungsroman* and the first part of *PS* explains and defines the nature and scope of *PS* as a whole; (2) the temptation to claim that the relation between *Bildungsroman* and *PS* can be extrapolated without qualification onto the Hegelian corpus as a whole. Neither temptation has evidential support; both must be regarded as potentially misleading. Even a cursory reading of the second part of *PS* would pose a serious challenge to the first claim, for clearly it is concerned less with biography than history, less with the individual than the community, and one almost wants to say, less with ontogeny than phylogeny. This is not to deny that the more social-historical trajectory of the second part displays a developmental pattern similar to that discernible in the first, indeed, that in broad respects the patterns are isomorphic. But the shift in the subject of inquiry from paradigmatic individual self to community and, more specifically, the shift in discourse from concern with the pedagogy of the individual to concern with the pedagogy of the community within which the individual is constituted is an important one. As well as correcting the individualist pretension of the modern age, particularly the Romantic focus upon genius, Hegel is convinced that the more encompassing socio-historic vision explicated in the second part can more nearly situate human being and, by doing so, can provide the broad lines of definition. The socio-historic concern, of course, is by no means original to Hegel. Ready at hand in his own cultural environment is Herder's Romantic view of the organic development of history,[63] as also is Lessing's eloquent depiction of the pedagogy of the human race over time.[64] Thus *PS* is not univocally determined by one narrative influence, but rather a number of narrative projects are there endorsed, assimilated, and, it could be argued, transcended.

Even allowing for a democracy of narrative interest and influence in *PS,* however, with respect to commitment to a particular narrative form or structure *Bildungsroman* may have a certain priority. Certainly, one cannot speak as if two culturally available narrative patterns simply existed side by side in Hegel's text. And the reason is not that the alignment of the individual and the socio-historic is in itself self-destructively incoherent, but rather that a fundamental difference exists on the level of narrative structure. While it is the case that, as attested by their respective exemplars, both pedagogic patterns with which Hegel's text is in conversation envisage movement from a raw, uninformed state of selfhood (individual and socio-historic) to fully complete selfhood, the narrative patterns unfold differently. In the case of *Bildungsroman,* the pattern is dramatic: negation, alienation, and pain constitute the detour which, it so happens, is the route of progress. By contrast, the available developmental models of history authorize no such drama in the organic unfolding of more complete, more fully self-conscious community. Commentators have remarked often enough on Hegel's difficulties in unfolding two versions of pedagogy in *PS;* yet such an enterprise would not be merely flawed in detail, or forced, but foundationally impossible unless a single narrative pattern elaborated itself in the distinct narrative fields. *PS* definitely decides in favor of the more dramatic account of the *Bildungsroman,* and, accordingly, in his commitment to this model Hegel has, at once, a lens in and through which to see contradiction as a motor of history and a way of envisaging the complementarity of individual and socio-historic becoming.

By way of summary, then, it could be said that, as a focus and concern having a different background and independent claims to attention, the presence of an account of socio-historic dynamics is not explained by viewing it without remainder as the extrapolation of *Bildungsroman* narrative onto the historical field. Yet the amended and more modest *Bildungsroman* thesis can be more plausibly sustained, namely, that Hegel's commitment effects, or helps to effect, a revision of perception regarding the narrative dynamic of history. It should also be noted that announcing the presence, and ultimate complementarity, of two narrative fields in *PS* in no wise implies that the narrative horizon of *PS* is exhausted by narratives of a thoroughgoing anthropological type. The profoundly theological or ontotheological dimension of *PS* is, for the moment, only put in parentheses. When the parentheses are removed, it will be seen that the ultimate subject of becoming is neither the individual nor the community but God and that, consequently, in addition to the individual and socio-historical narratives delineated above, Hegel, even in *PS,* is concerned with a narrative at once radical and absolutely encompassing, a narrative whose grammatical subject is the transcendental signified much deplored by deconstruction.

If there are serious problems regarding the first claim, i.e., the claim that *PS* represents a discursive translation of *Bildungsroman,* there are even more serious problems regarding the second. In unmodified form this is the claim that not only *PS* but the Hegelian corpus as a whole is best characterized as a species of *Bildungsroman.* Such a view, however, is patently unsupportable given even a résumé of the content of mature works like the *Enc, LPR, LHP, LPH,* etc. The lack of evidence has not deterred some Hegelian admirers from suggesting such a reading.[65] Caprice not being one of the more common features of Hegelian hermeneutic, unequivocal supporters are few. But an amended version of this second claim in which *Bildungsroman* is regarded, not simply as the rendering of a particular narrative of human development departing in significant ways from the traditional model or models,[66] but as the provider of a basic grammar of becoming applicable to socio-historic as well as individual process, is more plausible and thus clearly more supportable. On this reading, Hegel's depiction of the dialectical process of history is a symptom of a commitment to a narrative grammar of a dramatic type generated within the horizon of *Bildungsroman.*

Yet the amended version of the second claim may still be as antitheological in inspiration as the claim is in its unmodified form and may effectively amount to a decision to restrict narrative in Hegel to the anthropological horizon, even if the horizon is interpreted in the broadest way possible. The restriction normally cannot be taken for granted, given Hegel's theological elaboration of the becoming of the divine itself. Arguments against the hegemony of the theological, as has already been suggested, take a variety of routes, from claims that Hegel misunderstood himself to claims of willful deception. On the presumption of the antecedent improbability that a position asserted in varying circumstances over a period exceeding twenty years would or could be an attempt to deceive a suspicious public, let no further word be said concerning the last mentioned antitheological option. The first antitheological option is clearly the more plausible of the two, yet it also is not without defect. In the absence of specifiable criteria as to what would count as a proper understanding of one's own work, the charge of misunderstanding remains irrefutable but, precisely for that reason, not overly perspicuous. In any event, there is a thin line between Hegel's asserted misunderstanding of himself and the creative need to misunderstand Hegel, who may have understood himself all too well. The antitheologically aspirated form of the amended version of the second claim fails, therefore, to be persuasive. Failure, here, nevertheless leaves open an even more radical possibility, a possibility, I think, hinted at by Pannenberg,[67] namely, that Hegel's theological or ontotheological narrative is determined with regard to structure by the narrative grammar of *Bildungsroman*. This question will be broached shortly, though no definitive answer should be expected in this essentially introductory chapter. Before the question is raised, however, it is apposite to attempt some preliminary description of Hegel's ontotheological narrative vis-à-vis the two anthropological narratives we have been discussing.

The Hegelian view of the divine does not imply positing the existence of a third narrative field alongside the two anthropological narrative fields we have been discussing, but rather implies that the narrative field of the divine encompasses the others and determines them to be regions of its own elaboration. In other words, the becoming of fully developed subjectivity of both individual and community are elements of the becoming of divine subjectivity. Espousal of this view is marked in Hegelian texts. The Preface of *PS,* which identifies truth with God and Spirit, insists that truth is the whole (*das Wahre ist das Ganze*) (#20). And the whole is not a given but a reality constituted by an activity of alienation in and through the finite. The whole is a differentiated totality, not a simple unity. When Hegel critiques the attempt to render God in propositional form (#20), the non-narrative givenness of the divine is certainly not the only ontotheological presupposition disavowed, but it is clearly included. All of these points are repeated in later Hegelian texts. *LPR 1* is a good example. The divine cannot be grasped in non-narrative propositional terms (1824 E 308, G 212–213). At the same time, its narrative enactment is global rather than local (1821 MS E 230, G 139), encompassing everything within itself, the infinite, the finite, and the elevation of the finite to the infinite (ibid. E 221, G 130).

The encompassing nature of the divine narrative field and trajectory may be considered from two different points of view: (1)*horizontally,* that is, as existing on essentially the same level as the two anthropological narratives but fully inclusive of them, all reality is storied between the beginning and end of the becoming of the divine; (2) *vertically,* that is, the very fact that the narrative of divine becoming is the parameter within which all reality is comprehended, and that human becoming thereby is included as an aspect of divine becoming, places the narrative of the divine on a different level to the other two narratives. The first point is almost trivial, and even the second would hardly be worth mentioning were it not for the fact that certain Hegelian commentators, who see clearly Hegel's theological framing of history, do not equally clearly distinguish Hegelian narrative of the divine from a relatively simple first-order recapitulation of the Christian narrative of salvation history. A case in point is Mark Taylor. In *Journeys to Selfhood,* Taylor diagnoses the theological narrative commitment of Hegel and thereby dissociates himself from an anthropological reduction.[68] But Taylor seems to identify Hegelian narrative with the Christian narrative which has creation and eschaton as its alpha and omega, the drama of fall, alienation, and redemption as its center. In making this identification, however, Taylor perhaps does not pay sufficient attention to Hegelian ontotheological narrative's full extent or correctly assess its radicality: the former, because it is clear that, for Hegel, divine enactment is in process anterior to creation; the latter, because Taylor does not specify, as Hegel does, what the enactment of the divine in history has to do with the definition of the divine itself.[69] And it is only if Hegelian commitment to the Christian narrative is further examined and seen to be comprehended by an encompassing narrative that the full radicality of Hegel's position comes to light. Relative to the Christian narrative, or metanarrative, to use Bernstein's locution, the Hegelian narrative of the *Deus Revelatus* is a higher-order narrative which must be seen to reshape the Christian narrative and alter its theological or ontotheological implications. Substantively speaking, what reshaping and altering occur need not occupy us here, but narrative reshaping and theological alteration will be specified in detail in the ensuing chapters. For present purposes, the general point concerning the nonidentity of the Hegelian narrative of the divine and the Christian narrative of salvation history will suffice.

What commentators such as Taylor seem to have missed is set in relief by commentators such as Iwan Iljin and Eric Schmidt, both of whom comment in detail upon the encompassing scope and radicality of Hegelian narrative.[70] For both, the depth of Hegelian commitment to narrative is indicated only approximately by appeal to Hegel's understanding of the relationship of the divine to human history, which is the content of the Christian narrative. The commitment is authentically specified when the narrative of the divine is seen to *enfold* all other narrative fields, including the Christian narrative of God's acts in history and, just as importantly (if not more so), when the narrative of the divine is seen to *unfold* itself in all other narrative fields.

Earlier discussion of the possibility of hermeneutic imperialism with regard to *Bildungsroman* narrative put in parentheses the radical question of whether even Hegel's ontotheological narrative could be construed as a species of *Bildungsroman.* It is time to remove the parentheses. Again, as in previous rehearsal of the relation of *Bildungsroman* narrative to other narrative fields there are perspicuous and nonperspicuous ways of posing the question of relation. The question is posed nonperspicuously to the degree to which the obvious similarity of narrative structure of *Bildungsroman* and ontotheological narrative is read to imply that the real subject of ontotheological narrative is the individual self, with the theological frame being nothing more than a disguise. Without repeating numerous earlier arguments against theological exdenomination, it might be observed here that to read Hegel in this way is to make him look like an amended version of the Fichte of the *Wissenschaftslehre* and the prototype of Stirner's ego-philosophy, which charitably might be described as narrative Cartesianism.[71] By contrast, the question is posed perspicuously when, on the basis of observed isomorphism of narrative structure, the hypothesis is advanced that the elaboration of the becoming of the divine might owe something to the dramatic, agonic model of becoming advanced by *Bildungsroman.* The question or hypothesis has at least prima facie plausibility, given both the exactness of the match and the fact that it was, in principle, possible for Hegel to pattern the becoming of God in a unilinear, evolutionary way. The modesty of the hypothesis should be underlined. It in no wise implies that the narrative structure of the divine is *explained* by considering it an extrapolation from *Bildungsroman.* The depth and extent of Hegel's cultural appropriation forbids such a reduction, even if Hegel's debt to this forceful narrative proposal should not be shied away from on principle. The possibilities for specifically theological appropriation, for instance, were not exhausted by the unknown God of Kant and Romantic Intuitionism, the God of Wolffian natural theology or Spinoza's Substance. Available to Hegel from the Swabian speculative-mystical tradition was Oetinger's dynamic conception of God who is defined by act of manifestation. At the archeological bedrock of this tradition lay Jacob Boehme (1575–1624) and his view of the self-manifesting God who gains fully complete subjectivity or personhood by way of exile, alienation, and pain. And there is now something of a consensus that Hegel had access even to this archeological aspect of the speculative-mystical tradition before his entry into the public sphere of discourse.[72] Even superficial knowledge of Boehme's elaboration of the dramatic narrative of the divine would make extrapolation from *Bildungsroman* to ontotheology unnecessary, since a direct precedent for Hegel's nonstandard view already existed within the theological field. But there is no reason to suppose that two narrative proposals (with different subjects in mind) would not be experienced as mutually reinforcing, and that together they might not provoke Hegel into the narrative direction he took, without it being claimed, of course, that together *Bildungsroman* and Boehmian narrative proposals *determine* that narrative direction.

Anaclasis and Synclasis: Prolepsis and Analepsis

Rationale for the selection of the hermeneutic pair 'anaclasis' (narrative openness) and 'synclasis' (narrative closure), as well as the determination of their basic meaning, having already been tendered in the Introduction, obviates the need for introduction here. From the very beginning of Hegel's public intellectual career, anaclasis is considered a disvalue, synclasis a value. In texts such as *FK* and *DE*, Hegel's value scheme is worked out in terms of a comparison between the philosophical systems of Fichte and Schelling,[73] with Schelling, in effect being the yardstick by which Fichte is judged. Whatever the debits of Schelling's transcendental Idealism—and Hegel shows signs of intuiting a few even in this earliest period—disavowal of anaclasis is not one of them. Moreover, it is Hegel's view, and here he is supported by a sizable number of twentieth-century commentators and critics,[74] that the Fichtean system achieves its ultimate determination in the third and not in the first proposition of the *Wissenschaftslehre*. From Hegel's Schellingianly informed perspective, the third proposition, which formally specifies that A ought (*sollen*) to be equal to A + -A, signifies a radical anaclasis where no closure is reachable in principle. Thus, anaclasis points to the ineluctable horizon of finitude within which selfhood cannot come to full reflective transparence.[75] The not-A, the other-than-self, is never fully assimilated, and obscurity and opacity are inexcisable elements of the story of self. However congenial this view is to a Hegelian commentator such as Chapelle and post-Hegelians from Heidegger to Gadamer, Sartre to deconstruction,[76] Hegel deems the view to be seriously flawed. He rules that full self-transparence, full appropriation of the (ad)venture of self is, in fact, possible but is possible only on the basis of narrative closure or synclasis. The becoming of fully realized selfhood presupposes "the sense of an ending," to use Frank Kermode's felicitous phrase, and it is from the perspective of ending that all aspects of narrative (ad)venture are clarified.

Synclasis, for Hegel, may be understood in a minimal or maximal fashion. Minimally, synclasis is the condition of the possibility of the plenitude of meaning, whereas anaclasis secures only relative meaning. Maximally, synclasis affords the very condition of the possibility of meaning, where anaclasis subverts the very possibility. The maximal view represents Hegel's nonapologetic stance. As Seidel seems to have recognized, the anaclasis posited by the *Wissenschaftslehre,* or what he refers to as "the unrealizable eschatology" of the Fichtean system,[77] is ultimately accused of subverting meaning altogether by eschewing the context within which meaning is alone possible, i.e., a determinate horizon constituted by closure. For Hegel, a context bedeviled by semantic fracture, opacity, and constitutional lack of certitude cannot sustain meaning. *DE* seems to bear out Seidel's point. In a language redolent of his mature works, Hegel complains of the inability of Fichtean self-consciousness to complete a circle (E 45–46). The deficiency is, however, just as much the reverse. The inability to maintain circularity (constituted by closure) crucially undermines the possibility of self-consciousness or full-blown subjectivity. Hegel believes the deficiency to be endemic to the Fichtean system. In his view Fichte's translation of the problematic of closure from the theoretical to the practical level does nothing to correct what is at once a semantic and a narrative deficiency,[78] and the former because the latter. The suggestion that one approximates closure through act still leaves closure having more the status of heuristic idea than realized fact. The iteration of act evokes the sense of an ending, a realized eschatology; it does not bring it into being. We have suggested that narrative deficiency, specifically anaclasis, is at the root of semantic deficiency, a semantic deficiency which, on Hegel's maximal view, is radical. To this we might add the opinion that, just as there exist in Hegel maximal and minimal views regarding semantic deficiency, so also there exist maximal and minimal views respecting the depth of narrative deficiency. On the minimal view, anaclasis is a narrative deficiency, but one can still intelligibly speak of narrative. On the maximal view, anaclasis destroys the possibility of narrative, and where anaclasis is found narrative has been subverted. Again, when Hegel is not taking an apologetic stance, he seems to adopt the second and maximal view and, in so doing, speaks not only to his present but the future. The maximal reading certainly sharpens the debate and focuses choice: narrative or non-narrative, Hegel or Fichte, Hegel or deconstruction.

The pro and con of *FK* and *DE* concern basic foundational principles. The argument with Fichte continues in *PS* with Hegelian constructs such as 'circle', 'whole', and 'return' drawing a line of demarcation between sufficient and deficient narrative positions (#17–23). The base of the attack broadens in Hegel's logical works to include all proponents of anaclasis, though even here Fichte continues to be the exemplar (*Enc* #93–95; *SL* E 150–151). Against the anaclastic view of subjectivity Hegel submits that the realization of subjectivity requires *synclasis.* Thus despite Fichtean (and non-Fichtean) avocation of the narrative dimension of subjectivity, in the context of the omission of narrative closure, only the narratively degenerate subjectivity of finitude is articulated.

Hegel in neither *FK* nor *DE* provides a theological translation of the Fichetean self as subject of becoming and radical *anaclasis.* The Fichtean self is ambiguous between human and divine ascription, but finitude is, in either case, its ultimate mark.[79] With *PS* the debate between *anaclasis* and *synclasis* assumes theological form. The Hegelian articulation of Spirit as divine, self-differentiating activity clearly wishes to steer between the Scylla of non-narrative monism and the Charybdis of a divine, all process, no term, all journey, no arrival. Hegel insists upon process, yet equally insists on the result (#22–23). If God is a narrative, he is a narrative of homecoming. The image of the Odyssian adventure evoked in the Preface is a perspicuous one: Odysseus not only wanders but ends his journey by returning to the place he left. His peregrination shapes a circle. It is possible to journey without conclusion, to wander the labyrinth, to be erring in Mark Taylor's sense.[80] In that case, however, Odysseus would not be the appropriate figure, but rather a Theseus deprived of Persephone's salvific thread. The narrative matrix of the divine in *PS,* as supported by the odyssian figure, does not articulate the labyrinth in a process of erring. If *PS* manages to explicitly theologize the contrast between anaclasis and synclasis, Hegel's very general treatment of the 'spurious infinite' (*die schlechte Unendlichkeit*) in his logical works, it could be said, is unable to keep the theological factor repressed.[81] It is in *LPR,* however, that the theological framing of synclasis and anaclasis, and their opposition, receives definite expression. The critique of anaclasis predicated of the divine is to the fore in *LPR 1* (1824 E 308, G 212–213; E 422–423, G 305). The rich discussion of the 1821 manuscript is especially worth recalling. The 'mystical', which Hegel avers is nothing more nor less than the becoming of the divine (E 249, G 157; E 254, G 162), is both encompassing and of consummate shape and definition. Hegel writes:

> And when we say 'God', this word signifies the absolute all encompassing fulfillment (*allbefassenden Erfüllung*), the truth of everything [that subsists] as the world of finitude and appearance. (E 230, G 139)

The passage is compact. It certainly means that the divine is the telos of all finitude. This much Aristotle or Aquinas could assert. But, for Hegel, the divine is equally the telos of itself,[82] and it can be telos only in so far as one of its constitutive aspects is not becoming but the 'have become', the actuality of synclasis as realized perfection.

Affirming the ultimate prerogatives of synclasis, Hegel, nevertheless, should not be construed as positing it to the exclusion of anaclasis. On the contrary, anaclasis is the indelible foundation of all modalities of narrative becoming. Without that opening into movement and process, and movement and process themselves, synclasis is redundant. For Hegel, the mutuality of anaclasis and synclasis must be affirmed. The mutuality can be caught symbolically in the reciprocity of line and circle.[83] Line indicates narrative trajectory, circle, the coming to completion and plentitude of narrative trajectory that ties together end and beginning. A deficiency of anaclasis in the long run constitutes a deficiency of synclasis, whether the narrative field is that of individual subject, the human community in history, or divine subjectivity. From this perspective, any approval, even of a marginal kind, is withdrawn from Identity Philosophy,[84] just as approval is ruled out for any ontotheology that stresses closure outside of the context of a drama of alienation and exile. Thus, whatever circularity is attributable in the context of Identity Philosophy, lacking dramatic line, it must be deficient on general Hegelian principles. The following passage from the preface of *PS* specifies a general rule that, in principle, applies to fields as distinct as individual human subjectivity, community in history, and divine selfhood:

> The circle that remains self-enclosed (*der in sich geschlossen*) and, like substance, holds its moments togehter, is an immediate relationship, one therefore which has nothing astonishing (*nicht verwundersame*) about it. (#32, Miller p. 18, *GL2*:33–34)

The context of the passage suggests that the accent falls on the condition of divine becoming. The text clearly proposes the deficiency of any circularity that does not maintain a narrative line of a dramatic sort, for I take it that "nothing astonishing" can be read to imply dramatic line as a counterpoint. This point is consistently reinforced throughout *LPR*.[85]

For the various narrative fields deemed important by Hegel, above all the fields of individual, communal, and divine becoming, anaclasis and synclasis are structurally supporting principles. Our second narrative pair, prolepsis and analepsis, serve the same function, and, as with the first pair, these two principles are intimately related to each other, in fact, are reciprocal. If anaclasis and synclasis, as basic principles of narrative, are at the same time basic conditions of meaning or sense, the same also can be claimed for prolepsis and analepsis. Unless the given and unrealized form of subjectivity in any of its modalities anticipates development and development's conclusion, and unless the realized form of subjectivity not merely ends development but fulfills it by recollecting and maintaining the integrity of the developmental process, Hegel is convinced that the specter of nonsense will not have been exorcised.[86] Prolepsis and analepsis work together to guarantee that the narrative horizon is teleological through and through and without semantic waste. These two narrative principles are neither more nor less important than anaclasis and synclasis. If, in one sense, it seems plausible to claim that narrative openness and closure determine the narrative horizon that prolepsis and analepsis further specify, in another sense, it seems equally plausible to suggest that this pair is itself constitutive of narrative openness and closure. Thus, these two pairs are best regarded as coordinate and all four principles best understood as factors in the production of narrative field and constitution of meaning.

Discussion of the meaning and function of prolepsis and analepsis will be restricted to those texts in Hegel where the engendering of divine subjectivity is the explicit theme. But before presentation and comment upon specific texts, a few words ought to be said concerning Hegelian commitment to these principles as regulative of all narratively engendered selfhood whatsoever. Hegel's vision of selfhood in all its forms is of a reality intrinsically self-transcendent. Its posture of fixed givenness, what Hegel refers to as its 'immediacy' (*Unmittelbarkeit*), is but a bluff, and it holds within itself not merely the transgression of its givenness but the totality of transformations that constitute development. If, in one sense, *an-sich* (in-itself) is almost synonymous with *Unmittelbarkeit,* in another sense, it more clearly registers the anticipatory dimension within the given, for *an-sich* connotes the *implicit,* the to-be-realized of the not yet realized. Hegel could hardly be more definite that fully realized selfhood of any kind involves mediation (*Vermittlung*)[87] as an interconnected process of development and that this, in turn, signals the unity between process and result. Selfhood is fully real or actual only as the appropriation of the interconnected stages or moments that constitute it. One of the words used by Hegel to suggest this characteristic of appropriative preservation (formally suggested by the category of *Aufhebung*)[88] is the noun "recollection" (*Erinnerung*) and its verbal correlative "to recollect" (*sich erinnen*). Care, however, should be exercised here. Hegel uses the noun form in a number of different ways in a number of different contexts, not all of which are equally revealing. In *LHP 1 Erinnerung* is used to refer to Platonic *anamnesis.* In the *Enc* (#460–464) *Erinnerung* names a specific form of psychological operation inferior to thought.[89] Yet there are also contexts in which the noun (and verb) get associated with fully realized subjectivity. At the end of *PS* Hegel speaks of recollection as a property of Spirit itself (#808, *GL2:*619). It is this latter connection that most clearly suggests recollection as an infrastructural narrative principle. Since *Erinnerung* is informed by the other contexts of its employment, however, it is not suitable as a general narrative category. Nonetheless, analepsis can be understood as translating *Erinnerung* understood as a property of fully realized subjectivity.[90]

Enough has been said by way of the general situating of prolepsis and analepsis. Turning to our specific task of explicating the functioning of prolepsis and analepsis as narrative principles of divine self-constitution, the Preface of *PS* suggests itself as an important textual locus. There Hegel speaks of Spirit presupposing its end as its goal (*der sein Ende als seinen Zweck voraussezt*) (#18, *GL2:*23) and, lest we miss the implication of anticipation embedded in the teleological language, Hegel offers the analogy of the growth of the human embryo (#21).[91] As a narrative principle, analepsis is suggested in #20 where Hegel speaks of essence, i.e., divine essence, fulfilling itself through development. Paragraph 22 sums up the operation of both principles in the divine and their relation. Speaking of the divine under the rubric *Vernunft,* Hegel focuses upon the divine as 'self-moving'.[92] He writes:

> The result is the same as the beginning, only because the beginning is the purpose (*der Zweck*), in other words the actual is the

> same as its Notion only because the immediate, as purpose, contains the self or pure actuality within itself. The realized purpose (*ausgeführte Zweck*), or the existent actuality, is movement and unfolded becoming (*entfaltetes Werden*) (Miller p. 12, *GL2*:25–26).

Concerning the narrative principles of prolepsis and analepsis, *LPR* and the *Enc* remain within the *PS*'s pale of understanding, though in both cases the trinitarian interpretation of divine becoming, and thus the trinitarian contextualization of narrative principles, is more to the fore. In the 1824 Lectures on Christianity, Hegel speaks almost exactly as he does in *PS* of the entire process of divine self-development being presupposed in the beginning (*LPR 3* E 186, G 120). The 1827 Lectures specify that the movement of the self-determination of the divine is through otherness (*LPR 3* E 347, G 269). As all the Lecture series maintain, the term of movement is the actuality (*Wirlichkeit*) of the divine anticipated from the beginning, an actuality that does not, and cannot, annul the process which constitutes it. The *Enc* shows Hegel again, as in the *PS*, describing Spirit using images that have anticipative, teleological connotation. In *PS* it was embryo; in the *Enc* it is seed and germ (#379 *zu*). Paragraph 381 is especially interesting. There, speaking of the activity whereby the externality and foreignness of the finite is overcome, Hegel explicitly associates the process of appropriation, what he calls the inwardization of the object (*die Innerlichmachung des Gegenstandes*), with the recollection of Spirit (*die Erinnerung des Geistes*).

Section 1.3 Trinity as Adequate Theological Articulation

That the Christian doctrine of the Trinity is central to the Hegelian vision and articulation of the *Deus Revelatus* has come more and more to the fore in recent Hegelian scholarship, even if the basic recognition is as old as Hegelianism and its immanent and nonimmanent critique. More than the number, it is the calibre of those who recognize the pivotal role of the doctrine of the Trinity that is truly impressive. They include such scholars as Claude Bruaire, Piero Coda, Emil Fackenheim, and Michael Theunisen.[93] Interpretation of Hegelian ontotheology that places the doctrine of the Trinity at the center is thoroughly nontrivial, since it specifies: (1) that the relationship between Hegelian philosophy and Christianity is founded upon something much more determinate than a vague correspondence of theistic tendency; (2) that the grounds of congruence lie in the intellectual sphere of articulation rather than the affective sphere of nonarticulation or primitive articulation; (3) that despite rival claims of other Christian dogmas or theologoumena such as the Incarnation, the doctrine with nonobvious claims to scriptural warrant and least immediacy is, in fact, the link par excellence between religion and philosophy, Christian representation and Hegelian concept. These extraordinarily strong claims go beyond anything that could be justified by merely presenting passages in Hegelian texts in which the Christian doctrine of the Trinity is invoked and its importance underlined. The doctrine of the Incarnation, for instance, is invoked just as often. The issue is whether a particular Christian doctrine is regulative in the last instance. For the commentators cited, and for a significant number of others, it is the doctrine of the Trinity that is regulative, just as it is the case that as they understand Hegelian ontotheological optics the doctrine or theologoumenon of the Trinity is inclusive of all other Christian doctrine and theologoumena. The issue of inclusiveness will be taken up shortly.

At the outset, however, it can be said that Hegel regards the Christian doctrine of the Trinity as a perspicuous symbol of the self-revealing God or Spirit. *LPR* is typical in this respect. With due regard to inadequacy on the level of expression, the Christian doctrine of the Trinity discloses the real, that is, the self-revealing God. The following passage from the 1824 Lectures is typical: "Thus it is just this definition of God by the church as a Trinity that is the concrete determination and nature of God as spirit; and spirit is an empty word if it is not grasped in this determination" (ibid. 127, G 43). For Hegel, the Christian doctrine of the Trinity subserves a double function: negatively, it broadens and deepens the foundational, antinegative theology thrust of Christianity, positively, it offers a truly speculative, that is, truly synthetic, articulation of the *Deus Revelatus* which, for Hegel, is the ultimate subject of all reality and discourse. The trinitarian counter to negative theology, particularly its most recent romantic vintage, does not eschew the language of mystery, but by the use of such language Hegel should not be read as engaging in disingenuous support of the traditional supernaturalist view of the Trinity. Rather, as we said previously (chap. 1, sect. 1.1), Hegel should be read as making a revisionist theological move in which mystery is read antithetically to mean revelation. Thus, the generic repristination of the Pauline emendation of the meaning of mystery specifies itself on the level of Hegelian adoption of and elaboration of the Trinity. The following passage could not make the specification more clear:

> The Trinity (*die Dreieinigkeit*) is called the mystery of God (*das Mysterium Gottes*); its content is mystical (*der Inhalt ist mystisch*), i.e., speculative. But what is for reason is not a secret (*ist kein Geheimnis*). In the Christian religion one knows, and this is a secret only for the finite understanding, and for the thought that is based on sense experience. (*LPR 3* 1824 E 192, G 125)

Though Hegel will never deny the susceptibility of trinitarian discourse to various kinds of deformation, trinitarian discourse in principle, if not always in fact, is a discourse of *Vernunft* rather than a discourse of intuition or *Verstand*. The principled status of the discourse of the Trinity provides grounds for assurance that the pathology of the modern age, symptomed in the jointure of Pietistic irrationalism and Enlightenment rationalism, can be meaningfully transcended.[94] The jointure, however, is not hospitable to the theologoumenon of the Trinity or speculative ontotheology in general. Where the doctrine or theologoumenon has not been excised, it has been marginalized. And marginalization rather than excision is more descriptive of what has occurred within the high theological traditions of Protestantism. The continued presence and crucial role played by the doctrine in Roman Catholicism and the Orthodox tradition matters not a whit to Hegel. These religious traditions are not cultural forces in the same way as the Lutheran and Reform traditions, and it is the marginalization of the doctrine within these traditions which bears the brunt of Hegelian critique.

Marginalization of the theologoumenon of the Trinity is just the most blatant as well as the most serious example of the marginalization of all dogmas of which Hegel complains so bitterly, especially in *LPR* (*LPR 1* 1827 E 166, G 76) and the foreword to Hinrichs's apologetic text. There are various reasons for marginalization within the Protestant tradition as a whole, but within the Lutheran tradition it is quite clear that biblicism is the main culprit (*LPR 1* 1827 E 157, G 67; E 168, G 78). The antispeculative tendency to which marginalization attests Hegel presumes to be completely unfounded. Scripture after all, he declares, is a "wax nose" onto which any shape, i.e., any construal, can be introduced (ibid. 1824 E 123, G 39–40). Arguing against a primitive anticipation of Harnack's "acute Hellenization" hypothesis, Hegel insists that proof that a doctrine or theologoumenon evolves by the assistance of philosophical concepts does not in itself vitiate its potential truth value (ibid. 1827 E 157, G 67).

Hegel's rejection of the general thesis that dogmatic development of necessity implies corruption comes into exceptionally sharp focus when the dogma concerned is the one Hegel thinks axial. In *LPR 3* Tholuck's dismissal of the doctrine of the Trinity on the grounds that Platonic and/or Neoplatonic concepts are elements of articulation is the proximate provocation.[95] Hegel feels called upon to demur on grounds of general principle but also to argue that, despite apparent fidelity to Protestant Christianity, such a view, in fact, represents a betrayal. For Hegel, it is in Protestant Christianity that the revelatory aspect of Christianity is accorded its full due. This implies that Protestantism, Lutheran Protestantism in particular, is favorable to the elaboration of doctrine since such elaboration is a vehicle, perhaps the vehicle, of the continuation of revelation (*LPR 1* 1824 E 121–123, G 38–39). Though he fails to thematize the issue, Hegel seems clearly of the opinion that Lutheranism in principle involves no wholescale rejection of the doctrine of the Trinity. This does not mean, however, that Lutheran Protestantism must of necessity simply repeat the conciliar formula. The conciliar formula that emerged under specific circumstances at a particular time and place might, indeed,, suffer from serious flaws. Yet, while rehabilitation may be a desideratum, Hegel thinks the doctrine or theologoumenon is too important to be ignored. Ignored it is, however, in modern confession, and the doctrine of the Trinity is, in practice, not an effective theological principle or symbol (ibid.).

Hegel is almost certainly moving beyond Luther and Lutheran orthodoxy when he suggests that the theologoumenon of the Trinity is *the* Christian principle, the central symbol of the living God.[96] For Hegel it is a nonanxious extrapolation, and one for which he has precedent, albeit in the most heterodox wing of Lutheran confession. Among the many contributions to (or deformations of) the Lutheran tradition rendered by Jacob Boehme (1575–1624) can be counted his retrieval of the doctrine of the Trinity as an effective theological symbol.[97] In Boehme's hands Lutheranism entails more than notional assent to a doctrine detached from religious life and theological vision. The theologoumenon of the Trinity, albeit the theologoumenon as representing significant modification of conciliar understanding,[98] becomes the symbol of the living God who reveals, who encounters, who saves.

Marginalization of the doctrine of the Trinity in modernity is not a uniquely Lutheran phenomenon. That it is a general Protestant phenomenon is proved to Hegel by the case of Schleiermacher, who is not only the most theological member of that group of thinkers Hegel bands together under the label of "Intuitionist" but also the most conspicuous constructive thinker in early nineteenth-century Reform Theology. Hegel's diagnosis of the degenerate apophaticism of Schleiermacherian theology and his unveiling of theological difficulties based upon this radical fault have been touched on already (chap. 1, sect. 1.1). Here, Hegel's claim that the basic tendency of Schleiermacher's theology is inherently antidogmatic might be recalled. For Hegel, what prompts the claim is the recognition that for Schleiermacher discursive articulation is an attempt to adequate to a prediscursive given whose riches and depth cannot be exhaustively translated. Hegel believes just the opposite. Discursive articulation is not less rich but more rich than the pre-articulate given, not less deep but more deep. And doctrine is the ultimate form of discursive articulation within the realm of religion, the richest, the most deep, or, as Hegel would say, the most concrete. Doctrine is a species of representation (*LPR 1* 1821 MS E 106, G 24), a modality of discourse surpassed only by concept.

This foundational dispute is of obvious relevance for the doctrine of the Trinity. From Hegel's perspective, Schleiermacherian methodology sets intolerable restrictions on the role that can be played by the doctrine of the Trinity: meaningfulness can be asserted, truth cannot; something can be said about how the doctrine might illuminate Christian religious experience, nothing about how it might illuminate the nature of the divine.[99] But, as is well-known, Schleiermacher in the *Glaubenslehre* does more than make the doctrine of the Trinity derivative in the way all doctrines of the faith are derivative. The doctrines of sin, redemption, and creation are all derivative with regard to Christian experience and primitive expression. The doctrine of the Trinity is briefly attended to only at the very end of the *Glaubenslehre,*[100] and then only to suggest that it is derivative in quite another way to the derivativeness endemic to all doctrine in the Schleiermacherian theological scheme. Unlike doctrines such as sin, redemption, and creation, the doctrine is not extrapolable in any direct way from the nondiscursive given.[101] From a Hegelian point of view, Schleiermacher's theological methodology deforms all Christian doctrines or theologoumena that come directly or indirectly within doctrinal embrace. To the extent to which the doctrine of the Trinity admits of inclusion, and it does, it constitutes no exception. But the doctrine or theologoumenon of the Trinity suffers from a flaw quite specific to it, i.e., its marginal status (*LPR 1* 1824 E 127, G 43). The doctrine of the Trinity is thus, on Hegel's somewhat tendentious reading, rendered all but redundant. Marginalization of the doctrine of the Trinity, Schleiermacher's sincere intention to translate fundamental tenets of Protestantism notwithstanding, provides further proof, if proof be needed, of Schleiermacher's collusion with the forces of theological dissolution in modernity.

That the entire narrative development of the divine can be comprehended by the theologoumenon of the Trinity is a point made explicitly by Hegel in *PS* as well as in important post-*PS* works such as the *Enc* and *LPR*. In the chapter on Revelatory Religion in *PS,* having dealt with the Incarnation (*Menschwerdung*) as the term of the basic thrust of religious yearning and cultural need (#748–770), Hegel goes on to situate the Incarnation in a complex nontriadic narrative upon which Hegel then suggests the superimposing of triadic form (#771–787). Eschewing the traditional theological language of person, Hegel recommends a nonsubstance trinitarian discourse, a discourse of movement, where one speaks of three interconnected 'moments' rather than a Trinity of mutually relating entities (#771). As it turns out, these moments display a significant measure of internal differentiation. For instance, the first moment, that is, the moment of divinity in itself, is itself constituted by the complex intradivine dynamics of self-manifestation, a process proximally registered in the traditional language of Father, Son and Spirit. The second moment is even more obviously differentiated (#774–785) and embraces three moments of a subordinate kind, i.e., creation, opposition of good and evil, and incarnation. At least, on the surface, the third moment (#786–787), the moment of spiritually informed community within which the saving action of God is recollected, is the least internally differentiated.

Thus, at a minimum, one can speak here of a triadic subsumption of the activity of the divine as Spirit whose narrative unfolding exhibits a more complex, nontriadic structure. But one can say more. The mode of subsumption is not triadic in the abstractly philosophical way of a Kant or a Schelling.[102] Hegel interprets the subsumption in a theological manner. It is clear that he associates the Son with the second moment (#776), and Spirit, as realized self-conscious Spirit, with the third. Hegel, therefore, appears to be suggesting that the triad of moments subsuming the encompassing narrative of the divine is nothing more than the Christian Trinity rightly understood. And this Trinity is inclusive of the intradivine Trinity, which in the larger scheme of things, it seems safe to infer, corresponds to the Father.

In the dense but critically important section on Revealed Religion (*die geoffenbarte Religion*) in the *Enc* (#564–571) Hegel has achieved greater clarity about the triadic elaboration of the narrative of the divine, which includes all the elements treated in *PS,* i.e., the dynamics of the intradivine, creation, incarnation, salvation, and sanctification. The language within which triadic elaboration is couched is varied. In #566, where Hegel introduces his nonsubstance discourse, it is 'spheres' (*Sphären*) or 'media' (*Media*). In #567–569, where triadic subsumption is in operation, Hegel makes even more clear his process subversion of traditional ontotheological construal by availing of the dynamic language of moment. In his discussion Hegel does not seem particularly concerned to theologically identify the three moments he brings to the reader's attention. The language of description of divine revelatory dynamics constituted by three moments belongs more to the level of *Begriff* than *Vorstellung.* Universality (*Allgemeinheit*), Particularity (*Besonderheit*), Individuality (*Einselnheit,),* the labels Hegel gives to his triad of moments, clearly indicate that the Hegelian treatment of Revealed Religion in the *Enc* is already heavily informed by the problematic of relation between Christianity and philosophy and the conviction that philosophy will appropriate, translate, and save the essence of the Christian vision. Nonetheless, theological signals are not absent. The second moment seems to concern the Son as the moment of self-differentiation *ad extra.* The third moment also has a theological correlative, though here the mapping is more ambiguous or at least more complex. On the one hand, the third moment refers to Spirit as articulated in the self-conscious recollecting community; on the other, it points to the Son in his role of redeemer and reconciler. The first moment, as in *PS,* is read as the dynamic intradivine process (or procession) of Father, Son, and Spirit. Here again, as in the *PS,* Hegel is reluctant even to suggest a label for this narrative sphere. Yet reading #567 in the light of #246–248, where movement from the intradivine to the extradivine sphere of differentiation is described as having theological correlatives in God's creation of the world and sending forth of his Son, a correlation of the intradivine trinitarian sphere with that of the Father seems justified. Thus, in the *Enc* as in *PS,* implicitly if not explicitly, subsumption is perceived not merely as triadic but trinitarian.

Hegel's various lecture series on Christianity compiled in *LPR 3* provide, by far, the most detailed account of the triadic subsumption of the encompassing narrative of the divine that enfolds the intradivine dynamics of self-manifestation, creation, generation of evil, incarnation, salvation, and sanctification. In the 1824 and 1827 Lectures, Hegel speaks quite abstractly and formally of the triad consisting of three interconnected Elements. By contrast, in the 1831 Lectures the discourse is both more obviously theological and possibly more revealing of the trinitarian tradition to which he belongs. Hegel avails of the language of Kingdom (*Reiche*) and speaks of the triadic divine's self-elaboration as the dynamic unfolding of a trinity of kingdoms. The theological traditions evoked by this way of speaking of Trinity need not engage us for the moment, but the names of Joachim de Fiore and Jacob Boehme might be suggested by way of preliminary orientation.[103] In any event, Element and Kingdom do not exhaust Hegel's triadic envisagement. Hegel also avails of the abstract, i.e., conceptual, language of Universality, Particularity, and Singularity, which is his standard in the *Enc.* Moreover, the language of moment, which perhaps best captures the dynamism of divine self-development, crisscrosses these other kinds of discourse, even if it is not to the fore as an explicit organizing principle in the way it is in the *Enc.*

The trinitarian rendering of triadic subsumption is absolutely transparent in the 1831 Lectures. In the fragments we have from that Lecture series, the encompassing narrative of the divine is rendered as the movement from the kingdom of God the Father through the kingdom of God the Son to the kingdom of God as Spirit. If not as explicit in the 1821 Manuscript and 1824 and 1827 Lectures, assignation of Father, Son, and Spirit to the three moments of increasing determination of divine personhood is clearly justified. In Hegel's discussion of the second element or moment, he avails of Son language, and he does so in two different ways: firstly, to refer to the realm of createdness (1824 E 199, G 132; 1827 E 292–293, G 217–218); secondly, to refer to the incarnate Christ (1821 MS E 121–122, G 56). With regard to the third element or moment, Spirit appears to be unambiguously identified with the self-conscious recollective community that is the Christian church. As is the case in *PS* and the *Enc,* in *LPR 3* Hegel tends to avoid as much as possible giving the intradivine dynamic, itself interpreted as the *perichoresis* (but perhaps more) of Father, Son, and Spirit, a determinate name. That the only candidate is *Father* Hegel reveals when he discusses the movement from the intradivine to the sphere of the extradivine, the movement from the first trinitarian moment to the second. Hegel, harkening back to Jacob Boehme (1827 E 292–293, G 217–218), suggests that the movement corresponds to the descent of the Son from the Father.[104]

If the intensity of Hegel's commitment of the theologoumenon of the Trinity is best disclosed in his polemical poses, its extent can be discerned from the constructive ontotheological proposals of *PS, Enc,* and the *LPR* with which we have just dealt. It should be pointed out, however, that Hegel's commitment to what he regards as the quintessential Lutheran view of God as living, effective reality and revelation makes it unlikely that Hegel is simply repeating the patristic and medieval standard. As Hegelian texts make abundantly clear, in comprehending the encompassing narrative of the divine, the Trinity is invested with qualities of process and dynamism to a degree not matched anywhere in the mainline trinitarian traditions focused on hypostasis or person.[105] Though the difference between the Hegelian view and the standard classical view is not our topic here (see chapter 2, section 2.3), I wish to suggest at this point the prima facie implausibility of congruence.

In a way that other Hegelian terms such as 'element', 'sphere', etc., do not, 'moment' captures the process rather than entitative character of the divine. For Iwan Iljin the point is crucial, and he insists that Hegelian elaboration of the Trinity exemplifies at the infrastructural level a fully radical narrative commitment. The essence of Hegelian ontotheology, he implies, is nothing more than a theogenetic narrative trinitarianly subsumed, or, as we would prefer here, trinitarianly configured. This configuration presents a divine movement of three dominant epochs, the epochs of divine self-manifestation, divine differentiation, and divine return. In his use of the language of 'epoch', Iljin intends to underline not only the narrative commitment present in the Hegelian rendition of the Christian doctrine of the Trinity on the plane of representation but also, and especially, in the conceptual translation of Christianity and its pivotal theologoumenon. Dale M. Schlitt interprets the Hegelian enterprise in a similar manner. For Schlitt, Hegelian ontotheology has as its center the trinitarian articulation of the auto-constitution of divine personhood. *Hegel's Trinitarian Claim* nowhere sorts out the philosophical from the theological element in Hegelian depiction and suggests, perhaps, that the task would be time-consuming and wasteful, since Hegelian depiction of the Trinity is almost always philosophically informed. Hegel's use of terms such as Universality, Particularity, and Singularity are eloquent testimony of the essential rightness of Schlitt's intuition.

Hegelian rendition of the Christian theologoumenon of the Trinity within the confines of representation stretches representation to the breaking point. Here it might be said that Hegel is forcing representation to engage in a preliminary way in a critique of its own deficits, a critique that properly belongs to concept and is fully executed there.[106] Still, in principle, a distinction can be made between both spheres. On the level of representation the trinitarian elaboration of the divine auto-constitution is subject to narrative defects erasable on the level of conceptual articulation. The outstanding narrative defect is the propensity to suggest that the divine process of self-revelation is nothing but "a temporal and external sequence" (*Enc* #571). Hegel wishes to say that the notes of temporalization, external connection, and, we might add, contingency are effects of symbolic form and do not belong to narrative (qua story) as such, which may be construed as an indivisible coherence of moments (*Enc* #571). The transition from *Vorstellung* to *Begriff,* therefore, does not imply abolition of narrative so much as the erasure in both its express and mute forms of narrative indices such as the 'and-then' of narrative localization and the 'and' of narrative connection.[107] We will be returning to such considerations in chapter 7.

The mere recognition that the theologoumenon of the Trinity is central to Hegel's vision of Christianity, as well as the elaboration of his own ontotheology, has not satisfied those commentators who wish to render the complexity of Hegel's trinitarian proposal and evaluate it only on the basis of some knowledge of the options within the theological tradition in general, the trinitarian tradition in particular. In this laudatory attempt the analytic pair, Immanent Trinity—Economic Trinity, a pair commonly used in the interpretation of classical trinitarian theology, has been frequently assumed and sometimes invoked. It has been invoked declaratively by Peter Hodgson and Emil Fackenheim.[108] It has been assumed by Claude Bruaire and Albert Chapelle among others.[109] To the extent to which the distinction suggests that trinitarian articulation on the plane of the intradivine is other than trinitarian articulation on the plane of the nondivine, and that the former has a regulative status with respect to the latter, the distinction is not useless. But, as sensed by Schlitt, the distinction can only have relative value when applied to the Hegelian trinitarian scheme,[110] because the classical trinitarian model which it interprets and to which it is tied, differs radically from the Hegelian proposal. Three key decisions concerning the relation of the intradivine to the activity of the divine in the realm of the nondivine constitute the core of differentiation. In the classical scheme: (1) the intradivine Trinity is the ontological foundation of the activity of the divine in the sphere of the nondivine, in creation, in salvation history; (2) revelation dynamic is attributable to divine activity within the sphere of the nondivine and in no way to intradivine trinitarian reality; (3) revelation dynamic is *extrinsic* to the definition of the divine. The fundamental decisions constitutive of the Hegelian trinitarian model cut in a contrary direction. In contrast with the classical model, (1) the intradivine Trinity, while in some respect regulative of divine activity on the plane of the extradivine, is not regarded as *foundational;* (2) revelation dynamic is effective on *every* level of the divine, including the intradivine; (3) revelation dynamic is *intrinsic* to the definition of the divine. These differences, which are differences of a grammatical kind, render it very doubtful that the immanent-economic polarity of the classical scheme can be appropriately extended to the Hegelian scheme.

In any event, Hegelian texts are rife with signs betraying *décalage.* One such sign is the ascription, both implicit and explicit, of the term *Father* to the intradivine milieu *as a whole.* Within the classical trinitarian scheme this would be nonsense, for it would amount to nothing less than providing the intradivine realm of Father, Son, and Spirit with an *economic* qualification. Such a position is absurd if the intradivine Trinity is understood to be the ontological foundation of revelational activity *ad extra.* A similar and reinforcing subversion is operative in Hegel's use of the language of Kingdom. Kingdom language in the Christian theological tradition is economic language par excellence. Thus speaking of the intradivine Trinity as a Kingdom, even without the qualification *Father* or *of the Father,* would signify disturbance of the traditional model. Needless to say, the subversion of the classical frame of reference, which gives the analytic pair immanent-economic its determinate context of meaning, ought not to be understood as implying the reduction of the intradivine Trinity to the economic. If the intradivine Trinity is an epoch of revelation, it is not so in precisely the same way as is divine revelation on the plane of the nondivine. If the intradivine is seen to have a process, even a primitively narrative, character, given repeated affirmation of its eternal status, it cannot be said to be historicized. Hegel, therefore, in no wise compromises the specificity of the intradivine vis-à-vis the divine enactment in creation and salvation, even if he dramatically rethinks its meaning.

Yet it is not simply the case that the intradivine dynamic is not reducible to the divine activity *ad extra.* Even this activity, as unfolded in the narrative epochs of the Son and Spirit, is not economic, given the way 'economic' is understood in the classical scheme of things. In the classical scheme, divine revelatory activity, which presupposes divine aseity, adds nothing to the divine as such. Divine activity of revelation is *for us* and is constitutive of *our* knowledge of God. For Hegel, by contrast, divine revelatory activity beyond the milieu of the intradivine is constitutive of the very identity of God. As crucial to divine definition, it can, therefore, be said that trinitarian elaboration in its second and third epochs, as with the first, is not economic in any reductive sense.

All of this argues for the unsuitability of the immanent-economic Trinity distinction as an interpretive tool intended to lay bare Hegel's trinitarian proposal, and, accordingly, it should be dropped. This still leaves commentators with the task of constructing a less misleading interpretive vocabulary. Schlitt, who seems to have some intuition of the drawbacks of immanent-economic nomenclature, offers some hints towards refurbishing the vocabulary. As he sees it, Hegel's trinitarian scheme maps the autogenesis of absolutely inclusive divine subjectivity.[111] Nothing exists outside the process of divine self-determination. Though Schlitt himself does not make the move, on the basis of his keen analysis of the Hegelian trinitarian proposal in which 'inclusiveness' is a singularly important descriptor, it seems not unreasonable to recommend *Inclusive Trinity* as the title for Hegel's trinitarian elaboration as a whole. All that remains is the rechristening of the intradivine Trinity. The differences between the Hegelian view and the classical are marked, indeed, as we hope has been shown. Nonetheless, immanence in the sense of interiority is a word one would like to predicate of Hegel's intradivine Trinity, provided care is taken to avoid suggesting that the Hegelian and classical view are the same. Both of these duties are discharged in the recommendation that the intradivine Trinity be spoken of as the Immanent Trinity in an inverted comma sense.[112] That "Immanent Trinity"-Inclusive Trinity is a more adequate interpretive pair than the Immanent Trinity-Economic Trinity pair appropriate to classical trinitarian theology is simply illustrated by the following schemata.

I. Scheme 1. Immanent-Economic Classical Model

Imm. Trinity	Economic Trinity
F =S = Sp	Creation = Incarnation = Redemption = Divine Presence

II. Scheme 2. "Immanent"-Inclusive Hegelian Model

Inclusive Trinity						
"Imm. Trinity"	=	Creation	=	Incarnation	=	Divine Presence
F = S = Sp		Redemption				
Father		Son				Spirit

Two points might be noted before closing our discussion of what constitutes (in)adequate interpretive vocabulary. First, the classical trinitarian scheme availed of above is greatly simplified, and important differences of emphases between trinitarian thought of Western and Eastern Christianity are ignored. Second, the Hegelian scheme is similarly simplified and Hegelian oscillation in trinitarian distribution put in parenthesis. As we have already suggested, the distribution scheme of the *Enc* differs from that of *PS* and *LPR 3,* and scheme 2 offers the distribution scheme of these latter two texts only. We turn now to another theological move of some significance, i.e., Hegel's integration of trinitarian theology with a redescribed natural theology.

Hegel's endorsement of a theology of revelation is, as we have seen (chap. 1, sect. 1.1), uncompromising. Natural or rational theologies of a Wolffian sort are thoroughly deficient and issue ironically in apophatic commitment. Read in one way, Hegel seems to understand the theological situation as one of option: natural theology or a theology of revelation. When faced with the choice, Hegel resolutely chooses the latter. However, dismissal of natural theology does not fully define the Hegelian position, and a definite feature of Hegel's ontotheological enterprise is the integration of elements of natural theology *with* revelation theology, or rather *into* revelation theology, since it is the latter that provides the basis of integration. Given the Hegelian argument that a theology of revelation receives its determinative register in the theologoumenon of the Trinity, the integration of elements of natural theology implies the integration of these elements into the matrix of the Hegelian rendering of Trinity. A theory of divine names or predicates, and the so-called proofs of God's existence, especially the ontological proof, are the two most noticeable elements of natural theology Hegel sees as assimilable by his recasting of trinitarian theology.

His proposed assimilation of a theology of divine names in no wise implies that Hegel is hospitable to the way such a theology is presented by Wolff and others of his school. The tendentious tone adopted in *PS* (Preface) seems to indicate that no negotiation between natural theology and a theology which has the *Deus Revelatus* at its center is possible (#20, 61, 62). Hegel's dominantly negative attitude is also conspicuous in the *Enc* (#28,29). But *LPR 3*, the *locus classicus* of Hegel's treatment of divine names, evidences a more complex appraisal, at once thoroughly negative with regard to their role in natural theology, but positive about their principled status and the possibility of retrieving what is valuable and insightful in this articulation within the context of a trinitarian theology of a narrative kind.

With a clarity unrivalled by other Hegelian texts, *LPR 3* exposes the basic flaws of natural theology's articulation of divine names. Three flaws are especially significant: (1) the positing of a plurality of divine names which, as determinate and fixed, at best can be externally related to each other, at worst fatally contradictory; (2) the separation of divine names from the divine subject; (3) the proposal that divine names do not refer to divine qualities as such but rather to modes of God's relation to human being. All three flaws are mentioned in the various suits of the 1821 Manuscript, 1824 and 1827 Lectures, and Hegel is certain that these flaws are expressive of a thoroughly wrongheaded commitment to a finite modality of understanding.[113] A few words ought to be said about what precisely is at issue in each of those areas in which Hegel espies weakness. (1) If Hegel is sensitive to the deformation made possible by the narrative 'and-then' and 'and' of *Vorstellung,* he is even more sensitive to the deformation attendant to the *conjunctive* use of 'and' with regard to the divine which is the common practice of *Verstand* (1821 MS E 74–75, G 13–14). This conjunctive is both cause and symptom of the fragmentation of the divine into a plurality of predicates held together in the most external way and not held together at all when the predicates have the appearance of being contraries. From Hegel's point of view, the theological consequences are not easy to bear: lost is the unity of the divine, that is, the living unity that holds contraries together and reconciles them (1827 E 278, G 203). (2) Chapelle is undoubtedly correct when he sees Hegel diagnosing natural theology's position as inherently *nominalistic.*[114] The names of God do not really name the divine, since the divine is viewed in the scheme of natural theology as the ineffable subject of predication distinct from the predicates as such. Hegel attacks this view with the kind of vehemence marking Ludwig Feuerbach's later attack in which Hegel is the presumed guilty party. The gap that opens up between subject and predicates, the gap that constitutes the divine as the *Deus Occultus* and the divine predicates as *mere* names, also eviscerates the ontological power of language. Language in the theology that has *Verstand* as its underpinning may be accorded many estimable functions, but the function of disclosing the real and the true that is the divine is not one of them. The move from (2) to (3) is a fairly easy one. The move is a longstanding one and is part of the Christian tradition since Pseudo-Dionysius. Certainly its role in Dionysian tradition is more conspicuous than its role in Wolff and rational theology. Nonetheless, the mystical tradition once again remains unaccused. But, then, it also appears as if Wolff and his followers cease to be the main object of rejection given the more proximate target of Schleiermacher, whose *Glaubenslehre* advocated, according to Hegelian criteria, a phenomenalistic reductionist view of divine names.[115]

For Hegel, neither singly nor together do these criticisms count against the intelligibility of divine predication as such. They count simply against natural theology's specific practice. A theology of divine names is genuinely possible if the supporting theological context is such that the systemic flaws of natural theology's articulation can be overcome. Hegel is convinced that his narrative trinitarian theology provides such a context, a context within which names have ontological status, are authentically expressive of the divine as subject, and in which the contrariety of names does not vitiate the unity of the divine but suggests, rather, its richness and depth.

Hegel's refusal to completely sunder natural theology from a theology of revelation has been noted by scholars as different as Claude Bruaire and Jürgen Moltmann.[116] Of the two, it is the more academic Bruaire who has the keener grasp of the details and the limits of rapprochement. But it is, perhaps, Moltmann who sees more clearly the general theological and historical significance of Hegelian integration. In *The Crucified God* it is suggested that Hegelian integration represents an attempt to rid Lutheranism of a deformation consequent upon Luther's uncritical acceptance of the *De Uno-De Triuno* distinction of late medieval theology.[117] Luther's condemnation of the theology of divine names, which was accompanied by reserved acceptance of the theologoumenon of the Trinity, maintains, Moltmann suggests, the scholastic bifurcation. Moltmann's point can be further developed. Hegelian challenge to the separation of *De Uno-De Triuno* in the scholastic, Lutheran, and modern natural theology (Deism, Theism) traditions is, in effect, a challenge to any theological system that separates knowledge from revelation, making the former merely finite, the latter merely mysterious. Integration implies a theology where the mysterious is excised and knowledge is not merely finite and thus incapable of genuine access to the divine. In making this challenge, Hegel evokes another dispensation in theology where the theologoumenon of the Trinity was of vital religious, as well as doctrinal, substance and within which the theology of divine names was a partner rather than an antagonist. I am referring to the patristic and early medieval theologies of Pseudo-Dionysius, Maximus, and Duns Scotus Eriugena. This is not to suggest that the substance of Hegel's theology is identical to any of these Christian Neoplatonic theologies. Their emphasis on the mystery of the Trinity and their affirmation of a kind of transdiscursive knowledge as the only means of access to the divine separate them definitively from Hegel. Yet, on the most general level, they do more nearly approximate to the Hegelian position than scholasticism, Luther's own theology and modern natural theology. They are, however, not the only general approximates to the Hegelian position. If Alexandre Koyré is correct, that Lutheran reviser, Jacob Boehme, is involved in a very Hegelian-like operation of reconciliation. From his earliest works, Koyré insists,[118] Boehme sought to describe the becoming of the divine in which the emergence of the Trinity is inseparable from the emergence of divine qualities.

The second way in which Hegel refuses to sanction the split between natural theology and a theology of revelation is disclosed in his attempt to integrate the so-called proofs of God's existence into his trinitarian ontotheological scheme. Worthy of special attention is the ontological proof, which he sees, after Kant, as foundational for the other two proofs. Unlike Kant, however, he sees the proof as genuine. It is, in fact, Hegel insists, the only genuine proof (*LPR 3* 1831 E 352, G 271–272). The failure of the proof, he argues in the 1827 and 1831 Lectures, is merely conditional. The proof fails to work because of the limitation of the epistemological context within which the proof is inserted. If *Verstand* is the limit of cognition, then the proof in either its classical Anselmian or Wolffian-Leibniz influenced form must necessarily fail, for the concept of the divine is read as *merely* concept, that is, ideal. Thus the reality to which the concept reaches can be only notional. When this notional reality is confounded with reality as such, then theology exposes itself to the corrosive of Kantian critique. And this is unfortunately precisely what has happened in the classical formulations of the proof. The problem lies, according to Hegel, with the construal of the concept itself. The concept is understood in such an abstract—i.e., impoverished way—that, if reality is to be introduced, it can only be introduced surreptitiously. Hegel's reformulation of the proof—which is also a reformulation of the nature of proof itself—insists on the richest possible interpretation of concept. To interpret the concept richly means to see reality, all reality, as implicit in the divine as concept and to understand that the movement from concept to reality is not executed by the finite intellect but by the divine itself.[119] God is the movement in which otherness is constituted and in which is established 'negative relation to self' (*die negative Beziehung auf sich*) (1831, E 357, G 275).

The 1827 and 1831 Lectures make it abundantly clear that the ontological proof admits of entry into trinitarian articulation. The following passage in the 1827 Lectures, summed up by negative relation to itself, is clearly trinitarian:

> . . . as far as the concept is concerned, it is immediately this universal that determines and particularizes itself—it is this activity of dividing, of particularizing and determining itself, of positing a finitude, negating this its own finitude,and being identical with itself through the negation of this finitude. This is the concept as such, the concept of God, the absolute concept . . . (*LPR 1* E 436, G 325).

While scholars have debated whether Hegel views the ontological argument to be coextensive with the "Immanent Trinity" alone or with the articulation of Trinity in its full and global ambit—i.e., the Inclusive Trinity—the emerging consensus is that Hegel ultimately identifies it with the latter.[120] Positing coextensiveness in any form represents a radical theological or ontotheological move and flies in the face of post-Reformation theology in both its rationalist and pietist forms, which would keep the discourse of revelation and the discourse of argument completely separate. Moreover, the association of the ontological argument with trinitarian theology guaranteed, or at the very minimum reinforces, the non-Kantian ontological claims Hegel is prepared to make. Hegel eloquently argues the advantages of Anselm over Kant,[121] but acknowledges that he is going beyond Anselm in connecting the ontological argument with an ontotheology of divine self-constitution. This ontotheology bears plausible resemblance to medieval and Spinozist renditions of *Causa Sui.*[122] Yet, in associating the ontological argument with the Inclusive Trinity, Hegel departs from both medieval and Spinozist interpretation, though, in passing, it might be remembered that Spinoza is not always accorded a fair hearing. In any event, even on the most dynamic reading of Spinozist *Causa Sui,* the finite as such (i.e., mode) is not an essential element of the divine, though, after the fact, the finite cannot but express the divine. The assertion that the determined or grounded finite is constitutive of the self-determined, self-grounded infinite is a proposition for which medieval theology has no protocol. The assertion is nonsense of a self-contradictory, self-vitiating sort. In uniting trinitarian theology to the ontological argument, and relating the latter to interpretations of *Causa Sui,* Hegel manages to introduce a decisive shift in meaning with respect to the ontological argument and the notion of *Causa Sui.* On the basis of revelation Hegel feels entitled to propose that the God of Christianity, though not necessarily the God of Judaism, Islam, or the God of the philosophers, is a God of narrative elaboration who enters decisively into finitude if only to sublate it. The episodes of this narrative include creation, incarnation, etc., but Hegel submits the episodes of this narrative to a trinitarian configuration, for it is the theologoumenon of the Trinity that encapsulates the essence of the Christian vision.

The exposé of theological or ontotheological foundations has doubtless been summary in the extreme. Yet I am more or less convinced that the basic structures of Hegel's species of Christianity, or the basic principles by which he determines the object Christianity, have been identified. Hegel's rendition of Christianity is characterized by an absolute commitment to the *Deus Revelatus,* as this divine narratively unfolds and determines itself, and as this unfolding and determination submits to trinitarian configuration. It is the elucidation of the various episodes of unfolding and determination and their trinitarian context to which we now turn.

PART 2

The Trinitarian Structuration of the Epochal Divine

Part 2 of our text wishes to explore in detail the important, narratively related Christian theologoumena that in *LPR 3* and the *Enc* are subjected to trinitarian contraction and elevation under the auspices of the language of Father, Son, and Spirit, or Universality, Particularity, and Singularity. Chapter 2, the first chapter in a cycle of five, examines the immanent sphere of the divine which Hegel regards as exhausting the first trinitarian phase or epoch of divine autogenesis. Keeping in mind both Hegel's apparent anxiousness to correlate the first trinitarian epoch with the "Immanent Trinity" of the classical trinitarian tradition, and the difficulties of making such a presumption, the first trinitarian epoch will be identified as the "Immanent Trinity". The characteristics of Hegelian elaboration of the "Immanent Trinity" will be elucidated, as will its relation to and departure from the classical determination of the intradivine Trinity. Chapter 3 focuses on Hegelian rendition of the theologoumenon of creation as this theologoumenon is plotted as the narrative consequent of the first trinitarian epoch, the epoch of the Immanent Trinity. Paying attention to, but not overestimating, the fact that in the *Enc* the theologoumenon exhausts the second trinitarian epoch, whereas in *LPR 3* and *PS* it is the first phase of a two-phased epoch with incarnation and the passion narrative being the second, superficial examination of the theologoumenon reveals oddities sufficient to raise the question of just how closely Hegelian rendition corresponds to the avowals of the mainline Christian tradition or traditions. The observation of a considerable degree of swerve, a phenomenon noted also in the case of

Hegel's treatment of the immanent divine, encourages the search for precedent(s) within the ontotheological tradition. Acknowledging its somewhat different narrative locus, *Enc* (first movement of third epoch) on the one hand and *LPR* and *PS* (third movement of the second) on the other, chapter 4 examines Hegel's treatment of the theologoumenon of Christ and/or the Christ story. Just as Hegel's elaboration of the theologoumenon does not obviously replicate the conciliar view, its patent theology of the cross color situates it broadly within the Lutheran tradition. Yet this still leaves open the question of difference from or transformation of theology of the cross in the narrative, trinitarianly contexted Hegelian rendition of the theologoumenon of the story of Christ. Ideally, pursuit of the question of difference/transformation would not concern itself exclusively with the elements of Luther's christological deposit that are not absolutely faithfully recapitulated but also with uncovering any systemic structures of transformation, i.e., a transformational grammar, that might exist. Any such uncovering would greatly assist construing the specificity of Hegelian rendition of the christological theologoumenon. Any precedent that could be found in the ontotheological tradition for Hegelian-like transformation of Luther's theology of the cross, any evidence for a similar operation of a transformational grammar, would not only greatly assist taxonomic identification of the species of Hegelian Christology but Hegel's trinitarian elaboration as a whole. Chapter 5 examines the Hegelian rendition of the theologoumenon of Spiritual Community (*Gemeinde*) which, in *LPR 3* and *PS,* has sole occupancy of the third and final trinitarian epoch, but which in the *Enc* is identified with the third and last phase of the third and final trinitarian epoch. Elucidation of the salient features of Hegelian depiction raise doubts as to whether Hegel can legitimately claim to be recapitulating the Lutheran doctrine of the church. The patent evocation of the Christian mystical tradition raises the question as to whether the Christian mystical tradition (or traditions) might not be the circumambient context within which the Lutheran view is interpreted. Chapter 6 is, at once, continuous with the delineation of the theologoumenon of Spiritual Community of chapter 5 and provides a summary of the Christian theologoumena, trinitarianly contracted and elevated, whose narrative interlocking identifies the nature of the divine. As before, precedents are sought with regard to notable swerves observed in Hegelian treatment of a specific Christian theologoumenon. Here, however, the emphasis shifts to search for precedents regarding the complete narrative elaboration of the divine, at once an exhaustive narrative configuration of Christian theologoumena and an exhaustive narrative configuration of swerves that systematically disfigure basic Christian meaning.

2

THE FIRST NARRATIVE EPOCH: The "Immanent Trinity"

More than one locus of reflection upon a trinitarian divine outside the context of relational divine activities such as creation and incarnation can be found in Hegelian texts, but the key loci are undoubtedly the Hegelian hermeneutical rendering of the dogma of the Trinity in *LPR 3* and Hegelian logic's redescription in *SL* and the *Logic* of the *Enc.* Elucidation of Hegel's narrative understanding of Trinity will here concentrate upon these loci, though by no means exclusively.

The present chapter is divided into three sections. Section 2.1 deals with the theological and trinitarian essence of Hegelian logic which Pavel Apostel has christened *logica divina.*[1] In addition, some attempt is made to understand the unusual intersection of a theology of predicates and a theology of Trinity in the *logica divina* of *SL* and the so-called Lesser Logic, i.e., the logic of the *Enc.* Section 2.2 revolves around Hegel's hermeneutical presentation of the "Immanent Trinity" in *LPR 3,* though *PS* receives some attention. Isolated in this section are various narrative structural properties of Hegel's depiction of the self-referential trinitarian divine: its narrative proleptic character, its character of being at once closed (synclasis) and open (anaclasis). Given the incipient narrative locus of "Immanent Trinity", the question is raised with regard to ontological, gnoseological, axiological, and existential development as to what degree of adequacy is possible on this level of the divine. It will be argued that serious debits obtrude. Section 2.3 raises the issue of the theological status of the "Immanent Trinity" and asks: (1) does the Hegelian presentation swerve from the normative hypostatic understanding? and (2) what precedents exist in the Christian theological or ontotheological tradition for such swerve?

Section 2.1 Hegelian Logic as **Logica Divina**

An antitheological reading of Hegelian logic, while by no means exclusive to the Anglo-American scene of Hegel hermeneutics, is not untypical.[2] Where the *Weltanschauung* is one of conceptual modesty, and where, in addition, the question of method is crucial, whether that of logical method in the strict sense or that of the methodological foundation of science, metaphysical, or in Kantian terms 'transcendent', claims of a foundational sort are regarded with suspicion. If all transcendent claims are questionable, this is *a fortiori* the case with respect to claims about divine reality. Presupposition and suspicion dictate Hegelian apologetics in which Hegel is trimmed and important aspects of his vision shelved, misinterpreted, or explained away. The antitheological interpretation of Hegel, and of Hegelian logic in particular, represents an interpretive decision with respect to Hegelian philosophy that is more specific than the antimetaphysical, antiontological reading, though often this reading functions as a corollary of the antiontological stance. Alan White's *Absolute Knowledge* is but the most recent example of this trend. Extraordinarily sensitive to Hegel in some respects, White shows himself anxious to offer a transcendental, i.e., nontranscendent and nontheological, interpretation of Hegelian logic,[3] even if this means ignoring or exdenominating many passages that explicitly announce ontological and theological commitment.[4]

As argued earlier, the antitheological reading of Hegel corresponds neither to the evidence nor to the normative understanding of the Hegelian system as a whole. *Mutatis mutandis* with respect to the reading of Hegelian logic. In the more recent Hegel scholarship, the more normative appraisal has not gone without its champions. In the Anglo-American commentary the specifically theological essence of Hegelian logic has been most completely articulated by Malcolm Clark and Dale M. Schlitt, in French commentary and criticism by André Leonard and Claude Bruaire.[5] While it is recognized by German interpreters of Hegel that his philosophy as a whole and his logic in particular admit of a methodological interpretation, the irradicable theological faceting of Hegelian thought is generally not denied. Indeed, a host of Hegel scholars, including Reinhard Heede, Iwan Iljin, Walter Jaeschke, Walter Kern and Jörg Splett,[6] have gone out of their way to insist upon the necessity of a theological reading. Hegel's two logical texts provide ample evidence for the hermeneutical probity of the theological reading. These texts provide three *analytically* distinct kinds of evidence to support the asserted relationships between logic and theology: (1) evidence for the general relationship between logic and metaphysics, metaphysics and theology; (2) evidence for the more specific interconnection between logic and the Christian Trinity; (3) evidence for the specification of the thought-determinations (*Denkenbestimmungen*) of Hegelian logic as divine ideas, i.e., either divine predicates or archetypes or both. The briefest rehearsal of the evidence will be provided here. More detailed treatment of (2) and (3) will be furnished later in this section.

(1) Given the Hegelian critique of Kantian and post-Kantian dualism that has a multitude of aspects, the most important of which, the epistemological and ontological, were touched upon in chapter 1, one is forced to conclude that Hegel by no means excludes a transcendent dimension. Indeed, the Hegelian critique of Kant might be regarded as one of the most significant early post-Kantian attempts at rehabilitating the transcendent.[7] We have seen one clearly theological aspect of this rehabilitation in Hegel's restatement of the ontological argument in chapter 1. Another not so explicitly theological aspect is Hegel's correction of Kant's doctrine of the categories. For Hegel, Kant's doctrine of the categories is deficient in two especially important respects.[8] (1) Despite Kant's so-called transcendental deduction, the categories represent nothing more than a collection of Aristotelian and scholastic categories extrinsically and mechanically arranged to provide the appearance of system. This is Hegel's opinion form as early as *FK* where he complains of the mechanistic, rather than organic, character of the Kantian arrangement (*GL1:*322). Moreover, as Fichte had been the first to recognize, Kant had by no means thought through the relationship between the categories and the transcendental 'I' (*Enc* #42 & *zu*). (2) By placing the categories on the level of Understanding, and not on the level of Reason, the categories are denied full-blown ontological status (*Enc* #44–46). The categories serve as ineluctable conditions for the possibility of experience, but experience pertains merely to the phenomenal order and not to the noumenal order on the thither side of appearance. Hegel at once assigns the categories to Reason and opts for a more traditional, nonheurisitc interpretation of their nature, scope, and function (*SLE* 46; *Enc* #62).

In granting some kind of metaphysical or ontological status to logical categories Hegel is, at least formally, more nearly Aristotelian than Kantian.[9] Indeed, in correcting Kant, Hegel in a sense repristinates Aristotelian logic, though not with any level of exactitude. Excepting Aristotle's work on the syllogism, Aristotelian logic, specifically the Aristotelian elaboration of the categories, does not escape metaphysical assumption. While the *Categories* and *On Interpretation* may tend on some occasions to move in the direction of radicalizing what the scholastics regarded as the key *discrimen* between logic and metaphysics, i.e., the *de re/de dicto* distinction, arguably there exists in Aristotle an in-built declension towards the ontological.[10] Thus, despite hints in Aristotle that the articulation of the logico-categorial framework belongs to the metalevel of reflection upon first order discourse about the realm of beings, there is no absolutely radical divorce between logic and metaphysics or logic and ontology. For Hegel, also, no divorce can be maintained, though he has a much more acute sense of the metalevel property of logic that provides at least an aspect of its overall definition.[11]

In the *Logic* of the *Enc* Hegel declares this connection in the most ambitious way possible when he claims that, not only does his logic contain all previous logic, but that it is inclusive of all previous metaphysics (*Enc* #24). Yet Hegel is not content simply to make explicit a connection that was merely implicit in Aristotle; he also thematizes the intrinsic relationship between logic and theology. If, for Hegel, logic is ontological, it is also theological. Ontology and theology are inseparable; an avowal that brings Hegel closer to the scholastic than the Lutheran tradition. But, again, it is Aristotle who provides the ultimate precedent for this view. Excellent Aristotelian scholars such as Joseph Owens and Giovanni Reale have successfully countered attempts to excise the theological side of Aristotle's metaphysics.[12] This theological side is most clearly revealed in Bks. G, E, K of the *Metaphysics,* where first philosophy is not merely identified with the science of being qua being but with the science of primary substance or *ousia* Hegel is operating within the general ontotheological matrix of Aristotle when he writes in the Introduction to the above-mentioned text:

> The objects of philosophy, it is true, are upon the whole the same as those of religion. In both the object is Truth, in that supreme sense in which God and God only is the Truth. (*Enc* #1, *GL8:*41)

Though Hegel neither thinks nor treats of the matter syllogistically, the identification of the ontological essence of logic and the theological essence of ontology are steps in the elaboration of the full definition of logic. The fully adequate definition of Hegelian logic is, as Reinhard Heede observes an *onto-theo-logik* where the accent falls equally on each element of the complex term.[13] Reinforcing the passage cited above, and confirming Heede's definition, is another passage in the

Logic of the *Enc* where the development of the categories is understood as the elaboration of the metaphysical definitions of God (*Enc* #85). Passages announcing the theological (or ontotheological) nature of logic are also found in the *SL*. Hegel, for example, speaks of science (*Wissenschaft*) and divine concepts (*die göttlichen Begriffs*) as if they are synonymous, and logic is characterized as the immediate presentation of the self-determining God (*der selbstbestimmten Gottes*) (*GL5*:175).

(2) If there exists support for the general intervolvement between logic and theology in Hegel's logical texts, there exists almost equally strong support for the interrelation of logical development and trinitarian articulation. Splett correctly points to a passage in *SL* that introduces Hegelian reflection on the logical or ontological category of Measure (*Mass*) as providing one of the most overt assertions of connection between categorial genesis and the "Immanent Trinity."[14] The "Immanent Trinity" is understood as the theological (representational) correlate of the logical movement of Quality, Quantity, and Measure, though in the correlation the accent falls heavily upon Measure as the completing third moment: it is this moment that is responsible for the determinateness of development. Proximally, Measure (*Mass*) corresponds to the third moment of divine articulation, yet as such Measure can also summarize immanent trinitarian elaboration, since the third moment of trinitarian elaboration represents the recollection (*Erinnerung*) of the first two.[15] Hegel, it should be pointed out, regards the correlation of trinitarian and logical development as providing apologetic justification of the determinate, or self-determining, nature of God, symptomed in the Christian construct of the Trinity. Indeed, for Hegel, the trinitarian view, or a certain version of that view, provides an adequate construal of the divine, one, moreover, susceptible to logical translation. And, as logically translated, the trinitarian view may be summed up in the statement: God is Measure (*Gott ist das Mass*).[16] The Christian trinitarian view is contrasted to, and compares favorably with, the view of God as the indefinite and immeasurable (Spinoza), and the view of God as an incomplete development (Indian Trinity).[17]

Hegel's correlation of the "Immanent Trinity" with a narrow band of categorical development—development that takes place exclusively within the horizon of the logic of *Being* and not the logical horizon as a whole—renders the correlation more or less approximate. Hegel is not offering a logical *systematic* mapping of the Trinity, but rather is pointing to a strong *analogy* between trinitarian and logical or ontological development. While other kinds of evidence suggest a more adequate mapping that would correlate the movement of logic as a whole with the "Immanent Trinity", *SL* is somewhat less overt in making this suggestion than the *Logic* of the *Enc*. One can conjecture three complementary reasons for this. First, while *SL,* like its precursor *PS,* is a dazzling *tour de force,* the virtuoso performance is not conducive to great clarity. *SL* in a sense answers to the well-known characterization of Tolstoy's *Anna Karenina* as "a big, loose, baggy monster," and compares somewhat unfavorably with the more sharply focused, more concise logic of the *Enc.* The approximateness of correlation between the logic of Being and the "Immanent Trinity" thus might be regarded as being a reflection of a more generic approximateness and looseness. Second, Hegel's own understanding of his philosophy as providing an apologetic defense of Christianity, at one and the same time translating it and correcting its conceptual deficiencies, itself developed over time.[18] Such also is the case with regard to the correlation between logico-categorial development and the articulation of the "Immanent Trinity". This correlation also demanded a deeper, more coherent, and sensitive appraisal of the intrinsicality of trinitarian elaboration to all philosophical thought, including the logical. Where the desideratum is logico-theological mapping, *SL* might be regarded as a promissory note, with the *Logic* of *Enc* representing actual payment. The third point in a sense represents a corollary of Albert Chapelle's diagnosis of different emphases in Hegel's two logics. *SL,* Chapelle argues,[19] has an epistemological emphasis not found in the *Logic* of the *Enc* which, it is suggested, is more ontological in orientation. If one accepts the premise that the more ontological rendering of logic is more efficient in establishing and supporting theological liaison,[20] then the systematic differences between the logics may serve at least as one explanatory factor among others for the greater mapping precision of the second of Hegel's two logics.

Again, these three reasons are conjectural and, in any case, not exhaustive. Yet, it certainly appears to be the case that the so-called Lesser Logic suggests a more adequate and comprehensive mapping of the realm of logic and that of the "Immanent Trinity." The following passage is not atypical, though it is found not in the main text but in the *Zusatzen,* which in some sense provide a theological commentary upon the progression of logical categories:[21]

> The movement of the concept is as it were to be looked upon merely as play (*nur als ein Spiel*): the other which it sets up is in reality not an other. Or, as it is expressed in the teachings of

> Christianity: not merely has God created a world which confronts him as an other (*als ein Anderes gegenüber steht*); he has from all eternity begotten a Son, in whom he, as Spirit, is at home with himself (*bei sich selbst ist*). (*Enc* #161 *zu,* Miller p. 225. *GL8:*356)

This passage, which identifies Concept with Spirit, points, in the most general way, to the correlation of the entire logical movement of Being-Essence-Concept with Father-Son-Spirit. Supporting evidence is provided by Hegel's discussion of Reflection (*Enc* #112) which commences his treatment of the logic of Essence. This discussion strongly suggests the correspondence of Essence and Son. The complex details of Hegel's discussion, however, need not occupy us just yet. The clinching bit of evidence for a one-to-one mapping of the regulative categories of the Logic of *Enc* with the differentiations of the "Immanent Trinity" is provided not by the *Logic* itself but by Hegel's correlation of religious and philosophical syllogisms which close the *Enc.* There Hegel makes quite explicit the parallelism between the triadic elaboration of the *Logic* (*Enc* #575) and the trinitarian movement on the level of Universality (*Allgemeinheit*) (*Enc* #566–567).

(3) The well-known passage from *SL* that speaks of logical articulation as "the presentation of God in his eternal essence (*wie er in seinem ewigen Wesen*) *before* (*vor*) the creation of the world and finite spirit" (*GL4:*46) is most often cited as a proof text for the thesis of the general theological essence of Hegelian logic. The passage also supports, however, the more specific Hegelian determination that Hegelian logical categories correspond to divine ideas. The passage from *Enc* (*GL8:*201), cited already, might also be mentioned in this context, as might *SL* (*GL5:*175). Passages in which the essence of God is specifically determined as a noetic essence—passages, in other words, where the categories are either regarded as divine archetypes (*GL4:*46, 57) or divine predicates—undoubtedly provide the clinching evidence. Detailed treatment of the categories as divine ideas must await later discussion. Here two points will be touched on, the second considerably more important than the first.

Deciphering the ontotheological nature of logic implies that, even at the most general and formal level, Hegel was essentially moving beyond Aristotle. The identification of the categories with the divine ideas pushes Hegel more in a Platonic or Neoplatonic direction,[22] though, as I will have occasion to declare more than once, (1) there are other possible theological antecedents, and (2) similitude at this level does not imply similitude in every possible respect.[23] Even if this taxonomic identification were less provisional, however, it would be insufficient to clarify the specificity of the Hegelian elaboration. L. Bruno Puntel, D. M. Schlitt, and Iwan Iljin have all made contributions here. Puntel and Schlitt agree that logical method has both a structural and dynamic character.[24] Both underscore the element of development (*Bewegung*).[25] For neither is categorical framework constituted by a mere aggregate of ontologically empty logical forms, nor is structure divorced from development an exclusive determinant. Structure is intimately related to process and provides its direction and determinateness of movement.[26] Iljin, less precise on the technical details, is more overt in drawing definite theological conclusions. Categorial articulation from *Sein* to *Begriff,* or from *Sein* to *Idee,* is nothing less than a theogenetic process (*theogenitische Prozess*) of divine self-determination, self-actualization.[27] The sequence of logical forms is the necessary path from imperfection to perfection. Iljin suggests, in his vocabulary of process and his understanding of the logic as epoch, a peculiar narrative understanding of the divine that is by no means typical of the neoplatonic or Christian tradition or even the Christian Neoplatonic tradition.[28] By narrative understanding I do not necessarily mean temporal understanding, though Hegelian logic is open to the objection that its pattern of atemporal becoming is modeled after a *temporal* narrative pattern.[29] Narrative pattern connotes more than process: it connotes development, ontological, gnoseological, axiological, and existential increase.[30]

It is time to summarize our discussion. Both brief review of the textual evidence and appeal to hermeneutical authority have been employed as counters to the antitheological interpretation of Hegelian logic. The rejection of the antitheological stance by no means implies the rejection of the more or less logico-methodological interpretation of Hegelian logic,[31] nor does it imply that the theological perspective is the only legitimate one. Characterizing Hegelian logic after Pavel Apostel as a *logica divina* is in no way incompatible with the methodological reading, since Hegelian logic has both a semantic and functional density that neither interpretation exhausts. It is Iwan Iljin who argues for a complementarity of hermeneutic schemes, maintaining that Hegelian logic can support three different readings, i.e., a scientific-systematic; a theological-religious; and a cosmological.[32] All are necessary and true. All have aspects in Hegelian logic to which they respond and correspond. Moreover, all are irradicable. If Iljin emphasizes the theological, this is, in the main, determined by response to the danger of its interpretive excision or exdenomination.

Hegelian Logica Divina and the "Immanent Trinity."

The basic evidential grounds for correlation have already been supplied. The categorial articulation of the realm of 'pure thought' corresponds to some version of the Christian Trinity, though it cannot be decided at this stage whether Hegelian logic's onto-theological translation of a vision of divine reality more commonly elucidated within the sphere of representation either twists or deforms the standard presentation, or noninterferingly translates a specific nonstandard version of the Trinity that is accepted beforehand.[33] This either/or, of course, only can be properly investigated when all the available textual evidence, from *LPR 3* and elsewhere, has been gathered. When itemizing some of the more salient trinitarian passages in Hegelian logic, however, we mentioned *Enc* #112 but postponed discussion of its theological pedigree. Theological interrogation of this text is justified not only because of the reinforcement it supplies for the homology between the categorial movement, Being-Essence-Concept (Idea), and the trinitarian symbol of Father-Son-Spirit, but because of its anticipatory value. Theological exegesis will aid important later comparisons of Hegel and Jacob Boehme.[34] In *Enc* #112 and *zu,* Reflection and Essence are synonymous. Reflection is, of course, in the first instance a physical image. Both the identity of Reflection with Essence and its symbolic backdrop are apparent in Hegel's remark that:

> The point of view given by the Essence is in general the standpoint of 'Reflection'. This word 'reflection' is originally applied, when a ray of light in a straight line impinging upon a surface of a mirror is thrown back from it. (*GL8:*262, Miller p. 163)

Obviously, the theological component is here not on the surface. If such a component exists, it requires excavation. What is proposed, then, is a historico-theological reconstruction of the symbol complex, reflection-light-mirror, the reconstructive montage serving to destroy the obviousness of its physical-philosophical appearance.

From the first burgeoning of patristic trinitarian thought, the Son is symbolically represented as a ray of light emitted from the Father. Light often stood proxy for consciousness or mind. The Son, then, was the consciousness or mind of the Father.[35] The vocal image of the emitted word is the other patristic standard. The scriptural locus for both images was the Gospel of John (Prologue 1.1–3, 1.5 esp.), though with respect to the image of the ray of Light there is a conflation of John 1.5

with John 1.1–2, the latter communicating its dynamism and sense of emergence to the former. Undoubtedly most students are also cognizant of the post-Tertullian normative hermeneutical practice which dictated that Proverbs 8.22–23 be read in connection with the Prologue of the Fourth Gospel, and that the Wisdom (*Sophia*) of the former be correlated with the Word (*Logos*) of the latter.[36] As Ernst Benz has pointed out,[37] Meister Eckhart, the father of a great part of the working vocabulary of German philosophical thought, concurs with this general tradition. Eckhart, who is almost unique in escaping any kind of censure by Hegel, identifies Wisdom and Word in his Latin commentary on the Prologue.[38] Any ascription or description, metaphysical or otherwise, made of Wisdom applies also to the Word or Logos. Eckhart provides a mixed bag: "the pure emanation from God," "the brightness of everlasting light," and (most interestingly) "the unspotted mirror."[39] In Eckhart the refusal to distinguish the image of mirror from the image of light is coextensive with the refusal to distinguish between Wisdom and Logos. Obviously, this is the position Hegel adopts. Yet, equally obviously, there is a strain in the image's equation of mirror and ray. In so far as the mirror sends back the ray, it is *not* the ray. Moreover, mirror appears to suggest greater independence than the ray, which is quintessentially the image of the Son. Boehme, as we shall see, will take the literal declensions of these images seriously and will unite seriousness with respect to symbolic *tendenz* with hermeneutic seriousness; both moves will combine to disconnect Logos from Sophia and retreat back beyond Tertullian to those Gnostic modes in thought critiqued by him.[40] Thus there is theological normalcy in Hegel's use of 'reflection' despite the inner tension of 'ray' and 'mirror'.

What is of much greater general importance is the dynamism Hegel ascribes to the categorial realm. Alan White adopts the interesting procedure of providing an etymological analysis of key Hegelian constructs in order to enucleate their narrative character. White selects *Method* and *Bewegung*. Both *Method* and *Bewegung,* he suggests, imply direction and movement, even if direction is dominant in the former, movement in the latter.[41] *Method,* in Greek, *met'hodos,* means, literally, proceeding along a road; and *Bewegung,* or movement, has as its root *Weg* cognate with way or path.[42] For White, this dynamism connotes merely the autonomous development of one logical category from and through another, a kind of natural deductive logic, the movements of which are discoverable only in the process of thinking and the full results of which are available only to the logician who has run through the entire series of logical forms. In White the logico-methodological analysis forces the erasure of the ontotheological component. Ignored is the theological situating of the logician, who, as Alexander Kojève recognizes,[43] is human being raised to the status of the divine, human thought purged and elevated into the divine noetic circuit, the circle of thoughts constitutive of self-thinking thought—*noesis noeseos noesis*[44]—of the self-contemplative God. Moreover, as Hegel sees it, this self-contemplative God must be diagnosed as trinitarian and the unbroken process of ascent of categorical evolution correlated with trinitarian development.[45] Hegelian logic consistently posits a terminus to both processes and, as we shall see later, offers good reasons why this must be so. Whatever the kind or degree of correlation posited, the absolute Idea is the asserted terminus. As terminus it represents the full realization of subjectivity and personhood. A passage from *SL* eloquently expresses Hegel's general position:

> The richest is therefore the most concrete and most subjective, and that which withdraws into the simplest depth is the most powerful and all-embracing. The highest, most concentrated point is the pure personality (*Die Höchste, jugeschärfteste Spitze ist die reine Persönlichkeit*), which solely through the absolute dialectic which is its nature, no less embraces and holds everything within itself. (*SL* 841. *GL5*:349)

The equating of the development of the logic with the articulation of self is a constant feature of Hegelian logic. In addition to the one cited above, several passages endorse the view of the logic as descriptive of the autogenesis of subjectivity or personhood. Many register this process as triadic. Hegelian logic nowhere registers this more clearly than in its ontotheological treatment of the syllogism of Universality, Particularity, and Individuality, which syllogism correlates with the ordered series of the three members of the Trinity. But a syllogism is a process, even an action, and Universality is but the immediate (*an sich*), the starting point of a process that presupposes the difference of Particularity and its mediation, and the fully enriched, fully determinate conclusion of Individuality.[46]

For orthodox theistic and trinitarian thinkers, Hegel's view is as idiosyncratic as it is disturbing: all subjectivity and personhood whatsoever requires development, even if the subject referred to is God. The only modification Hegel makes in the case of God is that movement need not be understood exclusively in temporal terms. That Hegel is envisaging God under the lens of the Aristotelian metaphysical principles of potency (*dynamis*) and actuality (*energeia*) is unmistakable, though Aristotle—and in this he was followed by the scholastics—did not apply this metaphysical distinction to the divine. God, as primary *ousia* (Metaphysics), is identifiable with *energia,* just as the former is identifiable with *noesis noeseos noesis* (thought thinking itself) of the *Nichomachean Ethics* (Bk. 10). Here Hegel has not only brought personality into the Aristotelian God but potentiality also.

Categorial Genesis As Narrative Stringing of Divine Predicates and Prototypes. What is impossible for Kant is possible for Hegel. Categories, or "thought-determinations," are not simply empty concepts that admit of application to an intrinsically other material; they have as their legitimate domain of application the divine in its pure self-relation.[47] Categories are, thus, predicates of the divine or divine names.[48] Yet, as we have already seen, Hegelian criticism of natural theology forbids any retreat behind Kant to a precritical level of assumption. Kant's criticism of Scholastic and Wolffian theology of divine names hits the mark but only, Hegel opines, because of the latter's flawed epistemic basis. To the extent to which the epistemic foundation is provided by the understanding with its freezing and hypostatizing tendency, the theology of divine names is crucially undermined. A plurality of self-identical, intrinsically nonrelational categories constitute an aggregate with no underlying unity. Moreover, the categories, as predicates, are only extrinsically related to the degenerately mystical X it is impossible to disclose. The theology of divine names, whether implicitly or explicitly, operates within the apophatic horizon of assumption. Predicates are the best available discursive gestures for disclosing the divine, but, in a strict sense, all language and concept as finite is riddled with opacity and is forever surpassed by the reality it would name.[49] Hegel, who makes much more ambitious claims for language as well as concept and thought, recommends a shift from understanding to reason from *Verstand* to *Vernunft,* in which shift non-nominalistic predication of the divine becomes not merely possible but actual and the spectre of agnosticism—the subjective correlative of the evocation of the Unknown God—is exorcized.

The recommended shift implies, among other things, that (onto-theo-)logical categories, or divine predicates, illustrate a relationality with respect to each other that is internal rather than external, indeed, a relationality such that it can be said that relationality is constitutive of each and every category's identity or even self-identity. No (onto-theo-)logical category is either self-identical in some immediate fashion or different or other in some immediate fashion. Rather each category is related to all other categories (through difference internalized) proximately or ultimately, and these relations are constitutive of its complex, nonimmediate identity (*Enc* #32, 80–81, 86, 114, 119). Measure, for instance, is related proximally to Quality and Quantity in its own categorial band of Being and to the category of Essence outside it; it is related only distantly and ultimately with the Idea. Yet all these relations define it. And, for Hegel, the very possibility of meaning and truth is predicated upon the existence of a relational matrix with a determinate number of categorial forms constituting a totality.[50] Categorial structuration should and, in fact, does mirror the articulation of the divine as the true and the encompassing whole. In positing a relational matrix for categories, and determining that they form an integrated whole or totality, Hegel takes his distance not only from the scholastic and Wolffian traditions of natural or rational theology but also from Spinoza. From Hegel's perspective, the parallelism of exemplification in the finite of the two attributes or predicates, i.e., Thought and Extension, postulated by Spinoza, does not suggest genuine relationality, any more than Spinoza's suggestion that one may plausibly conjecture an infinity of attributes or divine predicates[51]—all but Thought and Extension unknown and unknowable—implies a totality. For Hegel, predicates are relational or are not at all; and as constituting and constituted by a relational matrix that is determinate, the number of predicates, it is insisted, must be finite. Even in the absence of any suggestion that almost none of the attributes or predicates of the divine is graspable, and thus potential items of discursive articulation, the postulate of an infinite number of predicates is, for Hegel, sufficient to traject Spinoza into the pale of negative theology and its nominalistic discourse of the divine.

If (onto-theo-)logical categories display relationality of an internal sort, this implies, in neither *SL* nor the Logic of the *Enc*, indifference regarding sequence or order. The series Being-Essence-Concept or the series Quality-Quantity-Measure are not interruptable without loss of meaning and/or truth. Not only would the series Being-Concept-Essence and Quality-Measure-Quantity fail to disclose the truth of reality or divine reality as truth or the true, they would signal the breakdown of the intelligibility of discourse, which is, of course, related in the closest possible way to the intelligibility of the divine. Order in sequence of categories is an ineluctable. Being-Essence-Concept constitutes the determinative categorial "string"[52] within which other strings such as, for example, Quality-Quantity-Measure and Essence-Appearance-Actuality are alloted an ordered place. From the point of view of reflection, it is possible to commence with relatively complexified categories such as Measure or Concept, but it is Hegel's view that, if one does so commence, thought would lead back to the ordered sequences Quality-Quantity and Being-Essence, respectively, as their presupposition. No matter what would be the categorial point of entry, the same set of ordered sequences or string of categories would eventually come to the surface. Whatever Hegel suggests about the nature of logical, as opposed to temporal, relations (*Enc* #565), it is clearly the case that relations between categories are not characterized by reversibility. There is a constitutive, normative order with respect to sequence on the level of *logica divina*. This constitutive order is, however, not simply a metalogical feature of Hegelian categorial movement. Considered in the light of Hegel's emphases on process and becoming, categorial stringing must be interpreted as categorial genesis, just as the latter must be considered as inextricably linked to the genesis of divine subjectivity (albeit limited to the measure of subjectivity possible on the level of divine immanence).

Explicit elucidation of categorial genesis, as constitutive of the development of divine subjectivity, is tied to Hegel's logical texts. Yet other, earlier, reflection on the nature of the categories and their relation to subjectivity anticipates Hegel's fully developed proposal. In Hegel's earliest philosophical texts, in *DE* and especially *FK*, categorial genesis is linked to the development of the Idea of Reason (*GL1:*311). The Idea of Reason, it should be noted, is no longer regarded as belonging to the heuristic order, but rather the constitutive order within which it has come to be identified with the self-positing, self-particularizing 'I'. In *PS*, categorial genesis and development of self (in the Preface, unambiguously *divine* self) are tied together by the notion of 'pure category' (*die reine Kategorie*) (*GL2:*269). The pure category, upon which all determination devolves, is an activity, in fact nothing more nor less than the process of actualization whose constitutive feature—and here Hegel is correcting Fichte to whom he is so much indebted—is a return into itself (*in sich zuruck gegangen*) (*GL2:*302). The return into itself, this synclasis that constitutes the circle and circuit of self-constitution, occurs in and through a determinate and necessary order of 'opposited determination' (*entgegengesetzen Bestimmungen*) (*GL2:*302).

Hegel could not be more clear, however, in his discouragement of the view that the stringing of ontotheological predicates fully defines the divine as such, or more accurately the divine considered as a process of self-constitution. Firmly grasping the ontotheological nature of the so-called logical categories, G. R. M. Mure is undoubtedly correct in insisting that the categories—and indeed their sum—offer only *partial* definition of the divine.[53] Though Mure more asserts than argues the point, it is clear that categories cannot be more than partial realizations to the degree to which they name or express the divine outside the context of relationality to the nondivine. Outside the context of engagement in and with the finite, the divine is not fully realized individuality or self-consciousness. Thus, categories or predicates, or even strings of such categories or predicates, name or express in direct fashion the *regional* autogenesis of divine subjectivity limited to the immanent milieu. If Hegel, rowing against the current of critical erosion of a theology of divine names, can legitimate such a discourse and determine it to be inherently non-nominalistic, in a certain sense this discourse is, and must necessarily be, nonfinal. The *Enc* as a whole introduces a host of nonlogical categories such as Space, Time, Organic Being, Consciousness, etc., to name, express, and interpret the noninfinite, nondivine order within which, nonetheless, the divine dwells. The nonlogical categories that express, name, and interpret nature and finite spirit are both continuous with, and represent concretizations of, logical categories, just as nonlogical categorial strings mimic logical categorial stings that reveal themselves as foundational.[54] But discursive continuity and mimicking of categorial structure and order is intimately related with, and might even be conceived as a function of, ontotheological continuity, for the sphere of divine immanence is not, in any *real* sense, outside of relation to the finite. The very use of the preposition *before* or *vor* to characterize the sphere of immanence betrays the fact that the putative nonreferentiality of the immanent sphere to the otherness of finitude is understood to be *hypothetical*.[55] To avail of our technical terminology of synclasis and anaclasis, it seems to be Hegel's view even in his logical works that any synclasis of the logical sphere, the sphere of the divine as pure self-referentiality, or the divine construed even as pure thought after Aristotle, is ultimately notional in the non-Hegelian, nontechnical, sense of not being fully real. Thus, what characterizes the (onto-theo-)logical sphere of the immanent divine is radical anaclasis. As we shall see shortly, *LPR 3* reinforces this stance taken by Hegel in his logical texts.

One very important corollary of the (infrastructurally) anaclastic nature of the immanent divine is that the categories or thought-determinations of the *SL* and the Logic of *Enc* are *archetypes* at the same time that they are predicates. Specifically, the categories (and their strings) point beyond themselves to exemplification, both discursive and nondiscursive, in the nonimmanent sphere. For instance, the category of Being is exemplified on the most primitive and undeveloped levels of nature and finite spirit,[56] as it gets exemplified in discursive formations that smack of immediacy and undifferentiatedness (e.g., Empiricism, Schelling, Schleiermacher). Similarly, the category of Concept is exemplified in the most differentiated aspects of nature and the most differentiated aspect of finite spirit.[57] In a sense, therefore, such logical categories are proleptic. As proleptic, they cannot be considered as divine predicates without remainder. They are, at one and the same time, divine archetypes.

Scholars prepared to grant the Hegelian logic can be understood as articulating a theology of divine names and/or divine archetypes sometimes suggest that Hegel's rendition of thought-determinations can usefully be read vis-à-vis Plato's theory of forms. And this is true even in the case of Mure who articulates the Aristotelian predilection of Hegelian logic.[58] Certainly, it is Plato, rather than Aristotle, who articulates the transcendent dimension of the forms (*Theaetetus, Sophist, Parmenides*) and who provides them with theological aspiration as archetypes of the created order (*Timaeus*). Needless to say, we are not dealing here with an interpretive either/or. As Mure's own commentary indicates, there are good reasons for believing that Hegelian reflection on the categories represents a synthesis of transcendent-Platonic and immanent-Aristotelian tendencies. Mure's point is a quite general one. Yet, I submit, the thesis of synthesis can be further specified and the claim advanced that Hegelian reflection on the categories, even in its most transcendent thrust, represents a synthesis of the Platonic theory of forms and the Aristotelian theological notion of *noesis noeseos noesis*.[59] Earlier we spoke on Hegelian thought-determinations as partial *definitions* of the divine. This, in itself, represents no more than a provisional description, for thought-determinations are generated within the milieu of an ever-present divine self-consciousness. For Hegel, thought is *not* without a thinker, and categorial genesis is not a species of categorial proliferation on automatic.[60] Effectively, what Hegel does is inset the categories, which in a Platonic world of assumption can exist *outside* the divine mind, *within* the divine mind whose provisional description is Aristotle's *noesis noeseos noesis*. In doing so, it could be said that, thereby, the thought-determinations offer not merely partial definitions of, but partial *self*-definitions, of the divine.

It is clear that, in making this particular synthesis, Hegel is engaged in an interpretive operation many scholars think typical of the Neoplatonic project.[61] In the *Timaeus* the forms are the givens that set limits to the creativity of the demiurgic mind. In that regulative text the relation between thinker and thought is external rather than internal. In Aristotle, divine mind, as *noesis noeseos noesis,* is puzzlingly empty. Neoplatonism sought to solve the aporias of both philosophies and their dissonance with respect to each other by identifying the self-thinking thought of the divine with the thinking of the intelligibles.[62] The synthesis is by no means one of perfect balance. In any of its forms, whether Jewish, Pagan, or Christian, the Neoplatonic synthesis is weighted heavily in favor of the Platonic contribution, particularly when dialectic becomes understood after the late Platonic dialogues as the study and discourse not of the *way* towards the forms but of the relation *between* forms, which relation is, in significant part, constituted by otherness.[63] The presence of this last element suggests, in the strongest way possible, Neoplatonism as the precedent of the general form of Hegelian articulation of the categories, at once predicates and archetypes. Can anything more determinate be said about the relation between Neoplatonic and Hegelian elaboration, such that Neoplatonic elaboration of the intelligibles in the horizon of *Nous* stands out as offering an approximate taxon of Hegelian elaboration of categorial stringing and genesis? Does Neoplatonic reflection offer any precedent for the overdetermination of the immanent divine milieu by trinitarian articulation and articulation by divine predicates- archetypes? The hypothesis I wish to test is that post-Fourth-century Neoplatonism does afford an approximate taxon and does provide a precedent for the theologically astonishing intersection of trinitarian and predicate-archetype articulation. Before testing begins, however, I will add the caution that the hypothesis does not imply that *no* other approximate taxa or precedents can be found. Though it is implied that *few* ontotheological configurations illuminate the Hegelian position as much as late Neoplatonism, and no ontotheological configuration illuminates it more.

Integration of Trinitarian Constitution and Categorial Genesis: Neoplatonic Precedent. By way of pursuing the taxonomic and precedent-setting credentials of late Neoplatonism, I will first examine the relation of Hegel's articulation of the transfinite divine with Proclus's sophisticated Neoplatonic synthesis and then pursue the question of relation between Hegel and developed Christian Neoplatonism as a simplifying emendation of the non-Christian Neoplatonism of the Proclean kind. We begin with the first-mentioned task. Proclus is not often mentioned or explicitly evoked by Hegel, but wherever Proclus is discussed (e.g., *LHP 2* E 432–450. *GL19*:71–92), or evoked (e.g., *LPR* 3 1821 MS E 80 Note 60, E 84 Note 71; 1827 E 280 Note 83), the estimate is appreciative. At one point in his fairly dry delineation of the basic elements of Proslus's ontotheolgical system in *LHP 2,* Hegel gives way to enthusiasm and issues a professorial commendation of *sehr gut* (*GL19*:85). While it is clear that Hegel is very positive about the more systematic order, more developed form (*LHP 2* E 435. *GL19*:73), and Proclus's replication of earlier Neoplatonic integration of the Platonic vision of the intelligibles with the Aristotelian conception of *Nous,* Hegel presumes Proclus's real achievement to lie in his understanding of the articulation of *Nous* (or idea for Hegel), an understanding that shows an unmatched clarity with respect to determinate stages of progression (*ein bestimmteres Fortschreiten*) and differentiation of spheres (*Unterscheiden der Spharen*) (ibid.). Proclus is not original in construing the Triad (*Trias*) as the basic structure of differentiation (*LHP 2* E 440, *GL19:79*), and, in fact, the Triad that Hegel places under consideration, i.e., the Triad of Being-Life-Intellect, recapitulates the Triad of earlier Neoplatonism that was influential in Neoplatonic Christian elaborations of the Trinity.[64] We noted earlier that Hegel is not allergic to the intersection of Neoplatonic philosophy and the exegesis of Christian revelation and presumes that theological formulation may have something to learn from a cogently developed system of philosophy, even if it is not surpassed by it. What is instructive in the developed Neoplatonic synthesis is that in recapitulation two crucial defects of the earlier rendition of the Neoplatonic Triad are obviated, i.e., (1) the failure to fully appreciate the self-constituting activity (*Tätigkeit*) of the divine (qua Triad) (*LHP 2* E 441. *GL19*:81), and (2) the failure to see the necessity for further differentiations (ibid.). Proclus's rendition of the Neoplatonic Triad avoids a Trinity of abstract moments (*LHP 2* E 440. *GL19:79;* also *GL19:*81).

As diagnosed by Hegel, under the aegis of two sets of formal universal principles that apply to the sphere of *Nous* or the Idea, the Neoplatonic Triad of Being-Life-Intellect is not merely rendered more dynamic but is differentiated into an *Ennead.* These two sets of formal universal principles are themselves triads of a sort and are correctly identified by Hegel as Limit, Infinity, and Mixture, on the one hand, and Remaining, Regression, and Reversion (Return), on the other. These triadic sets of principles overlap and in reinforcing ways illuminate the Triad of Being-Life-Intellect. Yet, while it is the case that Being exhibits the principles of Limit (Unity) and Remaining (Identity) in an exemplary way, just as Life exhibits the principles of Infinity (Multiplicity) and Procession (Difference) and Intellect exhibits the principles of Mixture (Totality) and Reversion (Identity and Difference), each of the hypostases exhibits both sets of principles in their entirety. Thus, whichever set of principles one selects, each of the hypostases differentiates into a triad. Proclus is credited with the discovery of a Triad of Triads (*LHP 2* E 448. *GL19:*90), and his complexification within the horizon of the Neoplatonic synthesis of Plato and Aristotle constitutes, for Hegel, an advance illuminating and instructive for both Christian trinitarian theology and a Christian philosophy founded upon such a theology. Hegel applauds the noetic register of Proclus, where the latter in the *Platonic Theology* understands the Triad of Triads as the self-thinking thought of the divine (*LHP 2,* E 448; *GL19*:90). Unlike Plato, there is divine thinking (*noeseos*) as well as divine thought (*Theos noetos*), and unlike Aristotle, divine thought is inexpugnable from divine thinking. For Hegel, the result is a divine self-consciousness that constitutes a noetic whole.

Hegel's appreciative response to Proclus's ontotheology cannot simply be dismissed as being of purely historical interest. A clear measure of espousal is suggested. The dynamic, process Triad of Being-Life-Intellect bears more than a superficial resemblance to the dynamic, process Hegelian Triad of Being-Essence-Concept, especially since Hegel does think his basic triad exemplary of identity, difference, and the union of identity and difference. Moreover, as triadic articulation in Proclus is determined to take place within the milieu of the divine mind, so also is this the case with Hegel who, as with Proclus, unites the *Theos noetos* and *Theos noeseos.*[65] And, for both, it is in the third element or moment that union is definitively realized. Perhaps an even more important basis of rapprochement lies in Proclus's construal that the primitive Triad undergoes further differentiation. Arguably, the real point of contact between Proclus and Hegel lies less in the enneadic structure thus constituted in developed Neoplatonic ontotheology than in the operation of differentiation itself as regulated by a triad of principles. From a Hegelian point of view, nothing forbids more than one application of principles such as remaining, procession, and reversion.

At a minimum, then, the non-Christian Neoplatonic system of Proclus, at least on the level of the immanent divine, is able to suggest a route whereby a Christian theologian-philosopher might heal the split between trinitarian theology and a theology of divine names. Needless to say, in retrieving the Neoplatonic insight of the dynamic self-differentiating of the divine Hegel will make a number of emendations. Beyond the obvious fact that, notwithstanding significant agreement in construing the immanent divine, identity of position cannot be affirmed, there are three emendations I would like to mention here. The first is an effect of that interpretive operation we earlier called apophatic erasure, i.e., repression of the apophatic element of certain ontotheologies of a speculative type. Hegel pays almost no attention to the *Henad* of Proclus's ontotheology and instead focuses upon the derivative Triad. And where he does seem to acknowledge the relation between the Triad and the *Henad,* it is interesting to see how the priority claim of the *Henad* is dealt with. Hegel confesses that the Triad announces the unimparted (*amethekton*) God. But it seems to be Hegel's point that, as imparting the divine, the Triad ought to be conceived exclusively as a matrix of manifestation and in no way as the matrix of mystery. As Hegel downplays any suggestion of a divine *behind* or *beyond* imparting, he also guards against any suggestion that the sphere of differentiation borrows ineffability from the unimparted divine. Concerning the three triads, which Proclus calls 'mystic' since they have an unknown (*agnostos*) cause, Hegel opines that mystic or mystery be read in a positive, kataphatic rather than negative, apophatic manner, though he concedes that, in the strict sense, this is the discovery of Christianity. For in Christianity *to mysterion* is no longer the hidden but, rather, the disclosed, the manifested (*LHP 2* E 448. *GL19:*91).

The second important Hegelian emendation—though it should be confessed that it is not fully explicit in Hegel's discussion of Proclus in *LHP 2*—concerns the value given to the order of differentiation. Whereas in Proclus the series Being-Life-Intellect is a series of descending value,[66] for Hegel, the series of Being-Essence-Concept is a series of ascending value. Therefore, differentiation on the plane of the divine outside of, or rather before, appearance in the finite order is upward not downward. Moreover, the principles that apply to the basic Triad and differentiate it further are also evaluated differently. Whereas in Proclus priority is given to the principles of unity and identity, in Hegel priority is given to the principles of synthesis and totality. Hegel is, therefore, convinced that if subordination is a reality on the level of the immanent divine, it goes in precisely the opposite direction to that announced by non-Christian Neoplatonic ontotheology.

The third and final point of departure concerns an aspect of Proclus's thought not thematized by Hegel. Comparison with Proclus will put into relief the latter's move beyond Neoplatonism and illuminate his radicality. As we have seen already, the differentiation of the basic Triads of Neoplatonic and Hegelian ontotheology puts us in possession of the predicates of the divine. Now, while not all Neoplatonists make a distinction between divine predicates and divine archetypes, the system of Proclus does. For Proclus, both the peculiarity of divine names as differentiation of hypostases and their active, process character make them unsuitable candidates as archetypes of the world of manifestation. For, as forms, archetypes should regulate rather than model process and becoming. Accordingly, archetypes as regulative static forms are placed in the third hypostasis of Intellect.[67] Hegel, by contrast, believing that archetypes regulate precisely by demonstrating the form of process, encounters no obstacle in considering the differentiations of Being-Essence-Concept to be, at one and the same time, archetypes as well as predicates.

I will address much more briefly the second of our two themes in this subsection, i.e., the relationship between Hegelian elaboration of a divine triad and categorial differentiation and what developed Christian Neoplatonism of the Pseudo-Dionysian tradition thought concerning the intersection of a trinitarian theology and a theology of divine predicates and archetypes. As we have seen, Hegel defended Neoplatonic Christianity against the biblical purism of a Karl Friedrich Göschel. This does not imply, however, that Hegel had a great deal of knowledge of Neoplatonism of the first Christian centuries. *A fortiori,* the same can be said of Hegel's knowledge of the Dionysian tradition, though Hegel shows some awareness of Eriugena.[68]

Without even attempting to decide the question of the relative proportion of Christian revelation and Neoplatonic philosophy in Christian Neoplatonism, it is clear that one of the ways of describing the relation between the Dionysian tradition of Christian Neoplatonism and Proclus is to say that the Triad of Being-Life-Intellect, which in the latter is derivative with respect to a First Principle, is in the former assimilated to the first principle itself.[69] From a Hegelian perspective, this emendation can be positive in a principled sense at least, since the emendation abolishes the *beyond* of an unnameable transcendent. Yet, the kataphatic advantage of excising a unitary beyond always can be offset by saturating the Neoplatonically influenced

Christian Trinity with the unknowability, unnameability, and ineffability of the transcendent one. And this is precisely what happens in the Dionysian tradition where the Superessential Godhead (*hyperousias Thearchia*) becomes identified with the Superessential Trinity.[70] The apophatic note with regard to the Trinity becomes so radical that it is arguable whether Hegel's tendency towards apophatic erasure might not find Proclus an easier target than the Dionysian tradition, given the former's association of ineffability and unity. If the triadic scheme of Proclus's ontotheology possessed a borrowed apophatic physiognomy, it also had a kataphatic dimension. Not yet manifestation in the nondivine order, nonetheless, it is on the way and provides the ultimate ground of such manifestation. The general issue here is the question of the various coefficients of resistance to kataphatic emendation within the Neoplatonic tradition and the specific issue or whether the Dionysian or the Proclean rendition of Neoplatonism is better situated to resist Hegel's operation of apophatic erasure. We will return to these issues again in section 3 when we treat of the relationship between Hegel's and Eckhart's trinitarian thought. The question I now wish to address, however, is somewhat different: what happens to the intersection of divine predicates and archetypes with a triad of hypotases in Christian Neoplatonism's emendation? The radically apophatic horizon of the Triad-Trinity of Christian Neoplatonism rules out further differentiation of Triad-Trinity, differentiation being possible if and only if a reality is in some respects knowable.[71] But the superessential Trinity is not known in any discursive way, and divine attributes, which can be ascribed to the Trinity as to the Godhead, become linguistic gestures of a nominalistic sort. Predicates point toward, but do not find their objective correlative in, the divine.[72] Moreover, Christian Neoplatonism of a Dionysian sort—the proximate foundation of both the mystical tradition of the Western and Eastern churches—solidifies and radicalizes the tendency in Proclus, namely, the tendency to distinguish between divine predicates and archetypes. In the Western Dionysian tradition it is Eriugina who is clearest on this. Whatever the incapacity of divine predicates to truly name God, it is evident that the basic horizon they intimate is the sphere of absolute transcendence. By contrast, archetypes, or what Eriugena refers to as 'primordial causes', belong to a posterior order this side of mystery.[73] If archetypes relate closely to the Trinity, their ontological status is, nonetheless, decidedly different.

In the light of the emendation of Christian Neoplatonism of a Dionysian sort, it can be said perhaps that the Proclean variety of Neoplatonism offers the best taxonomic credentials of the integration of a dynamically conceived trinitarian theology and a theology of divine predicates and archetypes observable in Hegel's logical texts. Of course, such integration is suggested elsewhere and is recommended in *LPR* but is carried out in a truly effective way only on the level of concept (*Begriff*) which belongs to philosophy proper. Nevertheless, what Hegel says in this realm is not irrelevant for his discussion of the Christian articulation of the theologoumenon of the Trinity on the level of divine immanence, and his logical portrayal of intersection, must be awarded regulative status.

Section 2.2 The "Immanent Trinity" as Speculatively Informed **Vorstellung: LPR** *and Other Hegelian Texts*

LPR occupies a middle ground between the full conceptual translation or rewriting of Christianity and dogmatic Christian theology that possesses a narrative base. Hegelian presentation is hermeneutical. As such, Hegel's presentation is multifaceted: it critiques traditional dogmatic forms and points towards a normative conceptual presentation which, however, remains in the margins. The *Lectures* centrally include exploration of the "Immanent Trinity," and Hegel's depiction is such as to facilitate mapping between development upon the level of logic and trinitarian articulation. The domain or region of the Hegelian "Immanent Trinity" is that of *Universality,* a meta-ascription that can be applied to logical articulation as a whole, though within logical articulation, as within the sphere of trinitarian divine immanence portrayed by *LPR 3,* three elements or moments, i.e., Universality, Particularity, and Singularity, are found.

Reinhard Heede has proposed a correlation between the *onto-theo-logik* of Hegelian logic and the religious *phaenomeno-theo-logik* operative elsewhere in Hegelian texts. While there is a sense in which *LPR* as a whole articulates a *phaenomeno-theo-logik, LPR 3,* in particular, might be construed as providing more, providing, in fact, an *onto-theo-logik,* though an *onto-theo-logik* that is hermeneutically involved with religious-theological presentation. The ontotheology of *LPR 3* has, of course, a scope more inclusive than the logic, and, indeed, the mapping of the complete articulation of the divine history that is the momentous subject of *LPR 3* is provided only by *Enc* as a whole.[74] The first element, region, moment of trinitarian ontotheological elaboration is the objective correlative of Hegelian logic. Moreover, both can be provided with essentially the same characterization. The "Immanent

Trinity," hermeneutically isolated by *LPR 3,* is the articulation of the intrareferential self-manifestation of God. For Iwan Iljin, what Hegel expressly states as the identity of the "Immanent Trinity" in his hermeneutical elaboration is also the appropriate theological characterization of the logic. Logic is the first epoch of the manifestation of God, the epoch of self-manifestation, self-revelation.[75]

Hegel's defense of the revelational essence of Christianity, his subverting of the apophatic tradition's hold on mystery by appeal to a Pauline revision of the notion, and his appeal to the trinitarian matrix of revelation were all discussed in chapter 1. *LPR* repeatedly reminds that trinitarian revelation is a dynamic that occurs on the level of the ahistorical, or, to use Berdyaev's locution,[76] the 'metahistorical'. The Lectures of 1824 succinctly underscore the metahistorical aspect of trinitarian revelation:

> In this field God is the act of self-revealing (*das Sichoffenbaren*) because he is spirit; but he is not yet the act of appearing (*das Erscheinen*). (E 190, G 123)

The contrast between self-revealing (*das Sichoffenbaren*) and appearing (*das Erscheinen*) specifies the difference between the two revelational matrices. A passage in the 1821 Manuscript in which the Hegelian revisionist sense of mystery is in operation on the metahistorical level of the immanent trinitarian divine is particularly worthy of attention:

> God is spirit—that which we call the triune God, i.e., the mystery of God (*mysterium Gottes*). God is spirit, absolute activity (*die absolute Tätigkeit*), actus purus, i.e., subjectivity, infinite personality (*unendliche Persönlichkeit*), infinite distinction of himself from himself (*unendliche Unterscheidung seiner von sich selbst*). (*LPR 3* 1821 MS E 78, G16)

Hegel's use of the language of mystery and the mystical with regard to the Trinity might plausibly be regarded as disingenuous apologetic. But Hegel here, as elsewhere (*LPR 3* 1824 E 192, G 125), is, in fact, making a systematic theological move of some import and not merely making a covert rhetorical appeal to his orthodoxy. The context of his move is a complex one. The revisionist Pauline acceptation of the essence of Christianity is, of course, foundational. Paradoxically, though Luther is not a central factor in Hegel's determination, he serves as a warranting presence. Neither Luther's prohibition on speculation, his severe demarcation between a theology of the cross and a theology of glory, nor his *relative* silence on the doctrine of the Trinity provides positive impetus to investigate the revelational context of the Trinity. Nevertheless, the fact that the context of Luther's theology of the cross is thoroughgoingly revelational; that Luther does, in fact, make *some* comments about the Trinity;[77] and that these are not absolutely corrosive all provide Hegel with *negative* capability for reflection upon the nonfinite, nonrelational, and noncreative domain of reality. And for Hegel, it appears as if negative capability is sufficient when justification is ruled out. Yet, if Luther cannot be categorized as part of the positive ambiance, Jacob Boehme, who faced, as with Hegel, similar problems with respect to his avowed Lutheran orthodoxy, certainly can. Hegel shows himself aware of the trinitarian contribution of Boehme in the *LHP 3,* and his own locution of holy Trinity (*heilige Dreieinigkeit*) in the Lectures of 1827 (E 275–276. G 201) appears deliberately to recall the *Ternarius Sanctus,* the "Immanent Trinity," of Boehme.[78] Boehme's mystical depiction of the Trinity, which underscored the ability of noetic vision, unfolded a Trinity of dynamic self-manifestation. But Boehme's depiction harks back to a previous mystic's treatment—a treatment which is perhaps ultimately responsible for Hegel's ultrakataphatic redescription of the revelational dynamics of the "Immanent Trinity." This mystic is Meister Eckhart, who was much admired by Hegel.

Now, a constitutive tension may be seen in Eckhart's envisagement of the relation between Godhead and Trinity. One pole is constituted by traditional apophatic theology's identification of the Superessential God and the superessential Trinity. This is the case with respect to two of Eckhart's main sources, Pseudo-Dionysius and Duns Scotus Eriugena. For the former the superessential Godhead (*Hyperousias Thearchia*) is defined by the superessential Trinity of Persons; and Eriugena applies to the Trinity the very same apophatic terms he applies to the Godhead.[79] The other pole consists in the tendency to emphasize the transcendence of the Godhead such that even the Trinity no longer properly belongs to, or defines, the Superessential Godhead but becomes separate from it. Michel Henry is particularly eloquent with respect to the second and, arguably, dominant strain in Eckhartian mystical theology.[80] Henry suggests a number of reinforcing reasons for this dislocation. One basic reason, according to Henry, is that Eckhart's conceptual need to distinquish between the nonrelational and relational divine gets codified in the distinction between the Godhead (*Gottheit*) and God (*Gott*). This has the effect of ontologizing what otherwise might have been regarded as a functional distinction. And when hiddenness, unity, and inactivity are associated with the unrelational Godhead, this forces the Trinity to the relational or God pole, since manifestation, differentiation, and action cannot be unequivocally eschewed. From the point of view of the effect it has within the Neoplatonic stream of theology, in Eckhart that Trinity undergoes a kind of kataphatic relativization that corrects the Dionysian tradition's correction of the ontotheology of Proclus we commented on earlier. In Eckhart trinitarian thought is brought back in the direction of Proclus, making easier Hegel's own emendation of the Christian mystical tradition's rendition of Trinity, a rendition which even more forcefully than Scholasticism and Lutheran orthodoxy protected its ineffability.[81]

Of course, in Eckhart the apophatic in the shape of the barren Godhead or the divine solitude (*Abgeschiedenheit*) still plays a dominant role. As we have seen, exactly the opposite is the case with Hegel. Yet, essentially presupposing the Eckhartian distinction between the Godhead and Trinity, Hegel's excision of the negative divine and his critique of monism leaves intact only the dynamic, essentially trinitarian revelational nexus. And this trinitarian articulation, while it is essentially intradivine, is thoroughgoingly *kataphatic.* Moreover, the kataphatic nature of the intradivine realm of manifestation associates the "Immanent Trinity" with the nonabsolutely transcendent *God* in an *intrinsic* way. This also, as we have seen, had been suggested by Eckhart, and in Eckhart this lead to the close relationship of what has to be regarded as the Trinity in itself with creation. In his exegesis of the Prologue of John's Gospel, the Trinity, or rather the Birth (*Geburt*) of the Trinity, relates in the closest possible fashion to creation. Creation and Begetting are, Eckhart suggests, two sides of a single act.[82] For Hegel also, and this is especially evident in *LPR,* the Trinity is connected with *God,* with what might be called the positive rather than the negative divine. [83] The Trinity is narratively proleptic and open with respect to the genuine otherness of finitude. This openness or *anaclasis* is an indelible feature of Hegel's "Immanent Trinity," while at the same time the "Immanent Trinity" represents a *provisional* closure or synclasis (*LPR 1* E 307–308, G 211–12).

The "Immanent Trinity" As Narratively Proleptic: Synclasis and Anaclasis

The "Immanent Trinity" is the realm of divine self- manifestation. Considered as anything more than ground-sketch of fully articulated divinity, however, the "Immanent Trinity" signals a truncated divine. From the vantage point of a complete vision of God's nature, which Hegel argues will not merely include but be defined by appearance or manifestation *ad extra,* the "Immanent Trinity" would describe a narcissistic divine incompatible with the perception of *Deus Revelatus* whose story is the content of the Christian *theological* narrative or metanarrative. But this story is understood by Hegel to be nothing less than an enactment or elaboration of divine personhood or divine self-identity. The narrative mutilation that would result from positing the "Immanent Trinity" as exhaustive of the divine would rule out personhood, which Hegel views after the model of *Bildungsroman* as requiring encounter, even antagonism, between virtual self and world. Personhood is possible only in and through struggle with, and ultimate victory over and appropriation of, the initially alien. *LPR 3* eloquently charts the self-transcending nisus of the divine beyond the pale of immanence and suggests there is nothing extrinsic in the 'ecstasis' of the immanent divine.[84] *LPR 3* also provides a clear map of the encounter between *virtual* divine, or *virtual* infinite, and the radical finitude of nature and finite spirit. For Hegel then, it can be said, personhood, even divine personhood, is only narratively possible.

Hegel does not envisage the "Immanent Trinity" as exhausting the divine. For him, a structural feature of the "Immanent Trinity" is that of *narrative prolepsis.* The "Immanent Trinity" anticipates further narrative adventure, and full realization of the divine only takes place in negotiation with the *counterdivine* of nature and finite spirit.[85] As with the sphere of logic, the "Immanent Trinity" depicted in *LPR 3* constitutes a whole or totality and, as such, may be symbolized by a circle. The parallelism of religious syllogism and philosophical syllogism in the *Enc* certainly appears to legitimate the use of circle symbolism. Thus, in a sense, the "Immanent Trinity", which in the Hegelian interpretation and redescription of the Christian *Vorstellungen* of Father-Son-Spirit denotes the self-reflexivity of divine self-consciousness, is synclastic or closed. But, with respect to the "Immanent Trinity", synclasis or closure is only provisional or relative. In absolute terms, the "Immanent Trinity," is anaclastic. From a Hegelian point of view, anaclasis with respect to divine immanence guarantees a divine whose goodness can be affirmed in the ontological generosity of self-communication. That Hegel selfconsciously intends to situate himself within the general parameters of a Neoplatonic definition of divine goodness, we have seen already in chapter 1 where Hegel appealed in his combatting of negative theology to the Neoplatonic construct of the nonenviousness of the divine.[86] Whether this contexting is ultimately revelatory of Hegel's structural allegiance will be an issue tackled later (chapter 3).

From a Hegelian point of view, the relativization of the synclasis that properly belongs to the domain or epoch of the "Immanent Trinity" avoids three invidious, closely related ontotheological possibilities: (1) a degenerate depiction of God as enclosed and self-involved, *Deus Incurvatus* or incurved divine,[87] (2) obliteration of the meaning of existence, and (3) reduction of the status of existence to that of accident.[88] In addition, this relativization of synclasis also ensures the relativization of the mode of differentiation proper to the sphere of immanence. To the extent to which this mode of differentiation is misunderstood as exhausting the divine, it, too, is diagnosed as degenerate. The mode of differentiation has a multitude of aspects, and the incapacity of this mode in and of itself to support divine personhood is similarly polyvalent, and applies to and is distributed over its various aspects of which four are especially important: the ontological, the gnoseological, the axiological, and the existential. We shall individually examine each of these aspects in the sequel, but, for the moment, our focus will be upon the general quality of this mode of differentiation as presented in *LPR 3*.

The following two passages in *LPR 3* are exemplary in taking the mode of differentiation proper to the immanent or universal sphere as an explicit theme. In the first, synclasis is relativized in the 'only' (*nur*), and thus metonymically the mode of differentiation is also relativized. In the second, a contrast is implied between two modes of differentiation, a less adequate mode on the level of the "Immanent Trinity" and a more adequate mode which is provided with a description but not given a name. Substituting the more philosophically informed Idea (*Idee*) for the more dogmatically informed Trinity (i.e., "Immanent Trinity"), Hegel writes:

> Eternal being-in-and-for-itself is what discloses itself, determines itself, divides itself, posits itself as what is differentiated from itself (*sich als Unterschiedenes seiner zu setzen*), but the difference is at the same time constantly sublated. Thereby actual being in and for itself constantly returns into itself (*in sich zurückgekehrt*)—only in this way is it spirit. What is distinguished is defined in such a way that the distinction immediately disappears, and we have a relationship of God, of the idea, merely to himself. The act of differentiation is only (*nur*) a movement, a play of love with it-

> self (*ein Spiel der Liebe mit sich selbst*), which does not arrive at the seriousness of other-being, of separation of rupture. (1827 E 291–292, G 216)

And again, the "Idea"

> is posited in its infinite differentiation (*unendliche Unterscheidung*), it has not arrived at darkness (*Finsternis*), i.e., being-for-itself, opacity (*Undurchsichtigheit*), impenetrability (*Undurchdringlichkeit*). . . . (1821 MS p 78, G 16)

Considered together, these passages make clear that Hegel is registering a distinction between a mode of differentiation (*unendliche Unterscheidung*) proper to the immanent milieu and a more adequate mode of differentiation, i.e., that *between* the finite and the infinite. Infinite differentiation, Hegel is suggesting, is *virtual* rather than *actual,* though the virtual status of this mode of differentiation is a fundamental deficiency only if its proleptic tendency is ignored. In Hegel's vision of the complete articulation of the divine, while adequate differentiation and adequate dialectic presuppose diremption (*Entfremdung*) and alienation (*Entäusserung*),[89] infinite differentiation does, indeed, provide the *formal condition* of genuine differentiation and dialectic (*LPR 3* 1821 MS E 87, G 24–25).

Hegel's registering of this very important distinction between two modes of differentiation mixes the conceptual and the symbolic. The conceptual and the symbolic in no way conflict and are, in fact, mutually reinforcing and revealing. Limiting interpretation to symbolic explication, it is clear that the implied distinction between *darkness* and *light* in the second of our two passages in turn implies the differentiation of *light* as the contrary. This implication is corroborated in *LPR 1* where Hegel clearly states that the immanent milieu or the milieu of the universal is the locus of transparency (1824 E 305, G 210).

A number of other passages reinforce this symbolic, but theologically dense, equation between light and the "Immanent Trinity", which Hegel in *LPR 3* still occasionally speaks of after the model of love (1821 MS E 78, G 17). Worth particular mention also is the passage from *Enc* (#112) discussed above, where the category of Essence is explicated through the metaphors of reflection and light. Given the theological core of the symbol of light, the relativization implies the relativization of the normative trinitarian complex that supported the logos theory of the Gospel of John with a metaphysics of light. Fully adequate revelation or manifestation demands appearance (*LPR 3* 1824 E 190, G 127). Put another way, revelation demands contrast, opposition of light and darkness. For Hegel, a God of mere light is just the opposite of the self-revelatory divine. And, for Hegel, the self-revelatory view of the divine is the only proper one, and this view is proposed in absolute clarity in the Christian Religion and is explicated in its theology, or at least ought to be so explicated.

Corresponding to the two modes of differentiation posited in *LPR 3* are two modes of *closure,* though such a correspondence is not written on the surface of Hegel's lectures. But before the correspondence is thematized, a brief reminder of Hegel's assertion of the ontotheological requirement of closure or synclasis is in order. This requirement is as generic as the requirement of differentiation and in Hegel is often pursued under the auspices of return (*Rückkehr*) or return into self (*Rückkehr zu sich*). The generic requirement of synclasis is present from the first burgeonings of Hegel's philosophical self-identity. The logic of the Enc, written over twenty years later, still reprises *DE* with respect to the necessity of closure, though the Hegelian view is couched in a language much less gnoseologically pronounced than the earlier text. Infinity, Hegel suggests in *Enc* #94, is never reached through the and-so-on of iteration. *LPR 3,* in its discussion of the "Immanent Trinity" and its closeness and distance from other varieties of trinitarian thought, consistently uses the synclasis of the "Immanent Trinity," its aspect of return (*Rückkehr*), as a criterion of distinction. Indeed, this is the specific difference of the Christian Trinity, what demarcates it from Spinozism or the Indian Trinity (*LPR 3* 1824 E 193, G 126–127).

With this we arrive at our distinction of two modalities of closure. These, in fact, correspond to the two modalities of differentiation already detailed. Synclasis is, certainly, in operation on the level of the "Immanent Trinity." Thus synclasis represents for Hegel nothing less than a formal property of the Christian thought system. But the closure or return on the level of the "Immanent Trinity" cannot be absolute, for the divine activity, or *actus* in the latinate form Hegel avails of in *LPR,* is more encompassing than that possible on the level of immanence. Absolute closure and return is predicated of the complete divine narrative, and this includes the divine history of creation, incarnation, and redemption. Undoubtedly, the Hegelian view of the narrative of the divine answers to the criterion, judiciously expressed in Frank Kermode's phrase, that a narrative express "a sense of an ending." But it should be recognized that it is only on the level of the

Inclusive Trinity as a whole that ending, that synclasis, is fully realized.

Modes of Differentiation. Let us return to the Hegelian distinction between modes of differentiation and the inadequacy of this mode on the level of immanence. I stated above that, differentiation being polyvalent, the inadequacy of infinite differentiation may be considered from four overlapping points of view, i.e., ontological, gnoseological, axiological, and existential. Three of these points of view may be dealt with here, and where convenient the measure of inadequacy on the plane of differentiation correlated with that on the plane of closure. The fourth point of view, i.e., the existential, can be more conveniently dealt with in a separate subsection of its own.

(1) *Ontological.* Chapelle has commented that a major rupture between Hegel and the mainline theological traditions (especially Neoplatonic and Scholastic) occurs in Hegel's envisioning of the immanent divine, not as the milieu of ontological richness, but under the sign of privation that it actively, and in a quite literal sense *creatively,* tries to overcome.[90] Put in different terms, the sphere of the "Immanent Trinity" is not the 'really real' (*ontos on*) that is only narratively possible,[91] narratively engendered and acquired. Mediation (*Vermittlung*) on the level of categorial immanence presupposes a certain poverty in the immediacy of the categories of Being and Nothing, and the nisus to further mediation beyond the realm of categorial immanence (and its explicit trinitarian correlate in *LPR 3*) points to a deficiency proper to the level of divine immanence or universality as a whole. The point may be made somewhat differently by focusing upon the category of actuality (*Wirklichkeit*). Actuality is a category *within* the immanent sphere of the divine, but the crucial point is that it is not a category that, as such, *applies* to a reality on the level of the immanent sphere. The Idea itself, as the terminus of the immanent divine dynamics, is actual (*wirklich*) in no more than an *ideal* sense. Actuality has but a proleptic status on the level of divine immanence and is fully possible only as the term of the complete, and completed, development of the divine infinite in and through the finite. The self-development, or self-determination, of the divine requires a divine history (*die göttliche Geschichte*) over and above the metahistory of development on the level of immanence. The developmental, one might even say, narrative character of Actuality is, perhaps, already coded in the category itself which, as adopted by Hegel, is quite Aristotelian. Actuality trans-

lates Aristotle's *energeia,* and *energeia* in the *Metaphysics* and *Physics* betokens becoming as often as Being, on-the-way to completion as completion itself.[92]

To be fully real or actual the elaboration of the divine requires not merely a more concrete modality of differentiation than that possible on the level of immanence, it also requires multiplicity.[93] It is an ontological rule that totality (*Totalität*) requires multiplicity. In a deficient sense, both multiplicity and totality belong already to the sphere of immanence. But in *LPR 3* Hegel is clearly of the opinion that the overall character of the "Immanent Trinity," as that of 'immediate identity' (*LPR 3* 1821 MS E 78, G 17), vitiates the claims to genuine adequacy of both. Thus, the multiplicity posited within the protological sphere—as also its mode of differentiation, i.e., infinite differentiation—is valid only in its aspect of prolepsis, i.e., of signaling and anticipating a narratively evolved more adequate instantiation. Similarly with *totality.* The incompletion of totality represented in the logic by the *Idea* has been pointed out by Jaeschke and, following him, by Schlitt.[94] Both reflect on the end of *SL* where Hegel explicitly declares that the terminus of categorial development on the level of logic is not the *absolute Absolute.* To the extent, therefore, that the Hegelian model of the divine is that of ontogenesis, or what might be called the model of *ontological increase,* ontological richness and depth is not realized on the level of divine immanence. It is hardly necessary to point out that, in this adoption, Hegel departs from the traditional view of divine as the *Summum Esse* fully complete from eternity and within eternity, and requiring no development, either atemporal or temporal. Aquinas obviously stands out as a major proponent of the traditional view, and even Eckhart, who introduces the linguistic term *Wirklichkeit* into German theological and philosophical thought,[95] notwithstanding his differences from Aquinas, stands much more solidly within the ambit of the tradition than does Hegel.[96]

(2) *Gnoseological.* The gnoseological aspect of differentiation is, of course, only analytically separable from the ontological, as it is from the axiological and existential. For Hegel, differentiation is an ineluctable condition of genuine self-consciousness and subjectivity. But Hegelian distinction between the two kinds of differentiations, belonging to less developed and more developed epochs of the divine, determines the kind of subjectivity and self-consciousness possible. On the level of the "Immanent Trinity" the 'play' of distinction does realize a divine subjectivity and self-consciousness. On the plane of immanence, knowledge of other is knowledge of self. But for the

gnoseological plenum to be realized, just as with the ontological, the more concrete form of differentiation, i.e., that *between* the infinite and the finite, is a requirement. Absolute subjectivity, what Hegel calls in the logic of *Enc* 'encompassing subjectivity', is not realized on the level of immanence.

For Hegel, then: (1) Differentiation is an ineluctable, if *any* self-conscious subjectivity whatsoever is to be possible. Differentiation specifies a condition that applies indifferently to the divine and the human. (2) Self-conscious subjectivity is more or less concrete depending upon the modality of differentiation and the narrative locus of its operation. Both of these assertions are theologically important. Neither is theologically uncontroversial. In advocating them, Hegel sets himself against such a major representative of the Christian theological tradition as Aquinas. A brief analysis of the *Summa* 1 a Q 14 shows up in a particularly striking way the differences between a more traditional understanding of God and its Hegelian revision. Two either/or's are examined in 1 a Q 14 that are important for determining Hegel's gnoseological revolution: (1) One must posit either the identity of the knower and the known in divine simplicity or the *return* (*rediens*) of knowing through the known to the knower. (2) One can hold the view that either infinity can have itself as object or that infinity is never graspable as object but merely approximated to through an indefinite number of finite cognitive acts. In both cases Aquinas chooses the either, Hegel does not. Let us turn to the first of Aquinas's *aut-auts*. In Q 14, article 4 Aquinas rules that God's act of knowing is his substance. God is self-identical and self-subsistent. Aquinas disputes the thesis of self-reflexive return, and the reason he does so is clear. Return must be denied, since return presupposes an initial separation. For Aquinas, there can be no separation. The divine simplicity does not have knowledge but *is* knowledge. For Hegel, by contrast, both divine knowing within and without the sphere of divine immanence is, as we have argued, construed after the model of *Rückkehr* and *Unterscheidung*.

In claiming the simplicity of divine knowledge, Aquinas is obviously drawing his conclusion from a theological tradition of divine simplicity that had major representatives in Augustine and Maimonides. The Neoplatonic tradition was, in many respects, also available as a support.[97] But Aquinas does not represent the only viable option within the ontotheological tradition, and the Hegelian model of divine knowledge cannot be regarded as a mere reflex of an idea found philosophically persuasive. Hegel's view of divine knowledge represents a not altogether uncommon, though ultimately strictly minority, theological option. A root of this *Unterscheidung-Rückkehr* envisioning may paradoxically be precisely that Neoplatonism which was one of the earliest and most powerful voices in the avocation of divine simplicity. The supreme principle or reality in the *Enneads,* for example, is totally beyond duality and multiplicity and is referred to, after the *Parmenides,* as the *One* (*to Hen*). Yet, when Plotinus raises the question as to whether the One has knowledge of itself after the manner of the *noesis noeseos noesis* of the Aristotelian God, he appears to oscillate between denying knowledge (gnosis), intellection (noesis) or self-consciousness (synaesthesis) to the One (*Enneads* 3.9.9) and maintaining that the One does, indeed, have knowledge of itself, but a knowledge that is qualitatively different (*katanoesis*) or qualitatively superior (*hypernoesis*) to that found on the level of *Nous,* where the latter presupposes a subject-object bifurcation.[98] As we saw earlier, the tendency in Proclus is to suggest that divine knowledge that bears the remotest analogy to human knowledge requires differentiation between *Theos Noetos* and *Theos Noesis.* This, he believes, is possible only on the nonabsolute level of the Neoplatonic triad of Being-Life-Intellect.

Both Plotinus's constitutive tension and Proclus's simplifying prescription undergo occasional reprise within the Christian theological tradition, particularly within the ranks of mystical theology. Eckhart presents a not totally exceptional case. As a good Thomist, Eckhart is quite prepared to identify being and knowledge in God.[99] Nevertheless, in distinguishing *Gott* from *Gottheit,* and even the "Immanent Trinity" from the barrenness of the Godhead, there is a tendency to posit gnoseological duality on the level of the "Immanent Trinity." The critical link in this chain of ontotheological precedents is, undoubtedly, Jacob Boehme, who came to evaluate the relative merits of Godhead and God, Godhead and Trinity in a way antithetical to Eckhart. If Eckhart espouses the hidden God, Boehme espouses the mystery of the self-revealing God. If Eckhart points to the supereminence of the non-knowledge or unknowing possible on the level of divine simplicity, Boehme posits the supereminence of divine knowledge possible on the level of trinitarian differentiation. It is, perhaps, Boehme who, in the theological tradition prior to Hegel, most radically posits the necessity of differentiation on the level of the divine. And it is Boehme, a self-professed Lutheran like Hegel, who also posits the necessity of return and the resolution of differentiation on the level of the divine. Two very short Boehmian texts provide perhaps the clearest expression of the two general desiderata of differentiation and return. In *Clavis* Boehme writes:

> For in the one only substance (*einem ewigen Wesen*) wherein there is no division (*darinen keine Schiedlichkeit*) there can be no knowledge. (E # 29, G #13)

In *Theoscopia,* or *The Divine Intuition,* the question is asked: "How can a single will have knowledge of itself?" (1,10). The question is somewhat rhetorical since Boehme has already declared in 1,8 that:

> Without contradiction nothing can become manifest to itself; for if it has nothing to resist it, it goes continually outward and does not return again into itself. But if it does not return into itself as into that from which it originally came, it knows nothing of the primal being.[100]

We can be a good deal briefer with regard to the second either/or. In article 12 of the same question (Q 14) Aquinas insists that the infinite can have the infinite as object and attacks the view put forward in Aristotle's *Physics* that the infinite at best can be approximated through an indefinite (or infinite) series of cognitive acts. Strictly speaking, Hegel's position is identical to neither that of the criticizer nor the criticized. While Hegel's construal of the immanent infinite divine does, in some sense, grant that knowledge of the infinite is possible through the infinite, he qualifies this knowledge as not being *actual* to the fullest degree. From Hegel's point of view, the Aristotelian view of the quantitative infinite is also flawed. Aristotle's view suffers from a narrative defect similar to that marring the *Wissenschaftslehre.* For Hegel, while knowledge *of* and *through* the finite is an inexcisable moment of the infinite's knowledge of itself, a terminal point must be reached in which knowing is adequate to the infinite as object. In a sense, the common defect of both Fichte and Aristotle might be regarded more strongly as a *defect of narrative,* for Hegel does appear to suggest that real knowledge is not possible unless we postulate closure (synclasis) or return. Boehme, as we have already seen, was Hegel's precursor in positing closure and return as ontotheological desiderata, but, though the point cannot really be argued for here, Boehme might also be thought to anticipate Hegel in maintaining that the itinerary of the differentiation and return of the infinite argues exile in the finite, and, more specifically, that divine knowledge is fully actual only if it has travelled the route of finite cognition.

(3) *Axiological.* Though Hegel does not, in all of his texts, shy away from predicating qualities of the divine, he does not in general, as we saw earlier (chap. 1, sect. 1.3), react in an unambiguously positive way to this relatively standard theological procedure. As presented in *LPR 3,* the theological procedure of divine names suffers from a number of flaws. For Hegel, these flaws, discussed in some detail in chap. 1, sect. 1.3, tell against using a predicate like goodness in any direct first order way of the divine. Yet the trinitarian divine does not go without characterization in Hegel. To the trinitarian divine is ascribable the fullness of reality and knowledge (later we shall examine the Hegelian ascriptions of Love and Life). These ascriptions, in a sense, might be regarded as belonging not to a first- but second-order level of reflection upon the trinitarian self-revealing divine that is summarized in the semantically dense notion of *Geist.* Accordingly, if goodness is not serviceable as a direct first-order attribute, this does not imply that goodness is not a legitimate characterization of the divine. As we shall see momentarily, the real question is not whether this characterization is legitimate; the question is what is its proper sphere of differentiation and the narrative locus of its application.

LPR 3 implies that, just as the sphere of the "Immanent Trinity" is the domain of the holy, it is also the domain of the good. In a passage from the 1824 lectures which will be treated in detail below (*LPR 3* E 194, G 127), Hegel maintains that one of the reasons he cannot advocate a personalist view of the "Immanent Trinity" is that, in his understanding of person, this implies the attribution of *evil* (*das Böse*) to the immanent divine. Leaving until section 3 examination of the rationale for this rather unusual position, Hegel can be construed as characterizing the "Immanent Trinity" as good. And making due allowance for the nonfinite nature of the "Immanent Trinity," Hegel, by extension, may be construed as applying 'goodness' to the divine that has not entered into relation with the other than infinite. But goodness ascribable to the "Immanent Trinity" is in the very same situation as the ascription of full actuality and developed subjectivity. It is, at best, proleptic. This means that, just as the "Immanent Trinity" cannot be identified with the *Summum Esse,* neither can it be identified with the *Summum Bonum.* The first epoch of the divine in describing a noninclusive infinite describes at the same time a noninclusive good. In Hegel's narrative depiction of God, rendered in *LPR 3* as a trinitarian elaboration, actuality, subjectivity and goodness (or the perfection of goodness) have all the character of being gained and nothing of the character of being given. Within the first epoch of the Inclusive Trinity, i.e., the "Immanent Trinity," it can, of course, be granted that the maxima of reality, self-consciousness, and perfection of goodness are *implicitly* present. To render the good fully explicit, however, requires the hiatus of evil that belongs to the second epoch of the trinitarian divine, the domain of the finite separate from the integrity of the infinite. The hiatus of evil will be examined in section 3.2 of the following chapter.

There is another, much more narrow, sense sometimes appealed to in the secondary literature in which Hegel might be understood as characterizing the "Immanent Trinity" as good. I pointed in chap. 1, sect. 1.2 to the fairly extensive rhetorical appeal Hegel makes to the Platonic construct of the non-enviousness of God, though it should be pointed out in passing that Valentinian Gnosticism also availed of the trope.[101] God, in Hegel's view, is thoroughgoing activity of revelation. An essential feature of this activity is the ecstasis of the "Immanent Trinity" and the positing of finitude. There can be little doubt that the Hegelian view of *ecstasis,* while it has much more approximate analogues within the Christian tradition, formally obeys Pseudo-Dionysius' theologically regulative idea of *Bonum diffusivum sui,* where diffusion in a sense, plays at once the role of exemplar and ultimate criterion of goodness.[102] It is questionable, however, whether the indicator *diffusion* can exhaustively define goodness. Yet, avoiding this question, another can be asked. Is the Hegelian appeal really Pseudo-Dionysian? Does the Hegelian epochal view of the divine really authenticate a Christian Neoplatonic view of goodness? On the surface this certainly appears to be the case, but in chapter 3 I hope to show the Boehmian and Gnostic precedents of Hegel's position.

The Apathetic Divine of the Immanent Sphere

Thus far we have discussed three fundamental aspects of the constitutive deficiency of the "Immanent Trinity." Here we address the fourth, i.e., what might be called the aspect of *existential* deficiency. In *LPR 3,* Hegel more or less indiscriminately applies the terms Love (*Liebe*), Life (*Leben*), and Spirit (*Geist*) to the immanent trinitarian dynamics of producing distinction and overcoming it. This is the case in the 1821 Manuscript, 1824 Lectures, and 1827 Lectures. In this aspect the notions Love, Life, and Spirit get implicated in the constitutional deficiency of the sphere. The deficiency of Love is merely tacit in the 1821 Manuscript's talk of Love consisting of immediate identity (*als unmittelbare Identität*) and negative reflection into self (E 78, G 17). The 1824 Lectures are less tacit. Still, the kind of deficiency divine Love and divine Life are involved in within the sphere of immanence is not fully determined. Love and divine Life both denote a process (*Prozess*), a process that is nothing so much as the play of self-maintenance and selfconfirmation (*nichts als ein Spiel der Selbsterhaltung, der Vergewisserung seiner selbst*) (E 195, G 129). The critical edge here is concentrated in the term *play* (*Spiel*). But Spirit (*Geist*) also gets implicated in the deficiency of the "Immanent Trinity." Immediately following his reflection upon Love in the 1821 Manuscript Hegel adds:

> God is Spirit, the one as infinite subjectivity (*als unendliche Subjektivität*), the one in the infinite subjectivity of distinction (*Einer in der unendlichen Subjektivität des Unterschieds*). (*LPR 3* E 78, G 17)

Yet the fact that Spirit also denotes the elaboration of the fully inclusive divine subjectivity, which necessarily involves divestment (*Entäusserung*) and alienation (*Entfremdung*) in and through the finite, and in consequence covers two domains, i.e., a relative and regional domain (the "Immanent Trinity") and an absolute and inclusive domain (the Inclusive Trinity), suggests, at the very least, the plausibility of the double extension of Love and Life. It must be admitted that the extension most often attributed to Love and Life in *LPR 3* is, indeed, the immanent sphere, but from this it should not be inferred that Hegel has completely shelved the parameter of alienation that was implied in his earliest use of these categories.[103] This parameter, which radically alters the sense of Love and Life and, perhaps, also defines Spirit, is implied in *LPR 3*. Thus, in a sense, it is not that Love and Life are in themselves flawed, but rather that their sense has not been adequately determined if the parameter is that of "infinite differentiation" constitutive of the domain of immanence.

LPR 3 reflection upon Love and Life or the divine Life can fruitfully be read against the background of determination Hegel makes in *PS*. There Hegel proposes an extension that centrally involves alienation and rules out or, at the very least, sets critical limits to the applicability of the categories of Love and Life to the immanent sphere. Moreover, it is *PS* that suggests the appropriate antithesis to play and, in its revisionist language, indicates the aspect of Spirit it most wishes to defend. All this is crystallized in the following pieces of rhodomontade:

> Thus the life of God (*Das Leben Gottes*) and divine cognition may well be spoken of as a disporting (playing) of Love with itself (*als ein Spielen der Liebe mit sich selbst*); but this idea sinks into mere edification, and even insipidity, if it lacks the seriousness (*der Ernst*), the suffering (*der Schmerz*), the patience, and the labor of the negative. In itself, that life is indeed one of untroubled equality and unity with itself (*die ungetrübte Gleichkeit und Einheit mit sich selbst*), for which otherness and alienation (*Entfremdung*), and the overcoming (*Überwindung*) of alienation are not serious matters. But this in-itself is abstract universality (*die abstrakte Allgemeinheit*), in which the nature of the divine life to be for itself, and so too the self-movement of the form, are altogether left out of account. (#19, Miller p. 10. *GL2:*23)

Presuming theological aspiration of the categories of Life and Love, Hegel argues against some unidentified opponent that Life and Love can and, indeed, must be interpreted in terms other that those of unity (*Einheit*), untroubled equality (*ungetrübte Gleichkeit*) and play (*ein Spielen*). The attack is polyvalent, but the central focus appears to be *existential.* To the *play,* which is supported by unity and untroubled equality, Hegel opposes suffering (*der Schmerz*) and the seriousness (*der Ernst*) possible only in a context of otherness and alienation. From a theological perspective, Hegel is launching a foray against the notion of divine unity, but the proximate target here is *divine impassibility,* which in the position he is attacking—and, perhaps, endemically—is regarded as an implicate of divine unity. In recommending that divine Love and Life can be only adequately construed within the parameter of alienation, Hegel is engaged in making a quite momentous claim: the existential aspect of the divine is *pathetic* rather than apathetic. Moltmann and Eberhard Jüngel, in particular, have commented on this theological revolution that distances Hegel from the mainline Christian tradition.[104]

The monistic rendering of Love and Life, the horizon of their extension, their existential typification, all found inadequate in *PS,* are reprised in Hegel's treatment of the "Immanent Trinity" in *LPR 3*. It is hardly too daring to draw the conclusion that some of the *PS*'s negativity is present in *LPR 3,* even if in a more implicit and more limited way. The play of the "Immanent Trinity" is certainly not a fully adequate depiction of the divine and is, at the very least, highly misleading with regard to the existential aspect of God. The more moderate tone of *LPR 3* is, in part, due to its more perspicuous narrative consciousness. The horizon of abstract universality (*Allgemeinheit*) is a moment in the process (*Prozess*), movement (*Bewegung*), of the inclusive subjectivity of the Inclusive Trinity. The moment is not, of course, absolute or defining, but, though followed by pathos and even 'the death of God', it is inexcisable. And within the overall trajectory of the divine defined by the Inclusive Trinity, it should be remembered that pathos and death are themselves surpassable moments. The Inclusive Trinity, or the trinitarian elaboration of inclusive subjectivity, which defines Spirit as such, also defines, or redefines, divine Love as having an ingredience of pathos, divine Life as having an ingredience of death. But pathos or death do not have the last word. Love and Life represent, as does Spirit, victory (*Überwindung*) over the negative.

To be able to construe the sphere of Universality and its modality of process and movement as a narrative phase within the larger movement itself rests upon the prior construal that the sphere of Universality is anaclastic, i.e., a sphere essentially *open,* open specifically to further narrative development. In *LPR 3* further narrative development is presented in terms of the Christian narrative of creation, incarnation, and reconciliation. This position is hardly explicit in the Preface to *PS,* and Hegel, mainly due to tone, appears to be engaged in an outright attack on Universality. Read in the light of Hegel's elaboration of ontotheological narrative in his section on Revelatory Religion, where Universality is homologized to the "Immanent Trinity" that devolves into creation and incarnation and into the spiritual community as the articulated presence of the Holy Spirit, one might infer that anaclasis, or lack of such, is also an issue here. Indeed, the deficiency of undramatic monistic views of the divine, the deficiency of the existential aspect in particular, could be a function of a synclastic view of the sphere of divine immanence. This closure of the divine absolutizes the immanent sphere, as it absolutizes the deficiencies that belong to this sphere. Historical excavation makes this more than likely.

The passage from the Preface quoted above is most often thought to be a further jibe at the expense of Schelling's Identity Philosophy.[105] That Hegel is attacking some variety of monism, here of a decidedly theological aspect, hardly merits comment. But given the language in which the monism is couched, it is doubtful whether Schelling or any particular work of his is the proximate object of scorn. *Leibe* and *Leben* are not central categories of Schelling's Identity Philosophy, nor is monism of Identity Philosophy, unlike the dualism which the essay *On Human Freedom* inaugurates, theologically aspirated in an *overt* way.[106]

The vocabulary of Love and Life, understood existentially to exclude *pathos,* suggests Fichte, not Schelling, not, of course, the Fichte of *Die Wissenschaftslehre,* but the later, radically different Fichte, represented above all by *Die Anweisung zum seeligen Leben* (*Anw*), which appeared in 1806, the year the bulk of *PS* was written.[107] The *Wissenschaftslehre* had a number of constitutional faults, which Hegel did not desist from pointing out in the *DE* and *FK.* Fichte's recognition of the necessity of opposition, however, was hardly one of them. *Die Anweisung* presents a totally different Fichte. Just at the point that Schelling is preparing to metamorphosize into a theological dualist, a Fichte sea-change issues in an ontotheology along Identity Philosophy lines.

One of the most salient features of this text is the central role of the concepts *Leben* and *Liebe* play in the elaboration of *philosophia perennis* that is unashamedly theological. The entire set of ten lectures essentially hangs upon two equations unequivocally opposed to differentiation, variety, and multiplicity. These equations are hinted at in the first and fleshed out by the succeeding lectures. At the risk of overschematization, they are:

(a) *Sein* = *Leben* = *Liebe* = *Seligkeit*
(b) *Sein* = *Leben* = *Liebe* = *Gedanke*[108]

Liebe, to speak of but one of our two terms, is in Fichte's succinct formula, "the affect of Being" (*der Affekt des Seins*) (*Anw* 110). The affect is not distinct from Being but supposes the unity of feeling rather than the differentiation of thought. This unity constitutes the divine Blessedness or Beatitude (*Seligkeit*). The association of Blessedness with the self-enclosed undifferentiated divine recalls the 'august repose' of the Plotinian One[109] and, if Michel Henry's intuition is correct,[110] the "Immanent Trinity" of Eckhart. In any event, in Fichte's ontotheology we are clearly dealing with an *apathetic divine.* Fichte thinks it possible, even given his decidedly monistic elaboration,[111] to hold on to a dynamic conception of Being and God. Speaking the language of ontology, he insists that Being is not fixed (*stehendes*), rigid (*starres*) or dead (*totes*) (*Anw* 113), and thus neither is Love. The same can be said of Life which is coextensive with Being and Love. Yet the Life and Love spoken of in *Die Anweisung* are regulated in the last instance by Fichte's determination that Being is structureless and thus possessed of those existential-ontological characteristics compatible with undifferentiation.[112]

In all of this it might be thought that Hegel is involved in a requital of minimal interest. The opposing ontology, even if theologically read, is simply too eccentric to merit attention. But this would be to ignore the union of components in Fichte's *philosophia perennis,* i.e., Greek ontology and Christian scripture.[113] On the textual level the Fichtean hermeneutics makes a deep cut in New Testament texts. The Synoptic Gospels and the Pauline epistles are excised because they do not contribute to a *philosophia perennis.* Only the Gospel of John can be brought into alliance with what is essentially a Neoplatonic ontology, and even here Fichte, in hallowing the preexistent Logos, excludes the strong incarnational thrust of that Gospel. Moreover, he initiates a Marcionite disjunction between the Old Testament and New Testament, ruling that the Logos passages of John and the creation story of Genesis, regarded by the normative Christian theological tradition as symbiotic, are mutually exclusive.[114] These two hermeneutic moves combine to cut off the immanent Logos from any self-transcending momentum. The circuit of the divine is closed. Synclasis on the level of the immanent sphere, therefore, dominates Fichtean ontotheology and points to what, from a Hegelian point of view, is nothing less than a narrative mutilation of the divine and a distortion of a definition that takes Christian representation seriously. Narrative mutilation issues in the loss of creative nisus and incarnational thrust. As a result pathos is excluded from the divine. For Hegel, as we have seen, pathos is a sine qua non in the elaboration of the divine, though pathos does not infiltrate the divine on the level of the "Immanent Trinity."

Section 2.3 Trinitarian Swerve: Dynamic, Narrative Modalism

Passages highlighting the dynamic aspect of the "Immanent Trinity" are by no means scarce in Hegel. We have already reviewed a few of the more trenchant formulations, particularly from *LPR.* The "Immanent Trinity" can be considered, after Iljin, as the first of the three narrative phases or epochs of divine history. Because it is merely a first phase, any completion within the immanent sphere is more or less relative with respect to the overall trajectory. Yet Spirit as Idea does represent a provisional terminus and appears to be ontologically, gnoseologically, axiologically, and existentially richer than that from and through which it is generated. It is both the terminus and summary of generation.

The relation of Hegel's dynamic narrative depiction of the "Immanent Trinity" to the more standard hypostatic view has not been addressed yet. Such a comparison is warranted by Hegel himself who clearly sees himself as correcting deficiencies in the traditional *Vorstellung,* which in essential respects, he believes, grasps the truth. Revisionary recommendations are made in *PS, Enc,* and above all *LPR 3.* In *PS* #771 Hegel argues that the language of Father and Son with its misleading implication of 'natural relation' (*die natürlichen Verhältnisse*) must be transcended. A similar embargo is placed on any view that treats of developmental phases "as isolated immovable substances and subjects instead of transient moments" (*für isolirte nichtwankende Substanzen oder Subjekte, statt für übergehende Momente*) (*GL2*:585, 586). But it is in *LPR 3* that Hegel offers his definitive views with respect to his revision of both popular and normative theological trinitarian views. Representation evidences different degrees of adequacy. At the most primitive level, the mystery of the Trinity is expressed in the language of Father, Son and Spirit, a way of speaking that labors under the quasi-biological cipher of 'generation' (1824 E 194, G 127–128; 1827 E 283, G 208–209). On a less primitive level of representation, the mode of discourse is that of person (1821 MS E 82, G 20). Nevertheless, as Hegel had already hinted at in *PS,* this language too is deficient in some way. For Hegel, traditional trinitarian discourse in its more primitive and less primitive, in its more popular and more sophisticated, form gives unhappy testimony to the reifying activity of the understanding, which changes moments into entities and transforms processes into static relations between entities. In Hegel's view, it is ultimately impossible for such a discourse to avoid the implication of Tritheism.[115] The constitutive fault is the kind of symbolic operation in action. Only on the level of concept or, at the very least, conceptually informed representation, can the invidious effects of the language of person, entity, and number (quantitatively understood) be avoided. From the conceptual point of view of the *Logic* (*Enc* #99–103) error with respect to number is more basic than error with respect to person and supports it; yet, within the horizon of representation, it is the notion of person that is more visible and consequently the more contentious (*LPR 3* 1821 MS E 82, G 20). *LPR 3* clearly suggests, and here the *Logic* serves a supporting role, that Hegel's view of the Trinity represents a decisive departure from the traditional, summed up for the Scholastic and post-Scholastic age by Aquinas:

> There are several real relations in God, and hence it follows that there are several realities subsisting in the divine nature, which means that there are several persons in God.[116]

The Hegelian revision, then, demands that the dominant be process rather than entity. In addition, though the point cannot be developed here, a new logic of *internal* supplants the old logic of external relations. Both aspects inform the new paradigmatic language of the Trinity, the language of moment.

The transparency of the Hegelian revision has not prevented a fairly lively debate as to whether Hegel conforms to, or deviates from, the normative Christian interpretation of the Trinity; or, otherwise expressed, whether he opts for a hypostatic or nonhypostatic interpretation. No critical consensus exists. Franz Grégoire has accused Hegel of modalism, while Bruaire and Chapelle have defended Hegel against the charge.[117] More unanimity exists among the German theologians, Moltmann, Pannenberg, and Splett, among others, thinking Hegel guilty on this count, his dynamic elaboration amounting to a *Geistesmonismus* whose basic model is the idealistic one of the autogenesis of subjectivity.[118] If both Pannenberg and Moltmann agree that the isomorphism between the Romantic idealist model of human becoming and the dynamic articulation of the divine is too close to be accidental, it is Pannenberg who makes explicit the charge of a *projection* from the human psychological order into the divine. Pannenberg writes:

> Now it is just this priority of the subject in relation to its articulation thus signified as auto-articulation which appears to be a projection of finite categories into the divine reality.[119]

The criticism clearly has merit. Even on the level of the "Immanent Trinity" there exists a narrative thrust that appears to owe something to the narrative model of *PS* which sums up for Romantic Idealism the ontogenetic and phylogenetic aspects of *human* becoming. And, of course, *a fortiori* this is the case with the full account of divine self-constitution which, in its more complex trinitarian elaboration, replicates the determinative process of self-development that is the theme of the *Bildungsroman*. Though Pannenberg may have overstated his case somewhat, the model Hegel employs to explain both human and divine Personhood is one of narrative becoming, the latter understood as a genesis and development of meaning. As a complete explanation, however, Pannenberg's account of extrapolation must be resisted as too reductionist. There were many reasons of a theological sort, including the estimable one of envisioning God in Pauline fashion as the living God, which urged Hegel in a dynamic direction.[120]

Theological Precedents

Both the thinker whom Hegel called "the first German philosopher" (Boehme)[121] and the mystic whom he thought crystallized his own vast theologico-philosophical program (Eckhart)[122] articulated modalistic Trinities. Critically, in neither case is modalism statically registered. Boehme's "Immanent Trinity" is dynamic through and through, as is the Eckhartian encapsulated in the semioxymoron 'the eternal birth' (*die ewige Geburt*). The existence of such a tradition encourages the question whether Hegel might not be usefully read against—if to be sure not reduced to—its backdrop. In any event, it certainly appears to be the case that the two pivots of the Hegelian enterprise are also essential to both Eckhart and Boehme. In both cases the "Immanent Trinity" is viewed under the aspect of the divine thrust toward manifestation, and in both cases emphatic dynamism tends to rule out hypostatic interpretation. The interaction of these two pivots is transparent in Boehme's great hexaemeron, *Mysterium Magnum*. Recapitulating the Eckharian trope of the Trinity as the 'eternal unbeginning birth' (*die ewige unanfängliche Geburt*), Boehme proceeds to obviate a possible confusion:

> Not that you are to understand that God thus receives a beginning, but it is the eternal beginning of the manifestation of God (*es ist der ewige Anfang des geoffenbarten Gottes*). (4, 7)[123]

The effect of this emphasis upon the dynamics of divine manifestation with respect to the traditional doctrine of the Trinity becomes clear some chapters later:

> There is no ground for calling God threefold in person, but that He is threefold in his eternal generation (*sondern er ist dreyfaltig in seiner ewigen Gebarung*). He begets Himself in Trinity; and yet in this eternal generation or begetting we are to understand only one essence and generation; neither the Father, Son or Spirit but one eternal life (*sondern das einige, ewige Leben*). (7, 11)

The significance of Hegel's revision of the traditional view is by no means mitigated by pointing out that the revision itself has a precedent. Given Hegel's own bias towards the traditional rather than the originary and his particularly high estimate of the two German mystics, Hegel in no way would be disturbed by this contextualization of his thought. Hegel consistently betrays a positive attitude towards Boehme as a trinitarian thinker. Hegel's appreciation is quite explicit in *LHP 3* where Boehme is credited with two major insights, i.e., the insight into the trinitarian structure of all reality and the dialectical conflict between yes and no that is reality's ground. And the approbation displayed in *LHP* is a late expression of a longstanding appreciation which dates at least from the early years of the first decade of the nineteenth century.[124]

Approbation notwithstanding, there exists only one place in *LPR 3* where the "Immanent Trinity" is an explicit theme that Boehme is discussed. Hegel's discussion is very brief and general and differs little from his equally general remarks in *LHP 3.* He points approvingly to Boehme's insight into the centrality of the Trinity, especially his vision of it as a dynamic reality enacted in the heart of man (a thought that Boehme ultimately owes to Eckhartian reflection on the *Gottesgeburt*). Very approving of the content, he is less than approving of the mode of expression, which, as in *LHP 3,* he suggests is wild and phantastic (*LPR 3* 1827 E 289, G 214). Given the apologetic context of his discussion, the generality of Hegel's remarks are understandable. Boehme is just one of a number of thinkers cited as justification for the general intelligibility of trinitarian thought in speculation. Some of those cited are non-Christian, e.g., Aristotle, Plato, Philo, and Proclus, and some trinitarian precedent-setting in Christianity—for instance, Kant's use of triads in *The Critique of Pure Reason*—is more formal-logical than explicitly theological. Given Hegel's specific agenda, namely to recommend the potential speculative respectability of trinitarian forms of thought rather than to point to previous speculative transformations of the dogma *within* Christianity, it perhaps should come as no surprise that Hegel betrays no awareness of the difference between the earlier hypostatic Boehmian view (*Aurora*), a view from which Hegel's own position is clearly swerving, and the more mature nonhypostatic Boehmian view, e.g., *Mysterium Magnum.*[125] From what is possible by way of source reconstruction, *Aurora* is the most likely source of Hegel's apologetically oriented remarks,[126]—a task for which, as the most trinitarian of all of Boehme's texts, it is admirably suited. It is to be admitted, then, that the passage in the 1827 Lectures provides no clear evidence that Hegel is actually basing his revisionist views on the nature of the "Immanent Trinity" upon the kind of speculative translation of the conciliar and confessional dogma of the Trinity evidenced in Boehme's mature period (1620–24), a revisionist view for which Boehme was roundly criticized by Lutheran orthodoxy.[127] Yet the coincidence between Boehme and Hegel, both with respect to the nature of the "Immanent Trinity" and its place in a larger narrative elaboration, which may itself be seen as possessing a trinitarian form (see chap. 6, sect. 6.1 below) or capable of being trinitarianly adapted, is astonishing. Limiting discussion to the Boehmian and Hegelian elaboration of the "Immanent Trinity," it can be suggested at the very minimum that taxonomically these two elaborations separated by a period of two hundred years belong to the same essential type, representing similar subversions of conciliar understanding and similar swerves from the Lutheran orthodox view that tied Luther firmly to the mainline Western trinitarian tradition.

In the 1827 Lectures Hegel rules that invidious numerical understanding and a highly substantive notion of Personality (*Persönlichkeit*) skew the version of Trinity that is, according to him, alone rationally intelligible (*LPR 3* E 287, G 212). Rational intelligibility for Hegel does not, of course, exclude mystery (chap. 1, sect. 1.1). Rather, it fully includes it. For the mystery (*mysterium*) of the "Immanent Trinity" is no longer the mystery of negative theology but mystery in the truly adequate Pauline Christian sense, i.e., open revelation or process of revelation. This view of mystery as the self-revealing dynamics of the divine—here dynamics that do not transcend the immanent sphere of the divine—puts the accent decisively upon the unity of process. Unity of process, and not the tritheistically endangered representation of three persons, represents the refurbished and speculatively defensible trinitarian view. The 1824 Lectures differ in few essential respects from the 1827 Lectures in which the positive appraisal of Boehme is found and are, if anything, more declarative of the valorization of the dynamics of divine unity. Hegel recommends that, with respect to the "Immanent Trinity," Personality must not be taken in the most intense sense of being for self but "as a vanishing moment" (*LPR 3* E 194, G 127). The narrative interpretation of the "Immanent Trinity" is transparent in the following passage, the narrative indices being provided by posited (*gesetz*), resolved (*aufgelöst*), and sublated (*aufgehoben*):

> It is precisely in the divine unity that Personality, just as much as it is posited (*gesetz*) is posited as resolved (*aufgelöst*); only in appearance (*in der Erscheinung*), does the negativity of Personality appear distinct from that whereby it is sublated (*aufgehoben*). (Ibid)

The resolution of Personality is necessary not merely to avoid tritheism but for another important, though ultimately related, reason. As Hegel sees it, if Personality is unresolved in the immanent milieu, then Evil is posited in the divine. Though Hegel in *LPR 3* and *Enc* makes it abundantly clear that he is prepared to state that evil is posited within the overall narrative elaboration of the divine, he is not prepared to suggest that it occurs on the level of divine immanence. Appearance (*Erscheinung*), the state of divine manifestation or revelation *ad extra,* is its appropriate narrative locus.

Hegel's understanding of Personality, or at least one crucial ontotheological determination of it, is sufficiently unusual to permit reconstruction of its source or sources. *LPR 3* (1824, 1827) provides abundant evidence that Boehme is the main source for the peculiar Hegelian view of Personality and his consequent refusal to posit it on the level of the "Immanent Trinity." In his justification of the Christian representation of Creation (*Erschaffung, Schöpfung*), which is, at the very least, a key constituent of the second narrative epoch of the fully inclusive trinitarian narrative, Hegel explicitly appeals to the Boehmian myth of Lucifer.[128] The self-centering imaginative activity of Lucifer leads to a fall and a materialization into a cosmos that is not merely extradivine but *antidivine* or evil. It is this self-centering activity, or involution, that is regarded as constitutive of independent Personality and that is at the heart of the finite antithesis to the infinite. In denying Personality to any narrative aspect of the "Immanent Trinity," Hegel is operating within the parameters of Boehme's ontotheological and mythological definition. To the extent to which Hegel regards this understanding of Personality as being in some way determinative, it follows that he would have tended to read even *Aurora* as denying Personality on the level of immanence, or at least have been logically required to make such a denial.

The forensic use of Boehme's negative appraisal of Personality to support his narrative redefinition of the "Immanent Trinity" is not the only or most subtle ploy adopted by Hegel in his critique of the normative understanding of the Trinity. Admittedly, some of this critique is logico-conceptual in nature, but critique also proceeds by way of immanent subversion. The theologoumenon of *divine self-emptying* or *kenosis* is enlisted, for instance, as an agent in the subversion of the hypostatic understanding of the "Immanent Trinity." In accord with its essentially biblical usage, kenosis in the Lutheran tradition belongs properly within the christological ambit. On a few occasions, most notably in *PS* and *LPR 3* (1821 MS), Hegel avails of the symbol construct on the level of the "Immanent Trinity." In *PS* #770 the context of the operation of kenosis is provided by a Logos theology that remains on the plane of the intradivine. The word (Son) uttered represents the emptying of the utterer (Father) (Miller 465, *G12:*285). In *LPR 3* the "Immanent Trinity" as a whole (otherwise put, the self-development of the concept) is to be understood after the model of self-emptying (*Selbstablassen*) (1821 MS E 83, G 21). Kenosis refers in the first instance to the self-emptying of the Father, or what Hegel in his refurbished vocabulary calls the Universal (*das Allgemeine*). To this extent, *LPR 3* overlaps with *PS.* But *LPR 3* contains an implication not found in the 1807 text, namely, that self-emptying equally applies to the second moment of the immanent trinitarian articulation, the moment of the Son (*Sohn*) or the moment of particularity (*Besonderheit*). Hegel in *LPR 3* suggests that Spirit, to the degree that it is realized on the level of divine immanence, is a result of the double kenosis of both Father and Son.[129] The transference of the theologoumenon of kenosis from its christological context to the level of the "Immanent Trinity" does not necessarily destroy the possibility of a hypostatic interpretation of the dynamics of divine immanence. Logically the theologoumenon of kenosis could support either a hypostatic or nonhypostatic reading. As a matter of fact, however, Hegel's use of the theologoumenon, which emphasizes the aspect of dissolution that is, at most, a *surface* feature of the semantics of kenosis, tends to critique hypostatic autonomy and subvert the Christian theological tradition from within by availing of one of its crucial theological counters.

Hegel's efforts to establish the pedigree of trinitarian thought in *LPR 3* betrays some unusual features. We have seen already in section 1.3 that, in opposition to Schleiermacher, Hegel regarded the dogma of the Trinity as crucial to Christianity in general and to Protestant Christianity in particular. Yet in *LPR 3* Hegel makes no use of conciliar definition, makes no explicit appeal either to Patristic or Scholastic trinitarian formulation and speculation and, most interestingly, makes no mention of any confessional or theological Protestant formulation he takes to be normative. The 1821 Manuscript and the Lectures of 1824 and 1827 show a Hegel involving himself with some strange company. In the 1821 Manuscript, in his attempt to establish the basic theologico-speculative credentials of the Christian Trinity, Hegel refers to Hinduism, Aristotle, Plato, Neoplatonism, Kant, and Gnosticism. The list remains pretty constant and is repeated with fairly minor alterations in the Lectures of 1824 and 1827. It is in the 1827 Lectures that Boehme receives a mention. Hegel's list is not a thoroughly undifferentiated one, and it is clear from his treatment that the thought of the philosophers, i.e., Plato, Aristotle, and Kant, is not taken to be as profoundly trinitarian as that which has a religious dimension, i.e., the thought of Philo, Neoplatonism (Proclus, in particular), and Gnosticism. The source for Hegel's knowledge of Neoplatonism and Gnosticism, it now appears, is August Neander's *Genetische Entwicklung der vornehmsten gnostischen Systeme* (Berlin, 1818).[130] It was through this text that Hegel came in contact with the thought of Basilides and Valentinus, though it should be remembered that as early as 1795 Hegel had come in contact with heterodox varieties of thought in the shape of Schelling's dissertation on Marcion.[131] Almost all of Hegel's trinitarian appeals are nonstandard; but the appeal to the Gnostics in the context of an attempt to justify and reappropriate the Christian dogma of the Trinity is not only nonstandard but truly extraordinary. Basilides and some vague general forms of Valentinian Gnosticism appear to be gestured to in Hegel's evocation. Hegel focuses upon Abyss as the *Propater* (Forefather) or *Proarchia* (Prebeginning) and the generation of *Monogenes* (First-Born) (*LPR 3* 1821 MS E 85, G 23). *Monogenes* appears to interest Hegel in a particular way, since *Monogenes* is the revealer of the Forefather. From Hegel's point of view this appears to establish that, the negative determination of the Abyss notwithstanding, *the immanent divine realm is a matrix of revelation* (ibid.). Once again we witness the Hegelian interpretive operation of apophatic erasure and the concomitant move of enlisting the thus corrected nontraditional system of thought to aid and abet a counterdogmatic program.

That the immanent divine realm is a domain of revelation, thus of speakability and legibility, could be granted by a considerable number of more orthodox Christian trinitarian thinkers, who regard the *Logos* as the rendering visible of the invisible Father. With the key textual warrant being provided by the Prologue to John's Gospel, this point was central to much of Patristic theology and even to the theology of Luther himself.[132] The importance of John's Gospel for the early Hegel, and the fact that the background for Hegel's ontotheology of the Word in *PS* #770 is a general Lutheran recall of the Johannine Prologue, make the Hegelian concern to exegete Gnosticism seem redundant. The apparent redundancy, however, is symptomatic: Hegel obviously feels that the revelation dynamics of the immanent divine sphere are much more explicitly declared in Gnostic modes of thought than in the conciliar definition that he acknowledges in *LPH 3* (part III, sect.

III, chap. II) to be regulative for the Christian community and its identity. The appeal to Basilides and what Hegel, following Neander, takes to be Valentinian Gnosticism certainly appears to be more positive than negative, though Hegel is not entirely uncritical. Gnosticism, in common with the entire ambit of representational thought, betrays a deficient hypostatic tendency (*LPR 3* 1821 MS E 86, G 23–24). In Gnosticism the process of divine self-revelation that characterizes the immanent milieu is reified into entities or aeons. In addition, Gnosticism makes it impossible for the divine realm to be fully constituted totality (*Totalität*) (ibid.). By totality in this context, Hegel means a narrative that possesses closure and return or, otherwise put, a narrative self-reflexive whole. The following passage has not often made its way into the secondary literature:

> In brief, the source of many so-called heresies lies purely in the turn of speculation, which, in the transition from the One, the universal, to the process of distinction, distinguishes this activity from the universal, hypostatizes it apart from the universal (*sie hypostasiert getrennt von jenem*), which [is supposed] to stand over against it as abstract. Considered more closely, however, this Logos has already itself the characteristic of return within itself (*ist dieser Logos schon selbst die Bestimmung der Rückkehr in sich*), since it contains a moment that must be distinguished in order to comprehend the distinction exactly. The resolution (*die Auflösung*) consists in the fact that Spirit is the Totality (*der Geist die Totalität ist*), and the first moment itself is grasped as first only because, to begin with, it has the determination of the third, of activity (*Tätigkeit*). (*LPR 3* 1821 MS E 86, G 23–24)[133]

Closure and self-reflexivity constitute the specific nature of the immanent realm of the divine. It is these features that, from Hegel's perspective, constitute the determinate nature of the Christian notion of the Trinity, even if many of the specific theological elaborations within Christianity tend to deform this. Of course, this truth of Christianity is only fully protected on the level of Hegelian concept or in what we are calling Hegel's speculative rewriting. Protected or not, reformed or deformed, these above-mentioned properties are sufficient to distinguish the Christian from all non-Christian versions of the Trinity, especially the Indian. Hegel remarks on the distinction between the Christian and the Hindu Trinity or *Trimurti* in *LPR 3* (1821 MS, 1824, 1827), but perhaps his most powerful articulation of the distinction had been made earlier in *SL* Book 1, Sect. 3. While acknowledging the common element (*ein gemeinsames Element*) (*GL4:*407), Hegel argues that there exists an infinite (*unendliche*) difference between them. The Third Principle is what crucially distinguishes the Hindu from the Christian. Hegel assets:

> This third principle is according to its determination, the dispersal (*das Auseinanderfahren*) of the unity of Substance into its opposite, not the return of unity to itself (*nicht die Rückkehr derselben zu sich*)—not spirit but rather the non-spiritual. (E 328, *GL4:*407)

Interestingly, Hegel in *SL* connects his denial of congruence between the Christian and Indian Trinity with his championing of the claims of Subjectivity over the Spinozist championing of Substance. Hegel offers in the introduction to Bk. 1, Sect. 3 a theologically biased reading of the three central categories of the *Ethics*, Substance, Attribute and Mode, and concentrates his critical attention on Mode, which Spinoza had defined as existing in and through something else.[134] In the vocabulary of the *Logic* this definition commits Spinoza to the position that the Mode as such is untrue (*das Unwahre*) (ibid.) If Hegel eschews a substance interpretation of the "Immanent Trinity" as a whole, and Spirit in particular, he is not prepared to countenance this form of modalism. For him, the third moment of the Trinity, as the summation of trinitarian dynamics, if it is not a hypostasis in the strict sense, is, nevertheless *not through* something else in an unequivocal way. If it can be considered as constituted in and through two determinate phases of becoming, it is more properly thought of as self-determining, specifically self-determining in and through these phases. Hegel's Trinity in a sense, therefore, is only negatively modal to the degree to which it is not hypostatic. It is definitely nonmodal if modalism implies either the submergence or undermining of all distinction within the divine. For Hegel, there are irradicable distinctions, and these are ultimately narrative in character. The attack on Spinozist modalism, which ultimately endorses the hegemony of Substance (undifferentiated), is far from mild. Hegel complains:

> . . . to it (substance) everything must be brought back. But this is only to submerge all content in the void, in a merely formal unity lacking all content. (E 328, *GL4*:407)

The critical hub of this attack becomes even clearer as he continues:

> In other words, the difference and the determinateness only vanish again but are not preserved, are not sublated (*nicht aufgehoben*), and unity does not become a concrete unity, neither is disunity reconciled (*die Entzweiung nicht zur Versöhnnung zurückgeführt*). (E 328–329. *GL4*:407–408)

The various strands of reflection and argument can now be brought together. It is clearly the case that the Hegelian presentation of the Trinity is nonstandard, which is indicated in the twofold way: first, by the outsider status of those trinitarian thinkers whom Hegel avails of in his apologetic appeal, and second, by his consistently explicit antihypostatic stance. Much of Hegel's presentation is occupied by recommendations of a logico-conceptual type, and, while this aspect of the Hegelian presentation, what might be called the reconstructive aspect, was touched upon, it was not elaborated in detail. The reason was to highlight the specifically *theological* nature of Hegel's trinitarian recommendation as a *first* stage, without in any way denying its (re)conceptualization.

Narrative Modalism

The position advanced here is that, judged within the parameter of a more traditional criteriology, Hegel's trinitarian elaboration be understood as a species of dynamic, narrative modalism. The dynamic quality of the Hegelian "Immanent Trinity" is an unassailable given. Such also is the case with regard to narrative quality. Hegel is clear that any development within the immanent divine sphere is atemporal, though the model of development on the level of the immanent divine does not appear to be radically different from the *Bildungsroman* narrative model that has its locus and exemplification in human temporality and history.[135] The important issue is whether it is taxonomically coherent to attribute modalism to the Hegelian rendition of the "Immanent Trinity" in conjunction with the qualifiers dynamic and narrative.

From a textual point of view, modalism is at least negatively suggested in Hegel's critique of the language of number, his general attack on the phenomenon of hypostatization, i.e., the transformation of process into entity, and his strenuous objection to the Augustinian personalist view of the Trinity. Yet, it might be argued that this need not imply an absolute swerve from the normative Christian trinitarian tradition, since the Augustinian personalist tradition represents but one of the major options, the more Greek, specifically, the Cappadocian, view representing the other.[136] Hegel, it could plausibly be claimed, does not swerve from this latter view, which explicitly uses the language of hypostasis, as he swerves from the Augustinian. Support for this position is certainly available in Hegel. He continually insists, for instance, that distinctions do exist in the divine and that these distinctions are noncollapsable. And the general assertion of distinction is certainly one of the regulative functions of the language of hypostasis. Hegel, in addition, while he makes no mention of the conciliar definition of the Trinity in *LPR 3*, does invoke it positively in *LPH 3*, though the invocation by no means sanctions the actual formulation of the dogma. Nevertheless, the main thrust of the Hegelian view still appears fairly definitely headed in an antihypostatic direction, even if it is understood that hypostasis is not necessarily the equivalent of person. There are still other reasons why Hegel cannot be identified as belonging to the hypostatic tradition. The first and second moments of the immanent dynamic of divine self-revelation do not appear to enjoy equality with the third moment of narrative terminus. As narrative terminus, the third moment, the moment of Spirit, is mediated, but Spirit also mediates the other two. And Spirit is identifiable with Substance (*Substanz*), though a self-mediating Substance.[137] This tends to leave two options open: (1) that no hypostases are posited in the self-differentiation of the divine; and (2) at most one hypostasis is posited, i.e., Spirit as narrative terminus.[138] In either case the Greek view of *one ousia* and *three hypostases* is subverted.

Mentioned above was Bruaire and Chapelle's defense of Hegel against the charge of modalism, though both of them comment on the originality of the Hegelian formulation of the "Immanent Trinity."[139] Throughout this section I have tried to argue that (1) without derogation to Hegel's originality, a positive, theological context can be supplied for his trinitarian formulation; (2) this context is decidedly heterodox, centrally including the German mystics, Eckhart and Boehme, and even Valentinian Gnosticism though to a much lesser extent; and (3) from a more standard or orthodox point of view, the incriminating association with the heterodox tradition insinuates that Hegel's ultimate allegiance is to a nonhypostatic Trinity. Though neither of his two French defenders seem able to offer a compelling defense of Hegel's traditional credentials on this score, it is true to say that Chapelle argues a weak case with some vigor. This defense is both historically thin and conceptually flawed: historically thin in that Chapelle does not attempt to place Hegel against the backdrop of specific and historically determinate varieties of trinitarian thought, conceptually flawed in that Chapelle tends to assume that a trinitarian elaboration that avoids static quality by this very fact avoids modalism.[140] Hegel's "Immanent Trinity," dynamic through and through, must thus, he reasons, escape traditionalist censure. But Chapelle's premise is hardly supportable. The historical thinness of his approach seems to lead him into transforming a historically relative feature of modalism, i.e., the static quality of the Trinity in Sabellianism, into its essence,[141] thereby encouraging him to accept an extrinsic as an absolutely intrinsic feature and criterion. The focus is, in consequence, directed away from the status of the trinitarian determinations, specifically, from the postulation of inferiority and superiority within the milieu of differentiation. Inferiority of an ontological kind, of course, in principle can be posited within a dynamic milieu of differentiation as within a static. And this appears to be precisely what happens in the Hegelian "Immanent Trinity."

The line of subordination in Hegel moves in the contrary direction to that typical in the Christian tradition. Hegelian subordinationism moves not from origin to terminus of generation, but rather from terminus of generation to origin, from Spirit to Father, Individuality to Universality, or again Concept to Being. It is not Spirit that is the most inferior, it is the Father as Universality and/or Being. Ontologically, gnoseologically, axiologically, and even existentially, the movement from Father to Spirit, or Universality to Individuality, or Being to Concept, is one of increment. Individuality or Subjectivity on the level of divine immanence is, however, constituted by a particular mode of generation, i.e., infinite differentiation. As Hegel pointed out, however, in his resolute criticism of both Spinoza's and Indian thought's failure to adequately articulate a divine Trinity, their deficit (one not apparent in the mainline Christian tradition we presume, and certainly not transparent in such thinkers as Proclus and Boehme) is that they fail to understand that synclasis is a condition of the possibility of a determinate Trinity and, what for Hegel amounts to the same thing, a determinate divine. Hegel validates the simple equation: no synclasis on the level of the divine, no realization, no perfection. Realization, however, by no means abolishes the moments of Universality and Particularity or Father and Son which are presuppositions. As the two moments of Universality and Particularity or Father and Son point towards Singularity and Spirit, Singularity or Spirit preserves these two prior moments. And these two prior moments are not merely preserved in some indefinite way but their identity and narrative order are preserved. Above, we said that Hegel does preserve distinction on the level of the "Immanent Trinity." We can now qualify that and say that, above all, Hegel preserves the narrative distinction of Father, Son, and Spirit as moments of divine self-constitutive process on the level of divine immanence. We might register this in our language of prolepsis and analepsis: as Universality and Particularity or Father and Son are narratively proleptic of Individuality or Spirit on the level of the immanent divine, the latter is narratively analeptic of them and in analepsis preserves their identity and narrative location.

Yet, it is important again to remember not only the narrative context *within* the "Immanent Trinity" but the narrative context *of* the "Immanent Trinity." In *LPR 3,* Universality is a descriptor of this sphere as a whole and of the first moment of the triadically or trinitarianly structured process of divine becoming on the plane of immanence. There is nothing really equivocal about this double use of the notion Universality, any more than there is anything equivocal about the implied double use of its representational equivalent Father. The concrete material meaning of Universality and Father are provided by the narrative contexts to which they refer. For Hegel, the use of the same linguistic term to describe narrative fields of process that are not identical appears justified on the grounds of isomorphism. Specifically, the realities they name are both first moments of triadic or trinitarian elaboration and, relative to further development, are characterizable by similar properties and similar deficiencies. In comparison with Universality and Father, Individuality or Spirit realized on the level of the "Immanent Trinity" signals perfection. Yet it appears to be Hegel's view that the entire sphere or epoch of the "Immanent Trinity" is deficient and is not able to constitute fully perfect subjectivity. Realization is, thus, relative rather than absolute in the third and final moment of divine autogenesis on the level of divine immanence. This means also that synclasis is relative, as is analepsis. The "Immanent Trinity" is foundationally narratively anaclastic and proleptic and must be so on pain of constructing a self that is a play of self-reference, a spectral romance devoid of those features that alone can bestow reality.

3

THE SECOND NARRATIVE EPOCH: Creation and The Epoch of the Son

The "Immanent Trinity" represents neither the full compass of the divine nor the full realization of personhood. To be sufficient divine subjectivity, what is required, besides ahistorical or metahistorical divine becoming, is becoming within the milieu of finitude, the divine history of creation, fall, incarnation, redemption, and salvation.[1] While divine history may have as its term the sublation of finitude, its province is, quintessentially, that of finitude and, above, all the matrix of history and temporality. The role of finitude in the self-development of the divine is impossible to overestimate. Crucially, the milieu of finitude makes possible the genuine contrariety that cannot be established on the level of the immanent divine. In short, it is the milieu of finitude that is responsible for the emergence of *real dialectic.*[2]

Both the theological proposals of *LPR 3* and *Enc* insert the emergence of finitude into an encompassing trinitarian context. If the immanent divine (or the "Immanent Trinity") becomes associated with the Father, finitude and its vicissitudes become associated with the Son. And just as in the former case we are not speaking of a hypostasis but rather of a narrative phase or epoch, so also here. The Son is more properly designated the 'epoch of the Son'. This epoch, as Chapelle, in particular, is anxious to underscore,[3] is by no means identifiable with the Son as the second moment of the intradivine generation, which, we insisted, only by courtesy could be identified with person and whose real logic was quite nontraditional.

As already pointed out above, the trinitarian mappings of *LPR 3* and *Enc* are not identical. Concretely, what this means is that whereas *Enc* only includes the creation of nature and finite spirit within the second epoch—in philosophical terminology, the sphere of particularity (*Besonderheit*)—*LPR 3* includes also the incarnation, passion, death, and reconciliation of Christ. It is important to remember that the underlying narrative which Hegel contracts into his trinitarian scheme is the same in both cases. Thus, no fundamental differences with regard to the construal of creation and Christ arise. This is not to say that the different trinitarian distributions of *Enc* and *LPR 3* are trivial. The distribution of the second epoch throws into relief determinate theological or ontotheological emphases with their attendant difficulties. For instance, the exclusion of the christological narrative from the ambit of the Son in *Enc* is certainly not without moment for normative Christianity, which identifies Jesus of Nazareth as the incarnate Son of God. From such a point of view, the trinitarian contexting notwithstanding, Hegelian avowals associating Son and created world at the very least would be discomforting. The following passage, which speaks of the immanent sphere in the act of self-transcendence, would be especially so:

> Theology, as we know, expresses this process in representation by saying that God the Father (this simple universal or being-within-self), putting aside his solitariness creates Nature (the being that is external to itself, outside itself), begets a Son (his other 'I'), but in the power of his love beholds in this other himself, recognizes his likeness therein and in it returns to unity with himself. (*Enc* 381 *zu*, Wallace 12, *GL10:27*)[4]

More seems to be claimed here than a mere association between creation (or the created sphere) and the economic activity of a particular trinitarian person. Some kind of ontological identity between the Son and the created sphere seems to be asserted, though the Son here is other, other in form, at least, to the Son who is the internal word.[5] More reserve is exercised elsewhere in *Enc*. Yet the fact that the created sphere exhausts the epoch of the Son continually forces estimates of proximity of the created sphere to the divine, and homologization of the activity of creation to the act of incarnation, that from a normative Christian point of view are exceedingly problematic. By contrast, in including the christological narrative within the epoch of the Son, *LPR 3* relieves Hegel's ontotheological proposal of some of its heterodox appearance.[6] Trinitarian distribution, however, represents merely the surface grammar. The depth-grammar of *Enc* and *LPR 3* is the same. If *LPR 3* is less heterodox-looking in including Christ within the epoch of the Son, this by no means implies that we cannot here find 'Son' language referring to the created sphere of nature and finite being.

In this chapter I wish, first, to rehearse Hegel's consistent legitimation of the *Vorstellung* of creation. In this rehearsal, the elements of the *Vorstellung* that Hegel accepts are set in relief, but the formal and material ways in which the Hegelian acceptation departs from or recommends departure from the *Vorstellung,* as traditionally conceived, are also noted. Particular attention is paid to Hegel's relationship to Luther and Lutheran orthodoxy and the degree to which Hegel swerves from Luther's own understanding and that of his scholastic-minded successors. This, in broad outline, is the task of section 3.1. I wish, second, to comment upon and analyze Hegel's extremely unusual (though not unique) characterization of the realm of creation by means of the ciphers of fall and evil. In doing so, I argue that, while Hegel does, indeed, stress that fall and evil belong more properly to finite spirit, ultimately his position is that the order of finitude as such is evil, thereby constituting the most intense possible contrast with the immanent realm of pure divine goodness. Accordingly, I feel it appropriate to avail of a Ricoeurian distinction and insist that Hegel, the modern Christian-philosopher par excellence, elaborates at a fundamental level a *theogonic* rather than *anthropogonic* account of the emergence of evil.[7] Though it is the theogonic nature of Hegel's account that decisively distinguishes him from Kant's anthropogonic account, nevertheless, the broad measure of overlap in regard to their anti-Enlightenment sense of evil in the human sphere—evil's radicality as well as its teleological, eschatological overcoming—justifies more than casual mention, especially since Kant's *Religion Within the Limits of Reason Alone* (*Religion*) was an important text for Hegel and, arguably, the first Kant-text he read.[8] This agenda is made visible in section 2. Considering the amount of swerve from the more standard Christian positions apparent in sections 3.1 and 3.2, third, and last, I wish to pursue the question as to what, in fact, is the appropriate taxon of Hegel's creation position. The general suggestion is made that Hegel's view belongs broadly within the general parameter of the Boehmian-Gnostic view. Now clearly there are considerable difficulties not only associating Hegel with each of these heterodox strands vituperatively denounced by the emerging orthodoxy of the second and third centuries, on the one hand, and emergent Lutheran orthodoxy of the seventeenth century, on the other, but also the special methodological difficulty of the congruence of these particular heterodox modes of thought—the kind of congruence that would justify hyphenation. The first difficulty can be easily met. Hegel shows an interest in, and familiarity with, both species of heterodox thought.

While his familiarity with the great speculative mystic of his own religious tradition goes well beyond his knowledge of historical Gnosticism, that he had some knowledge of Gnosticism, albeit within the limits of nineteenth-century thought, is now taken as an interpretive given.[9] Moreover, the approval rating Hegel gives to these thinkers, both in general and especially with regard to the problem of the finite other, is quite high. The second difficulty is somewhat less easily met. I should confess up front that, while some indications of congruence of Boehmian ontotheology and Valentinian Gnosticism will be supplied, to keep the text at something like reasonable length it is simply not feasible to present the kind of full-scale argument that I would ideally like to mount. For Hegel at least, however, they seem to name not only an alternative to the mainline Christian traditions, his own Lutheran tradition in particular, but also an alternative with superior credentials. Indeed, it is the view proposed here that the Boehmian and Gnostic—and their jointure—view of creation, as construed by Hegel, possesses taxonomic advantages over those other surrogates for the standard Christian view, influential in Hegel's own day, i.e., the Spinozist and Neoplatonic renditions of *creatio ex Deo*. It will turn out that the most conspicuous advantage of the heterodox modalities of thought is, in the last instance, a narrative advantage or set of narrative advantages.

Section 3.1 Hegelian Legitimation of the Representation of Creation

Hegel's legitimation of the representation of creation as central to Christianity and to his own enterprise as a Christian philosopher is agreed upon in substance by a host of Hegelian commentators and critics. Chapelle, Fackenheim, Iljin, Kern, Koslowski, Lauer, and Schmidt constitute but a cross section of a more extensive list.[10] The evidence in Hegel is not at all recessed. It is implied in *SL*'s characterization of the realm of pure thought as God in his eternal essence before the creation of the world and finite spirit (*GL4:*46, *SL,* 50) and clearly stated in the *PS*. The following passage deserves to be quoted in full:

> Thus the merely eternal or abstract Spirit becomes an 'other' to itself, or enters in existence, and directly into *immediate* existence. Accordingly, it *creates* a world. This 'creating' is representation's word for the concept itself in its absolute movement; or to express

> the fact that the simple which has been asserted as absolute, or pure thought, just because it is abstract, is rather the negative, and hence the self-opposed or 'other' of itself. (#774, Miller, p. 476, slightly revised translation)[11]

In addition, express commitment to the Christian representation of creation is voiced in a number of important passages in *Enc* (esp. the *Zusatzen* of #246–248, and 381, 568). *LPR 3,* however, provides by far the clearest and most extensive endorsement of the Christian representation of creation with *LPR 1* providing a supporting role, just as it is *LPR 3* which is the key proof-text of Hegel's trinitarian contexting.

LPR 3 triumphantly confirms Chapelle's assessment that, for Hegel, creation (*Schöpfung*) as the appearance (*Erscheinung*) of the divine is internally complex and covers both the coming into being of nature and finite spirit.[12] Considered under the rubric of *Logos* or discourse, as Chapelle tends to recommend, the order of finitude as a whole testifies to the essential bilingualism of the divine. Hegel renders this complexity in his 1821 Manuscript, as in his later 1824 and 1827 Lectures, in the speculatively revised language of differentiation (*Unterscheidung*) and alienation (*Entfremdung*), with the latter referring to the difference between finite spirit (*endliche Geist*) and the divine infinite of the "Immanent Trinity," the former the difference between the materiality, externality, and fragmentation of nature, and the immateriality, interiority, and unity of the immanent sphere.[13] Appearance vouchsafes a determination of manifestation (or revelation) and modality of differentiation that both contrasts with—and, in important respects, is superior to—the self-referential manifestation of the "Immanent Trinity" and the mode of differentiation proper to it. Distinct as self-manifestation and appearance are—and some kind of hiatus is a desideratum—a measure of continuity must also be asserted. Were no continuity posited between the "Immanent Trinity" and the created order, this would imply, among other things, that the infinite sphere as such is closed off, or, in our technical narrative terminology, that the "Immanent Trinity" is synclastic. But, as we have already shown, the "Immanent Trinity" is only hypothetically synclastic; it is, in fact, anaclastic, i.e., open and receptive to determination beyond the epoch of self-reference. Though the foundational logic of relation, specifically of *Essence,* is more perspicuously rendered in *Enc,* it can be said that, even in *LPR 3,* Hegel is well aware of the distinction between *appearance* (*Erscheinung*) and *illusion* (*Schein*). In contrast to appearance, illusion isolates essence (here, divine essence) and devalues the multiplicity of finite objects.[14]

The anaclastic nature of the "Immanent Trinity" is, thus, inseparable from creation's status as appearance, appearance, in turn, underscoring a relationality that is nonextrinsic. From the Hegelian perspective, appearance—dependent upon the narrative openness of the "Immanent Trinity"—symptoms the specificity of the Christian view of creation and distinguishes it from all other views. Chapelle, in fact, suggests that central to the Hegelian elaboration is a structural contrast between the Christian and the Judaic view, the Judaic view coming under the rubric of *Schein* or illusion.[15] No one-to-one correspondence between Judaism and illusion-position exists, however, and oriental views can be equally characterized as belonging to the manifold of illusion.[16] Thus, *Schein* is a broad category, with Judaism, at best, providing an exemplary typification. That the Hegelian contrast Chapelle averts to is more functional than theoretical is aptly illustrated by Hegel's critique of Spinoza's illusion view of creation. Hegel, fairly indiscriminately, labels Spinoza's view (Judaic) (*Enc*) and oriental (*SL*) as suits his purpose.[17] The illusion view betrays certain systemic features: (1) it is characterized by a gap between the divine and the nondivine which renders the two spheres incommensurable; and (2) it is characterized by the merely accidental character of a relationship between the divine and nondivine, where the status of the latter can only be that of brute fact.[18]

Hegel's derogation of any creation theory regulated by *Schein* is intimately connected with his ultimate disavowal of *creation from nothing.*[19] The doctrine of creation from nothing is not thematized in either *LPR 3, Enc,* or *PS,* the main textual sources of our knowledge of the Hegelian view of what constitutes (descriptive) or ought to constitute (prescriptive) the Christian view of creation. The doctrine does come up for explicit discussion, however, in *DE* (E 93–94) and *SL* (E 84, *GL4*:90). In both cases, Hegel appears to give verbal assent to the quasinormative Christian dogmatic position. Nevertheless, in neither case can verbal support be taken as an unequivocal endorsement of the position that has been standard in the Christian tradition since Augustine and representative of the mainline trend since Irenaeus.[20]

In the case of the passage from *DE,* where the general context of discussion is trinitarian, creation from nothing is identifiable with creation from the abyss of the Father. Here it seems to be the case that one comes upon that curiously recurring phenomenon in the Christian tradition, that is, the providing of the *creatio ex nihilo* doctrine with a *creatio ex Deo* interpretation.[21] The passage from *SL,* the second of our two passages, illustrates the same phenomenon. On the surface Hegel appears to give wholehearted support to the Christian doctrine in directing a frontal attack on Spinoza's critique, which ultimately is summarized in the formula: *ex nihilo nihil fit* (*GL4*:90–91). In critiquing Spinoza's critique, Hegel does anything but mount a fundamental challenge; rather, he surreptitiously shifts the basis of the argument. Spinoza construes nothing as absolute nothing, the very contrary to reality, and insists upon the unthinkability of the creation from nothing position.[22] In his riposte, Hegel does not argue that something (determinate being or *Dasein*) can come from absolute nothing,[23] but rather that something can come from Becoming (*Werden*), where Becoming is understood as intermediating, or representing the synthesis of, Nothing and Being.[24] Whatever the status of the nothing with which Hegelian logic starts, no warrant is provided for interpreting the nothingness of Becoming in anything other than a relative sense. Availing of the form of categorial distinction, which begins to surface in modernity in Berdyaev and Tillich, between *oukontic* (absolute or Parmenidean) and *meontic* (relative or non-Parmenidean) senses of nothing,[25] it is clear that Hegel and Spinoza are at cross-purposes. Two different senses of nothing are in play: Spinoza is reflecting on oukontic nothingness and its possibilities, Hegel on meontic nothingness and the possibilities that belong to it. Denial of creation with respect to oukontic nothingness does not imply denial with respect to meontic nothingness, no more than affirmation with respect to meontic nothingness implies affirmation with respect to the oukontic modality. Spinoza rightly understands the creation from nothing position in both Judaism and Christianity to be operating with, and in terms of, the oukontic sense of nothing, and he disputes the intelligibility of presupposing that a determinate finite order can emerge from nothing understood in this way. When Hegel, on the other hand, defends the Christian position against Spinoza, he is, in fact, not defending the Christian position as Augustine, for instance, would understand it,[26] but from a revisionist view in which the sense of nothing has subtly, but dramatically, shifted from an oukontic to a meontic determination. Acceptance of this revisionist view enables Hegel to avoid some of the difficulties endemic to the normative Christian view with its stress on the power and sovereignty of God, the externality of relation between the divine infinite and the nondivine finite, and the contingency and ultimate unimportance of the world.[27] Only if creation from nothing is understood to imply creation from God can Hegel rescue the doctrine from the invidious realm of illusion that implies both a worldless God and Godless world.

The legitimation of the Christian representation of creation is not uncritical and is not exhausted by the contrast between the Christian and competing Judaic and oriental views. Implicit criticism of the normative Christian presentation of creation from nothing is insinuated, as we have shown, in Hegel's very championing of the doctrine. But there is a much more explicit, and much more fundamental, criticism of Christianity that bears directly upon the Christian doctrine of creation and a much more basic correction recommended. To the extent that it operates exclusively within the sphere of representation or *Vorstellung,* Christianity is in danger of obscuring its proper content. Correction entails countering the declension or leaning in the language of representation to suggest that the emergence of nature and finite spirit and their preservation (*Erhaltung*) (*LPR 3* 1821 MS E 89–90, G 27–28) is a consequence of discrete divine acts, either identical to temporal acts or viewed after a temporal model. From Hegel's point of view, temporalizing divine manifestation into a series of discrete acts represents one of the most serious dangers to a speculatively authenticated Christianity that sees divinity and act as one and that sees the divine as one integrated act of epochal manifestation or revelation. This thought is axial in *LPR 3* and achieves a correlatively intense asseveration in *Enc* (#378–388). Yet, it is perhaps *LPR 1* that supplies the best example of Hegel's corrective proposal. The unity of God's activity, Hegel insists, is the norm by which symbolization should be judged, and here representation is found to be wanting. Hegel writes:

> . . . the [logical] coherence between elements of content appears in representation as sequential. This coherence does not appear in its necessity, which can be apprehended as such only through the concept; hence in religion it is narrated that "such and such has happened;" and what has happened, which is an essential part of the content of the life of God, then appears figuratively, as a natural occurence, something that happened in time, and the next moment of the determinate content seems then to follow after it. (1824 E 334, G 235–236)[28]

It is clear that Hegel believes Christianity to be susceptible to what James Yerkes has elegantly christened the 'punctiliar' view. In the background of Hegel's attempt to correct theological skews resulting from the inadequacy of *Vorstellung* lies Spinoza's critique of theological voluntarism in his *Ethics* (Bk. I). Hegel attacks, as Spinoza did, the notion of creation as eternal decree (*LPR I* 1821 MS E 249, G 158), as he attacks any view of efficient causality underpinned by the optics of event or decision (ibid.). Yet, the critique of theological voluntarism is more local than the critique of punctiliarity. It is Hegel's view that theological voluntarism is epiphenomenal to storytelling punctiliarity endemic to Judeo-Christian representation in general, Christian representation in particular. Judeo-Christian representation finds its primitive, privileged, and foundational expression in the biblical narrative, with Genesis providing the paradigmatic representational account of the creation of nature and finite being. The critique of punctiliarity thus extends beyonds that pale of theological opinion that is the main focus of Spinoza's destructive attack, i.e., Descartes and the late scholastic tradition, to include critique, or at least critical correction, of the biblical account or any relatively first-order interpretation of this account. In his *Commentary on Genesis,* Luther presents one such account. Thus, in advising correction of the biblical view by advising correction of the modality of discourse—an operation gestured but not fully executed in *LPR*—Hegel also must be understood as advising correction of Luther.

In his *Commentary on Genesis,* Luther supports an extreme case of the punctiliar view.[29] Exegeting the biblical creation account, he attacks St. Augustine and Hilary, who shared the view that the universe was created instantaneously (Vol. 1, pp. 4, 69). While Luther agrees with Augustine and Hilary that creation is an act, and regards the theory of the eternity of the world as anathema, he insists that creation is successive, as plainly described in the biblical text. Moreover, these acts are works that occur *in time.* Speaking explicitly of the creation of Adam and Eve, Luther sums up his punctiliar optics *in nuce:*

> These are works of time, that is, works that require time and are not performed in one moment, they are works requiring time and they are performed on the sixth day. (ibid., p. 69)

The substantive conflict between Luther and Augustine and Hilary is associated with, and perhaps ultimately determined by, a distanciation on the level of hermeneutics. Central to Luther's attack is his espousal of the literal sense. The failure of Augustine and Hilary rests in large part, according to Luther, on the failure to stick to the literal sense and their propensity to indulge in allegorical speculation (ibid., p. 15). Hermeneutically, the difference between Hegel and Luther corresponds to the perceived differences between Augustine and Luther. Hegel eschews the literal sense, hoping thereby to avoid the theological debits that go with the punctiliar declension of the narrative surface of representation, as well as any kind of heteronomous authority system, be it institutional or textual. Scripture, Hegel constantly asserts, is open to the witness of spirit. Spirit is self-validating. Redolent of Luther's own tactic, Hegel appeals to 2 Cor. 3:6: "the letter kills, the spirit gives life" (*LPR 3* 1827 E 260, G 187). But with Hegel, more in continuity with the stridently pneumatic wing of the Reformation that included the so-called Spiritual Reformers and Jacob Boehme than with Luther or the tradition of Lutheran orthodoxy which tried to rein in Lutheranism's pneumatic impulse,[30] the pneumatism of interpreting subjectivity is absolutized and authority decentered from text to interpreter. The interpreter is not in any reductionist sense a rationalist but, illuminated by spirit, a correcter of biblical representation. This correction, which cuts against the grain of the literal sense by erasing the punctiliar declension, opens up the authentically *mystical* content of scripture, indeed, of Christianity as a whole (*LPR 1* 1827 E 254, G 162):[31] the mystical content consists not in the acts of the divine, but rather in the divine as act of continuous, differentiated, and fully inclusive manifestation.

For Hegel, then, the scriptural rendering of creation, as well as any relatively first-order interpretation, are deficient with respect to form. As species of representation, they cannot but obscure the content they seek to disclose, i.e., God as integrated act of manifestation. The question naturally emerges whether scripture and first-order reflection on scripture do more than obscure, but actually falsify and deform, the mystical content. This question, it should be noted, leaves open the possibility that there exist highly developed forms of representation that escape deforming content, when more basic forms are indictable. Decisions on these matters are postponed until later.[32] Suffice it to say, at the moment, that Hegel thinks rather differently of the representations of speculative theology than he does of the biblical or more biblically normed position.

To round out this account of Hegel's act of distanciation from the standard Judeo-Christian perception of creation, it ought to be recalled that Hegel not only departs from scripture and first-order reflections on it but also has decisive objections to the theologico-philosophical cipher of efficient causality. Like the two previously mentioned positions, the cipher of efficient causality, in Hegel's view, misrepresents the truth of the divine as integrated *actus,* in which creation or appearance is a moment, and the relation between God and creation as internal rather than external (*LPR I* 1821 MS E 248–249, G 157). Against the cipher of efficient causality Hegel has this to say:

> "Creating" is not a "grounding" or "causing": it is something higher than these limited thought-categories and contains the speculative relationship,the producing by the idea. (ibid. E 249, G 157)

Hegel's critique here is thoroughgoing and extends to any and every articulation of this position, whether Aristotelian, Cartesian, Scholastic, or Wolffian. In contesting the legitimacy of the cipher of efficient causality, Hegel, in principle, is also questioning the legitimacy of its use in Lutheran orthodoxy for whom it played a major role in the elaboration of the doctrine of creation. For Hegel, however, the questioning of Lutheran orthodoxy's view of creation, as codified in the great dogmatic treatises of the seventeenth century, does not constitute a fundamental act of betrayal of Lutheranism, anymore than does the contesting of the ontotheological adequacy of Luther's own first-order rendition of the Christian narrative. No fundamental act of betrayal need be involved, since Hegel assumes a speculative precedent in Lutheranism that does not admit Aristotelian or Scholastic categories of analysis. This speculative precedent, it will be made clear in the next section, is none other than that of Jacob Boehme, whose thought system continued to be critiqued well into the seventeenth century, not only for its non-Aristotelian method, but for its nonstandard view of creation.[33]

To sum up our discussion thus far: as a foil, then, to the various deficient formulations, Hegel proposes his view of the divine infinite as act, process, and becoming. The divine infinite is not worldless but includes in its fully encompassing scope the reality of the world as a fundamental moment of its expression. Encompassing aspect of the divine infinite is fully rendered in the following passage:

> And when we say "God," this word signifies the *absolute, all-encompassing fulfillment* (the truth of everything [that subsists] as this world of finitude and appearance). (*LPR 1* E 230, G 139)

Section 3.2 Creation as Fall and Evil

All of the flavor, much of the grammar, and not a little of Hegel's real speculative allegiance is betrayed when he proposes the following as a legitimate theological exegesis of something stated much more formally and compactly in the main body of *Enc* text:

> Nature is the Son of God, not *as* (*als*) the Son however, but as abiding in otherness (*im Anderssein*), (in which) the divine Idea is alienated from love and held fast for a moment. Nature is self-alienated spirit (*der sich entfremdete Geist*); spirit a bacchantic god, innocent of restraint and reflection has merely been let loose (*ausgelassen ist*); in nature the unity of the concept hides itself. (*Enc* #247 *zu, GL9:*50)[34]

Hegel's real elective affinity becomes fully explicit in the *Zusatz* to #248, when he endorses Jacob Boehme's vision of creation:

> Nature is the negative because it is the negative of the Idea. Jacob Boehme says that God's first born is Lucifer, and this Son of Light (*Lichtwesen*) centred his imagination on himself (*habe sich in sich hineinimaginirt*) and became evil: that is the moment of difference (*das Moment des Unterschiedes*), of otherness held fast against (*gegen*) the Son, who is otherness within the divine love (*der das Anderssein in der Liebe ist*). (*GL9:*57)[35]

For Boehme the most formal, but at the same time the most substantive, note of creation is that it is a tragic fall,[36] where a part of divine reality splits itself off from the divine milieu and engenders an antitype, a no to the divine yes. Much of what Hegel writes in the Introduction under discussion, but possibly also in those passages relevant to creation in the *PS* (#774, 776–777), tends to corroborate Schelling's tardy snipe that the Hegelian vision of creation has the mythopoetic Boehmian version as its precursor.[37] Schelling is obviously doing more than merely suggesting claims of anteriority-posteriority or engaging in an act of hermeneutical revenge when he makes Hegel, in Harold Bloom's sense, Boehme's 'ephebe'.[38] He is aware that the alliance in some way compromises the religious orthodoxy of Hegel's theological-philosophical proposal.

The heterodoxy of Hegel's view of creation and its dependence upon Boehmian reflection is averred by Hegelian scholars such as Peter Koslowski and H. S. Harris. Both point to the *PS* #776–777 as an early crescendo of Boehmian impact. Koslowski argues in an important essay that Hegelian thought, just at the point at which it begins to reflect upon creation, postulates a fourth hypostasis, a hypostasis that is the ultimate origin of finitude.[39] Moreover, finitude does not appear to be unequivocally characterized as good. While not totally explicit, Koslowski appears to suggest that the paragraphs in *PS* be read in connection with those passages in *Enc* where Jacob Boehme is granted the status of precursor. Further support that the Boehmian *mythos* of creation is not an adventitious phenomenon but a constant allegiance in Hegel is provided by the research of H. S. Harris into the pre-*PS* Hegel. Harris implies in *Night Thoughts* that Boehmian influence is much more considerable than previously thought.[40] This influence is responsible for the identification of 'earth' and 'evil' in *FK,* as it is constitutive of Hegel's envisioning of creating as *fall* in the important fragments of the "Triangulation of the Trinity" which remain in Rosenkranz's account of the development of Hegel.[41]

While Koslowski and Harris provide evidence for Schelling's hypothesis, they do not go so far as to suggest that the Boehmian view is *the* determinant of the quite heterodox-looking Hegelian view, essentially providing its taxonomic identification. But, despite some Hegelian scholars' deep aversion to the Schellingian proposal, it appears to have some warrant.[42] Both the general form of the Boehmian view of creation as antithetical formation of aggressive antitype and its telescoping in the ciphers of fall and evil (*das Böse*) are systemic features of the Hegelian view. Creation is, for Hegel, neither a punctiliar act of the divine, nor the sequence of such acts, nor an undisturbed emanation of finite being from infinite being or substance, nor the limit and point of exhaustion of divine devolution or diffusion.[43] Creation is the generation of the contrary of and for an immanent milieu, which milieu, as generally envisaged, is constituted by the dynamics of the "Immanent Trinity."

The presence of the ciphers of fall and evil, as explicit or implicit, is a constant throughout Hegel and does not cease with the *PS*. While the emphasis appears to be on evil as the result, the cipher of fall gets expressed in *LPH* where Hegel, in an important passage noted both by Kojève and Heidegger,[44] remarks on spirit falling into time. It gets expressed in *PS* when Hegel insists that the created world is fallen spirit (*geworfende Geist*).[45] It appears legitimate also to infer that the *ausgelassen* of *Enc* #247 *zu* (also #256) connotes fall, though, read in connection with other passages in *Enc* (e.g., #378–386), one is not entitled to read the fall in a deterministic or fatalistic way. Such a fall,[46] a fall into pain (*Schmerz*) and fall into evil (*das Böse*), is a phase of the self-determination of the divine, which self-determination provides the adequate definition of freedom. The pivotal use of the cipher fall occurs in *LPR 3* (1827) in a passage paralleling *Enc* #248 *Zusatz* quoted above:

> Jacob Boehme expressed this transition (*Übergang*) inherent in the moment of the Son as follows: the first only begotten one was Lucifer, the light bearer, brilliance and clarity, but he inwardly fancied himself (imagined into himself) (*in sich hineinimaginiert*), i.e., he posited himself for himself (*sich für sich gesetz habe*) he strove to be, and thereby he *fell* (*abgefallen sei*) . . . that (first) other is not the Son but rather the external world (*äusserliche Welt*), the finite world, which is outside the truth. . . . (*LPR 3* E 293, G 218)[47]

The presence of the cipher of evil in Hegelian texts, particularly as it operates in *LPR 3,* will be thematized shortly. But before we get to this, we might gesture to the broader matrix of the Hegelian view, as well as the full circuit of allegiance. Schelling's charge that the Hegelian view of creation is in its basic grammar Boehmian finds more than a little support in Hegelian text. Harris, in his excavation of the thought of the early Hegel, adds the interesting suggestion that Hegel's use of the cipher of fall associates him at the same time with Gnostic modes of thought.[48] This characterization, however, is not intended by Harris to be anything more than a loose comparison, moreover, a comparison with a quite specific textual focus. Nothing in Harris would justify extrapolation from this overlap of view to the use of the Gnostic view of creation as a *comparandum* and taxon of the mature Hegel—nothing, that is, except further evidence in Hegelian texts. But such evidence does exist. As mentioned earlier chapt. 2, sect. 3 (*2.3*), Hegel has some second-hand knowledge of Gnosticism and profers Valentinian Gnosticism with Boehmian theosophy as supplying theologically interesting accounts of an immanent sphere, dynamic, wholly pure, and without evil. Hegel, in another passage in *LPR 3* (1821 MS), appears to have the Gnostic creation account or, in general terms, the transition from the infinite and pure to the finite and evil explicitly in mind.

Hegel praises the Gnostics for being especially insistent upon the separation of the spiritual and material orders of being and their championing of the independence *(Selbständigkeit)* of *hylé* (*LPR 3* MS 1821 E 87–89, G 25–27). Hegel is not, in any absolute sense, affirming dualism. He is making the point that the antithetical, antitypical character of finitude—a characteristic emphasized in Gnostic myth— is an indispensable moment of narrative economy. Independence in Gnostic (and Boehmian) myth is flagrantly asserted, but, in the context of the narrative of the whole, independence is seen as a relative item. *Hylè* is, at the same time, the opposite of the independent, nothing but a moment of positedness (*das Moment des Gesetzseins ist*) (ibid. E 87, G 26), whose existence consists solely in sublating itself and being a moment in a process (*sich aufzuheben und Moment des Prozesses zu sein*) (ibid. E 89, G 27). Nevertheless, even if the independence is de-absolutized, one might even invoke the locution "de-created," *hylé* is antitype. It is important to remember that this antitype, which appears to be invested with some kind of deficient selfhood, is not just matter pure and simple. Matter, it appears to be Hegel's view in *LPR 3* at least, is itself a narrative result and thus finds its explanation elsewhere. Matter is derived from spirit; it is engendered *by* and *from* the immanent divine, and, as such, it is nothing but spirit in an alien, opaque, and concealed form.

The Boehmian and Gnostic parallels with Hegel's view of creation are especially important for defining its basic taxon. At a minimum, they appear to offer basic ontotheological contexts from which the Hegelian view of fall and entrance into evil might be viewed. While many commentators have been particularly blasé with respect to this aspect of Hegel's thought, and certainly quite abstract, the strangeness of Hegelian statements and their extraordinary appeal to mythic modes of thought has not been lost on all. We have already mentioned Harris and Koslowski as exceptions. Erik Schmidt in his *Hegels Lehre von Gott* also rises above the common denominator in being struck by the oddness of Hegel's account of creation: first, that it is described in terms of a fall and second, that the fall appears to be internally complex and under the governance of the mythologem of Lucifer. Schmidt notes that *PS* does not present the Christian standard but, rather, promotes a view of double-fall, a two-stage engendering of evil.[49] The *locus classicus* of this ontotheological oddity is #776:

> . . . the becoming of Evil can be shifted further back out of the existent world even into the primary realm of thought. It can therefore be said that it is the very first-born Son of Light [Lucifer] himself who fell because he withdrew into himself or became self-centered. (Miller p. 468)

Schmidt's remarks would clearly apply also to Hegel's more mature texts. *LPR 3* certainly seems to corroborate the two-stage theory of fall and engendering of evil. As in the case of *PS,* the movement from the sphere of the immanent divine into evil is, in the first instance, a self-concentration or entrance into personhood (1824 E 184, G 127) anterior to the anthropological upsurge of involution or self-centeredness anathemized by Paul, Augustine, and Luther. Of course, the postulate of involution in a higher realm before its human appearance is itself authorized by the mainline Christian traditions. Augustine and Luther provide representative examples of the traditional view of the fall of Lucifer and the relation between the Luciferian and Adamic fall.[50] In both cases, the Luciferian fall into self-concentration provides the prototype of human self-concentration, which is thus understood as imitation and repetition. In both cases, also, while the creation of the world is intimately associated with the Luciferian fall, creation is good and represents a narrative interregnum between the two-stage positing of the self-centeredness of evil. Yet the Hegelian position is not an innocent recapitulation of this standard adjustment of two Christian mythologems. It is marked by very noticeable swerve. In Hegel, Luciferian involution is not identified as the act of the *other* of God, but rather as the act of the *othering* of God. Moreover, the Luciferian fall appears, not merely to *narratively precede* the creation of the world of nature and finite spirit, but is *actually identified with* it. This peculiarity evokes the heterodox traditions, Valentinian Gnosticism implicitly, Boehme explicitly. Indeed, mention of Boehme in *Enc* and *LPR 3,* as well as implicit appeal in *PS,* suggests that Hegel is not only recapitulating the Luciferian motif but a highly specific version of that motif. And that specific version that Boehme supplies in *Aurora* (1612), as elsewhere, in identifying the fall of Lucifer with the creation of the world is, as the Boehme scholar Hans Grunsky implies, quite nonstandard.[51]

Together, nature and finite spirit define the twin poles of the antithetical milieu, though it is in the pole of finite spirit that antithetical excess is fully realized. Finite spirit is the acme of evil whose defining characteristic is self-centeredness. The following passage from *LPR 1* could not be any clearer. Evil belongs to the *worldly* sphere as a whole but, in the deepest possible way, to finite spirit. The passage from the 1821 Manuscript reads:

> God [is] the absolutely positive; therefore what differs from him [is] the negative. This negative appears on the side of worldly essence, of human being. This negative of God is evil, or wickedness in general. (E 194, G 104)

While evil refers in a supreme way to finite spirit, it does not refer uniquely. Evil possesses a cosmological, or more accurately, a *cosmogonic* aspect, which is hardly surprising given that Hegel speaks of the generation of nature as involving a fall. And fall from the pure sphere, dominated by unity, to the not-so-pure realm, dominated by division, alienation, and contradiction involves a translation into the realm of evil. For Hegel, there is an asymmetry of level. It is in finite spirit that the immanent divine finds its true other or other-being (*Anderssein*), a self-consciousness capable of introverting singularity, a self-consciousness capable of and actually executing refusal, of being no to the eternal yes of universality. No doubt with the distinction between the two poles clearly in mind, Hegel sometimes appears to renege on the categorial inclusiveness of evil. An example of such a conceptual wobble is presented in the following *LPR 3* (1821 MS) text, where Hegel is engaged in exegesis of the Genesis account of the fall:

> The more precise way of representing this evil [condition] is to say that human beings become evil by cognizing, or, as the Bible represents it, that they have eaten of the tree of knowledge of good and evil [Gen. 3.5–6]. Through this story cognition, intelligence, and theoretical capacity come into a closer relationship with the will, and the nature of evil comes to more precise expression. Against this it may be said that it is in fact cognition that is the source of all evil, for knowledge or consciousness is the only act through which separation is posited at all . . . it is cognition that first posits the antithesis in which evil is to be found. Animals, stones, and plants are not evil. . . . (E 205–206; G 137–138)

Hegel, here, in the most declarative way appears to disassociate createdness and evil. Evil is, above all, the alienation and rupture introduced on the level of finite spirit, and experienced on that level. Before this is taken as Hegel's definitive word on the issue, however, it should be remembered that Hegel does not clearly distinguish between a religious representation of approximate value and his own position with respect to this representation. Moreover, it is plausible that what is of interest to Hegel in the above passage is the relationship of finite spirit and nature, and, comparatively speaking, as the center of a subjectivity that can say no, finite spirit is incomparably *more* evil than nature. But this is not to claim, or at least not be entitled to claim, that nature is not evil in *any* way. When the interest is less the relationship of nature and finite spirit and more that of creation as a general form of contrariety, all of creation appears to be characterized as fallen, all creation appears to be characterized as evil, and, indeed, all creation appears to be characterized as self-centered and involuted. As I have suggested, these characterizations, which do not fundamentally discriminate between nature and finite spirit (even the last), are explicable against the background of theogonic narrative of a Boehmian-Gnostic type. Against this background, any distinction between nature and finite spirit is a distinction *within* the order of evil.

Though there are revisionist features in Hegel's hermeneutic rendering of Genesis in *LPR 3* (also in the *Enc* 24 *zu*), as we shall see shortly, the very fact that the exploration of evil is carried on via a reading of the Adamic fall appears to center his interpretive account more firmly within the normative Christian and Lutheran traditions. The contexting may be deliberate on Hegel's part, and passages such as the one cited above point in that direction. There are times, in fact (e.g., *LPR 3* 1827 E 305, G 229), when Hegelian explanation hovers in the vicinity of a then contemporary rendering of the Adamic myth of fall, which, while it departs from the punctiliar and historical element of myth, nonetheless, remains within the normative Christian tradition's general ambit. The account I have in mind is that of Schleiermacher. In Schleiermacher's perspectival rendition, nature is not evil in itself but is perceived to be so in human being's alienated and fallen condition.[52] Through explicit confession, through focus on the Adamic myth of origin, and affinity with a specific anthropological view of origin and locus of evil, Hegel appears traditional. But all of this tends to mask the nonanthropological background of the emergence of evil and the real tradition or traditions to which the Hegelian view belongs.

While the appearance of orthodoxy is, perhaps, a motive for Hegel's account of origin, it is not *the* motive. The pivotal motive in the Hegelian alignment to biblical narrative is forensic: to draw a critical line of demarcation between the specifically Christian view and the naive Enlightenment view of human being's aboriginal goodness and innocence (*LPR 3* 1827 E 296, G 221). Human being as such, that is, human being as spirit, who supposes differentiation from the natural environment, is aboriginally evil (ibid. E 298–299, G 223).[53] In making this appraisal, via a hermeneutic of the Adamic account of origin, Hegel at once incorporates the Kantian critique of the Enlightenment summarized in the notion of 'radical evil' and points the way forward (ibid. E 305–306, G 229–230) to Kierkegaard's psycho-theological rendition of sin and sinfulness in the *Concept of Anxiety*.[54] Hegel's relationship to Kant—particularly the Kant of *Religion*—illustrates in a particularly revealing way his continuity with the anthropologically biased tradition accounting for evil's genesis.[55]

The Hegelian account overlaps with the Kantian in three closely interrelated ways, though distinctions also exist. (1) The Hegelian account of the emergence of evil in *Enc* and *LPR 3,* as with the Kantian account in *Religion,*[56] provides support for the biblical account of origin. (2) In and through his allegiance to the content revealed in the biblical narrative, Hegel, after the precedent of Kant in that text decried by Goethe as a betrayal,[57] essentially breaks with the Christian dogmatic tradition of original sin.[58] (3) Hegel, following Kant, places goodness and perfection in a teleological-eschatological perspective.[59] Each of these three areas of overlap requires some explicatory comment.

(1) For Hegel, as for Kant, the biblical account of origin possesses not merely symbolic richness but truth (*LPR 3* 1821 MS E 100, G 36–37), which, if elucidated, exposes the shallowness of the Enlightenment view that human being is essentially and aboriginally good. Both discern a primordial ground of evil in human being, and both remark on the inherent tendency of evil to be concretely realized. In his description of the ground, however, Hegel parts company from Kant. Hegel is prepared, as in the passage cited above from *LPR 3* (1824), to implicate will in the emergence of evil (E 205–206, G 137–138; also E 203–206, G 135–136). But it is knowledge that is the real root of evil and that provides its basic motor. It is knowledge that is ultimately responsible for human being's alienation from nature, God, and itself.[60] Will's role is marginal. Hegel's distance from Kant and the marginalization of will are both indicated in Hegel's word choice. Hegel uses *Wille* rather than *Willkür,* suggesting that, for him, will has no transphenomenal connotation and, in no wise, can be identified with the transcendental ground of self.[61] While circling within the orbit of the normative Christian anthropological account, in making knowledge rather than will the ground of origin, Hegel distances himself from the dominant voluntarist strand of interpretation which stretches from Augustine to Kant through Luther. One cannot expect in Hegel anything more than a relative validation of the biblical suspicion of knowledge, but a relative validation is supplied. Knowledge is the agent of rupture and pain and provisionally, at least, must be perceived under the lens of pathology. In an image that Nietzsche later uses,[62] knowledge is a 'disease' in finite spirit, indeed, a disease that *is* human spirit (*LPR 3* 1824

E 206, G 139). The pathogenic or pathological characterization of knowledge, it should be pointed out, is not specific to *LPR 3*. It is also very much to the fore in *Enc* (#24 *zu*).

(2) Paradoxically, precisely because both Kant and Hegel take the symbolic account of *Genesis* so seriously, they swerve from or, at the very least, suggest serious revision of, the normative dogmatic account of original sin. The ground strokes of both subversions lie in the deindividualization and dehistoricization of the biblical narrative. Adam, for both, is not a proper but a common name. It denotes not the first historical being but humanity. Moreover, it is the case for Hegel, as for Kant, that, despite its surface grammar, the biblical account of fall does not uniquely refer to the past.[63] For both, therefore, evil does not come into the world once and for all through a specific individual and thereafter proceed, as the Augustinian or traducianist tradition had thought, through biological or quasi-biological transmission (*LPR 3* 1827 E 301–302, G 225–226). Though neither Kant nor Hegel are fully explicit on the point, they both seem to think that the biologism of hereditary sin is a consequence of a punctiliar optics governing the construal of the emergence of evil in a concretely unique individual—a construal both regard as philosophically unsound.

(3) Similar to Kant, Hegel situates evil within a teleological-eschatological perspective.[64] For Kant goodness can be realized eschatologically in the human community that instantiates the Christian symbol of the kingdom of God. Of course, Kant, unlike Hegel, also posits goodness as the truly archeological substratum.[65] For Hegel, however, it is the former and not the latter posit that can be affirmed, and that legitimates the counterthesis of human being's essentially evil nature. Evil is not merely radical; it is the absolutely radical. This position is insisted upon in *LPR 3* but also finds an expression in the collateral hermeneutic of the biblical account of origin carried on in *Enc* #24 *zu*.

> For the very notion of spirit is enough to show that man is evil by nature (*das der Mensch von Natur böse ist*) and it is an error to imagine it otherwise. (Miller, p. 44. *GL8:96*)[66]

Eschatologically, however, human being is indeed good (*LPR 3* 1827, E 296, G 221),[67] and thus the Enlightenment proposal can be accepted in some measure—yet only with appropriate revision, revision determined by the biblical view or, at least, some interpretation of this view. Hegel in *LPR 3* dismisses as thoroughly jejune the good-on-the-one-hand-evil-on-the-other compromise of those who flirt with both the Christian and secular options with respect to perspective on the human essence. For Hegel, not all contradiction is fertile, and the adoption of both options as being equally and simultaneously true is expressive of a contradiction of a conceptually sterile sort. Both positions, indeed, can be asserted, but only if they are placed within a narrative whose trajectory moves from evil to good. The goodness of human being must be accorded its eschatological narrative location, as it must be teleologically indexed. Human being is destined to overcome alienation and the disproportion between what is and what ought to be. The therapeutic agent in this process, just as it is also the pathogenic agent, is knowledge. *LPR 3* (1824 E 206, G 138–139) and *Enc* (24 *zu*) are once again in concord. The passage in *Enc* is especially worthy of citation:

> The spiritual is distinguished from the natural, and more especially from the animal, life, in the circumstance that it does not continue a mere stream of tendency, but sunders itself to self-realization. But this position of severed life has in its turn to be suppressed, and the spirit has by its own act to win its way to concord again. The final concord then is spiritual; that is, the principle of restoration is found in thought, and thought only. The hand that inflicts the wound is also the hand which heals it. (Miller p. 43. *GL8:*93)

The focus will return to knowledge momentarily. Before this, however, a few concluding observations with respect to Kant's and Hegel's teleological-eschatological reading of the Adamic fall of a general kind are in order. Though one should be loathe to dismiss the influence of the Enlightenment in the case of either Kant or Hegel (this is particularly so with regard to Kant), the teleological-eschatological reading of the Adamic fall is not without precedent within the theological tradition. As Laurence Dickey has pointed out, the German religious tradition that provides the proximate context for Kantian and Hegelian articulation was pedagogical and eschatological in intent and substance. Seeing the analogy between this widespread supposition that got parsed in different ways in Bengel, Lessing, Kant, Hegel, and Christian Neoplatonism, Dickey suggests that a perspicuous way of understanding this widespread teleological and eschatological supposition is to see it as something of a retrieval of an Alexandrian view of the early centuries of the Christian era.[68] While by no means questioning the general suitability of the Alexandrian taxon, Dickey's suggestion can be qualified helpfully in two ways: first, the Alexandrian taxon should not be construed so narrowly as to exclude the potential illumination that might be provided by Irenaeus, who, in his own way, provides an early, highly teleological rendition of the Christian narrative;[69] and second, it should not be construed so broadly as to rule out the search for the best possible analogue within the Alexandrian tradition. With respect to the latter point, the Cappadocian, Gregory of Nyssa, has particular claims to critical attention. For instance, Nyssa's *On the Making of Man* provides a superb example of a teleological-eschatological reading that tends to moderate the accent of loss and exacerbate the accent of gain.[70] Of course, in a certain sense the eschatological horizon is never totally absent in Christian interpretation of redemption and salvation. Augustine's *City of God* presents a classic account of the more standard Western Christian position. Within the horizon of the entire Christian narrative the fall into evil is indeed a *felix culpa.* The *felix culpa* valence of the fall in Augustine, however, does nothing to ameliorate its momentousness and horror. Indeed, it could be argued that the Augustinian rendition of *felix culpa* cannot, in principle, alleviate, since fortunateness is not fully *internal* to the fall itself; or, otherwise expressed, the fall is not invested with a fully fledged teleological logic. Matters stand otherwise with the Nyssan rendition with which Kant and Hegel have more in common. For Kant and (especially) Hegel, as for Nyssa, fortunateness does appear to be *internal.* Fall does appear to be invested with an intrinsic teleological logic. Thus, it could be argued that in Hegel and Kant one is dealing with (1) a fall whose logic is only superficially a fall *downward* but which, in principle, is a fall *upward,*[71] and relatedly (2) a fall where the teleological-eschatological horizon introduces a *felix culpa* modality that has theological warrant, though not a warrant found appealing throughout most of the history of Western Christian theology.

The teleological-eschatological reading of the Adamic fall evidences a kind of hermeneutic in important respects less faithful to the literal sense than the reading of Augustine or Luther. This is clear in Kant's allegorizing exegesis in *Religion,* as it is transparent in the Hegel of *LPR 3* and *Enc* (#24 *zu*), who, though in a very general way suggesting that representation norm interpretation and concept, nevertheless, in practice, recommends an eschatological-futural reading of biblical narrative that cuts against the grain of the literal sense. Moreover, Hegel's particular eschatological-futural reading is associated with other hermeneutic practices that do not find exemplification in the more standard Christian traditions, whether Patristic, medieval, or modern, or even in Kant's far from standard *allegoresis*.

The single most important illustration of hermeneutic revision is provided by Hegel's reading of those passages in Genesis which concern knowledge. As stated earlier, Hegel is prepared to partially validate the biblical suspicion of knowledge. His determinative view of knowledge's status, however, is rendered in his exegesis of *Genesis* 3:5 and 3:22. The comparison with Luther is truly instructive. Luther's response to Gen. 3:5 where the serpent says to Eve,"You will be like God," is to exclaim, "This is Satanic oratory!" (Vol. 1, p. 155). By contrast, conforming 3:5 with 3:22 where Yahweh states, "Behold Adam has become like one of us, knowing good and evil," Hegel concludes in *LPR 3* and *Enc* (#24 *zu*) that the serpent told the truth.[72] For Hegel, the serpent as a *dramatis persona* is not, as for Luther, the symbol of Satan, the father of lies, but a discloser of the unrecognized truth. The general issue that divides Luther and Hegel is the status of knowledge, its role negative or positive, the question whether it is, in principle, damning or salvific. For Luther, as indeed the tradition of Lutheran orthodoxy that Hegel made an early acquaintance with in the *Stift* at Tübingen, knowledge, specifically self-centering knowledge, is satanic. For Hegel, by contrast, the evil of knowledge is, at once, a provisional narrative state and a partial description. In principle, knowledge, knowledge of good and evil in particular, is divine. The Hegelian reading is quite extraordinary. It bears some resemblances to Christian Neoplatonic readings of Genesis in that, in both cases, knowledge is regarded positively. Christian Neoplatonism, however, cannot be posited as an adequate *comparandum* or taxon since, in the Neoplatonic interpretive scheme, knowledge of good and evil is not regarded as a sign of divinity but a sign of loss of aboriginal image.[73]

Arguably, the real hermeneutical precedent for the positive reading of knowledge, even in its fallen situation, and the accompanying strange affirmation of the serpent, is to be found in Gnosticism. Knowledge may be a pathogenic agent in so far as it alienates, yet it is also the soteriological agent par excellence, and the serpent, for Hegel, is clearly in the service of knowledge (gnosis) and is instrumental in revealing its possession to the not yet fully self-conscious spiritual beings. Moreover, Hegel is also more nearly Gnostic in the consistency with which he interprets the serpent image. In contrast not only to Luther and Lutheran orthodoxy but also to a long Christian tradition that included Christian Neoplatonists as well as Augustine and Irenaeus, Hegel, after the fashion denounced by the first of the great heresiologists, effectively assimilates Genesis 3.1 with Matthew 10.16, where Christ enjoins the disciples "to be wise as serpents." The hermeneutic bivalence that characterizes Augustine (*Contra Julianum* 4.3.20) is typical of the main Christian traditions. The Genesis serpent passage admits only of a negative reading, the Matthaean only of a positive, for, if in the former the serpent connotes diabolic cleverness, in the latter the serpent connotes humility and preparedness to repent. Augustine's reasoning, as with Irenaeus before him, is essentially that only in such bivalent reading is the truly dramatic character of revelation vouchsafed. The serpent provides the type for the Redeemer who is the great antitype as well as thoroughly definitive *dramatis persona.* Within Augustine's traditional reading, the problem with hermeneutic monovalence regarding the serpent image is not only that it sanitizes the power-seeking dimension in knowledge but that it also undercuts the decisive and gratuitous intervention of Christ. Within the general ambit of what emerging orthodox Christianity presumed to be an arrogant and uncontrollable revisionism, Gnostic hermeneutics was, in particular, condemned. One area in which the revisionism of Gnostic hermeneutics showed itself in particular was in the interpretation of the fall story of Genesis. In the context of the revisionism that Irenaeus attempts to capture in the technical term *metharmottein,*[74] that is, disfiguration-refiguration, fall is read comically rather than tragically.[75] Disobedience is the condition of possibility not of deformation but of the realization of perfected selfhood, or, in other words, the divine dimension of the self. In this act of emblematic disobedience that breaks the circuit of heteronomy, the serpent in Gnostic texts is, at a minimum, both hero and truth teller, at a maximum, the saviour as the figure of gnosis.[76]

The Gnostic-like revision in Hegelian philosophy of religion of the more standard, and more Lutheran, reading of Genesis 3.1. takes place, it must be admitted, within the horizon of a reading whose parameter is teleological-eschatological. The divinity of human being or the divine image, both essentially constituted by knowledge, is fully real eschatologically rather than aboriginally. This dictates the eschatological twisting of the 'has become' (*ist geworden*) of Genesis 3:22. The has become, Hegel writes in *LPR 3*

> gives expression to the particular moment: [not that] of the first and original likeness of God, but of the likeness that is to be regained. (1821 MS E 108, G 43–44)[77]

The image of God, therefore, does not lie in the archeological past but in the eschatological future. Because this is so, innocence (*Urschuld*) has no special prerogatives.[78] From a noetic perspective, innocence is tantamount to ignorance, if, indeed, it can properly (even if privatively) be classified under thought. On Hegel's view, it is thought that makes possible the vocation of human being and, in a certain sense, is identical with this vocation.[79] Hegel's assessment of the inferiority of feeling in the context of a clear evocation of the Adamic mythos is fully registered in the following passage:

> A natural unity of thought and intuition is that of the child and animal, and this can at the most be called feeling (*Empfindung*), not spirituality. But man must have eaten of the tree of the knowledge of good and evil and must have gone through the labor and activity of thought in order to become what he is. . . . (*Enc* #246 *zu,* Miller p. 9)

Almost identically the same point is made in the famous passage in *LPH* where paradise is said to be a park fit for animals but not men (*GL11:*413).[80] The undifferentiation and complacency of paradise is not for human being, who is always and already quest. On this view, the fall of man or original sin is "therefore the eternal myth of man's becoming man" (*der ewige Mythos des Menschen, wodurch er eben Mensch wird*) (ibid.). Therefore, whatever the Gnostic element in the text, there does exist a future-oriented surplus that calls for a different description. This future-oriented surplus will come in for explicit discussion in chapter 5. But, as we shall see momentarily, eschatological twist in a Christian metanarrative need not be historical or historicist in orientation, and it well could be the case that either Gnosticism, Boehme, or the depth grammar that explains their unity can assist further in understanding the nonstandard nature of Hegel's view of a perfection of knowledge that can only be gained.

Hegel's exegesis of the Adamic account of the origin of evil, as well as the Kant-Hegel liaison, has been explored in sufficient detail. This liaison is by no means perfect, and differences obtrude themselves. But the fundamental difference between Kant and Hegel has not been broached yet. In the *First Critique* Kant forbade transregulative knowledge of God. From the beginning, Hegel disputed Kant's epistemological premise and thought such knowledge not merely possible but actual, actual at once in Christianity and philosophy, which is, or at least ought to be, Christianity's speculative rewriting. As we saw in chapter 1, Hegel aligned himself with the mystics in regard to gnoseological claim but also suggested that the ultimate mystical content is the englobing narrative of trinitarianly structured divine. Though Kant in *Religion* goes beyond the restrictions of the *First Critique,* and his mixed discourse of transcendental investigation and symbolic exegesis go beyond the merely heuristic,[81] he never unequivocally legitimates transcendent discourse about the divine.[82] Kant clearly shows himself capable of aligning transcendental philosophy and Christian narrative. Hegel does also, and, arguably, the bond is much closer. But more importantly, and definingly, Hegel aligns philosophy with an account of the divine that narratively elaborates itself. Hegel offers *transcendent* rendition of the narrative of the divine, a rendition he takes to be faithfully Christian. In doing so, Hegel also validates Ricoeur's suspicion, voiced at the end of *The Symbolism of Evil,* to the effect that, in the subtle and refined ontotheologies of German Idealism, one can witness the recrudescence of the *theogonic* account of evil.[83] The theogonic account represents a departure from the normative Christian tradition's espousal of anthropological origin for which the Adamic account is regulative.[84]

In Hegelian texts the anthropological narrative is involved in a double relationship to the narrative of the divine: (1) it is formally isomorphic with it; (2) the anthropological narrative is a phase or moment of the narrative of the divine. Both relationships are important. The fact of isomorphism dictates the identity of dramatic structure in the evolution of subjectivity and personhood from the merely implicit and potential (one might say 'irreal') to the fully explicit and actualized. Narrative development in both cases proceeds by way of exile and alienation. It is this fact of isomorphism that provides a motive for the humanist reading or rather misreading of Hegel. Hegel, indeed, serves as something of an *agent provocateur* in his own misreading in that he appears to affirm in the *Zusatzen* to *Enc* that *either* God or human being can be supplied as the referent to the highly formal dynamics presented in the main body of the text. Yet, in the last instance, the ultimate referent is, indeed, the divine and not human being, though in Hegel their relation is much closer than in the normative Christian tradition. Hegel, who makes numerous appeals to Aristotle, and at the very least appropriates Aristotelian technical terminology,[85] might usefully have appealed here to Aristotle's *pros hen* formulation and openly determined the divine narrative to be the prime analogate. Nevertheless, even in the absence of such an explicit assertion, no fair-minded reading of *LPR 3* and *Enc* could conclude that the anthropological narrative has dominance or even parity. Both these texts make it clear that the becoming of human being is a narrative phase or moment of the becoming of the divine. The insertion of anthropological narrative into the larger theogenetic framework is hardly inconsequential. In fact, insertion relativizes conclusions whose truth appears apodictic within the anthropological horizon. Within that horizon, it is human being alone that is evil or appears to be so. Within the encompassing narrative frame of divine becoming, however, nature itself is also so determined.

We turn now to a narrative element that, at once, reflects the isomorphism between the anthropological and theogenetic narratives, as well as the material differences that are the consequences of the encompassing of one narrative field by another. The element, or trope, to which I refer is that of *felix culpa,* whose functioning on the level of anthropological narrative has already been examined. Within a narrative matrix where the determinative properties are teleological-eschatological, the overall quality of fall and evil is transformed. While the surface grammar of fall still maintains *downward* directionality, the depth grammar is antithetical, and fall paradoxically is, in principle, a fall *upward.* The overall quality of evil also undergoes metamorphosis when evil is not viewed exclusively as it is in itself but with regard to its purpose and place in a narrative that requires and presupposes it.

Though the point has not been made in precisely this way by Hegel scholars, some version of this reading would not be unacceptable to a sizeable number. It is plausibly the case that more resistance would meet the suggestion that, as Hegel elaborates a theogonic account of evil, he also elaborates a *felix culpa* appropriate to the notion of divine fall, divine engendering of evil, a *felix culpa* whose horizon is not the anthropological narrative but the englobing narrative of the divine. The only Hegel scholar who, to my mind, touches on this idea is H. S. Harris in his magnificent account of the early Hegel and his sources. In *Night Thoughts* Harris points to *FK* as indicating a correction to theogonic fall and theogonically engendered evil.[86] Whereas religion expounds evil as a necessity of finite nature, as one with the concept of finite nature, philosophy sees evil in its *fortunate* aspect as a precondition of the realization of the infinite. Fortunate aspect is not an affect; rather, it is that dimension added to the religious (or Christian) view when fall and evil are resituated in a teleological-eschatological setting. Resituation, however, is not a phenomenon restricted to this early Hegelian text but, it could be argued, is recurrent, throughout the Hegelian corpus. Despite the rather crude division between religion and philosophy announced in the passage from *FK,*[87] resituation takes two essential forms. It is executed in the Hegelian hermeneutic of Christian representation in the section on Revelatory Religion in *PS,* as also, of course, in *LPR 3.* Explication on the level of philosophy proper, understood as interconnected conceptual framework, is offered in the concluding sections of both *PS* and *Enc.* In the latter case, the teleological-eschatological resituation is accompanied in the main text by the effacement of the theological language of fall and evil and their replacement by the language of negation and contradiction.[88]

Only two texts will be discussed here and then only briefly, i.e., *LPR 3* and *Enc.* As *LPR 3* presents it, the "Immanent Trinity" enters into the finitude of nature and finite spirit, divesting itself thereby of the infinitude proper to it. Entrance into finitude, in turn, implies an entrance into evil, and, if our appeal to the centrality of the Boehmian-Gnostic cipher of fall as *explanans* is apposite, entrance into evil has fall as its generative modality. In *LPR 3* it is Hegel's view that nature and finite spirit, even as 'fallen forms' of the divine, contain a potentiality for infinitude that will not be denied. The order of creation as a whole (fallen nature and fallen finite spirit) represents a nadir that points upwards and initiates a new direction of narrative movement that ultimately issues in the divinization of the human community (*Gemeinde*). For Hegel in his hermeneutic of Christian *Vorstellungen,* the incarnation is an indispensable step on the upward trajectory, without which human being's entrance into infinitude cannot be realized. The narrative and theological status of the Hegelian view of the Incarnation will be explained in the immediately following chapter.

Even within the context of the anthropological narrative, the teleological-eschatological perfection posited in *LPR 3* possesses a cosmic, as well as specifically anthropocentric, aspect. Nature and human being are, indeed, fully reconciled, yet Hegel, though he appears to evoke Schleiermacher's perspectival view of the goodness of nature, seems to go beyond Schleiermacher and suggest something like an *ontological* transformation of nature occurring in and through Christ. In making this suggestion, Hegel brings *LPR 3* into the vicinity at least of the view of the early Church fathers, especially the Cappadocians and Christian Neoplatonists,[89]—though the peculiarities of his view of evil and its transformation have perhaps more in common with another revisionist Lutheran, Jacob Boehme, and even some Valentinian

Gnostic texts than with any species of Christian Neoplatonism.[90] This point will be thematized shortly. In any event, in the Hegel texts we are exploring, the overcoming of finitude and evil and entrance into infinitude and goodness is neither definingly human in terms of agency nor referent. Divinization of the pneumatic community, united in worship and contemplation of the divine, is indispensable to divine self-determination and definition. The selfhood or personhood of the divine is itself teleological-eschatological, as are the perfections that go with them, axiological, ontological, gnoseological, and existential. And, while evil and good are determinations that properly belong to the axiological axis of narrative trajectory, yet these axes are only analytically distinguishable. In practice, evil and good not only associate with, but at times condense, ontological, gnoseological, and existential properties.

With respect to the place of evil in the narrative of the divine, *Enc* does not differ in any significant respect, though, arguably, the teleological-eschatological thrust of the narrative is more to the fore. The obstacle character of finitude and evil plays an indispensable functional role in the elaboration of a perfection germinally there from the beginning (*Enc* #379 *zu*). Moreover, neither evil, alienation, nor their overcoming, is happenstance. They are necessary (*notwendig*) and not merely possible (*möglich*) elements of a narrative which possesses a teleological grammar.[91] The telos is, of course, fully divine selfhood that involves a return (*Rückkehr*) of the divine into itself—a return which, however, brings with it the whole narrative of development and actualization. *Rückkehr* is not a return into the same; it is a return into the *more*.

Section 3.3 Hegelian Swerve from the Normative Christian Tradition

Hegel's swerve from the more standard Christian traditions is multifaceted. The truly vital aspects have already been covered in this chapter, and all that needs to be presented here is the summary list. Five aspects of swerve stand out. (1) First among equals is Hegel's explicit critique of the punctiliarity of biblical representation and also, though less explicitly, of any theological representation, either directly normed by biblical narrative optics (Luther) or normed by it in the last instance (Augustine). The punctiliar critique also applies to any creation view that has the notion of efficent causality at its center (Aquinas, Descartes etc). (2) Hegel's notion of creation as divine manifestation parts company from the creation from nothing view that, from Augustine on, was regarded as both a biblical extrapolation and desideratum of Christian theology and which, most certainly, was a fundamental dogmatic point of Lutheran orthodoxy from the seventeenth century into Hegel's own day.[92] (3) Hegel's view of human being as essentially evil diverges from the biblically normed view (Luther and Lutheran orthodoxy, Augustine) that goodness is human being's prius. Hegel, also, departs from the more indirect, or more mediate, biblically-normed view such as found in Kant's *Religion.* (4) Hegel's vision of creation as fallen and evil represents a major departure from that understanding of creation represented by figures as disparate as Irenaeus, Augustine, and Luther, and theological trends as widely separate as Christian Neoplatonism, medieval Scholasticism, and Lutheran orthodoxy. (5) If Hegel's questioning of the absolute hegemony of the literal sense cuts against the grain of Luther's express intention and Lutheran orthodoxy's consistent attempt to exclude speculative interpretation, it is, nonetheless, not unprecedented. The most generous interpretation that can be proposed is that, read from the standpoint of strict Lutheran confessionalism, Hegel is involved in a regression to a proto-Catholic hermeneutic regime that placed considerable value on the nonliteral, ultimately mystical sense of the text. Hegel's actual exegetical practice, however, shows more than that he favors a more flexible, more nearly Alexandrian mode of exegesis: it reveals specific hermeneutic features and results nowhere sanctioned by the less hermeneutically restrictive Catholic tradition. Within the Catholic tradition, while anagogical was distinct from tropological exegesis, nevertheless, these respective modes of exegesis issued in complementary, not conflicting, results.[93] Hegel's pneumatic reading of the role of the serpent is, however, theologically brazen in a way without precedent within the most mystically inclined of the Christian traditions. Irenaeus's determination of the more significant features of second-century Gnostic revisionist exegesis as a rereading of the Genesis creation and fall stories in general, the role of the serpent in particular, as a singular mark of heterodoxy, provides an interpretive clue as to the typological placement of Hegel's extraordinary exegesis.

The elements of swerve here are, I take it, far from incidental. They are, in fact, of such importance that throughout this work we shall have occasion to return to many of them, offering further clarification and development. For the moment, however, the summary can serve as a set of lapidary formulations that capture important differences between the Hegelian and mainline Christian view or views.

I should like to make just one exception with respect to provisional adequacy and focus more carefully upon the second of these swerves, i.e., Hegel's notion of creation as divine manifestation. The purpose here is not to insist upon the difference between Hegel and the more mainline Christian view—this has been determined already—but rather to provide a more definite taxonomic identification of Hegel's view.

Above (sect. 3.1) we saw that despite express allegiance to the Christian standard of creation from nothing, Hegel, in fact, commits himself to the creation from God model. This, indeed, implies that the Hegelian model of creation is, in the final instance, emanationist. Yet, it should be reminded that this claim remains purely indeterminate at best, and erroneous at worst, unless emanationism is further differentiated and Hegel matched with the right species. Historico-conceptual simplification of the riot of particulars is hardly easy, yet a strong case can be made that the Western religio-philosophical tradition exhibits three distinct varieties: (1) the Spinozist, (2) the Neoplatonic, and (3) the Gnostic-Boehmian.[94] Our treatment thus far has shown significant overlaps between Hegel's view and that of Boehme and Gnosticism. The case for this complex taxonomic identification is further strengthened if it can be shown that the taxonomic credentials for the two other, better-known emanationist's varieties can be shown to be wanting. This, I think, can be demonstrated, though, as we shall see shortly, it is considerably easier to impugn the taxonomic credentials of Spinozism than Neoplatonism. We will start with a brief analysis of the not overwhelming credentials of the Spinozist option and, from there, proceed to the examination of the Neoplatonic option that in Hegel's day, and once again in contemporary German scholarship, enjoys a considerable measure of currency.[95] Having shown that Neoplatonism also ultimately fails to be satisfactory as a taxon, we will proceed to sketch the positive taxonomic advantages of Valentinian Gnostic and Boehmian renditions of creation from God.

Spinozist and Hegelian Creatio Ex Deo

Spinozism is one of the best known versions of emanation within the Western philosophico-theological tradition. Though the exact view of the relationship between the infinite and finite presented in *Ethics* Bk. 1 does not fully exhaust the possibilities of the Spinozist creation from God view in its broadest reach,[96] for practical purposes the view advanced there and Spinozism as a more inclusive and more structural category here may be regarded as the same. While it is anything but a majority view that Hegel's creation position is adequately described by the Spinozist label, the tradition of commentary and criticism certainly supplies examples of this proposal. Perhaps, still the most significant example from the point of view of normative Christianity is Franz Anton Staudenmaier's *Hegelsbuch,* i.e., *Darstellung und Kritik des Hegelschen Systems. Aus dem Standpunkte der christlichen Philosophie* (1844).[97] In condemning Hegel for pantheism (pp. 149 ff), Staudenmaier associates, if not identifies, Spinoza's and Hegel's position. As an orthodox defender of the creation from nothing position, Staudenmaier is intensely conscious of the subversion of the ontological difference between infinite and finite consequent upon denial of what he takes to be the normative creation view. Yet, in his attack upon the creation from God position, which he deems to be an illegitimate surrogate, Staudenmaier is just as much (if not more) concerned with the destruction of the finite that this position involves as with the reduction of the infinite to the finite. He argues that the contravention of ontological difference leads to the volatization of the world in the Godhead (p. 48), and this issues in an acosmism (p. 49) said elsewhere to be typical of Spinozism.

The textual evidence makes it extremely difficult to agree with Staudenmaier's estimate. Passages from *LPR 3* and *SL,* cited above,[98] clearly show a Hegel distinguishing himself from Spinoza not only with respect to the nature of the infinite as such, but also with respect to the relation between the infinite and finite. An especially relevant objection made to Spinozist creation from God is that the finite (Mode, in Spinoza) is swallowed up by the infinite (Substance). Other passages from these texts confirm what we have learned already. In the section on Being in *SL,* for example, Spinozist Substance is accused of not being genuinely self-transcending. In Hegel's view, Substance does not reach out beyond itself into finitude. As Hegel puts it: sameness dominates, difference is ignored (E 113). Interestingly, on this point Hegel contrasts Spinoza rather unfavorably with a Christian philosopher-theologian, Boehme, who, apparently, has not forgotten the principle of difference necessary to an ontotheology of subject (ibid. p. 114). Staudenmaier's collapsing of Hegelian creation from God into Spinozist emanation is especially surprising given Hegel's rather loud and triumphant demarcation in *SL* from any and all species of Spinozist monism. And acts of dissociation still dot the more urbane *Enc.* But it is undoubtedly in *LHP 3* that Hegel most definitively and comprehensively draws the lines of demarcation.[99] The rich detail of Hegel's analysis need not be repeated here. It suffices to outline the three criticisms that are at the core of Hegel's act of differentiation. (1) The Spinozist view of the infinite, i.e., Substance, is such that the infinite is understood as a static identity which eschews difference (E 261, 286–289). Thus, infrastructurally, Substance discourages, if not rules out, relationship between the infinite and other than infinite. (2) The separation of the infinite and finite, the emphasis upon the absolute character of the former, and the nonabsolute character of the latter debilitates the finite and robs it of its independent character (E 270, 288). (3) The absorptive character of the infinite, which Hegel believes to be the most salient feature of Spinozist Substance, in turn, implies that, far from Spinoza being guilty of having too little God (the atheist charge), Spinoza is, on the contrary, guilty of having too much God (E 282). Spinoza's position, in Hegel's view, is best described as *pantheistic* and *acosmist.*

Staudenmaier's reading of Hegel's creation-position goes directly contrary to Hegel's own understanding of his relation to Spinozist creation from God. Staudenmaier accuses Hegel of pantheism and acosmism, whereas Hegel, in accusing Spinoza of these flaws, presumes himself totally innocent of the charges. Of course, this need not in itself mean that Staudenmaier is wrong. Hegel, after all, could be self-deceived with respect to his distance from Spinoza's position. Certainly, Hegel tended to magnify the static character of Spinozist Substance, thereby accentuating the contrast between it and the putative thoroughgoing dynamism of Spirit. Modern Spinoza scholars have rightly complained that this all too common reading ignores the hints of dynamism and openness contained in Spinoza's construct of *Natura Naturans.*[100] Nonetheless, most Hegel commentators and critics have been persuaded that Spinozist and Hegelian creation from God do not overlap, and Pierre Machéry and Raymond Keith Williamson have been especially successful in teasing out the structural differences.[101] Not consenting to the Hegelian reading on every detail, both think, nevertheless, that in fundamentals Hegel's depiction of the depth grammar of both positions can be validated. Thus, the critical consensus would appear to be that Hegel's swerve from the normative Christian position does not in itself put him into the Spinozist camp. Staudenmaier's strategy here reveals itself as not being particularly subtle. Rightly sensing that, despite disclaimer, Hegel's creation position does not support a creation from nothing view, he then presumes a monolithic creation from God view that is sufficiently elastic to include not only Spinoza but the Eleatics and Neoplatonism. Furthermore, Parmenides and Bruno are accused of the same debits as Spinoza (p. 141). And even Boehme does not escape inclusion in the charge of pantheism (pp. 111–114). The presumption of essential identity between all these views cannot be sustained. The differences are simply too glaring. Thus, it is a desideratum to shelve the view of a univocal creation from God view in the Western tradition, while at the same time trying to bring order into choas by suggesting basic types and identifying each type's distinguishing taxonomic marks. Only if this is done can we achieve some determinacy of definition and, perhaps, be put in a situation where we can analyse the *quality* and even degree of swerve of Hegel's position from that which came to be the Christian standard. We turn now to the second candidate for taxonomic identification of Hegelian *creatio ex Deo.*

Hegelian and Neoplatonic Creatio Ex Deo

Though not many scholars would be prepared to join with Walter Bröcker in asserting that Neoplatonism in the shape of Plotinus and Proclus is determinative for Hegel,[102] quite a few would acknowledge a significant presence of Neoplatonic ideas in Hegel's major texts, especially as these relate to creation from God.[103] A solid measure of textual support definitely could be advanced. Much of the theological language of the *Zusatzen* in the Introduction to the *Philosophy of Nature* is redolent of Neoplatonism. In the *Zusatz* to *Enc* #246, for instance, the 'I' (*Ich*) othered in nature is said "to pervade all things" (*durch Alles Hindurch-gehende*), and Plato is explicitly evoked as supporting the idea.[104] Schelling's view of the Absolute in its estranged state as "petrified intelligence" (*versteinerte Intelligenz*),[105] which is also enlisted, similarly tends to place Hegel's remarks in a Neoplatonic field. Again, Hegel's designation of the realm of otherness (*Anderssein*) and externality (*Äusserlichkeit*) as nonbeing or 'non-ens' (*Enc* #247–248) conspicuously evokes the nothing (*meon*) of the *Sophist* (248–252) and the *Enneads* (1.8). Perhaps of even greater significance in the establishment of Neoplatonic pedigree is Hegel's consistent evocation of the Platonic-Neoplatonic theme of the nonenviousness of the divine infinite, examples of which have been cited above (chap. 1, sect. 1.3). The candid assertion of this theme, together with Hegel's flirtation with identifying the logical Idea with the Idea of the Good (*SL* 818–823, *GL5:*320–327) and his insistence that the divine is without need,[106] constitute a complex of ideas that seems to indicate the presence of the core *Bonum diffusivum sui* idea,[107] an idea central to the emanationist scheme of both non-Christian and Christian Neoplatonism.

On the basis of the Hegelian view of creation already presented in this chapter, I would like to propose that there are a number of marked differences between the Hegelian and Neoplatonic schemes and that these differences are fundamental, referring, as they do, to elements that belong to the depth grammar of both positions. The five major points of demarcation, which reveal different grammatical elements and ultimately different narrative constellations, concern differences in: (1) fundamental characterization of the milieu of the immanent divine that is presupposed in the activity of engendering the nondivine; (2) the presence and level of negativity in theophany, specifically, whether the reality engendered simply contrasts with or is in flagrant contradiction to its source; (3) the kind of narrative momentum that contextualizes the creation from God views, specifically, whether the movement from divine to appearance is gradualistic or dramatic; (4) the kind of narrative rhythm that contextualizes the creation from God view, specifically, whether this rhythm is dyadic (two-beat) or triadic (three-beat); (5) the interpretation of finitude as evil, specifically, whether finitude as appearance is defined privatively, that is, as being simply the exhaustion of the divine goodness, or positively as an inherently aggressive force. Forming a criteriological set, each of these elements are clearly very closely related to each other. It is not difficult to see that the first narrative criterion relates very closely to criteria (3) and (4), since differences with respect to understanding the immanent divine will tend to affect what we have labelled narrative momentum and rhythm. Similarly, it is not difficult to see that criteria (2) and (5) bear a particularly close relation, since positing either a privative or positive view of the finite as evil will depend upon a decision regarding the presence and level of negativity in theophany. We will treat briefly in turn each of these five potential points of discrimination between Hegelian and Neoplatonic *creatio ex Deo.*

(1) First, despite Hegel's avowal of the sufficiency of the divine—a commitment that supports the core Neoplatonic idea of *Bonum diffusivum sui*—Chapelle, as noted above (chap. 2), offers a timely remainder that, looked at more closely, Hegelian texts support quite another view of the divine infinite. He suggests that, if we take Hegelian logic as our clue, the immanent sphere of the divine is better characterized by *lack* than fullness.[108] The diagnosis of ontological lack as the motor of divine dynamic in turn challenges the credibility of casual identification of Hegelian creation from God by means of a theme or trope first registered in Christian Neoplatonism by Pseudo-Dionysius and thereafter a constant. For, in the context of Christian Neoplatonism, the *Bonum diffusivum sui* idea derives its meaning from the sense of the superabundance and lack of need in the divine defined

as Good. Put in terms of the construal that Hegel seems to be recalling only to subvert, Hegel seems to have placed *eros* at the heart of the divine. For *eros,* as had been definitely set forth in the *Symposium,* belonged to the nondivine sphere characterized as much by lack (*penia*) as fullness (*porus*).[109]

(2) Second, if Neoplatonic creation from God is theophany or divine manifestation, this manifestation is essentially characterized by likeness and contrast rather than by flagrant unlikeness and contradiction.[110] The Hegelian view, which equally stresses theophany, gives every evidence of the latter and thus, as we shall see shortly, finds a more adequate *comparandum* in the schemes of Jacob Boehme and Gnosticism, both of which are explicitly evoked by Hegel. This important difference so far has been more or less ignored by Hegelian commentators and critics. Guy Planty-Bonjour constitutes a notable exception. In his important essay, "La bonté de Dieu," Planty-Bonjour stresses the distinction in the order of negativity within the two theophanic schemes, particularly as this distinction gets registered in Hegel's use of the term *Urteil.*[111] Very much on the right track, Guy Planty-Bonjour, unfortunately, does not see the need to argue for the distinction. Assertion does not suffice, for at least on the formal-ontological level, it is not easy to argue for a distinction between Hegelian *Urteil* and Neoplatonic *diachresis* (division or differentiation). I think a distinction can be made, however. Hegel's notion of *Urteil* is a concentrate of meanings. In addition to its obvious logical aspect, and the formal-ontological aspect just mentioned, *Urteil,* in reference to the order of creation, bears something of the sense of finitude being under divine judgment and wrath, and thus, in some sense, evil. 'Wrath', with which differentiation is associated in *PS* and *LPR,* connotes both a separateness of the divine milieu from the nondivine manifestation and real conflict between them. Differentiation in the Neoplatonic scheme, by contrast, does not imply this measure of separateness. Neither is the nondivine manifestation regarded as antithetical in a fundamental, even if provisional, way to the divine source. The level of negation in manifestation in Hegelian texts, therefore, surpasses that found in the classic texts of Neoplatonism that some scholars have regarded as most nearly providing the precedent for Hegel's view of the relation between divine source and manifestation. Indeed, it surpasses it to such an extent that here one ought to speak of a qualitative difference rather than a mere quantitative one. This difference with respect to the level of negation gets specified fur-

ther in the respective applications of the term "evil" to designate the otherness of the manifestation.[112]

(3) Our third criterion of distinction also exposes a major difference between the would-be taxonomic identifier and Hegel's own view. Manifestation within the Neoplatonic creation from God scheme is *gradualistic*.[113] A long passage in *SL* shows that Hegel clearly understands this to be a grammatical feature of the Neoplatonic scheme. Speaking of the 'oriental' representation of emanation, that is, the Neoplatonic view, Hegel declares:

> . . . the absolute is the light which illuminates itself. Only it not only illuminates itself but it also emanates (*sondern strömt auch aus*). Its emanations are distancings from its undimmed light (*von seiner ungetrübten Klarheit*); the successive productions are less perfect than the preceding ones from which they arise. The process of emanation is taken only as a happening (*Geschehen*), the becoming only of progressive loss (*Verlust*). Thus being increasingly obscures (*So verdunkelt sich das Sein*) itself and night, the negation, is the final term of the series, which does not first return into the primal light (*das nicht in das erste Lichte zuerst kehrt*. (538–539, *GL4*:675)

The context of the passage clearly suggests that the oriental view is intended as a foil to Hegel's own position. Two related elements in Hegel's general rejection of the Neoplatonic generation scheme are especially worthy of mention: (1) Hegel distances himself from the Neoplatonic view that the relation between the infinite and finite, or metaphorically light and darkness, is indirect and that there exists some kind of transitional continuum. The transitional continuum or gradualistic view is patently critiqued when Hegel complains that darkness or finitude in the Neoplatonic scheme does not directly metamorphose into light or infinity. And surely it is a defensible extrapolation that, if Hegel is prepared to criticize Neoplatonism with respect to the reversion of dark into light, he can be understood to criticize the gradualistic movement from light to dark. (2) In commenting upon the serializing feature of 'happening' (*Geschehen*), Hegel can be read as pointing to a punctiliar view of narrative that supports Neoplatonism's vision of a transitional continuum from the infinite to the finite. In separating himself, as he does in this passage, from the Neoplatonic view, Hegel is clearly suggesting an antithetical understanding, an understanding of creation from God more dramatically direct, more having the quality of a tragic fall that is, nonetheless, not quite a tragic *accident.*[114]

(4) The fourth criterion of distinction, which relates closely to the previous, as well as depending vitally for its sense on criterion 1, also shows up a significant difference regarding the narrative scheme that contextualizes creation from God. Taking account of the Neoplatonic scheme in its entirety, in its completing reversion (*epistrophé*), as well as emanating (*proodos*) pattern, it can be seen that, if what has been said in (1)–(3) is accepted, then the basic rhythm of Neoplatonic narrative differs from the Hegelian. The rhythm of Neoplatonic narrative is more simple than the Hegelian. The rhythmic pattern is dyadic or two beat: *descent-ascent.* In contrast, the rhythmic pattern in the Hegelian narrative (the Hegel scheme is broadened here to include reversion) is triadic or three beat: *ascent-descent-ascent.* The first ascent aspect of the Hegelian rhythmic scheme specifies here the relevant element of difference, though obviously, given what has been said in (3), there also exist importance differences in stress. A brief examination of the logical Idea—Hegel's speculatively informed translation of Spirit as Spirit operates on the level of the "Immanent Trinity"—will help illustrate the level of progression that occurs on the plane of immanence prior to any movement into the extra-immanent divine. If the ontotheological interpretation of Hegelian logic supplied in chapter 2 is correct in essentials, then the move from Being to Idea through Essence is not simply a movement of categorial differentiation but a movement of the divine, a kind of metahistory, outside of divine engagement in the finite order as such. The Idea represents the optimum, that fullness possible on the level of divine immanence. For Hegel, as we have seen, this sufficiency is anything but absolute. Yet a *qualified* perfection does precede descent and provides descent with its character of *fall.* Thus, an ascent movement precedes descent which, in turn, gives way to ascent. The difference isolated here, admittedly, appears quite formal, but, as an integral element of a constellation of differences, the difference is not unimportant. Not only does this narrative difference assist in highlighting the dramatic, even agonistic, relation between manifestation and its source, it tends to suggest that no higher-order resolution can dissolve or erase the agon crucially necessary for the independence of manifestation or appearance.

(5) This brings us to our fifth and last difference concerning the various ways in which creation from God schemes apply the label of

evil to the realm of manifestation. For a start, it must be granted that Hegel was neither always careful to distinguish his own position from that of Neoplatonism nor to distinguish between the Neoplatonic and historically related but, nevertheless, distinct religio-philosophical views. This is certainly the case with respect to his typifying of the order of finitude. Hegel shows himself capable of designating the finite as nonbeing and evil, without raising the issue of the relation between these two categories or exploring their possible differences. In *LHP 2* Hegel attributes the former view to Neoplatonism,[115] without giving any notice that he is fully conscious of their relation-distinction, the normative rendition of which is supplied in the *Enneads* (2.6) of Plotinus. Nevertheless, there exist counters to this smudging in Hegel's texts. A passage from *SL* provides at the very minimum the basic outline of a distinction between the Hegelian and Neoplatonic determination of finitude, as well some criteriological assistance in distinguishing between the Neoplatonic view of finitude and other religio-philosophical views that look superficially similar. Discussing contradiction (*Widerspruch*), Hegel makes a distinction between two kinds of negative, a negative that is nonpositive, that is, a *privative* negative, and a *positive* negative.[116] Though Hegel sometimes shows himself capable of associating evil with the negative negative or the privative negative, in the section on Contradiction he quite clearly implies that evil in the proper sense is only associated with the positive negative. This association flagrantly contradicts Plotinus's normative view elaborated, interestingly enough, in the context of a discrimination between Platonic orthodoxy and the invasion of Platonism by Gnostic modes of thought. Plotinus can accept only the connection between a privative negative (*Enn* 1:8) and evil (*Enn* 2.6). In contradistinction, evil, Hegel maintains, is a thoroughly positive negative that consists in being self-poised against the good (*besteht in dem Beruhen auf sich, gegen das Gute*) (E 437, *GL4*:543).

Even if finally there exist profound grammatical differences between Hegel's depiction of the divine infinite and finite and that of Neoplatonism, it has to be admitted that Neoplatonism, especially the narrative Christian variety exemplified by Duns Scotus Eriugena's *De divisione naturae,* provides a more than superficially plausible taxon for the Hegelian view. In this respect Neoplatonism distinguishes itself from the Spinozist view whose taxonomic candidacy, even on the most superficial level, is glaringly weak. Despite its patent taxonomic unsuitability, however, Spinozism is one of the charges most often levelled by Christian orthodoxy against the Hegelian position. Given that the charge is devoid of the most elemental of textual supports, Christian apologists gain little credit for their own positions by this strategy.

The dismissal of the taxonomic candidacy of Spinozism (immediately) and Neoplatonism (ultimately) does not in itself prove the legitimacy of the Boehmian-Gnostic candidacy. Given the measure of correspondence and even actual influence already brought forward in our presentation of Hegel's position, however, and granting my premise that there exists a quite determinate number of creation from God types in the Western ontotheological tradition, the candidacy of the Boehmian-Gnostic type is greatly enhanced. Indeed, unless we are prepared to argue that Hegel's variety of creation from God is *sui generis,* the case, albeit less than direct, for Boehmian-Gnostic taxonomic determination becomes quite persuasive. We now turn to a more positive constructive account of the taxonomic advantages of the Valentinian Gnostic and Boehmian schemes of creation from God. Let it be said at the outset that it will not be possible in the time available to go into any great detail, nor to present these heterodox systems in such a way that their taxonomic advantages show themselves. Apologizing up front, therefore, for the necessarily schematic character of what I am about to present, I suggest that perhaps the most economic way of getting at the taxonomic advantages of these closely related heterodox modes of thought is to consider these systems essentially in the light of the criteriological set that enabled us to expose weaknesses in the apparently strong taxonomic claim of Neoplatonism.[117]

Hegelian and Gnostic-Boehmian Creatio Ex Deo

Now, while it is the position adopted here that the Boehmian and Valentinian Gnostic models of creation from God are two prime examples of what Ricoeur suggests is a higher-order logicization of a mythic narrative of an essentially theogonic kind,[118] thus justifying their use in a complex taxonomic category, some effort will be made, as I proceed, to assess the taxonomic power of both of these elements. Though F. Ch. Baur's *Die christliche Gnosis* does not provide the only reason for pursuing both lines of taxonomic inquiry, it does provide a precedent. It does so because it suggests both that Hegelian ontotheology finds its proximate modern precursor in the mythic ontotheology of Boehme and that both Hegelian and Boehmian ontotheology find their ultimate precedent in the heterodox Gnostic systems of the first centuries of the Christian era.[119] Though Baur's work is inadequate from a number of different points of view—for instance, his lack of sources, as well as his penchant of including under gnosis just about anything outside the mainline religious tradition of the first centuries[120]—his classic text, nevertheless, provides an indispensable entre, even for twentieth-century interpreters of the heterodox traditions, whose sources are considerably superior to anything available in the nineteenth century.

As we have seen, Hegel appeals as enthusiastically to Valentinian Gnosticism's creation from God view as he does to its trinitarian predilection. Yet, if the interpreter is to make more of this than that Hegel is indulging in his penchant for tweaking the nose of Christian orthodoxy, Lutheran orthodoxy in particular, by suggesting the relative superiority of heterodox varieties of thought, then the following interpretive difficulty must be faced head on. At first brush, the Valentinian Gnostic view that can be gleaned by the modern scholar from the texts of Nag Hammadi and the reports of the heresiologists only shows a modest improvement in the ratio of correspondence over Neoplatonism when subjected to the criteriological set elaborated in the context of our discussion of the taxonomic credentials of Neoplatonism. On the level of express intention, at least, Valentinian Gnosticism seems to suggest that the immanent divine is a fundamentally complete, even perfect configuration that is not in principle—though it turns out to be in fact—open to the nondivine. Valentinian Gnosticism excises from the realm of perfection (*pleroma*) any suggestion of need.[121] Thus, Valentinian Gnosticism and Hegel do not respond in the same way to the first criterion. Neither is it clear that they are fully at one regarding the second criterion, and this despite the fact that Gnosticism, like Hegel, posits the independence of the nondivine, an independence that defines it not as a mere contrast with the divine plenitude but as its dramatic contrary.[122] The lack of full correspondence lies in the tendency of Gnostic texts to (1) regard nature or matter not so much as the realm of the negative manifestation of the divine as the realm of nonmanifestation,[123] and (2) to admit that the divine plays a role in the genesis of nature and matter, while at the same time disavowing any suggestion of genuine divine activity—the world is an accident that happens to the divine.[124] Some problems also exist, therefore, with respect to the second criterion, and these problems have to be seen to affect the interpretation of the *prima facie* congruence of Hegel and Gnosticism regarding the fifth criterion. What evil means when applied to the nondivine milieu will differ depending on the determination of the intrinsicality or extrinsicality of the negative relation between the divine and the nondivine. The situation is not remarkably different with respect to the third criterion. Unlike Neoplatonism, there is nothing gradualistic in the Gnostic visioning of the move from the realm of divine fullness to the extradivine realm characterized by lack and sometimes meriting the title of 'nothing'.[125] The quintessential abruptness of the move, it could be said, defines its fall character. Valentinian Gnosticism enjoys a considerable taxonomic advantage here, for, if we were correct in our exegesis in the first two sections of this chapter, then Hegel defines the narrative movement from the divine to the nondivine as dramatic rather than gradualistic. From a Hegelian point of view, however, there would be an important problem with the Valentinian Gnostic affirmation, namely, that the fall would necessarily be characterized as being extrinsic to the divine. If anything, there appears to be even greater divergence with respect to criterion (4). Full agreement seems to be ruled out on the basis of what appears to be the express Valentinian posture that, just as no development of the divine is conceivable in the extradivine sphere, no development of any kind, whether ontological, gnoseological, or otherwise, is thinkable on the level of the pleromatic divine milieu. The divine milieu expresses; it does not develop. Since the immanent divine sphere does not develop, the triadic or three-beat rhythm of Hegelian creation from God is ruled out.

Cardinal Newman said somewhere: "A thousand difficulties do not constitute a fundamental objection." Newman was not advocating interpretive capriciousness; he was simply suggesting that we do not succumb to the tyranny of the *prima facie*. That Baur, and even Hegel himself, saw a much closer relation between the Gnostic and Hegelian rendition of creation from God than that permitted by the above-cited objections ought to count for something. Just what it is to count for, however, is problematic, given both the state of Baur's and Hegel's actual knowledge of Gnosticism, as well as the state of knowledge available in the first part of the nineteenth century. But one thing can be said: whatever the warrants, Hegel and Baur suggest that the *real* drift of the Gnostic myth is more teleological than usually thought and that the episodes of the Gnostic narrative are, in some real sense, determinative of the nature of the divine. When Hegel considers the relation between the divine and matter in Gnosticism, for instance, he does not read the relation as being extrinsic. Matter is the othering of divine spirit, an othering that is constitutive of the divine. Baur generalizes this Hegelian strategy and insists that before the modern period Gnosticism provides *the* example of a religio-philosophical regime that insists against the classical tradition on becoming and development in the divine.[126] All of this might be merely of historical interest had not Hans Jonas, arguably the foremost Gnosticism scholar of the twentieth century, suggested that interpreters look beyond the surface narrative features of Gnostic texts to their depth commitment. And Jonas makes a strong case that the depth commitment of Gnostic texts is to the transcendental genesis of divine self in which all episodes, including the episode of creation from the fallen divine, play a role.[127] One way of understanding this is to suggest that, from a much superior source situation and a more disinterested methodological focus, Jonas confirms the essential intuitions of Baur and Hegel. Indeed, one could say that Jonas is even prepared to suggest, after Baur, that Gnosticism provides the benchmark for Hegel's great insight into the historicity of Being.[128] While it is not possible to provide the kind of analysis of texts that would demonstrate the truth of Jonas's view, at least there is one extremely important text in the Nag Hammadi Library that seems to testify loudly that the depth commitment in Valentinian Gnostic texts is other than its surface implication. The text to which I refer is the *Tripartite Tractate*.[129]

If this Valentinian text makes comparison with Hegelian texts a little easier by identifying the agent of fall into matter as *Logos* rather than the more usual *Sophia,*[130] the real significance of the text lies elsewhere. More explicitly than other Valentinian texts, the *Tripartite Tractate* invests its narrative of tragic fall from the perfect divine into the world of matter and extreme alienation—and the overcoming of that alienation—with a teleological logic. The text suggests that the fall is not an unmitigated disaster but serves, rather, a providential purpose for the divine—a purpose that is essentially enriching.[131] Not only, therefore, is the divine seen to be more or less open to otherness, thus agreeing fundamentally with Hegel's parsing of criterion 1, but the created order is supplied with positive value despite, or even because of, its antagonistic relation to the divine fullness or pleroma. Of this work one can say that, whatever the case with other Valentinian texts, it (1) endorses the view that the fallen order is not so much nonmanifestation of the divine as negative manifestion, and (2) shows no signs of disavowing the genuineness of divine action in the engendering of an other, antithetical, antitypical realm. This important Valentinian text seems, thereby, to remove those barriers that got in the way of the claim that Valentinian narrative satisfied criterion (2) in the same way as Hegelian texts. The removal of these barriers with respect to criterion (2) also implies a removal of the barriers with respect to criterion (5). For the *Tripartite Tractate* is not only prepared to identify in a typically Gnostic way the extradivine order with evil and with a nonprivative nothingness,[132] but is prepared to see the economic role played by evil in constituting a richness of divine expression that cannot but have some consequence for divine self-definition. Again, as is typical of Valentinian texts, the move from the sphere of fullness to the extradivine, characterized explicitly by lack, is construed by the *Tripartite Tractate* as dramatic rather than gradualistic. In this respect, of course, the text is of a piece with Valentinian Gnosticism in general which shows a greater rapprochement with the Hegelian view than does classical Neoplatonism. But this philosophically sophisticated Valentinian text is not exposed to the objection, as more purely mythic Valentinian texts are,[133] that the relation is conceived after the fashion of pure happening or episode and thus—as is the case with Neoplatonism—from a Hegelian point of view, in need of narrative correction. This brings us to criterion (4). If it would be going too far to suggest that this text suggests a narrative that is isorhythmic with that elaborated by Hegel, the general teleological drive makes Logos a positive figure vis-à-vis anterior intrapleromatic expressions. One cannot legitimately talk of a pleromatic ascent preceding the alienating entry of the divine into the nondivine. Yet, at the same time, one can no longer think of the aeon, responsible for the generation of the nondivine, as situated, even before the fall, simply on the cusp of the divine, thereby conveniently disimplicating the divine from its own degradation.

If it is fair to read the *Tripartite Tractate* as providing an exemplary representation of the depth grammar of Valentinian Gnosticism that, Jonas believes, is obscured by its surface implications, then it is evident that one has a powerful taxonomic tool for Hegelian creation from God. The narrative criteriology certainly shows up a range and depth of correspondence with Hegel's articulation lacking in Neoplatonism. Moreover, the thoroughgoing telelological drift of the *Tripartite Tractate* provides strong evidence for the presence in Valentinian Gnosticism of a theogonic *felix culpa:* the fall of the divine turns out to be a fall upward; the nothingness that is introduced when the divine goes beyond the realm of divine fullness has a greater reality as its prospect. Asserting that the *Tripartite Tractate* provides declarative evidence for the kind of nonanthropological *felix culpa* found in Hegelian texts also suggests a fundamental alteration in the surface meaning of divine fullness or pleroma for which one can find a definite analogue in Hegel. For the implied claim that the pleroma that completes the Gnostic narrative gains through the 'tragic' interregnum suggests, not only that the eschatological pleroma rids the extradivine system of lack of reality, but evidences more reality, more genuine fullness, than the archeological pleroma. And this implies that, contrary to the more or less explicit claims of perfection without remainder made on behalf of the archeological pleroma, some relative lack must logically be posited. In contrast to Neoplatonism, therefore, it can be said that, in one of its exemplifications at least, Valentinian Gnosticism posits eros at the very heart of the divine. What this means on the most general level is that this text points to a phenomenon of a revisionist sense of pleroma, coexisting in the same text with the more traditional. The traditional Gnostic sense—the literal sense, if you like—of pleroma speaks of it as a substantive reality given once and for all.[134] The revisionist sense points more nearly to an activity, specifically, to an operation of fulfilling that is better registered as *plerosis.*[135] It will become evident throughout the rest of the text how this trope assists in the interpretation of Hegelian texts. But perhaps it would be helpful to lay out almost in a philological sense the double sense of pleroma that is effectively rendered in Valentinian Gnosticism with the view to throwing light on the double sense of the perfection of the divine in Hegel.

Despite the major differences between Valentinian and New Testament texts, the term pleroma is a New Testament borrowing. In the New Testament the term has two related but different meanings, neither of which, of course, is particularly technical. In Col. 2:9 and Eph. 1:23 pleroma means simply "fullness of the divine," Here, a reality rather than an activity is implied. Matt. 2:3 and Rom. 13:10, however, suggest another meaning that is more nearly that of activity than a given state. In the more metaphorically dense Matthaean passage, pleroma has the sense of "filling a hole." Romans, by contrast is less metaphorical, and there pleroma simply has the sense of "that which fills." In borrowing the New Testament term of pleroma, most scholars would agree that Valentinian Gnosticism technicalized the first sense of pleroma. What I am suggesting is that it also appropriated the second sense, even if in some texts that second sense is recessive. This sense does come to the surface, however, in the longest text in the Nag Hammadi Library. Pleroma takes on the sense of filling a lack, ultimately the lack which the divine itself is as a given rather than a result. In short, it takes on the meaning of plerosis. The relevance of this for Hegel is not hard to find. Hegel, as we saw especially in chapter 2, was prepared to claim that the immanent divine sphere is the realm of configurational perfection. Thus, at one level he endorses, as Valentinian Gnosticism did, something like a substantive notion of pleroma.

But he does so only to critically relativize its would-be claims to absoluteness by suggesting deficits that only can be narratively and eschatologically negated. As *PS* (#53) explicitly states, the initially abstract concept requires a filling that in turn is in need of cognitive mastery. That is, Hegel proposes that what is determinative in the last instance is the second sense of pleroma adapted by Valentinian Gnosticism as an explanation for a theogonic narrative where the teleological drift puts the accent on a gain that ruptures pure circularity.[136] The divine both recuperates to a point that is beyond its initial state of health, as it recoups more than its own particular investment.[137] It is time to turn to the Boehmian side of the complex taxonomic category.

As we saw in the earlier sections of this chapter, in his elaboration of his creation from God view, Hegel makes a number of appeals to Boehme as precursor. Everything in the appeals suggests that Boehme is being taken absolutely seriously, even if it should be accepted that Hegel has to be read as advising correction of Boehme's dense mythological language. But the requirement of discursive correction, i.e., demythologization, does not traject Hegel outside the general zone of the Boehmian view on the engendering of the nondivine by the divine—a view that, in its own era, was similarly chastised by Christian orthodoxy for betraying the Christian standard of creation from nothing.[138] Placed under the lens of our narrative criteriological set, the Boehmian articulation of creation from God shows a measure of correspondence with the Hegelian view that is as broad as that of Valentinian Gnosticism and, arguably, nearer the surface. We can deal in summary fashion with criteria (2), (3), and (5), since in the elaboration of his own views Hegel tends to invoke, and at a minimum evoke, his heterodox Lutheran ancestor. By insisting, contrary to the Neoplatonic rendition of criterion (3), that the movement from the divine to the nondivine is characterized as a dramatic fall, Hegelian texts, as we saw, consistently evoked the authority of Boehme. It is also the case that Hegel accepted the essentially Boehmian point that the nondivine manifested the divine by being its dialectical counter—indicating, thereby, if not actual Boehmian influence regarding criterion (2), then a fundamental structural correspondence. Hegelian determination of the nondivine as evil [criterion (5)] also involves an essential recall of Boehme. This leaves us with criteria (1) and (4), both of which demand a somewhat more detailed treatment.

In chapter 2 we indicated that, in the last analysis, Hegel considers the immanent divine to be infected with what we can call, following Milan Kundera, the unbearable lightness of being. Though the metaphor of weight comes to the surface only once in Hegelian texts (*PS* #60), it is an implication in many of the passages that describe the dialectical transition from divine Logos to nature and finite spirit. What is especially interesting about the *PS* passage is that it suggests that the process of overcoming the lightness of being does not commence with the order of finitude that plays the role of being the contradictory of the divine; it already begins, or has begun, in the formal sphere of being. The general upshot of this is that need and/or eros characterizes the divine even on the level of the "Immanent Trinity," despite Hegel's fairly consistent recall of the classical aseity tradition. Interestingly, Boehme not only erotically characterizes the immanent divine, as Hegel does; there is an overlap even on the level of metaphor. From an ontotheological point of view, the immanent divine is 'thin' (*dun*).[139] To be thin has the technical sense of being ineffable and spiritual. Yet it is unmistakably the case that Boehme goes with the metaphorical drift of thin, for the thin divine seeks or hungers for substance, for fulfillment.[140] It seems fair to say, therefore, that there is an overlap of a remarkable sort regarding criterion (1).

The level of correspondence with regard to criterion (5) is equally high. Before Hegel, and in contradistinction to Neoplatonism, Boehme, the heterodox Lutheran, presumes that differentiation at the level of the immanent divine represents a genuine development, albeit a development that needs to be complemented by the even more real development made possible in and through alienation in the nondivine. This has the consequence that, with respect to narrative rhythm, Boehme has a right to be called Hegel's proximate precursor. For with him, as with Hegel, an ascent movement precedes the movement of descent, its narrative placement exacerbating the descent movement and providing it with its character of fall. The extra stress or beat makes the Boehmian narrative genuinely three beat in the way few narratives are in the ontotheological tradition.

4

EPOCHAL OVERLAP: Incarnation and the Passion Narrative

What the above title intends to suggest is that Hegel in his key texts assigns the incarnation and passion narrative to different trinitarian spheres. Whereas in the *PS* and *LPR 3* incarnation and the passion narrative are assigned to the second trinitarian sphere and twinned with creation, in *Enc* incarnation and the passion narrative are assigned to the third trinitarian sphere and twinned with the constitution and development of the community of spirit. While, undeniably, trinitarian distribution has some effect on the material, i.e., narrative material, distributed, nevertheless, it would be going too far to suggest that, in and of itself, trinitarian distribution exercises theological imperatives of a truly radical kind. The fact that *PS* and *LPR 3* bring out more clearly than *Enc* the underlying structural similarity between creation and incarnation neither implies that *PS* and *LPR 3* disavow a pneumatological horizon for Christology, nor that *Enc* excludes any and all suggestion of structural similarity. *Ex hypothesi,* differences, and important differences, may exist between Hegelian texts on christological as well as other theological issues, but such differences cannot simply be read off from differences in trinitarian distribution.

Not noted for even marginal agreement, the Hegelian renaissance of recent years has once again pushed Christology to the center of investigation in a way not matched since Baur and Strauss.[1] Indeed, the suggestion is not at all uncommon that it is Hegel's view of the incarnation and passion narrative that represents Hegel's most important theological contribution, as well as representing the key to the comprehension of Hegelian ontotheology as a whole.[2] While this judgment itself must be regarded as partisan, its truth partial, it is certainly true that Hegel's reflection on christological matters is important, representing one of the very oldest and most enduring strands of his multifaceted theological exploration.[3] One must be grateful for the christological retrieval and happy about the level of scholarship and interrogation. Diagnosis of Hegel's major christological tendency has been essayed, Hegel's major christological tenets explored, and the relation of Hegel's christological position to the positions normative for the confessional traditions laid bare. In addition, it is in the context of this particular literature that the question of continuity-discontinuity of Hegel's theological enterprise is raised in an especially acute form.[4] Emilio Brito's *La christologie de Hegel* thankfully, releases us from the genetic task, but does so only with the proviso that we, in principle should be mindful of shifts of christological position and emphasis as well as continuities, a hermeneutic reminder also reinforced by Jaeschke and Hodgson both in their editorial practice and their commentary on *LPR*. For the most part, therefore, I will follow a structural tack and offer analyses of texts from Hegel's mature period. Now, while for purposes of symmetry it would be good to examine the christological component of *Enc,* since it is this text that offers the alternative trinitarian distribution to *PS* and *LPR,* for the sake of richness of detail I will confine myself to *PS* and *LPR,* both of which exemplify the same trinitarian distribution of narrative. The fact that examples of both trinitarian distributions are not put under scrutiny need not be of any great moment, provided one keeps in mind the different emphases—and they are hardly more than that—that are consequent to the adoption of a specific trinitarian distribution of narrative.

The exegesis of Hegel's mature christological view, prosecuted in section 1 of this chapter, will set the basis for the taxonomic analysis of Hegel's Christology in the more interpretive second section where, not only is Hegel's view situated within the general coordinates of Luther's theology of the cross, but investigation is made into what makes the Hegelian rendition so odd. It will be argued that if the peculiarities of the Hegelian rendition seem to indicate allegiance at some ultimate level to Valentinian Gnostic patterns of thought, at a proximate level, it is the intra-Lutheran christological emendations effected by Jacob Boehme that sets the precedent for Hegelian transmutation of Luther's theology of the cross.

Section 4.1 Hegel's Mature Christological Position: Trinitarian Contexualization of **Theologia Crucis**

That Hegel's thought does not offer the perfect example of Athena springing from the head of Zeus is eloquently testified to in the

German Idealist's recurring reflection on the nature and function of Christ. Commencing with his Kant-inspired view of Jesus as the supreme moral teacher in the "Positivity" essay (1795),[5] Hegel's early christological reflection points to a movement in which Hegel thinks himself more and more deeply into basic christological symbols. In this movement Hegel gradually achieves a deeper appreciation of the Lutheran tradition's appraisal of Christ. In "The Spirit of Christianity and its Fate" (1799), the ethical interpretation of Christ gives way to the mystical[6] one in which the focus is on the role of Christ in constituting human beings as 'sons of God' and in bringing about the 'kingdom of God'.[7] In continuity with the emphasis of Luther himself, and to a somewhat lesser extent the tradition of Lutheran orthodoxy,[8] Hegel's own emphasis is upon the work of Christ rather than his person, an emphasis that makes Hegel impatient with the ontological modes of christological discourse. In a move that smacks more of the early than of the later Luther, and not at all of Lutheran orthodoxy, Hegel shows particular impatience with the two nature/one person classical and conciliar view of Christ.[9] Hegel is as clear in this text, as he will be in *PS,* that the historical Jesus must be surpassed in the Christ of faith, the Christ that is appropriated in Spirit. If the christological tendency of this early theological essay is pneumatological, it is also eschatological. At the very least, it can be said that the heavy stress on the kingdom that is to be brought about by Christ's life and teaching, and even more importantly, by Christ's death as it opens up the space for appropriation of Christ's meaning, suggests some move away from the realized eschatology view that was not solely the prerogative of Catholicism but found its way into Lutheran orthodoxy. *FK* can be regarded as the penultimate moment in the development of his christological position, if only from the point of view that it is in that particular text that Hegel introduces the 'death of God' theme which retrieves the fundamental agonic construal of Luther while adding a cultural diagnostic twist. As we shall see shortly, when the theme is integrated in mature works like *PS* and *LPR* with a constellation of other christological elements, it also shows revisionary features via-à-vis Luther's own position and Lutheran orthodoxy's standard.

The Phenomenology of Spirit

Hegel's mature view is first realized in *PS.* In that text, there exists a dialectical relationship between the christomorphic, dominantly crucimorphic, symbolization of the differentiation of subjectivity and the plotting of Christianity on a historico-developmental axis within the general parameter of subjectivity. Put another way, the passion-narrative of Christ serves as a lens through which the differentiation of subjectivity is viewed, while Christianity is but a figure or *Gestalt* of the many figures that articulate and are articulated by Spirit, which, at the very least, bears the closest possible relationship to the theological construct 'God' (*Preface* #23, 60–66). What makes possible this relationship is openly disclosed in the section on Absolute Knowledge. An intimate bond exists between Christianity as the revelatory religion (*die offenbare Religion*) and philosophy. As Hegel puts it: religion, revelatory religion in particular, expresses sooner in time than philosophy absolute content or truth as Spirit (*PS* #802, Miller p. 488, *GL2:*614).

Explicit christomorphic metaphors are not plentiful in PS, yet from them PS derives much of its tone and flavor. Not all of the explicit christomorphic metaphors are of a crucimorphic type, but the most riveting certainly are: (1) "Stations" (*Stationen*) in the *Introduction* clearly evokes the stations of the cross (#77, Miller p. 49. *GL2,*71); (2) "Way of Despair" (*der Weg der Verzweiflung*) similarly refers to Christ's passion (#78, Miller p. 49. *GL2,*71); (3) "The Calvary of Absolute Spirit" (*die Schädelstätte des absoluten Geistes*) (#808, Miller p. 493. *GL2,*620), which closes *PS,* is perhaps the most famous, as it is the most gripping. It insinuates in a superlative way the relationship of passion and death, a theme that dominates in the *Preface* (#19, 32 esp.), but which is not there provided with *explicit* christological signature. While the christomorphic ensemble has as its dominant focus the *via crucis,* noncrucimorphic images also surface. 'Throne' (*Throns*), found in the last paragraph of *PS,* is a regal image and evokes more the transcending of suffering than suffering itself. Despite the resolutional, even the eschatological, force of the image, however, throne associates with, and is informed by, the crucimorphic image of "the Calvary of Spirit" and thus does not loosen itself completely from pathetic suggestion. 'Chalice' (*der Kelch*) is another image, again in the closing paragraph of the text, whose central thrust is other than pathetic. Nonetheless, the celebratory and consummatory significance of this essentially eucharistic image cannot but evoke as its background the sacrificial passion and death of Christ. Thus, one can say that the images of transcendence and resolution in a sense recollect the *via crucis*. Similarly, a strong case could be made for saying that the crucimorphic images point forward to, and are proleptic of, resolution, even if they do not explicitly announce it. In general terms, then, though the christomorphic images of PS reflect different surfaces, they all, in some way, condense the agonic process and completion that is nothing short of the central theme of that baroque text.

If christomorphic images color the differentiation of subjectivity, it is also the case that Hegel's presentation of the person of Christ, the christological narrative, and the appropriation of the significance of Christ's person and life, are constrained by their insertion into a multi-dimensional developmental scheme within the general horizon of the differentiation of subjectivity (section 7). Yet, the constraining effect of the subjectivity horizon does not, as Emilio Brito is inclined to argue,[10] imply by this very fact the vitiation of the christological project of the *PS*. Certainly, from a normative Christian point of view there are problems with Hegel's christological presentation, but those problems are not peculiar to the *PS*. Similar if not identical problems emerge in almost all of Hegel's texts. Thus, at best, one is entitled to claim that the subjectivity horizon angles and, at a limit, exacerbates christological oddities systemic to the Hegelian position.

In *PS* Christianity is plotted as the acme of the developmental dynamics of religion. Beginning with natural religion and proceeding through the Religion of Art, religious consciousness and expression finds its term in Christianity. The most successful and most coherent articulation prior to Christianity is found in the various forms of Greek art. Indeed, in many respects Greek art anticipates the revelation of the mystery only fully rendered in Christianity. According to Hegel a good example of such anticipation is presented by Dionysian ritual. Dionysian sacrifice unmistakably points forward to christological consummation:

> Spirit has not yet sacrificed (*nicht geopfert*) itself as self-conscious Spirit to self-consciousness, and the mystery of bread and wine is not yet the mystery of flesh and blood. (#724, Miller p. 438. *GL2*:551)

Here evoking Hölderlin's problematic of Dionysius or Christ,[11] Hegel recalls none of the poet's equivocation. Dionysius is not a possible contender to the religious hegemony of Christ. Dionysius is but a stepping stone to Christ, as Dionysian ritual is Christian celebration in a more or less inadequate form. Hegel will allow for no Nietzschean substitution for Christ. In Christ the absolute content becomes manifest:

> This incarnation of the divine Being, or the fact that it essentially and directly has the shape of self-consciousness, is the simple content of the absolute religion. (#759, Miller p. 459. *GL2*:577)

In the developmental dynamics of religious experience and expression, Christ represents a solution to an impasse, specifically the alienation, grief, and self-dispossession that is the outcome of the turn to self. The 'happy consciousness' of reliance upon self reveals itself as the Unhappy Consciousness that has lost all supports of self. The Unhappy Consciousness of which Hegel speaks in Section 7 (#752) is not the same as the Unhappy Consciousness of which he has spoken earlier in the text (#207 ff.). If the Unhappy Consciousness of the earlier moment in the text is identifiable with Judaism, the Unhappy Consciousness of Section 7 refers to the Unhappy Consciousness of the Hellenistic world as a whole that provides the (negative) condition of the appearance of Christ and consciousness of or faith in Christ.

The epiphany of absolute content in a single individual is not accorded the status of a brute fact but is posited as the dialectical outcome of previous religious configurations that achieve their realization and apotheosis in this definitive manifestation. Pannenberg and Schlitt,[12] as with Kierkegaard before them, feel that here Hegel is dangerously close to an *Erscheinungslogik.* Schlitt is here especially apropos and argues fairly convincingly that the single most determining factor in the affirmation of concrete empirical subjectivity is epistemological.[13] Given the epistemological consistency of the finite subject, which the first part of *PS* plots, the determined order of the appropriation of religious meaning follows within, as without, Christianity the patterned sequence: sense-perception; representation-understanding; thought. Still, the epistemological conditions of appearance are not absolutely determining. They cannot, for instance, legislate that there be but *one* instantiation of absolute content. Hegel seems simply to accept this claim made by Christianity, just as he seems simply to accept Christianity's claim with respect to the unsurpassability of Christ. This is not to suggest that everything in Christianity is unsurpassable. Jesus Christ may be granted an unsurpassable status, but, just as with the early theological writings (*ETW* pp. 266–268, 271–273), *PS* underscores the limitation of the empirical form of manifestation. Moreover, less negatively, and more clearly, than the early oeuvre, *PS* charts the process of religious consciousness weaning itself from the authority of the discrete subjectivity bound by conditions of space, time, and culture—a process which Hegel regards as nothing less than the actualization of the full significance of the incarnation. The *Dasein* of Christ (#757, 758)—though not Christ as an ontological power in history—is a stage to be overcome, and a stage which, in point of fact, Christianity has overcome.

In contradistinction to his earlier christological reflections, Hegel does not consider the movement of the disappearance of the discrete subjectivity of Jesus as a movement beyond faith (*ETW* pp. 266–267). The movement is a movement within faith and of faith. But even revised in this direction, Hegel's position to a large extent justifies the association made by Michel Henry of Hegel's earlier christological proposal with that of Eckhart. For, as Henry points out,[14] in the Eckhartian scheme that seems to be recapitulated in Hegel, for Jesus not to point beyond himself to the christic potency of all is for the would-be saviour to become the main source of spiritual opacity. Since Jesus is the quintessential ground of the unlimited in human being, it is essential to the meaning of Jesus that he surpass his determinate mode of existence. Though Hegel in *PS* does not recall the scriptural, specifically Johannine, warrant that he recalled after Eckhart in his 1799 essay, it is evident, given his relaxation regarding the assertion of this position, that he regards his position not simply as philosophically but theologically supportable.

Having already argued against one Brito misinterpretation of *PS,* by way of introducing our exposé of those vitally important concluding paragraphs of the Hegelian treatment of Christianity, i.e., #772–789, it is appropriate to argue against another. Brito boldly asserts that Hegel's christological presentation excludes dogmatic content.[15] Brito does not openly declare the criteriological basis for such a view, yet it is clear that he holds to classical-ontological Christology as norm and paradigm. In itself, there is nothing fundamentally wrong with availing of classical Christology as a criteriological and hermeneutic tool. It is one way among others of assessing christological presentation, one way among others of exposing the unique features of the Hegelian view. In section 4.2 of this chapter we ourselves will avail of the Patristic-medieval standard as a hermeneutic tool. Yet the evaluative element in Brito's evocation of a standard is so high that it effectively closes off the possibility of a proper contexting of Hegelian Christology essential to the task of interpretation. For classical-ontological Christology is but one option, albeit an extremely important one, within the christological tradition as a whole. Other, less codified, but not totally undogmatic, christological presentations are hardly rare. If I cite Irenaeus and Luther, it is not because these are the only representatives of a non-ontological theological style, but because they provide two of the clearest instances.The case of Luther is particularly illuminating, since Hegel presumes himself not to be deviating from the spirit of Lutheran confession.

It can be claimed plausibly that, while Lutheran orthodoxy attempted some mediation of Luther's own view and the classical tradition, Luther himself, except in his very latest works, departed from traditional modes of christological discourse.[16] Such a departure, however, did not in itself so much signify the disavowal of all dogmatic formulation, as such, as the correction of the theoretical and ontological bias of the classical tradition. Luther was anxious to redirect Christology back in a practical-existential and soteriological direction. Certainly, compared with the classical christological systems and codifications, Luther's Christology comes off as dogmatically thin but with such regulative notions as *deus absconditus, sub contrario specie,* and *communicatio idiomatum,* Luther's Christology hardly can be claimed to be dogmatically empty. The case appears to be similar with Hegel. Hegel's soteriological revision of classical Christology is apparent in his refusal in his early theological writings to countenance the classical ontological view of hypostatic union. *PS* evidences an equally thorough trimming of dogmatic vegetation of an ontological sort. Nevertheless, no more than in the case of Luther does this mean the surrender of all dogmatic content. Like Luther, Hegel's Christology is more that of a *picture* than a set of propositions. The picture, however, is by no means ontologically innocent. It makes implicit ontological claims—claims which, as we shall see later, run counter to the explicit ontological claims of the classical christological tradition. To the extent to which such claims are being made, Hegel should be regarded as involved in a dogmatic or counterdogmatic enterprise.

In *PS* #772–787 are condensed Hegel's narrative dogmatic revision of nothing less than the entire conceptual matrix of classical theology. It is the global revision undertaken by these paragraphs that provides the context for the more local revision of classical Christology. As in the earlier paragraphs in this section on Christianity, the incarnation is an important element, but it is in itself no longer the central preoccupation. Hegel's christological presentation here is distinguished by three features: (1) presentation of the incarnation as itself a moment of a larger encompassing narrative that has a trinitarian form; (2) presentation of the incarnation as intrinsically connected with the passion-narrative; and (3) presentation of the incarnation as intimately associated with the community (*Gemeinde*) as the vehicle of appropriation of the meaning of the incarnational event. Of the three features, the one that is in most need of explication is the second. Since a briefer treatment suffices for the first and third features, it is appropriate to start with them and then move to a more developed analysis of the key second feature.

The narrative, trinitarianly figured in #772–787 of *PS,* is in essential respects the global Christian metanarrative that finds a more extensive expression in *LPR 3* and an equally dense, but more lucid, expression in *Enc* (#564–571). Specifically christological matter is assigned there to the episodically complex second sphere (#784–785), and occupies the third moment of this sphere connecting to the representation of creation (#774–775) by way of the representation of evil (#776–783). The trinitarian contexting involves an essential correction of the almost overwhelmingly incarnational surface of *PS* and suggests that, if from a phenomenological point of view Christology has priority, from a properly ontotheological point of view priority must be granted the 'trinitarian figure', to evoke Hodgson's felicitous locution.[17] Trinitarian figuration, however, is not innocent regarding theological commitment in general, christological commitment in particular. For one thing, the inclusiveness of the trinitarian figuration, which dismantles the distinction between the inside and outside of the divine, dictates that the emptying that Hegel is prepared to speak about on the level of the immanent trinitarian divine (#770) achieves its term in the emptying manifested in the incarnational event and especially in its passional center. This, in turn, suggests that the christological drama does not, as in the classical narrative trinitarian construals of an Augustine or even an Irenaeus, merely exemplify the divine but rather defines it, defines its what and who. This point is important, and it will be returned to throughout this chapter. A few words should be said about the third distinctive feature of the christological presentation of *PS.*

The trinitarian distribution of *PS* is the prototype of *LPR 3* rather than *Enc,* in that creation and incarnation are included within the second element or epoch, with community alone occupying the third element or epoch—the element or epoch of Spirit. The point could not be stated more clearly:

> Spirit is thus posited as the third element, in universal self-consciousness (*im allgemeinen Selbstbewusstsein*), it is in community (*er ist seine Gemeinde*). (#781, Miller p. 473. *GL2*:417)

That community is the sole occupant of a specific narrative frame, while it certainly highlights the pneumatic bias in Hegel's trinitarian rendering, by no means implies that it is in any real sense, i.e., any *narrative* sense, cut off from the christological trajectory of the second element. It is the community, after all, that is the agent of appropriation, thus full actualization, of the reconciliation implicit in the death of Christ, where reconciliation implies the overcoming of the mutual separation of the divine and the human. Though Hegel will at least formally insist upon the mediation of pathos and death, his presentation in *PS* supports the Patristic view of the deification implication of incarnation. In the community, the divine infinite becomes fully rendered as it becomes explicit and self-conscious. *PS* argues, then, not merely for the intervolvement of Christology and Pneumatology but suggests, as in the case with other Hegelian texts, that Pneumatology provides the fundamental horizon of Christology. The grain of this Christology, as a host of commentators and critics have pointed out, is, however, thoroughgoingly agonic. If Hegel in his discussion of pneumatological appropriation cannot avoid deification implication, in line with the suggestions in the Preface that the way can be only the way of the cross, he suggests that the inbreathing of the spirit is intimately related to the cross (#785). This brings us to the vitally important *theologia crucis* valence of Hegel's christological presentation in *PS* and Hegelian radicalization of the 'death of God' theme that makes a brief appearance at the end of *FK*.

While Jean Wahl has provided the general hermeneutic contours for analyzing the death of God theme in *PS*,[18] commentators such as Asendorf, Brito, and Link have broadened and deepened his actual analysis.[19] All agree with Wahl that at the center of the death of God theme is what might be called the phenomenon of double divestment, i.e., the divestment of the concrete existence or *Dasein* of the historical human being, Jesus, and, at the same time, the divestment of the abstract divine essence unexposed to suffering and death. Of the three, it is perhaps Link who most clearly sees the cultural-diagnostic overplus in Hegel's evocation of Lutheran confession. Otherwise stated, it is Link who points to *atheism* as an intrinsic element of the death of God theme. Eberhard Jüngel and Hans Küng have both commented upon the importance and continuing relevance of this Hegelian superaddition over and beyond any specifically theological changes Hegel may, or may not, ring on this Lutheran trope.[20] The latter point will be a focus of section 4.2 of the present chapter. Here the concentration will be upon the interconnection of absence and atheism that some commentators have read not only to represent the subversion of a specific theological view or set of views but the subversion of the very possibility of a theological view.[21]

In pointing to the divestment or emptying of the abstract universality of the divine, Hegel, as Jüngel and others have argued,[22] suggests as absolutely crucial the subversion of traditional theism's view of the uninvolved and invulnerable deity, and insinuates in contradistinction a version of atheism. The context, however, determines that the attack against traditional theism does not represent an attack against Christian substance. Indeed, the version of atheism endorsed by Hegel in #785 has positive theological value and forms an essential element or moment of Christian self-definition. Thus, it can fairly be said that essentially, and not merely diagnostically, Hegel asserts the privilege of the absence of the divine over the givenness and obviousness of the divine presence. Or, more carefully stated, he asserts within the Christian context and for the Christian community the privilege of the absence of the divine over the givenness and obviousness of a *particular* mode of divine presence. The reasons why Hegel refuses to endorse this particular mode of divine presence, that is, theistic presence, are easily extrapolated from the text: theistic presence is rejected on the grounds that (1) it is inherently fetishistic, i.e., it makes divine presence into an object, albeit an object that is beyond (*Jenseits*), and (2) it hides a real absence, the absence of the divine from the world and history. Yet, if Hegel refuses to countenance theism's fetishism of presence, he also refuses to endorse the fetishism of absence, i.e., atheism as an unequivocal substitute. The restricted, hence nonfetishistic, atheism that Hegel feels able to endorse involves, therefore, a modality of absence at once more dramatic, or dramatically equivocal, and more dynamic than that offered by Christianity's critics. It is far from the pure absence diagnosed by the Enlightenment. It is, in fact, absence as occluded presence, or presence operating under the sign of contradiction. Thus, contra any purely atheistic or a/theological proposal, the death of God always points to the implicit presence of the divine. Textually, this is declared by the fact that death is always at the same time the death of death pointing the way forward to reconciliation. Absence, in this context, it can be said, has a dramatically inbetween or *metaxic* character.[23] It is absence only insofar as it is the inbetween state of a divine presence not fully arrived, a particular mode of divine presence having been left behind. But if absence is interstices and presence on the way, atheism can only be interregnum.

If Jüngel has best captured the dramatic modulation of absence and atheism, Küng has, perhaps, best captured its dynamic character.[24] The absence, unveiled in the night of the death of God, gets its latent presence quotient fully explicated in the Christian community illuminated by spirit whose existence and development is coextensive with the third trinitarian epoch. The Christian community represents divine presence, yet, it is important to point out, not in its original theistic and transcendent form, but rather in that undisclosed form that subverts and corrects a presence of deficiency, or a deficiency of presence, if presence is rightly, that is, nonfetishistically understood. As coextensive with the third trinitarian element or epoch, the Christian community is thus the term of a movement that begins with the divine presence hiding a real absence, proceeds through an apparent absence hiding a real presence, and culminates in a fully disclosed and fully wrought presence that is nonobjectifyingly lived and experienced. This dynamic movement within a narrative trinitarian context implies a rereading of emptying or divestment of presence. The real logic of emptying appears to be that of the covert filling of presence, the healing of its lack. The movement of *kenosis* of presence is in consequence an agent of *plerosis.* If this interpretation is correct, then clearly Hegel cannot be claimed to be involved in a thoroughgoing deconstruction of the ontotheological tradition. Rather, he has to be understood, not only as remaining within the ontotheological tradition in a genetic sense, but deeply embedded in the Christian rendition of that tradition. This is not to deny, of course, that Hegel may be engaged in a profoundly significant intratextual revision of this Christianly-rendered tradition.

The intratextual revision seems to involve more than a shift of legitimacy from the divine presence of *Jenseits,* exclusive of the human, to the divine presence of *Disseits,* inclusive of the human. Involved also is an essential rethinking of other traditional assumptions. One such assumption, already gestured to, is the notion of divine *apatheia,* which from the first burgeonings of theology was regarded as an implicate of divine transcendence and infinity. In any event, apart from some early challenges to this essentially Platonic logic in the name of the scriptural view (e.g., Noetus)—challenges, incidentally, pronounced heretical by developing orthodoxy—the passionlessness of the divine functioned in theological discourse more or less as an axiom or ineluctable principle. On the surface in #784–785, Hegel, like Luther, seems merely to challenge docetic thrust in Christology. In the most rhetorically powerful way, he wishes to insist on the reality of the suffering and death of Christ. At a depth level, however, something much more radical appears to be going on. Hegel reasonably can be construed as mounting a direct challenge to the apathetic axiom as such. As Hegel presents his christological views in #784–785, he does not have available to him the late Luther's or Lutheran orthodoxy's recourse of appeal in the last instance to the personal locus of suffering in Christ—a strategy calculated to exempt the divine nature as such from suffering and death.

Lectures on the Philosophy of Religion

By far the most detailed and complete christological presentation in the Hegelian corpus is to be found in *LPR 3*. As previously mentioned, this text and *PS* are linked insofar as they share a common trinitarian distribution of encompassing ontotheological narrative, with creation or differentiation (*Unterscheidung*), incarnation (*Menschwerdung*), and reconciliation (*Versöhnung*) occupying the second trinitarian sphere or epoch and with community the sole occupant of the third. While the various lecture series do not fail to reveal some differences among themselves, as Hodgson has rightly pointed out,[25] as well as some movement beyond the very compact statement of *PS*, the christological presentation of *LPR 3* is, nevertheless, internally coherent and its position generally congruent with that of *PS*. Not all equally complete, and evidencing different shades and emphases, the 1821 Manuscripts and 1824 and 1827 Lectures are united by their common, complex, and integrated agenda. Put in its most general and abstract form, the agenda has three aspects: (1) provision of a rationale for incarnation and reconciliation; (2) account of the significance of the figure of Jesus Christ; and (3) account of death as at once the summation of the incarnation and the pivot of reconciliation. Proceeding to an examination of each of these three aspects in turn, we begin with (1) the general rationale for incarnation and reconciliation.

The foundational theocentric argument that the divine infinite necessarily expresses itself in the finite is basic to the christological presentation of *LPR 3*. The argument, common to 1821 Manuscript and 1824 and 1827 Lectures, is throughout given a more or less explicit trinitarian confession, with the finite, as the otherness of the divine Idea, being identified with, or rather by, the representation of the Son (1824 E 215, G 146; 1827 E 311–312, G 234–235). Hegel in his foundational argument makes even more explicit what is already apparent in the basic structuring of encompassing narrative into spheres. And, as we shall see later, Hegel offers further reinforcement of the basic trinitarian matrix of Christology by insisting upon the trinitarian horizon of the suffering and death of Christ.

If the theocentric argument is central to incarnational rationale, *LPR 3* sometimes offers an additional foundational argument of a more anthropocentric and phenomenological kind. The incarnation, in this view, answers to the need for overcoming the alienation and disunity that is, at once, the note of a deficient religious perspective and a deficient culture. This second, and arguably ancillary, argument is most clearly expressed in the 1824 Lectures and may be regarded as homologous with *PS*'s account of Christianity's dynamic of emergence predicated upon the confession of Jesus of Nazareth as the incarnate Christ. Certainly, the vision expressed there of the coincidence of most intense alienation and its solution, the maximum disunity promoting the maximum unity (1824 E 211, G 143), recalls *PS*'s account of the fateful Unhappy Consciousness that is the condition of the emergence of reconciliation. Neither singly nor together can these foundational arguments provide a completely sufficient rationale for the incarnation. The theocentric argument, for instance, can only indicate the necessity of finitude for divine determination but cannot further specify finitude with respect to aspect. Finitude ambiguously covers creation and incarnation, or, in its trinitarian modulation, Son refers ambiguously to creation and the incarnate one.[26] To provide something like a sufficient rationale, one must proceed in a determinative order of investigation to raise and answer three questions of increasing specificity. It is only with the last question and answer that one completes what might be called 'the circuit of transcendental questioning'.[27] These three questions are: (a) Why does the divine infinite express itself in finite spirit or concrete human being? (b) Why does the divine infinite express itself in *sensible intuited* empirical human being? (c) Why does the divine infinite express itself in a *single* sensible intuited empirical human being?

It is 1821 Manuscript that broaches (a) in a fully explicit way. Hegel's treatment is extremely brief, almost cryptic, and seems to presuppose his account in *LPR 2* of the differentiation dynamic of religion, at once historical and qualitative.[28] While the text simply denies that either a material object or ideal individual can serve as the proper revelatory medium of the divine (E 113–114; G 48–49), and provides no motive for rejection, it can be inferred from what Hegel has written in *LPR 2* that both material object and ideal individual evidence deficiency in manifestation ability. In the first case, the relation between what is manifested, i.e., the spiritual divine, and what is doing the manifesting is so extrinsic that the latter cannot present divine reality without at the same time fatally obscuring it. In the second, though the ideal individual presents the divine in a much more adequate way than the material object, despite such greater transparence there still exists a gap between, as it were, medium and message. The ideal individual, itself an abstraction of qualities, is too lifeless to fully represent, or fully present, the dynamic narrative actuality of the divine. Thus, according to Hegel, it is only in the concrete human being or finite spirit, dynamically and narratively structured, that one finds the appropriate medium of manifestation.

In essence question (b) reprises the epistemological restriction we saw operative in *PS*. Appearance depends upon the cognitive structure of the epistemic subject, and Hegel believes, with Aristotle and Aquinas, that a definite *ordo cognoscendi* is an ineluctable feature: finite subjects move from natural consciousness to spirit, from given sensible fact to produced spiritual actuality. Given this epistemic restriction, appearance can occur in no other mode than that of natural fact or existence sensibly intuited. The milieu of sensible intuition (*Empfindung*) is also the milieu of primitive certitude (1821 MS E 110–111, G 47; 1827 E 313, G 237). But the milieu of *primitive certitude* might also be called the *primitive milieu* of certitude. This form of certitude, as with the modality of natural consciousness or sensible intuition in general, is but an archeological prius and thus destined to be surpassed. Hegel, however, seems to be aware that the specification of sensibly intuitable finite existence is itself not sufficiently determinate. The possibility remains that a *plurality* of instantiations could be posited. In (c) Hegel wishes to cut off this option. Arguing from the premise of the uniqueness of the individual, Hegel concludes that only one such instance is possible (1821 MS E 114, G 49). Whatever the cogency of Hegel's argument here, it is perfectly clear that he is as anxious as orthodox Christian theologians before and after him to distinguish the Christian espousal of incarnation from the non-Christian. With this we come to the second of the three aspects of Hegel's complex and integrated agenda: his account of the significance of the figure of Jesus Christ.

It was a point with (a) to posit the unsurpassability of the unique individual, Christ. The *when* of his appearance, however, admits of no deduction, transcendental or otherwise, and must be read off from history (1824 E 215, G 147). Though Hegel's prescription seems at first clear and simple, on investigation it turns out to be ambiguous and perhaps quite complex. Does reading off from history imply that while a deductive procedure cannot be adopted with respect to Christ, nonetheless, the historico-phenomenological examination of cultures and their constitutive religious frameworks in a general way can establish the privileged credentials of the temporal locus of the appearance of Christ? Hegel's account of religious trajectory in *LPR,* specifically *LPR 2–LPR 3,* as elsewhere,[29] shows some evidence of such a commitment. Or, does reading off from history imply advocacy of the irreducible historicity of the Christ event?[30] It might be hazarded that really Hegel does not see an either/or here and that he wishes to maintain both options in tension with each other as aspects of a more complex, differentiated position. Stated more concretely, it is plausibly the case that Hegel wishes to hold onto, at one and the same time, the historico-phenomenological position that Christ appeared when the time was ripe and the view that this appearance contains unpredictable, even refractory, features, features such as Jewishness, unletteredness, features whose rightness can be only retrospectively understood and validated.

Willing to concede in some respect at least the historicity of Christ, Hegel shows himself more anxious to isolate those elements in Christ which, if they do not traject him outside his culture and its historico-temporal conditioning, do enable him to transcend it. Hegel is clear that a defining feature of the unique individuality of Christ is his teaching, and he concentrates upon its double aspect: its polemical (*polemische*) thrust in subverting the established ethical order (*Sittlichkeit*) (1827 E 319, G 242); its positive thrust in its annunciation of the kingdom of God (*das Reich Gottes*), which, as Hegel points out, is not so much God as the living actuality of God (1824 217, G 148), the presence of God (1827 E 322, G 245). Hegel is not heavy-handed in suggesting the this-worldly locus of Christ's teaching, yet it is clearly implied. The positive-constructive, as well as th negative-polemical, side of Christ's teaching has this world as its horizon. The empowerment preached by Christ has its locus not in the world beyond but in the here-and-now which can, and ought to, undergo transformation.

Nevertheless, for *LPR 3,* in continuity with Hegel's early movement beyond the Kantian-moral view of Christ, teaching is a universal or abstract descriptor and cannot in itself establish the *who* of Christ. Something more concrete is required, and Hegel thinks he has found it in the 'narrative enactment' of Christ (1821 MS E 165, G 50).[31] Though Hegel is prepared to announce the superiority of narrative over teaching, he is not anxious to introduce a wedge between them. Teaching and narrative are best thought of as mutually reinforcing. Moreover, the narrative enactment as simply and lucidly rendered in believing consciousness, while foundational, is not fully regulative. When Hegel speaks of the narrative (*Geschichte*) available to believing consciousness, it is not infrequently accompanied by a relativizing note, since narrative is clearly correlative to 'immediate consciousness.' This need not, indeed ought not, be taken to imply that the depth element is non-narrative. Hegel's early theological writings chart his weaning from meaning as incorrigibly atemporal and static. The form or shape of meaning, even ultimate meaning, for Hegel is dynamic. If the mediation of immediate consciousness corrects its simple-minded episodic or punctiliar appraisal, the eternal that is the issue is itself narratively qualified. Jesus Christ is uniquely disclosive of the 'eternal history of God', a history which is nothing less than the history of love open to suffering. With this we come to the third and crucial point: death as the consummation of incarnation and the pivot of reconciliation.

Death is nothing less than the full explication of the finitude inscribed in incarnate life. As a theme, 'death' rarely fails to provoke Hegel to eloquence:

> However, the pinnacle of finitude (*die höchste Endlichkeit*) is not actual life in its temporal course, but rather death, the anguish of death (*der Schmerz des Todes*); death is the pinnacle of negation (*die höchste Negation*), the most abstract and indeed most natural negation, the limit (*die Schranke*), finitude in its highest extreme. The temporal and complete existence of the divine idea in the present is envisaged only in Christ's death. (1821 MS E 124–125, G 60)

The language of this 1821 Manuscript text is unexceptional and confirms the general theocentric perspective of Hegel's theological approach as well as the 'descent' predilection of his Christology. This theocentricism rules out death functioning as confirmation of the authenticity of Christ's life and teaching. Death is the extreme of finitude, finitude's realization, and finitude is a crucial element or moment of the trinitarian unfolding of the divine. Death, accordingly, can be predicated of the divine. There is, thus, nothing excessive in the continual invocation throughout the Lectures of the Lutheran theme of 'the death of God'. "*Gott selbst ist tot*" renders a complex phenomenon, centering around a double divestment or kenosis (*Entäusserung*). In essential respects recapitulating the position of *PS*, the experiential emphasis in *LPR 3* is, nevertheless, somewhat more mute. The double divestment of death concerns at one and the same time: (1) the divestment of finitude; (2) the divestment of the eternally complete, invulnerable, apathetic divine (1821 MS E 124–125, G 59–60; 1827 E 325–326, G 249–250).[32]

While Hegel insists upon both aspects, *LPR 3* seems to make the second its focus. The first aspect's christological importance seems to lie in establishing the ground-condition for appropriating the mystery of Christ. It is absence rather than presence, disappearance rather than appearance,[33] which opens the gap enabling a new beginning of Christ's definition not available on the level of the *hic et nunc* of his earthly existence. The divestment of finitude, clearly the more experiential of the two aspects of the *Entäusserung* of death, thus points to the inalienable pneumatic horizon of Christology. At the very center of Hegel's death of God provocation, however, lies a kenotic theology or ontotheology that bears at the very least some family resemblance to the positions advanced in the mainline Christian tradition(s). Just how close or how distant these resemblances may be will occupy us in the interpretive section which follows immediately. But, even by way of description, the following can be said: Hegel clearly wishes to block off the escape route from the kenotic radicality he sees in the traditional Christology of two natures (1821 MS E 110, G 46; 1824 E 211, G 143; E 214, G 146) and in dualistic Christology of a Gnostic type (1824 E 219, G 150). The assertion that "God himself is dead" implies nothing less than predicating pathos and death of the divine itself. Drawing attention to the Lutheran matrix of the assertion, as well as, perhaps, making covert appeal to Lutheran warrant, Hegel could not be more explicit in teasing out its radical implications:

> . . . the human, the finite, the fragile (*das Gebrechliche*), the weak (*die Schwäche*), the negative are themselves a moment of the divine (*göttliches Moment selbst sind*), that they are within God himself (*dass es in Gott selbst ist*), that finitude, negativity, otherness are not outside of God (*nicht ausser Gott*) and do not, as otherness (*als Anderssein*), hinder unity with God. Otherness, the negative, is known to be a moment of the divine nature itself. This involves the highest idea of spirit. (1827 E 326, G 249–250)[34]

Yet, if pathos can be posited as an ineluctable element of the divine, this implies a redefinition of divine love or agape (1821 MS E 125, G 60; 1824 E 219–220, G 150–151). As Hegel already suggested in *PS* (#19) agape does not achieve full actuality on the level of immanence. An enclosed, or synclastic, divine love would, at best, instantiate the formal structure of love, i.e., union-in-disunion, in a purely *ideal* way, and, at worst, shorn of proleptic tendency, divine love would fail to manifest itself altogether, since disunion would be absorbed by union.[35] Truly real, that is, truly effective agape is predicated upon the union of genuine contraries and thus can only take place in the milieu of otherness (*Anderssein*), or more accurately *through* the milieu of otherness. While the milieu of otherness can be said to lie outside the immanent divine or the "Immanent Trinity," it does not, as the above text makes pellucidly clear, lie outside the divine as such. Put another way, otherness cannot be said to lie outside the narrative explication of the divine which defines the divine as divine (1821 MS E 132, G 68).

As we have averted to already, the narrative explication of the divine is, of course, trinitarian. Hegel explicitly asserts the trinitarian ambiance of the death of God, and he does so in contexts which appear to involve patent revision of two major traditional theological interpretations of the passion and death of Christ, i.e., the theory of 'satisfaction' and the theory of 'sacrifice'. If the revision of the theory of satisfaction occurs in the 1824 Lectures, the revision of sacrifice occurs in the Lectures of 1827. Against the background of the traditional reading of satisfaction with its strong juridical emphasis, the following Hegelian passage can only seem strange:

> In this death, therefore, God is satisfied. God cannot be satisfied by something else, only by himself. The satisfaction consists in the fact that the first moment, that of immediacy, is negated; only then does God come to be at peace with himself, only then is spirituality posited. God is the true God, spirit, because he is not merely Father, and hence closed up within himself, but because he is Son, because he becomes the other and sublates this other. (E 219, G 150)

Here, Hegel recalls the satisfaction theory of atonement only to subvert it. First, it is noticeable that, while satisfaction can still in some general way be said to be rendered *to* God in the suffering and death of the God-man, nowhere is it implied that satisfaction is rendered to God in his aspect of justice. Moreover, the rendering of satisfaction does not appear to be for the sake of human being but, oddly, for the sake of the divine itself. Second, traditional theories of satisfaction like those of Tertullian and Anselm speak of satisfaction in terms of its soteriological effect of repairing or *at-oning* the broken relationship between the human and the divine. There is not the slightest suggestion of the divine itself being *at-oned* in the offer to humanity which involves the passion and death of Christ. Within the anti-Gnostic horizon of presumption within which theories of satisfaction have been found, the assertion of the divine as being anything other than one with itself is absurd.[36] Hegel clearly seems to be suggesting this absurdity, for oneness is not a given but a process, a process which is thoroughly agonic. In doing so, Hegel can be read as offering an ontological or ontotheological redescription of a theological construct of some importance in the Western Christian tradition.

The subversion of the Christian theologoumenon of sacrifice (1827 E 327, G 251) is more complex, since sacrifice may be viewed either in association with satisfaction or in separation from it.[37] Seen in the former light, the theologoumenon can be viewed as twisted, or at least vulnerable to twisting, after the manner of the construct of satisfaction. Seen in separation from satisfaction, that is, culled of juridical association as instanced for example in Irenaeus's so-called classical theory of atonement,[38] the traditional rendition and the Hegelian do not seem to differ quite so readically. Two elements found in the classical but not in the juridical view, to invoke a version of Gustav Aulen's distinction, are responsible for the greater degree of proximity: the mythic-dramatic character of atonement; the exaggerated emphasis upon divine agency accompanying the deemphasis upon the substitutionary nature of atonement. Yet, again, no ultimate identity between the Hegelian and classical view can be posited. In Irenaeus, the drama of redemption is proposed from the perspective of first-level confessional description. In Hegel, by contrast, the perspective is the second-level one of ontological or ontotheological redescription. Put simply: if Irenaeus is anxious to attest to *what* is, Hegel is equally anxious to tell us *why* it is. The consequences of the perspectival shift are significant. First, the soteriological aspect of sacrifice undergoes sublation. It is denied insofar as Hegel shifts reflection from the order of salvation to the order of being, i.e., divine being; it is preserved to the extent that reality itself now takes on the note and shape of sacrifice. Second, the narrative of freedom is transformed into the narrative of necessity.[39]

The Hegelian revision of the notions of satisfaction and sacrifice as traditionally understood and accepted point to the specificity of the of the Hegelian concept of reconciliation. The passion and death of Christ reconciles the divine with an alienated humanity which displays opacity to the divine in its defiant independence (*Selbständigkeit*). But, and this point can hardly be stressed enough, the reconciliation of the divine and the human, and the reconciliation of the divine with itself, are not antithetical. Indeed, it is possible to go further. It was contended in our discussion of *LPR 3* in chap. 3 that, while Hegel apparently endorses the Adamic or anthropological account of the origin of evil, in fact, the ultimate context of the genesis of evil is the divine process of self-determination. Similarly here: while in an obvious sense reconciliation concerns healing the breach between humanity and the divine, in a nonobvious but infrastructural sense, reconciliation refers to the divine, healing its own breach within itself. What this amounts to is nothing less than Hegelian endorsement of what may be called a *theogonic* account of reconciliation to pair with a *theogonic* account of the emergence of evil. This pairing, in turn, reinforces Ricoeur's citing of German Idealism as authorizing a theogonic account of evil in a transmythic conceptuality. Of course, in *LPR 3,* as in *PS,* reconciliation is implied in the death itself. Death is already the death of death waiting its appropriating by the pneumatic community. At one level Hegel is being, at once, Johannine and Lutheran in seeing the glory of the cross as the great *coincidentia oppositorum,* but the relative contraction of the resurrection into the cross seems to go beyond that of the Johannine Gospel and that found within Luther and Lutheran orthodoxy. There is no denying, however, that in *LPR 3,* as in *PS,* the Johannine Gospel and Luther both function as provocation and warrant.

We now leave exegesis behind and turn to interpretation. The line of investigation is complex. The attempt will be made to critically assess Hegel's agonic Christology in the light of Luther's theology of the cross. The investigation, however, is undertaken with the view that, if differences become apparent, it is not sufficient merely to note them. Rather, the unearthing of differences provokes deeper hermeneutical inquiry in which the question is asked whether there is any underlying logic of transformation of Lutheran *theologia crucis.* The proposal is made that Valentinian Gnosticism and Boehmian Gnosticism provide examples of a logic that could structurally account for the swerving of Luther's theology of the cross evident in Hegel's texts. The case of Boehme is especially important, for it is Boehme who, within the Lutheran field per se, provides the precedent for an interlocking set of transformations that, in the last instance, are narrative in kind.

Section 4.2 **Deus Patibilis:** *Hegel and Luther: Agreement and Swerve*

There exists something of a consensus among modern Hegelian commentators and critics that Hegel's theology in general, Christology in particular, represents a serious attempt to come to terms with, if not render, Luther's vision of the *Deus Patibilis* in an encompassing ontotheological framework. The positive judgment for Hegel-Luther liaison is made by scholars with such varying theological tendencies as Ulrich Asendorf, Emilio Brito, Eberhard Jüngel, Hans Küng, and Christian Link.[40] None of these scholars presumes Hegel to be involved in mere transcription. Of the five, it is the first two, Asendorff and Brito, who appear to be the more convinced that Hegelian ontotheology connotes an intratextual translation within Lutheranism, whereas Jüngel, Küng, and Link emphasize to different degrees the atheistic or Nietzschean element in Hegel's rendition of *theologia crucis,* particularly as this theology finds its symptom and summary in the theme of the death of God. For the latter three, the human experience of the devastating absence of God is a crucial moment of the Hegelian rendering of the christological narrative. It is also a narratively surpassable moment, however, for the loss of belief correlative to divine absence is transcended by the community's attestation of divine spirit as its own regulative principle. In any event, whatever the divergences on this point, and my distribution does tend to flatten out responses which are as nuanced as they are complex, all five are agreed in thinking that Hegelian Christology is best understood as qualifying a theological frame whose basic contours are Lutheran. In this, they could not be more different than Thomas Altizer and Richard Solomon, the former suggesting that Hegel's deipassionist language is subversive of the theological tradition in general, the Lutheran tradition in particular, the latter proposing a Hegel of masquerade, a Hegel who disguises his atheistic-humanist intent by availing of ready-made, but threadbare, theological clothes.[41] For both, but especially Solomon, nothing could be clearer than that the announcement of the death of God renders Nietzsche's atheistic diagnosis and recommendation belated.

To insist here with Brito, Jüngel, and others, on the overall theological frame of Hegel's position, even its overall Lutheran frame does not, anymore than in our previous examination of Hegel's treatment of Trinity and creation, imply the bestowing of orthodoxy.[42] The affirmation that Hegel's Christology is determined in broad outline by the theology of Luther precludes neither the affirmation of non-Lutheran features nor the claim that the Lutheran frame has suffered substantial alteration. Since no principled incompatibility exists between these determinations, interpretation of Hegel's Christology, as it revolves around the notion of the *Deus Patibilis,* can, and perhaps ideally should, enfold (and unfold) all three. Here, therefore, the hermeneutic task is not exhausted by charting a significant degree of overlap between

Hegel and Luther. Some account is rendered of the non-Lutheran features both theological and nontheological. Furthermore, any metamorphosis of the Lutheran rendition of *Deus Patibilis,* is acknowledged and clearly displayed.

The emergence of the deipassionist element in Hegel, as Jüngel points out,[43] does not predate *FK.* Still very much of the work of a neophyte, *FK* renders itself memorable in the christomorphic allusion of 'speculative Good Friday' (E 191) and the ringing cultural-theological announcement of the death of God (ibid. 190). Yet these remain but broad gestures of a more positive-constructive, if more *agonic,* construal in a text that is preponderantly negative and destructive in tone. For, if anything is characteristic of the text, it is its attack on the 'negative theology' of Kant and post-Kantian Romanticism and Idealism. A more positive-constructive proposal is presented in *PS*. The Jena text broadens the christomorphic base and, in so doing, insinuates that Hegel is more dominated by christological vision. More importantly, the text explicitly determines a theological context for the agonic view of the whole that briefly surfaced in *FK.* Hegel contends that Christianity, especially in its christological aspect, reveals, albeit in the deficient mode of *Vorstellung,* the agonic center of reality. The passion and death of Jesus is the axis upon which reality, which is to say divine reality, turns. The locution *death of God* has a more prominent place than in the earlier text, and again it is summary, not only of the experience of the apostolic community or communities, but of an experience enduringly relevant even into modernity, and perhaps there present in acute form. Yet, as previously pointed out, what we might call the experiential aspect of the death of God furnishes but one pole of a complex rendition that also has a more properly theological or ontotheological aspect. At the center of Hegel's theological vision is the divestment of the divine splendor, the descent of the divine infinite into the nadir of the finite and human. From our rehearsal of Hegel's later christological position, it is clear that his overall view does not undergo substantial modification over time. The death of God theme resounds throughout the different lecture series of *LPR 3* and is understood in the complex existential-ontotheological way of *PS* of, at once, referring to a particular experience of God and to an actual change of form by divine-infinite reality.

Hegel's existential-ontotheological rendering of passion and the death of God does not in itself imply a distantiation from the Lutheran understanding. Granted that the cultural-diagnostic element in Hegel's usage of the death of God finds no correlative in Luther,

Luther's theology of the crucified Christ seems to suggest the double faceting of Hegel: the believer is enjoined to enter in a deeply experiential way into the decisive moment of the passion while, from a theological point of view, the cross, death in particular, is the epitome of divine self-abandonment. Hegel's jointure of *agape* and *pathos,* presented perhaps most impressively in #19 of *PS,* is also certainly of Lutheran theology of the cross vintage. The agonic view, rhetorically rendered in the Preface, carries essentially the same theological cargo as the Lutheran conjunction in play from the *Heidelberg Disputations* on, i.e., the calling into question of the apathetic view of the divine which had been axiomatic since the Patristic period.[44] Luther's theology of the cross also provides the precedent for the Hegelian view of the indissoluble bond of death and life, the implicitly redemptive and life-giving power of death, as well as the quite noticeable editing out of the resurrection that is a salient feature of Hegel's theological appraisal in *PS* and *LPR 3* in particular.[45] In Luther's elaboration the cross represents the paradoxical *simul* of life and death, just as the life-potential of death on the cross is a function of the divine power that is present *sub contraria specie.*[46] If the resurrection tends to be marginalized, this represents less a decision with respect to its theological redundancy than a new or renewed concentration of focus upon the dramatic and decisive transformation of the human estate crystallized in the cross. Though Luther shows himself capable of telling or retelling the Christian story of the death *and* resurrection of Jesus Christ on the narrative line Good Friday/Easter Sunday, there are many texts where his highly dramatic lens—one might say Johannine lens—which sees redemption already in *pathos,* tends to make Easter Sunday a mere implicate of Good Friday.

The degree of overlap between Hegel's and Luther's Christology is as systemic as it is significantly large. Yet, even in those areas where the overlap is greatest, subtle but important differences begin to emerge.[47] Leaving in parentheses for the moment the axial structural overlap of experiential and theological poles, the three last-mentioned points of connection, when explored in greater detail, reveal that Hegel swerves in important respects from the Lutheran tradition. This is especially the case with respect to the first and, from our point of view, regulative point of overlap, i.e., the coincidence of death and life.

Hegel certainly recollects the Lutheran simul of life and death. His two most important articulations of the death of God theme in *PS* and *LPR 3,* as well as his talk in the *Aesthetics* of death as negation and death as reconciliation (*GL13*:129, 148), certainly appear to be magnificently faithful to the Lutheran rendition. And though Kierkegaard, forever an agent of suspicion, is not always a reliable witness, here the opinion he elaborates in *Philosophical Fragments* and *Concluding Unscientific Postscript* should give us pause. Kierkegaard argues that Hegel transforms paradox into *mediation.*[48] While obviously Kierkegaard's attack on this transformation is a function of his attack on what he deems to be a global philosophical transformation, in his view disfiguration, of Christianity, nevertheless Hegel's christological core seems to be under specific scrutiny and accusation. In Kierkegaard's view, Hegel's use of *coincidentia oppositorum* seems focused on the issue, the product of tension and contradiction. In other words, while it is the case that in Hegel's ontotheological elaboration pairs such as pain and joy, life and death, and finite and infinite are indissolubly bound together, Hegel often implicitly, sometimes explicitly, establishes the order of narrative anteriority and posteriority. The establishing of narrative order between the finite and the infinite is of special interest to Kierkegaard but in itself is merely symptomatic of a phenomenon that is thoroughly systemic. Concerning the above mentioned pairs, not only is infinity (determinate infinity) narratively grounded upon finitude, but joy is narratively grounded upon pain, as life is upon death. *PS* #32 is admirably explicit about the *narrative relation* of death and life:

> But the life of Spirit is not the life that shrinks from death (*das sich vor dem Tode scheut*) and keeps itself untouched by devastation (*und von der Vermüstung rein bewahrt*), but rather the life that endures it and maintains itself in it (*in ihm sich erhält*). It wins (*er gewinnt*) its truth only when, in utter dismemberment (*in der absoluten Zerrissenheit*), it finds itself (*sich selbst findet*). It is this power, not as something positive, which closes its eyes to the negative, as when we say of something that it is nothing or is false, and then, having done with it, turn away and pass on to something else; on the contrary, Spirit is this power only by looking the negative in the face, and tarrying with it. This tarrying with the negative is the magical power that converts it into being. (Miller p. 19, *GL2*:34)[49]

We shortly will be called upon to offer a more complex judgment with respect to the above passage. For the present, however, it is sufficient to propose it as an example of Hegel's *narrative punctuation* of a key aspect of Luther's Christology.[50] Now, to suggest that Hegel narratively punctuates the Lutheran *simul* of life and death is not without bearing upon Hegel's regulative construal of the life-potential of death. To render death the narrative ground of life is to go beyond the insight that redemption and salvation are compacted in the contraries of Godforsakenness and death. For Luther, further elucidation would destroy the paradox of coincidence and indicate the presence of the ratiocinative intellect. Whether Hegel exemplifies the ratiocinative intellect is certainly a moot point;[51] but it is undeniable that Hegel does not rest with paradox. In Hegel, death becomes the narrative nadir that is the condition of the possibility of the zenith of life. Death is a narratively surpassable stage. Viewed from the vantage point of the final and consummate affirmation of life, death is a stage overcome and appropriated.

If *narrative punctuation* can be seen to subtly alter both the Lutheran *simul* of life and death, and the avowal of life-in-death, a more complex explanation is required to account for differences between the Lutheran and Hegelian marginalization of the resurrection. As we noted already, Luther's marginalization does not connote any rejection of resurrection as a datum of belief for Christian faith. Yet, as has been suggested, Luther's theology of the cross restricts its independent assertion. Resurrection is implicated in, but at the same time thoroughly dominated by, the *pathos* and death of the cross. To this extent it is not improper to speak of Luther's *theologia crucis* as implying a *narrative contraction* of the christological story whose terms are Good Friday and Easter.[52] Hegel avails of this contraction, for in it is highlighted the intimacy of opposites in a way unsurpassed in the confessional theological tradition. Hegelian acceptance is, however, complex, for in his hands the Lutheran rendition of *coincidentia oppositorum* at the same time undergoes immediate narrative punctuation. One might conjecture that such a narrative operation would have the effect of rehabilitating the role and status of resurrection in the christological narrative. What actually happens is different. Life is shifted away from Christ and becomes rather the prerogative of the Christian community enlightened by spirit.[53] Narrative punctuation is so informed by the pneumatic contexting of the christological narrative that resurrection could be said, not only to be marginalized, but to be effectively excised altogether. Instead of resurrection being a major element of a soteriological complex to be appropriated as a whole, pneumatic appropriation becomes itself a substitute for resurrection. Luther is nowhere as radical as this,[54] and nowhere do we find this association between pneumatic translation and narrative punctuation.

This statement must, for the moment, function as something of a dogma, until the next chapter, which has Hegel's notion of *Gemeinde* as its express theme. There the details and bases of Hegel's pneumatic translation will be laid out, facilitating, thereby, a deeper assessment of Hegelian swerve.

A final word with regard to resurrection in Hegelian ontotheological texts. Whereas pneumatic translation and narrative punctuation point to the process whereby resurrection is excised and replaced—one might say elided—they do not provide an account of concrete motive. A primary motive, it might be argued, is Hegel's dissatisfaction with the empirical-rationalist advocacy of the resurrection appearances and the phenomenon of the empty tomb.[55] For him, a post-Lessing and thus a post-Reimarus theologian, it is not possible to think of either as providing unambiguous historical validation. Moreover, Hegel is thoroughly convinced that if, *per impossibile,* unambiguous proof were forthcoming, it would be thoroughly useless.[56] The testimony of spirit crucial to faith admits of no proof. Hegel's use of the 'empty tomb' in no wise signifies the breakdown of the consistent anti-proof stance. Rather, the empty tomb serves as the cipher for the failure of any and all empirical-rationalist verification.[57]

I wish to return briefly to the passage from *PS* (Preface) quoted above. The passage, we argued, announces a systemic difference between Luther's and Hegel's christological presentation, a difference that is confirmed elsewhere in Hegelian texts. The same passage, however, also might be thought to announce a different kind of rapprochement. Celebratory of the overcoming of death by life, *PS* #32 appears redolent of the Lutheran theme of *Christus Victor.* Interestingly, Hegel speaks in this passage of 'winning', just as in the other passages in *Enc* he evokes an *agonic* construal in which the emphasis falls upon victory. With his theological figure of *Christus Victor*—some Lutheran commentators would suggest mythologem[58]—Luther reinstates a bona-fide narrative component that tends to be eclipsed in his christological rendition of *coincidentia oppositorum.* In a sense, then, *PS* #32 can be read *both* as the narrative punctuation of Luther's paradoxical *simul, and* as registering the victory of the positive divine in and by Christ over evil, wrath, and death. Assertion of this second aspect will appear far fetched only if *PS* #32 is disconnected from Hegel's compact rendition of Christianity in Section 7. There, in his outline of the Christian narrative, Hegel associates, if not identifies, wrath and evil,[59] and death is regarded as the midmost between evil and redeemed life, at once the epitome of alienation and finitude and the point of transformation into life. If this reading is correct, then we are dealing with a Lutheran recall in Hegel that is multidimensional and semantically dense. Needless to remark, this density can only complicate the determination of degree of swerve of Hegel from Luther. Notice only of this complication is offered here; what real effect, if any, it has in reducing the gap between Hegelian and Lutheran christological rendition is best discussed after we have broached Boehme as Hegel's proximate and intratextual Lutheran precedent in compacting two distinct elements in Luther's overall christological ambiance, i.e., the themes of *coincidentia oppositorum* and of *Christus Victor*.

It is time now to study in more detail the overlap of a structural kind between Hegel's agonic christological rendition and that of Luther and determine its degree as well as its limit. As a preliminary observation, it should be noted that, while Hegel recapitulates Luther's existential-theological presentation, he does expand the existential pole beyond anything found in the reformer. It is certainly not true to claim, however, that the existential emphasis, in certain texts as least,[60] thoroughly dominates the more properly theological aspect. As Jüngel points out, the *theocentric* aspect of Hegel's agonic Christology is to the fore even in such a text as *PS*,[61] where its presence provides some evidence that by no means has Luther been thoroughly dispatched. But, of course, the affirmation of seriousness of recall does not amount to the affirmation that Luther's *theocentric* core is *faithfully* recalled. Since kenosis is at the core of Luther's theocentric Christology, as it is at the core of the Lutheran avowal of the death of God, investigation into the measure and limit of correspondence will be pursued under the auspices of this theological presentation.

Whereas for Luther the ineluctable and only locus of kenosis is the incarnational sphere,[62] Hegel, by contrast, authorizes a number of different loci. Based upon our examination of Hegel's texts in the previous section we can say that, in addition to availing of the category in the incarnational sphere, Hegel also uses the category in the context of his elaboration of the immanent sphere and the sphere of creation.[63] On this point a scholar such as Brito has been anxious to underscore the differences between Luther and Hegel.[64] Needless to say, the Hegelian extension of the category of kenosis beyond the incarnational sphere does not in itself imply that Hegel departs from the Christian tradition considered in its fullest extension. Though Brito can find no precedent for use of the category in the immanent sphere, he does confess a Patristic precedent for a creational use of the category.

The assertion of congruity between Hegel and the Patristic tradition with respect to their common capacity to extend the category of kenosis beyond the incarnational sphere by no means implies an identity. If our elaboration of Hegel's view of creation was correct, then it is impossible not to differentiate between two quite opposed intentions. If the Patristic usage is guided by the notion of *Bonum diffusivum sui,* the Hegelian view is guided by the mechanism of lack that continually asserts itself.[65] Though the divine infinite, which takes on finite form, can be regarded in some *relative* sense as a fullness, in an absolute sense the immanent divine is a *lack* in need of satiation, an indefinite infinite in need of definition and determination. Hegel may, indeed, on occasions approach the Christian and Scholastic definition of the divine infinite as *nulla re indiget ad existandum* (*Enc* #246–247), yet the gratuitousness which is at the center of the Christian vision is noticeably absent, as has been recognized by Barth and von Balthasar.[66]

Two further points of departure are worth mentioning. The first point is that it cannot be claimed that in the Patristic tradition the category of kenosis is applicable in precisely the same way to creation as it is to incarnation, a position Hegel's texts do not disavow. In the Patristic period the general unity of scripture implied a general unity of view. Thus, Philipians 2.9 and the Genesis creation accounts could not fail to resonate with each other, just as the creation accounts resonated with the Prologue of St. John's Gospel. The application of the category of kenosis to creation was a function of this scriptural resonance and in no wise entailed the theological decision that the category applied in *exactly* the same way to creation as it did to Christ. Indeed, given the authority of the doctrine of creation from nothing from the end of the second century on, application of the category could only have been *analogical.* To say that the divine is emptied in Jesus Christ, or the form of Jesus Christ, is quite different from saying that the divine is emptied in finite reality as such. Jesus, after all, is understood to be divine in a way the order of nature is not. Though the Patristic writers did not explicate the difference, they seemed to recognize that, whereas kenosis in the incarnational order implied a gap in the order of form or appearance, with respect to the sphere of creation kenosis implied an insurmountable ontological difference, since between God and creation lay the abyss of nothingness.

Hegel's peculiar narrative view of the "Immanent Trinity" issues in a second major departure from the Patristic tradition. While Hegel and the Patristic tradition agree in extending the category of kenosis to cover creation, they disagree not merely with regard to theological or ontotheological import but also with respect to the identity of the kenotic agent. Whereas the Patristic tradition identifies the kenotic agent with the Logos or Son, Hegel in his major texts identifies the kenotic agent of agent-patient with the *Concept* or *Idea* which represents Hegel's speculative transformation of Spirit,[67] traditionally understood as the third person of the Trinity. Thus, in Hegel there is a global, dramatic shift from Son to Spirit. However, given what we have learned earlier in regard to Hegel's understanding of "Immanent Trinity," we are not entitled to say that the shift involves a displacement from the second to the third person for, having gone beyond the traditional language and conceptuality, the shift has to be construed as focusing upon the locus in the immanent divine where the maximum incidence of personhood is realized, even if the Idea itself, as a translation of immanent Spirit, does not *fully* realize it. The Idea is the summary of intradivine becoming, but of this alone. Divine becoming extends beyond the infinity of divine immanence. This extension provides the backdrop of the Hegelian view of kenosis. Kenosis, it can be said, is in Hegel a function of the anaclasis of the immanent divine.

Luther's determination of the sphere of incarnation as the only proper, that is, scripturally warranted, locus of the categorial use of kenosis can be read as a function of a double need: (1) to provide absolute univocity in predication; (2) to wean the theological tradition from the tendency to conflate the orders of creation and incarnation. The two needs are, of course, related, since categorial extension suggests, at the very least, a strong likeness between the spheres of creation and incarnation. The theological motives here are sound, even if the theological tradition in general, and the Patristic tradition in particular, can be exonerated of the charges of absolute univocity in predication and, in principle, of confounding the two spheres. The Hegelian extension of categorial use, by contrast, remains much more vulnerable to Luther's critique, since Hegel explicitly rejects the substance of the doctrine of creation from nothing, thereby determining all kenosis to involve a transformation of form. The important question that has not yet been addressed is whether, in the more local application to the incarnational or christological sphere, Hegel is at one with the Lutheran understanding of kenosis.[68] It is to this question that we now turn.

Though Lutheran christological themes are regularly evoked and invoked in Hegelian texts, even here noticeable differences come to the surface. Whatever the differences between Hegel and the Patristic tradition[69]—and the differences, as we have seen, are quite major—they are in agreement insofar as they identify the kenotic agent as divine without reserve. The case is quite otherwise with Luther. It is almost a commonplace of Luther scholarship to insist that for Luther the agent of kenosis is not the divine Logos but rather the incarnate Christ.[70] The variety and complexity of the reasons why Luther made such an identification cannot be enumerated here, though Luther's wish to preserve *in some measure* the apathetic axiom of the mainline theological tradition, even while criticizing it, certainly can be postulated as a factor. True, divinity is fully revealed in Jesus Christ, above all in his suffering and death, yet Luther is hardly radically deipassionist in his insistence that the divine as such does not suffer. This point has been underscored by such reputable Luther scholars as Ian Kingston-Siggins and Marc Lienhard. Even in kenosis the divine form is not set aside. Luther is quite explicit:

> He has not so laid aside the divine form to the point that he can no longer feel it, or see it. If that were so no divine form would remain. But he does not take it up nor use it to lord himself over us, rather he serves us with it.[71]

Here a Luther commentator such as Lienhard shows himself keen to disassociate Luther from kenotic theologians of the nineteenth century such as Frank and Thomasius. Though Lienhard may be giving these creatures of a post-Hegelian *Weltanschauung* something of a forensic reading when he suggests that their version of kenosis implies full suspension of divine power and glory,[72] this view is certainly instanced in Hegel, who must be regarded as the primogenitor in modernity of the espousal of a thoroughly radical interpretation of kenosis.

Clearly, then, in his presentation of kenosis Luther shows himself unprepared to make the move a number of post-Hegelians enjoin, i.e., the move from the crucified Christ to the crucified God.[73] Luther remains traditional in this respect. The theological construct that facilitates this traditionalism is ironically the very construct with which Luther critiqued christological schemes that were docetic because of the fervor with which they protected the divine from all commerce with suffering and vulnerability, i.e., the construct of *communicatio idiomatum*.[74] This construct, which Luther believes is not his invention but a regulative principle in Patristic theology, dictates that while suffering and death can be predicated of the person of Jesus Christ they cannot be predicated of the divine nature as such. As Lienhard, for instance, has pointed out,[75] Luther resolutely insists upon the *personal* locus of the communication of attributes. Though communication between the divine and human natures is resolutely declared to be possible, nevertheless, Luther ultimately insists with the mainline Christian tradition that the human nature of Christ can no more acquire the attributes of omnipotence and omniscience than can the divine nature acquire the attributes of weakness, suffering, and death—a position that is codified in Lutheran orthodoxy where, if the hypostatic union suggests authentic *perichoresis,* it is ultimately not theologically proper to speak without reservation of the divine nature in terms belonging to the human nature of Christ. Thus, if Luther takes issue with the ontological style of classical theology, regulative notions such as the *communicatio idiomatum* join him to the classical tradition. Moreover, his version of the communication of attributes is unintelligible without the presupposition of the classical two nature/one person theory, and in his later works Luther explicitly makes the connection,[76] a point that becomes increasingly obvious in the trajectory of Lutheran orthodoxy.

Since Hegel provides a different identity for the kenotic agent or agent-patient, it makes sense that he nowhere appeals to Luther's classical theological supports. Ironically, Luther himself is perhaps an agent in his own dismissal, for it was the Reformer who called for the shift from a theory-laden ontological Christology to a soteriological Christology unloaded of most of the former's theoretical cargo. Hegel's dismissal of the two nature/one person classical Christology can be seen as redolent of Luther's attempt to restore christological ballast. Yet from a retrospective vantage point Hegel's early dismissal of a christological view, which the later Luther in essentials adopted and Lutheran orthodoxy developed in some detail, might be seen as the prefiguration of a self-conscious theological stand that in Hegel's mature works is systemic. Whatever Luther's vacillations and occasional flirtation with monophysitism, the category kenosis operates ultimately in a christological context that is definitely Dyophysite. This does not seem to be the case with Hegel. Eschewing Luther's regulative christological principles, the overall context of Hegelian kenosis can be labelled Monophysite. Hegel does not say, like Luther, that Christ is human *and* divine, that kenosis consists in the *relative* masking of the divine by the human which is intrinsically other than it. It is, rather, Hegel's view that the human *is* the alienated form of the divine and that suffering and death are nothing but the extreme of such alienation. Kenosis, here, consists not in a relative but an *absolute* masking of the divine, even if Hegel suggests that this masking itself is not fully definitive of the divine.

Given its monophysite background or commitment, Hegelian kenosis is radical in a way it is not in Luther. And radical kenosis implies deipassionism.[77] No more than Luther is Hegel prepared to insinuate suffering and death into the immanent divine. But, for Hegel, the divine is not sequestered in a pure infinity. The divine is *as* present, indeed *more* present, though in disguised form, in the radical finitude of suffering and death. Before Moltmann, before Berdyaev, Hegel makes the momentous move from the suffering of Christ to the suffering of God. Moltmann's broad interpretive judgment on his two precursors, first, that the stress on the agonic brings Luther and Hegel together and, second, that Hegel's trinitarian contexting of suffering and death specifies the difference,[78] seem in essential respects to be valid. It is Hegel's trinitarian contexting that determines, for instance, that his deipassionism cannot be confounded with the patripassianism of the Patristic period.[79] Yet the Hegelian variety of deipassionism is neither that of *The Crucified God* nor *The Trinity and the Kingdom*. For in Hegel, in contradistinction to Moltmann, the trinitarian context of suffering and death is not the milieu of the "Immanent Trinity" or any surrogate thereof, but rather the fully embracing trinitarian movement which unfolds the entire prospectus of divine becoming—infinite and finite, atemporal and temporal.

Boehmian Transformational Precedent

There is sufficient agreement between the Lutheran and Hegelian vision of the Deus Patibilis to enable confirmation of the supposition that Hegel's presentation can be broadly situated in the tradition of Luther's theology of the cross. Yet, as we have also seen, there are weighty disagreements. How are we to adjudicate between agreement and disagreement? which is supereminent? These questions, however, may prove misleading to the extent to which they elicit either an accounting procedure in which debits are assessed against credits or the assigning of different weights to various elements of agreement or disagreement, in order to tip the scale to one or another side. Though the latter procedure is certainly to be preferred, it suffers, like the former, from the disadvantage that it risks the banishment of counterpositive information which thus is never respected in and by the final result. By contrast, the question to which this section offers itself as a partial answer can be stated: granted general agreement, how do we account for disagreement? Here differences are accorded the status of transformations, sometimes of a quite radical sort, of christological themes basic to Luther. What I wish to do now is deepen the analysis by suggesting a precedent within the Lutheran field for the transformative operations upon Luther's theology of the cross that appears to be at play in the Hegelian rendering of the Deus Patibilis. The precedent to which I draw attention is that radical intratextual metamorphosis of Lutheran Christology that occurs in Jacob Boehme.

Were it not for Heinrich Bornkamm's *Luther und Boehme,* it would be nearly impossible to find an audience for the claim that Boehme functions as a mediator of Luther.[80] While quite a few insightful nineteenth-century thinkers were prepared to see a connection between Boehme and German Idealism, von Baader and F. Ch. Baur being not the least distinguished,[81] none was prepared to see that Hegel's relation to Boehme was not necessarily separate from his relation to Luther. For Bornkamm, this separation implies a false either/or.[82] Nevertheless, the obstacles to seeing the connection were many and obvious. Two were especially significant according to *Luther und Boehme.*[83] (1) While Boehme's ontotheology is not adequately defined as a *Naturphilosophie* in the tradition of Giordano Bruno, it does have a core *Naturphilosophie* component that has no precedent in Luther; (2) to the degree to which Boehme's thought is, in general, saturated by the symbols and ideas of Alchemy, it does not appear to belong to the same linguistic and ideational field as Luther. Here Bornkamm is acknowledging but softening objections to Boehmian theosophy made by Lutheran orthodoxy in the seventeenth century (e.g., Calov, Frick).[84] Nonetheless, these obstacles, Bornkamm insists, should not be allowed to disguise important continuities between Boehme and Luther. Yet Bornkamm is less interested in providing an interpretive account antithetical to the nineteenth century than in providing a rationale for differences it would be difficult, if not impossible, to gainsay. In short, the real value of Bornkamm's antithetical reading lies in his account of the transformation (*Umbildung*) of key structural elements of Luther's Christology that he sees taking place in Boehmian ontotheology. In presenting this account of metamorphosis, Bornkamm at once provides the model for the kind of analysis pursued here, as well as offering as yet unsurpassed descriptions of the *terminus a quo* and *terminus ad quem* of the Lutheran themes involved in transformation. My own analysis, however, will go beyond Bornkamm in a number of respects. First, it will slightly enlarge the area of christological focus. Second, it will concentrate upon and thematize, in a way Bornkamm does not, the basic mechanisms of transformation. These amendments of Bornkamm are dictated by our agenda, i.e., the attempt to expose massive correspondence between the Boehmian and Hegelian transformation of Luther's theology of the cross to the point where Hegelian transformation is seen to replicate the transformation executed by Boehme. In line with our presentation of Hegel, we will address three transformations accomplished by Boehme: (1) The *narrative punctuation* of Luther's christological coincidence of opposites; (2) the exacerbation of Lutheran dualism; and (3) the radicalization of the Lutheran conception of kenosis. We begin with the first transformation mechanism.

In his commentary on *Psalms* Luther writes:

> In Christ there coexisted both the highest joy and the deepest sorrow, the most abject weakness and the greatest strength, the highest glory and the greatest shame, the greatest peace and the greatest trouble, the most exalted life and the most miserable death. (*WA* 5, 606, 22)[85]

The above passage is thoroughly representative of Luther. Opposites belonging to quite different poles, a pathos-death pole and a joy-life pole, are conjoined in a christological vision regulated by the Gospel narrative and the Pauline Epistles. Nothing like this is found in Boehme, when the theosophist has in view the Christ that appeared at a certain point in history and radically altered it. Boehme's account of Christ, massively and perhaps decisively, influenced by Alchemy and Schwenckfeld as it is,[86] does indeed avail of the language of coincidence of opposites, but his discussion seems to be regulated by the mythic motif of androgyny rather than by the coincidence of suffering and exaltation, death and life. Boehme's overall christological scheme, and with it the incidence of correspondence between Boehme and Luther, alters dramatically, however, when Boehme pursues his investigation into the heart of eternity. Among the relevant christological polarities uncovered in Boehme's speculative-visionary account, the following are to the fore: poisonous life/healthy life; wrathful source/merciful source; evil source/source of good; darkness/light; pain/beatitude; sinking-down/exaltation; death/life. Mature Boehmian texts such as *Mysterium Magnum* (1623) are replete with examples of such polarities, but even a less mature text such as *De Signatura Rerum* (1622) displays some effort to recapitulate Luther's christological coincidences. In a stunning section of the latter text, which goes under the alchemical title of "The Sulphurean Death," Boehme conjoins a host of opposites, the most potent being that of life and death, as he envisions a cross being formed at the center of eternity. For Boehme, the event of Golgotha, locatable at a certain time and place, is but the emblem of the eternal event of Golgotha which is constitutive of the very nature of the divine. We shall in (3) comment on the radical deipassionist implications of Boehme's elevation of the cross into eternity, but the point to be made now is that the Lutheran christological nexus of the coincidence of opposites does get recapitulated, albeit in a *Naturphilosophie* context. A single citation will serve to illustrate the close correspondence between the Boehmian and Lutheran coincidence of opposites, as well as the crucial rupture between presentations. The text is from *Six Theosophic Points:*

> Life proceeds out of death, and death must therefore be the cause of life . . . were there no poisonous fierce source, fire would not be generated, and there would be no essence, hence there would be no light, and no finding of life.[87]

It is not necessary here to explicate the Boehmian symbol of fire or construct of essence. The basic polarity is the recognizably Lutheran one of death and life. But notice that Boehme does not insist on their paradoxical *simul* as Luther does. Rather he insists upon a definite order of narrative anteriority (death)-posteriority (life). Boehme is engaged in the *narrative punctuation* of a coincidence of opposites vital to Luther.

Yet, the Boehmian corpus here forces us to face a difficulty. While the overwhelming majority of Boehmian texts, freely interweaving and substituting an entire gamut of christological polarities, manifest this phenomenon of narrative punctuation, certain other texts seem to go in a contrary direction. This text from Boehme's magnum opus provides one of the very best examples:

> The wrathfulness and painful source is the root (*Wurzel*) of joy (*Freude*), and (the) joy is the root of the enmity of the dark wrathfulness. So there is a contrarium, whereby the good is made known and manifest that it is good. (*MM* 4,19, G 4,17)

On the surface, at least, this passage seems to renege on Boehme's general narrative punctuation of christological polarities, where the negative is always narratively anterior. That joy (*Freude)* can be asserted as the root (*Wurzel*) of wrath plausibly dismantles the irreversibility of the narrative order. Yet, before this conclusion is reached, a few points should be noted that argue for distantiation between the Boehmian and Lutheran coincidence of opposites. First, the emphasis in the conclusion as well as the opening of the passage falls upon the narrative order of negative to positive. Second, the reversibility of narrative order declared in the first two sentences does not ultimately evoke Luther's christological *simul* so much as suggest the phenomenon of reciprocal determination, thus pointing forward in a quite remarkable way to Hegel. That this phenomenon is at play in Boehme should at once make Hegel's praise of Boehme's vision of contrariety in *LHP 3* more significant, as well as determine for Boehme a much more important place in the manifold of precedents to Hegel's dialectic than a Hegelian scholar such as Croce would grant.[88] Indeed, it could be argued that, unlike any of the other precursors listed by Croce, i.e., Heraclitus, Plato, Cusa, Bruno, and Kant, Boehme combines the double emphasis of Hegelian dialectic: reciprocal determination of opposites plus affirmative reconciling conclusion.

Boehme's precursorship here, however, no more establishes the credibility of the of conjunction than it establishes the credibility of Hegelian dialectic. The question still remains how narrative punctuation, implying narrative irreversibility, is consistent with the affirmation of reciprocal determination. It is, of course, one of the essential tasks of Hegelian logic to demonstrate in formal terms precisely such compatibility. But a much less formal, and much more explicitly ontotheological rationale, is fortuitously at hand in another exegetical resource of German Idealism which is thoroughly at home in Boehme's agonic world. In his post-Identity Philosophy text called *The Ages of the World* (1815),[89] Schelling discusses in almost an identical ontotheological context the conundrum raised by Boehme's *Mysterium Magnum* text and argues for a reconciliation. He suggests that the mutual determination of wrath and joy signatures what he calls their 'existential equality'. But existential equality, he goes on to point out, never overrides the 'necessary sequence of revelation',[90] which concretely means the sequence of negative to positive. On pain of demonism or nihilism, the narrative 'sense of an ending', to evoke Kermode's locution once again, is affirmative rather than negative. If Schelling's exegesis of Boehme is persuasive—and I think it is—then one can conclude that narrative punctuation is never suspended in the Boehmian recapitulation of Luther's christological coincidence of opposites. And it is this narrative punctuation that provides the precedent for an operation we diagnosed as active and effective in Hegel's redescription of Luther's Christology. It is time to say a few words about Boehme's exacerbation of Lutheran dualism, the second operation of emendation discerned to be at work in the move from the christological universe of Luther and Lutheran orthodoxy to that of Boehme.

As we pointed to earlier, there exists in Luther something of a tension between his exposé of the christological *simul* and the strong narrative tendency crystallized in the mythologem of *Christus Victor*. In that mythologem, however, is focused much of what is dualistic in Luther, for at its core is the fundamental opposition between the negatives of divine wrath, evil, and sin, on the one hand, and the positive of Christ's overwhelming, redemptive love, on the other.[91] The dualism embedded in the mythologem is dramatic and narrative rather than static. If we suggested a Hegelian recollection, in Boehme the recollection is even clearer and helps in isolating the formal mechanism of transformation. An important emblem of Boehme's recollection is provided in the famous eschatological declaration of *Mysterium Magnum* that in the victory is the joy (*in die Uberwindung ist die Freude*) (*MM* 40,8).

The theological context and agenda of Boehme differs considerably from that of Luther and effects a profound transformation even in recollection. Whereas Luther's mythologem, in line with the warp and woof of the christological tradition, was a compact kerygmatic rendering with soteriological rather than ontological import, Boehme's speculative-mystical explication of the narrative genesis of the divine dictates the *ontologization* of a non-ontological distinction.[92] In ontologizing, Boehme exacerbates Luther's dualism. Boehme's exacerbation, however, in no way implies, pace Lutheran orthodoxy, the introduction of a Manichaean-like dualism, for it is axiomatic for Boehme that undergirding all duality is a fundamental unity which is involved in narrative explication. And any and all opposition in such a unitive, narrative horizon can be finally only relative. Now, in essence, the difference between Hegel and Luther that remains recalcitrant in Hegel's recapitulation of the *Christus Victor* mythologem can be similarly explained as an exacerbation of dualism by ontologizing a non-ontological distinction. Boehme, then, provides the precedent for an operation that is perhaps more convert in Hegel, an operation, which, among others, would be considered as inducing a pseudomorphosis of Lutheran Christology.

Exacerbation of Lutheran dualism effected by ontologization is attended by a side effect that quite astonishingly makes its appearance in Hegel, most noticeably in *PS*. Though Luther's thoroughly compact language fails to differentiate them, realities named as providing the negative backdrop to the dramatic victory of Christ—realities such as divine wrath, evil, and sin—are by no means identical in principle.[93] For Bornkamm the point would be trivial, were it not for what he sees as a major point of discontinuity between Boehme and Luther pointing to a Boehmian transformation. Boehmian ontotheology effects an emendation whereby these in principle distinct realities become collapsed into each other. Put another way, realities that in Luther are at worst insufficiently linguistically differentiated are reread as ontologically undifferentiated. Thus, evil and the devil not merely associate with divine wrath but essentially name one and the same reality.

The phenomenon of collapsing what in Luther are distinct realities is faithfully recapitulated in Hegel. Against the background of Boehmian transformation, Hegel's startlingly odd identification of divine wrath and evil in PS #775–777 and the tendency to associate both with a personification of evil (*Enc* #246 *zu*) ceases to be a theological surd.[94] Moreover, the phenomenon of collapse accompanying ontologization enables us to see more clearly the specifically theological basis of the association of *Urteil* with evil and Lucifer in the *Enc* and *LPR 3,* for, if *Urteil* has primarily a logical or ontological connotation, the juridical element of judgment associated with divine wrath is not fully erased. Thus, even in Hegel's most mature texts Boehmian transformational operations seem to be in play, transformations that radically alter Lutheran Christology. It simply remains to discuss the third structural element of transformation: the radicalization of Lutheran kenosis.

A major difference between Luther and Boehme, not addressed in Bornkamm's brilliant study of relation, concerns the category of kenosis. This difference is quite complex and should be regarded as a function of more specific disagreements with respect to: (1) extension of the category; (2) integrity of locus; (3) identification of kenotic agent; (4) ontological foundation. We shall deal in summary fashion with each of these four areas of disagreement that symptom Boehmian transformation.

(1) It is worth recalling that for Luther the ineluctable, indeed, the *only,* locus of categorial use of kenosis was christological. Luther did not support the Patristic extension of the category, and one can only conjecture that he would have found any use of the category on the level of divine immanence quite unintelligible. We have already seen how Hegel makes both extensions. With him the category now has application to a process that belongs to the epoch of the "Immanent Trinity" as well as the emergence of nature and finite spirit that conceals their divine origin and prerogatives. The extension to the latter was un-

derlined as being of particular significance, since it effectively pits Hegel with the Patristic tradition against Luther. The case is similar with Boehme. There is the same double extension of categorial use, though the extension is much more overt with respect to the finite sphere.[95]

(2) Anxious as Luther was to avoid the kind of categorial extension of kenosis in evidence in the Patristic writers, in fairness it must be said that the Patristic extension in principle never undermined the integrity of the creation and incarnation loci. If we were correct in our interpretation of the Patristic extension, the *analogical* status of extension was never fully lost. The case is different with Boehme, who once again provides the precedent for Hegel. Kenosis univocally covers the ineffable divine's descent into the birth throes of nature (eternal nature) and the agony and death of Christ (the eternal Christ).[96]

(3) Whereas Luther identified the kenotic agent as the incarnate Christ, Boehme identified the kenotic agent with the as yet unincarnate divine. If Boehme had identified the kenotic agent with the preexistent Christ, he would have merely recalled a position by no means unrepresented in the Patristic tradition. But this Boehme does not do. For him, no more than for Hegel, is the divine kenotic agent equatable with the preexistent Christ. Rather, the divine kenotic agent is identified with that reality representing the narrative consummation of divine process on the level of divine immanence. Sometimes this reality is identified with Spirit as the third moment of a narrative trinity of a modalistic type—and here Boehme could not provide a more exact anticipation of the Hegelian swerve from and transformation of Luther. At other times, Boehme seems to identify narrative completion on the plane of immanence with Sophia, and here, whatever the process of historical filiation, Boehme aligns himself in an extraordinarily intimate way with Gnosticism.[97] Admittedly, Boehme's assertion of Sophia as an additional narrative element on the level of the immanent divine specifies a difference between Boehme and Hegel, but not a crucial one, since both are in fundamental agreement that it is the immanent divine in its most narratively realized aspect, whatever the label, that is the agent or agent-patient of kenosis. Moreover, as Koslowski has pointed out,[98] Hegel flirts in *PS* with the idea of an element other than the "Immanent Trinity" occupying a place on the level of the immanent divine and crucially responsible for creation.

(4) Though Patristic and medieval elaboration of God as the Supreme Good struck Luther as unnecessary, nevertheless, Luther does not materially diverge from these traditions in taking for granted that

the ontological foundation of kenosis is the divine goodness as consummate love, power, and fullness. To the departure from and redescription of Lutheran kenosis Boehme adds another precedent-setting move in suggesting a new ontological foundation. Instead of the fullness maintained by Luther and the mainstream theological tradition, *lack* is suggested as ontological foundation.[99] Certainly, the kenotic agent-patient must be characterized by qualities of a superlative kind, and Boehmian texts do not shy away from such attribution. Yet Boehme is especially insistent that the counterpositives of alienation, finitude, pain, agony, and death add new qualities to those operative on the immanent sphere and translate those operative within the immanent order onto new and higher levels of effectiveness and determination.[100] The Boehmian position represents at once a local mutation of Lutheranism and a mutation of the traditional consensus. With the arguable exception of Valentinian Gnosticism, Boehmian revision with respect to the ontological understanding of kenosis stands out as unique. When German Idealism in general, Hegel in particular, attempt theological or ontotheological construction in modernity, this revision is retrieved.

It is important to recall the purpose of what might appear to be a somewhat esoteric rehearsal. While, undoubtedly, Boehmian transformations of Luther's theology of the cross, and especially the mechanisms of transformation, are interesting in themselves, they are recalled here because they seem to establish the precedent within the non-orthodox Lutheran field for the presence in Hegel's texts of more or less identical transformational mechanisms or operations that explain the degree and angle of swerve of Hegelian ontotheology from its desired retrieval of Luther's theology of the cross. As attention, up until now, has been focused for the most part on the basic mechanisms of transformation, it seems appropriate here to round off our explication of the relation between Boehme and Hegel by highlighting a few material theological implications.

For Boehme, kenosis, considered both generally and in its christological aspect, is primarily, if not exclusively, a reality or operation whose proper locus is eternity. Hegel does not recapitulate this particular Boehmian predilection. Prepared to see eternity as a scene of operation, considered in its christological aspect kenosis does involve time and temporality, for kenosis involves the descent of the eternal into the temporal and the establishment of communion. Nevertheless, formally there appears to be quite an extraordinary amount of agreement. Boehme and Hegel agree in thinking that what from a Lutheran point of view are mutually exclusive categories, i.e., metaphysical and properly theological categories, can be posited together, just as both think narratively of the Lutheran coincidence of opposites and, in general, tend to narratively reconstruct Luther's theology of the cross. This narrative reconstruction is not calculated to leave all aspects of Luther's christological proposal intact. One important christological aspect undergoing revision, as Lutheran orthodoxy accused Boehme,[101] is Luther's *ultimate* Dyophysite presupposition.[102] It is Boehme who establishes the revisionary precedent; it is Hegel who follows.

If few Christian philosopher-theologians have emphasized duality and oppositions as much as Boehme, this by no means implies that Boehme is a dualist in the strictest sense. To predicate becoming and destination of the divine infinite is to imply its narrative identity. Thus, despite massive opposition between evil and good, suffering and joy, death and life, dualism is never radicalized. Boehme may invoke the Manichaean language of two principles, as he suggests a conflict between two natures in eternity, yet the postulate of underlying narrative identity specifies a crucial difference between Boehmian and Manichaean varieties of dualism. Thus, despite, or perhaps because of, Boehmian dualism, Luther's Christology is twisted in a Monophysite direction. When Boehme speaks of the coincidences of pathos and joy, death and life, his view is that terms that name opposites do not refer to different realities but rather to different aspects or manifestations of a single, underlying reality that is narrative in kind.

Boehme's precedent-setting status extends beyond the transformation of Lutheran Dyophysitism to ontotheological rereading of the personhood of Christ, indeed, of personhood in general. Luther does not display a great deal of interest in investigating the consciousness of Christ, not even in the premodern way of Aquinas in Part 3 of the *Summa*. Luther is equally uninterested in presiding over the definition of the person of Christ, and the definition of personhood in general, though he does in the most general way consent to the personal, hypostatic view of Christ countenanced by the mainline theological tradition.[103] Luther is neither prepared to propose the Boethian definition of person as an individual substance of a rational nature, nor its medieval revision by Hugh of St. Victor.[104] No conceptual counterposition is offered, Luther simply remaining skeptical with respect to what, in his view, is a metaphysical and not a properly theological enterprise. Boehme shows no such hesitation. As he views it, the Personhood of Christ, as with personhood in general, is not, as in the Patristic and medieval-Scholastic tradition, an ineluctable given. Personhood is the narrative result of a process of overcoming, requiring alienation, suffering, even death. Negativity is an indispensable narrative condition in the constitution of personhood, though this constitution is fundamentally realized on the level of eternity and does not require time and temporality in the way the Hegelian model does.

A further point of overlap between Hegel and Boehme, where Boehme plays the role of precursor, is worthy of mention. Boehme's narrative ontological translation of kenosis, which supposes a single subject underlying all manifestation, even contrary forms of manifestation, implies a deipassionist revision of Luther. While Luther's theology of the cross may suggest such a position, his notion of *communicatio idiomatum* in the last instance serves as an effective theological bulwark against such a move. The cross is at the center of one's vision of God, yet Luther does not wish to say, as Boehme is prepared to say, that the cross and its pathos are at the heart of eternity. For Boehme, and not for Luther, there is an eternal as well as temporal Golgotha, a position that Lutheran orthodoxy roundly rejected and regarded as a misinterpretation of Luther's view.[105] Boehme, however, does avoid the Patripassian pitfall, as he avoids, like Hegel after him, imputing suffering to the immanent sphere of the divine. But the fact that the immanent divine does not and cannot suffer is a sign of deficiency, a deficiency that must be, and in fact is, overcome in the full narrative elaboration on the divine that for Boehme, as for Hegel, admits of a trinitarian figuration or syncopation. Here is not the place to elucidate the relationship between Boehmian and Hegelian figuration. The topic will receive somewhat detailed treatment in chapter 6.

Valentinian Gnostic Precedent

The rationale for introducing Valentinian Gnosticism into a taxonomic discussion regarding Hegel's nonstandard Christology seems somewhat slight at best, and presumptive at worst, given the profoundly antidocetic character of his construal and his assumption that an authentic understanding of the cross permanently invalidates the axiom of divine *apatheia*. Moreover, despite his relative appreciative estimate of Gnosticism in his elaboration of other Christian theologoumena, Hegel does not seem to sense the possibility of rapprochement concerning christological articulation. Basing his judgement of Gnostic Christology largely on Neander's presentation,[106] Hegel is assured in *LPR* that his position and that of Gnosticism are more nearly like contraries. The obstacle provided by Hegel's own assessment cannot be ignored, anymore than it can be avoided by appealing to the formal correspondence between Hegel's early espousal of a pedagogic Jesus and the teacher-of-gnosis, Jesus of Gnosticism. Even if a case for strong material correspondence could be sustained—and this is by no means certain[107]—it would, in any event, be beside the point, since the *comparans* that is of interest is the Christology of the mature Hegel. Nevertheless, Hegel's own view of the matter does not constitute an ultimate impediment, granted the stipulation of two hermeneutic rules that informed our treatment of creation from God in the preceding chapter: (1) the attempt to show a Valentinian Gnostic precedent is not intended to suggest the redundancy of the of the Boehmian precedent, which continues to be regarded as the proximate precedent within the Lutheran and modern field; and (2) the new text situation permits one to reopen investigation regarding Gnostic tendencies in modern thought, German Idealist thought in particular. In the next few pages the focus will be on the second of our two points, though I will conclude with a few brief words about the first.

The Hegel of *LPR* cannot be blamed for considering the essence of Gnostic Christology as docetic, and, perhaps even more than traditional and orthodox theology, as wedded to an ontological dualism between the infinite and finite that mandates the thesis of the invulnerability of the divine. Neander is completely dependent upon heresiological sources, especially Irenaeus's account of Ptolemy's Valentinian system. According to Neander's reprise, the general thrust of this Christology is almost archetypically docetic. Within this context of assumption, it makes perfect sense for Hegel to accuse Gnosticism of a dehistoricization of the incarnational event as a whole and of a specific neglect of the passional and thanatological components of the infinite that has fully entered into the finite. Ultimately, on the authority of Irenaeus, Hegel feels that he is dealing with a representative example of the christological tendency of Gnosticism. If this were truly the case, investigation would have to stop immediately. But given even relatively superficial acquaintance with heterodox texts from the early centuries, Hegel can be thought to simply recapitulate a pastiche, which effectively disguises correspondences that go much deeper.

First, it should be said that important Valentinian texts from Nag Hammadi, such as the *Gospel of Truth* and the *Tripartite Tractate,* do not, as a matter of fact, elaborate Christologies of an unequivocally docetic type, thus giving the lie to the obviousness of Valentinian Christological understanding. The *Gospel of Truth,*[108] for instance, shows genuine respect for the historicity of Christ (18.10–26) and faithfully recalls the synoptic narrative of Christ's life, suffering, and death, as well as his teaching. The suffering and death of Christ by no means appear to be the colossal embarrassment they obviously are in Ptolemy's system, though it is the case that suffering and death are expressly denied the kind of soteriological significance that theologians of the orthodox party like Irenaeus enjoin. Suffering and death are, however, at once paradigmatic for those who live on the exoteric level and emblematic of the pathos that attends that transmundane fall of the divine. The *Tripartite Tractate,* an important Valentinian text broached in chapter 3, is not significantly different. Despite its obvious philosophical predilection, the text manifests a considerable degree of fidelity to the Gospel narrative, including the suffering of the saviour. As in the case of the *Gospel of Truth,* however, the suffering of the saviour has no salvific force, though once again the suffering is both paradigmatic and emblematic. Denial of soteriological significance to suffering with respect to both the christological sphere and the prior narrative sphere to which the christological sphere refers back as its signification is definitely part of the surface logic of both texts. The question arises, however, whether a distinction between the surface logic and the depth logic might not be made. The question is spurred by two considerations: first, Hegel's own profoundly theological reading or rereading of Ptolemy's articulation of the immanent divine; and second, the radically teleological dimension of the *Tripartite Tractate,* in which the would-be negatives of the extrapleromatic universe admit of a positive interpretation. These two points will now be expanded.

When Hegel avails of Neander's presentation of Ptolemy's system in *LHP,*[109] he makes a point that could be extended well beyond its specific reference to the immanent divine. Subverting the archeological priority of the ineffable divine by the narratively posterior *Monogenes* that reveals and reflects the divine, Hegel suggests that the Gnostic narrative makes more sense read teleologically. While Hegel's intention to correct the dominance of the episodic is by no means as apparent in his discussion in *LPR 3* of the fallen divine of Gnosticism,[110] his validation of *hylè* in conjunction with a general recommendation to view *hylè* as setting the stage for its sublation, suggests that he has by no means renounced his self-consciously revisionary proposal. Needless to say, to be consistent, Hegel, had he explicitly considered the issue, also would have stipulated that anything that attends the real embeddedness of the divine in the nondivine, including suffering, has to be validated if the narrative result is to be validated. But there is also some evidence that this corrected version of Valentinian Gnosticism's surface commitment is part of Valentinian Gnosticism's emerging understanding.

In the teleological Valentinian narrative of the *Tripartite Tractate,* the emblematic interpretation of the suffering of Jesus at once remains faithful to the docetic thrust of Ptolemy's system by denying soteriological capacity to the suffering of the saviour and, at the same time, suggests that the real signified of suffering, the extra-immanent or extrapleromatic suffering of the *Logos,* is not pure waste. In the teleological field of divine filling or *plerosis,* suffering itself is an economic factor: it, too, pays dividends.

Nothing that I have said here about the Hegel-Gnosticism connection forswears Hegel's more intimate connection with Boehme. Yet it does serve to broaden the taxonomic field and open up the question of ultimate precedent for the eccentric christological and specifically deipassionist moments in both post-Reformation metaphysical theologians. Boehme, in any event, performs, more directly than Hegel, a hermeneutical correction of Valentinian Gnostic narrative that makes fully explicit correction unnecessary for Hegel. On internal grounds it seems evident that Boehme had some access to Ptolemy's system. Not only is it the case that the agent-patient of fall can plausibly be identified with Sophia, but the guise of fallen Sophia, that is, Nature, is also the same.[111] But, for Boehme, Nature, as well as the angst and death that belong to it,[112] fulfills an indispensable function in the divine's coming to itself. The temporal Christ functions merely as a symbol of a cross that plays an essential role in the definition of the extra-immanent divine as such. In a real sense, Boehme reads Ptolemy from the point of view of another Valentinian text to which he could not have had access, i.e., the *Tripartite Tractate.* What can be said of Boehme explicitly and Valentinian Gnosticism by implication is that they set the stage in Hegel for what Bataille called 'restricted economy': there is no expenditure without reserve, no suffering that is not a way station to a higher order of being and enjoyment, no sacrifice that does not recoup its gift and, in this case, add to the store of the divine self.

5

THE THIRD NARRATIVE EPOCH: The Moment or Kingdom of the Spirit

In Hegel the determination of God as Trinity is semantically ambiguous and may refer to either the sphere of divine immanence or to the sphere of the divine as fully inclusive of all reality, finite and infinite. Adequate trinitarian definition, however, ultimately involves all of reality, the "Immanent Trinity" or 'the holy Trinity' (*die heilige Dreieinigkeit*) *LPR 3* 1827 E 275–276, G 201) not being sufficient and requiring completion in and through its exile in the finite. Though we have adopted Iljin's language of 'epoch' as an interpretive tool, Hegel, it should be remembered, uses a variety of terms to capture what we have called the Inclusive Trinity, e.g., 'element', 'kingdom', 'moment'. Of these terms, kingdom is the most historically dense and theologically evocative, moment, the most narratively suggestive. Good examples of Hegel's use of the latter idiom are not lacking:

> The first moment is the idea in its simple universality for itself, self-enclosed, having not yet progressed to the primal division, to otherness—the Father. The second is the Particular, the idea in appearance—the Son . . . The third element, then, is this consciousness—God as the Spirit. (*LPR 3* 1827 E 331, G 254; see also 1824 E 230, G 161)

Spirit here defines a moment of union not possible on the level of the "Immanent Trinity" and not attributable to the holy Spirit (*der heilige Geist*), whose matrix is essentially that of infinite differentiation. Finitude (*Endlichkeit*), in *LPR 3* both opposited or created being and the finitude involved in the incarnation, passion, and death of Christ, in the *Enc* merely the former, is a moment or epoch without which fully determinate Personhood, fully concrete subjectivity, is not possible.

Though *LPR 3* and the *Enc* unfold different trinitarian distributions, their underlying narrative is identical, and both texts include the community (*Gemeinde*) of finite spirit in its elevation into the infinite as belonging essentially to the third and last trinitarian epoch. Distributional difference accentuates certain aspects of the underlying narrative, repressing others. *LPR 3* puts the community and the development of its religious potential at the center of the epoch of Spirit in a way not matched by the religious syllogism(s) of the *Enc.*[1] In the religious syllogism(s) of the *Enc,* the third syllogism essentially defines a movement that has its origin in the incarnation, passion, and death of Christ, continues in the appropriate *imitatio* of the Christian community, and concludes in the elevation of this community into authentic relation with the divine. In contrast to the distribution of *LPR 3,* the distribution of the *Enc* is more emphatically christological. Nevertheless, it ought to be pointed out that the greater christological emphasis of the *Enc,* and any theological advantage that might attach to this, is but the complement of surrendering the epoch of the Son to creation. Thus, any theological advantage with respect to the third epoch is balanced by theological disadvantage with respect to the second. Similarly, the theological disadvantage of the trinitarian distribution of *LPR 3* with regard to the third epoch is balanced by the obvious advantage it enjoys over the *Enc* in regard to the second epoch. In any event, while it must be admitted that the incarnation is not thematically central to the third narrative epoch of *LPR 3,* it is, nonetheless, its objective foundation.

If on intrinsic grounds it would be suspect to argue that the theological or ontotheological significance of the third narrative epoch, and *Gemeinde* as the central theme of that epoch, surpasses in significance the two other epochs and all theologoumena that reflect antecedent narrative phases, this is because the Hegelian ontotheological narrative is an integrated one where all narrative phases are codetermined. The third narrative epoch does, indeed, complete the other two, as *Gemeinde* closes, to all intents and purposes, the articulation of theologoumena, yet it is true to say that, in the very act of completion, the third narrative epoch, and *Gemeinde* in particular, depends upon its antecedents. Nonetheless, the teleological thrust of Hegel's ontotheological narrative does tend to highlight the final, actualizing stage and set it in relief. In any event, whatever the strict intentions of Hegel, perceptually at least, the third narrative epoch of Spirit has tended to assume the mantle of first among equals, since it is seen to provide, as terminus, the recollective summary of previous narrative stages. An additional factor in its promotion is that here the hermeneutic agon reaches its crescendo, with some interpreters arguing that Hegelianism finally reveals its naked secular intent, while others mount a rear guard action to defend Hegel's orthodoxy. In continuity with our treatment of other elements of Hegelian ontotheology, the position adopted here insists upon a theological reading of Hegel, even if this insistence is accompanied by the persuasion that, as Chapelle has remarked, it is too late to baptize Hegel.[2] A theological reading of Hegel need not suppose or promote the view that Hegel can be placed squarely within the frame of the mainline Christian tradition or any one of its more mainline confessions. Indeed, as was the case in previous chapters, it is important to attend to swerve, in this case, swerves from confessional pneumatology and ecclesiology that are marks of the Hegelian view. Yet, such an approach is, in and of itself, too negative. The positive complement is pursuit of the appropriate theological ambiance of the Hegelian depiction. It is decided that there is no simple way of talking about this ambiance but that it proves illuminating to regard Hegel at once against the background of Christian mysticism—or rather various strands within a complex, multiverse tradition—and the Lutheran tradition where this tradition is interrupted by interlacing strands of mystical varieties of thought.

Hegel's depiction of the third narrative epoch is sufficiently complex to deserve not one but two chapters, the first (chap. 5) focusing upon the Hegelian presentation of *Gemeinde* as it is regulated by the symbols 'the kingdom of God', 'the kingdom of Spirit', the second (chap. 6) focusing upon the third narrative epoch as the synclasis or closure of divine becoming which raises, among other issues, the important question of the relation between the kingdom of Spirit and the "Immanent Trinity". The first of these two chapters, which is our immediate concern, is divided into two sections. Section 5.1 concentrates upon Hegelian elucidation of the theologoumenon of *Gemeinde,* primarily as it is rendered in *LPR 3*, though other Hegelian texts are called forth in support. The analytic procedure is in the main descriptive, but an interpretive minimum is also present. Description includes presentation of the ensemble of elements Hegel presumes to be constitutive of the theologoumenon, that is, its condition, defining characteristics, modes of expression, development, and terminus, or concretely, incarnational presupposition, divine-human intimacy of an *ontological* sort, cultic, doctrinal and ethical expression, representational and doctrinal elaboration over time, and eschatological fulfillment of the developmental dynamics of Christianity in Lutheran Protestantism and its secular extension. The interpretive side represents a first response to the fairly naked alignment Hegel makes between the mystical union and mystical vision and *Gemeinde*, particularly *Gemeinde* in its realized aspect as Lutheran Christianity. Section 5.2 is almost exclusively interpretive. It articulates the bold claim that Hegelian presentation indicates the presence of not one but a number of varieties of mystical thought and that, together, these varieties can be said to be determinative of Hegelian *Gemeinde* and *explanatory* with regard to noticeable swerves of the Hegelian rendition from the normative Christian position(s), particularly from the Lutheran position. The three varieties of mysticism which, it is claimed, co-constitute Hegelian presentation, are the Eckhartian, the Joachimite, and Boehmian, all of which insinuated themselves into Hegel's intended Lutheran profile. It should be noted that the claim of co-constitution does not imply equal constitutive power and that an order of level of such power can be established, an order which accords to Eckhart the lowest level, to Joachim de Fiore the intermediate and to Jacob Boehme the highest level.

***Section 5.1 Spiritual Community* (Gemeinde): Corpus Mysticum**

> The community is made up of those single, empirical subjects who are in the Spirit of God. But at the same time this content, the history and truth of the community, is distinguished from them and stands over against them. (*LPR 3* 1827 E 329, G 252)

The Kingdom of the Spirit is, in general terms, identifiable with the spiritual community, and this identification points to the remarkable consistency of Hegel's thought. For, as H. S. Harris has pointed out, Hegel had formulated his notion of the Kingdom of God in his Stuttgart years and clearly expressed it in Tübingen.[3] The Kingdom of the Spirit represents, in essence, a trinitarianly grained translation of the earlier locution. Consistency, however, does not exclude evolution, and a decidedly less antagonistic attitude with regard to the visible church manifests itself in Hegel's mature religious reflection. There is nothing in *LPR* comparable to the neophyte's separation of the visible from invisible church (*die unsichtbare Kirche*) and his identification of the Kingdom of God merely with the latter.[4] In *LPR* the invisible church, while not coextensive with the visible, represents its legitimate extension, and the spiritual community is an embracing unity that includes both. In the earliest period of his theological reflection Hegel not only made the unilateral distinction of visible and invisible but portrayed himself as being very much under the shadow of Kant's Enlightenment-influenced version of the kingdom as the kingdom of universal rationality.[5] Hegel always remains an apostle of reason, and his kingdom is always of *Vernunft*. But, in his evolving thought, the definition of reason becomes more complex, and the notion of community becomes interpreted according to a more organic model. Reason no longer excludes feeling and intuition, but it is inclusive of them and under the influence of Herder and Lessing the notion of community takes on a historical dimension. The community is a historically contexted whole in which individuals live, move, and have their being, where their relations to each other and to the whole are determined by the whole. If *DE* and *FK* represent expressions of Hegel's discovery of the ambit of reason—though as yet the contrast *Verstand-Vernunft* is not made—*PS* represents the first major watermark of Hegel's mature 'Romantic', but also fully *religious,* conception of community.[6] Hegel insists on the Christian definition of community and regards it as a fundamental moment in the trinitarianly interpreted elaboration of God. The spiritual community, which Hegel at the end of his section on Revelatory Religion in *PS* interestingly calls 'the universal divine Man' (*der allgemeine göttliche Mensch*), is identifiable with the Spirit as the third moment of a triadic elaboration of which Hegel had spoken a little earlier.[7] The community is neither simple nor complex, neither unity nor multiplicity; it is a *totality,* the unity of a multiplicity. Hegel provides an emblem of this in the closing dithyrambic lines to a bravura test. These lines, an adaptation of the closing lines of Schiller's *Die Freundschrift,* are celebratory in their depiction of multitude that has a common divine source: "From the chalice of this realm of spirit foam forth for Him his own infinitude" (Miller, p. 493). The notion of spiritual community does not go without mention in the *Enc,* but it is in *LPR 3* that Hegel's decisive reflection is found. Accordingly, even if reference to other textual loci in Hegel is not eschewed, *LPR 3* provides the overarching structure of analysis. There Hegel's analysis breaks down into three parts: (1) the origin; (2) subsistence; and (3) realization of the spiritual community.[8] The scheme of *LPR 3* represents an attempt to respond adequately to the developmental dynamics within Christianity. Christianity in general, the Christian community in particular, portrays different degrees of religious differentiation over time, and it is only in Lutheran Protestantism that authentic spiritual community, implicitly in Christianity from the beginning, becomes fully explicit. If the Christian community is in a general way identifiable with the third trinitarian epoch, this is the case in a qualitatively unique way with the spiritual community made possible by the pneumatic saltus of Luther.

(1) *Origin:* The founding condition of the Christian community is obviously, for Hegel, the incarnation. But, in Hegel, the *purpose* of the incarnation stands out in high relief, and this purpose is nothing less than the constitution of the Kingdom of God, the bestowal of sonship upon finite beings. If the incarnation provides the *objective* condition for the unity of infinite and finite, sonship provides the subjective conclusion. But it is a constant in Hegel's religious reflection, manifested in his early antipositivity theological stance and corroborated in *PS* (#763), that the existence of Jesus, while revelatory of the divine and the indispensable condition of reconciliation of infinite and finite, constitutes at the same time a potential source for spiritual opacity. John 16.7 points to Jesus' own understanding of his mission and intimates his death. And it is withdrawal or death, as the epitome of vanishing or disappearance of the 'sensuous unit', that makes possible the commencement of the elaboration of spiritual autonomy.[9] In the chapter on Unhappy Consciousness (*das unglückliche Bewusstsein*) in *PS* Hegel describes the unspiritual search for the incarnate beyond (*Jenseits*) (Miller, 131–132, *GL2:*172–173) that is Jesus. The historical quest is completely wrongheaded, for it fails to recognize that the vanishing of Jesus is a condition of the presence of Spirit. The quest for the body of Jesus (Crusades) issues, of course, only in the empty tomb, eloquent and ironic confirmation of the fallacy of the quest. As related in *LPR 3*, the Pentecostal experience is at once the pneumatic substitute for the concrete existence of Jesus Christ and the term of Jesus' vocation which was to make persons free and children of God (1821 MS E 142, G 78).

For Hegel, sonship is at the very centre of Christianity and crucial to salvation. This point is underscored in *LPR 3* but also finds an airing in *LPH.* Hegel, in the latter work, is especially clear:

> It was then through the Christian Religion that the Absolute Idea of God, in its true conception, attained consciousness. Here man, too, found himself comprehended in his true nature, given in the specific conception of "the Son" (*die in der bestimmten Anschauung des Sohnes gegeben* ist). Man, finite when regarded from himself, is yet at the same time the image of God and a fountain of infinity in himself (*ist zugleich auch Ebenbild Gottes und Quell der Unendlichkeit in ihm selbst*). He is the object of his own existence—he

> has in himself an infinite value, an eternal destiny. (E 333, *GL11*:427)

Sonship is not intended to suggest the exclusion of the finite. Indeed, in the trinitarianly elaborated narrative of the divine, the Son proximally refers to the spheres of nature and finite spirit. But where, as in the above passage, sonship is associated with an Image theology, sonship tends to be identified with humanity's *infinite* aspect.[10] The finite aspect of humanity is never absolutely erasable in Hegel, though it is a narratively surpassable moment. The principled identification of sonship with image and, in turn, with infinity is reinforced by Hegel's reflection on image in his hermeneutic of Genesis in *LPR 3* and the *Enc*. Such identification counters his more dialectical proposal in *LPR I* (1824 E 212, G 120) and elsewhere,[11] where infinity and finitude are codeterminants of humanity, constituents, in fact, of an unresolved and essentially irresolvable tension.

One profound consequence of this double identification which belongs, Hegel insists, to the very essence of Christianity and is present, though *latent*, from the very inception of Christianity, is that Hegel separates himself from the mainline Augustinian theology of image based on resemblance rather than identity.[12] For Hegel the presence of the divine conforms or transforms the human into the divine. *Ab origine*, the infinity or divinity of humanity is merely potential, or at least potential as a general property of the community. Or, to use the Aristotelian terms Hegel avails of in *LPH*, the divinity of the human is a *dynamis* that requires the explicatory activity of *energeia* (E 334, *GL11*: 427). For Hegel, it is axiomatic that Christianity is not a revelation once and for all, but rather, a movement of revelation that is not merely *continuous* but *progressive* and, at a limit, *universalistic*. This means that revelation has a history and that time is an indispensable vehicle of the articulation and concrete appropriation of human being's divinity and sonship, an insight not lost on twentieth-century theology and philosophy.

(2) *Subsistence:* Hegel distinguishes the subsisting (*bestehende*) community from the emerging (*entstehende*) community.[13] The subsistence of the Christian community is the determinative historical existence of the Christian churches constituted by faith and the doctrinal elaboration of faith, and cultic observance and sacrament. Underpinning both, Hegel observes, is the objective content referred to by both, i.e., trinitarian narrative. In *LPR 3* the Christian churches mentioned are Catholicism, Lutheranism, and the Reform tradition. The Eastern

Orthodox churches are noticeable for their absence. Elsewhere (*LPH*), Hegel's talk of the Christian churches tends to polarize into a contrast between Catholicism and Lutheran Protestantism (sect. 3, part 3, chap. 2)

As we discussed at some length in chapter 1, Hegel shows no allergy to doctrinal codification, thinking that doctrine represents the explication of faith. That it is the *community* rather than the individual that is the real subject of religion fortifies Hegel's doctrinal bias (*LPR 3* 1827 E 333–334, G 256–257). He argues that the religious community is not constituted by faith as intuition or feeling but by doctrine which is normative and directive for the community (ibid. 1824 E 233–235, G 164–165). Granted doctrines initially stand over against the religious believer and are maintained solely through authority—or expressed in an earlier vocabulary, doctrines are initially positive—yet doctrines can be appropriated and in their appropriation lies rebirth (*Wiedergeburt*) (ibid. 1824 E 235, G 165). While, in availing of the language of rebirth, Hegel is nodding in the direction of Pietism, he is, in fact, siding with Lutheran orthodoxy in insisting against Pietism that rebirth is not immediate but doctrinally mediated. In any event, Hegel is convinced that rebirth constitutes the rite of passage from the natural to the spiritual self.

Again Hegel seems to side with Lutheran orthodoxy in insisting that cultic observance and sacrament are equally constitutive of the existence of the Christian community (ibid. 1824 E 236, G 166–167; 1827 E 337, G 260–261). Hegel makes the important and unsubstantiated claim that the differences among the Christian denominations are ultimately cultic and sacramental rather than doctrinal (ibid. 1821 MS E 154, G 89). The question of the legitimacy or illegitimacy of this view need not detain us here. Two points, however, can be made. First, the postulate of ultimate doctrinal correspondence, which tends to suggest that perceived differences between any Christian system and another are merely phenomenal, in turn, undermines the possibility of arguing a principled distinction between orthodoxy and heterodoxy, between, for instance, normative presentation and Hegel's own rendition.[14] Second, Hegel seems to imply that different cultic practices, or differences in understanding the sacraments, expose, in an unsurpassed way, distinct perceptions or understandings of the divine and divine mediation. In this respect, cultic and sacramental differences are theologically more decisive than purely doctrinal differences, though this is not to say that cultic and sacramental differences are adoctrinal.

In his treatment of the sacramental difference between the Christian churches, Hegel takes the eucharist as his example. Staying as close as possible to the confessional Lutheran understanding of the matter, Hegel's discussion in *LPR 3* is hardly unevaluative. The Catholic view is too objectivistic in conceiving the real presence of Christ to be contained in the material sensuous reality of the host. The Reform view is too leveled and historical in that the host is considered as mere memorial. Against these inadequate interpretations, Hegel opposes the Lutheran view of presence (*Gegenwart*), where presence is not valid in itself but authenticated by faith (*LPR 3* 1827 E 338–339, G 261–262). Jaeschke has rightly pointed to the generality of Hegel's retrieval here.[15] Certainly, nothing like a full-fledged sacramental theology is offered, and the specific marks of the confessional Lutheran view are absent. In a sense, Hegel is not so much defending a particular sacramental doctrine as indicating support for a particular understanding of a sacramental *principle* that may very well apply to all reality. Hegel sees clearly that the general drift of the Reform tradition on sign is to emphasize absence, thus, in a sense, to constitute a kind of negative theology and, in turn, ground the negative theology of modern thought. Against this view, he has no problem supporting the Lutheran interpretation of sign as indicative of presence and of the power of language in general, and not simply a specific set of biblical words, to provide access to the divine. His discussion of sign in the *Enc* (#458 ff) clearly provides a significant measure of philosophical support for a Lutheran view of presence. Though there is no reference to the Catholic doctrine of transubstantiation in Hegel's *LPR 3* discussion, from Hegel's compact remarks it is safe to assume that, in continuity with the Lutheran tradition, he would have found that the doctrine smacked of the ratiocinative intellect and that, furthermore, it offered additional support to the mechanistic, even magical, aspect of the Catholic interpretation of eucharist, summed up in the theory of *ex opere operato*. Perhaps a further reason is also in play. Granted that the generality of Hegel's discussion suggests a larger canvas than sacramental theology in its more narrow sense, it could be argued that what Hegel is problematizing is the ubiquity of the divine that is the central explanatory trope of Reformation sacramental discussion and offering a particular interpretation of ubiquity. The failure of the Catholic view of transubstantiation, as this view is now understood more as principle than specific doctrine, is that, on the one hand, it fails to emphasize the preservative element in the divine process of idealization and transfiguration and, on the other, does not place signification in the sphere of the subject.

Advocacy of the superiority of the Lutheran sacramental view—albeit in a highly generalized guise—concludes in *LPR 3* with a move that confirms, indeed accentuates, its pneumatic thrust. It is a standard in Lutheran confession to insist on the appropriative context of faith while insisting on real presence. If not absolutely constitutive, the faith emphasis points to a *discrimen* between it and the presumedly deficient Catholic view. In *LPR 3*, however, the appropriative element gets exaggerated beyond anything sanctioned by Luther or later Lutheran orthodoxy, such that it suggests that, if Hegel is to continue to be regarded as best interpreted within the Lutheran trajectory, then he must be assumed to belong to a nonorthodox wing. Some indication of Hegel's allegiance is indicated in his heavy insistence that the Lutheran view of the sacraments is the truly mystical view. Indeed, for Hegel, the sacramental presence of Christ constitutes nothing less than the mystical union. The following passage is less well-known than it ought to be.

> The subsistence of the community is completed by sharing in the appropriation of God's presence [i.e., the *communion*]. It is a question precisely of the conscious presence of God, of unity with God, the *unio mystica,* [one's] self feeling of God, the feeling of God's immediate presence within the subject. (*LPR 3* 1827 E 337, G 260; also 1824 E 236, G 166)

Thus, not only historically and structurally, but ideationally and sacramentally, Christianity, for Hegel, has a mystical center. The mystical center, present from Christianity's inception, is most declarative in the pneumaticism of Lutheran Protestantism that Hegel, in line with standard Protestant polemics, represents as the overcoming of the externality of Catholicism. In Lutheran Protestantism the rebirth of the self—presumably unnecessary in Catholicism—is validated, as is the witness of spirit which indicates fully self-conscious freedom and authentic sonship. *LPH* succinctly sums up these two related maxima. The passage on sonship has already been quoted. A page later, speaking of the appearance of "the principle of absolute freedom in God" (*das Princip der absoluten Freiheit in Gott*), Hegel puts forward a doctrine of participation or *methexis:*

> Man no longer sustains the relation of dependence (*Verhältniss der Abhängigkeit*), but of love—in the consciousness that he partakes of the divine essence (*dass er dem göttlichen Wesen angehört.*) (*GL11:*428)

Hegelian participation and Hegelian mystical union are one and the same thing, and if Hegel's passage, interconnecting sonship and Image Theology, is to be regulative, then participation ought to be interpreted not merely in an existential fashion but as involving a claim of ontological commensurability between the divine and human, a claim made, for instance, in Eckhart and, arguably, in Jacob Boehme, but not absolutely *typical* of the Christian mystical tradition,[16] and definitely not typical of the Lutheran tradition.[17] This pneumatic-mystical interpretation of Christianity in general, Lutheran Christianity in particular, effects a definite move away from a theology of justification to a theology of sanctification. And, even if one accepts the view that a theology of sanctification is not absolutely proscribed by Lutheranism, from the confessional point of view, Hegel could hardly be deemed to have set sufficient blocks to its radicalization. We will be returning to this point shortly. Talk of pneumatic Protestantism implies that, in the strict sense, we are dealing not merely with (2) but with (3), i.e., the *realization* of the spiritual community. It is to this that we now turn.

(3) *Realization*: Catholicism is not merely inferior sacramentally to Lutheran Protestantism; it suffers from a more generic defect. It sunders reality into the spheres of the holy and nonholy. The Catholic holy, it is Hegel's view in *PS* (#223–230), *LPH* (E 414), as well as *LPR* (1831 E 473, G 361–362), is completely negative and self-isolating and has monkishness as its existential-ethical expression. By contrast Lutheran Protestantism subverts the Catholic split and avoids the corruption of the holy by the nonholy that is the inevitable consequence of the split (*LPR 3* 1824 E 238, G 168). In insisting on the recoil of corruption, Hegel foreshadows, in some way, Nietzsche's insight into the nemesis or autorevenge of the exclusivist repressive holy.[18] The nature of Lutheran holy is integrative:[19] it avoids the deformation of the holy because it transforms the unholy. In transforming the unholy, it recovers the ethical realm (*Sittlichkeit*) and religiously sanctions the substitution of the civic virtues of economic activity, marriage, and the undergirding virtue of rational autonomy for the so-called religious virtues of poverty, chastity, and obedience.[20] For Hegel, Lutheran Protestantism as the *religion of the integrative holy* represents the culmination of the development of Christianity and the term of the evolution of religion as a whole. In Lutheran Protestantism, religion is finally fully adequate to its concept.

The conceptual telos of Lutheran Protestantism will be taken up momentarily. A few words, however, ought to be said about the *practical* determination of Protestantism in general, Lutheranism in particular. While in the most general sense it is the Reformation's own self-avowal that provides the basic warrant for the practical rather than contemplative and sacramental interpretation of Christianity, it is also interesting to speculate on the 'history of effects' of the Reformation avowal. Within the eighteenth-century field of conflict between Pietism and Lutheran orthodoxy that determines the basic contours of religious discourse, it would seem that, in Hegel's mature work at least, Lutheran orthodoxy has the advantages, given Hegelian criticisms in *PS* and *LPR*. Yet, as Laurence Dickey has convincingly shown, Pietism not only represented the shift from a theology of justification to a theology of sanctification observable in Hegel, but also represented the hallowing of the ethical-political sphere, a hallowing that has to be seen to be reflected in Hegel's championing of *Sittlichkeit*.[21]

If, for Hegel, Lutheran Protestantism is the telos of religion, philosophy is the telos of Lutheran Protestantism.[22] Despite Luther's own explicit disjunction between faith and philosophy, Hegel argues that they possess the same content, and this content is *mystical*. For Hegel, mystical content has both a synoptic and more elaborated extension. Synoptically, it is the conjunction of the finite and the infinite; non-synoptically, it is the movement of the infinite wherein the infinite attains full determination (and full personhood) in and through the finite. In either case, the *mystical* is especially attuned to knowledge. Thought (*Denken*) is, for Hegel, the essential thrust of all religion. *A fortiori,* this is the case with respect to theology. As we have seen already (chap. 1, sect. 1.2), Hegel is prepared to make the claim that devotion (*Andacht*) is but a degenerate form of thought (*Denken*), and theology nothing more, nor less, than what its etymology suggests, i.e., knowledge of God who is reality and truth. In this sense, while mystical is implied in the mystical union of religion, whose symbolic mode is that of representation, mystical vision is fully and adequately realized on the level of concept. But representation is itself on the way towards thought and concept and is itself implicitly vision, i.e., vision that has not yet come to full neotic transparence. Hegel, then, is engaged in providing Christianity with a thoroughgoing mystical definition and takes account of existential, ontological, and gnoseological aspects of religious relation. Hegel's interpretive decision here is, to put it mildly, surprising. When, however, he adds that Lutheran Christianity represents the apogee of the mystical center of Christianity, the most phlegmatic of readers has the right to be shocked. For does not Lutheran Protestantism provide the ethico-religious paradigm for Christianity? Hegel can agree with this characterization, as we have just seen in *LPR*

3 (the position is reinforced in *LPH*) and yet maintain that the *ethical* and *mystical* are not mutually exclusive. Protestant Christianity is ethico-practical not merely in spite of, but because of, its full appropriation of the mystical content of Christianity, a content that proposes divinity, infinity, sonship, image and participation, and freedom. The ethico-practical, either within the sphere of churchly influence or without, is but an expression of this center.[23]

As construed by Hegel, Lutheranism is founded upon spirit. Spirit, he argues, with one fundamental drift of the Reformation, is the final authority, not church institution (*LPR I* 1827 E 166–167 G 76–77). And it is precisely because of the authority of spirit that Lutheran Protestantism undergoes caricature in the *sola scriptura* doctrine. It cannot be defined through norming biblical text or the *sensus literalis* that reneges on the Pauline warning that the letter killeth, the spirit maketh alive (*LPR I* 1827 E 167, G 77). For Hegel, Lutheran pneumatism and Lutheranism's eschatological qualification are thoroughly in agreement. Their liaison, however, in no way implies any devaluation of the mystical essence of Christianity, Lutheran Christianity in particular. Pneumatism, eschatology, and mysticism in Hegel's interpretation all peacefully coexist, codesignate and codefine Christianity's acme. Lutheranism utters in the *eschaton,* the *eschaton* ultimately being the realization of *Gemeinde* as *corpus mysticum* and thus the realization of the kingdom of God qua kingdom of spirit.[24]

With respect to Hegel's rather fateful interface of pneumatology and eschatology, two moves he makes are worth of brief attention. First, there is a sense in which Christianity as the religion of Revelation (*Offenbarung*) implicitly gets associated with apocalypse. Second, despite the principled equality of members in the eschatological spiritual community, Hegel suggests a de facto differentiation and hierarchization. Whether defined as *die geoffenbarte Religion* or *die offenbare Religion,* Christianity is an exegesis of revelation, a revelation consummately given in pneumatically informed *Endzeit.* Though the historical trajectory is, from the incarnation to the realization of the *corpus mysticum,* the *point d'aperçu* is that of revelation eschatologically granted, first in Lutheran Protestantism, and in Hegelian ontotheology via its explication in modernity. The content of this revelation has already been addressed, but to the content discussed might be added the depiction of historical exegesis itself, including the eschatological term. Hegelian revelation associates with apocalypse (this reflection will be developed below) in that revelation unveils a content—in the first instance the content of mystical union. But revelation, which is conditioned by the coming into being of *Endzeit,* also has revelation as one of its *topoi.* Revelation as apocalypse, therefore, accounts for its own genesis. The second point can be dealt with even more briefly. For Hegel, as a good Lutheran, the *corpus mysticum* is a democracy of spirit. At least on the surface, such appears to be the case. Indeed, Hegel seems to reinforce the democratic proposal that translates the Lutheran theme of the priesthood of all believers by refusing to validate one mode of existence, e.g., worship, over ethico-practical life. Yet, despite the eulogy granted to *Sittlichkeit,* Hegel does appear to validate one kind of asymmetry that could prompt one to speak of the hegemony of the contemplative. If Hegel's definition of thought as *authentic* worship points in the direction of an asymmetry, Hegel's talk of philosophers constituting an isolated order of priests declares it loudly (*LPR 3* 1821 MS E 162, G 97). Hegel, then, appears to introduce a differentiation within the *corpus mysticum,* granting a qualitatively superior place to those who have mystical vision in the proper sense, i.e., those who have elevated themselves beyond representation into the pure realm of concept.[25] In doing so Hegel replicates a long-standing practice in the mystical and heterodox traditions of Christianity to authorize a two-tiered Christianity, an exoteric version that includes the sacramental and ethical forms of life, and an esoteric mode which, if it does not surpass the exoteric in every respect, seems to surpass it at least in one fundamental respect.

A few words ought to be said about the place of *Gemeinde* in the context of Hegel's elaboration of the Inclusive Trinity or, what amounts effectively to the same thing, Hegel's depiction of the non-synoptic mystical. Christianity is fundamentally the religion of *unio mystica.* The full communal realization of the *unio mystica* is not a given but an attainment, and, accordingly, realization is situated by Hegel in a narrative field. The narrative field to the foreground in *LPR 3* is the historico-temporal narrative of Christianity, which strictly speaking, begins with the pentecostal experience and is consummated in pneumatic Lutheranism. Yet this narrative field can be thought of as inserted in ever more inclusive narrative fields: firstly, within a field that has the incarnation as the alpha; secondly, within a field that begins with the creation of human beings, within which the incarnation represents the momentous point of transformation of the possibilities for human being; and thirdly and finally, within a narrative field that commences with the divine, specifically the "Immanent Trinity." The omega in the first two cases is the constitution of the *corpus mysticum.* In the case of the inclusive narrative field, the *corpus mysticum,* which now belongs to the divine self-definition itself, is brought into close relationship with the "Immanent Trinity." Precisely what the nature of this relationship is will be treated in chapter 6. It is the inclusive narrative or the Inclusive Trinity that is the content of the nonsynoptic mystical. And whereas *LPR 3* provides the explicated version of the nonsynoptic mystical, the religious syllogisms of the *Enc* present the nonsynoptic mystical in condensed form.

Before proceeding to interpretation, the basic elements of the Hegelian picture of *Gemeinde* are worth recalling. Insisting in general upon the mystical essence of Christianity, Hegel explicitly states that mystical union is axial. Mystical union is the interpretive substratum that informs the appeal to, and exegesis of, a number of ciphers Hegel believes central to Christianity: sonship, image, participation, freedom, divinity, infinity, knowledge. Lutheran Christianity represents the acme and telos of Christianity, thus, of its mystical thrust. Lutheran Christianity also represents the eschatological fulfillment, the coming of the kingdom. Eschatology, pneumatology, and mysticism are indissolubly intervolved in Lutheranism. Lutheranism ushers in the kingdom, the kingdom of spirit, a kingdom that may legitimately be called the *corpus mysticum*. The claims for Lutheran Christianity are quite momentous. To the above, Hegel adds another: Lutheran Christianity is the acme of a revelation, continuous, progressive, and eschatologically *universal*. In Lutheran Christianity a revelation is vouchsafed which is, in principle, unsurpassable. This aspect of Hegel's thought that I have suggested (justification comes later) borders on apocalyptic. The determinative content of the differentiation of Christianity and the differentiation of the Christian community specifically—Hegel refused an individualistic interpretation of Christianity—is, for Hegel, not the differentiation of religion, nor human differentiation, but the narrative of the divine's self-differentiation that is the nonsynoptic content of revelation, i.e., the nonsynoptic mystical.

Section 5.2 Complex Mystical Determination: Complex Mystical Inflection

In his exegesis of *Gemeinde* Hegel's view may, indeed, swerve from standard ways of both Christian and Lutheran envisagement, yet this calls more for explanation than provide warrant for his perfunctory dismissal. What is required is a taxonomic analysis of the Hegelian position which, at one and the same time, takes account of the mystical varieties of thought that get registered in his analysis and of the way in which these mystical varieties interfere with anything like a pure retrieval of Lutheranism. The two-front interpretation undertaken here complements the kind of historical proposal made by Laurence Dickey, for even if the Pietistic dissolution of Lutheran discourse in the eighteenth century provides the proximate horizon for the Hegelian rendition and obvious departures from the position of Luther and Lutheran orthodoxy, this still leaves the task of identifying the various mystical strands that are conspicuous in Hegel's complex braid. The interpretive hypothesis entertained in this section is that at least three varieties of Christian mysticism, influential in Protestantism, mark or inflect Hegel's account of spiritual community and, singly or together, are responsible for notable swerves in Hegel's account from standard Christian accounts, the Lutheran view of the *corpus mysticum* in particular. These three varieties are Eckhartian mysticism, Joachimite mysticism, and Boehmian mysticism, respectively.

Eckhartian Determinant: Eckhartian Inflection

Modern research has validated the historical fact of interaction between Hegel and Eckhartian thought. H. S. Harris convincingly argues that K. Rosenkranz's claim that Hegel excerpted Eckhart as early as 1795 (flush in his antipositivity period) be regarded as accurate.[26] E. Benz and Malte-Fues have both accepted as fact Hegel's sustained dialogue with von Baader over the winter of 1823/24 concerning Eckhartian mysticism, its significance with respect to religion, philosophy, and general culture.[27] For both, von Baader is a credible witness, and his narration of Hegel's enthusiastic reception of what he took to Eckhartian epitome: "The eye with which I see God is the same eye with which God sees himself. My eye and God's eye are one eye," which issues in the breathless *"da haben wir es ja, was wir wollen,"* is not regarded as apocryphal.

At a minimum then, relation between Hegel and Eckhartian mysticism has some historical basis, and Hegel is declaratively involved in conferring upon Eckhart, even if retrospectively, the status of precursor. A variety of interpretive options remain open, but, using Occham's razor, they reduce to two: Either one dismisses the historical connection as unimportant and the conferral as aberrant, or one takes seriously both historical connection and avowal as Benz does in *Les sources mystiques*.[28] Our own analysis is decidedly in agreement with the latter interpretive posture but insists equally upon a *critical* estimation of limits. Two factors are crucial for interpretation. First, it should be noted that Hegel, in his avowal, is not so much making a *causal* as a *taxonomic* claim, and accordingly it is the latter kind of claim that should be regulative. Second, granting the sincerity of avowal, and even that the liaison possesses a significant measure of cogency, the question of the *exact* measure should be raised. Is there an element of misreading in Hegel's reading, misvision in vision? In short, does Eckhartian mysticism provide an adequate taxonomic description of Hegelian depiction of the divine-human relation?

The fundamental horizon of Romantic-Idealist interpretation is set by Franz von Baader.[29] For Baader, Eckhart's sermons exemplify the true significance of Christianity, i.e., the discovery of the infinite worth of the individual. Infinite worth he considers a function of a relationship established *by* the divine *between* the human and divine, the finite and infinite. The divine understood in this way can only be understood as Spirit (*Geist*).[30] In speaking in this manner Baader sounds extraordinarily Hegelian. He is no less Hegelian sounding in decrying the modern separation of the finite from the infinite which, for him, connotes a derailment of the authentic Christian view, and in his denunciation of the devaluation of knowledge and speculation associated with this separation.[31] Mysticism in general, the mysticism of Eckhart in particular, is a sign of authentic Christianity in a time of decadence and forgetfulness.

Within Baader's widely scattered reflection on Eckhart one notices that, despite the textual limitations under which he operated, he is familiar with, and regards as crucial to Eckhartian theological anthropology, both the cipher of the 'divine birth' (*Gottesgeburt*) in the soul and the associated cipher of the 'divine spark' (*Fünklein*), though Baader tends to substitute 'breath' (*Hauchs*) for spark.[32] If these two ciphers are pivotal, and already involve a theology of sonship, they are associated in Eckhart with a particular theology of Image and notion of participation that brings out the radicality of the Christian position. Though Baader is capable of speaking of the mystery (*Geheimnis*) of the infinite-finite unity, his emphasis with regard to the divine birth and the related notion of breath tends to be more or less ketaphatic. He underscores their connection with reason (*Vernunft*) and rationality (*Vernunftigkeit*), where reason and rationality are to be understood in the post-Kantian manner as *transcendent* knowledge of self and God.[33] The interrelation of the divine birth and gnoseological capability of a fully radical sort is thus asserted by Baader. On the basis of passages like the one declaring the identity of God's and the self's vision that so moved Hegel (*LPR I* 1824 E 347, G 248), Baader is prepared to speak of the divine birth as implying the elevation of the consciousness of the divine to the state of divine self-consciousness. Fully radical gnoseological capability, which has its foundation(s) in the divine birth and breath, in turn, grounds, Baader seems to suggest, a particular theology of image that goes well beyond the Augustinian model of resemblance, indeed, implies a divinization of the self.

It should be pointed out that, with the exception of a moderate deemphasis of the apophatic side of Eckhart, Baader's presentation of the overall thrust and basic contours of Eckhart's theological anthropology is extraordinarily perspicacious. Modern scholars such as Ebeling point to the centrality of the divine birth,[34] and, though the cipher of divine spark can be construed as representing a different strain of reflection, it is, in fact, aligned in Eckhart's sermons with the divine birth.[35] Furthermore, there is no lack of evidence that Eckhart explicitly connected the doctrine of the divine birth with reason[36] and that the divine birth in particular is foundational with respect to his non-Augustinian Image theology. Interestingly, however, the principle of Baaderian interpretation is consistently *theistic.* He insists, for instance, that, for Eckhart, reason does not come from human being but from the divine.[37] In addition, he rules that whatever the particular nuances of Eckhart's theology of sonship and Image theology, no identity is postulated. Speaking of the human self, he insists that 'the divine reason' (*die göttliche Vernunft*) is only represented or reproduced rather than being originary in human being. It is, then, axiomatic for Baader, as it is for the normative Christian tradition, that the superb level of intimacy between the self and God in no way implies the breakdown of their unbridgeable difference.[38] Though Eckhart functions as the yardstick by which to judge modern deformations of Christianity, given Baader's hermeneutic principles, Eckhart's full critical potential is hardly set free. In a real sense, this is more nearly Hegel's achievement than Baader's.

If we opened with Baader's relationship to Eckhart rather than Hegel's, it is because Baader inscribes the *upper limit* of Hegel's knowledge of Eckhart. The *lower limit* is set by the single citation that appears in his collected works (*LPR I* 1824 E 347, G 248). From the historical evidence (see Benz, Malte-Fues), it is Baader who is ultimately responsible for the citation. The context of the citation makes it clear that Hegel is putting Eckhart to forensic use against those who would deny gnoseological capacity to human being. Hegelian use resembles in the strongest possible way Baader's own use and with much the same targets in view. The passage cited by Hegel, however, does not contain explicit reference to the doctrine of divine birth which Baader seemed to imply was the hub of Eckhartian anthropology. Neither can an echo be heard, nor a trace reconstructed, of the ciphers of divine spark and breath, in Hegel's mature thought, though Hegel shows himself committed to the view that the self has an infinite dimension. Evidence of this commitment in *LPR* and *LPH* has already been brought forward. The Preface and the concluding two sections of *PS* also feature this idea. In the third part of the *Enc* the idea is, of course, pivotal. The idea dominates *Enc* #377–384 and #564–574. Hegel here articulates in a decisive way the interconnection between Christianity and the infinite dimension of the self, interpreted primarily in a gnoseological way. He asserts:

> . . . the Greeks were the first to grasp expressly as spirit what they opposed to themselves as the divine, although they did not attain, either in philosophy or in religion, to a knowledge of the absolute infinitude of Spirit; therefore with the Greeks the relation of the human spirit to the divine is still not one of absolute freedom. It was Christianity, by its doctrine of incarnation and of the presence of the Holy Spirit in the community of believers, that first gave to human consciousness a perfectly free relationship to the infinite and made possible the comprehensive knowledge of Spirit in its absolute infinitude. (*Enc* #377 *zu,* Miller, p. 2)

It appears to be the case that, for the mature Hegel, what is of most importance is the general reality of mystical union and the mystical vision with which it is associated rather than the ideational scheme into which it is inserted. He is profoundly interested in the mystical vision and associates it, as Baader does, with the self-consciousness of the divine. Hegel has absolutely no problem endorsing a position he finds in Göschel.

> God is God only so far as he knows himself: his self-knowledge is, further, a self-consciousness in man and man's knowledge *of* God, which proceeds to man's self-knowledge in God. (*Enc* #564)[39]

Just as Hegel's single citation does not contain explicit mention of a theology of sonship, neither does it correlate mystical vision with an image theology. Nevertheless, to the degree to which Hegel does elaborate an image theology, the emphasis upon the self's divinity and power of knowledge is isomorphic with the gnoseological rendition of mystical union and his championing of Eckhartian mysticism with authentic Lutheranism as essential Christianity.

As Malte-Fues observes,[40] unlike Baader, Hegel, in his presentation of mystical union, does not take the trouble of insisting upon the absolute division between the divine and the human. Indeed, it could be argued that much of Hegel's enthusiasm for Eckhart is based upon his perception that in Eckhart one finds a religious thinker brave enough to announce not merely commensurability between the divine and human but actual ontological identity.[41] For Hegel also, mystical vision is without remainder the self-consciousness of God, whereas for Baader such an assertion can only be made accompanied by the grammatical rider that such an assertion not controvert the axiom of the unbridgeable difference between the divine and the human. Both Baader's and Hegel's general interpretive positions are internally consistent. For the former the nexus of concepts or ciphers—divine birth, divine spark, breath, sonship, image, child of God—must be interpreted in such as way so as *not* to entail the overcoming of the infinite-finite distinction. Contrariwise, for Hegel, mystical union and mystical vision point to a divinization so radical that the ontological difference between finite and infinite can be thought to be overcome, even if Hegel does not commit himself to such a thoroughgoing relativization of the finite as that evidenced in Eckhart's less dialectical texts.[42]

Without in any way succumbing to the nineteenth-century interpretation, which made of Eckhart an "antediluvian Hegel" (Franz Rosenkranz) and Hegel a "pantheist" in Eckhartian mode (Carl Schmidt),[43] it would appear that Hegel in his principle of interpretation more nearly approximates the real Eckhart, i.e., the textually and critically verified Eckhart. It can be plausibly claimed that a pivotal Eckhartian notion such as the divine birth clearly points in the direction of overcoming the ontological difference that Baader believes to be axiomatic for Christianity. A host of passages in Eckhart suggest this revision.[44] Sermon 6 in the *Deutsche Werke* (*DW*) is emblematic in this respect. In that important text, the ontological identity of self and God is implied via the subversion of the (onto)theological distinction axiomatic from the Patristic period, i.e., the distinction between generation and creation. The divine birth constitutes the radical divinization of self. In *DW* 6 Eckhart finds scriptural warrant for the operation of divinization in 2 Cor. 3:18 but goes beyond the mainline Christian tradition in reading it to imply removal of all distinction between the human and the divine. Eckhart sums up the major thrust of his reflection on the divine birth and divinization:

> I am so changed into him [God] that he produces his being in me as me, not just similar. By the living God this is true . . . There is no distinction.[45]

The concept or cipher of the divine birth defines Eckhart's theology of image. Indeed, the divine birth might be said to constitute the self as image. Moreover, the concept of the divine birth provides ultimate theological support for, and definitive theological interpretation of, the Johannine symbols of 'friends' and 'children' of God.[46]

Thus, while it is the case that no *explicit* reminder of the *Gottesgeburt* is extant in Hegel, nevertheless, there exists a remarkable correspondence between Eckhart and Hegel with respect to the ideas of divine sonship, image of God, child, and friend of God, the basic outline of which we presented in our interpretation of Hegel's concept of *Gemeinde*. By way of rounding off discussion, I should like to comment briefly on a common subversive corollary drawn by both Eckhart and Hegel from similar articulations of mystical union and mystical vision. This corollary suggested by Hegel and articulated in his own day and just after his death by his defenders—and to an extent by his detractors—posed a challenge to normative Christian construal, both traditional and Protestant, that was met with something like dismay.[47] I am referring to the revision of the common representational view of immortality implied in an understanding of Christian mystical vision and union that does not seek the security of Baader's essentially grammatical stricture. In suggesting Hegel's overlap with Eckhart here, I am neither suggesting that Eckhart is Hegel's actual historical source, nor that Hegel's view does not bear a significant relation to Spinoza's reflection on the mystical state in *Ethics* BK 5. My point is that Hegel thought—and rightly thought—that he had found in Eckhart Christian intratextual warrant for a way of understanding immortality that would not be as vulnerable to critical rationality as the standard Christian view. Providing the view of immortality with critical ballast implied at one and the same time (1) a dismantling of the absoluteness of the distinction between this life and the next life, where this gets specified in a radicalization of the soteriological function of mystical union and (2) a revisionist and critical understanding of the durational representation of immortality. (1) The soteriological implications of the Eckhartian mystical union and vision are radical not merely with respect to the Christian tradition, in general, but with respect to the mainline mystical tradition. As a protagonist of mystical union and vision, Eckhart shares with the mystical tradition the understanding that deification already involves one in a relation to divine presence that the nonmystical traditions, especially the tradition of Lutheran orthodoxy, declare belongs properly to the next life.[48] But Eckhart radicalizes the mystical position when he suggests the mystical union functions as *the* eschatological state, or otherwise put, as the *surrogate* for the eschatological state. (2) Also undermined is the durational construal of the soteriological state, common to the high theological traditions of the West and popular religious imagination. Eckhart's view of mystical union and vision excludes positing durational properties since, as the passage Hegel liked so well indicates, the vision of the mystic is God's own vision which has to be understood in nondurational terms. Though Spinoza necessarily must be regarded as the main philosophical proposer, it is Eckhart that suggests for Hegel a definition of eternity as the transcendence of time and not (as in Augustine, arguably Luther, and definitely popular imagination) as indefinite temporal extension, i.e., everlastingness.

Hegel appears to draw precisely the same soteriological conclusions on the basis of the elevation of the self into the divine this side of death in his own mature work. The subversion of the pre-eschatological/eschatological distinction is implied in the sections on Revelatory Religion and Absolute Knowledge in *PS,* the conclusion of the *Enc* where the self undergoes apotheosis, and in *SL* which presupposes a divinized subject. Hegelian consideration of the Christian envisioning of the eschatological state is most patent in *LPR.* In the following passage, revision is indicated by use of the distancing "to begin with":

> This absoluteness and infinitude of self-consciousness is represented in the doctrine of the immortality of the soul. To begin with, the outstanding characteristic of the latter is duration in time; and in this way immortality, the fact that spiritual self-consciousness is itself an eternal, absolute element, is represented as a sublimation or elevation, a being snatched up out of time. (*LPR* I 1821 MS E 195, G 105)

"Eternity," as Hegel says elsewhere, "is not mere duration—on the contrary it is knowing (*ist nicht blosse Damer . . . sondern sie ist Wissen*)" (*LPR 3* Fragments E 386, G 305).[49]

Hegelian appeal to Eckhart not only points to the putative Christian pedigree of Hegel's vision of the deification potential in human being that can get actualized in a variety of ways in modernity but, at the same time, to an intra-Christian resource of criticism. This criticism in the main is directed at dominant modes of symbolization that call for correction. In a sense then, Hegel's enthusiasm for Eckhart rests, in part, on the fact that the medieval religious thinker provides the warrant for considering iconoclasm an internal Christian procedure and event and not simply an introjection from the outside. As Bataille has recognized,[50] however, Hegel passes over the obvious difference that in Eckhart's case the iconoclasm is unrestricted and applies to concept as well as religious symbol. At the very least, such a recognition would have complicated matters; it would certainly have rendered the invocation of Eckhart ineffective in Hegel's attack against modern negative theology. But even substantively, it would not be wise to accept Hegel at his word that the Eckhartian vision of the mystical provides the model for his own articulation of the mystical, even where the mystical is considered in its purely synoptic extent. Eckhart cannot carry the burden of exclusive precursor, since, from a Hegelian point of view, the conditions of the possibility of divinization have not been adequately thought through. Though Hegel does not, in fact, attend to Eckhartian deficits—it is unnecessary, since he can pick from other quarters in the mystical tradition or mystically inflected Lutheran tradition—two deficits are particularly conspicuous, i.e., Eckhart's view of time and history, and his view of the role of Christ.

With regard to the first point, it can fairly be said that, in the textually verified Eckhart, time and history not only do not identify the soteriological domain, as is the case in Hegel, they bear no soteriological index whatsoever (e.g., *DW* 2, 5b, 30). Looked at from an individual or communitarian perspective the Eckhartian view of mystical union and vision, associated with salvation, has *eternity* as its content. Importantly, given Eckhart's and Hegel's common subversion of temporalizing tendency of popular religious imagination and significant trends within the theological tradition, eternity in Eckhart is not understood as the sublation of the temporal and the historical; it is Platonically or Neoplatonically conceived as their negation (e.g., *DW* 11, 13, 29). The thoroughgoing devaluation of time and history obviously leads to the erasure of the eschatological dimension of Christianity, dependent on value being ascribed to the temporal-historical dimension. *LPR 3* and *LPH,* examined earlier, could not provide clearer evidence that any and all renditions of Christianity, even mystically inflected versions, must protect Christianity's essentially historical and eschatological essence. Moreover, though it is true that when Hegel defines time as 'the abstraction of consuming' (*Abstaktion des Verzehrens*) (*Enc* #258 *zu*), he could plausibly be read as recalling Eckhart's Platonic dismissal, it is important to point out that this is not Hegel's last word on time. Hegel makes a distinction that Neoplatonists with the exception of Augustine did not tend to make, i.e., a distinction between cosmological time and human temporality. And, for Hegel, human temporality belongs to a much more differentiated stratum of reality (*Enc* #440–465). If the former is the pure antithesis to eternity, the latter, belonging to *Mind,* shows itself capable of genuine growth and development, a development that presupposes the eternal as *telos.* In Hegel, as in Eckhart, while the basic determinant of temporality inscribed within the parameter of creation is undoubtedly that of finitude, finitude here is not finitude indelibly mired, but finitude on its way to its own transcendence. Mystical union and vision represent the apotheosis of finitude. Achieved communal apotheosis, achieved communal elevation into infinitude, is the prerogative of the eschatological age, i.e., the modern age founded upon Lutheran Protestantism, which itself, of course, is from Hegel's perspective the exegesis of the revolution of Christianity. This brings us to the second area of rupture—albeit unacknowledged by Hegel—different understandings of the nature and function of Christ.

Assertion of a significant degree of correlation between Hegel's and Eckhart's christological reflection would not be a wholly shocking thesis. Certainly there is in both cases an overriding divinization interest, and the horizon of their respective Christologies is unabashedly pneumatological. Michel Henry, for instance, has pointed to their common selection of John 16.7 as a scriptural passage in which the necessity of the historical Jesus' withdrawal is coded.[51] Henry has the antipositivity of Hegel in the early theological essays explicitly in mind, but it is still true of the mature Hegel, as we saw in chapter 4, that he focuses heavily on the pneumatic appropriation of Christ, which, it turns out, is constitutive of human divinization. Thus, while in one sense Hegel is doing no more than recapitulating the Lutheran *pro me,* the pneumatic emphasis begins to recall the more overtly divinization-friendly Christology of Pietism than the position of Lutheran orthodoxy. And Pietism, as is well-known, was considerably more hospitable to expressly recapitulating the mystical tradition,[52] since it did not polarize in the way Lutheran orthodoxy tended to do, a theology of sanctification and a theology of justification. Still, at least on the level of intention, the christological position of the mature Hegel differs in two important respects from that of Eckhart. The first difference concerns the issue of the uniqueness of Christ, the second has got to do with the issue of the incarnation, the point at which the eternal touches the temporal.

Though Hegel's positing of the uniqueness of Christ might be regarded as satisfying a purely formal criterion, still in *LPR* no adequate Christology or even Pneumatology can proceed without it. Eckhart, that is, the historically verified Eckhart, from a Hegelian point of view fails this crucial transcendental test. While the scriptural roots of Eckhartian reflection tend in general to count against express dogmatic statement, when Eckhart does rise to the metalevel of properly theological discourse, he is not shy about repeating the Athanasian formula crucial to the deification tradition within Christianity: God becomes human in order that the human become divine (*DW* 29, 43). Yet, despite this commitment to the Athanasian formula, Eckhart's theological presuppositions in general, his concept of the divine birth in particular, do not support a consistent or coherent christological focus. Jesus Christ is not the indispensable condition of the divinized self. Divinization is secured in a nonmediated event in which self and soul play the role of virgin-mother (*theotokos*) giving birth to the Word (*DW* 2, 22). In the determinative context of the divine birth, Jesus can serve only the role of model or exemplar, a position abandoned early in Hegel's career as inadequate. From the standpoint of Hegel's mature theological reflection, the equalizing of every self and Jesus (and every self and Mary),[53] or even the palliative of Jesus as model, vitiate the normative and correct understanding of the *qualitative uniqueness* of Christ that *LPR* in particular is anxious to defend.

The first deficit is only analytically separable from the second. The divine birth that determines each self as son also dehistoricizes the Christ-event in a way unacceptable to the mature Hegel, smacking of the doceticism that he sees most glaringly displayed in Valentinian Gnosticism. The divine birth does not connote the generalization of the incarnational event—a generalization of which Hegel has sometimes been accused notwithstanding his insistence on the uniqueness of Christ. It is an event that operates exclusively on the plane of eternity, where eternity and uncreatedness are regarded as synonymous. A radical disjunction between the eternal and uncreated order and the temporal and the created is thereby implied and renders the possibility of irruption of the eternal into the temporal totally unintelligible. As in Fichte's later practice, incarnation becomes assimilated to the generation of the Logos; John 1.14 is hermeneutically disconnected from John 1.1[54] If Hegel is to find warrant in the mystical tradition for the *kairotic* dimension of the incarnation, the *hic et nunc* of the incarnational event, and the soteriological dimension of history, then he must necessarily look elsewhere. 'Elsewhere' here effectively means, if we are right about our triple mystical determination proposal, turning to the Joachimite and Boehmian mystical traditions. But before we get to this, there is a question of some importance to be dealt with. What is it in Hegel's reading of the history of Christianity that allows him to assume a harmony between the Lutheran Christianity he confesses and the Eckhartian mysticism that, at one point at least, Hegel suggests provides the lapidary summary of his own ontotheological program?

Hegel's enthusiastic reception of Eckhart's trenchant affirmation of mystical union and vision as summary of Christianity, philosophy, and their alliance; his determination of the mystical essence of Lutheran Protestantism; and his bold interpretation of a number of important Christian ciphers such as sonship, image, participation, cumulatively force a strong alliance between Luther and Eckhart. Admittedly, the hermeneutic intelligibility of this alliance is far from obvious, with many scholars, particularly those of Lutheran persuasion, finding these religious horizons to be fundamentally incompatible.[55] The prospective range of mismatch is extensive, with some scholars suggesting that alliance may be ruled out quite simply, since Luther and Lutheranism reject precisely that divinization commitment that marks the mystical tradition in general. Indeed, it is argued, this is at least partly the issue between Lutheran orthodoxy and Pietistism throughout the eighteenth century. Yet this distinction may be too crudely drawn, with some scholars claiming that Luther does not exclude divinization altogether, no more than he is totally inhospitable to the mystical tradition.[56] Nevertheless, even on the most benign reading, Hegel's alliance of Eckhart and Luther in his self-conscious championing of Lutheranism as the acme of Christianity has to meet some serious difficulties. Two are especially conspicuous, i.e., Eckhartian subversion of the ontological difference between the human and the divine, and Eckhartian emphasis upon *transcendent* knowledge of a *radical* type. Both of these points require brief explication.

With regard to first point it should be said that, even if Luther is not best read as forswearing his early interest in the mystical tradition, his taste, be it Tauler—whom Hegel is reported to have read in his early years—or the *Theologica Germanica,* is not only dominantly practical-existential, rather than speculative-ontological, but does nothing to challenge his basic Augustinianism. This Augustinianism dictates that any view of principled commensurability and any suggestion that commensurability is realizable through human agency is to be rejected. Here Luther departs from Eckhart, and Hegel can be seen to make a both/and out of an either/or. With regard to the second point, we can be even briefer. Whatever Luther's affirmation of mystical vision in his early work or in his sacramental elaboration, he did not regard it after conventional mystical fashion as an esoteric event or esoteric knowledge that represented an essential foretaste of the eschatological state. Eckhart's radicalization of this idea, namely that mystical vision can legitimately substitute for the eschatological state—a position Hegel cannot logically deny to Luther—for Luther himself would have been anathema. Moreover, though the Christian iconography of the afterlife may not pass the bar of reason, there exists in Luther's view no warrant for theological ideology-critique, since one can rely on the word of God. Hegelian support of Eckhart on these points suggests his disagreement with Luther and the mainline Lutheran tradition that followed him.

That there are serious barriers, therefore, to the allying of Eckhart and Luther cannot be doubted. Yet an alliance is forged by Hegel. The alliance or rather mésalliance of Lutheran Christianity and Eckhartian mysticism might be explained (or explained away) by asserting Hegel's ignorance of the specificity of these Christian phenomena (thus a pardonable error) or by willful deception. Neither approach, however, does justice to the importance of the alliance and the hermeneutic mechanism(s) in and through which it gets asserted. Two hermeneutical moves are of especial importance: (1) Hegel's *synecdochical* interpretation of Christian representation as well as philosophy,[57] (2) Hegelian *selection of a core* of a Christian thought-constellation which *peripheralizes* other elements and at a limit *erases* them. The first hermeneutical move manifests itself when it becomes clear in Hegelian texts that every rendition of Christianity presents a part to the whole vouchsafed in the Hegelian presentation, just as every previous philosophical formation represents a part to the whole elaborated in and by Hegelian philosophy.[58] Hegelian reading of the tradition of Christian representations and interpretations through the trope of synecdoche is the ground-condition of the blurring of their distinctiveness. Every presentation is considered only to the extent to which it *anticipates* Hegelian presentation. And while the horizon of anticipation does not absolutely neutralize distinction, it tends to encourage blurring. If this is true in general, it is particularly true of those presentations selected from the stream of tradition that Hegel in an especial way regards as having the status of precursorship.[59]

With regard to the second move, it can be said that the attestable pneumatism of Lutheran Protestantism is accepted by Hegel as *the* core. Considered thus, pneumatism provides the warrant for the peripheralizing of other elements of the Lutheran ensemble and, at a limit, erasing them altogether. One can see both sides of this operation in action with respect to the Lutheran stress on the radical finitude and sinfulness of human being and human being's gnoseological incapacity. Where human being's finitude, sinfulness, and ignorance are granted by Hegel (and they are conceded in *LPR 3* and *Enc*), they tend to be shorn of their radicality and peripheralized to the degree that they become mere way stations on the road to infinity, perfection, and absolute knowledge. They are erased when Hegel, less careful about narrative context, outrightly asserts the infinity, perfection, and fully radical gnoseological capacity of human being. The alliance between Lutheranism and mysticism of a decidedly Eckhartian type is aided and abetted by the complementary selection of the core of Meister Eckhart. Selection of the ontological and gnoseological center is ipso facto selection of a kataphatic horizon. Pseudo-Dionysian apophatic element in Eckhart is at least peripheralized and arguably erased.[60] No trace of such an element, which sets restrictions to the kind of knowledge possible, is revealed in the eye passage that forced the exclamation: *da haben wir es ja was wir wollen.* In an apophatic context, which one could reasonably determine as its regulative horizon—and one registered though somewhat weakly in von Baader—vision or knowledge can only be intuitive and nondiscursive. And the nondiscursive restriction prevails, even if the iconoclastic element in Eckhart is affirmed, perhaps especially when the iconoclastic element is affirmed. Images are looked on with more than a degree of suspicion, but concepts are hardly in a better position. Hegel manages to authorize a much more restricted iconoclasm that can be either found in or extrapolated from Meister Eckhart.

Before we proceed to our second mystical determination, it should be made clear that the presence of these hermeneutic operations by no means determines that the Hegelian alliance can be usefully classed in Bloomian fashion as willful misreading. That his Lutheranism does not correspond to that of the historical Luther or Lutheran orthodoxy does not imply that Hegel is involved in pure invention or the testing of his imaginative powers. More plausibly, it points to the possibility that Hegel is dredging a stream of Lutheran tradition that preceded the rise of Lutheran orthodoxy and maintained itself in different configurations in Pietism in the seventeenth and eighteenth centuries, a tradition not as despairing about the human condition or the possibility for enjoying the divine presence, even when human sinfulness is acknowledged.[61] Yet, at the same time, Hegel is drawing conclusions from Lutheran sacramental theology that are there to be drawn but historically were not drawn in the matrix of Lutheran orthodoxy. Similarly, Hegel's Eckhart, if truncated, is not unrecognizable. Eckhart's view of the mystical easily could be seen to harmonize with the generalized version of Lutheran sacramental theology one finds in Hegel. For this view not only suggests that divine presence can be encountered in manifold modes of being but in a sense deconstructs the privilege of the sacrament as such by shifting attention onto the pneumatological condition of constitution and also by making all of reality intrinsically sacramental.

Joachimite Determinant: Joachimite Inflection

That Lessing's *The Education of the Human Race* exercised considerable influence on the thought of Hegel is a point generally agreed on by Hegel scholars.[62] The extent of this influence is, however, open to debate, since, if that text evokes the *evangelium aeternum* of Joachim de Fiore, it contextualizes it within a developmental view of history that represents something of an Enlightenment thinning of the kind of *Heilsgeschichte* scheme found in the Calabrian abbot.[63] And it is argued, in Hegel, the mature Hegel in particular, the religious impulse goes deeper, and modernity finds a thinker who religiously replenishes the attenuated eschatological scheme of the Enlightenment and Enlightenment-influenced account of historical development. Morphologically, therefore, Hegel's eschatological position more nearly resembles the position of Joachim than that of Lessing, and historically Hegel can be regarded as representing a deeper and more comprehensive retrieval of a tradition that bears a Joachimite stamp. Surprisingly, however, there has been little attempt at either morphological or historical analysis of the relationship between Hegel and Joachim or Hegel and the Joachimite tradition. On the historical front, the work of Henri de Lubac constitutes an exception. His *La postérité spirituelle de Joachim de Fiori* argues a case with style and conviction. The interrelated elements of de Lubac's complex historico-conceptual thesis may be schematized as follows: (1) Joachimite ideas decisively infiltrate Lutheran thought; (2) Lutheranism is the main agent of mediation of Joachimite ideas into the eighteenth century; (3) Jacob Boehme is a particularly significant courier of this tradition; (4) major couriers of this tradition in the eighteenth century include Bengel and

Oetinger; and (5) both Hegel and Schelling are heirs to the Joachimite tradition.[64]

As stated, the thesis is as vulnerable as it is complex, and no single aspect of it would go unchallenged. Yet most of the assertions have more than superficial warrant. (1) It is a commonplace that Joachimite ideas inform the radical Reformation,[65] just as it is a commonplace that Luther's own insistence upon the primacy of spirit over structure establishes elective affinities between Lutheran pneumatology and Joachimite apocalyptic. (2) Though not a commonplace, there exists a persuasive argument to the effect that apocalypticism did not die out with the radical wing of the Reformation but remained close to the center of late sixteenth- and early seventeenth-century Lutheran piety.[66] (3) That Boehme is a major courier of the Joachimite apocalyptic tradition in the seventeenth century is a point I expect to establish shortly. (4) Something like a consensus exists among scholars that Silesian figures such as Bengel and Oetinger were involved in a reprise of Joachimite apocalypse.[67] (5) That Hegel and Schelling owe a debt to the Silesian mediators has been suggested by such a considerable scholars as Ernst Benz.[68] While the position adopted here is in essential agreement with de Lubac's historical thesis as a whole and the parts that constitute it, two modifications are recommended. First, substituting for de Lubac's causal reading, it is suggested that the trajectory is best understood as a continually revitalized matrix of eschatological discourse to the side of mainline Lutheran confession, and this discourse can trace its ultimate pedigree back to the medieval monk who played a significant role in the ideology of the Reformation. Second, the strong version of de Lubac's historical thesis, namely, that Joachim or the Joachimite tradition is the exclusive determinant of Hegelian ontotheology, is rejected in favor of his weaker proposal, i.e., that it is this tradition in interaction with the German mystical tradition that exercises determinative impact. Rejection of the stronger version of de Lubac's thesis is indicated, of course, in the attempt here to see Hegel's view of *Gemeinde* as mystically determined and inflected by various brands of mystical thought within the modern Lutheran tradition of which the Joachimite is simply one.

Since my taxonomic intention is not fulfilled by a historical account—however emended—this section, which attempts to bring out the Joachimite element in Hegel, will have a morphological, as well as historical, aspect. The morphological aspect is in play in the first two subsections where, after a brief outline of the apocalyptic mysticism of

Joachim with its intersection of trinitarian reflection, pneumatology, and eschatology, I proceed to present Joachimite registration in Hegelian texts. A third subsection deals with the historical trajectory of Joachimism within the Lutheran field and, specifically, how this species of thought, while differing considerably from the noneschatological brand of Lutheranism, provides the basic frame for Hegelian eschatological discourse.

Joachim: Trinity, Pneumatology, Eschatology. Though modern scholarship on Joachim goes to some pains to emphasize that the abbot of Fiore's works unfold not one but two distinct patterns of history,[69] the omega or dyadic pattern of Father-Son that dominates Joachim's two main early works, *Concordia Novi ac Veteris Testamenti* and *Expositio in Apocalypsim,* and the alpha or trinitarian pattern of Father-Son-Spirit that dominates *Psalterium Decem Chordarum,* it is undoubtedly the case that the originality of Joachim is more clearly evident in the trinitarian pattern of history and that this pattern was responsible in large measure for Joachim's later influence. Moreover, the alpha or trinitarian pattern is by no means absent from Joachim's earlier works where the omega pattern is to the forefront. *Concordia* Book 2 provides just one such example. That text presents Joachim's more or less standard periodization of history.

I Tempus of the Father: Adam–Christ
II Tempus of the Son: Christ–St. Benedict
III Tempus of the Spirit: St. Benedict–Consummation

'Tempus', 'aetas', and *'status'* are the periodization terms most often used by Joachim in his elaboration of his trinitarian theology of history. *'Regnum'* or 'kingdom' is not, in fact, a textual assignation used by Joachim, but rather, a Joachimite development. The development is, however, very much in contact with the inspiration of Joachim himself, and thus may be regarded as synonymous with *tempus, aetas,* and *status.*[70]

Joachim's trinitarian periodization specifies a trajectory of qualitative differentiation on a number of different axes, three of which are crucially important: (1) religious apprehension and religious relation; (2) incidence of freedom; and (3) incidence of knowledge. Differentiation is not open-ended; it has a terminus in the *tempus* or kingdom of Spirit or Holy Spirit that represents the perfection of religious relation and apprehension, realization of freedom, and knowledge. All of the modalities of differentiation, as well as the attainment of the goal of differentiation, are captured in the following passage from *Concordia* found important by Jürgen Moltmann:

> The mysteries of Holy Scriptures point us to three orders (states or conditions) of the world: to the first, in which we are under the Law; to the second, in which we are under grace; to the third, which we already imminently expect, and in which we shall be under a yet more abundant grace. . . The first condition is therefore that of perception, the second that of partially perfected wisdom, the third, the fullness of knowledge. The first condition is in the bondage of slaves, the second, in the bondage of sons, the third in liberty. The first in fear, the second in faith, the third in love. The first in the condition of slaves, the second of free men, the third of friends. The first of boys, the second of men, the third of the aged. The first stands in the light of stars, the second in the light of dawn, the third in the brightness of day. . . The first condition is related to the Father, the second to the Son, the third to the Holy Spirit.[71]

The passage is more or less self-explanatory, but perhaps it would be useful to underscore the following points. First, the age of kingdom of Holy Spirit (*Spiritus Sanctus*) represents the coming into being of perfected relationship with God, a relation that has the character of equality. For Joachim, as for Eckhart, fellowship has scriptural warrant, but, in contradistinction to Eckhart, Joachim understands fellowship in an *existential,* and not at all in ontological, manner. Unlike Eckhart then, Joachim does not belong to the deification tradition. The individual self is not divinized, and whatever else we are to think of 'the new people of God' of which Joachim speaks in *Concordia,* it cannot be taken as implying transmutation of the ontological state of a group. Secondly, the kingdom of Spirit represents the perfection of human autonomy. History in Joachim's view is nothing more nor less than the providential exegesis of freedom implicitly granted in Christ. Thirdly, the kingdom of Spirit represents not merely the perfection of faith but also knowledge. The *plenitudo intellectus* of which Joachim speaks in *Concordia* points not merely to a shift in the *level* of knowledge but also knowledge's comprehensiveness and power of integration.

The gnoseological element can be more precisely determined. Two remarks are in order. W. Schachten in her fine work, *Ordo Salutis,* notes how, though deeply indebted to Augustinianism Joachim undoubtedly is, he, nevertheless, breaks from it in refusing to countenance any unilateral distinction between *'fides'* and *'ratio'*, or, if you will, any distinction between *'fides'* and *'intellectus'*.[72] There is then in Joachim none of Luther's Augustinian sense of the irreconcilable conflict between faith and knowledge, and thus it would make sense that in interaction with the Joachimite tradition Lutheranism would temper, if not annul, the difference. The second point is independent of Schachten. It could be argued that the reason why the Augustinian division between faith and philosophy collapses in Joachim is that ultimately both are dependent upon revelation. Joachim's thought is apocalyptic in the obvious sense that it is committed to the imminent end of history. But Joachim's thought is apocalypse-bound, not merely in the weak sense that process and end of history can be, and are, exegeted through an *application* of the symbols of *Revelation,* but in the strong sense that all disclosure whatsoever has the form of revelation. Revelation now is no longer identifiable with the historical event of Christ or even with revelations that occurred in apostolic times, yet it is still scripturally bound in that vision or revelation is a function of a specific kind of hermeneutic (i.e., anagogic-futural) of scripture,[73] and insofar as Christ is the pattern and promise of fellowship with God and authentically free existence. Revelation, or *apokalypsis* in the Greek sense, is, at once, the sign of the new age and testimony that within the age of Spirit disclosure is fully transparent, thereby undercutting the necessity of the distinction between faith and knowledge.

The revolutionary implications of Joachim's trinitarian *Heilsgeschichte* scheme are noted and critiqued by Aquinas. Central to Aquinas's attack on the Joachimite periodization in *Summa Theologica (S Th* I, Q 106, art. 4) is both a particular view of the christocentric basis of Christianity and a particular understanding of the *operationes ad extra* of the Trinity. The gospel of Christ, he argues, is the gospel of the kingdom and is not transvalued by another gospel (i.e., the so-called eternal gospel). Moreover, the *parousia* is not an event in the future; the parousia was given as soon as Christ was glorified in the resurrection.[74] Aquinas's nonapocalyptic cast of thought receives its ultimate expression in the insistence that existence in history is structured in a fully determinate and exhaustive way by the Old and the New Law. Aquinas shows clearly that he understands the third age or kingdom of Spirit to be Joachim's historico-temporal reduction of the eschatological state by arguing that the eschatological state points in a vertical rather than horizontal direction, that is, it belongs not to a period of history but to heaven.[75] It might be said in passing that Aquinas's anxiety here seems to bear a family resemblance, at least, to an anxiety expressed by the orthodox defenders of Christianity of Hegel's own day with respect to his rendition of the eschatological state.

As is evident from the presence of two patterns in his texts, Joachim does not intend the radically heterodox shift ascribed to him. Under the lens of the dyadic pattern, Christ is both the beginning and end of all history. Even in the articulation of the alpha pattern, Christ must be regarded as the *objective condition* of the third age where the dispensation of the gospel is fully and perfectly appropriated.[76] What is surpassed, it might be said, is not Christ but rather deficiencies of religious relation that are not in conformity with the kerygma and that require the explication of history for their removal. Indeed, it can be argued that the perception that the age of Spirit does not, and cannot, exclude a christological backdrop greatly aids the liaison of Joachimite and Lutheran pneumaticism, this liaison, in turn, facilitating a Lutheran self-perception in which the eschatological view of history is not regarded as foreign but essential to its definition. It remains to be seen to what extent this hypothesis helps account for a particular inflection in the Lutheranism Hegel offers as the apogee of Christianity and religion in general.

If in *S Th* I, Q 104, art. 4 Aquinas's main concern is the preservation of the christocentric basis of Christianity, his correction of what he sees as a deficient view of the *opertiones ad extra* of the Trinity plays a supporting role. Aquinas is a clear witness that trinitarian periodization in Joachim provides no warrant for the claim that ultimately what is afoot in Joachim is a thoroughgoing historicization of the Trinity. On the evidence of *S Th* I, Q 39, art. 1, it is clear that Aquinas recognizes the presence of the Trinity *in se* in Joachim's thought, this in no way being reducible to the *operationes ad extra* in creation and history. Formally, Joachim like Aquinas remains within the parameter of the Immanent Trinity/Economic Trinity distinction,[77] though no agreement exists as to the relation between the two trinitarian modalities or the morphology of the Trinity *in se.* And though Aquinas's thought is caricatured when it is severed altogether from the scheme of salvation history and the narrative working out of God's divine plan, it is certainly the case that the relation between the divine *in se* and the divine in its operations is much more intimate in Joachim. From a Joachimite perspective the condition of intimacy rests upon the morphological structure of the Trinity. For a morphology of Trinity that is essentially an equal distribution of personal energy and power could be conceived as crucially more *open* to time and history than a Trinity whose *una essentia* defines the basis in which the persons participate.[78]

Trinitarian periodization and an eschatological view of history are inextricably intertwined in the thought and symbolism of Joachim. Eschatological thrust was clearly evident in the passage from *Concordia* cited above. Eschatological thrust is also evident, though in a slightly different manner, in *Expositio in Apocalypsim* where through interpretation of *Revelation* Joachim suggests a correlation between the eschatological aspect of the *tempus* of spirit and the seventh period of the Augustinian scheme of salvation history.[79] And just as Augustine perceives himself at the end of the sixth period and at the dawn of the seventh, Joachim sees himself at the close of the second trinitarian *tempus* and intuiting the stirrings of the third. The eschatological reign of the Spirit inaugurates 'the eternal gospel'. In *Concordia* the inauguration is connected with the coming into existence of the new people of God. This new state of existence and community will not be such as to eschew differentiated functions, but the emergent community is as a whole pervaded by the presence of the Spirit. Indeed, as Bernard McGinn suggests, the new people of God, which in a certain sense points to a transvaluation of the old order and old church hierarchy, more positively points to the authentic Church. In fact, the community of the new people of God might be regarded as Joachim's translation of the classical idea of the Church as the mystical body of Christ announced in Ephesians 4.13.[80] As observed before, trinitarian periodization certainly puts the christological basis of the *tempus* of Spirit under pressure. *Mutatis mutandis* with Joachim's presentation of the mystical body. This symbol tends to suggest a community of pneumatic fellowship that *in some respects* transcends its christological basis. Yet, despite the suggestion of an age free from the moorings of Christ, and a mystical body equally independent, Christ, for Joachim, is, nevertheless, the objective basis of both.

The basic Augustinianism of Joachim is well documented.[81] We have just commented on Joachim's conservative attempt at correlating his trinitarian model of history with the sevenfold model of Augustine. This is not to say, however, that there are not real Joachimite innovations. For instance, whereas Augustine does, indeed, see human being as the image of the Trinity, it is to Joachim that is owed the discovery of the idea that the Trinity is the archetype of historical process where humanity comes to perfect itself. Moreover, a crucial rupture occurs in the Joachimite model of salvation history that renders it particularly congenial to post-Reformation assimilation. While the narrative span of both salvation history schemes is similarly global, stretching from creation to eschaton, it is clear that Joachim breaks with the Augustinian two-tier construal in which sacred history only covers a drama that has a vertical reference. The rest of history—institutional, political, cultural—is excluded, an exclusion which, in a sense, encourages creation of modern secular history. By contrast, Joachim suggests an inclusive salvation history scheme that refuses the Augustinian dichotomy and, in principle, recognizes all movement in history as relevant. But this means less a dilution of the sacred than the rehabilitation of the profane—an idea that again seemed destined to find a home in an ideational environment that refused to accept the dismissal of the non-sacramental modes of private and public life and represented a *Heilsgeschichte* alternative in modernity to secular history.[82]

Joachimite Constellation in Hegelian Pneumatology. Though there is undoubtedly an abstract and mechanical aspect to such a rehearsal, it might be useful to list the constellation of elements constituting the Joachimite core recapitulated in Hegelian ontotheology. At a minimum there are seven such elements: (1) time and history are vehicles of the exegesis of knowledge, freedom, and religious relation where the subject of differentiation is more the community than the individual; (2) the conviction that the eschaton and the kingdom of God is at hand; *(3) the assertion that the Trinity is both open to and involved in the historical process; (4) the association of the eschaton with the Spirit or Holy Spirit; (5) the dismantling of the sacred-profane history distinction; (6) despite the stress introduced by massive pneumatic emphasis the positing of Christ as the objective condition of the kingdom of God; and (7) the centrality of the role played by revelation in the sense of revelation of secrets granted in *Endzeit*.

All of these features are present in some way in the Hegelian elaboration of *Gemeinde*, the most complete version of which is presented in *LPR 3*. All of these features with the exception of (3) are there unproblematically recollected, a recollection we shall shortly see operative also in *LPH*. The asterisk on (3) points to the fact that though Joachim and Hegel posit an interface between Trinity and history, there exists a fundamental difference in their perception. Since it will be discovered that Hegel's split with Joachim here is a function of an allegiance to a different kind of narrative envisagement, the description of the nature of the difference will not be attempted here but will be postponed until chapter 6 where some of the basic features of this narrative commitment will be thematized.

Exact mapping between Hegel's elaboration of the Christian community in *LPR 3* and Joachim's trinity of Kingdoms is not to be found. The elaboration of *Gemeinde* excludes that sphere (or those spheres) of religious relation that antedate Christianity. As will be argued shortly, the triadic differentiation of Christianity represents a Lutheran application of the Joachimite scheme, with Lutheranism posited explicitly as the eschatological realization of the historical dynamics of Christianity. Hegelian elaboration of religion as a whole (*LPR 2-LPR 3*) brings Hegel at once closer and further from Joachim: closer, in that Hegel posits modalities of religious relation prior to Christianity, of which Christianity is in some respect the issue; further, in that the trinitarian scheme becomes inapplicable when one religion, i.e., Christianity, constitutes the kingdom of both Son and Spirit, with all other religions more or less unsuitably being assimilated to the Father.[83] Nevertheless, the insertion of the development of Christianity within the broader development of religion as a whole tends to introduce greater commensurability of narrative span. The inscription of the developmental dynamics within the broader narrative of the development of humanity, which in *LPR 3* spans from creation to eschaton, also aids narrative commensurability even if trinitarian periodization must be ruled out.

This is not to say, however, that no direct echo of the Joachimite scheme can be found in Hegelian texts. The typological mode of discourse notwithstanding, Hegel's presentation in the chapter on Unhappy Consciousness in *PS* of three kinds of religious relation suggests Joachim's *historical* schema. The Hegelian schema runs as follows: (A) The most deficient mode of experiencing and construing the relation between the unchangeable (*das Unwandelbare*) and the changeable (*das Wandelbare*) is that of opposition, the unchangeable being everything, the changeable nothing. Experienced thus, the relation with the transcendent beyond (*Jenseits*) is oppressive and destroys the integrity of the finite (*GL2:*167). (B) In a still deficient mode of construal and experience, having assumed the form of individuality the unchangeable relates to the changeable again as a beyond and in the mode of opposition. The beyond this time, however, is historical in character, and the opposition is a horizontal (*GL2:*168).[84] (C) Only in a third modality of religious relation beyond the religion of the transcendent and historical beyond is the opposition between the unchangeable and changeable implicitly overcome. Reconciliation, however, demands development and pneumatic appropriation. In and through appropriation, reconciliation is explicated, and the sphere of the changeable elevated. The affective registering of this elevation which supposes overcoming of opposition and alienation is joy (*die Freude*). Read against the background of his early theological texts, Hegel's typological schematization translates into the series: Judaism as a world-denying religion offering obedience to a God who, if he is a father, is also a tyrant; Christianity that misplaces religious authority by attempting to find legitimation of the incarnation of the Son in mere historical fact; and Christianity in its pneumatic aspect where religious responsibility as well as authority are centered in the appropriative activity of the community. Not only, therefore, does Hegel's schematization in *PS* tend to recall the Joachimite developmental movement from Father to Spirit through Son by unfolding a pattern of relation between the human and the divine that connotes increasing validation of the finite, like Joachim he tends to connect increasing validation of the finite with vertical shifts in the incidence of freedom.

Qualification, perhaps, having dulled somewhat the real presence of a Joachimite constellation of ideas in Hegel, let us turn to *LPH* which surely displays most, if not all, of the features of the Joachimite constellation. History, as Hegel makes clear in his famous *Introduction,* implies the differentiation of freedom (*Freiheit*) over time. At the same time history is the differentiation of self-consciousness (*Selbstbewusstein*), for, as Hegel points out, self-consciousness and freedom are intrinsically connected. While the purview of *LPH* is by no means identical to that of religious differentiation over time, historical differentiation as a whole is interpreted through the lens of Christianity. Christianity is the only candidate as interpretant, since, in Christianity, God has revealed himself for the first time. If the self-revelation of God does not appear a sufficient lens with which to interpret history, it should be remembered that the disclosure of the infinite in finite human spirit is at the same time a disclosure of the true nature of finite spirit and its positive relationship to the infinite divine. Hegel's real interest in *LPH* is the differentiation of human spirit throughout history. But it is Christianity, or the incarnation in particular, that provides history with a meaning, for the incarnation reveals the truth of humanity. The incarnation also provides the objective condition for the realization of true humanity, fully defined human spirit. It does not itself, however, represent the realization that is nothing less than the coming into being of the Kingdom of God. The human dimension of the Kingdom of God is underscored in the *Introduction:*

> One may have all sorts of ideas about the Kingdom of God; but it is always a realm of Spirit to be realized and brought about in men. (E 20)[85]

The human dimension, however, is not the dimension of 'the all too human'. Earlier in the chapter we offered an illustration from *LPH* of Hegel's use of the Pauline cipher 'sons of God' (E 333, *GLII*:427). The human dimension is at the same time the divine. In explicating the son of God theme, Hegel accents human being's gnoseological capability, which is the correlative of the self-revelation of the divine. The suggestion of such capability clearly indicates human commensurability with the divine, as does freedom, which is the other aspect of correlation. Both knowledge and freedom because realizable possibilities only in the self-revelation of the divine focused in the incarnation.

In addition to its complex human-divine structure, the Kingdom of God, defined by Hegel as a realm of Spirit, is both communitarian and eschatological. The Kingdom of God does not consist in a solipsistic atom or congerie of such atoms. The Kingdom of God, for Hegel, is an organic unity or totality. Moreover, Hegel agrees with Joachim rather than Aquinas in thinking that the Kingdom is not contemporaneous with Christ. With reference to the christological narrative of incarnation, passion, death, and resurrection, the Kingdom is futural and requires the explication of history as the pedagogy of spirit and vehicle of appropriation. The need for appropriation as well as its promise is compacted in the symbol of pentecost. Giving no indication that the view might be controversial within as without Lutheranism, Hegel announces Lutheran Protestantism as the realization of the pentecostal experience. Thus defined, pneumatic Lutheranism invites explication and, in a manner of speaking, the redemption of its validity claims in Hegelian philosophy.

A few additional words ought to be said about Hegel's view of the pedagogy of freedom and the narrative background of this pedagogy. In his discussion of the emergence of Christianity in the main text (part 3, sect. 3, chap. 2), Hegel speaks of Christianity as introducing for the first time in history 'the principle of absolute freedom in God'. This implies that freedom in Christianity is not merely superior to the freedom attainable in other religions and other cultures on the model of more or less but that it is *qualitatively* distinct and unsurpassable. Hegel's bon mot therefore in the *Introduction* to the effect that in the Orient *one* was free, in the Graeco-Roman world *some* were free, while in Christianity *all* are free (E 23) is thoroughly misleading to the extent to which it suggests a *quantitative* model of more or less. Hegel shows himself aware of the possibilities of misinterpretation by immediately having recourse to qualification. Freedom in the Orient, he argues, is not in any event genuine freedom (i.e., freedom-as-self-determination) (E 24). In the *Introduction* the presence of freedom in the Graeco-

Roman world is not questioned, but the main body of the text provides evidence enough that freedom does not achieve fully valid determination in that culture. That its mode of freedom is qualitatively distinct from and inferior to that realized in Christianity does not mean that it is not a *qualitative approximation*. Hegel certainly permits this. Indeed, history as a whole is a differentiation of freedom, knowledge, and relation to the divine in which *qualitatively* distinct steps can be distinguished. Of central moment is the differentiation of Christianity or Christian culture over time, but the inchoate stirrings of freedom, knowledge, and fully adequate divine-human relation predate Christianity and must be included in the span covered by Hegelian history. Thus the differentiation of Christianity is a phase of a larger narrative of differentiation. The span covered by Hegel in his periodization does not match in any exact way that of Joachim. Indeed, it is only in some respect triadic.[86] Moreover, it does not extend beyond classic cultures or civilizations in a way the Joachimite schema does which commences with Adam.

In any event, whatever the lack of match here, it seems clear that Hegel, like Joachim, dismantles the *historia sacra/historia profana* distinction. Hegel does so by appealing to the theologoumenon of *Providence (Vorsehung)*[87] that provides a rationale for the teleological character of history. The eschaton in Hegel is an intrahistorical gestation. If everything is under providential sway, then everything, for Hegel, is sacred or holy. This means, among other things, that no essential separation exists between the religious and secular spheres. This insight, Hegel believes, essentially belongs to the self-understanding of Lutheran Protestantism. Lutheran Protestantism sanctions no divorce between cultic practice and the secular activity of the State. It is axiomatic in *LPH* that the State has as much right to be identified with the Kingdom of God as the sphere of Church Christianity. The same elevation beyond the finite is constitutive of both, and thus both can be regarded as aspects of the spiritual community or even aspects of the mystical body. The mystical body is a body of spirit, but a body which has its objective foundation in Christ.

It is time to offer a summary of Joachimite elements in *LPH*. History is a process of differentiation that occurs simultaneously along three analytically separable axes, i.e., freedom, knowledge, and divine-human relation. History has an eschatological terminus that is at hand, and this terminus represents the realization of the dynamics of history, the parousia of the Holy Spirit, the guarantee and promise of which is provided by the pentecost experience. If history has its eschatological terminus in Lutheran Protestantism and its secular extension, this implies the coming into being of the *integrative holy.* In another respect the providential structuring of history constitutes all history as *historia sacra.* The community issuant upon historical differentiation is the realization of the Kingdom of God wherein human being has definitively realized the state of divine sonship. The Kingdom of God constitutes the mystical body, a body of selves who have elevated themselves to the infinite. The mystical body is, of course, in the most general sense the mystical body of Spirit as the self-developing, narrative divine. In a more narrow sense, a sense normed by the Christian *Vorstellung* of Trinity, the mystical body is, in the first instance, the mystical body of Holy Spirit, since *subjectively* Christ must be transcended. In the second instance, the mystical body is the mystical body of Christ, since Christ cannot be *objectively* surpassed. A crucial difference exists, however, between the Hegelian and Joachimite reading of religious relation and the mystical body, a difference that, in part, at last, may be ascribable to the presence in Hegel of an element that has been provisionally defined in a taxonomic fashion as Eckhartian. In Hegel the manner of relation is at least as much ontological as existential. This view is not specific to *LPH;* it is consistently maintained throughout all of Hegel's work.

Joachimite Inflection of Lutheranism: Eschatological Weave. The Lutheranism reprised by Hegel, according to Henri de Lubac, hardly can be classed as orthodox. As *La postérité* has it, what is reprised is a mythical Luther that has undergone something of a Joachimite contamination between the sixteenth and early nineteenth centuries.[88] Given the strong evidence of Joachimite themes in Hegelian texts, de Lubac's thesis, supported by a complex, somewhat sketchy, but nevertheless cogent historical argument, has much to recommend it. The thesis of inflection advocated here proposed presupposes the general lines of de Lubac's argument, with an important modification. The thesis of inflection is in agreement with de Lubac's contamination thesis in supposing (1) that Hegel presupposes a Lutheranism that is a complex forged from the blending of Lutheran Christianity and Joachimite ideas and that, in this blending, Lutheranism undergoes a mutation, and (2) that Hegel, presuming such a complex, thinks it faithful to the original inspiration of the Reformation. The thesis of inflection differs from de Lubac's thesis of contamination, however, in taking account of the conditions *within* Lutheranism that make possible significant departure from the position of the historical Luther and that of Lutheran orthodoxy. A brief historico-conceptual account of the dynamics of mutation will now be proposed.

It belongs to the self-interpretation of Lutheran Christianity as a whole that the Reformation ushers in a new unsurpassable age. Eschatological self-appraisal is endemic and tends to issue in a triadic schematization of the history of Christianity, whose trajectory moves from original Christianity qualified by spirit, through Catholic Christianity determined by structure, institution, and power politics, to terminal Christianity, once again qualified by spirit. Though generic eschatological self-appraisal in the sixteenth century found its most blatant expression in the radical Reformation,[89] that is not to say, as Robin Barnes has pointed out, that that eschatological self-interpretation did not carry on well into the seventeenth century in Lutheran quarters that could hardly be counted as fringe.[90] Throughout, of course, the figure of Joachim was evoked, though Joachim evocation was no guarantee that Joachim's work was known in great detail. Thoroughgoing eschatological reading of the Reformation is then the *proximate* condition for the Joachimite transfiguration of Lutheranism. Pace Asendorf,[91] no such thoroughgoing eschatologization occurs in Luther himself. In quite general terms it can be said of Luther's writings that they exhibit a tension between the eschatological motif (which at a limit suggests a surplus of pneumatic potency of final over original Christianity) and the motif of repristination, i.e., the motif of reassimilating and recorresponding belated Christianity to its original fresh and potent condition. Still, whatever the dominance-recessive relation between these two tendencies in the thought of Luther himself, Luther rightly can be seen to represent the *ultimate* condition of Joachimite transformation. He is the ultimate condition in the weak sense that, despite the elevation of the repristinative motif in Lutheran orthodoxy, the eschatological element in Luther could not be fully excised. And Luther is the condition in the strong sense if the eschatological thrust is taken as the dominant, as many scholars have recommended it should. The Joachimite tendency in Lutheran thought, while under serious constraint because of orthodox Lutheran attack, was kept alive in the seventeenth century by Jacob Boehme among others and in the eighteenth century continued to have currency in Pietism, which was the matrix and conduit of a complex weave of different discourses marginalized by School Theology. In Bengel and Oetinger, the eschatological dimension of Lutheranism once again found powerful voices.

In *LPR 3* Hegel places himself within the above-mentioned eighteenth-century field of discourse that insists on the eschatological definition of Lutheran Christianity and reactivates the original Reformation understanding of Protestantism's eschatological role. Christianity is a triadic elaboration, beginning with the pentecostal experience, proceeding through institutional Christianity (i.e., Catholicism), and ending with Lutheran Christianity. In continuity with the eschatologized Lutheranism, the adopted model bears, at once, a tensional relation to Luther's own understanding of the triadic scheme and is clearly at odds with the view of Lutheran orthodoxy. True, in one sense, Hegel, after Luther, appears to assert some kind of correspondence between the pneumatism of origin and pneumatism of end, with Catholicism the more or less spiritual trough intervallied between. And in Hegel's contrast of Catholicism and Lutheranism are echoes of Luther's own polemics against Catholicism as a religion of externality. Nevertheless, the Hegelian rendering of Christianity's trajectory suggests a merely formal correspondence between end and beginning, and Hegel nowhere suggests, as Luther does, that original Christianity represents the unsurpassable instance of Christianity in addition to providing its basic *eidos*. For Hegel, original Christianity provides the eidos; it does not represent the supreme instance. Though in Hegel, as in Bengel and Oetinger, not every trace of repristination can be effaced, his depiction of Christianity reprises and validates a thoroughly eschatologically twisted species of Lutheranism, first rendered with clarity in the radical Reformation, continuing in Boehme, and finding expression again in significant currents of eighteenth-century Pietism.

When Hegel speaks in *LPR 3* of the development of Christianity occurring simultaneously along the three merely analytically separable axes, he is providing evidence of the kind of acute Joachimite surplus that is hardly matched by Bengel and Oetinger in their more eschatological moments. Hegelian reprise of this conspicuously Joachimized Lutheranism specifies his swerve from the position of the historical Luther and that of Lutheran orthodoxy. From an orthodox perspective, Joachimized Lutheranism represents a species of a theology of glory that mistakenly thinks of time and historical development as having something like soteriological capacity. Moreover, this variety of religion is flawed in each of its three aspects: relation between the divine and the human is constitutionally asymmetrical, with the possibility of relation being exclusively dependent on the justification imputed to sinful human being by Christ, and filial obedience being the normative form of relation; freedom in human history not only does not grow but is a chimera that leads astray; and knowledge in the present sinful dispensation is constitutionally questionable, since, unlike faith, it tends toward self-centered pride and boasting. Though each of these more specific rejections are worth elaborating in some detail, I will confine further explication to Lutheran orthodoxy's rejection of knowledge and by implication any emphasis within the boundaries of Lutheran confession on the possibility of knowledge and its basic value.

The eschatological or Joachimite inflection of Lutheranism is marked by its legitimation of knowledge. Luther himself affirms a more or less absolute disjunction between faith and knowledge, and this is codified within the Lutheran orthodox tradition. Yet it is important to point out that Luther is not followed all the way by the Spiritual Reformers or the radical wing of the Reformation. Indeed, as has been eloquently demonstrated by Robin Barnes, it is part of the sixteenth-century dynamic of Lutheranism that such a disjunction undergoes blurring.[92] The stretching of Lutheranism turns to overstretching, and, in a figure such as Jacob Boehme (seventeenth century), while faith is opposed in orthodox fashion to worldly wisdom, no real distinction between faith and transworldly knowledge remains. In fact, as we shall shortly see, Boehme accepts the Joachimite view of their coincidence in the eschatological age thoroughly qualified by spirit. Joachim himself announces no fundamental distinction, appearing to regard the development of faith and knowledge as collateral and in the eschaton the *plenitudo intellectus* to be no different than the perfection of faith. The category in Joachim that finally undermines distinction is the category of revelation, revelation *qua* apocalypse, i.e., eschatological disclosure of the secrets of history and the becoming of the *corpus mysticum*. That Hegel's position not merely authorizes the Joachimite rather than the specifically Lutheran view of the relation between faith and knowledge, but also tends to recapitulate the Joachimite condition of their indistinction, becomes clear through a brief contrast of the Lutheran and Joachimite categories of revelation.

The Lutheran category of revelation may get expressed in a variety of ways in Luther's works, yet it can be said that, centrally, revelation denotes disclosure through scripture of the nature of Christ as embodied in the scriptural narrative of incarnation, passion, death, and resurrection. Luther's view is every bit as soteriological as Joachim's, yet for him revelation is once and for all, or *was* once and for all, though at the same time enduringly pertinent. For Joachim, by contrast, the content of revelation is primarily the historical process that has its pivot in Christ but where the accent is shifted onto the coming of the kingdom characterized by spirit. Moreover, for Joachim, revelation is (was) not once and for all, but continuous, progressive, and eschatologically perfect and universal—features that are stunningly replicated in the Hegelian account. As chapter 4 brought provisionally to attention, it is undeniably the case that Hegel endorses the Lutheran view of revelation in some measure. Luther's *theologia crucis* and christological narrative are too important for him not to do so, and this commitment is lexically registered in Hegel's designation of Christianity as *die geoffenbarte Religion.* It appears that Hegel wants to assert a once/once-only, yet in his description of *Revealed Religion* he attributes to revelation characteristics that more properly belong to the Joachimite complex and thus tends to displace not merely the scriptural but also the christological center. Christ does not provide the point of view from which everything is seen. The vantage point is rather the realization of the kingdom as disclosed in revelation *qua* apocalypse. The christological narrative of Luther remains an important content disclosed. But the mode of disclosure is not scriptural in the full sense, and the direction of interpretation is from the future-present rather than the past.

Boehmian Determinant: Boehmian Inflection

Of the three varieties of mysticism claimed here to determine the Hegelian rendition of the Christian theologoumenon of Holy Spirit or *corpus mysticum,* the case for the widest and most direct acquaintance is strongest in the case of Jacob Boehme. Moreover, our own analysis of Hegel up to this point has indicated that, with regard to Hegelian rendition of crucial Christian theologoumena, Boehme plays essentially two roles: the role of illuminating precedent when the ontotheological field is taken in its widest possible (i.e., Western) span, and arguably the proximate taxon when the ontotheological field narrows to that of Protestant theological investigation. Now, while this fact, perhaps, legitimates the antecedent presumption that Boehmian theosophy has also an important taxonomic role to play regarding the theologoumenon of Holy Spirit, needless to say, it does not logically imply its taxonomic superiority over Joachimism or even Eckhartianism. Any claim to taxonomic superiority must be demonstrated. And it is important to point out that two difficulties attend any such demonstration in the context of this chapter. The first is methodological; the second is substantive. Methodologically,

Boehme is put at a disadvantage by the decision in this chapter to prescind from taking into account the relation of the notions of Holy Spirit and mystical body to encompassing ontotheological narratives that are spoken of in the language of kingdom. Only when this is taken into account, as it shall be in chapter 6, can an adequate judgment be rendered as to taxonomic superiority. The second point is substantive. As proved in the vitriolic impeachments of his orthodoxy in the seventeenth century, Boehme is not only viewed as purveying theosophical renditions of Christian theologoumena that do not correspond to the canonic symbols, he is also seen as a conduit of radical eschatological ideas of a Joachimite stripe now found unacceptable and of a mystical theology tradition whose voice is not easily assimilated to a confession tradition.[93] This makes his situation vis-à-vis the other two mystical determinations discussed fairly complicated, for if, on the one hand, he represents a distinct strand of mystical discourse, on the other, he represents a weave of discourse encompassing and modifying the other two.

What I propose to do in concluding my interpretive account of Hegelian swerve from the mainline Christian pneumatology, Lutheran pneumatology in particular, is to first discuss those elements of the Hegelian account of Holy Spirit and mystical body that can be intelligibly argued to find their precedent in Boehme and, then, proceed to brief examination of some specifics of the Boehmian inflection of Lutheranism that made it a religious option for some religious thinkers in the eighteenth century and, if we are correct, for at least one in the nineteenth.[94] With respect to the first-mentioned task, there are at least six elements of Boehmian reflection that might be thought to be reprised in Hegel. These elements fall naturally into two groups. The first consists of Boehme's reflection on rebirth, his views on biblical hermeneutics, the nature of doctrine, the nature of the sacraments, eucharist in particular. The second has to do with Boehme's theology of history and image and the degree to which he can be said to be a conduit for both Joachimite and Eckhartian ideas and symbols. In discussing this second group, the issue of taxonomic superiority-inferiority suggests itself naturally, and the issue will be treated, albeit in the preliminary fashion that is dictated by the methodological decision we mentioned above.

Boehmian Constellation in Hegelian Pneumatology. In *LPR 3* we saw that in his account of Holy Spirit, specifically his account of the developmental dynamics of mystical community, Hegel makes an effort at something like ecclesial acceptability by eschewing neither sacrament nor doctrine. Though his pneumatism is obvious, it seems that he wishes to expand the horizon and interpretation of church, rather than insinuate either a sectarian alternative or a global substitute.[95] Good intentions notwithstanding, what Hegel indicates in his understanding of biblical hermeneutics, the nature of doctrine and sacrament and the significant role he accords rebirth serves to place him in a different tradition than that of Lutheran orthodoxy. Though it is undoubtedly the case that, at first acquaintance, the positions and emphases Hegel adopts suggest nothing more specific than a siding with the general Pietistic critique of orthodoxy, it is the case that all of the Hegelian positions and emphases can be found in Boehme and that Hegel's proposal recapitulates the Boehmian attempt at reconciling pneumatic and doctrinal exigencies.

As is the case in Hegel, Boehme consistently takes a negative attitude to the orthodox insistence on the primacy of the literal sense. In *Aurora,* which was read by Hegel, and in his other texts, Boehme inveighs against the more or less absolute hegemony of the literal sense and argues that there are good biblical grounds to pursue mystical or anagogic exegesis, not least of which he takes to be an injunction in Paul to search into the deep things of God. Boehme's attitude towards the sacraments, the eucharist in particular, arguably illuminates the criticism implied in Hegel's resolute insistence on the necessity of appropriative faith that marked his discussion in *LPR 3*. While officially supportive of the Lutheran view, Boehme takes issue with the dominant emphasis in interpretation that effectively reintroduces the *ex opere operato* Catholic view that Lutheranism is supposed to have surpassed. As Boehme puts it trenchantly at one point: "As the mouth is, so also is the food belonging to the mouth."[96] And rebirth is a central theme in Boehme and is to a considerable extent at the base of his pneumatic critique of the dominant Lutheran emphases in biblical interpretation and understanding of the sacraments. Moreover, though Boehme is anxious not to interpret rebirth in such a way that it is set loose from the theological jurisdiction of justification,[97] there are certainly times when rebirth suggests a context of sanctification that has liberated itself from the restrictive *ordo salutis* of confessional Lutheranism as indicated especially in the semi-Pelagian tone of much of Boehme's discourse.[98] Boehmian followers in the eighteenth century will by no means show the same scruple. But, perhaps, it is the salient Boehmian tendency—a tendency that distinguishes him from most Pietists—to balance the subjective dimension of faith (*fides qua creditur*) by an objective dimension (*fides quae creditur*) that most clearly announces Boehme's claims to precursorship. While Hegel's insistence in *LPR 3* on the necessity of doctrine might be explained by suggesting that he is attempting to balance his overall Pietistic tendency with a concession to Lutheran orthodoxy, there are some limitations with this explanation. Hegel's argument is for the general necessity of doctrine; he does not argue for the necessity of the doctrines of the normative Christian tradition; he does not argue in particular for the necessity and normativity of Lutheran doctrine as such. Hegel seems to be arguing at once for a space of theological or doctrinal formulation—a space he himself is articulating in *LPR 3*—and suggesting heterodox alternatives. Something similar is going on in Boehme, who we have argued supplies the proximate precedent for some of Hegel's material theological revisions. In Boehme's self-understanding, he is offering a nondoctrinal Lutheranism; in fact, however, his view has itself an objective, or *fides quae creditur,* dimension that is absent from the Pietistic tradition of the seventeenth century. The freedom he displays from normative Lutheran symbols seems to be the ground, not for a nondogmatic, but rather a counter dogmatic enterprise.

We turn now to the second group of Boehmian ideas that provides reasonable grounds for the recapitulation claim, i.e., his theology of history and image. As mentioned earlier, it is here that the taxonomic issue suggests itself and gets complicated, for it is here that the role of Boehme as a mediator and courier of the mystical strains of his taxonomic competitors is most in evidence. The theology of history rendered in *Aurora* and other texts is eschatological through and through. Even if Boehme does not provide the eschatological age with the technical title of Spirit, after the manner of Joachim, much in his account is of Joachimite vintage. Something more than generic recall, however, is afoot; there are a number of quite specific borrowings. Though his periodization is septenarian after the Augustinian model, he does not fail to recall Joachim's 'natural triads' that suggest the trinitarian schema of Joachim.[99] Two important symbols, i.e., aurora and lily, name the third term of specific triads in Joachim and play an important role in Boehme's first text. The former, which provides the title for Boehme's literary debut, is a symbol of apocalyptic breakthrough, whereas the latter is more nearly the name for the eschatological age as a whole. Endtime is the time of the lily (*Aurora,* chap. 12). Though Hegelian texts such as *LPR* and *LPH* do not explicitly recall either these or other symbols, such as that of Enoch, that belong to the Boehmian eschatological framework, there is, nonetheless, a good measure of reprise. It hardly needs to be said that Hegelian reprise of Boehme in his theology of history is, at the same time, the reprise of the Joachimite tradition he is mediating. In any event, with this caveat, it can be said that three Boehmian emphases are repeated in Hegel's texts. (1) The shape of history, including its teleological or providential drift, becomes transparent from the standpoint of a revelation or illumination fully granted only in endtime. (2) The pneumatic character of eschatological revelation effectively dismantles, without and within Lutheranism, the distinction between faith and knowledge. (3) Christ is still regarded as the objective condition of the pneumatic vision of the eschaton. It is, perhaps, not unfair to say that, with regard to the theology of history, Boehme is more important as a courier of Joachimite eschatology than as offering a unique contribution of his own. Indeed, wherever Boehme actually departs from Joachim, he does so to his taxonomic disadvantage. For instance, following the examples of Augustine and Luther, Boehme has a two-tiered view of the unfolding of salvation. If time is the milieu of the exposé of the drama of salvation, it contributes nothing. Hegel, as we have pointed out already, assumes with Joachim that time and history can carry a heavier soteriological burden, and, in this, Hegel has been followed by a host of twentieth-century philosophers and theologians.[100]

Enough has been said about Hegel's reprise of Boehmian theology of history. It is time now to say a word about Hegelian reprise of an idea whose natural context is that of mystical theology but in Boehme's case, as indeed in Hegel's, can be only artificially segregated from a theology of history. Three important aspects of Boehme's theology of image find expression in Hegel's texts: its narrative quality, the movement of actualization as a process of divinization, and the image's communitarian nature.[101] One might think of this view of image setting the ideological terms for Herder and *Bildungsroman,* as one might also note its similarity to the Alexandrian model of progression in Pietism that some Hegelian scholars wish to suggest set the terms for Hegel's own discourse. The point I wish to emphasize here, however, is a slightly different one. The Boehmian articulation of image possesses distinct taxonomic advantages over the theology of image of Eckhart, notwithstanding Baader's pious misreading and his own recall of the medieval mystic in his use of the language of spark. The image theology of the historical Eckhart is not especially narrative in orientation; neither is it particularly communitarian. Yet for all his taxonomic disadvantage here, Eckhart does surpass Boehme in at least one respect. If Boehme thinks a transcendent form of knowledge possible, he does not, like Eckhart, presume that this in itself amounts to salvation and, in effect, a substitute for the eschatological state as envisioned by the Christian community from the earliest centuries. Hegel agrees with Eckhart.

Boehmian Inflection of Lutheranism. From the vantage point of late eighteenth-century religious thought Boehme could be looked on as a significant, even representative, figure who had kept alive the pneumatic essence of Lutheranism that threatened to be forgotten in the dominance of Lutheran orthodoxy. He was a significant witness for many in the Pietist camp that Lutheranism avowed the ultimate authority of Spirit, not scripture, dogma, ritual, church institution, but also not the individual self as such. Within the context of pneumatic avowal, Boehme was distinguished by his insistence not only on the divinization but on the eschatological dimension of Lutheranism. The inflection of Lutheranism comes more from the resoluteness of the insistence than the sheer fact, for it has been cogently argued that Lutheran orthodoxy itself by no means represented a pure continuation of the message of the historical Luther, repressing, in fact, the noticeable divinization and eschatological tendencies in his thought. One can speak of Boehme's divinization view swerving and inflecting Lutheranism insofar as in Boehme the mystical union that Lutheran orthodoxy is prepared to speak of only on condition of its being normed by the theologoumenon of justification seems to be gaining a measure of autonomy. And one can speak of Boehme's eschatological view swerving or inflecting Lutheranism in that for him the post–Reformation period possesses a religious potential that surpasses the apostolic age. Boehme, therefore, provides for German religious thought a mode of Lutheranism which, if dense and rich, is out of tune with the scholastic tradition in Lutheranism and has a much more relaxed attitude to heterodoxy. But Boehme makes another critical contribution. He is, arguably, the figure who showed eighteenth-century religious thought how different strands of mystical discourse can be held together in a pneumatic brand of Lutheranism. As we have pointed to more than once, Boehme's complex weave of mystical discourse is able to unite Joachimite and Eckhartian discourse and add his own relatively unique theosophic discourse.[102] Moreover, in this complex weave the Joachimite and Eckhartian discourses are subtly but decisively modified: Joachim's *Heilsgeschichte* discourse is ontologized to the extent that the problem of existential relation between the divine and the human is seen as an aspect of the problem of the ontological relation and the ontological status of terms, the human in particular; and Eckhart's fairly static ontological view of image is historicized, which has the effect of making the Boehmian theology of image more dialectical than that found in Eckhart. This precedent-setting move is of crucial importance, for it signals that the question of the mystical impulse in German Idealism very well may not be a question of the search for a pure type but, if figures like Oetinger are anything to go by, a question of a highly complex, highly hybrid species.

6

THE THIRD NARRATIVE EPOCH: The Inclusive Trinity

Having outlined the complex Hegelian configuration of spiritual community, it is time to thematize the relation of spiritual community, or as Hegel sometimes suggests, Holy Spirit (*LPR 3* 1821 MS E 140–142, G 75–77), with *Spirit* as fully inclusive trinitarian articulation of divine subjectivity. Such thematization calls to our attention a range of issues that a considerable number of Hegelian scholars and critics have found important, e.g., (1) the issue of whether the Hegelian elaboration of spiritual community, as essentially constitutive of the third trinitarian epoch, represents an immanentization of the divine in a reductionist sense, or whether some measure of transcendence is preserved,[1] (2) the issue of what relation, if any, the "Immanent Trinity" bears to the third trinitarian epoch, for where commentators and critics do argue for a measure of transcendence, it is most often Hegelian commitment to the existence of a divine sphere that may be construed outside of any actual relation to the finite and nondivine (i.e., the "Immanent Trinity") that carries the bulk of the argumentative freight.[2] It is perhaps also the case that, in the context of thematizing the relation between Holy Spirit and Spirit, two other issues of a more general type, issues of some import for the characterization of Hegelian ontotheology as a whole, can be best examined. The first of these concerns the question of the existence and precise nature of apocalypse commitment in Hegel and is proximally motivated by the palpable presence of Joachimite and Boehmian ideas in Hegel's articulation of spiritual community and its genesis. The second and related issue concerns theodicy commitment in Hegel. Here the question is perhaps less the existence of such a commitment—this largely been agreed upon[3]—than the issue of the basic grammar of the theodicy type involved.

In this chapter, we will make ourselves responsible for all the above issues. To fulfill this intention a tripartite organization is proposed. Section 6.1 focuses in a general way on the relation between

Spirit and "Holy Spirit" and the crucial interpretive and theological issues involved therein. In addition, a more specific examination of the relation of the "Immanent Trinity" to the third trinitarian epoch as well as its relation to trinitarian elaboration as a whole is offered. An important result of this more specific examination, it will be contended, is that as the "Immanent Trinity" is understood by Hegel to initiate the narrative enactment of the divine, it also must be understood to close it, or, put in other words, the "Immanent Trinity" exists in two quite distinct narrative modalities. Sections 6.2 and 6.3 focus upon what might be called 'genre' questions, though genre is not intended here as a literary category. Section 6.2 is essentially an investigation into the genre of Hegelian apocalypse, given the confirmed presence of apocalypse commitment in Hegel's ontotheological elaboration, whereas section 6.3 attempts to define the genre of Hegelian theodicy. The latter attempt is motivated by the desire to offer as much specificity as possible when speaking of Hegelian theodicy, given the plurality of theodicy types in the ontotheological tradition.[4] Before we proceed, however, I should like to advise that this particular chapter with the possible exception of section 6.3 will be more textually thin perhaps than previous chapters.

Section 6.1 Holy Spirit—Spirit: Spirit—"Immanent Trinity"

As Louis Dupré has rightly argued, spiritual community, or Holy Spirit, is not identifiable in any empirical way with Spirit,[5] even if it is the case that Spirit to be Spirit, that is, to be fully rendered intensive and extensive subjectivity, requires an integrated plurality of members actually elevated, or in principle elevatable, into the nonfinite realm. Without such an integrated plurality, Spirit, in Hegel's view, is abstract and lifeless. In some obvious sense Hegel's narrative account of Spirit is organisimic, where an organism, for Hegel, is nothing more nor less than a self-differentiating, self-realizing totality. But this still leaves much room for ambiguity. Is totality predictable of Holy Spirit or Spirit as such? However apparently innocent the framing of the question, it is deceiving to the degree to which it suggests an either/or. The integrated plurality of members constitutive of Holy Spirit as the mystical body is nothing other than a totality. But then, Spirit in its own way is also a totality, and Holy Spirit qua totality is, in the final analysis, predicable of it.

Yet, it appears that there are more approximate and more ultimate ways in which Holy Spirit or spiritual community as mystical body is predicable of fully realized Spirit. The point has been made in a number of different ways by Hegelian commentators as diverse as Brito, Fackenheim, and Theunissen that there exists a clear distinction between Holy Spirit, operating on the level of cult and representation, and this community, or members of this community, operating on the level of thought. In the former case, though the theological drive towards full intimacy of the human with the divine is realized, the relation of intimacy (perhaps identity) is not fully appropriated, since cult (*Andacht*) and representation (*Vorstellung*) determine that human being remain *this* side of the divine-human relation. It is only in the elevation of some privileged members of the spiritual community—their sum constituting the 'isolated order of priests'—to thought (*Denken*) that human being passes beyond to the infinite divine side of divine-human relation. Such elevation (*Ehrebung*), however, is by no means constitutive for participation in the divine, as the eschatological spiritual community can be said to participate already in a superlative way in the divine. And, in a sense, all of finite spirit and nature participates in some way in the divine. But the ultimate level of participation is reached when consciousness of God is divine consciousness of itself, where self-consciousness and divine consciousness coincide. And this coincidence occurs only in thought, a fact noted above all by the Christian mystics and superbly rendered by Meister Eckhart: "The eye with which God sees me is the eye with which I see him; my eye and God's eye are one and the same" (*LPR 1* 1824 E 347, G 248). Nowhere else in Hegel, perhaps, is the ontological identity of the human and divine so clearly asserted, even if identity is asserted in a gnoseological register. Of course, Hegel implies as much in his discussion of the movement from *Vorstellung* to *Begriff* in the *Enc* (#564 ff) and in his understanding of the relation of the absolute knowledge, realized as the end of the *PS*, to the 'pure thought' presupposed by *SL*. The elevation of a privileged group into the divine infinite not merely distinguishes between two orders within the field of spiritual community, between nonphilosophers and philosophers (*LPR 1* 1827 E 180, G 88; *Enc* #573), but suggests nothing less than that the groups of elevated thinkers are in some way determinative of thinking on the level of the divine infinite or, at the very least, determinative of any concreteness predicable of divine thinking.

Yet even if we presume such a split within Holy Spirit and concede that Hegel posits a detachable select group elevating itself out of the *kairotic* present of eschatologically realized community into the eternity of the divine infinite, this still leaves the status of transcendence in Hegelian depiction highly problematic. Certainly Hegel is correct in presuming that the further saltus of pneumatically informed human spirit argues against any immanentist reduction of the divine infinite to the nondivine finite, finite spirit in particular. To such reductionism he gives the name, *pantheism* (*LPR 1* 1824 E 346, G 246–247; *Enc* #573),[6] and against such a view Hegel is anxious to underscore the reality of *difference* between the finite as nonelevated and the divine infinite into which, however, a portion of finite spirit is elevatable, and in eschatological time elevated, having then joined with the divine infinite in the most intimate relation. Hegel, therefore, wishes both to announce difference and to underscore the reality of deification which he interprets just as radically as Meister Eckhart. But if Hegel is against what he presumes to be the false charge of pantheism and is willing to argue for transcendence, it is interesting to note that his talk of elevation puts under pressure any proposal of transcendence ultimately predicated on the purity of the divine-infinite sphere. In his discussion of region and philosophy (esp. #566, 574, 577) in the *Enc* as in *LPR 1* (1827 E 414–441, G 308–330) Hegel suggests that elevated finite spirit enters into the divine milieu as such, which consequently becomes occupied, its putative simplicity abrogated.

Furthermore, recourse to the purity and essential otherness of the divine milieu before (*vor*) the creation of the world of nature and finite spirit is not a hermeneutic vista in and through which the claim of transcendence in the strong sense (i.e., theistic sense) can be plausibly sustained. For this claim to have value it would not be sufficient to have warrants for asserting that mature Hegelian texts posit a sphere or moment of the divine unengaged in manifestation in and through the finite. It would be necessary to add that this 'beyond' be characterized by perfection (or perfections) of a superlative kind. But, if our explication of this sphere in chapter 2 was correct, imperfection or imperfections characterize this sphere. Admittedly, the imperfection or structural set of imperfections is only *relative,* but it is crucial to observe just why this is the case. Imperfection is relative precisely because the milieu of the immanent divine *before* the creation of the world and finite spirit is not independent (*Selbständigkeit*) in the classical sense of the term. For it to be so, the immanent milieu would have to be closed off from and in no way anticipatory of the milieu of the finite. But, as we learned, while the immanent milieu represents a circle and thus is characterized in some way by synclasis and analepsis, nonetheless, not being the circle of circles but rather a circle within a circle, it is in the last instance exemplary anaclasis and prolepsis. And it is only as anaclastic and proleptic that the divine of the immanent sphere can sustain itself against the imperfection or structural set of imperfections which typify this sphere. What is true *within* the milieu of the immanent divine of the "Immanent Trinity" is true, as chapter 2 brought out, also *of* this milieu: it is lack seeking fulfillment. Arguing against any interpretation of Hegel that would locate transcendence in the "Immanent Trinity" *before* divine manifestation *ad extra* does not rule out the possibility of making some more modest affirmation of transcendence, nor entail the conclusion that those who intuit that, somehow or other, the "Immanent Trinity" is the only viable locus of transcendence are wrongheaded. That Hegel validates some kind of transcendence and that the *primary* locus of this transcendence is the "Immanent Trinity" both can be affirmed, but affirmation requires at a minimum that clarity has been reached respecting the different values of the "Immanent Trinity" dependent upon narrative locus in the elaboration of divine subjectivity or personhood.

Modalities of the "Immanent Trinity"

Major textual sources for suggesting the existence of the "Immanent Trinity" in an analeptic, as well as proleptic, mode include Hegel's discussion of religion and philosophy in the *Enc,* the discussion of absolute knowledge in *PS,* and its presupposition in *SL.* If Hegel in #566 of *Enc* suggests that the immanent sphere is Spirit's terminus as well as origin when he speaks of the 'infinite return' (*unendliche Rückkehr*) of the divine from manifestation as a withdrawal (*Zurückgehen*) into the unity of its fullness (*in die Einheit seiner Fülle*) (*GL10:*455), in #574, where Revealed Religion (*die geoffenbarte Religion*) has undergone speculative redescription in philosophy as the articulation of *Begriff,* Hegel could not be more explicit. There Hegel touches upon the logical sphere of articulation which, it has been shown, is coextensive with the articulation of the "Immanent Trinity." Crucial is the way in which the logical sphere gets qualified. Whereas before the logical sphere was treated as the sphere of the immediate (*unmittelbares*), here Hegel understands it:

> with the sense (*Bedeutung*) that it is Universality validated (*bewährte*) in concrete content in its actuality (*in seiner Wirklichkeit*).

> In this way science has gone back to the beginning (*in ihren zurückgegangen);* and the result (*Resultät*) is the logical (system) as a spiritual principle (*als das Geistige*). (*Gl10:*474)

The concluding sentences of *Enc* (#577) confirm the basic tendency of #566 and #574 in speaking of the Idea, not merely as ground of process, as implicit, or in Hegel's technical terminology as *ansich,* but as *an und für sich,* as terminus having required development and activity of explicitation. Hegel speaks even of Idea, i.e., absolute Idea, as enjoying (*geniesst*) itself, by which Hegel means enjoying its self-possession. Such self-possession is, of course, impossible without the detour in and through manifestation as appearance.

The textual case for the hypothesis for an analeptic mode of "Immanent Trinity" is, admittedly, by no means as obvious in *PS*'s and *SL*'s treatment of the nature of absolute knowledge, yet clearly a case can be argued. Whereas it is a commonplace in Hegel scholarship to link *PS* and *SL* and to understand the 'absolute knowledge' with which *PS* terminates to coincide with that knowledge that runs through the categorial genesis of Being-Essence-Concept (and their differentiations), the consequence of the entrance of the philosopher into the immanent divine has not been as often understood. The presence of the philosopher as divine thinker—one who has given up the name of the love of wisdom and become coincident with wisdom itself—is betrayed throughout *SL* in that the movement of categories, or what we have called earlier categorial stringing (chap. 2), is not automatic but is, rather, accompanied by a commenting voice whose assurance derives from the fact that, in principle, the entire process of categorial genesis on the plane of divine immanence has been already run through. But the fact that the movement or "Immanent Trinity" is thought by the philosophers cannot be without consequence with respect to the immanent movement or "Immanent Trinity," for the philosopher as finite spirit elevated is in principle 'after' not 'before' the dynamism of the immanent sphere. Moreover, it is the philosopher who, in a superlative way, is the locus of recollection (*Erinnerung*) of the entire sum of finite experience and its trajectory. This does suggest that the sphere of immanence, either as trinitarian articulation or categorial stringing, cannot be considered exclusively as a domain of prolepsis; to it also must be attributed an analeptic aspect. The attribution does not imply that the immanent sphere or the "Immanent Trinity" is analeptic and proleptic in one and the same respect. It suggests rather that, as foundation of divine becoming the "Immanent Trinity" is operating as narratively proleptic and as completing divine becoming, which crucially includes the engagement of the divine in the finite, the "Immanent Trinity" is operating as narratively analeptic.

In addition to the above textual evidence, there are grounds of a more general sort for believing that it is not Holy Spirit as such that terminates the trinitarianly elaborated narrative of the genesis of divine subjectivity, but rather the "Immanent Trinity" as realized and analeptic with respect to the entire process of genesis. I would like simply to make two points in this connection. First, given Hegelian commitment to return (*Rückkehr*) as a constitutive feature of the synclasis of narrative formation, it is difficult to see how return is complete unless Spirit, as encompassing narrative process, in fulfilling itself on a linear axis also bends the line to shape a circle. Hegel is transparently clear about this desideratum from *PS* on, and his account of theogenesis, as Mark Taylor has rightly observed, is neither that of line nor circle, but of line/circle.[7] Origin and end, arché and telos, unite to figure a dynamic self-constituting circle. Without the element of return, the identity of the grammatical subject of becoming is not made fully perspicuous, and the teleological dimension of divine genesis is not captured in its full radicality.

We have already made so bold as to connect Hegelian ontotheology with mythic, specifically theogonic, varieties of thought (chap. 3). In this connection it is interesting to note Hegelian departure from that kind of theogonic account which finds an exemplary instance in the Babylonian creation hymn, or *Enuma Elish,* not merely with regard to the level of symbolism, but with regard to the narrative commitment involved. No more than Aristotle does Hegel want to commit himself to a theogonic view which describes the differentiation of a sphere of divinity illuminated by consciousness, self-consciousness, and discursive power out of a stratum of vague, subjectless, literally oceanic divinity. This theogonic view regards the subjectivity and discourse of the divine as displacement of the night of divinity, whereas Hegel in all his major texts wishes to suggest that the process of differentiation is undergirded by fundamental identity. This fundamental identity guarantees that the movement is not from the absence of subjectivity to its presence, from nondiscourse to discourse, but rather undeveloped subjectivity and discourse to their fully developed form. The departure from this kind of theogonic account, however, by no means signals Hegel's principled liberation from all and every variety of mythic-theogonic account. There exist other, more sophisticated theogonic accounts that much more nearly preserve the identity of grammatical subject in process and that even go so far as to posit return as the consummation of narrative identity. Hegelian ontotheology's rapport with theogonic varieties of thought rests on Hegel's replication of the basic structure or grammar of these more sophisticated mythic renditions of which Jacob Boehme (unarguably) and Valentinian Gnosticism (arguably) supply two of the more significant exemplifications.[8]

The second of our two general reflections bolstering the textual evidence that the "Immanent Trinity" subsists in an analeptic, as well as proleptic mode, is not nearly as important as the first and basically plays a supporting role. This reflection centers on the play of connotation contracted in the locution *Holy Trinity* (*die heilige Dreieinigkeit*) sometimes used by Hegel to name the "Immanent Trinity." Earlier in the text (chap. 2) we noted that there was nothing casual in Hegel's use of the epithet 'holy' in connection with the "Immanent Trinity," that, indeed, it recalled a quite specific use in the ontotheological tradition. Boehme was suggested as Hegel's precedent, since it is in his theosophic system that the "Immanent Trinity" as holy gets explicated in such a way as to suggest deficiency, deficiency, moreover, which is only relieved when the so-called pure divine opens itself to the finite and enters into its impurity, finally, of course, subjecting it to transmutation. The deficiency of the pure "Immanent Trinity," which at best anticipates the order of nature and finite spirit in Boehme, is insinuated into the term holy. Holy here has the connotation of noninvolved exclusivity. Mark just how different is the connotation of holy when holy is connected with spiritual community as it is in the locution of Holy Spirit. Here holy bears not the slightest trace or note of inadequacy or exclusivity. The connotation is simply that of complete adequacy and inclusiveness.

Clearly then the epithet holy does not have an univocal sense in Hegelian texts. In itself there is nothing anomalous in this provided attention is paid to the specific narrative locus upon which the sense of holy depends. Applying to the milieu of the divine considered as either outside of, or at best proleptic, of divine encounter in the finite and human, holy will have one sense; applying to the fullness of divine presence in the spiritual community as terminus of divine encounter and proximal condition for fully concrete divine subjectivity, it will have another. But I would here like to go one step further. Granted this distinction of sense dependent upon narrative location, there exists the strong possibility that with respect to the "Immanent Trinity" Hegel's use of the epithet is overdetermined. Hegel's insistence time and again in *LPR 3* on the inclusive dimension of holy is so blatant as to suggest inclusiveness as a defining feature. This warrants our taking another look at the use of holy in connection with the "Immanent Trinity." That holy can and indeed does have a negative sense cannot be reneged on. But if holy also is to have a positive sense with regard to the "Immanent Trinity," how can it apply without contradiction? One way out of the impasse is to say that the negative Boehmian sense applies to the "Immanent Trinity" considered as narratively proleptic, with the positive sense being a secondary connotation. As applied to the "Immanent Trinity" considered as the divine fullness that presupposes narrative exegesis in and through exile (*Entäusserung*) in the world of nature and finite spirit, however, holy would evoke the integral of ontological, gnoseological, axiological, and existential perfection constitutive of divine subjectivity (*Subjektivität*) and personhood (*Persönlichkeit*). Specifically, holy as evoking fullness implies the "Immanent Trinity" as the really real (*ontos on*), as divine self-consciousness enriched by finite consciousness, as divine goodness made determinate by agon with evil, and as divine love made concrete by exposure to and sharing in the pain and suffering of the other, i.e., the created sphere. Fullness, as the compact of these qualities, is a gain, not a given, a victory, not a possession. Constituted in and through particular narrative epochs, the fullness of the "Immanent Trinity" would not be reducible to any of its stages of formation. In it all stages of divine formation are recollected (*Erinnerung*), or, to use our technical language, all stages of divine formation are analeptically maintained. But analeptical maintenance does not imply, thereby, that the "Immanent Trinity" on the plane of the infinite is thereby finitized. The divine history is analeptically preserved as 'past' in the eternity of the "Immanent Trinity," exemplifying the consummate self-presence of the divine.[9]

Hopefully, we have established at least a prima facie case for the existence of the analeptic as well as proleptic modality in the case of the "Immanent Trinity." While Hegel scholars have not traditionally put matters in this way, it could be argued that this position represents the tendency of a significant group of German commentators and critics. It is surely implied in Iwan Iljin's talk of 'theogenetic process', plausibly so in Falk Wagner's account of the genesis of divine subjectivity or personhood.[10] And if I interpret him correctly, despite serious misgivings as to 'too theological' an interpretation of Hegel, Walter Jaeschke in an important essay tends to confirm the presence of a double modality of gnoseologially registered infinite.[11] In Jaeschke's essay this takes the form of analyzing the connection between Aristotle's *noesis noeseos noesis,* which Hegel recalls (*Enc* #577), and Hegel's view of divine self-consciousness. While Jaeschke points to obvious overlaps between the two, particularly as this relates to the logical sphere outside of or 'before' the creation of nature and finite spirit, in the last instance, he is of the opinion that the Hegelian view of divine self-consciousness departs decisively from the Aristotelian view—and, we might add, any emendation of this view. The departure is based upon the Hegelian understanding of what constitutes the necessary conditions of fully determinate divine self-consciousness which are not realized on the level of (onto-theo)-logical immanence conceived as anterior to engagement in the finite. For Jaeschke, it is clear that in Hegel the self-contemplative circuit of the divine does not eschew the non-divine, but presupposes it as its basis, 'recollects' it.

To conclude the first section of this chapter, I would like to return once again to the question of transcendence in Hegelian depiction of the trinitarianly scaped narrative unfolding of the divine. In a number of his most important texts Hegel explicitly argues against any immanentist reduction of his conception of the divine as Spirit, a reduction which he presumes in his eloquent disavowal of pantheism in *Enc* #575 to take the form of either materialist equation of the divine with the mereological sum of things or religiously motivated reduction of a monist sort where the absolute is not adequately differentiated from the phenomena within which it inheres (e.g., Hinduism). Yet, if Hegel in *Enc* as elsewhere dismisses radical immanentization, it is important to gain clarity concerning the specific form of transcendence countenanced. On the interpretation offered here it is indeed true that it is in the "Immanent Trinity" that we discover the true locus of transcendence. But it is *only in the "Immanent Trinity" in its analeptic modality that transcendence in the full and proper sense is found.* Undoubtedly, a kind of transcendence characterizes the "Immanent Trinity" even in its proleptic mode. At the very least, it is irreducible to the finite, and, moreover, it subserves the positive functions of establishing divinity as the ultimate grammatical subject of Hegelian ontotheology and being the ultimate condition of the constitution of realized subjectivity or personhood achieved in the "Immanent Trinity" in its analeptic modality. Nevertheless, as we have already argued, the "Immanent Trinity" in its proleptic modality exemplifies inadequacies that determine that the kind of transcendence it displays is ultimately degenerative in kind.

Not all commentators and critics who see that Hegel does not authorize a theistic version of transcendence such as found in the mainline biblical and theological tradition of Judeo-Christianity have concluded that Hegel consequently can be interpreted in a thoroughgoing immanentist fashion. Dupré, Fackenheim, Iljin, Schmidt, and Williamson, *inter alia,* have all argued against pantheistic interpretation,[12] and a number have suggested that Hegel's position be characterized as *panentheism,* since his position steers between the Scylla of theistic avowals of the absolute separation of the finite and infinite, on the one hand, and the Charybdis of their conflation on the other.[13] Though the label is potentially misleading unless care is taken to dissociate the term panentheism from too close an association with a particular modern form of construing the relationship between the infinite and finite, i.e., Process Theology,[14] the label does accurately capture both Hegelian commitment to the divine as ultimate definition of reality and the close proximity of the finite to the divine infinite by which it is subtended.

The addition of 'dialectical' as a qualifying epithet, suggested by some supporters of the panentheism label,[15] obviates some of the difficulties in application by specifying that becoming is characteristic of ultimate reality and not merely relative reality and that becoming proceeds, not by way of unilinear progression, but by way of contradiction and contrariety. 'Dialectical panentheism,' therefore, provides a relatively illuminating description of Hegel's ontotheological view of divine Spirit. Yet, perhaps one further step is required, since even under this complex rubric it is possible to confound Hegel's view with another view from which, nevertheless, Hegel's view ultimately decisively departs. Nothing prevents, for instance, the inclusion of the Heraclitean view of the Logos under this rubric, for, as Heraclitus perceives it, *polemos* (conflict) and *diapheron* (division) are determining characteristics of Logos as *kinesis* (becoming). Few Hegelian commentators would be prepared to deny rapprochement between Hegel and Heraclitus regarding the validation of change and becoming. Indeed, there is even a measure of truth in the suggestion that, in a sense, Hegel rescues Heraclitus after the long dominance of Parmenides throughout the Western ontotheological tradition. Yet it would be a mistake to construe Hegelian ontotheology as representing any pure recrudescence of Heraclitean becoming. Sticking to the limited categories of Parmenidean advocacy of Being (circle) and Heraclitean advocacy of Becoming (line), it is transparently clear in all of Hegel's major texts, in *PS, SL, LPR,* and especially in the *Enc* that Hegel does not unconditionally opt for one over the other.[16] Hegel senses the particular deficits of both ontotheological schemes: if Parmenides fails to introduce the richness and dynamism of appearance into Being thereby leaving it impoverished (*LHP 1* E 256, GL19:314), Heraclitus fails to provide Becoming with an underpinning of determinate form that would guarantee meaning and intelligibility. The complementary deficits of Parmenides and Heraclitus also might be understood as an excess of circularity (as with Schelling) in the case of the former and excess of linearity (as with Fichte) in the case of the latter.

In his articulation of the autoconstitution of Spirit, Hegel wishes to overcome Parmenidean and Heraclitean deficits and their complements, and in so doing move beyond an either/or to a both/and. In Hegel's synthetic framework, Being is the being of Becoming, and Becoming is the becoming of Being considered as the most developed, most concrete totality. In Hegel's synthetic framework, also, the nonencompassing circularity of Parmenidean Being is relieved of its deficient synclasis and opens up to the dynamic linearity of the progression of appearance, and the 'bad infinite' of the linearity of Becoming is overcome in an synclasis that enfolds all determination. Hegelian synthesis points to the specific kind of qualification necessary to add to the rubric *dialectical panentheism*. The portrayal of the Spirit as the identity-in-difference of Being and Becoming, circle and line, implies that the form of panentheism espoused by Hegel is not merely dialectical but *narrative*. Dialectic gains its meaning from a narrative context in which anaclasis and synclasis, prolepsis and analepsis are depth-narrative structures. For Hegel, the domain of narrative is not simply the domain of change but the domain of increment, in which the divine as grammatical subject achieves definition and self-consciousness, a self-consciousness in which all previous moments of narrative trajectory are analeptically maintained.

Section 6.2 The Genre of Hegelian Apocalypse

Explicit assertion of a general connection between Hegelian ontotheology and apocalyptic thought is nonexceptional in Hegelian commentary and criticism.[17] It is crucial, for instance, in Eric Voegelin's analysis of Hegel in *From Enlightenment to Revolution* where Hegel is read as assimilating, redescribing, and secularizing apocalyptic thought.[18] But Voegelin nowhere defines apocalyptic thought or attempts to present its ensemble of elements. With respect to the diagnosis of Hegelian content, if not with respect to evaluation, Voegelin's interpretation does not represent a significant advance on Löwith's thesis that Hegelian ontotheology represents a redescription of Judeo-Christian eschatology.[19] In fact, Voegelin's lack of specificity is the fruit of a double hermeneutical failure. To the failure to adequately distinguish Judeo-Christian apocalyptic from Judeo-Christian eschatology is wedded the failure to raise the question whether there might not be a number of apocalypse types of which apocalyptic is only one. Yet Voegelin insists on speaking as if Judeo-Christian apocalyptic is exhaustive and definitive of apocalypse as such. Voegelin's failure is a failure of proof as it is a failure of conceptual clarity The avowal of the intimate relation between apocalyptic and/or apocalypse and Hegelian ontotheology is, however, not thereby falsified. Indeed, provided conceptual clarity is reached with respect to the relation-distinction of eschatology and apocalyptic, and some preliminary decision made with regard to the possibility of there being more than one type of apocalypse, the claim of connection between Hegelian ontotheology and apocalyptic plausibly can be both sustained and qualified.

Before embarking on this foundational task, a few methodological recommendations are in order. Given the almost bacchanalian revel of interpretation and interpretive methodology currently in operation, and the obvious fact that the phenomena of apocalyptic and apocalypse, however defined, extend far beyond the Judeo-Christian field and even its margins, it is necessary to restrict the extension of these categories to this field (i.e., Judeo-Christian) and its margins; to legislate that *apocalypse* be defined predominantly (though not exclusively) in terms of content;[20] to legislate that the category 'apocalyptic' be normed by the mode of thought and thought-content evidenced in the apocalypses of the mainline Judeo-Christian tradition.

In the attempt to unearth Hegel's apocalypse commitment and expose the apocalypse type that is in operation in his ontotheology, I will adopt the following procedure: (1) provide a résumé of the evidence of apocalypse commitment in Hegel; (2) attempt a definition of Judeo-Christian apocalypse and itemize some of the more salient marks of Judeo-Christian apocalypse as these feature in (a) canonic and noncanonic texts of the biblical period and (b) in the more self-conscious, postbiblical literature in the Christian tradition; (3) outline the ways in which Hegelian ontotheology overlaps with the primary and secondary exemplars of the Judeo-Christian apocalypse tradition; (4) explore the ways in which Hegelian ontotheology departs from the primary and secondary exemplars of the Judeo-Christian apocalypse tradition; and (5) propose some precedents for the kind of apocalypse evidenced by Hegel's ontotheological texts, particularly as this kind of apocalypse has an effective history in the trajectory of Lutheranism until the early nineteenth century. The brief remarks that follow sketch the merest outline of this fivefold procedure.

(1) In establishing the credibility of the application of the category apocalypse to Hegelian ontotheological texts, a number of pieces of evidence suggest themselves as important. First, Hegel's insistence on revelation as constitutive of Christianity, or more especially his insistence that in the revelation matrix of Christianity the mysterious and the mystical do not imply the occlusion of the secrets of the divine and the relation of the divine to nature, humanity, and history but rather their disclosure, corresponds at least in a formal way to apocalypse as *apokalypsis*. Second, there is some evidence that Hegel had direct contact with apocalypse literature. As H. S. Harris points out, one of the courses taken by Hegel as part of the theological curriculum at Tübingen concerned Revelation, perhaps the root text of the Christian apocalypse tradition.[21] While there is no reason to suppose that Hegel was any more attracted to the tone, style, or imagery of the text which D. H. Lawrence characterized as the work of a second-rate mind[22] than he was to the teaching of Storr, nevertheless, such reading would have challenged the facile Enlightenment view of natural historical progression and facilitated movement beyond theologically thin eschatological accounts provided by a figure such as Lessing. Moreover, through Storr it is possible that Hegel came in contact with various commentaries on the text, some of which, like Bengel's, were as apocalyptic in their interpretation as the *Urtext* itself and involved the application of the symbols of Revelation to modernity.[23] Third, like Bengel before him, Hegel presumed that a vitally important aspect of the content of revelation is the providential action of God in history, where the latter moves inexorably towards the eschaton and full disclosure of divine secrets one sees or knows only in the last days. If David Walsh suggests this point, James Yerkes makes the point with some force.[24] Texts such as *LPH* and *LPR* display a Hegel who clearly construes the present age as *Endzeit*. A particularly good example of such expectation is provided by the strange section closing the 1821 Manuscript of *LPR* which addresses the passing away of (*Vergehen*) of the community (*LPR 3* E 158–162, G 93–97). Though relative to other Hegelian accounts in *LPR* and elsewhere, the section in the 1821 Manuscript is anomalously pessimistic about the present age and decries the decadence of egoism, intellectualism, and voluntarism Hegel sees everywhere; nonetheless, decadence, as with progress in other texts, here figures 'the signs of the times' (*LPR 3* 1821 MS E 159, G 94). As Hodg-

son rightly points out, the sign of the times locution is classic apocalyptic discourse.[25] Fourth, we learned in chapter 5, Hegel viewed Lutheran Christianity as representing the decisive revelation of the divine, a revelation not fully consummated in the pneumatic event of the Reformation itself but unfolding in modernity both within the realms of thought and praxis. In taking his stand on the dynamics of completing the Reformation, Hegel was, in fact, retrieving a major strand in late sixteenth-century Lutheran self-interpretation and validating the effective history of the apocalyptic dimension to Lutheran thought not completely silenced by the emergence of Lutheran orthodoxy. The fifth point relates closely to the fourth. The effective instruments of keeping the apocalyptic dimension alive within Lutheranism in the centuries of scholastic dominance were the Joachimite and Boehmian apocalyptic traditions, whose systemic presence in Hegelian texts was discussed in the previous chapter.[26]

(2) Judeo-Christian apocalypse focally concerns a revealing or uncovering in a vision physical, imaginary, intellectual, and, at a limit, hermeneutical of what is or has been hidden or secret.[27] The content of apocalypse may extend beyond history and its patterning, expectation of the imminent end, and transfiguration of the order of existence, and may include heterogenous material, e.g., the upper world, angels, the nature of good and evil, creation and even meteorology and astrology; nonetheless, the central focus is historical in general, eschatological in particular.[28] Still, it is important to insist from the outset that Judeo-Christian apocalypse is not exhaustively defined by eschatology. Moreover, demarcation does not rest exclusively upon the kind of content disclosed. An important differential is the formal characteristic of Judeo-Christian apocalypse as revelation to a privileged seer who is initiated into the secrets of the divine ordinance. In addition to this formal characteristic, important differentials of a material kind include: (a) the *cosmic* or *universal* perspective on history (Dan 2:31–45, 7; Baruch; Enoch); (b) the emphasis upon the inexorable working out of the divine plan within history, appearances to the contrary; (c) periodization of history; (d) exaggerated contrast between the negativity of the present aeon and the *new* which is expected; (e) the positing of an end to history and the existence of a post-historical period; (f) a heightened dualistic perspective wherein there is a distinction of a near absolute sort between those who are good and those who are evil; (g) the quasi-absolutization of dualistic perspective in the positing of an eschatological judgment whereby salvation is granted to the good, damnation to the wicked.

All of the above features are structural elements of canonic and noncanonic apocalypses of the biblical period (e.g., Daniel, Enoch, Revelation), however baroque the imagery, however rhetorical the text. These very same structural elements can be said to be recapitulated in Judeo-Christian apocalypse texts of a secondary or metalevel type, granted the necessary qualification that the more self-conscious hermeneutical regime of the latter may tend to attenuate somewhat the heightened dualistic emphasis and temper both the baroque imagery that, at once, expresses the nonordinary state of vision and the difficulty of expression and the rhetorical urgency predicated upon the perception of the breaking in of the new and eschatologically decisive victory of good over evil. It is perhaps the texts of Joachim de Fiore that provide the classic example of secondary, rather than primary, Judeo-Christian apocalypse.

At this juncture it is apposite to recall the third methodological stricture with which we opened the present section. The structural elements which we have suggested as constitutive of Judeo-Christian apocalypse define Judeo-Christian apocalypse as apocalyptic. The relation between apocalypse and apocalyptic is nontautologous, and apocalypse and apocalyptic are not interchangeable terms unless we rule out beforehand the possibility of the existence of other apocalypse types, which, while formally constituted by the announcement of the revelation of secrets of the divine hitherto undisclosed, are not materially dominated by focus upon history, God's providential enactment within history, and the eschaton. Until it has been conclusively proven that no other, essentially nonapocalyptic type of apocalypse enters into the Western ontotheological tradition, apocalypse operates as a more inclusive category than apocalyptic, though apocalyptic translates to all intents and purposes the mainline primary and secondary production of the Judeo-Christian tradition. If alternative types of apocalypse (or an alternative type) exist, therefore, in the Western ontotheological tradition they must (logically) exist on that tradition's margins. We shall return to this point in (4) and (5).

(3) On the basis of previous examination of Hegelian texts, especially in chapter 5, it should not be difficult to conclude that Hegelian ontotheology evidences *almost all* the features of Judeo-Christian apocalypse or apocalyptic. Formally, Hegelian ontotheology is based upon a revelation of the divine mystery, possible in a definitive way in the *end time* within which the modern Christian theologian-philosopher already lives. Significant material overlaps exist between the Hegelian construal of history and Judeo-Christian apoc-

alyptic: (a) while history in Hegel is looked at from a variety of perspectives which tend to focus upon a limited or regional slice, in its fully universal and encompassing extent it stretches from Adam to eschaton; (b) history in Hegel is theologically interpreted as the exegesis of divine providence in contradistinction to nontheological rationalist views of historical progress; (c) history in Hegel displays definite signs of periodization, both trinitarian and nontrinitarian; (d) history is regarded as having reached its term, and a new world is experienced as irrupting into the old; and (e) while history is regarded as concluded in one sense, it is not in another. The term of history does not terminate the temporal dimension of individual and social communitarian existence. Time is transformed, transfigured not abolished.[29] The eschaton opens up the *kairotic* dimension of time, which approximates, though it is not totally identifiable with, Hegel's revisionist notion of eternity, no longer understood, or misunderstood, as being reducible without remainder to timelessness.[30] Hegel recapitulates all these five material elements of Judeo-Christian apocalypse without reserve or equivocation. This is not the case with respect to structural features (f) and (g) which, if recalled, are recalled in the way not unusual in apocalypse discourses of a secondary, metalevel type superbly instanced in Joachim, that is, with an attenuation of the absoluteness of the dualism of good and evil and the stress on judgment which reifies this dualism. Nonetheless, the measure of recall is such as to give considerable evidential support to the thesis that Hegelian ontotheology recapitulates the apocalyptic thought of the Judeo-Christian tradition. It might be noted, however, that recapitulation of major *topoi* of the apocalyptic tradition may not necessarily exclude the presence of other *topoi* which seem to signal another apocalypse matrix and that, consequently, the recall of Judeo-Christian apocalypse cannot be logically assumed to define Hegelian ontotheology's apocalypse commitment.

(4) If there is an extraordinary measure of overlap between Hegelian ontotheology in its apocalypse commitment and Judeo-Christian apocalypse, there are also departures—and here I am not speaking of amendments that leave the basic grammar of Judeo-Christian apocalypse or apocalyptic intact—wherein the basic disposition of Judeo-Christian apocalypse is altered. Three departures are, in my view, significant, and all three relate to narrative dimension, specifically, (a) whether the narrative disclosed admits of direct ontological interpretation, (b) the span or reach of the narrative disclosed, and (c) whether one can speak of *radical narrative* or *radical narrativity,*

that is, whether one can speak of the divine as being constituted or defined by narrative enactment.

(a) The salient narrative dimension evoked in the discourse of Judeo-Christian apocalypse is 'economic', by which I mean, the primary focus is not upon the divine as such, either nature, attribute, or the configuration of the celestial or supercelestial world, but upon divine action in history and the divine providential plan for humankind. Where reflections about God's nature, etc, do occur, such reflections should be understood as largely functional: they set the stage for God's relevancing relation to human being embedded in the temporal stream. While the disclosure of God's acts in history cannot but in some way reveal who God is, the point is that the reality of God, God's being, is disclosed only by indirection and by implication. Thus, the discourse of Judeo-Christian apocalypse, if it cannot fail to have some ontological implication, is, nonetheless, not ontological discourse of a first-order type. By contrast, the discourse of *LPR* and *Enc,* as well as other Hegelian texts that disclose the divine activity, is explicitly and directly a discourse of the reality of what it discloses. And the what of which it wants to speak is nothing more nor less than Being itself but now conceived in its most concrete depth and fullness. But the what of which it wants to speak explicitly and directly is a who, *the* Who that as fully concrete, fully enriched Being is constituted in and through narrative enactment.

(b) While the span of the narrative disclosed in Judeo-Christian apocalypse is, in the last instance, universal in scope, the universality of narrative span is, nonetheless, restricted to history strung between genesis and eschaton. In the case both of primary and secondary apocalypses, the narrative of history is bounded by a nonnarrative alpha and a nonnarrative omega—though there may be a variety of ways in which the nonnarrative poles are construed. The contrast with the apocalypse commitment of Hegel could not be more stark. The transhistorical alpha and omega that provide the bounds of history, and which in the Judeo-Christian apocalypse tradition are ineluctably nonnarrative, in Hegel are themselves subject to process. Whereas in primary apocalypses alpha is construed as the sovereign Lord not subject to our processes of growth and decay, and in the classic secondary apocalypses of Joachim as the nonprocess Trinity that is the foundation of all process, worldly and historical, in Hegel the sphere of the transhistorical alpha is itself process. This process that submits to rendering as the articulation of divine attributes and the "Immanent Trinity," it might be said, is not merely foundational with respect to the divine history (*LPR 3* 1824 E 186–187, G 120) in nature and history but has to be understood as prologue and even first act of divine history. Similarly, whereas in the primary apocalypses of the Judeo-Christian tradition omega is understood as the confirmation of God's absolute power and righteousness that brings the drama of creation to conclusion, and in the classic secondary apocalypses of Joachim as human being sharing in the nonnarrative life of the Trinity of persons, the apocalypse of Hegelian ontotheology construes omega as the elevation of human being into the narratively disposed "Immanent Trinity" as both epilogue and last act of divine history. For Hegel, as we indicated in the previous section, the "Immanent Trinity" is alpha and omega, alpha in its proleptic, omega in its analeptic mode.

(c) From what we have seen in (a) and (b), it follows that narrative commitment in Judeo-Christian apocalypse is nonradical in that it does not touch the divine, as such, who is the nonnarrative alpha and omega of actions that intersect time and history and provide history with meaning. By contrast, Hegelian narrative commitment is absolutely radical, since in Hegel's view the various phases of self-manifestation and manifestation *ad extra* of the divine are constitutive of divine identity and personhood. Thus, by contrast with Judeo-Christian apocalypse, Hegelian narrative depiction is ontological or ontotheological, of absolutely encompassing scope or span, and absolutely radical. It is possible to crystallize the Hegelian swerve from the classic metalevel Judeo-Christian apocalypse by noting the different *semantics of kingdom* in Hegelian ontotheology and Joachimite apocalypse—the difference in semantics here showing up the taxonomic superiority of Boehme. As elaborated in detail in chapter 5, the content of Joachimite revelation is primarily the serially succeeding kingdoms of Father, Son, and Spirit in history, with the latter identified as the eschatological kingdom of God. This trinitarian elaboration of kingdom is an elaboration of divine acts and the changing context of such acts. And, while it can be said that divine acts and their qualitatively changing contexts cipher the reality of the divine, they cannot be said to name the reality or being of God in any direct way. Again, while trinitarian elaboration of history is universal in scope, reaching from creation to eschaton, the fact is that history is the context of trinitarian elaboration. Trinitarian elaboration is, thus, in Joachim synonymous with trinitarian periodization. Lastly, in the Judeo-Christian apocalypse of Joachim, trinitarian elaboration is in no way understood to be constitutive of the divine. In line with the mainline Christian tradition, Joachim conceived the divine to be fully self-sufficient even if open to the world, time, and history in particular. This fully self-sufficient, yet open, divine is the intradivine Trinity.

The merest glance at the Hegelian semantics of kingdom as elaborated, for instance, in *LPR 3* gives every evidence of *rupture*. The 1831 Lectures offer this classic example of Hegel's trinitarian schematization:

1. The idea in free universality, or the pure essence of God—the kingdom of the Father;
2. The inward diremption of the idea, held fast for a moment in its differentiation—the kingdom of the Son;
3. The reconciliation of this finite spirit with spirit that has being in and for itself—the kingdom of the Spirit. (*LPR 3* E 362, G 280–281)

Kingdom language, which is as static in surface implication as the language of 'element' that it replaces and the language of 'sphere' with which it associates, in Hegel has to be read in the light of the self-revealing divine whose structure of elaboration it names. As such, there is nothing static in the trinitarian elaboration of kingdom. In the above passage trinitarian elaboration is understood to touch upon the very *being* of the divine and its *who,* for the very *being* of the divine and its *who* is not rendered without the process of manifestation *ad extra* in and through the finite both natural and spiritual. While Hegel, like Joachim, does not exclude the activity of the divine in creation and history from his semantics of kingdom, the other-referencing activity of the divine is not treated as a phenomenon only indirectly indicating the being or who of the divine. If the language of Father refers to the *being* or *who* of God, so also does the language of Son and Spirit. Father, Son, and Spirit thus function ontologically or ontotheologically in the 1831 passage. The narrative span of the trinitarian elaboration of kingdom is absolutely encompassing and reaches into the divine immanence or the "Immanent Trinity" itself. Thus the trinitarian elaboration of kingdom is not, in the strict sense, the same as trinitarian periodization which refers to the temporal and historical as such. The "Immanent Trinity," which is the equivalent of the 'idea in its universality', and which is named by the symbol Father, does, as other *LPR 3* texts show up more clearly (1821 MS E 76, G 15) have a process-narrative character, but its milieu is, nonetheless, not that of time and history. While it is possible to accuse Hegel of directly narratizing the Trinity, it is not possible in the same way to accuse him of directly historicalizing it.[31] None of this means, however, that Hegel has no interest in history or that some of the kingdoms are not historically indexed. A measure of such indexing is clearly in operation in the case of the kingdoms of the Son and Spirit. One final point: Hegelian apocalypse's commitment to ontological or ontotheological discourse and its insistence on inclusive narrative span dictate that narrative commitment is radical, that is, the divine activity of self-manifestation and manifestation *ad extra* constitutes the divine. No aspect of the divine is nonnarrative; all aspects of the divine are constitutive.

(5) Hegelian ontotheology's appropriation of the eschatological and apocalyptic tradition cannot be gainsaid, but then, neither can the novelty of a position that considers the content of revelation to include description of the extrahistorical divine, that sees all reality as circumscribed by an encompassing narrative, and that posits the divine itself as narratively constituted. Hegelian departures from the Judeo-Christian apocalypse tradition are sufficiently significant to insinuate that we are dealing with a different genre of apocalypse. But the further question necessarily suggests itself: is the apocalypse genre of Hegelian ontotheology radically new? is it without precedent within the Western ontotheological tradition? If the mainline tradition of Judeo-Christian apocalypse is as we declared it to be, no precedent is possible from within this tradition. Still, this leaves the margins of this tradition. Can any precedents be found here? I believe the question can be answered in the affirmative, and that two precedent-establishing ontotheologies whose focus is revelation can be espied on the margins of the Western tradition. I am referring to the ontotheologies of Jacob Boehme and Valentinian Gnosticism. I am aware that such a suggestion is provocative; more importantly, in the absence of detailed analysis of Boehmian and Valentinian Gnosticism, this suggestion cannot rid itself of all trace of assertion. Nevertheless, even in the absence of what might pass as proof, the prima facie plausibility of such a hypothesis can be established. Though, such establishing can, at best, function only as an unfulfilled intention, even this is important.

As we hinted in chapter 5, Jacob Boehme appropriated Joachimite images of the progress of history and its end and, with some revision, committed himself to Joachim's apocalyptic understanding of God's operation(s) in history. Moreover, for Boehme, Revelation was a key text whose meaning is hermeneutically unveiled when submitted to a pneumatic, i.e., mystical, interpretation. But the difference between Joachim and Jacob Boehme does not lie in their different periodization schemes or the different degrees of chiliastic expectation,[32] but rather in the nature and scope of content revealed and the understanding of the character, narrative or otherwise, of the content revealed. In contradistinction to Joachimite apocalypse, Boehmian apocalypse is absolutely universal in scope. To avail of a word Boehme himself borrowed from the alchemical tradition, Boehmian apocalypse is *pansophistic.*[33] Revelation is quite literally a revelation of *all* things, eternal and temporal, divine and human, invisible and visible. Though Boehme's mature texts cut deeper than *Aurora* with which Hegel was familiar, it is clear that, even in that text, revelation is fully inclusive. A difference in emphasis accompanies the difference in scope, that is, in a way unparalleled in Joachim; Boehme concentrates on the nontemporal, nonhistorical dimension of the totality. Moreover, as we have seen in the case of the apocalypse variety of Hegelian ontotheology, Boehmian thought as *theo-sophos* envisages all of reality as narratively dynamic, even the Trinity of the immanent sphere,[34] which Joachim in a more traditional posture excepted. Since the 'being of beings' is in Boehmian texts identified without reserve with the divine,[35] the narratization implies the narrative constitution of the divine. Put in another way, Boehmian apocalypse unveils the narrative self-constitution of the divine or, as the great Boehme scholar Alexandre Koyré put its, unfolds the conditions of possibility of divine personhood.[36] If our analysis is correct, then these conditions are nothing more nor less than narrative conditions.

I would like to make just one further point. To the above alterations of the Joachimite apocalypse tradition, Boehme adds another. Boehme submits the narratively self-constituted divine to trinitarian interpretation. The divine life is understood as the unfolding of three kingdoms which can be proximally identified with the symbols Father, Son, and Spirit. What is decisively different about the Boehmian construal is that, unlike Joachim, only *one* of the kingdoms, i.e., the kingdom of the Spirit, refers in a direct way to the temporal order. The first two kingdoms refer to narrative episodes on the plane of eternity. Boehme, in effect, radically alters the Joachimite semantics of kingdom. Trinitarian elaboration is now ontotheological in the strict sense and not merely economic; it now concerns epochs of the divine as such and not the periodization of divine acts, or the context of such acts. The alteration of semantics of kingdom accompanying the mutation of apocalypse is of profound import for German Idealism in general.[37] What is suggested here is that, in the context of German Idealism in general, 'kingdom' language (Hegel) and 'age' language (Schelling) symptom the victory of Boehmian apocalypse over Joachimite apocalyptic with which it had shared the seventeenth-century field of Lutheran apocalypse. Another way of making the same point is to say that German Idealism in general, Hegel in particular, accepts the Boehmian emendation of Joachim, for the Boehmian meta-apocalypse does not define itself antithetically to Joachimite apocalyptic; rather, it subsumes it. Because the mode of relation is subsumption rather than exclusion, this means that the Joachimite elements still may be conspicuous without being constitutive.

For many scholars Valentinian Gnosticism would not appear to be an especially good candidate for inclusion under the category of apocalypse or any specification thereof. Clearly Valentinian Gnosticism is antithetical in most fundamental respects to Judeo-Christian apocalyptic with its valorization of time and history.[38] Thus, if it is ruled a priori that apocalyptic exhaustively defines the possibilities of apocalypse, then Valentinian Gnosticism is definitely outside the pale. But, as I claimed at the beginning of this section, such apriorism should be challenged, and the possibility of other varieties of apocalypse not be legislated out of existence. Beyond this methodological objection does any evidence exist in the Gnostic texts of the first centuries of the common era suggesting that Valentinian Gnosticism merits inclusion under the apocalypse category? Again, conscious as with Boehme that we are here operating from a taxonomic point of view at the level of unfulfilled intention, I would like to suggest that it does. First, a number of Valentinian Gnostic texts are explicitly called apocalypses on the basis that at their center is *revelation* to a privileged seer.[39] A nonordinary event of communication occurs in which a divine messenger—but also a divine prototype of oneself—unveils the secrets hitherto sealed from mankind and still perhaps incomprehensible to certain classes of humanity. Moreover, even where Valentinian Gnostic texts do not adopt the title of apocalypse, a central feature of such texts is either explicit reference to or allusion to a decisive moment of revelatory communication in which the seer or knower plumbs the depths of the arcane mysteries.[40] The knower 'sees the light' as it were. Second, *what* is revealed is fully comprehensive in scope and includes complete description of the transcendent, the drama of the upper world, creation, etc. The focus and emphasis of

Judeo-Christian apocalypse is other than this, as we have observed from the beginning. Casual acquaintance with Valentinian Gnostic texts would be sufficient to mark this important difference in scope of content revealed. The situation is more complex with respect to the two other features of the apocalypse variety of Hegelian ontotheology, namely, *inclusive narrative span* and *narrative radicality*. If present, these features are not on the surface. Indeed, many scholars would exclude narrative talk from discussion of Gnosticism. Yet, as we pointed out in chapter 3, with the help of Baur and Hans Jonas, a relatively powerful argument can be constructed that makes narrative the infrastructural tendency in Valentinian Gnosticism. And looked at from a narrative perspective, Valentinian Gnosticism not only evidences a narrative span that is absolutely inclusive, it shows eminent signs of suggesting that the divine loudly asserted to be immune to change and becoming is in fact a divine that undergoes a process of perfecting as it traverses the drama of fall, exile, and return. Valentinian Gnosticism, therefore, seems to supply the first instance of this nonapocalyptic kind of apocalypse that finds later instances in Boehme and Hegel.

From the point of view of the present work, Valentinian Gnosticism and Boehmian theosophy represent, therefore, plausible precedents of the apocalypse variety illustrated by Hegelian ontotheology. This brings us to the question of labelling the specific type of apocalypse of Hegelian ontotheology. Of course, it is possible to use the locution *Hegelian apocalypse* with the understanding of its specificity and the understanding that there exist at least adumbrations, if not fully determinate illustrations, of this variety of apocalypse in the Western ontotheological tradition. Alternatively, one might label this variety according to its emergence in the ontotheological tradition, and here Gnosticism has pride of place. Accordingly, the genre of Hegelian apocalypse is the genre of *Gnostic apocalypse* in contradistinction to Judeo-Christian apocalypse or apocalyptic. Any use of the category of Gnostic apocalypse, however, is here proleptic given the unfulfilled intention of the present diagnosis. Yet over the similar suggestion of Voegelin,[41] my own account possesses the clear advantage that it supplies definite criteria whereby the adequacy of locution such as 'Gnostic apocalypse' can be assessed.

Section 6.3 The Genre of Hegelian Theodicy

The recognition of suffering, death, crime, frustrated ambition, destruction, war, the pain of change is not absent in Hegel. Evil in its many manifestations is seen to course through history and, thus, cannot be erased from description; the impact of these manifestations are such that they cannot be shunted aside as trivial. Yet, if history is primarily the scene of the sacrifice of human being's happiness, in fact nothing more, as *LPH* puts it, than a "slaughter-bench" (E 21), is any exoneration of human being possible, since human being is the prime reason for human misery? is any exoneration of the divine possible, since the divine presumptively permits both human atrocity and natural catastrophe? Hegel expressly forbids peremptory gestures of consolation, and yet cannot resist raising the question: "to what final aim these enormous sacrifices have been offered?" (*LPH* E 21)

In posing the question in this way, Hegel brings to full explicitness the issues of anthropodicy and theodicy and suggests a teleological-eschatological context as, not merely the best situation from which to pose the question of the meaning of evil, but the situation within which a solution can be found. According to Hegel in *LPH,* it is only from the vantage point of the end of history, the apocalyptic last days, that "the ill that is found in the world may be comprehended and the thinking spirit reconciled with the fact of the existence of evil" (E 16). Without such a vantage point, without historical synclasis, it is impossible to answer the question whether evil has a meaning and, thereby, it seems, a justification. The proximate foundation of the eschaton, which is characterized by the unparalleled relation of human beings to the divine and to each other, is Lutheran Christianity. As we saw chapter 5, Hegel saw Lutheran Christianity as representing the principled overcoming of separation of human being from the divine and one human being's separation from another. Lutheran Christianity, or rather its historical exegesis in modernity, makes possible the constitution of the spiritual community (*Gemeinde*) of *Endzeit* in which duality and exclusivity is replaced by intimacy and integration. In the sphere of eschatologically realized spiritual community, or in general in the context of Holy Spirit, it becomes possible to affirm that "all the sacrifices that have ever and anon been laid on the altar of the earth (are) justified for the sake of *this* ultimate purpose" (*LPH* E 477) where the demonstrative "this" points, at the very minimum, to the existence of Holy Spirit in which the divine potential of freedom and knowledge in human being reaches its fulfillment. Thus, despite Hegel's own suggestion that no consolatory result abolishes, or should be allowed to abolish, the extravagant reality of suffering and evil, eschatological consummation and eschatological vantage point encourage the teleological graphing of all events, even the most monstrous, which thereby are measured and distilled into a scheme of meaning. Semantic thrust and intention are retroactively bestowed upon suffering, evil in general, insuring, thereby, its legitimation.

War, as it functions as an ontic category in Hegelian ontotheology, provides an excellent example of retroactive legitimation from the vantage point of the perceived synclasis of history. More important than Hegel's impatience with would-be empiricists who refuse to acknowledge that war subserves any function whatsoever, either physical or ethical, or the contradictions within Kant's critical liberal view, is Hegel's positive point that war provides a singular opportunity for examples of individual and communal transcendence of the egocentricity and opportunism of civil society.[42] Both the sacrifices of individuals in acts of heroism and that higher-level bonding that distinguishes community from a mere aggregate of individuals give testimony to an aim and interest that surpasses the commonplace. Aside from such local justification, there is the nonlocal justification of war as one of the main motors of historical development as such. To the nonapparent meaningfulness of each and every war, i.e., the propulsion to transcendence, Hegel adds the nonapparent meaningfulness of the historical repetition of outbreaks of war. Appearances to the contrary, the sequence of conflicts are not without a rational kernel. In fact, war is nothing more nor less than an exemplar of the 'cunning of reason' (*List der Vernunft*) or, in a more theological idiom 'divine providence'. Shlomo Avineri, one of the best commentators on Hegel's political thought, could not be any clearer regarding the eschatological-teleological conferral of meaning:

> Thus even war itself, with all its negativity, does finally receive a meaning within the wider scheme of things. Out of the vortex of clashes characterizing international relations, an inner order emerges and reason appears in history not as something given *a priori*—as an axiomatic system of norms—but as the end product of a long, arduous and sometimes seemingly meaningless process.[43]

From the eschatological point of view that insinuates a teleological aspect to the narrative of history, nothing in history constitutes a rupture of sense or meaning, or, in Hegel's own vocabulary, nothing in history is "accidental," mere "show" (*Schein*).[44] Within the eschatological perspective of realized Christianity (and Hegelian philosophy as the ultimate discourse of this historically generated possibility), all events, however negative, take on the character of necessity (*Notwendigkeit*) (*PR*

E 344) or even fate (*PR* E 324). They are nothing less than authentic appearances of the plan of God.

Still, war as an ontic phenomenon is only a single mode of evil's manifestation. Not only war but every other manifestation of negativity, as eschatologically transcended, is teleologically justified. This attitude provides an interpretive context for the famous if somewhat unfortunate aphorism of *PR*: "the rational is the real, and the real is the rational" (E 10).[45] Coincidence is only fully evident in the parousiac present of the *eschaton* but can be read back into the developmental dynamic of history in which all events can be regarded as adumbrations of this coincidence. It is the eschatological vantage point in its imposition of teleological grammar that decisively divides Hegel from Kant on this point. Hegel recognizes, as with Kant, that, looked at from anything other than an eschatological perspective, there exists a disproportion between what is, in fact, the case (*Dasein*) and what ought to be. From the perspective of the consummation of history, however, disproportion is reread as the merely surface script. In every event, no matter how monstrous from a moral point of view, is compacted the is and ought that together constitute reality or actuality (*Wirklichkeit*) as such. One important effect of this rereading is to deprive of any possible validation the ought of protest and complaint. The following passage makes explicit the relativization of Kantian *Moralität:*

> For the history of the world moves on a higher level than that proper to morality. . . The demands and accomplishments of the absolute and final aim of Spirit, the working of Providence, lie above the obligations, responsibilities and liabilities which are incumbent on the individuals in regard to their morality. . . It is irrelevant and inappropriate . . . to raise moral claims against historical acts and agents. They stand outside of morality. . . World history . . . could on principle altogether ignore the sphere of morality and its often mentioned difference with politics. It could not only refrain from moral judgments. . . .(*Reason in History,* 82–83)

The Kantian ought makes sense only within a pre-eschatological or noneschatological perspective, but, even on this level (as is signaled clearly in his opposing of *Moralität* by *Sittlichkeit,*) Hegel finds endorsement extremely difficult. Certainly, to the extent to which ought suggests in Kant a transhistorical criterion of judgment without possible instantiation in history, Hegel rules that ought voids itself of semantic potential.[46] And, for Hegel, the voiding of semantic potential is simultaneously the voiding of ontological potential.

Read back from *Endzeit,* the application of ought to historical reality is not only useless but meretricious. Transparently, the depotentiation of ought that is a consequence of retroactive collapsing of is and ought in the actual (*wirklich*) transgresses the imperative latent in the indicative statement of Merleau Ponty: "History never *confesses.*"[47] For Merleau Ponty history has a plasticity, a receptivity to editing and abbreviation. In Hegel the abbreviation is such that history not only comes to make sense but comes to make *complete* sense. That it is the synclasis of history that provides the basis of the legitimation of evil has been recognized by thinkers as distinct as Levinas and Adorno, who accordingly protest against the tyranny of a thus constituted totality (Levinas) or the elevation of the universal (Adorno) that deprives the victims in history of the validity of their witness and protest, their *No.*[48] For the latter, who, perhaps more perspicuously than any Hegelian critic before Derrida, focuses upon the synclasis of history, all protest in the Hegelian ontotheology of history will be eschatologically invalidated as ephemeral and reread as affirmation. Every no is transmitted into a yes. The indictment in *Negative Dialectics* is eloquent:

> Just as the general concept, the fruit of abstraction, is deemed above time—and just as the loss which the subsumed suffers by the process of abstraction is entered into the profit column, as a draft of eternity—so are history's allegedly supratemporal moments turned into positive. Hidden in them is the old evil, however. To agree to the perpetuation of the status quo is to discredit the protesting thought as ephemeral.[49]

Transfiguration donated by the realization of totality effects a transfiguration of evil, suffering, and the voice of protest raised against both. Transfiguration effectively implies the nonbeing (*meon*) of evil and suffering and the speechlessness of protest.[50] Adorno seems to suggest an intimate connection between this kind of transfiguration and the mode of Hegelian recollection. Whatever the general connection between Hegelian and Platonic ontotheology, Adorno appears to recognize, as Ernst Bloch does, that Hegelian recollection—what we have called analepsis—and Platonic *anamnesis* are not identical.[51] Recognizing the specificity of the Hegelian view, Adorno argues that, in the fully secured totality guaranteed by synclasis, the agent of re-collection, ultimately the transmundane universal, gathers together all previous moments, including those moments of nonidentity, fracture, and surd. Were Hegelian analepsis to do so with integrity, then the history of World-Spirit would be nothing more than the history of evil and suffering. But, of course, Hegelian analepsis is not, from Adorno's point of view, unadulterated, and the critical negative element is edited out as marginal, as redundantly individualistic and perspectival. If synclasis suggests a teleological grammar for history, analepsis confirms it and, in doing so, represses the tragic, introduces sense where no sense existed. The contrary to the salvific modality of Hegelian analepsis, however, lies not in Platonic anamnesis, which skips over time and history altogether, just as Hegelian validation ultimately subverts their integrity and reality. The contrary—the thought is originally Benjamin's—is anamnetic solidarity with the victims who have lost everything, even the right to speak.

Avowal that at least part of his project, i.e., delineation of the salvation history of divine interaction with the human is in fact a theodicy, is made fully explicit by Hegel in *LPH*. Granted eschatological vantage point, Hegel is in no doubt that the so-called negatives in the narrative of historical becoming will disclose themselves as positives, thereby releasing God from accusation. God is justified, if you like, by the charges being dropped. Hegel equally has no doubt that granted eschatological vantage point, insight into the true shape of history, is more a matter of knowledge than faith, more a matter of *Nachdenken* than hope. With respect to the issue of theodicy, as with other important theological issues, Hegel disobeys Kantian restrictions regarding the limits of knowledge. Where Kant announces the impossibility of a speculative theodicy of a 'constitutive' kind in an important later essay and proposes instead a heuristic theodicy where one *hopes* for the overcoming of evil which indicts God,[52] Hegel suffers no epistemological impediment, announcing complete confidence, not simply with regard to the possibility of a constitutive theodicy, but its actuality, and proposing the redundancy of hope, for evil is, in fact, overcome. In proposing the reality of the eschatological victory, evil is retroactively deprived of its negative charge and accusatory power. Moreover, hope is short-circuited, and any and all affirmation of a Joban 'in spite-of' character is transmitted into a 'because of'.

As Kant and Hegel differ regarding their specific types of theodicy commitment, if Michel Despland is correct in his reading of Kant's historical investigations,[54] they differ also with regard to who is the prime subject for legitimation. For Kant, according to Despland, the prime subject for legitimation is human being and only secondarily God; thus

Kant's focus is primarily an *anthropodicy* and only secondarily theodicy. In the context of other works such as *LPR* and *Enc, LPH* gives us every reason to believe that just the opposite is the case with Hegel, that what Hegel ultimately offers is, in the first instance, a legitimation of the divine and only in the second instance of human being or the human species. In suggesting such a legitimation Hegel will have to imply the intersection of absolute power and goodness in the divine,[55] though it is clear beforehand that the kind of good predicable of the divine is of a nonmoral, and certainly of a non-Kantian character. We will be returning to this point later, but at the moment our task is to enable a more specific type of determination of the genre of Hegelian theodicy than that made possible by the contrast between constitutive and heuristic modalities of theodicy and the primary or secondary status of theodicy vis-à-vis anthropodicy.

By way of executing this task, let us commence by making the obvious point that not only is the Hegelian brand of theodicy nonheuristic, and thus condemnable for this very reason on Kantian grounds, but, more specifically, the Hegelian rendition is marked by the kind of metaphysical appeal typical of the proximate speculative tradition in theology condemned by Kant in his essay on theodicy. Metaphysical appeal, as it occurs in Hegel, it should be granted, does not take the form of a recapitulation of the logico-metaphysical bases of Leibniz's thesis of this world as the best of all possible worlds or Wolff's attempt at a modified, apologetic version of such bases in his rational theology. Rather, if the metaphysical bases of any theodicy exercise influence, these bases are provided by a thinker who, while looming large in German Idealism, did not figure prominently in Kant's reflections. I am speaking of Spinoza. Spinozist presence is betrayed in a number of theodicy-relevant ways in Hegelian texts. These include: the posit of the in-principled identity of freedom and necessity in the divine as such and in divine self-expression; the idea that the assertion of the evil of world, finite spirit, and history is but a consequence of a partial perspective; and the notion of the ultimate nonbeing of evil when considered in the context of the whole that is really real.[56]

The Spinozist elements are hugely important and determine not a little of the tone as well as the substance of Hegel's view of the problem of evil and how evil reflects or fails to reflect upon the goodness and power of the divine, particularly the former. Despite, but perhaps ultimately because of, Hegel's high estimate of the potential of human being, human perception of the world and individual human being's place in the total order of things is relativized. In a number of texts Hegel inveighs against the caprice of human being regarding itself as the center of reality and especially, if not exclusively, worthy of concern (*FK* E 180–181, *PS* #570–581). Whatever differences exist between Spinoza's and Hegel's view of the finite particular human being, Hegel agrees with Spinoza that the finite particular human being does not have absolute value, indeed, that its value is a function of its relation to the divine infinite, whether Substance or Spirit. When Hegel enjoins the finite particular human being to transcend, à la Spinoza, the egocentricity of its own case with its specific, if not idiosyncratic, desires, needs, etc., and to look at things *sub specie aeternitatis,* in which case the whole or totality becomes the sole object of interest and concern, it is important to attend to the effect that this has on all moral or ethical claims upon the divine infinite. In the case of *FK* and *PR,* as with Spinoza's *Ethics,* the effect is a neutralization of all claims whose origin is the finite partial perspective. In Hegel's case, as in Spinoza's, all ethical or moral discourse is reducible, in principle, to egocentric discourse. As Levinas and Adorno in particular have complained, Hegel here sanctioned the victory of metaphysics over ethics.[57] The expressiveness of the divine infinite is beyond ethical jurisdiction and provides itself with its own justification. Hegel's recommendation that what alone should be looked at is Spirit and its trajectory opens up the possibility of a justification of God. At the same time, the intelligibility of theodicy is subverted when the absolute perspective becomes normative for the interpretation of the evidences of evil, and ethical criteria are debarred. And the barring of ethical criteria is particularly acute in Hegel's case, since we have no reason to question divine power given the luxuriant manifestation of divine expressiveness in nature and finite Spirit.

Hegel, who perhaps never adequately acknowledges the range of his overlap with Spinoza, nevertheless, is right in assuming that the *context* of his ontotheological program constitutionally differs from that found in the *Ethics*. For Hegel this takes the form of insisting time and again, in *PS, Enc, LHP,* and *LPR,* on the prerogatives of the ontotheology of the subject over that of substance and the Christian base of the former. The differentiation presupposes at an infrastructural level decisions regarding the possibility of predicating process and becoming of the divine, even more, the possibility of predicating narrative becoming of the divine. For Hegel, and clearly Hegel has submitted the standard Christian view to a specific form of interpretation—many commentators and critics would argue specific form of misinterpretation—the Christian construal of the divine, i,e., the divine as Spirit, is nothing more nor less than a vision of the narrative becoming of the divine whose terminus is fully realized subjectivity or personhood. Furthermore, the Christian vision of the narrative becoming of the divine is not permitted to remain inchoate but is the theme of the central Christian theologoumenon, i.e., the theologoumenon of the Trinity (in Hegel, the Inclusive Trinity) which represents a synopsis of the complex narrative of the activity of divine self-development. The point I wish to make in recalling these infrastructural distinctions is that it suggests a critical line of demarcation between the modalities of Spinozist and Hegelian theodicy. The modality of Spinozist theodicy is metaphysical through and through. That there is a metaphysical element in Hegelian theodicy already has been admitted, but of Hegelian theodicy it can be said to be metaphysical only because it is at the same time a self-consciously Christian narrative theodicy. Since the reality status of the intended construct 'Christian narrative theodicy' is by no means so established that it can be taken for granted, it is necessary to make some kind of case for its taxonomic protocol.

One would have to be naive in the extreme to presume unequivocal acceptance of the view that the mainline, more or less first-level theological reflections on the Christian narrative as rendered in the jointure of the Old Testament and New Testament represents a theodicy. And yet the claim that such reflection and, indeed, the narrative that provokes (and at the same time is permitted to norm) reflection has theodicy implication is surprising only granted the antecedent presumption that a theodicy proposal must be a fully explicit answer to equally explicit question, precisely the kind of proposal one would expect to find in a Leibniz or a Hume. The rejoinder to those philosophers and theologians who would mete out such stringent requirements involves invoking the commonsense reminder of Samuel Johnson that prose, even good prose, is spoken previous to use of prose as a category naming a certain genre of writing with grammatical and stylistic rules. The correlative here is that the theodicy issue is implicated in religion and religious texts, particularly in Christianity and Christian texts, long before judicious and elegant formulation of the question. And Christianity and Christian texts, as with Gnosticism and its texts, both shape and are shaped by a narrative that carries the burden of hope for human being plunged in finitude and evil and filters the exoneration of the divine who in different ways is discharged of responsibility for the tragic plan of existence. The Christian narrative is centrally the narrative of history as salvation history, stretching from genesis to eschaton, a narrative that has its pivot in the passion and death of Jesus Christ, the eschatological revelation of God. The narrative as a whole discloses the goodness of God, first in creation, then in God's providential action in history, as well as superlatively in the drama of salvation focused in the person and activity of Jesus Christ. In the drama of salvation, God reveals the what and who of God by sending the Son of God to atone for human sin and heal the breach that alienates human being from the divine. Christ enters into the agon with sin and death and defeats them. Of course, what is revealed quintessentially in this drama is that the divine is nothing other than love. Christian narrative depiction has a complex motivation, but the theodicy effects of this depiction hardly can be put in doubt: the divine is exonerated from being the cause of evil; and the divine is exonerated from exhibiting sanguine indifference regarding human affairs. Perhaps, the classic example of a first-level theological rendition of the Christian narrative where the theodicy implication is near the surface is provided by Irenaeus, who is engaged in combatting what he views as an alternative narrative pattern distorting the Christian account and with a quite different theodicy implication to that extrapolatable from Christian scriptures. Furthermore, of Irenaeus it can be said that it is he who establishes the limits of the kind of claim that can be offered by a Christian theology which allows itself to be normed by scriptural witness. The theodicy implication of the Christian narrative that it is the duty of theology to explicate is a matter of faith (*pistis*), not knowledge (*gnosis*), where faith is, not so much a matter of belief which lacks the certitude of knowledge, but a matter of trust in the redemptive event and Christ as the one who saves.[58] The event decisively transforms history and our place in history, though history continues to be the history of free human being who can say yea or nay to the redemptive event and Christ the Redeemer.[59]

Though the conclusion of our argument will place Hegel quite definitely in another narrative camp than Irenaeus, there is a considerable degree of congruence. In one of his earliest texts (*FK* E. 180–181) Hegel reminds the Romantics and their epigones, who base judgment concerning the world and God on caprice and personal proclivity, that the Christian view is based upon a positive estimate of the world and, correlatively, a positive estimate of the divine. The positive nature of the divine could not be more eloquently declared than in the redemptive activity of Jesus Christ. For Hegel in *FK*—and he will repeat the point in later texts, especially *LPH*—the Christian view happily coincides with the Platonic-Neoplatonic view of the benevolent preserve of the divine in the cosmos. Bemoaning in both earlier and later texts the fact that modern culture only sees evil in the world, he proposes in *FK* a retrieval of Plato's more benign but truer estimate in the *Timaeus* (34b), i.e., the world is a blessed God, and in *LPH* a retrieval of Anaxogoras's notion of the Nous and the Neoplatonic intuition of the *anima mundi.*[60]

Of course, in talking of Christian theology's commitment to the Christian narrative, we are not talking about a homogenous tradition. It should come as no great surprise that not every theological perspective will faithfully replicate Irenaeus in every detail. The later Augustine, for instance, is so convinced regarding the human incapacity not to sin that human being is granted no role, even in the postincarnation *tempus,* in cooperating with the divine in salvation. Moreover, the theodicy center in Augustine is no longer, as it is in Irenaeus, the incarnation and the salvific passion and death of Jesus Christ, but rather the eternal will of the divine which gratuitously elects some souls to salvation out of the mass of perdition of corporate sinfulness and guilt.[61] Again, Luther's theological commitment to Christian narrative is complex and shows evidence of strain in a way that Irenaeus's theological commitment does not. Specifically, Luther's commitment to the Christian narrative displays at one and the same time allegiance to a christocentric (Irenaeus) and theocentric (Augustinian) perspective, both of which, however, from a theodicy point of view are complementary, since they function together to impart blame for the condition human being so vociferously complains about on human being's own stubbornness, ungratefulness, and self-centeredness. Lastly, there is an apocalyptic strain in the Christian narrative theology tradition that corrects the standard Christian scheme in a number of different ways. In the classic example of such correction provided by Joachim de Fiore, the most important elements include: (1) a decentering of focus from Christ to eschaton; (2) the according of revelation status to *Endzeit*; (3) the legitimations of the prerogatives of *Endzeit* as the consummating movement of the economic activity of the Trinity in history in which, both the relation of human beings to each other and the relation of human being to the divine are, is brought to perfection; and (4) the reduction of the gap between faith and knowledge.

In Joachimite apocalyptic emendation, arguably, it is (3) that carries the bulk of the theodicy freight, though it is the Christian narrative, submitted to the ensemble of emendation, that constitutes the specificity of the Joachimite apocalyptic modality of theodicy. If Hegelian texts evidence congruence with the classical Irenaean rendition of the Christian narrative, *a fortiori* this is the case regarding the Hegelian texts' relation to Joachimite trinitarian theodicy of history. As with Joachim, in texts such as *LPH* and *LHP,* while remaining the privileged center of theodicy, (3) is nonetheless reinforced by the other three elements in a way that effects a recentering of the narrative field. As we have pointed out already, Hegelian legitimation of divine presence in history is from the eschatological point of view. Such a view permits retroactive interpretation of the evil, pain, and negativity of history in which the hidden positive charge of all events is brought forth. Events, however apparently negative, are positive when viewed in a means-end relation to what will be, i.e., the existence of the pneumatic spiritual body. It is not being too fanciful, I believe, to think of many objections to Hegelian theodicy, for example, those of Adorno, Horkheimer, Levinas, Merleau Ponty, as responses to Hegelian reprise of Joachimite apocalypse's eschatologically swerved version of the Christian narrative. It is time, however, to draw a critical line of demarcation between the Hegelian modality of theodicy and that espoused in the theological tradition which took seriously the Christian narrative. In the present context, this means focusing upon the ultimate difference of narrative environment between Hegelian theodicy and classical Christian, e.g., Irenaean, theodicy, and Hegelian theodicy and Joachimite apocalyptic theodicy. I will be as brief as possible concerning both, especially the second.

While the Hegelian narrative, indeed, could be said to involve a commitment to history as salvation history, and to the christological movement as axial in God's dialogue with world and human being, Hegel's ontotheological rendition the Christian narrative is not told or retold as the drama of God's freedom and generosity vis-à-vis a creation without claim, and beholden to such freedom and generosity for its very existence. Rather, the accent switches from God in relation to world and the inadequacy of one's knowledge concerning the divine nature—as is the case in a classical rendition of the Christian narrative offered by Irenaeus—to the nature of the divine as such which is now directly available to thought. Faith, as Hegel understands it in *FK, PS, LPR,* and the *Enc,* is but the anticipation of knowledge that defines it, and knowledge unveils a divine that exhibits dynamism and movement outside of relationality with the world (the "Immanent Trinity"). Nevertheless, the divine does enter into relation with the world, and, indeed, such relationality appears to be a desideratum if the divine is to become actually what it is potentially. The mark of becoming in Hegel even, or especially, in the case of the divine is alienation and conflict. The infinite undergoes the pain and alienation of immersion in nature and finite spirit, though finite spirit, in principle, represents the locus of the divine coming to consciousness of itself. Finite spirit or human being exhibits also a tendency towards involution and no that renders opaque the manifestation of the infinite as infinite. This tendency must be overcome if the divine infinite is to be liberated. As with Irenaeus, Hegel sees Christ as the decisive eschatological victory, which victory is consummated in *Endzeit*. But it is vitally important to note the huge changes rung by Hegel's ontological recontextualization of the Christian narrative. First, it cannot be said any longer that human being falls, but rather the divine falls in or *as* human being. Second, and correspondingly, redemption concerns no longer only finite spirit or human being but rather the divine in or *as* finite spirit or human being. Christ now appears to be just the contrary of what Irenaeus thought him to be, in fact, to all intents and purposes, not so much the Redeemer as the Redeemed Redeemer of the Gnostic sects he deemed antithetical.[62] These changes, in turn, symptom a shift in theodicy type. In the classic scheme of Irenaeus, retelling of the narrative is a theodicy that still pays respect to the perspective of the human being burdened by sin and death who wants to know that the world and life can be provided with a hopeful description. And human being is told something very hopeful: God loves us and redeems. Hegelian retelling, by contrast, in switching the focus exclusively to divine self-constitution effectively ignores the claim of human being to be entitled to an explanation. In a manner homologous to Spinoza's metaphysical theodicy, Hegelian ontotheological rendition of Christian narrative might be thought to supply, at one and the same time, a thoroughgoingly theocentric theodicy and an undermining of the very possibility of theodicy, since human being's complaint by definition is not to be taken seriously.

Similarly, the three elements we proposed distinguished the genre of Hegelian apocalypse from that of Joachim, i.e., its direct ontological intent, its inclusive narrative span, its determination of a radically narrative divine, dictate a fundamental shift in theodicy taxon. While it is certainly true that within the perspective of history Hegel shows himself anxious to combat the low estimate of some who only see bad or evil in the world (a degenerate form of Romanticism), Hegel's more positive estimate of history occupies no more than the foreground of his theodicy. On a more radical level than pointing to the eschatological and teleological impulse of history, which has the effect of legitimating all that has happened, is the pointing beyond human concern as such, including humanly generated ethical imperatives. Hegel recommends the adoption of a theocentric perspective in which the divine process of self-constitution becomes the measure of value as well as truth. In recommending such a point of view, Hegel is no longer simply saying that we may come to a different value determination when we look at the full sweep of history, but rather suggesting that all ethical judgments which focus upon God's goodness and justice should be dropped. They should be dropped since the divine process of self-constitution qua Inclusive Trinity is self-legitimating. Hegel may be more ponderous in his expression than William Blake in his *The Marriage of Heaven and Hell,* but like Blake he is committed to the view that without contraries there is no progression and insistent that this rule of life apply to the divine. The divine, therefore, is subject to the most dramatic contraries of pain and joy, no and yes, death and life, good and evil. In recommending the shift into the theocentric level and the self-legimitating ontogenesis of the divine, which must necessarily include negativity and evil, Hegel is harkening back to one of Blake's own masters, i.e., Jacob Boehme.

Theogenetic Theodicy: Ontological Proof. If what we have argued thus far is correct, then the true *proprium* of Hegelian theodicy is represented in Hegel's articulation of the Inclusive Trinity as coextensive with the radical narrative of the divine, notwithstanding the appeals of a patent economic sort Hegel makes to Providence (*Vorsehung*) and *Nous.* If this conclusion is joined to another we arrived at earlier (Chap. 1 sect. 1. 3), namely, the coextensivity of Inclusive Trinity and Hegel's rendition of the ontological proof, it follows automatically that within the Hegelian world of assumption the ontological proof illustrates the specific character of Hegelian theodicy, indeed, provides its resumé. Since Hegel's discussion of the ontological proof and theodicy is a good deal richer than that likely to be encapsulated in a syllogism, before the theodicy status of the ontological proof is specifically addressed, it might be useful to attend to the general theodicy status of the proofs of God's existence and excavate the specific theodicy commitments of the teleological and cosmological proofs.

The *locus classicus* of Hegel's treatment of the so-called proofs is *LPR 1* (1827 Lectures) where Hegel shows himself willing to concede the Kantian point that the proofs fail on a ratiocinative level, i.e., the level of *Verstand,* but in the mood to countercharge claims that Kant has failed to appreciate what is really going on in the proofs (1827 E 414–441, G 309–330). For Hegel, this is nothing more nor less than the mind's elevation to God. Hegel is saying more than that the proofs have existential force by way of complement to ratiocinative force (or lack thereof); he is saying, in fact, that the proofs, epistemically or gnoseologically considered, have mystical force. When it comes to the matter of ontotheological content, Hegel seems to be of the opinion that the proofs refer to overlapping but nonidentical, narratively situated realities. Limiting our focus for the moment to the teleological and cosmological proofs, the precise ways in which Hegelian ontotheology supports these proofs in light of the Kantian critique is worthy of discussion.

In the case of the former, Hegel avails of Kant's own refashioning of the nature and scope of teleology in the *Critique of Judgment* to positively reframe the teleological proof rejected by Kant in the *Critique of Pure Reason* (E 428–429, G 320).[63] In doing so, Hegel self-consciously anonounces himself to be in agreement with those in the ontotheological tradition prior to Kant who adopted an *internal* rather than external view of teleology. The list includes Anaxagoras, Plato, Neoplatonism, and Aristotle. In the *LPR 1* text there is no mention of the Christian symbol of Providence, but Hegel does bring explicitly into view the notion of *Nous* (E 430, G 321), which he reads as the principle in the whole of the finite irreducible to the finite. In doing so, *LPR 1* cannot but succeed in resonating with the Introduction to *LPH* where a similar espousal of *Nous* is explicit. And, in the *LPH* text, *Nous* clearly associates with a theodicy reading of the historical trajectory of finite spirit at once dramatic and narrative. Implied in the following passage is a theodicy reading of the thrust of the finite which eschatologically achieves its satisfaction:

> For that reason the genuine form is as follows: There are finite spirits but the finite has no truth; for the truth of finite spirits and its actuality is instead just the absolute spirit. The finite is not genuine being; it is implicitly the dialectic of self-sublating and self-negating, and its negation is affirmation as the infinite, as the universal in and for itself. (E 431, G 322)

Compared with his discussion of the teleological proof, Hegel's discussion of the cosmological proof in *LPR 1* is content-thin (E 426–427, G 318). In questioning the common ratiocinative use of the proof, he points to the polarity of contingency and necessity as inherently self-defeating (E 426). While it is clear that Hegel in *LPR 1* is involved in revisions of the cosmological proof that will deflect the brunt of Kantian critique, there is a paucity of detail. Nevertheless, a reconstruction of Hegelian rehabilitation is not impossible, provided the textual ambit is extended. One element of Hegelian reconstruction is his support of the view of nature and finite spirit as theophany and his correlative rejection of efficient causality (E 430, G 321). The kind of manifestation offered by nature, it must be admitted, is obscure and happens only in the context of a surface denial of theophany. As pointed to in chapter 3, by contrast with the mainline Christian traditions, Neoplatonic, Scholastic, and otherwise, divine manifestation has a dramatic 'in spite of' rather than an undramatic 'because of' character. With this difference goes another: whereas in the dominant traditions signature points vertically, in the case of Hegelian ontology it points horizontally and eschatologically. A wonderful expression of this is found in *Enc* #381. Hegel writes:

> For us, spirit has nature as its presupposition. It is the truth of nature, and therefore its *absolute prius.* (Wallace, p. 8)

Hegel goes on to specify that nature in its radical finitude is but a surpassable moment whose otherness (*Entäusserung*) is overcome (*Enc* #381 *zu*). Nature, Hegel suggests, is the *reality* ground of the ideality which wins out as process of idealization or sublimation. One perspicuous way of construing the move from nature to finite spirit is that of liberation, in which nature and spirit are correlatable with necessity and freedom, respectively. Given the equation of nature and evil endorsed in *PS, LPR,* and *Enc,* liberation from nature also means liberation from evil. It is with respect to this process that Christianity and philosophy have privileged access. To the degree to which the divine carries the burden of liberation, Hegelian reconstrual of the cosmological proof is also a theodicy enterprise.

The above rehearsal allows us to see with greater clarity the theodicy dimension of the ontological proof. As pointed to in chapter 1, whatever his disagreements with Kant, Hegel agrees that the ontological proof is the foundation of the other two. But, if in Kant the ontological proof is foundational because it is logically implied by the other two, in Hegel's case the ontological proof is foundational because it specifies in a fully complete manner the theocentric perspective within which investigation of nature, finite spirit, and history takes place or ought to take place and because the narrative field referred to in the ontological proof is fully global, encompassing the more regional narrative fields referred to in and by the cosmological and teleological proofs. With regard to the first point, it can be said that the epistemic surplus of the ontological proof over the other two is largely a function of the fact that in this particular proof the divine is exposed as *arché* as well as *telos*. In a sense, therefore, the ontological proof places the elevation (*Erhebung*) of self to the divine in the context of the divine and radicalizes the mystical aspect present in all the proofs. With regard to the second, it can be said that in *LPR 1* Hegel is quite aware of the totalizing dimension of the ontological proof in contradistinction to the other two proofs. In that text he communicates his insight by way of his symbol of *Begriff*. And *Begriff*, Hegel asserts, is "this totality, this movement or process of self-objectifying" (E 438, G 327). Hegel makes abundantly clear, a point which Mark Taylor is anxious to underscore,[64] that creation is an indelible moment of the ontological proof (E 427, G 326–327). But the *descensus Dei in mudum* dose not exhaust the narrative enactment of the devine and the *ascensus* of the nondivine finite to the divine infinite constitutes an equally important moment or set of moments. In fact, the ontological proof exhaustively maps the complete trajectory of the divine whose sum of narrative moments is captured in Hegel's interpretation of a key set of narratively related Christian theologoumena. And this narrative and the theologoumenon of the Inclusive Trinity that summarizes it elaborate a peculiar narrative theodicy which at once subverts the theodicy enterprise by enjoining a radical theocentric perspective and provides a theodicy of an eschatological type, but an eschatological type not reducible to time, history, and its processes (*LPR 1* 1827 E 423, G 316; also *Enc* #386 *zu*).

PART 3

Narrative and Logico-Conceptual Articulation

A considerable number of points in part 2 could use amplification. The relation between Boehmian and Hegelian narrative—as these narratives are trinitarianly schematized—demands further explanation, as does the relation between Hegelian and Valentinian narrative. In addition, it would be appropriate to raise the issue of whether the category *Valentian Gnostic narrative* is applicable, not only to the second-century field of esoteric narrative, but also applies to Boehmian and Hegelian narrative. Finitude dictates, however, that the case presented thus far will here have to suffice as a good enough explanation, with the amplification being postponed to the sequel of this text. What is not a candidate for postponement is the issue of the relation-difference of representation and concept and the relation-difference of their respective spaces, 'narrative space' on the one hand 'logical space' on the other. Throughout part 2, I concentrated on the often suggested compatibility between representation and concept, especially to the extent that representation was identified with a trinitarian synopsizing of an encompassing ontotheological narrative. But Hegel does not simply assume such a relation; he thematizes and problematizes it. This thematization and problematization marks Hegel's mature oeuvre. *PS, LPR,* and *Enc* all equally point to the difference between representation and concept, a difference between their respective spaces that is most conspicuous when the level of representation does not reach the kind of heights that would make it possible to speak of the narrative sphere as being a structure of Universality, Particularity, and Individuality.

Even where philosophers have not been especially exercised about the issue of the relation-difference of religion and philosophy that is the privileged context in Hegelian texts for the issue of the relation-difference of representation and concept, there is a real sense that it is an issue of crucial philosophical importance insofar as it has something to say about the relation between narrative and knowledge, *mythos* and Logos. Theodore Gereats is one Hegelian commentator who thinks that, not only is the issue crucial for Hegel, but that despite enunciation of distinction, in the last analysis Hegel suggests the continuity of narrative and concept, the fundamental narrativity of concept, the fundamental conceptuality (if not of narrative in general, and even all versions of the Christian narrative) at least of some thinkable versions of the Christian narrative.[1] Needless to say, Gereats's view that Hegel ultimately supports the case for the inextricability of narrative and thought—that some narratologists assume to be announced in the Sanskrit word for knowledge, i.e., *gnâ*[2]—cannot be taken as an answer to the question of the relation-difference of representation and concept. Yet it does help to focus the issue on the relation between these various spaces, neither of which may in the long run remain insulated from each other. The crux of the issue is whether, on analogy with modern structuralist attempts to dechronologize narrative,[3] Hegel's articulation of concept represents an attempt to denarratize or logicize narrative. As with even the very best of analogies, the analogy has to be contextualized and limited. First, the substitution of denarratize for dechronologize is necessary since, if it is clear that Hegel understands most narratives, both Christian and non-Christian, to have an explicitly chronological element, it is not clear that all narratives necessarily need be defined by their chronological implication. Hegel seems to except, for example, the kind of trinitarian narrative he proposes in his mature oeuvre, which at once represents his normative proposal and, at the same time, finds instantiation in the margins of the Western ontotheological tradition in general, the Christian ontotheological tradition in particular. Second, the analogy should not be taken to imply any exact one-to-one correspondence between the logical space pointed to by structuralism and that of Hegel. Even if logical space in Hegel transcends the temporal features that Marcuse,[4] for instance, finds present in Hegelian texts, this neither means that all narrative features have been erased, nor that some erased narrative features are not palimsestically recoverable. Though the thrust of our investigation is on the difference between narrative and logical space to the extent to which this specifies the difference between representation and concept, one cannot immediately rule the Derridian suspicion of 'white mythology' to be meritless.[5] It is this suspicion that informs chapter 7 and determines the use of the locution *speculative rewriting*.

Needless to say, in neither the case of Derrida's metaphor about the metaphorical implication of philosophy, nor my own metaphor about metaphor, do I intend to unmask the foundational pretensions of a philosophy that finds itself ironically succumbing to the law of one metaphor too many. Philosophy may not be necessarily emasculated when it discovers that it indelibly consorts with metaphor, no more than philosophy need be totally undone when it is forced to recognize with Gödel the fundamental truth that no semiotic or semantic system can be simultaneously consistent and complete. Moreover, the category of 'speculative rewriting' is not intended as a code insinuating that something like Derridean *archiwriting* represents the legitimate focus of Hegelian concept, whose difference from traditional conceptuality specifies its transcendence of Logos as speech. Whatever differences pertain between the Hegelian view of the sphere of concept and that of the tradition—select differences will be touched on in chapter 7—they will not be such as to remove Hegelian thought from logocentric gravitational pull; indeed, they may not be such as to persuade that Hegel is not the apogee of the ontotheological tradition that has the Word at its center. For is not Hegelian *Geist* the Word uttered and the Word heard in the autodialogue that both constitutes and is supported by a trinitarian frame?

7

REPRESENTATION AND CONCEPT: Speculative Rewriting

Given the sheer quantity of the writing, one reasonably might be persuaded that the issue of the relation between representation and concept has become exhausted. One certainly could be excused for thinking that further treatment seriously risks redundancy. Part of the problem, admittedly, lies with the extant treatments. Too often discussion has amounted to little more than a presentation of passages where Hegel speaks to the issue. Such textual rehearsal is not of much help, for the best that could be expected is the determination of Hegel's intention, and determination of authorial intention has long been a discredited hermeneutical procedure. In any event, in the absence of criteria to adjudicate between passages that tend to emphasize continuity between representation and concept, and other passages that emphasize discontinuity, there is no way to explain one's valuing continuity statements above discontinuity statements or vice versa. To agree that Hegel thinks of the relation of concept to representation under the auspices of *Aufhebung* does not solve anything, for the issue is what precisely is the relative degree of preservation and cancellation in the movement of translation. Moreover, Hegel's insistence that transformation involves really only a transformation of symbolic form leaving intact representational, that is, narrative, substance ought to set the terms of discussion, not be the presumed solution. And, even if it were the solution, the solution would have to be understood and defended. What is certain regarding the move from representation to concept is that narrative construal is corrected. It is important to note, however, that narrative space is not homogenous. Not only do narratives belong to more than one field of discourse, for example, art as well as religion, within the field of religion there exists a hierarchy of discourse reaching from religions Hegel regards as primitive to Christianity, regarded as consummate religion. Indeed, the field of Christian discourse is itself multileveled, with Hegel thinking that some versions, i.e., trinitarian versions, are significantly superior to many more popularly and confessionally-embraced forms. The present chapter is an attempt to move beyond these oversights which have seriously hindered exploration of what is involved in the movement from representation to concept. In doing so, it is guided by the question whether in the movement all narrative commitment is excised, a conclusion that obviously would have serious consequences regarding the achievement of part 2 of our text, which specified the trinitarian ontotheological narrative commitment of Hegelian discourse in general.

In the three sections of the present chapter, I wish to build the case for the ultimate perdurance of narrative and thus a last line of defense for the legitimacy of the kind of taxonomic enterprise undertaken in part 2. In section 7.1, I will outline Hegel's own reflection on the relation-difference between representation and concept, as the terms for discussion are set by Hegel's mature texts. Though a crucial aspect of the deficiency of all representation, and even Christian representation as its epitome, is its narrative character, it is interesting that Hegel undertakes something like a discursive redemption of narrative in the Universality-Particularity-Individuality schema which marks the highest reaches of Christian representation. Section 7.2 focuses on the actual move from representation to concept, as this move involves a number of operations or operators exacting correction of narrative predilection. For present purposes these operators may be referred to as 'denarratizing operations' or 'denarratizing operators.' This section is the critical hub of chapter 7, and thus of part 3, for there the crucial question is pursued whether these denarratizing operations are radical in subverting any narrative tendency whatsoever, or nonradical in affecting the form not the matter of narrative, affecting what might be called narrative indices rather than narrative substance. Answering this question involves raising the issue of the relation between denarratizing operations and narrative operators, like anaclasis, synclasis, prolepsis, and analepsis prominent in Hegel's consistently teleological discourse. In addition, this section raises the issue of the principled compatibility of the view that the concept is genetically dependent on representation—or that Hegelian 'logical space' is constituted by a refiguration of 'narrative space'—and the view that the concept is autonomous—or that narrative space constitutes a discursive projection of logical space. Section 7.3 attempts to draw broad-ranging conclusions from the analysis of sections 7.1 and 7.2. It insists that what typifies the Hegelian position is the centrality of narrative, its perdurance in the logical space of concept. It underscores the fact that this narrative, or better, metanarrative, finds its proximate analogies more at the margins of the Western ontotheological tradition than at the center. Most importantly, it tries to show that the oddity of the kind of metanarrative Hegel is committed to is not incidental to understanding his discursive enterprise. Specifically, it points to (1) the demise of the currency of the standard Christian metanarrative which, agreeing with its critics, Hegel thinks is no longer viable, (2) Hegel's reluctance to go the route of some modern philosophers and theologians who, if they reject metanarrative, think that local narratives are the solution to the metanarrative enterprise that was always *de trop,*[6] and (3) Hegel's conviction that the metanarrative enterprise as such has not failed and that what remains to be done is to construct a viable alternative to the Christian monomyth.

Section 7.1 Representation and Concept in Hegel's Mature Works

Throughout Hegel's mature work the intimate relation of absolute religion or Christianity and philosophy is asserted. In the language of *PS,* Christianity and absolute knowing (*absolut Wissen*) share the same content (#788, 802), the mystical or the self-revealing divine that, ultimately, is the subject as well as object of discourse. In Christianity, by comparison with primitive religion, i.e., natural religion (#684–698) and with other more aesthetically inclined religious modalities (#699–747), the absolute content has been interiorized to such a degree that it is possible to conceive of the faith-appropriation in and by the spiritual community as the self-consciousness of God (#787) and not simply as a consciousness of the divine as a transcendent 'beyond,' symptoming Christianity's Unhappy Consciousness. For Hegel in *PS* (#803), the only difference between religious representation and philosophy as science or wisdom is that, in the latter case, the conceptual mode of symbolization proper to it is more adequate to the content as Spirit (#762–624). While Hegel does not offer a systematic survey of the debits of *Vorstellung* vis-à-vis *Begriff,* it is evident that *PS* draws a map that later works such as *Enc* and *LPR* will fill in. Though Hegel at various points will tend to suggest that *Vorstellung*'s debits belong to either the subjective or objective pole of the medium of symbolization, the fact is that representation is flawed in both subjective and objective dimensions.

While some commentators on *PS* have expressed puzzlement with regard to the role that religion in general, Christianity in particular, plays in *PS*,[7] those who have been less puzzled still have had to grapple with the fact that, while it is appropriate to think of Christianity, even in its representational mode, as essentially involving the self-consciousness of the divine (#782), the subjective genitive here has not yet come to the fore, and representational consciousness treats the divine *as if* it were in the mode of consciousness (#795, 798).[8] This means, from a Hegelian point of view, that the full incidence of Spirit has not been experienced, since it only can be experienced if the individual or community fully appropriates, and is fully appropriated by, the divine as inclusive subject. There are deficits on the objective side as well: if representation does not abrogate the task of revealing the divine content, one cannot deny the dangerous flirtation with anthropomorphizing the divine embedded in the sensuous imagistic tendency of its mode of symbolization. A token of such danger is the representation of the Trinity that Hegel shows himself anxious to defend against its modern rationalistic and pietistic detractors. The language of Father and Son, and especially the way of construing the manner of relation is, Hegel observes, thoroughly naturalistic (#771) and is in need of correction, one might say demythologization. For Hegel, as for Ricoeur later,[9] however, there are hostile and nonhostile forms of demythologization, and his recommended form is representation and Christianity-friendly in a way the other modern forms are not. Indeed, his demythologization—a demythologization which if started on the level of representation is only fully complete on the level of pure thought—is necessary to subvert the hostile demythologization that Hegel thought was well under way in his own day. One obvious deleterious effect of the imagistic inclination in representation is its tendency to fragment the unity of mystical content (#771, 788) that Hegel suggested in the Preface alone could be regarded as true (#20). In this respect, representation, despite its sensuous predilection, colludes with *Verstand* the reifying, hypostatizating understanding. Effectively, what this means is that the decomposition of the whole brings with it the elevation of moments of a unitary process into entities (#771).

Both the subjective and objective debits of representation are to the fore in Hegel's discussion of the speculative proposition, particularly, the speculative proposition as the divine, and the divine as the speculative proposition (#23, 61 ff). On the objective side, Hegel questions the classical view that would separate the subject of predication from the predicates that articulate it and think of the former as having a significant measure of priority. Ironically, Hegel agrees with his critic Feuerbach in critiquing the view of the empty substrate beyond its determination by attributes. The predicates do not simply identify a subject; rather, their presence provides the grammatical subject of predication with any reality it has. Without predicates into which the grammatical subject flows, as in 'the actual is the universal' (#62) and 'God is Being,' the grammatical subject would be an empty subject. The subject-predicate relation, therefore, only can be maintained in the rehabilitated form of a dynamic movement from grammatical subject to its completion as real subject in and through the determination by predicates. The classical view of the subject-predicate relation also has the further deficit that it cannot register the modern turn to the subject initiated by Kant. Thus from the subjective side, Hegel questions the dissociation of consciousness from the movement of articulation. The articulation of content is, at the same time, the differentiating activity of the subject, the activity of the subject the articulation of content. The speculative proposition is the subjective-objective unity (#63–64). Expressed less formal-logically, the speculative inclusive proposition of the divine discloses the differentiating and definitional activity of the divine, while, at the same time, showing the place of knowledge in this divine activity of differentiation and definition.

Many scholars have recognized the originality of Hegel here, agreeing that Hegel at once subverts the classical Aristotelian tradition and departs in significant ways from the Kantian tradition that is its modern contender.[10] It subverts the classical Aristotelian tradition by undermining the view that the grammatical subject of predication is a real *hypokeimenon* underlying the attributes that inhere in it. For Hegel in *PS,* the real subject is the grammatical subject only as articulated in and by the predicates. Of course, Hegel in the Preface also might be thought to be moving beyond the Aristotelian framework by suggesting that the epistemological subject perceiving this movement of articulation is constitutive also of the movement or is a moment of it. Lastly, Hegel radicalizes Aristotle by bringing the theological dimension to the center. Not only is the self-articulating divine of Hegel quite different from the God of Aristotle—a difference touched on in chapter 2—and not only does Hegel include, as an instance of his revised view of the proposition, propositions where the grammatical subject is the divine, the speculative proposition is a proposition that has the divine as both its subject and object. Undoubtedly, in making his move beyond Aristotle, Hegel, as a host of commentators have recognized, more nearly belongs to the Kantian tradition of the transcendental turn to the subject. But the differences are, in the final analysis, equally conspicuous. If from Hegel's perspective the Kantian turn to the subject has to be validated, this is not to say that the Kantian theory of judgment will pass muster. It suffers from a number of systemic flaws. First, Kant does not depart decisively from Aristotle in presuming the extrinsicality of the relationship between the subject of predication and the predicates; second, the Kantian *synthetic a priori* can find no place for a proposition about the divine, not to mention a proposition that has the divine as both subject and object. In insisting that thinking is constitutive of the divine as object, Hegel not only undermines the Kantian position on the ontological argument[11] but fully radicalizes the subjective turn by refusing to accept the limits imposed by Kant on human knowing. Discursive knowing need not necessarily be a knowing with no claims to divinity.

It is in *LPR* and *Enc* that Hegel offers his definitive view of the relation between *Vorstellung* and *Begriff* and the debits of the former, even in its supreme instance in Christianity, vis-à-vis the latter. There is a good deal of continuity with the view sketched in *PS* but also a considerable amount of clarification and amplification. The continuities can be dealt with fairly briefly; the issue of clarification and amplification requires a somewhat more extended treatment. Continuity is maintained in the resolute insistence on the shared content of religious representation, Christian representation in particular, and conceptual articulation (*Enc* #573; *LPR 1* 1824 E 333, G 235; 1827 E 396–397, G 292); in the insistence that absolute religion and philosophy participate in the 'self-consciousness' of God (*Enc* #564; *LPR 1* 1827 E 276–278, G 182–183; E 334–335, G 236); in the insistence that the transition to thought as concept is, not only not destructive to absolute religion (*Enc* #571; *LPR 1* 1821 MS E 239–240, G 149–150; 1824 E 333, G 235; 1827 E 397, G 293), but calculated to protect Christianity from the subjective tendency wherein the divine becomes opaque regarding discourse (*Enc* 82+*zu*; *LPR 1* 1821 MS E 247, G 156); and in the insistence that the divine content apprehended by both representation and concept is not simple but internally differentiated. A significant amount of continuity is also preserved with regard to the more general and specific debits of religious representation vis-à-vis concept. As mediating between image and concept in general, the symbolization of the divine that is wholly dominated by image (art, lower order religion) on the one hand, and a symbolization of pure thought on the other, it is difficult, if not impossible, for representation to throw off all vestige of image. Representation is infiltrated by image that provides it with its mythic element (*LPR 1* 1821 MS E 238, G 148). The Berlin texts also agree with

PS in believing that imagistic thinking associates with the hypostatizing of the understanding (*Verstand*). The *Enc* is particularly apropos. In the concluding paragraphs Hegel complains of the fragmentation of the 'indivisible coherence' of Spirit into parts bearing an external relation to each other (#571) and the entifying of the abstract, universal divine, thereby cut off from an articulation that constitutes it as subject (#565).

The clarifications and amplifications of the position of *PS* are as important as the repetitions. The negative and positive aspects of evaluation that in *PS* exist side by side are seen in these later texts to be grounded in the 'inbetween' status of *Vorstellung*. In *LPR* and *Enc*, religious representation forms a tensional field that, in principle, accounts for a whole spectrum of varieties of religious symbolization both within and without Christianity.[12] Within this field, some varieties of Christianity gravitate more nearly to the image or the thought-pole. And from what Hegel suggests about the superiority of speculative theology over purely biblical theology, the religious stance of Pietism, Romantic Intuitism, and theology of a rationalistic stripe, differences in Christian symbolization are accounted for as actualizations of the various possibilities of the dominance-recessiveness of image and thought. Interestingly, Hegel does not seem to think that a self-consciously antimythic or demythologizing rendition of Christianity is necessarily nearer the thought-pole. At the very least, he believes there exist similarities in the depth-structure of rationalist and imagistic thought, inside as well as outside the Christian tradition (e.g., *LPR 1* 1824 E 254–255, G 162–163)).[13] Another clarification provided by the works of the Berlin period is Hegel's belief that the inner articulation of the divine, demanding reflection in discourse of a more nearly logical type for its completion, is more adequately indicated by the reenvisagement of the Aristotelian theory of the syllogism than the proposition, an envisagement that goes hand in hand with a reenvisagement of the divine as absolute idea (*Enc* #564–574; *LPR 1* 1821 MS 119–120, G 36–37). Thus, not only is there a theologization of the syllogism, there is a sense in which the syllogism is not external and formal in the way the Aristotelian syllogism is (*Enc* #181–183),[14] for it is part of the logic of the Idea (*Enc* #213 ff) that it connotes an interiorization of syllogism.

The fundamental amplification of the view of *PS* exerted by *Enc* and *LPR* concerns the systemic debits of representation vis-à-vis concept. Three debits are particularly important, with the first two being the more conspicuous. Though *PS* does speak of annulment of time (*die*

Zeit tilgt) (#801, *GL2:* 613) enacted in absolute knowing, this is, at best, only formally similar to what in *Enc* and *LPR* amounts to an injunction that, in order for the divine to be adequately rendered, the sequential mode of registering the divine marking representation necessarily will have to be transcended (*LPR 1* 1824 E 334, G 236; 1827 E 400, G 295). The *locus classicus* of the expression of representational disadvantage and corresponding conceptual advantage is to be found in the *Enc.* Paragraphs 565 and 571 are of exemplary importance. In the former Hegel complains about successiveness being introduced into the divine; in the latter he complains of the 'indivisible coherence' of the divine being sundered by a mode of construal in which 'a temporal and external sequence' is to the fore. Representation's manner of illicitly temporalizing the divine is intimately related to the second defect of symbolization, i.e., the problematic introduction of 'happening' and 'accident' into the depiction of the divine that affects the kind of coherence required to constitute the divine as truth (also science) (*Enc* #1, 9; *LPR 1* 1821 MS E 247–248, G 156; 1824 E 334, G 236). This coherence is guaranteed if and only if what Hegel refers to as 'the connectional matrix' (*LPR* 1821 MS E 248–249, G 156–158) is structured by necessity rather than by contingent event (*LPR 1* 1821 MS E 255–256, G 163; 1827 E 401–402, G 296). This point is something of a refrain in Hegel's interpretation of the various episodes of the Christian narrative which he wants to save and rehabilitate. It marks, as we saw in chapters 3 and 4, his treatment of the theologoumena of creation and incarnation. As a whole, the Berlin texts bring to explicitness a view already broached in *PS* (#769), where Hegel recommends the replacement of a discourse of happening by a discourse of necessity. Throughout, his treatment of Christian theologoumena Hegel is severe on the consequences the discourse of happening has for the view of the divine and the possibility of science. Interestingly, however, the debits of representation do not typify all theological accounts. In his appeal to speculative mystics such as Eckhart and Boehme, Hegel seems to suggest that correction of this inherently negative tendency is a property of the Christian tradition itself.

Though it is the first two deficits that dominate Hegelian attention in *LPR* and *Enc,* there exists a third, more specific, tendency manifest in Christianity that also comes in for attention.[15] This is the tendency to see events as discrete actions dependent upon discrete acts of divine volition subject to no restraint (*LPR 1* 1821 MS E 249, G 159). In *Enc* there are a number of different ways in which this is combatted on the most general level: (1) determining that logic, with its system of divine predicates and archetypes, articulates a rational field that sets restrictions on the divine; (2) authorizing the use of the language of 'will,' but having this language qualified in the context of mind with 'rational' (#445); (3) feeling comfortable, like the later Schelling, with speaking of the divine in terms of will (#232–233) without being a theological voluntarist in the strict sense;[16] (4) welcoming the attribution of freedom to God, while insisting that freedom properly understood cannot be rendered as *liberum arbitrium* (#183 ff); and (5) suggesting that reality is constituted by a rationality drive that expresses itself in increasingly adequate forms of syllogism that are anything but ontotheologically empty (#181–213; also *SL*, 664–665).[17]

Two points stand out in the amplification and clarification in Hegel's Berlin work of *PS* concerning the relationship between representation and concept and the deficiency of the former vis-à-vis the latter. First, it does seem as if the general drift of Hegel's mature work is toward moving beyond narrative discourse in religion, specifically, narrative discourse in Christianity, at least to the extent that this discourse is episodic. Second, there seems to be some warrant for the view that, despite a relatively clear demarcation of the boundaries of concept and representation, Hegel seems to suggest that representation is capable of approximating to concept to the extent to which it already is involved in a critique of its more imagistic and episodic intention. We shall be returning to this point momentarily, as we attempt to formalize those operations of critique that must necessarily attend the movement from *Vorstellung* to *Begriff* and which are, to some extent, constitutive of the latter.

Section 7.2 Agents of Speculative Rewriting

The guiding question here is whether a metabasis occurs in the movement from representation to concept, involving a shift from a narrative to a nonnarrative form of discourse. A specification of this issue is the question whether the maximum of narrative coherence insured by the four narrative operators (anaclasis, synclasis, prolepsis, analepsis) as these function nomologically in Hegel's rendition of the limit-possibility of *Vorstellung* within Christianity—and are seen to be appropriate to heterodox modes of thought in a way they are not for more nearly orthodox modes—can be seen to approximate at least the kind of logical coherence validated by *Begriff.* The question can be asked because Hegel, not only does not unilaterally criticize representation, but he thinks that it reaches much higher than Christianity's detractors and even defenders presume. The question ought to be asked, since whatever 'logical' means for Hegel, it does not mean analytic in Kant's sense. *A fortiori,* it cannot be identified with modern logic which, motored by logical operators, proceeds by means of strict logical implication. Connected with this specification is another that revolves around the issue of the principled replaceability, thus redundancy, of narrative relations. This issue is crystallized in the question whether narrative relations of anteriority-posteriority are dismantled in the elevation to the level of logical relations with their requirement of reciprocal determination.[18] In what follows I will offer a bifocal perspective, i.e., a look at the effect the movement to *Begriff* has on *Vorstellung* not worked over by the narrative operators, anaclasis-synclasis, prolepsis-analepsis, and *Vorstellung* as it has been so worked.

As is evident from our textual rehearsal of the movement from representation to concept, a number of what might be called 'denarratizing operations' are crucially involved. These operations suggest the presence of threshold operators responsible for the protection of the integrity of conceptual space. Now these operators, which can effect both the upper as well as lower reaches of representation, can be divided into two groups: the first, most obviously affecting lower-level renditions of the Christian narrative, the second, affecting all rendition equally. The first group consists of three denarratizing operators with one operator apparently having something like regulative status. This operator, most clearly rendered in *Enc* (#565, 571) but not absent from *LPR* (e.g., *LPR 1* 1824 E 334, G 236), might be referred to as the *antipunctiliar* or *antiepisodic* operator, i.e., its function is to remove any hint in discourse that the divine movement can be viewed as a sequence of discrete actions strung together on a temporal line. This involves expugning all punctiliar or episodic indicators such as 'first,' 'then,' 'and then,' etc. The second and third members of the first group of denarratizing operators relate closely to the group's regulative member. the second operator, which also is well represented in *Enc* (#1, 9) and *LPR* (e.g., *LPR 1* 1821 MS E 247–248, G 156), effects the erasure of suggestions of contingency, deconstructs the language of happening and accident. The third operator, which from a logical point of view can be regarded either as a corollary of the other two or an operator in its own right, receives a somewhat more sketchy instantiation in *Enc* and *LPR.*[19] This operator erases the tendency in representation to construe divine activity in terms of discrete acts of will. This operator isdirected, therefore, against any and all forms of theological voluntarism, whether biblical or otherwise.[20]

The second group of denarratizing operators consists of a single member. A text such as *Enc* (#574) suggests at one crucial point that a condition of the possibility of the move to *Begriff* is the subversion of the narrative order of posteriority-anteriority and the corresponding strict maintenance of the equipotency of any of the major spheres or epochs of the Christian trinitarian narrative at filling any place in a sequence that moves toward the condition of an unsurpassably teleologically wrought syllogism. Specifically, as one moves to the level of the concept proper, it becomes a matter of indifference as to which of the spheres of Universality, Particularity, or Individuality mediates and is mediated, and which of the terms is regarded as presupposition, which as conclusion. Thus one way of reading Hegel's discussion at the end of *Enc* is to take him to suggest that, in the language of *LPR,* a connectional matrix is maintainable without regard to particular sequence. If this reading were to be sustained, it would amount to a radical destruction of the narrative character of the Inclusive Trinity to which Hegel gives general support and endanger any and all claim that Christianity, albeit in a highly swerved form, is the presupposition of Hegelian philosophy or, indeed, that it can be legitimately claimed that Christianity and Hegelian philosophy share the same content. For the absolutely minimal condition of narrative is an ordered, irreversible sequence. The apparent presence of this second kind of operator challenges in a way that, arguably, the first group of denarratizing operators do not, the possibility of any ontotheological continuity between penultimate and ultimate levels of symbolization. It is hoped that our discussion will make clear that, if this denarratizing operation is suggested by Hegel, it does not have the kind of unrestricted scope that would cut off all continuity between the different levels of symbolization. This crucially important matter will be attended to in due course. Before we get to it, however, there is much to say about the first group of denarratizing operators that traject symbolization into the sphere of the concept proper. Our discussion begins with the regulative member of the first group.

Hegel's opposition to the punctiliar dimension of Christian representation is well-known and has received its fair share of commentary in the secondary literature.[21] Consistently throughout *LPR,* and especially in his discussion of the religious syllogism in *Enc* (#565, 571), Hegel complains about representational optics fragmenting what from the conceptual point of view is the unity of divine activity into discrete episodes with a distinct temporal connotation. He calls for a vision that respects the indivisible coherence of the three spheres of the inclusive Christian Trinity and suggests that such coherence has its proper domain in the realm of *Begriff* by substituting the language of Universality-Particularity-Individuality for the standard Christian representational language of Father, Son, and Spirit. Still, it is hugely interesting that Hegel can talk of such coherence at the level of *Vorstellung*. Needless to say, this does not imply that *Vorstellung* itself has the full resources to exercise correction of the insidious general tendency of Christian representation to sunder the whole identifiable with the divine. Hegel might be after all simply mixing levels or, perhaps more likely, be looking forward to the correction of the negative tendency of *Vorstellung* in *Begriff*. Certainly, it is the case, as Schlitt has perceptively pointed out, that Christian *Vorstellung*, at least to the extent that it is championed by Hegel, is already speculatively informed.[22] The issue is, however, whether the resources for removal of the episodic belongs properly to the sphere of representation, or whether this power is loaned to it by *Begriff*. If the continuum, even tensional, field view advanced in section 1 of this chapter is correct, then it implies that a significant measure of denarratization can occur at the level of *Vorstellung*, as *Vorstellung* begins to approximate to its higher thought-pole and move away from its pictorial pole (*Bild*). That it cannot fully escape the gravitational pull of *Bild* does not mean that it cannot approximate to such escape.

Hegel's point is, at once, a systematic and a historical one: a systematic one in that he wishes to allow for the possibility of an intra-Christian discourse that is largely pruned of the episodic and punctiliar; a historical one in that Hegel's appeal to instances of heterodox species of speculative theology suggests a tradition for the discursive practice he recommends. In order to function as such, heterodox varieties of thought such as that of Boehme and Valentinian Gnosticism either have to be seen as perspicuous instances of, or at least to harmonize well with, thoroughly thoughtful representation. And if our reading of Hegel throughout is correct, then thoughtful representation is guaranteed by a significant incidence of the four narrative operators that provide the Christian narrative with a more than episodic or punctiliar narrative coherence. As a matter of fact, Hegel's actual interpretive practice seems to oscillate between suggesting, on the one hand, that heterodox varieties of thought represent supreme instances of the kind of thoughtful representation he recommends and maintaining, on the other, that they are distinguishable from the more orthodox specimens of representation by being more easily rehabilitatable. For instance, if he complains loudly of the sensuous, imagistic element in Boehme, he also praises the Boehmian rendition of the Trinity as a Trinity of the divine as subject—an envisioning impossible unless the conception involves, both on the level of discourse and reality, the explicit activity of the narrative operators, synclasis and analepsis, and, implicitly, the narrative operators, anaclasis and prolepsis. By contrast, in the case of Valentinian Gnosticism, as we saw in chapter 2, Hegel gently corrects what he thinks is an underemphasis on the narrative operators of anaclasis and prolepsis in the Valentinian account of the original triad. Though Hegel insists that these operators must be seen to inform discourse and effect the articulation of a divine on pain of the articulation of the divine being an abstraction, by comparison with his treatment of more standard Christian renditions he is extraordinarily gentle. This gentleness very well may be systemic. Certainly, it is symptomatic of long-held elective affinities. In his thank-you note to Schelling for having received a copy of his dissertation, "De Marcione Paularum epistolae emendore," Hegel felt able to deliver himself of the opinion:

> I have at once found confirmation in it of a suspicion I have harbored for a long time, namely, that it would perhaps have done more credit to us and to mankind if no matter what heresy, damned by council and creeds, had risen to become the public system of belief, instead of the orthodox system maintaining the upper hand. (Aug 30, 1795)[23]

We turn to the second denarratizing operator. In *LPR,* in particular, Hegel inveighs against the character of mere happening attributed to episodes of the Christian narrative like creation and incarnation (e.g., *LPR 1* 1824 E 334, G 236, also *LPR 3* 1821 MS E 89–90, G 27–28). Though understandable as an attempt to respect the biblical narrative's registering of divine sovereignty, much of Christian theology has, in Hegel's view, mistakenly thought of divine activity as expressing itself in acts that are gratuitous or contingent, i.e., not truly definitional of the divine. From Hegel's perspective, this construal fatally divorces the divine and nondivine world (*LPR 3* 1821 MS E 248–249, G 157) and leaves the world not with the status of mystery, as the later Schelling suggests,[24] but with the status of accident that voids it of ontological substance. While the distinction of *Schein* as illusion and *Erscheinung* as genuine appearance receives its definitive treatment in Hegel's logical works (*Enc* #131 ff, *SL* E 394 ff), it is in operational use in *LPR* (*LPR 3* 1821 MS 64–65, G 4–5). As such, it assists in Hegel's redefinition of the meaning of mystery as the disclosed and the intrinsically related, rather than the hidden and extrinsically related (*LPR 1* 1821 MS E 230, G 139). However we may symbolize the divine and the God-world relation, this divine cannot be regarded as hidden, nor this relation be understood as extrinsic to the divine.

For Hegel, the best of the Christian tradition conceives of God who, as discourse, is open to the speech-acts of illuminated human being. Thus, if philosophy involves a polemical relation to Christianity, this is not systemic but signifies both a continuity with and a development of the critical impulse of Christian tradition functioning at its highest level. Critical impulse implies speculative redescription, and this involves the removal of all traces of contingency and accident. But again, even if it is granted that the proper horizon for the removal is *Begriff,* does this means that the operation is in no wise under way in the horizon of *Vorstellung?* Though Hegel does not appear to be as clear about the prerogatives of *Vorstellung* here as he was with respect to the first denarratizing operator, it seems reasonable to infer that, as *Vorstellung* evidences some ability to erase episodic indices, it also evidences some ability to correct the suggestion of accident. For example, Hegel is of the opinion that the Christian theologoumenon of creation rightly understood moves beyond the suggestion of accident; it is intrinsically superior to the view of efficient causality that canonizes the externality of the relation between the divine and the world and makes the latter purely contingent (*LPR 1* 1821 MS E 249, G 157). A similar point might be made about the incarnation. Though his notion of reason differs *toto caelo* from that of Anselm, Hegel agrees with him in thinking that something of a rationale can be provided for an event that has the marks of a contingency that seems to resist reason. Like Anselm, Hegel wishes to avail of a broader view of necessity than the contrary of freedom and a more generous view than that mandated by modal logic. Again the point would have both a systematic and a historical side: systematic, in that Hegel would be suggesting that it is a property of *Vorstellung* in its upper reaches to provide the narrative object with the kind of unbroken coherence possible only on condition of the expunging of accident; historical, in that Hegel would see that certain nonstandard renditions of the Christian narrative (Eckhart, Boehme, Valentinian Gnosticism) either approximate in fact, or could conceivably be thought to approximate in principle, a speculative-conceptual rendition in which all suggestion of accident is removed. Nevertheless, it is still true that the horizon of the concept provides not only the space in which accident is definitively removed, it provides the self-reflexivity wherein such a move is logically mandated by redefining the meaning of necessity such that it can function as a Christianly legitimate candidate to replace chance, accident, and contingency (*Enc* #167 ff).[25] More about the warranting or justifying function of philosophy shortly, but it is time now to turn to the third and final denarratizing operator of the first group.

The third denarratizing operator represents a block on any and all varieties of theological voluntarism. For Hegel, theological voluntarism represents, on the one hand, the way in which the episodic makes impossible the discourse of the divine that is intrinsically divine discourse and, on the other, an independent dispensation that recognizes 'divine good pleasure' as the condition of both divine sovereignty and, paradoxically, the possibility of science.[26] Particularly to the fore in *Enc,* though not absent from *LPR,* this block does not so much put an embargo on the language of 'will' regarding the divine as suggest the inadequacy of viewing the divine in terms of discrete acts of will considered outside rational articulation and discourse. As *Enc* (#443 ff) shows clearly, both will and reason interpret and interpenetrate each other. Hegel's account appears to be engaging at once Descartes's connection of will and imagination and Kant's suggestion in *Religion* on the primacy of will over reason.[27] Wishing to avoid the either/or that structures early modern philosophy from Descartes on, Hegel, following the early Fichte,[28] insists on the interpenetration of will and intellect. And against Kant, Hegel does not wish to provide will with the kind of primary transcendental status Kant provides it with in the text where he makes his peace with Christian *Vorstellung.* From Hegel's perspective, this gives too much autonomy to will and makes the relation between will and reason more extrinsic than he can countenance.

Now, as with the other denarratizing operators, though the block on theological voluntarism only can be fully guaranteed by concept, still representation in its highest reaches, at a minimum, institutes a resistance to degenerate voluntarism and, at a maximum, promotes its erasure. The possibility of such restriction and critique is grounded, of course, in the ability of some versions of Christian *Vorstellung* to limit and commence erasing the episodic element that is an endemic feature of popular imagination and many of Christianity's theological and even philosophical traditions. The excess of philosophy lies in philosophy's ability to conceive the unity of will and reason in the divine and the ability to reconceive the notion of divine freedom in such a way as to distinguish it from acts of divine good pleasure (*Enc* #158–160). In taking issue with the common religious view of divine will, Hegel is obviously taking issue with the nominalist view of absolute power (*potentia absoluta*) that funded much of Luther's discourse and the tradition of Lutheran orthodoxy. But, as Chapelle has pointed out,[29] in a certain sense this species of theological voluntarism is tied also to nominalism in the broad sense, i.e., the inability of discourse to form a science, which is only guaranteed if will does not have free play and the miraculous is not the mysterious but the rational, or, at least, reasonable, exegesis of the divine plan coextensive with the divine itself.

A way of further illuminating the first group of denarratizing operators, as well as showing up Hegel's agreement and disagreement with other modern philosophies that debated the merit of representation (or its facsimile) and philosophical concept, is to address (1) Hegel's debt to and departure from Spinoza, and (2) the different ways in which Hegel and Schelling adjudicated the merits of the symbolic matrix of religion and philosophy. We start with an account of the Spinozist background of the first group of denarratizing operations and the Hegelian emendations.

While from a historical, as well as systematic, point of view, there very well may be adumbrations of these denarratizing operations on the level of *Vorstellung,* it certainly is the case that, at least as elaborated in the *Enc,* Hegel's account is in constant negotiation with the view provided by Spinoza in the *Ethics* and the *Tractatus Theologico-Politicus,* if not dependent on it. In proposing the superiority of the philosophical over the nonphilosophical mode of construing reality—which for Sponiza is divine reality—Spinoza puts himself in opposition to the episodic mode of construal.[30] For Spinoza, the episodic mentality, which has the effect of totally fragmenting the divine, is indicated by the use in religious and theological discourse of such give-away punctiliar indicators as 'when,' 'before,' 'after.' In *Ethics* BK 1 Proposition 36, Spinoza expressly rules that properly philosophical envisagement—which, it subsequently turns out, is really mystical knowledge—rules out episodic optics: in eternity, there is no before or after. The injunction extends to any and all episodic indices, whether aspirated, as in biblical narrative, or nonaspirated, as in nonnarrative accounts of creation that feature efficient causality. In the *Ethics,* the first denarratizing operation—belonging in Spinoza's view only in the domain of philosophy—is connected to the second and third; for the barring order on successiveness is joined to barring orders on considering the divine activity of self-expression as exposing itself to contingency or voluntarism in any fashion. In *Ethics* BK 1 Propositions 33,

35, Spinoza rules that an envisagement of divine self-expression as contingent essentially reduces divine act to chance. A fully wrought philosophical view, by contrast, sees that all things proceed necessarily from God. Moreover, this does not make the divine subject to fate; rather, on the basis of the definition of freedom provided, i.e., the absence of external determination, freedom and necessity coincide. Spinoza's conjunction obviously funds Hegel's assertion in *Enc* (#158 ff) of the interdefinability of freedom and necessity. As Spinoza puts the matter to his philosophical and theological enemies in his letters to Boxel, the appropriate contrary to necessity is not freedom but chance.[31]

At a very obvious level, Spinoza's reenvisagement of the demands of philosophical discourse that avoids empty formalism dictates an attack against every species of theological voluntarism. The targets include the popular religious imagination of Judaism and Christianity normed in the last instance by the biblical narrative, nominalistic thought, and Cartesian voluntarism. Again, the *locus classicus* is the *Ethics* which rules that envisioning divine activity as a series of discrete divine acts, incomprehensible even after the fact, and totally unpredictable from a prospective point of view, at once misconstrues the integrity of divine expression and makes science impossible.[32] Again Spinoza's concerns are Hegel's. In practice, if not in principle, Spinoza thinks that voluntarism is so insidious that he is prepared to banish all reference to will as an appropriate term for the divine. In this, he is not followed by Leibniz, who, if anitvoluntarist in principle,[33] presumes will can be rehabilitated by integrating it with wisdom. Hegel follows Leibniz's lead here. In doing so, Hegel wishes to suggest the principled coincidence of will and wisdom in the divine in such a way as to reenvisage the famous either/or of the *Eutyphro* rather than leave it intact as Leibniz tends to do.[34] Not caring for the moral appeal Leibniz has recourse to, Hegel refuses to authorize the language of choice when it comes to the divine. For Hegel, such discourse involves backsliding into the very voluntarism that the suggestion of the coincidence of will and wisdom or reason is meant to undermine. Accepting Leibniz's emendation of Spinoza, i.e., the reintegration of the language of will into the divine, Hegel might be thought of as correcting Leibniz back in a Spinozist direction, without, however, ever coming to fully endorse a Spinozist position.

Hegel's minor, but not insignificant, departure from Spinoza here raises the question of more systemic Hegelian departure. Given earlier discussion (in chapters 2 and 3, in particular) of the ontotheological differences between Spinoza and Hegel, it is clear that the denarratizing operators Hegel finds ready at hand in Spinoza function in a more unrestricted way in Spinoza's system than in his own. For, as we pointed out there, the general drift of Hegel's movement beyond Spinoza lays in his affirmation of narrative operators that structure the divine as discourse, as well as discourse of the divine. Unless we wish to presume that Hegel is being frivolously inconsistent in also supporting Spinoza's set of denarratizing operators, this implies, at the very least, that the denarratizing operators do not necessarily interfere with the narrative operators that guarantee narrative coherence and severely limit the episodic tendency in representation. It may also imply, at the maximum, that the exercise of the denarratizing operators actually presupposes the exercise of narrative operators. Denarratizing operators, in any event, play a more restricted role in Hegel's case than they do in Spinoza. This greater restrictedness of role is connected with a considerably more positive estimation of the limits of religious discourse. For Spinoza, the upper and lower limits of Judaism and Christianity coincide. Religion may have its positive, essentially practical force, but it is, as the *Tractatus* points out, systemically unable to view reality in the proper perspective. At least when considering Christianity, Hegel perceives a spectrum of accomplishment, with speculative theology at the upper levels of representation approximating to what is possible on the level of concept. And if we have been correct in our analysis, upper level *Vorstellung* is constituted by the functioning of narrative operators. Extrapolating this suggests three hypotheses worthy of attention. (1) *Vorstellung* is not separated from conceptual thought in Hegel, as it is in Spinoza, by an absolute divide.[35] (2) From a Hegelian perspective, Spinozist denarratizing operators may be dependent in some way upon the functioning of narrative operators that help unite what is divided and engender continuity in the noncontinuous. Where such narrative operators are not actually functioning in religious representation—and Hegel assumes that they are not functioning in much of the Christian ontotheological tradition—the denarratizing operators function with the same lack of restraint as they do in Spinoza. Their function is thoroughly critical and iconoclastic. By contrast, where such narrative operators are functioning in discourse, the denarratizing operators simply augment a critical process already under way. (3) It is plausibly only the union of narrative and denarratizing operations that, at the level of being as well as knowing, guarantees the dynamic self-differentiating activity that defines Spirit. I feel obliged to explicate the last mentioned point, even at the risk of overcomplicating an already complicated discussion.

The assertion of the irradicability of narrative operations as against Spinozism takes not one but two forms. The form emphasized in (2) is the form we are familiar with since chapter 2, where we discussed in some detail Hegel's criticism of Spinoza's account of the finite as mode. Put simply, Hegel criticizes Spinoza for a radical finitization of reality, for mode is a principle of difference without unity. And it is the task of narrative operators to introduce coherence into a field of difference that otherwise would be a glorious example of a bad infinite. The presence of such operators in Christianity, Hegel believes, above all in the Christian doctrine of the Trinity, specifies the superiority of Christianity not only over Spinoza in particular but over Judaism in general. Hegel's other form of defense seems to take an entirely different tack. Here narrative operations are defended, not insofar as they guarantee unity in difference, but insofar as they guarantee the reality of difference that is being threatened by Spinoza's monism. Narrative operations insure an articulated divine and a divine articulated as discourse. Though it may seem to be an example of Freud's kettledrum logic, Hegel is not being inconsistent in making these apparently unrelated accusations. From his point of view, the two accusations are different sides of the same coin. The dynamism and finitism of Spinoza's depiction of mode is directly related to his tendency to conceive Substance in static terms, since their relation is extrinsic. The denial of a principle of unification to the field of mode bears directly on the denial to Substance of intrinsic differentiation.

To round out this set of contrasts, it is apposite to return to the distinction between Hegel and Spinoza made above regarding the appropriateness of speaking of the divine in terms of will. Hegel appears to be considerably less traumatized than Spinoza when it comes to discussing will in the context of the divine (*Enc* #443). Hegel's subversive conclusion supposes that he accepts Spinoza's assertion of the intrinsic relation between the divine and reason but opposes Spinoza's exclusion of will from reason. Hegel, of course, can be more sanguine about will than Spinoza, since he does not have to respond directly to Cartesian voluntarism, though it and other species of voluntarism continue to bedevil philosophical and theological discourse. Spinoza, therefore, is seen as being a little too reactionary and not having thought through the intrinsic relation between thought and will, where thought and will relate closely to Spinoza's own pair of necessity and freedom.[36] Much detail could be added to this very broad outline of the distinct ways in which Hegel and Spinoza think through the relation between concept and representation, the nature of the discourse of the divine, as well as the divine as discourse. It is because of the close relation between the demands of narrative and conceptual coherence that Hegel at once can challenge the appropriateness of the geometrical method to articulate the divine and question the Euclidean reading of the relation between the divine and its expression. We turn to the second topic for discussion the relation between Hegel and the later Schelling.

It is interesting for two quite distinct reasons to compare Hegel and Schelling, particularly the later Schelling, regarding their validation or nonvalidation of what we have called denarratizing operations. First, the validation or nonvalidation of these operations may be the hinge upon which a distinction between the two ontotheological projects is made. And second, it may show up the different ways in which Hegel and Schelling ultimately respond to the demands of conceptual discourse laid down negatively in Spinoza's inchoate outlining of a set of denarratizing operations. Of Schelling's later philosophy it especially can be said that, while it validates those narrative operations espoused by Hegel,[37] it questions the need for philosophy as such to be defined by the presence of denarratizing operators that are both prescribed and exemplified in Hegel's work. In a sense, one way of distinguishing a positive from a negative philosophy is precisely the relaxation of denarratizing operations thought necessary to distinguish philosophical from religious discourse, on the one hand, and presumed necessary to preserve the integrity of philosophical discourse, on the other.[38] Though the later Schelling is of a piece with his earlier self in thinking that popular episodic understanding of the divine is deficient, this does not imply for him that a *temporal-like* discourse is totally out of the order with regard to the divine, provided the analogical nature of this discourse is kept in mind and narrative coherence is at an optimum. This means that he is prepared, albeit with appropriate reservation, to countenance the language of past, present, and future with respect to God.[39] Yet if the language is not literal, it is not quite as metaphorical as Hegel's one concession to this nomenclature given in the *Enc* (#112 *zu*), where Hegel discusses the etymological connection between essence and past or *Wesen* and *gewessen*.[40] Again, with the intention of not reverting totally to the level of biblical construal, or to those theological systems critiqued by Spinoza and Hegel, Schelling nevertheless feels called upon to modify the Spinozist identification of freedom and necessity adopted by Hegel, which in his earlier incarnation he supported.[41] Freedom, he suggests, must be understood to involve some measure of contingency, just as, similarly, not all elements of compulsion can, or ought to, be excised from necessity.[42] A code for this departure in his *Philosophy of Revelation*, which, as with Hegel, insists on the presupposition of Christianity for philosophical thought, is Schelling's talk of 'the more than necessary development' on the level of the divine.[43] Third and last, Schelling takes issue with the need for as thoroughgoing an excision of voluntarism as that announced by Spinoza and recapitulated in Hegel. For Schelling, the Christian tradition was right in talking about God in voluntarist terms, not Spinoza in his excision or Hegel in his rationalist co-option. Will logically involves choice. Here, Schelling agrees with Leibniz and feels it necessary to continue to use the traditional and popular language of choice. Nevertheless, actual choice, even in the divine, must submit to a sequencing tied to the teleological goal of the engendering of a divine personality.

Now the teleological matrix of divine self-constitution is guaranteed by narrative operations of the kind evident in a speculative theological thinker like Jacob Boehme.[44] From Schelling's point of view, it is redundant at best, and falsifying at worst, to go beyond that realizable at the upper limits of representation and to give unrestricted employment to denarratizing operations that logicize all discourse and introduce a false closure. It is not difficult to imagine Hegel's reply to the later Schelling had he deigned to do so. On the most general level, he would undoubtedly have felt that positive philosophy not only betrays the critical impulse that in his view—as is the case in post-Kantian philosophy in general—is constitutive of philosophy, but that it exposes religion to the potential, even actual, abuses of popular religious imagination that have not held Christianity in good stead over the centuries. Because it is not calculated to rehabilitate, neither can it protect Christianity from deformation from both its friends and enemies alike. Furthermore, positive philosophy can do nothing about the establishment of a scientific method or super-science that will provide a coherence-network for the particular sciences. Philosophy represents both the condition of the healing of the split between religious and conceptual discourse and the guarantee that the fragmenting scientific disciplines have a unifying center. This center is, of course, from the vantage point of a variety of postmodernisms, the apotheosis of the ontotheological illusion that haunts Western philosophical discourse and that has had before Hegel exemplary instantiations in the classical ancient philosophy of Plato and Aristotle, as well as Aquinas. From Hegel's perspective, such a unifying center is absolutely necessary not only on the pragmatic grounds that without the presence of such a unifying function culture falls apart—an argument that is vulnerable to the Nietzchian riposte that such a presence is, in the end, precisely the cause of fragmentation—but also because it is this unifying ontotheological ground that validates the vocation of truth—a vocation that is similarly dismissed by Nietzsche and post-Nietzschian connoisseurs.

On a purely theological level, Hegel would also see problems with Schelling's narrative construal of the divine. First, in his discussion of the requirements of narrative coherence, thus narrative operators, Schelling does not break free from a more traditional voluntaristic understanding of the divine, even if he seriously modifies it. From a Hegelian point of view, Schelling's discourse is marked by the ghosts of nominalism, Cartesian theological voluntarism, and, above, all a voluntarist Luther. Indeed, it is precisely to prevent backsliding into a more traditional voluntarist rendition that denarratizing operators become a theological necessity. What unites Schelling, therefore, with Walter Kasper and Eberhard Jüngel divides him from Hegel.[45] Second, there is the issue of whether all four narrative operators are present in the work of the later Schelling. This issue is logically distinct from the issue of whether narrative operators are, indeed, present but rendered somewhat ineffective by elements of the borrowed picture of traditional theism. In the work of the later Schelling, it is certainly the case, for example, that a 'sense of an ending' is hinted at. Yet, since history, as a scene of divine definition, is not closed, the level of teleology is such that it remains vulnerable to Hegel's objection to the early Fichte: failure of circularity implies the failure of teleology and thus, ultimately, of narrativity. And failure of narrativity has the consequence that the divine as discourse does not become fully actual, and thus not fully ontologically, existentially, and axiologically reliable. Third, the constitutive error of the Schellingian revival of what amounts to an unredeemed Boehmianism is that it places too little trust in philosophy, just as Spinoza had placed too much. More specifically, in his aversion to denarratizing operators, Schelling fails to understand the supplementary character of these operators intended to protect—and not at all to undermine—the dynamic character of the divine. Moreover, Hegel believes that such protection can be provided the discourse of the divine, while at the same time guaranteeing that divine discourse has gnoseological and epistemic validity. Sacrificing the latter is a function of sacrificing the former. The sacrifice is as unnecessary as it is undesirable.

We come now to the second group of denarratizing operations and thus operators. This second group, which consists of merely one member, presents the most serious challenge to the thesis of continuity between representation and concept. For if this operation, which because of the resemblance it bears to structuralist treatments of narrative may be called *structuralization,*[46] can be proven to be unrestricted in scope, then any and all narrative analysis of Hegel can only claim to be illuminating up to a point. Put negatively, 'structuralization' suggests that in the move from religious *Vorstellung* to *Begriff,* the sequenced order that is the indelible property of even that higher-order Christian representation schematized in the structure of Universality-Particularity-Individuality, is breakable in principle. Put more positively, structuralization suggests the indifference of placement with regard to the mediating or the mediated role of the three spheres of Universality, Particularity, and Singularity. Each of the spheres can legitimately play the role of the mediating term—and not, as in the speculatively informed rendition of Christian representation, Particularity alone; each of the three spheres can play the role of first or third term of a movement that, for Hegel in his more mature work, is better captured in a revision of the classical view of the syllogism than in a revision of the classical view of the proposition.[47] The *locus classicus* for the suggestion of this denarratizing operation is Hegel's account of the movement from religious to philosophical syllogism at the end of *Enc* (#564–574).

There is considerable discussion in the secondary literature of how the three syllogisms of philosophy match the three syllogisms of religion.[48] Often the discussion proceeds as if there were a one-to-one correspondence between each of the three members of both kinds of syllogisms. And while, indeed, there is a measure of formal correspondence between the first, second, and third of the religious and philosopohical syllogisms, the fact is that, from a content point of view, the three philosophical syllogisms do not so much translate the ontotheological content of the three religious syllogisms into a more adequate idiom as represent three renditions of the first religious syllogism, synonymous with the "one syllogism of the self-mediation of the Spirit" (#571). This syllogism rightly may be referred to as the master syllogism of consummate religion coextensive with the Inclusive Trinity. When Hegel suggests, therefore, in the various philosophical renditions of the master syllogism that the realms of Universality, Particularity, and Individuality in the sphere of concept can break the narrative order provided by the master syllogism, something profoundly subversive may be afoot—something that relativizes any narrative based conclusions that might be drawn. What this essentially means is that the necessity of a connectional matrix and sequence is maintained, but no order in the sequencing is thought, in principle, to have priority over another sequencing. Now, if this were truly the case, then Hegel would have introduced a radical denarratizing move breaking the link between concept and representation in a way the first group of denarratizing operators cannot. The apparent announcement of such an operator at the close of *Enc* is of such importance that it encourages the search for corroboration in other Hegelian texts. Some corroboration seems to be offered by Hegel's insistence, for example, in the *Philosophy of Nature* that the emergence of nature can be understood—presumably legitimately understood—from an evolutionalist, as well as emanationist, perspective. Or, put in the language of Universality, Particularity, and Individuality that allows religion an entrée into the confines of a conceptual matrix, nature as Particularity can be construed either as a first term mediated by the Individuality of noetically and practically mastering historical human being with its destination being Universality as an illuminated and illuminating self-consciousness transcending the limited conditions of empirical and historical knowledge; or, nature as Particularity can be regarded as the mediating term with Universality the first and Individuality the third term, respectively. Of course, when Hegel suggests this he is not doing a great deal more than what Schelling did in his early work when he paired philosophy of nature and transcendental philosophy. Still, the equal plausibility of distinct theories based upon the equipotency of each realm to occupy a different place in a narrative sequence that in Christianity has an irreversible order certainly appears to pull the rug from under any and all commitment to Christian narrative, no matter how heterodox that commitment ultimately turns out to be.

Still, I want to argue that, in the final analysis, Hegel does not fully commit to structuralization or commit himself, at least, to an unrestricted view of structuralization. If the order, Universality (U), Particularity (P), Individuality (I), is given priority in *LPR*, it is not clear that the *Enc* ultimately withdraws the hegemony of this ordered sequence. And the reason for saying this is not that, as a simple matter of fact, *Enc* proceeds from Universality through Particularity to Individuality; it is more that, in order to indicate from the outset that the grammatical subject of becoming is the divine, Hegel is, in fact, constrained to commence with the sphere of Universality. If, in order to gesture to the circularity that is the prerogative of science, Hegel wishes to complement the syllogistic form, First Philosophical Syllogism (hereafter PS1), i.e., U-P-I, with Second Philosophical Syllogism (hereafter PS2) or P-I-U and Third Philosophical Sylligism (hereafter PS3), or I-U-P, this does not endanger the primacy of the theological syllogism which informs and regulates the other two less obviously theological syllogisms. Outside the context of regulation by PSI as the direct translation of the theological syllogism, PS2 would render a materialist-evolutionist Hegel that would be in no need of Feurbachian, Marxist, or even strictly evolutionist transformation. Though the fact that Hegel was read in the nineteenth century as if his entire philosophy had the divine as the grammatical subject of his discourse—and the divine itself as the real subject of his discourse only as articulated by a reality that is discourse—does not in itself prove, of course, that PS1 is regulative, still,at the very least, it encourages the questions of whether PS2 and PS3 should be read as ontotheological substitutes for PS1 and, if they are not to be so read, what purpose or purposes do they serve.

By way of answering the first question it is important to distinguish between what might be called ontotheological and perspectival structuralization. Ontotheological structuralization suggests that in the move form *Vorstellung* to *Begriff* the ordered sequence of the master religious syllogism can be broken and the terms made free-floating and susceptible to rearrangement. If ordered sequence were a matter of the form and not the content of religion, ontotheological structuralization would be inconsequential, that is, if it were not an impossibility. But, if as I interpet it to be the case, particular ordered sequence is not only important to the content of Christianity but constitutive of it, ontotheological structuralization would have the effect, not of sublating the content of Christianity summarized in the master syllogism of U-P-I, but anihilating it. By contrast, perspectival structuralizaiton suggests that the three syllogisms of philosophy represent three perspectives on the master religious syllogism, with only PSI directly translating it. Considered perspectively, neither PS2 nor PS3 would involve the deconstruction of the master religious syllogism directly translated by PS1; they would, in fact, represent different entrées into the shared narrative of religion and philosophy. Their presence would announce that however one entered the ontotheological narrative, the narrative would tend to get reconstructed. For instance, one might enter the narrative at P, but the relation between P and I would bring U into the reckoning. Needless to say, multiple points of entry are possible also within the context of representation. In fact, there is no reason to suppose that representation is less adept at reconstituting the narrative from points of entry not coextensive with the arché of the ontotheological narrative. Indeed, given the christological focus of Lutheranism that Hegel attempts to reprise, it very well may be fated to do so. The christological nodal point places the believer in the sphere of Particularity or Individuality, depending upon which of Hegel's two narrative schemes are in operation. It is from this epistemic vantage point that it sets about the task of excavating the trinitarian metanarrative. Nevertheless, religion suffers from the disadvantage that it is less able than philosophy to distinguish between narrative differences of a perceptual and a real sort. As such, it is also less capable of seeing infrastructural similarities beneath phenomenal differences. It is philosophy, therefore, that is the organ for deciding on difference of narrative structure; it is philosophy that is the site of true ecumenism. A further advantage of philosophy is that within a conceptual framework the primacy of the ordered sequence U-P-I is dissociated from the temporal first and last. We will return to this advantage momentarily.

If Hegel really only supports the perspectival version of structuralizaiton, what advantages does such perspectival variation have over the simple straightforward translation of the master religious syllogism by PSI? Three advantages come to mind. (1) One effect of structuralization has been suggested already: variation ultimately protects the theological primacy of the ordered sequence, U-P-I. Yet such protection has a number of useful ontotheological consequences. First, it serves as a block against representational consciousness lapsing into the comfortable theistic presumption that, since U is the grammatical subject of the religious master syllogism, this implies that it is a fully constituted actor. The second and third syllogisms suggest that the real subject of discourse, of which the grammatical subject represents the abstraction, is Spirit. Second, it exacerbates the teleological dimension insisted on in Hegel's account of the speculatively informed religious syllogism.[49] Variation exacerbates the teleological dimension constitutive of the divine Idea by suggesting that the connections within the master syllogism are so deep and internal that they are not undermined by having different starting, end, and middle points. (2) Perspectival variation also suggests a kind of free play that is only possible in the context of a conceptual matrix that can be legitimately spoken of as the self-consciousness of the divine where the subjective-genitive aspect is not repressed, as it tends to be in much of Christianity. Not only can the thinking self in its move to concept speak about divine freedom, it can exemplify it. If Spinoza is the ultimate ontotheological source for Hegel here, it very well may be the case that it is Schiller's view of the interpenetration of freedom and inevitability in aesthetic production that most nearly informs Hegel's view of the free, but nonarbitrary, disposition of the absolute Idea. (3) Perspectival variation also could be thought to serve a methodological purpose for the organization of the sciences. For if commentators such as Petry go too far in suggesting that the *Enc* should be read as if were only a methodological treatise,[50] it is nevertheless true that this is one of its major aims as witnessed in the divisions of *Logic, Philosophy of Nature, Philosophy of Mind,* which methodological divisions, as *Enc* #574 points out, translate the more ontotheologically laden vocabulary of Universality, Particularity, and Individuality. The important point here is that, in contradistinction to Petry, there is no need to make an either/or of the ontotheological and the methodological. Iljin remains the standard of sobriety in this regard, insisting on their complementarity.

To sum up then: granted its perspectival nature, structuralization is restricted and consequently does not have the effect of dismantling the ontotheological narrative preserved in PS1. As we saw earlier, the same can be said of the first group of denarratizing operators, i.e., the punctiliar operators. The upshot of all of this is that, far from abolishing narrative, *Begriff* is a witness to its perdurance in a form that escapes, on the one hand, the inhospitable friendship of popular religious imagination and various classical as well as modern forms of theology and, on the other, the hospitable enmity of rationalism and atheism. Together these two groups of denarratizing operators represent the site of Christianity's narrative protection and rehabilitation. That Christianity is in need of such protection and rehabilitation is a deeply held view of Hegel, since Christian representation by and large gravitates toward the lower image-pole of representation. Yet protection and rehabilitation also must be seen to be under way within representation itself to the extent that it moves toward its own thought-pole, and Hegel is convinced that Christian speculative theology provides quite a few instances. Within the speculative theology tradition, however, the protection and rehabilitation tends to be twofold. It can—and does, to a certian extent—exemplify the critical denarratization stance of philosophy; but it also prepares for the exercise of such critical correction by highlighting the teleological manifold of the Christian narrative by means of the narrative operators this text has spoken about so often. Still, even these narrative operators become conceptual property in the sublation of representation into concept. The union of such operators is calculated to provide a narratively enacted trinitarian divine that is, in the classical Patristic sense, *adiastematic,* i.e., without division.[51] The Hegelian revolution is not hard to see. Whereas in Cappadocian thought such an attribution can be made only of the "Immanent Trinity", in Hegel it can be made of the inclusive trinitarian process that embraces the immanent divine and its relations as but a moment.

On the basis of what we have said thus far, it would seem that concept is inextricably tied to representation as philosophical syllogism is inextricably tied to ontotheological narrative. But this raises the critical problem: what happens to Hegel's oft-made claim for the autonomy of the speculative thought? This issue is brought sharply into focus by Michael Rosen who opposes and adjudicates between the rival claims of what he calls the 'transformational' and 'generative' approaches to the nature of concept and philosophical discourse in general.[52] If the former assumes that concept implies a working on representation such that its metaphoricity and lack of necessity is corrected, the latter insists that thought or concept generates its own content. Not having an ideological axe to grind, Rosen acknowledges that there exists substantial textual evidence for both positions. Though Rosen's textual examination largely restricts itself to *Enc,* the passages he mentions are, indeed, representative and adequately serve the role of suggesting a tension in Hegelian texts between two different positions. Enlarging the textual domain beyond the Hegelian system in the strict sense does not resolve the issue by producing a preponderance of the evidence in one direction rather than another, for other texts of Hegel's mature period variously emphasize at different points that philosophy presupposes other discourses—particularly religious discourse—and independently constitutes its content. Forced to adjudicate, however, Rosen opines that the more telling evidence points in the direction of the generative thesis. He counts as especially telling a passage in *Enc* (#163)[53] where, ironically, religion itself is invoked to warrant the position that thought is generative. The Christian doctrine of *creation from nothing* is the basic metaphor for the untrammeled creativity of the concept. This important question is so lucidly posed by Rosen, and handled so soberly, that there is a certain awkwardness in cavilling. And while on the basis of section 7.2 it would be unlikely that we would accept his conclusion that the essential drift in Hegelian texts is in a generative direction, the cavilling really concerns Rosen's either/or that forces a more or less definitive choice between the transformative and generative approaches. Now, it well may be the case that Hegel is not entitled to have it both ways. But the fact that there exists substantial evidence for both approaches may just as nearly suggest that *Begriff* can be thought of as being transformative and generative at once, as that Hegel felt pulled in two mutually exclusive directions. This implies among other things that the apparent championing of the transformative thesis, explicitly in the last section and implicitly throughout the text, by no means entails the denial that Hegel consistently considered thought as concept to be generative.

Viewed from the vantage point of other commentators, Rosen's dualistic logic, which rules that philosophical concept either presupposes *Vorstellung* or is presuppositionless, is unnecessarily restrictive. Hegel's thought, it has been argued, exemplifies a genuinely third type: conceptual discourse has the ability to recursively account for its own presupposition.[54] And in this ability to account for its own genesis lies its autonomy. It is in Hegel, therefore, and not Marx, as presented by Louis Althusser,[55] that science breaks the vicious circle of the illusion of no-presupposition and the ghost of dependence and thus relativity. This correction—plausibly also endorsed by Habermas—clearly has force. It more nearly corresponds to the textual situation, does not assume that Hegel is speaking out of both sides of mouth at once, and does not construct a myth of agon between a Hegel 1 and a Hegel 2. The only addition I should like to make is to highlight the fact that it is religious *Vorstellung* that is the key presupposition among a complex series of presuppositions hierachically arranged. It is the task of *PS* to articulate this hierarchy. Moreover, in *SL,* as in the logic of *Enc,* concept is spoken of as inherently active, despite the insistence that it is genetically dependent. The relation of the concept to its own categorial presuppositions help inform how the relation between representiaton and concept is to be construed. As concept depends upon other categories for its genesis, Hegel is convinced that, as the telos of these less adequate categories, it is appropriate to think of the concept as grounding the very categories it presupposes. Similarly with the relation of concept to representation, what is presupposed genetically is, from a truly structural point of view, constituted by that which presupposition made possible.

In many of his texts Hegel does appear to be able to declare, almost in the same breath, the autonomy of the concept in its relation to *Vorstellung,* which thus becomes its constituted correlative, and the genesis of *Begriff* via the sublation of *Vorstellung,* which involves serious emendation to the form of symbolization. A good argument could be put forward that this is precisely what is happening in *Enc* #163, cited by Rosen as proof that Hegel gives the lie to the transformative position. It may be ironical, as Rosen notes, that religion announces the autonomy of philosophy and thus its nondependence on religion, but the announcement is also profoundly revealing. What Rosen does not seem to notice is that the irony cuts both ways. If religion is appealed to rather than philosophy as providing warrant for the autonomy of philosophy, this could just as easily point to the constitutive power of religious representation. At the very least, then, #163 is compatible with a view that surfaces in *PS* and elsewhere, i.e., if religion expresses sooner in time than philosophy the absolute content, and adequate conceptual articulation may be dependent upon religion, this does not mean that, from another point of view, religion in general, Christianity in particular, cannot be regarded as an expression of the fertility of concept, a kind of discursive projection that demands the kind of division between subject and object at the level of representation so that it can have the kind of nondivision—but not pure identity—at the level of concept interpreted as divine self-consciousness. Happily this reading seems to have the support of Ricoeur in his well-known essay on Hegel, where he emphasizes the activity of self-presentation (*Selbst-Darstellung*).[56] This position certainly seems to be advanced by *LPR*. Indeed, in a sense the very structure of the movement from idea to concretization in *LPR* seems to suggest that the text is conceived at once as verifying the generative thesis insofar as representation functions to open up the subject-object difference and transformative inasmuch as this bifurcation is constructively overcome in the self-consciousness of the divine. Thus, after the Heraclitean dictum(Fr. 60.), the way up is the way down (*hodos ano kato mia kai houte*). Between philosophical concept and representation, it could be said, there is a special kind of dialectical shuttle. The philosophical concept is arrived at through religious representation, yet the concept that presupposes representation, reconstructs, even redescribes, the genetic moment that made it possible.

Given the analysis prosecuted in part 2 of this text, one may draw the conclusion that Hegel ultimately allows us to see that not all Christian representation is equally privileged. Specifically, there are more than superficial reasons for thinking that Hegel recognizes a distinction between upper and lower Christian representation, with upper level representation manifesting to a considerably higher degree the presence of narrative and denarratizing operators as well as liberating, to a significantly greater degree, the subjective-genitive in the 'self-consciousness' of God. This liberation, which Hegel wishes to affirm of Lutheran Christianity and modernity as a whole, however, turns out to be instantiated only in the heterodox margins of the mainline Christian traditions. In chapter 5 we went to some effort to suggest that Hegel saw such a tendency clearly announced in the speculative theology of Meister Eckhart. Though Hegel's focus when discussing Boehme is more nearly on the objective content than on gnoseological interiorization, nevertheless, Boehme too is regarded as representing a prime historical example of the kind of pneumatic Christianity Hegel is endorsing. Hegel's view, however, is that this tendency in Christianity, a tendency also not lacking in Valentinian Gnosticism, is only fully guaranteed in a conceptual framework that, not only as a matter of fact is engaged in some iconoclastic action with respect to representation in its degenerative mode, but is able to account for its distinction from representation and articulate the complex demands of a discourse that reflects on itself as it reflects on what it is about, i.e., that is, at once, first and second level. In this it represents in spirit, if nothing else, the precursor of Husserl's view of the apophantic and formal ontological role of logical discourse.[57]

With a little help from Paul Valéry I would like to construct a model of what a purely generative account of discourse would look like: this with a view to showing that Hegel does not sanction any such account. In describing mind defined by intellectual autonomy, Valéry retrieves the French word *implexe,* common until the seventeenth century and deriving from the Latin *implexus,* the past participle of *implectare,* meaning to entwine, to twist, to plait.[58] Mind acquires the sense of a distinctly complex configuration. Moreover, as Valéry conceives it, this configuration is independent of empirical reality, if not cut off from it. Applied to Hegelian mind, 'rational implex' signifies the network of interlocking concepts constituting autonomous discourse. As 'enclosed', such discourse lacks an inlet from and, arguably, an outlet to, all nonautonomous forms of discourse including representation. Understood in this way, conceptual articulation would not be truly semantic, having no material, not even formal, ontological intent. Indeed, after a certain tendency in Saussure, it might be possible to think of it as a field of intersignification.[59] This conceptual field would be at once *langue* and *parole,* code and message, combinatory logic or syntax and propositional and syllogistic formation, or a kind of formal semantics. Of course, in Hegel this field would be less open than that sanctioned by Saussure which, in turn, conspicuously fails the Derridian test.[60] Logic in particular, the Hegelian system in general, in this view would be more nearly semiotic than semantic.

Yet this view flies in the face of Hegelian texts suggesting that Hegelian conceptual discourse is open at both ends, that is, that conceptual discourse is passively or receptively open to *Vorstellung* upon which it enacts those denarratizing operations we spoke of at some length and is actively open to the extent to which it constitutes or reconstitutes representation as its passive presupposition. However tendentious Derrida's interpretation of Hegel may be, it is true that Hegel's system evidences a semantic bias of a more than formal kind and, as with the Romantic interpretation of language in general, a self-consciousness of the metaphorical basis of concept. Derrida is far form being obtuse here. It is the case, as Clark and Dupré point out,[61] that Hegel's account of the relation between symbol and sign in *Enc* provides the interpretive underpinninng for the relationship between representation and concept. Moreover, the alignment of symbol with metaphor suggested by Derrida has some textual sanction in Hegel's work (*Enc* #3). Now, while to go on to say that the elevation of symbol to sign implies the searing away of metaphor, its degradation into dead metaphor or catachresis, may be interpretively overloaded, still the density of symbol is finally and completely unpacked in the move from representation to concept. Bataille on the one hand, and Ricoeur on the other, seem entitled to complain about the lack of excess.

Hegel appears to confirm the Derridian understanding in his interpretation of thought and myth in Plato in *LHP*. Platonic myths may have some residuum of the sensuous, but they are obviously more transparent to thought and open to refiguration than compact myth exhibiting a significantly higher degree of sensuousness and a significantly lower level of self-consciousness. Platonic myth and Platonic philosophy, therefore, have a kind of intertranslatability that is not, and cannot be, present between philosophy and more compact myth. Hegel's obvious attraction to this kind of higher order myth—in contradistinction to the later Schelling—indicates that his view of productivity of symbol is no more that of overdetermination than his view of metaphor is that of creative semantic pertinence.[62] The nearer symbol is to concept the greater its productivity, the more noticeable its semantic pertinence. Though the point never surfaces in Derrida's texts, arguably, something else is also indicated here: the ability of thought to construct its symbolic correlative. With this addition, Derrida's view that Hegel not only does not fully escape the pale of metaphor can be granted, but it also can be granted that Hegel does not fully escape

Aristotle's view of the distinction implied in metaphor between the proper and the improper. Hegelian circulation within the parameters of Aristotelian rhetoric determines that Hegel is not a good candidate for a revisionist view of metaphor such as that offered by Ricoeur and the protest made on behalf of other discourses against the imperious claims of the univocity of philosophy. Of Hegel, at least, it is difficult to deny that concept involves the lexicalization of metaphor, as it is difficult to affirm that philosophy avoids the lexicalization of narrative.[63] But Hegel is perfectly clear that lexicalization does not put philosophy in the position of surpassing metaphoric discourse as narrative. Metaphoric discourses have purposes that philosophy cannot serve. Philosophy's superiority is not first-order, as the Englightenment believes, but second-order. It saves metaphoric-narrative discourse by assimilating it, while at the same time supplying the reflective argumentative warrants that metaphoric-narrative is incapable of supplying.

Section 7.3 Hegel and the Perdurance of Narrative

An important conclusion that can be drawn from section 7.2 is that for Hegel ontotheological narrative perdures in the logical space of the concept. It if is true that perdurance is possible only because of the complete stripping away of narrative indices, it is also true that narrative not only is tolerated by logico-conceptual space but is intrinsic to it. Indeed, this stripped ontotheological narrative identifies Hegelian logical space to such an extent that it is not woefully inaccurate to think of Hegelian logical space as a kind of contracted narrative. Conversely, however, the narrative space that is the property of upper-level representation endures a preliminary logicization that essentially makes it an expanded syllogism. Both spaces are, therefore, systemically impure and are infected, if not inflected, by each other. Among other things, this means that knowing can no more shake off its narrative implication than narrative can dispose of its claim to knowledge. Here, it could be said, that Hegel, in principle, if not in fact, recognizes the ancient Indo-European intervolvement of narrative and knowledge. Of course, there is nothing like an unreflective reprise of their nondistinction in Hegel. Hegel fully accepts the distinction between *mythos* and Logos that is the achievement of Greek thought, an achievement, moreover, that for all the insistence on the nonprimacy of the rational, Christian theology does not forswear. While agreeing with Creuzer and Schelling on the intimacy of myth and thought richly considered,[64] Hegel neither dissolves the distinction, nor dismisses reflexive knowledge of this distinction. The constitutive problem of modernity, however, is not the confusion between narrative and concept, the reduction of logico-conceptual to narrative space. Within the Western ontotheological tradition, which until the modern period had been regulated by the Christian metanarrative, the real problem is the validity of any narrative construal, including Christianity's construal, which is relatively self-conscious of the difference between its narrative content and its epistemic justification. In challenging the rupture between narrative and knowledge, Hegel is arguing against purely formal and transcendental interpretations of knowing at the same time that he legitimates the claims of narrative to knowledge. The legitimation of narrative, indeed, a particular metanarrative, involves Hegel in laying bare a revisionist view of knowledge that has more in common with the mystical and esoteric traditions of Western thought than with the empiricists, Descartes or Kant.

Now if Hegel is able to establish the prima facie case for a real relation between the Christian narrative discourse and the discourse of conceptual thought, this does not mean that Hegel manages to save and rehabilitate anything like a standard version of the Christian metanarrative. The exhausting tour of the theologoumena structuring the Christian metanarrative conducted in part 2 showed that the metanarrative actually reprised by Hegel deviated sufficiently from the standard versions of the Christian metanarrative to provoke some investigation into its narrative taxon. In addition, we have drawn attention above to the fact that, while Hegel criticizes standard versions of the Christian metanarrative for being overly episodic, nonstandard versions of the Christian metanarrative, or reconfigurations of the Christian metanarrative, come in for significant praise, since they either avoid the defect or are intrinsically more capable of avoiding such a defect. Thus, the relation between narrative and logical space in Hegel is, in the final analysis, a relation between a pseudomorphosis of the Christian narrative and the concept that speculatively rewrites it.

That Hegel feels the need to reconfigure the Christian narrative, or adopt a reconfigured version, as a condition of its reclamation and subsequent conceptual validation shows that he is sensitive to the cultural crisis of Christianity. This crisis is symptomed above all by the lack of purchase of standard renditions of the Christian narrative, critiqued from without on the basis of Enlightenment dictates and hollowed out and compromised from within by apologetic efforts that articulate Christianity on the ground ceded to it by its despisers. The religious and cultural crisis is the mark of modernity. Hegel presumes that denial of decomposition is useless and defensive posture, regressive. Neither is despair an option, for this would involve not only the acceptance of the crisis of the Christian narrative but the conviction that there is no possibility of repair. Despair would involve nothing less than the abandoning of the narrative or metanarrative enterprise itself. And this Hegel will not concede. For him the narrative enterprise has not been falsified, either experientially or epistemologically. Standard renditions of the Christian narrative were vulnerable to criticism and, in due course, came to be criticized. What is called for is a reconfiguration of the Christian narrative that is validated by the very knowledge it grounds. In short, the failure of standard versions of the Christian narrative point to a need for the construction of a mythology of reason that is, at the same time, a mythology for reason.[65] From the perspective of this demand, neither the narrative responses of Kant nor Schleiermacher are radical enough. In their hands, knowledge is either respected too much or too little, and the narrative is respected much too little. Its full dimensions are reduced. Crucially, in both cases, the trinitarian element of the Christian metanarrative is excised. Kant makes of it an adiaphora; Schleiermacher, agreeing with Kant, determines that it is not a primary component of the Christian metanarrative. For Hegel, the exclusion of the Trinity from theological reflection is mistaken, not only because a profoundly important doctrine of the Christian community has been surrendered without sufficient warrant, but because its exclusion cuts off the possibility of a narrative or metanarrative reconfiguration that alone can stem the tide of Enlightenment hostility and stanch the serious internal hemorrhaging of Christianity.

Self-styled postmodernists are not particularly exercised by the distinction between the self-conscious metanarrative enterprise of the nineteenth century that reached its crescendo in Hegel and Schelling and the premodern situation of the Western ontotheological tradition, where the Christian metanarrative not only held pride of place but was an indelible part of its assumptive world. The threshold that is of interest to a postmodern such as Lyotard, for instance, is the emergence of a new situation in which disbelief in the legitimacy of the metanarrative enterprise accompanies the disenchantment of particular, regulative metanarrative.[66] This has the effect of relativizing the distinction between premodernity and modernity by rhetorically making both the foil of the novum that has emerged, though not all have recognized the fact. Lyotard is thoroughly nonexceptional here. Indeed, for the considerable number of postmoderns who depend upon Heidegger's genealogy of modernity, the relativization of the premodernity-modernity distinction is systematically called for, since modernity represents only the carrying out of the basic inspiration of the premodern Western tradition. While thinkers like Derrida and Mark Taylor may differ, for instance, with regard to the respective roles religion and philosophy played in this tradition, both are agreed that modernity represents the apotheosis of a premodern, even ancient deformation. While the general rubrics of this deformation, logocentrism and ontotheology, are broader than narrativity, sometimes the denunciation of the Western tradition as logocentric and ontotheological does bear on the endemic narrativity of this tradition. The function of narrative or metanarrative in the Western tradition is to convict reality of meaning and convince the human subject of reality's irradicable intellegibility. And narrative is often more capable of this task than philosophical thought because it is better able to take account of the experience of counterfactuals. Phenomena, which apparently deny meaning and intelligibility, are, on examination, ultimately revealed to affirm them. Narratives turn out to be scenes of recuperation in which meaning, while delayed, is ultimately extracted. In a narrative milieu, the alogical always turns into the logical, and the opaque is always rescued by the transparent. Following Bataille, the narratizing phenomenon, for both Derrida and Taylor,[67] is a recognizable incident within the Western tradition.

More interested in the Western theological tradition than Derrida, Taylor is prepared to think of the narrative deformation as constitutive. This is hardly in itself an unusual thought, given the centrality of narratives in the Christian canon. The specificity of the modern period is undermined by implicating the narrative project of the quintessential modern, i.e., Hegel, with the narrative project of ancient Christianity that finds its supreme instance in Augustine. Thus *PS* completes the narrative project of Augustine's *Confessions,* as *Philosophy of History* completes the *City of God.* Here Taylor takes his cue from Derrida; Augustine and Hegel are apostles of the 'book',[68] since if meaning can be disturbed, equally it can be won. A deconstructive position will necessarily contest the closure of meaning and intelligibility, indeed, this very vocation. In associating *Enc* with the Bible, Taylor radicalizes the narrative objection. Reprising the Heidegger of *Introduction to Metaphysics,* he makes explicit the connection between the enterprise of philosophy and *to theion,* a connection that represents a fatal alliance. In making the association Taylor does not so much as raise the possibility that scripture itself may be a disruptive force vis-á-vis the ontotheological tradition. Heidegger's highly general and procrustean genealogical scheme of deformation is never questioned. Moreover, it is instructive that, in prosecuting his argument about the ontotheological tradition, whose reflective alpha and omega are represented by Augustine and Hegel, respectively, Taylor invokes the Bible without ever making truly clear the relation between the Bible and Augustinian texts. Indeed, it seems as if part of the reason is that Taylor is not sure of the Augustinian analogue of *Enc.* Of course, the analogue is *De Trinitate.* But to acknowledge this would require that Taylor get more clear than in fact he is about the the various dimensions of standard renditions of the Christian narrative. A narrative of the self's journey to the divine is more restricted in scope than an account of the historical acts of God, just as the latter is more restricted than an account that features prominently a discussion of the nature of the divine *in se.* Any ranking of Augustine's texts in terms of narrative comprehensiveness, therefore, must place *De Trinitate* at the top. This is the key ontotheological text, since it identifies the trinitarian subject that is at the basis of history and the self. Admittedly, Taylor could accept that this very well may be the case but wonder what precisely is the force of the criticism. The point is essentially this: It is in texts like *De Trinitate* that the ontotheological tradition achieves its ultimate registering. It could be said (1) that it is only by reference to texts that not only suggest a subject underlying a global narrative but fully identify it that we are in the vicinity of the hot core of ontotheology, and (2) attention to both the trinitarian identification of this subject as *hypokeimenon* and the explicit and implicit ways in which this subject is logocentrically registered focus the connection between Augustine and Hegel in such a way that one is no longer dependent on Heideggerian and Derridian generalities. The essential flaw in Taylor's discussion is that he does not make clear when he is denouncing the narrative function in the Western theological tradition and when the Christian metanarrative is the object of critique. These are at least analytically separable issues.

The reaction of Hegel and his Romantic and Idealist contemporaries to the loss of authority of the Christian metanarrative is nothing less than a paroxysm of metanarrative construction. Whereas a poet like Hölderlin tried to construct a syncretistic religious myth incorporating elements of Christianity and Greek religion, Hegel and Schelling argued for a synthetic myth which however open to non-Christian elements would be, in the final analysis, Christian. How

Christian the synthetic myth was in both cases is open to question. And if we have been accurate in our depiction of Hegel, then one can safely conclude that Hegel's metanarrative departed decisively from standard trinitarian versions. The result should not surprise. Hegel shared with his contemporaries some of the criticisms of standard renditions of the Christian metanarrative. Certainly, he questioned their supernaturalist drift, and was made anxious by their epistemological assumptions. For him, rehabilitation implied that metanarrative and knowledge were related in an intrinsically positive way that the standard Christian proposals denied. Knowledge was not simply a set of restrictions that safeguarded the priority of the nonknowledge of narratively encoded, and thus narratively decodable, revelatory discourse. And this was the case whether the form epistemic restriction takes is that of Kant, Luther, Augustine, or Irenaeus. Knowledge completes the disclosure dimension of narrative. In other words, knowledge, or its essentially logical space, does not dismantle *apokalypsis.* It becomes rather the figure of apocalypse, the rendering of divine enactment that is truly radical in character. Yet if the analysis offered in chapter 6 is accurate, then, despite the suggestion of standard Christian precedents for this view, the precedents lie elsewhere. The trinitarian metanarrative that articulates the upper reaches of *Vorstellung,* and which lies between confessional *Vorstellungen* and concept, indeed constitutes the between, more nearly recalls the heterodox traditions of Valentinian Gnosticism and Boehmian theosophy. Moreover, the move from the highly articulated trinitarian narrative to that of concept not only confirms an apocalypse content that has the divine becoming as its object, it confirms apocalypse form. What is rendered in and by trinitarian apocalypse can be known and not simply believed. Hegel takes seriously the knowledge implication in the ocular metaphor. The rustle of the trinitarian metanarrative is seen not heard, consequently known and not simply believed. The movement to *Begriff,* therefore, serves to provide the seal of approval for the gnoseological claim of apocalypse. It is within the context of concept that the narrative enactment of the divine justifies itself. This justification or demonstration proceeds, without appeal to extrinsic logical rules of deduction or derivation, by showing itself. Justification is therefore *apophantic.* Conceptual discourse shows that the narrative semantic impulse is at one with the syntactical movement of Logos. Syntax and semantics are mutually reinforcing. If it is semantics that sets the kind of narrative limit to syntax abjured by Derrida and deconstruction, it is syntax that suggests that narrative divine self-enactment is underwritten by logical grammar. In short, Hegel represents a provocation to postmodernism, not because of apocalyptic tone, but because of apocalypse substance.

Were Hegel to reply to the Nietzschian wing of postmodernism that thinks it worthwhile to engage him, arguably, he would not be particularly disturbed by the accusation that he had given in to the lure of meaning and truth. For him, the exigence of the lure is a function of the possibility of its demands being met. The semantic and alethiological vocation is neither illusion nor delusion. Nevertheless, the vocation is not realizable within the ordinance of standard Christian symbolization. And this is so not simply because Christianity's predominantly narrative mode of biblical and dogmatic discourse does not meet philosophy's denarratizing demands. It is so because the dominant modes of narrative construal in Christianity are deficient from a narrative point of view. Though it is rarely referred to, this recommended and second corrective to standard representation is as important as the first. Among other things, it has the hugely important function in speculative rewriting of preventing religious discourse from being transformed without remainder into a nonnarrative Spinozism. The nonnarrative imperatives of conceptual discourse, adopted by Hegel from Spinoza, are to work in the context of a narrative formation that successfully negotiates the threshold dividing narrative and logical space. The denarratization demanded by concept is internally limited by the functioning of narrative operations that configure reality and discourse in such a way that it is not rejected within the logical field of concept.

Neither would Hegel be particularly disturbed by the accusation that his reconstructed metanarrative functions as a form of consolation. Entering a guilty plea, he would further incriminate himself by suggesting that, as the logical space of *Begriff* both justifies and provides the consummate figure of apocalypse, it also justifies the divine and provides the consummate figure of theodicy. Of course, the theodicy modality or genre justified in speculative rewriting, and raised to ultimacy in a speculative figure, will bare only a distant resemblance to the standard types of Christian theodicy that Kant found epistemically groundless and postmoderns convict of existential turpitude. Chapter 6 argued that because of the encompassing scope of the narrative envisaged and its radical nature Hegel's theodicy would have to be regarded as exemplifying a different genre to the mainline Christian standards. Needless to say, this does not get Hegel off the theodicy hook, for within postmodernism, in particular, any and all versions of theodicy, narrative or nonnarrative, anthropogonic or theogonic, religious or philosophical, on the surface of discourse or deeply embedded within it, are objects of the same suspicion and subject to essentially the same accusation. Hegel would likely reply that postmodernism is guilty of the dogmatism of which it charges its enemies. Postmodernism of a Nietzschean stripe consistently conflates the legitimacy of suspicion with the authoritarian legislation of guilt. And, if discourse does console, this may say less about the nature of human wish-fulfillment than the nature of discourse—indeed, not simply the nature of discourse but the nature of reality. In any event, whatever consolation is proposed by a trinitarian reconfiguration of the Christian narrative and justified within the field of concept, it is hardly facile. For, if sense in the first instance is haunted by the death of God, stalked by the reality of horror and the possibility of despair, in the second instance, meaning is proved by the shadow of nonsense and knowledge tempered by the prerogatives of skepticism. This Hegelian rejoinder, of course, would hardly suffice for postmodernism. Postmodernism would point to the triumph over horror and despair and the final victory of sense. The agon would continue, the battle simply played out on a different level. This itself, however, would be eloquent. Hegel would continue to be the hallowed enemy worth fighting, postmodernism's named other, perhaps the angel with which it wrestles to be blessed at daybreak.

☙ Notes ❧

Introduction

1. Jorge Luis Borges in *A Personal Anthology,* ed. foreword Anthony Kerrigan (London: Pan Books/Picador, 1972), pp. 54–58. This story is translated by the editor.

2. Ibid., pp. 55–56.

3. See Borges's fascinating pseudo-encyclopedia of fictional beings, *The Book of Imaginary Beings* or *El libro de les Seres Imaginarias* (1967) in *OBRAS Completas De Jorge Luis Borges: en colaboracion* (Buenos Airs: Emece Editores, 1979), pp. 569–714. I am reading Borges's book as if he is repristinating Coleridge's distinction between phantasy and imagination in the thirteenth book of the *Biographia Literaria,* and suggesting that the hybrid belongs not to the superior order of *imagination* but the lower order of *phantasy* that does not evoke the real or the really real.

4. Wilhelm Raimund Beyer, *Hegel-Bilder: Kritik der Hegel Deutungen* (Berlin: Akadamie Verlag, 1970).

5. For this judgment against the absoluteness of knowledge, see Gadamer's judgment of Hegel in *Truth and Method,* trans. ed. Garrett Barden and John Cumming (New York: Seabury Press, 1975), p. 319. For a similar judgment, see "Hegel and Heidegger" in *Hegel's Dialectic,* trans. P. Christopher Smith (New Haven: Yale University Press, 1976), pp. 103–116, esp. p. 110.

6. Karl Löwith, "Hegel and the Christian Religion" in *Nature, History and Existentialism,* ed. A. Levison (Evanston, IL: Northwestern University Press, 1966), p. 163. See also Martin Heidegger, "The Onto-theological Nature of Metaphysics" in *Essays in Metaphysics: Identity and Difference,* trans. Kurt F. Leidecker (New York: Philosophical Library, Inc., 1960), pp. 35–67. Heidegger makes a number of important statements on the issue in his *Hegel's Phenomenology of*

Spirit, trans. Parvis Emad and Kenneth Maly (Bloomington and Indianapolis: Indiana University Press, 1988), pp. 98–100, 124–126.

7. Löwith uses the term *ontotheological* to point to the de facto connection between religion, i.e., Christianity, and philosophy in Hegel's work. By contrast Heidegger is pointing to an intrinsic connection that occurs at the infrastructural level of Hegelian thought wherein Being is identified with 'the ground of Being' and consequently hypostatized. Hegel is not, of course, the first to make the connection. According to Heidegger's reading of the Western intellectual tradition, in Plato, the father of Western philosophy, the connection is inaugurated. It continues in Aristotle and the medieval tradition, with Hegel representing, in a sense, the culmination of the process of equating Being and *to theoin.* See *Hegel's Phenomenology of Spirit,* pp. 98, 126.

8. To say that Hegel identifies God with *Geist* is to say the same thing.

9. See *The Essence of Christianity,* trans. George Eliot (New York: Harper & Row, 1957).

10. Alexandre Kojève, *Introduction to the Reading of Hegel,* trans. James H. Nichols Jr. (New York: Basic Books, 1969). Lecture 7, chap. 8, pp. 112–120.

11. Theodor W. Adorno, *Negative Dialectics,* trans. E. B. Ashton (New York: Seabury Press, 1973). See Part 3: "The World Spirit and Natural History," which has as its subtitle, "An Excursus on Hegel."

12. Derrida self-consciously understands himself as coming to grips with the legacy of Hegel, who represents for him, as for Heidegger, the apogee of the ontotheological tradition. Derrida's translation of Heidegger's objections to the Western intellectual tradition leaves intact Heidegger's basic objection that this tradition is marked by the identification of a ground of reality that functions as the source of meaning, value, and truth. Hegelianism not only remains within the parameter marked by this identification but represents in its pretension at absolute transparence and full self-appropriation through reason the apotheosis of the Western, that is, the logocentric, tradition. Derrida in his texts shows himself particularly anxious to attack Hegelian notions such as contradiction, difference, *Aufhebung,* as these operate in Hegel's logocentric and totalizing framework. Frontal attack on Hegel is evident in a number of texts, though even where Hegel is not mentioned he can be assumed to be a conversation partner or a partner in an argument. See *Positions,* trans. Alan Bass (Chicago: University of Chicago Press, 1981), pp. 43–44, 101 (note 13); "From Restricted to General Economy: A Hegelianism without Reserve" in *Writing and Difference,* trans. Alan Bass, (Chicago: University of Chicago Press, 1978), pp. 251–277, esp. 271–273; *Dissemination,* trans. Barbara Johnson (Chicago: University of Chicago Press, 1981), pp. 4–6.

13. Richard Solomon, *In the Spirit of Hegel: A Study of G. W. F. Hegel's Phenomenology of Spirit* (Oxford: Oxford University Press, 1983).

14. Alan White, *Absolute Knowledge: Hegel and the Problem of Metaphysics,* (The Ohio Press Series in Continental Thought) (Athens, Ohio: Ohio University Press, 1983).

15. Barthes's notion of 'exdenomination' is equivalent to ideology where the emphasis is not so much upon ideology as a system of beliefs as ideology as an operation of repression or excision of alternate discursive items. Thus an ideology is just as much constituted by what is excluded as what is included.

16. See especially Ferdinand Christian Baur, *Die christliche Lehre von der Dreieinigkeit und Menschwerdung Gottes in ihrer geschichtlichen Entwicklung,* 3 vols. (Tübingen: 1841–1843), specifically on Hegel, see vol. 3, pp. 886–933; Franz Anton Staudenmaier, *Darstellung und Kritik des Hegelschen Systems: Aus dem Standpunkte der christlichen Philosophie* (Mainz: Kupferberg, 1844); reprint ed. (Frankfut am Main: Minerva, 1966).

17. Albert Chapelle, *Hegel et la religion.* 3 vols. (Paris: Éditions Universitaires, 1966–1971); *Annexes* 1967; Emil L. Fackenheim, *The Religious Dimension in Hegel's Thought* (Bloomington: Indiana University Press, 1967); Iwan Iljin, *Die Philosophie Hegels als kontemplative Gotteslehre* (Bern: Francke, 1946).

18. This integrated series of questions is vital, if one is to get a secure hermeneutic grip on Hegel.

19. Jörg Splett, *Die Trinitätslehre G. W. F. Hegels* (Freiburg, Munich: Karl Albert Verlag, 1965); Dale M. Schlitt, *Hegel's Trinitarian Claim: A Critical Reflection* (Leiden: E. J. Brill, 1984); Piero Coda, *Il negativo e la trinità: impotesi su Hegel* (Rome: Città Nuova Editrice, 1987).

20. The view that divine self-constitution takes place through a series of epochs or narrative stages is axial in Iljin's work.

21. Here I side with Kant as well as Hegel in opposing a modern style in philosophy. What Kant inveighed against in the 1790s and Hegel in the 1800s is still worth inveighing against. A good example of Hegel's criticism of aperçu is found in Hegel's criticism of Jacobi in *Faith and Knowledge* treated below in chapter 1, sect. 1.1.

22. Walter Jaeschke, "Christianity and Secularity in Hegel's Concept of the State," *The Journal of Religion* 61, No. 2 (April 1981), pp. 127–145. For quotation, see p. 127.

23. 'Swerve' is a term I borrow from the literary theory of Harold Bloom. In Bloom's work, the term denotes the posture of contrariety a later author may adopt towards an earlier experienced as significant with respect to one's own literary output. The purpose of the posture of contrariety is to free oneself from influence, thereby creating a space for the exercise of one's own creativity. Bloom's literary theory is basically psychological in orientation. At its center

is Freud's Oedipus complex. Swerve or negation is, according to Bloom, one of the strategies of nulling the primal (literary) father. See Harold Bloom, *The Anxiety of Influence: A Theory of Poetry* (London, New York: Oxford University Press, 1973); *A Map of Misreading* (Oxford, New York: Oxford University Press, 1975); *Agon: Towards a Theory of Revisionism* (New York, Oxford: Oxford University Press, 1983).

24. For an excellent account of this baptism, the various stages of this baptism, and the figures involved, see John Edward Toews' fine *Hegelianism: The Path Toward Dialectical Humanism, 1805–1841* (Cambridge: Cambridge University Press, 1980), esp. part II, chaps. 4–6.

25. *The Essence of Christianity* speaks to the theologoumenon of the Trinity in chap. 6 of the text. In addition, however, that text speaks of the incarnation (chap. 4), resurrection (chap. 14), creation (chap. 11), and providence (chap. 10).

26. For a succinct expression of Schlitt's thesis see "The Whole Truth: Hegel's Reconceptualization of Trinity" in *The Owl of Minerva* 15, 2 (Spring 1984), pp. 169–182.

27. See Mark C. Taylor, *Journeys to Selfhood: Hegel and Kierkegaard* (Berkeley: University of California Press, 1980), pp. 77 ff.

28. Taylor, op. cit.

29. That development can occur on the level of the nontemporal is an important point and is treated in detail in chap. 2.

30. Gerard Genette, *Narrative Discourse: An Essay in Method,* trans. Jane L. Lewin, foreword Jonathan Culler (Ithaca, N.Y.: Cornell University Press, 1980), chapter 1: Order, pp. 33–85; Analepsis, pp. 48–67; Prolepses, pp. 67–79; and for definition of analepsis, prolepsis, and problems of vocabulary, see p. 40, note 11.

31. See Hayden White, "The Value of Narrativity in the Representation of Reality" in *On Narrative,* ed. W. J. T. Mitchell (Chicago, London: University of Chicago Press, 1980), pp. 1–23.

32. See Daniel L. Cook, *Language in the Philosophy of Hegel* (The Hague: Mouton, 1973), pp. 134 ff.

33. Herbert Huber, *Idealismus und Trinität, Pantheon und Götterdämmerung: Grundlagen und Grundzüge der Lehre von Gott nach dem Manuscript Hegels zur Religionsphilosophie* (Weinheim: Acta Humaniora, 1984).

34. To the extent to which anamnesis connotes the retrieval of a state of full ontological realization and full gnoseological awareness that is, or was, given *ab initio,* anamnesis is quite other than analepsis. If, however, anamnesis is

read to mean, not the retrieval of a pregiven realized perfection lost by some irrational event that brings forgetfulness and ignorance, but rather the preservation of each stage of partial realization of ontological and gnoseological perfection in the plenitude of subjectivity, then anamnesis and analepsis mean essentially the same thing.

35. The central insight of August Von Cieszkowski's important but neglected *Prolegomena zur Historiosophie* (Berlin, 1838) is that Hegelian dialectic has trapped history in the present and the past and cut off the future. The future is the proper preserve of philosophy which should risk what Hegel least wants it to risk, i.e., being synonymous with prophecy.

36. See Hans George Gadamer, *Reason in the Age of Science,* trans. Frederick G. Lawrence (Cambridge, MA: MIT Press, 1981), pp. 40, 59; see also Eric Voegelin, "Wisdom and the Magic of the Extreme: A Mediation," *Southern Review* 17 (1981), pp. 235–87.

37. This avowal is basic to deconstruction, which does not see itself to be in the business of offering another and competing foundational theory. The spirit of deconstruction has certainly something in common with the later Wittgenstein who similarly denied foundationalism.

38. See Mark C. Taylor, *Erring: A Postmodern A/theology* (Chicago: University of Chicago Press, 1984), p. 70; also pp. 54–56, 66.

39. Jacques Derrida, *Positions,* op. cit., p. 77.

40. Prior to deconstruction this position was advanced by Jean Hyppolite in *Logique et existence: essai sur la logique de Hegel* (Paris, 1953).

41. See *Erring,* pp. 52–73 for a find discussion from the point of view of deconstruction of the Hegelian end of history; also Jacques Derrida, *Glas* (Paris: Éditions Galilee, 1974), p. 122, where Derrida points to the soteriological significance of the end of history.

42. For Heidegger, see especially *Hegel's Concept of Experience.* See also Emmanuel Levinas, *Totality and Infinity: An Essay on Exteriority,* trans. Alphonso Lingis (Pittsburgh: Duquesne University Press, 1969); see also Derrida's essay on Levinas called, "'Violence and Metaphysics: An Essay on the Thought of Emmanuel Levinas'" in *Writing and Difference,* pp. 79–153.

43. There is an obvious thetic quality to Taylor's *Erring* not found in the work of Derrida, though even in Derrida's case it is difficult to avoid the conclusion that he thinks his own proposal to be 'right' in the way the ontotheological tradition is not.

44. Frank Kermode, *The Sense of an Ending: Studies in the Theory of Fiction* (New York: Oxford University Press, 1967).

45. Jürgen Moltmann, *The Trinity and the Kingdom: The Doctrine of God,* trans. Margaret Köhl (London: SCM Press Ltd., 1981).

46. *Trinity and the Kingdom,* pp. 171–178, esp. pp. 174–176.

47. This point is central to both Iljin and Schlitt, though Schlitt's language is that of 'process' and 'becoming'. 'Epoch' is more nearly narrative language.

48. This point is suggested in Quentin Lauer's *Hegel's Concept of God* (Albany, N.Y.: SUNY Press, 1982).

49. Hegel's relationship to Spinoza will be touched on in a number of places below, particularly in chaps. 2, 3, 7.

50. Letter to Tholuck (514 b) *Briefe,* IV:9 (Hoffmeister edition).

51. Ulrich Asendorf's *Luther und Hegel. Untersuchungen zur Grundlegung einer neuen systematischen Theologie* (Weisbaden: Steiner, 1982).

52. James Yerkes, *The Christology of Hegel* (Albany, N.Y.:SUNY Press, 1983).

53. Ernst Benz, *Les sources mystiques de la philosophie romantique allemande* (Paris: Vrin, 1968). H. S. Harris, *Hegel's Development: Towards the Sunlight: 1770–1801* (Oxford: Clarendon Press, 1972); *Hegel's Development: Night Thoughts (Jena 1800–1806)* (Oxford: Clarendon Press, 1983).

54. Fredrick Copleston, "Hegel and the Rationalization of Mysticism" in *New Studies in Hegel's Philosophy,* ed. Warren L. Steinkraus (New York: Holt, Rinehart and Winston, Inc., 1971). This view is suggested also in the work of the English Hegelian commentators J. N. Findlay, G. R. G. Mure, and Stace. Similar suggestions have been made by Hegel continental scholars such as Louis Dupré.

55. See F. Ch. Baur's great dogmatic works, particularly *Die christliche Gnosis oder die christliche Religionsphilosophie in ihrer geschichtlichen Entwicklung* (Tübingen: 1835).

56. Jean Hyppolite, *Genesis and Structure of Hegel's Phenomenology of Spirit,* trans. Samuel Cherniak and John Hechman (Evanston: Northwestern University Press, 1974), pp. 542–543.

57. Malcolm Clark, *Logic and System: A Study of the Transition from 'Vorstellung' to Thought in the Philosophy of Hegel* (The Hague: Martinus Nijhoff, 1971), p. 208.

58. For a succinct account of Walsh's thesis, see his "The Historical Dialectic of Spirit: Jacob Boehme's Influence on Hegel" in *History and System: Hegel's Philosophy of History,* ed. Robert L. Perkins (Albany, N.Y.: SUNY Press, 1984), pp. 15–35.

59. See *Science, Politics and Gnosticism: Two Essays* (Chicago: H. Regnery Co., 1968), pp. 68–73, 77–80; *From Enlightenment to Revolution,* ed. John H. Hallowel (Durham, N.C.: Duke University Press, 1975), pp. 240–302. Here Voegelin discusses Marx as a gnostic thinker but argues that he represents the immanentization of Hegel's gnostic outlook.

60. Baur's *Die christliche Gnosis* may seem dated when looked at from the point of view of modern critical scholarship, though it still may be in its syncretistic way the best thing on Gnosticism in the nineteenth century.

61. The different methodological starting points do not necessarily invalidate the basic results of Baur (and his twentieth-century successor Hans Jonas). While one may need a good deal more concrete detail than Baur, it seems unlikely that, in any general typification of Gnosticism, one could avoid asserting the importance of the fall from the realm of pure perfection (*pleroma*) into the evil world of matter, the dualism of spirit and matter.

62. Primary texts of Gnosticism are now available to all since the great find at Nag Hammadi. These texts have found a convenient English translation in *The Nag Hammadi Library,* ed. James Robinson (San Francisco: Harper & Row, 1977). There tends to be a relatively good match between these texts and the reports of the heresiologists, especially the greatest of these, i.e., Irenaeus.

63. This is a point forcefully made by Claude Bruaire in *Logique et religion chrétienne dans la philosophie de Hegel* (Paris: du Seuil 1964), pp. 66 ff.

Chapter 1 Hegelian Rendition of the Deus Revelatus *of Christianity*

1. I hope to touch on all of these allegiances throughout the present work.

2. See, for example, *LPR 1* 1821 MS E 186, G 96; E 203–207, G 112–116.

3. See *LPR 1* 1824, E 115–116, G 33; E 120, G 37.

4. An emblem of this is suggested in *LPR 1* 1821 MS E 84, G 4, where Hegel suggests that God is beginning, middle, and end of all things. Hegel goes on to exegete this by saying that everything flows from God and everything returns. As the 1821 Manuscript and subsequent Lecture series make clear, the exit-return of everything from God or Spirit is also the exit-return of God or Spirit. See 1824 E 143, G 56–57.

5. See chap. 3, sect. 1 for Hegel's criticism of systemic narrative deficiencies in Judeo–Christian thought.

6. See *Faith and Knowledge* (*FK*), trans. Walter Cerf and H. S. Harris (Albany, N.Y.: SUNY Press, 1977), pp. 97–153; see also *Lectures on the History of Philosophy, Vol. 3 (LHP 3),* trans E. S. Haldane and Francis H. Simpson (London: Rut-

ledge and Kegan Paul, 1974), pp. 410–422; also Erik Schmidt, *Hegels System der Theologie* (Berlin, New York: Walter de Gruyter, 1974), pp. 13–14, 28–30.

7. As H. S. Harris makes clear, Hegel had access to Hölderlin's play *Empedocles* at this time. This play was a martyrology of sorts. Empedocles makes the ultimate sacrifice by throwing himself into the cauldron of Mt. Etna. See *Night Thoughts,* p. 9 note.

8. Compared with his attitude towards Jacobi, Hegel's attitude towards Schelling in both these early texts is positive. If Jacobi is an example of a philosophy of 'reflection' (understanding), Schelling provides an example of a philosophy of 'speculation' by which it is judged. It should be pointed out that *FK* was, in fact, one of the numbers of *The Critical Journal of Philosophy,* edited jointly by Hegel and Schelling (Vol. 2, No. 1). For an account of the overridingly positive appraisal of Schelling in *FK,* see Walter Cerf's essay which prefaces his and Harris's translation: "Speculative Philosophy and Intellectual Intuition: An Introduction to Hegel's Essays," XI–XXXVI. The *Differenzschrift,* or the *Difference Essay* (*DE*), similarly is founded upon the axial contrast between 'reflective' philosophy and 'speculative' philosophy, with Fichte more or less corresponding to the former (not Jacobi) and with Schelling again the prime example of the latter.

9. Werner Marx, *The Philosophy of F. W. J. Schelling: History, System and Freedom,* trans. Thomas Menon (Bloomington: Indiana University Press, 1984). Marx thinks Hegel incorrect when he claims in the *Phenomenology* that it is the nature of intuition to "go no further than just where it is." He asserts to the contrary that the term *intuition* or *self-intuition* "not only entailed a necessity to proceed to finitude but also to proceed to a systematic presentation of everything that is known as well" (p. 38).

10. See *LHP 3,* pp. 512–545.

11. The first two speeches provide particularly apt illustration of the alliance of a form of 'pantheistic' mysticism and a view of religion that separates it from theology and philosophy. For a convenient English translation, see *On Religion: Speeches to its Cultured Despisers,* trans. John Oman (New York, San Francisco, London: Harper & Row (Harper Torchbooks), 1958).

12. See *On Religion,* Speech 2, pp. 51, 59.

13. Peter Hodgson is correct, it seems to me, in advancing this position. See his introduction to *LPR 1* pp. 2, 3, 6, 7, 61. See also p. 136 note 52.

14. Hodgson reminds us that, despite Hegel's refusal to announce a distinction between Jacobi's *Empfindung* and Schleiermacher's *Gefühl* in *LPR 1* 1824 E 268–269, G 177; E 273, G 178–179, they are not, as Hegel well knows, the same. As Hodgson points out, Hegel himself distinguishes between them in *Enc*

#402–3, where he brings to light the more empirical, more sensible nature of *Empfindung*. See *LPR 1* E 268–269 note 20.

15. Without presupposing anything like Heidegger's existential analytic of *Dasein,* I would like to avail of his distinction of ontological-ontic to suggest a distinction of level between feeling and other modes of selfhood such as thought and action. For Schleiermacher, feeling is radical in a way thought and action are not. See Speech 2 in *On Religion,* pp. 36, 45, 54 and also 98 where Schleiermacher seems to equate feeling and imagination. It must be admitted, however, that Schleiermacher's assertion concerning the 'passive' nature of feeling somewhat jeopardizes its radical status by seeming to counterpose passivity and activity (p. 45). Furthermore, Schleiermacher's disjunction of religion and ethics (act) seems to put passivity and activity on the same level. In the *Glaubenslehre* the distinction of level is spelled out so clearly that the feeling of dependence in no wise can be conflated with passivity understood in the normal sense as contrary of activity.

16. While Hegel does critique Schleiermacher in *LPR,* in *PS,* and even in *FK*—see, E 150–152 (*GW 4:* 385–386)—the *locus classicus* of Hegel's critique is to be found in his preface to H. W. F. Hinrichs's *Die Religion in innern Verhältnisse zur Wissenschaft* (Heidelberg, 1822). For an English translation of this preface by A. V. Miller, see appendix to *Beyond Epistemology: New Studies in the Philosophy of Hegel,* ed. Frederick G. Weiss (The Hague: Martinus Nijhoff, 1974), pp. 227–244. For a critical edition of the Hinrichs's text, a new translation of Hegel's foreword and comprehensive study of its importance, see Eric von der Luft, *Hegel, Hinrichs, and Schleiermacher on Feeling and Reason in Religion: The Texts of their 1821–22 Debate,* Studies in German Thought and History, Volume 3 (Lewiston & Queenston: The Edwin Mellen Press, 1987). Page numbers in text are from *Beyond Epistemology.*

17. See *Glaubenslehre,* #16–19; also English translation, *The Christian Faith,* trans. H. R. Macintosh & J. S. Steward (Philadelphia: Fortress Press, 1928), pp. 78–93, where Schleiermacher makes a fairly definitive statement concerning theology as second order reflection upon primary experience and primitive expressions of faith, and consisting of second order propositions of a didactic type systematically held together. Theology, that is, dogmatic theology, as regulated by primary experience and confession, consequently excludes propositions of a speculative kind, though small vocabulary borrowings are not, according to Schleiermacher, illegitimate.

18. Hegel underscores the Anselmian nature of his theology in a variety of ways, some implicit, other explicit. *LPR 1* provides examples of both types. Implicit support of the Anselmian vision of theology is offered when Hegel, affirming the inwardness of faith (1821 MS E 192–193, G 101), nevertheless maintains that there is an internal dynamic which trajects faith (as inward-

ness) beyond itself to dogmatic expression, i.e., *Vorstellung* (1821 MS E 217, G 125–126). The self-transcendence of faith, however, does not receive its term in dogmatic theology, but rather in philosophy or thought (see also *LPR 1* 1821 MS E 243–244, G 152–153). Explicit support of the *fides quaerens intellectus* formula is evoked in *LPR 1* (1827 E 154, G 65–66). See Hodgson's interesting note on p. 154, note 9. That Schleiermacher belongs to the Anselmian tradition is clear from the axial presupposition of the *Glaubenslehre* that all theological articulation is based upon the primitives of feeling and nondiscursive expression of feeling as this feeling refers to a divine whence.

19. This is the way at least Barth frames the distinction between Hegel and Schleiermacher. See Barth's *The Theology of Schleiermacher,* trans. Geoffrey W. Bromiley (Grand Rapids, Mich.: Eerdmans, 1982), esp. pp. 186–188, 232–233. Barth regards Hegel's foreward to the Hinrichs text not only to be Hegel's most vitriolic response to the *Glaubenslehre* but the most vitriolic response to the text between the time of the text's appearance in 1821–1822 and 1830 (p. 186).

20. Of course, in a certain sense spiritual content is not fully articulate in the *Vorstellungen* of dogmatic theology either. Nevertheless, *Vorstellung* has been somewhat successful in pruning religion of *Bild* (image) and sensuous or sensible habits of response that hinder full disclosure of spiritual content. For an example of the attested superiority of *Vorstellung* over *Bild,* see *LPR 1* 1821 MS E 238, G 148. The difference between *Bild* and *Vorstellung* lies in the universality of the latter.

21. See also *LPR 1* 1824 E 208–211, G 117–119.

22. This point is made forcefully by Tom Rockmore in his *Hegel's Circular Epistemology* (Studies in Phenomenology and Existential Philosophy) (Bloomington: Indiana University Press, 1986).

23. Schleiermacher was at least convinced in his own mind that neither in the *Glaubenslehre* (see #93) or in *Das Leben Jesu* had he evaporated the historicity of the revelation of Christ and replaced the *hic et nunc* of Jesus of Nazareth by an ideal.

24. Gotthold Ephraim Lessing offers his famous image of the irreconcilability of accidental truths of history and necessary truths of reason in his essay "On the Proof of the Spirit and the Power." In *Lessing's Theological Writings,* trans. Henry Chadwick (Stanford, California: Stanford University Press, 1956), pp. 51–56, see esp. p. 55. Lessing, of course, was not being original. He owes the distinction to Spinoza, specifically the Spinoza of the *Tractatus Theologico-Politicus* (Bk. 10).

25. Hegel insists upon the preservative element of *Aufhebung* when he defines it in the *Enc* #96 zu (Miller p. 142).

26. Hegel here seems to be retrieving the view of religion captured in the Latin word for the phenomenon, i.e., *religare,* to bind or bond together. What is crucial for Hegel about religion is the bonding or connecting of the divine and human.

27. See esp. *LPR 1* 1821 MS E 243–244, G 152–153.

28. See James Collins, *The Emergence of Philosophy of Religion* (New Haven: Yale University Press, 1967), pp. 111–117 for the use of this term.

29. See *The Emergence,* pp. 117ff. See also Quentin Lauer, "Hegel's Critique of Kant's Theology" in *God Knowable and Unknowable,* ed. Robert J. Roth (New York: Fordham Press, 1973), pp. 85–105.

30. *FK* offers many of the same substantive criticisms of Kant which later works such as the *Enc* and *LHP 3* repeat, especially Kant's dualism of the finite and infinite, what can and cannot be known. Yet, compared with his treatment of Jacobi, the tone Hegel adopts with regard to Kant is respectful. See *FK,* pp. 67–96. For a fine descriptive account of Hegel's relation to Kant, see Stephen Priest's introductory essay to *Hegel's Critique of Kant,* ed. Stephen Priest (Oxford: Clarendon Press, 1987), pp. 1–48, esp. pp. 2–17.

31. If Hegel had a polemical side when he came to Kant, he equally had an appropriating or synecdochial side. That is, many of Kant's ideas were not regarded as wrong so much as partial instantiations of Hegel's fully developed view of the same, at once Christian and Idealist. Hegel's treatment of Kant in the *Enc* (#37–60) still shows some evidence of the latter tendency. W. H. Walsh in his essay "Kant as Seen by Hegel" in *Hegel's Critique of Kant,* pp. 205–220, seems to suggest the presence of the appropriative, synecdochical tendency.

32. In *LHP 3* Kant, it is suggested, provides the horizon for the Romantic Intuitionists. Hegel does not say what he almost said in *FK:* through the Romantic Intuitionists even the strengths of Kant are caricatured.

33. This is perhaps the central thesis of Hyppolite's *Logique et existence.*

34. See Chapelle, *Hegel et la religion,* vol. 2, pp. 44–45, notes 74–76.

35. Chapelle thinks that a correct understanding of the Hegelian negative implies that not everything is brought to complete transparence. Whatever its prescriptive value, descriptively Chapelle is incorrect. Hegel does suggest complete transparence. Here I side with Gadamer in his essay on Hegel and Heidegger. See *Hegel's Dialectic,* p. 110.

36. See Chapelle, *Hegel et la religion,* vol. 2. pp. 61, 66, 69, 70.

37. See Louis Bouyer, "Mysticism/An Essay on the History of the Word" in *Understanding Mysticism,* ed. Richard Woods O. P. (New York: Doubleday & Co. Image Books, 1980), pp. 42–54, esp. p. 46.

38. For this point, see Anders Nygren in *Agape and Eros* (Philadelphia: Westminister Press, 1955), p. 706.

39. For this point see Ernst Benz, *Les sources,* p. 17.

40. While, in the two volumes of Hegel's biography that have thus far appeared, Harris does not explicitly address the question of terminological change, nevertheless, during the period 1801–04 Hegel was prepared to use the radical apophatic term *Ungrund.* This term makes its appearance in *DE* and in Hegel's unpublished MS "The Triangulation of the Trinity." See *Night Thoughts,* p. 165. By the time of *PS* such terminology has disappeared.

41. I define 'apophatic erasure' as the operation whereby apophatic vocabulary, and thus the implications of such a vocabulary, are excised from a religious or theological proposal, leaving only a positive nonmysterious content to be appropriated. Practically this means that Hegel relates positively to such mystics as Boehme and Eckhart only to the degree to which he ignores, or better, systematically represses, the apophatic vocabulary and the suggested limits of cognition.

42. See Joseph Maréchal, *Studies in The Psychology of Mystics,* trans. foreword Algar Thorold (Albany, N.Y.: Magi Books, 1966), pp. 55–145.

43. Hermann Samuel Reimarus and Lessing exposed the ahistorical pretensions of Christianity and pointed to its historical conditionality and the contingency of much of its discourse. Kant accepted much of the critique but tried to rehabilitate what he presumed to be Christianity's core in *Religion Within the Limits of Reason Alone* (1792). Fichte's text, *Attempt at a Critique of All Revelation,* which bore such a striking resemblance to Kant's presumed view on Christianity to have been mistaken for a work of his, is, in fact, considerably less hospitable in tone than Kant's text. For Fichte, the rational kernel must be extracted, leaving the husk of historical revelation behind. Revelation is entirely relative and economic. See *Attempt at a Critique of All Revelation,* trans. Garrett Green (Cambridge: Cambridge University Press, 1978), pp. 144ff.

44. For examples of Hegelian reflection on divine freedom, see *LPR 3* E 270, G 196; *Enc* #382. For an example of Hegel's defining God as love see *LPR 3* 1827 E 276, G 201.

45. For Oetinger's definition of God as *Ens manifestativum sui,* see his tract to Princess Antonia. Benz in *Les sources* sees Oetinger's view of the divine as highly influential in the case of Schelling and Hegel. See Friedrich Christoph Oetinger, *Sammtliche Schriften,* ed. K. C. E. Ehman (Stuttgart, 1855–1864, 11 vols. in 2 parts. See Part 2, *Theosophische Schriften,*"Die kabbalistisch Lehrtafel der Prinzessin Antonia" (1.1–246).

46. See Alexandre Koyré, *La philosophie de Jacob Boehme* (Paris: Vrin, 1929), pp. 329ff. In Part 2 of *Sammtliche Schriften,* Oetinger's commentary on Boehme is significant.

47. Mark Taylor, *Journeys to Selfhood,* chap. 6.

48. See Gerard Schmidt, *The Concept of Being in Hegel and Heidegger* (Bonn: Bouvier, 1979), pp. 23, 28–29, 32–33; Schlitt, *Hegel's Trinitarian Claim,* pp. 82 ff.

49. See Schmidt, *The Concept of Being,* p. 113.

50. *SL* pp. 826, 842; *Enc* #83. On the more inclusive level of Spirit that transcends the formal ontological sphere of the logic, see *Enc* #386.

51. With regard to this important move, see George Seidel's *Activity and Ground: Fichte, Schelling, and Hegel* (New York: George Olms Verlag, 1976).

52. When Aquinas identifies God as *actus purus* in the *Summa* (1. Q. 10. Art. 1), his description is informed by his view of divine simplicity (Q 23) and divine self-sufficiency (Q 28 Art. 1; Q 33 Art. 1). To define God as *Pure Act* is to exclude potentiality and thus privation or lack from God (*Summa Contra Gentiles* BK 1, chap. 16, 43). In the case of Hegel, *actus purus* seems connected with a necessary drive to manifestation which puts the notion of divine self-sufficiency under pressure. The link with act (*Thatigkeit*) and pure act and divine manifestation is not original to Hegel. In the Romantic period before German Idealism it is first made by Oetinger in his kabalistic tract to Princess Antonia.

53. Michel Henry in *The Essence of Manifestation* underscores this point. See pp. 689–737. Henry suggests that this fundamental presupposition of Hegel is found also in Boehme.

54. The identity of thought and being is characteristic of Schelling circa 1800. It is pivotal in his *System of Transcendental Idealism* (1800) Part 1, Sect. II, and is still a basic axiom in *Bruno* (1802). For an accurate and thoughtful account of Schelling's Identity Philosophy, see Alan White, *Schelling: An Introduction to the System of Freedom* (New Haven & London: Yale University Press, 1983), pp. 50–81. Hegel, of course, only definitely broke from Schelling with the publication of *PS* (1807). His estimate of Intellectual Intuition in *DE* is still quite positive (pp. 28–29).

55. The point of view of completion is a structural element of Hegel's account of the narratives of individual, history, and the divine. In *PS,* while various, more or less inadequate, perspectives on reality are described: first, they are described with their *telos* of full adequacy clearly to the fore, and second, realization of full adequacy (i.e., the absolute perspective of the philosopher who achieves full cognitive transparence) is the condition of the possibility that one can espy *telos* and map the trajectory of perspectives within which *telos* is the power of movement. For this point, see Werner Marx, *Hegel's Phenomenology of Spirit: Its Points and Purposes: A Commentary on the Preface and Introduction* (New York: Harper, 1975). Similar points can be made with respect to the narratives of history and the divine. With respect to the latter, see Chapelle, *Hegel et la religion* vol. 2, p. 154.

56. See Errol E. Harris, *Salvation From Despair: A Reappraisal of Spinoza's Philosophy* (The Hague: Martinus Nijhoff, 1973), pp. 48–51.

57. See H. S. Harris, *Night Thoughts,* pp. 222–223, 561; Walter Kaufmann, *Hegel: A Reinterpretation,* p. 158; John H. Smith, *The Spirit and its Letter;* Mark Taylor, *Journeys to Selfhood,* pp. 77 ff. Novalis had said "Der Roman ist Leben als Buch," and life for Novalis, as for F. Schlegel, was development. If Novalis and Schlegel were major exponents of the genre of *Bildungsroman,* Goethe, who combined the stress on the explication of self with the stress on the conditioning of development by the social and ideological forces, was its most distinquished exponent. For a good account of *Bildung* as the pedagogy of self through formative encounter, see W. H. Bruford, *Culture and society in Classical Weimar 1775–1805* (Cambridge: Cambridge University Press, 1962).

58. That Goethe provides the model of *Bildungsroman* in his *Wilhelm Meisters Lehrjahre* (1796) was put forward most forcefully in the German Romantic environment by F. Schlegel. This view, however, was not universally accepted—Novalis, for instance, thinking its style too prosaic and its content not sufficiently lofty in inspiration. Modern scholars tend to divide along the lines of Schlegel and Novalis.

59. See Ronald D. Gray, *Goethe the Alchemist* (Cambridge: Cambridge University Press, 1952). Gray stresses Goethe's use of both alchemical symbolism and the determinate influence of alchemy regarding the figure of metamorphosis on both the level of nature and self.

60. The development that *Bildungsroman* addresses is not narrowly rationalistic. In this, *Bildungsroman* differs decisively from the novels and novellas of the Enlightenment period where the accent falls on education in the sense of the expunging of ignorance and achieving cognitive mastery. *Bildungsroman* has the entire sensibility as its frame of reference and fully comprehensive and integrated selfhood as its goal.

61. The influence of the alchemical tradition, particularly Paracelsus, on the early Hegel has been touched on by H. S. Harris. See H. S. Harris in *Night Thoughts,* pp. 274, 276–279, 438–439. David Walsh in "The Esoteric Origins of Modern Ideological Thought" suggests that the influence is considerable. If one twins Paracelsus and Boehme and largely construes both as examplars of the alchemical tradition—both Harris and Walsh would permit this—then Walsh very well may have a point. Hegel does, in fact, use the locution *caput mortuum* in his mature work. In alchemy, *caput mortuum,* literally, "dead remains," refers to the precipitate that remains after spirit has been extracted. Hegel uses the locution in *Enc* #42 to refer to the abstract hidden God of Kant which truly represents a residuum of a cognitive process of comprehending reality.

62. One of the truly important structural elements of *Wilhelm Meisters Lehrjahre,* as prototypical *Bildungsroman* text, is the debate, implicit as well as ex-

plicit, in the novel, as to whether everything occurs under the sign of chance (*Zufall*) or fate (*Schickung*). Goethe does not unequivocally decide the issue, but, as one Goethe scholar has suggested, it is extremely unlikely that Goethe supported the view that *Bildung* was a totally rational and necessary process (see Eric A. Blackhall, *Goethe and the Novel* (Ithaca and London: Cornell University Press, 1976), p. 136. Nevertheless, if chance is not expunged, life does turn out to have pattern and coherence. Hegel's support of the *Bildungsroman* view and his incorporation of it into philosophy as discursive articulation shows its metalevel character in the excision of the element of chance and happenstance. The pattern and coherence of development displays nothing accidental. Hegel would have thought talk of fate too deterministic and thus inappropriate, but it is clear that in *PS,* as elsewhere, development proceeds in a patterned sequence that appears in some way to be necessary.

63. Herder in his *Philosophie der Geschichte der Menschheit* (1784–1791) broke with the Enlightenment view of history as a record of events referring to human being conceived as a static given. Herder saw human being as historically constituted, and more, constituted by a specific culture. On this revised view, history is thus the movement of culturally constituted being. If Herder departed in certain respects from the *Aufklärung,* in others he did not. He still was a believer in the progressive movement of history.

64. Lessing's text is, of course, the famous *The Education of the Human Race.* See *Lessing's Theological Writings,* pp. 82–98.

65. The tendency to suggest such a reading is most widespread in students of Romantic literature. Yet, perhaps Mark Taylor in his *Journeys to Selfhood* also tends in this direction.

66. In addition to the Enlightenment model one might add: (1) the medieval model which tended to ignore history and acknowledged becoming only in the most formal, metaphysical fashion; (2) the Augustinian model which, while dynamic and mindful of salvation-history, nonetheless excludes cultural history as worthless and validates the absolute of God's election.

67. See Pannenberg's essay "Die Subjektivität Gottes und die Trinitätslehre. Ein Beitrag zur Beziehung zwischen Karl Barth und die Philosophie Hegels." *Kerygma und Dogma* 23 (1977), pp. 25–40. Pannenberg does not say in this essay that the genre of *Bildungsroman* influences Hegel in an explicit way, but for him it is clear that, in his elaboration of the divine, Hegel has projected a certain model of narrative becoming into the transcendent sphere.

68. See *Journeys to Selfhood,* chaps. 4, 5.

69. To be fair to Taylor, he is quite clear that Hegel is involved in a subversion of the classical view of a worldless God and a godless world. Yet, he does not make transparent whether Hegel elaborates an ontotheology with a pro-

found economic emphasis or whether something deeper, i.e., a *radical* subversion, is afoot.

70. See Iljin's *Die Philosophie Hegels* and Erik Schmidt's *Hegels Lehre von Gott.*

71. By amended version of the *Wissenschaftslehre,* I mean a reading of the text that would view it as elaborating a philosophy of finitude whose referent is unequivocally human being and not indifferently human being and the divine. Whatever the merits of such a reading, and a strong case can be made as shown by Alexis Philonenko in *Le liberté humaine dans la philosophie de Fichte* (Paris: Vrin, 1966), nevertheless, Hegel does not read Fichte, nor his own philosophy, as implying an anthropological reduction. His critique in *DE* and *FK* of Fichte's championing of the Third Ground-Proposition that suggests that subject-object unity is a matter of infinite approximation is not an argument against perceived Fichtean humanism: it is an argument against the Fichtean requirements of what a self-consciousness definitively realized would look like.

72. H. S. Harris has pointed out in *Night Thoughts* that, while Hegel did not purchase Boehme's collected works until 1811, he had some knowledge of Boehme as early as 1794.

73. This is explicitly so in the case of *DE,* implicitly so in the case of *FK.* While the basic outline of the contrast between the systems of Fichte and Schelling covers only 20 pages approximately (E 71–89) in *DE,* Schellingian speculation is opposed to Fichtean reflection (understanding) throughout, just as Schelling's authentic understanding of Identity is opposed to Fichte's inadequate understanding (E 2–3, 43, 71–72). Hegel's critique of Fichte's deduction in the *Wissenschaftslehre* in *FK* is premised on the view that Fichte has not risen to the point of view of genuine speculation in which the Absolute is the beginning, middle, and end of all thought. At the foundation of the identity axiom is the surreptitious presence of the empirical reality which had been abstracted from in order to arrive at the identity. This ground-proposition, which is really a residuum of abstraction, masquerades as a positive. But, argues Hegel, Fichte, in a sleight of hand, has merely changed the signs, has made a minus into a plus (E 159–162).

74. See Philonenko in *La liberté humaine,* p. 85; Seidel, *Activity and Ground,* p. 96.

75. See *DE,* E 3, 39, 43, 50–51; *FK* E 172.

76. See Chapelle, *Hegel et la religion,* vol. 2. p. 47. For Heidegger's and Gadamer's affirmation of the finitude of knowledge against Hegelian pretension to the contrary, see *Intro* note 5. Sartre's *Being and Nothingness* is in close dialogue with Hegelian ontology. While this dialogue is, in many respects, positive, there is also dispute. Sartre's foundational argument with Hegel concerns the possibility of coincidence of subject and object, consciousness and be-

ing. In the assertion on noncoincidence Sartre proves himself more Fichtean than Hegelian. For a very good account of the contrast between Hegel's and Sartre's ontology, see Klaus Hartmann, *Sartre's Ontology: A Study of Being and Nothingness* (Evanston, IL: Northwestern University Press, 1966), chap. 6, pp. 126–145.

77. Seidel, *Activity and Ground,* p. 96.

78. *DE* E 48; *FK* E 172.

79. The fact that finitude is *the* mark of the Fichtean self does not *logically* imply that reduction of self to the human self. There are reasons why one might feel compelled to argue for such an identification as Philonenko does in *La liberté humaine,* but as yet I am unpersuaded.

80. "Erring" is a word for process which, contra Hegel, has no teleological or eschatological drift. Taylor defines it as "a wandering, roaming, deviating from the right or intended course, missing the mark." See *Erring,* p. 12.

81. See *Enc* #93–95; or *SL* E 121–122.

82. In Aristotle and Aquinas, God is the final cause of the world. Since to be the final cause of something is to suggest that something achieves its full definition, perfection and sufficiency in something other than itself, this rules out the possibility of speaking intelligently of the divine as the final cause of itself. For Aristotle's exegesis of final cause inserted into a theological context see *Metaphysics* 988 b, 994 b, 1072 b; *Physics* 194 b–195 b, 258 b–260 a. Aquinas, as is well known, is directly indebted to these texts for the elaboration of his own view.

83. See Mark Taylor, *Erring,* p. 70.

84. Vis-à-vis openness of a radical sort, Identity Philosophy perhaps can be partially validated, since it could be regarded as validating closure. After 1802, Hegel submits this view to reappraisal and increasingly begins to think that, without some measure of openness, progress and differentiation, one cannot legitimately speak of closure. If Hegel's position is that of a circular line, Fichte's of a straight noncircular line, Schelling's position, on Hegel's post-1802 (and possibly tendentious) reading, is a point not a circle.

85. See *LPR 1* 27 E 423, G 316.

86. One does not need to be an advocate of deconstruction to concede that Hegel is a logocentric thinker for whom the unintelligible and the accidental are banished. We have already spoken of Hegel's commitment to discourse, whose imperialism is underlined by Heidegger when he analyzes the Greek form of dialectic or dialogue as *dialegein,* i.e., gathering together of that which is between. Everything is gathered, saved, as it were, by discourse. Nothing merely factitious occurs.

87. The classic treatment of the notion of *Vermittlung* is still Henri Niel's *De la médiation dans la philosophie de Hegel* (Paris: Aubier-Montaigne, 1945).

88. *Enc* #96 *zu* (Wallace p. 142).

89. *Erinnerung* belongs to the general symbolic modality of *Vorstellung* which has not totally pruned itself of image and externality. *Denken,* by contrast, is "imageless" and displays maximum inwardness.

90. That there exists a distinction between unrealized and realized subjectivity on the level of the divine is underscored by Walter Jaeschke in his article "Absolute Idee-absolute Subjectivität. Zum Problem der Persönlichkeit Gottes in der Logik und in der Religionsphilosophie." *Zeitschrift für philosophische Forschung* 35 (1981), pp. 385–416. While *Erinnerung* is certainly a property of *Geist* as process, it is also (and especially) a property of *Geist* as result, as fully realized, fully inclusive subjectivity.

91. Hegel has recourse to physiological and biological analogies of growth throughout his work. See *Enc* #379 *zu* for images of germ and seed.

92. Here one has, at one and the same time, an evocation and an emendation of Aristotle's Unmoved Mover (*Physics* 258 b–259 a). The emendation is, of course, momentous, and, by suggesting that movement belongs to God, Hegel not merely is departing from Aristotle but the theological tradition, which explicitly (as in Aquinas) and implicitly (as in Luther, Rational Theology) bases itself upon this Aristotelian axiom.

93. Claude Bruaire, *Logique et religion chrétienne dans la philosophie de Hegel* pp. 65 ff.; Piero Coda, *Il negativo e la trinita;* Emil Fackenheim, *The Religious Dimension,* chap. 6; Michael Theunissen, *Hegels Lehre vom absoluten Geist als theologisch politischer Traktat* (Berlin: Walter de Gruyter & Co., 1970), pp. 216–322. Other very useful contributions include: Walter Kern, "Dialektik und Trinität in der Religionsphilosophie Hegels: Ein Beitrag zur Discussion mit L. Oeing-Hanhoff." *Zeitschrift für katholische Theologie* 102 (1980), pp. 129–155; Peter Koslowski, "Hegel—'der Philosoph der Trinität?': Zur Kontroverse um seine Trinitätslehre." *Theologische Quartalshrift* 162 (1982), pp. 105–131; L. Oeing-Hanhoff, "Hegels Trinitätslehre. Zur Aufgabe ihrer Kritik und Reception." *Theologie und Philosophie* 52 (1977), pp. 378–407.

94. Needless to say, Hegel does not believe that the modern age is pathological as such. Indeed, Hegel has, in principle, a profound respect for the possibility of modernity. But with the actualization of the essence of the real spirit of modernity based upon Christianity went deformation of various types.

95. See Hodgson's valuable note, *LPR 1* 1827 E157 note 17 where he points out that F. A. Tholuck had argued the thesis that Platonic and Neoplatonic borrowings vitiated the doctrine of the Trinity.

96. Bruaire underscores this point in *Logique et religion chrétienne,* pp. 66 ff. For similar statements such as God as activity and process, see *LPR 3* 1821 E 78, G 16; 1827 E 270–271, G 196.

97. While the doctrine of the Trinity undergoes a number of important changes from Bohme's earliest text *Aurora* (1612) to his latest (1624), the Trinity plays an important part in all. The vicissitudes of Boehme's elaboration of the doctrine of the Trinity will be touched on in section 2.3 of chapter 2. All I wish to point out here is that just as Boehme more and more articulates the ineffable context of the Trinity and authorizes apophatic discourse, Hegel does precisely the opposite.

98. Important elements of Hegel's departure from conciliar understanding will be traced in chaps. 2 and 6. That Hegel does depart from conciliar understanding is a point suggested by Hessen and argued by Splett in the *Die Trinitätslehre.*

99. For Hegel's insistence that dogma does reach the real and true as such, see *LPR 1* 1821 MS E 106, G 24–25; E 243, G 152; *LPR 3* 1821 MS E 150–151, G 86; 1827 E 333–336, G 256–258.

100. See *Glaubenslehre,* #170–172; *The Christian Faith,* pp. 738–751. Despite the *Glaubenslehre's* seemingly explicit marginalization, some Schleiermacher scholars are prepared to argue that the great Romantic theologian does propound a substantive doctrine of the Trinity. See, for example, Robert R. Williams's *Schleiermacher the Theologian: The Construction of the Doctrine of God* (Philadelphia: Fortress Press, 1978), Ch. 6, pp. 139–159.

101. See *Glaubenslehre,* #170, *The Christian Faith,* p. 735.

102. One of the many accusations Hegel makes against Schelling's philosophy in the Preface of *PS* is that Schelling's triadic scheme is abstract and lifeless, i.e., is not imbued with, and regulated by, the content with which it deals. Kant's own triadic schemes in the First Critique are similarly objects of scorn.

103. See chaps. 5 and 6 for an examination of the background of Hegel's language of kingdom.

104. The nontraditional nature of Boehme's and Hegel's descent view will be explored in chaps. 3 and 4 below.

105. Ruusbroec, perhaps, constitutes an exception. See Louis Dupré, *The Common Life: Origins of Trinitarian Mysticism and its Development by Jan Ruusbroec* (New York: Crossroad, 1984).

106. As Hegel suggests in most texts (e.g., *LPR*) and formalizes in the *Enc* (#451–464), *Vorstellung* exhibits some variety in expression: it has, as its minumum sensible image, its maximum approximation to pure thought. Different

Vorstellungen and integration of *Vorstellungen,* therefore, may hover closer to one pole than the other. For a good discussion of the parameters of *Vorstellung,* see *LPR 1* 1821 MS E 238–250, G 148–159; 1827 E 396–403, G 291–298.

107. By narrative "and-then" and "and," I mean to suggest those narrative indices that symbolize reality as a sequence of events or happenings of before and after, connected externally and temporally and not logically and intrinsically. See *Enc* #565, also *LPR 1* 1824 E 334, G 235–236; 1827 E 400, G 295; 1831 E 467, G 356. In addition to the overt or covert use of story indices, see Hegel's related objection to the conjunctive "and," which simply ties together in the most external way possible divine attributes or predicates) *Enc* #20; *LPR 1* 1827 E 401, G. 296).

108. See Peter Hodgson's editorial introduction to *LPR 3,* pp. 16, 27–28; Emil Fackenheim, *The Religious Dimension of Hegel's Thought,* Appendix 3, pp. 218–219. I am interpreting the double Trinity of which Fackenheim speaks as corresponding to the Immanent Trinity and Economic Trinity.

109. See Chapelle, *Hegel et la religion,* vol. 2. p. 59; Bruaire, *Logique et religion chrétienne,* pp. 71–72, 113 ff.

110. Schlitt, *Hegel's Trinitarian Claim,* p. 45, notes 168–169.

111. For a summary of Schlitt's view, see *Hegel's Trinitarian Claim,* pp. 267–273.

112. I am here following Schlitt's strategy in *Hegel's Trinitarian Claim,* p. 42, note 160.

113. *LPR 3* 1821 MS E 75–76, G 14–5; 1824 E 185–186, G 119–120; 1827 E 277–278, G 202–203.

114. Chapelle, *Hegel et la religion,* vol. *2,* pp. 41, 47.

115. See *LPR 3* 1827 E 277–278, G 202–293. See also Hodgson's note 75 on p. 277. That attributes only refer to modalities of God's relation to the world but in no wise to God *in se* constitutes Schleiermacher's reduction.

116. Bruaire, *Logique et religion chrétienne,* p. 67; Moltmann, *The Crucified God: The Cross of Christ as the Foundation and Criticism of Christian Theology,* trans. R. A. Wilson and John Bowden (New York, San Francisco, London: Harper & Row, 1974), pp. 235–249.

117. *The Crucified God,* p. 239.

118. Koyré, *La philosophie de Jacob Boehme,* pp. 397–400, 409–414.

119. Hegel, of course, departs decisively from Kant. The various aspects of departures receive detailed treatment in Harold Knudsen's *Gottesbeweise im deutschen Idealismus: Die modaltheoretische Begründung des Absoluten dargestellt*

an Kant, Hegel und Weisse (Berlin and New York: Walter de Gruyter, 1972), esp. pp. 168–203.

120. See Bruaire's *Logique et religion* and Schlitt's *Hegel's Trinitarian Claim,* E. Schmidt, *Hegels Lehre von Gott,* pp. 111–140, *inter alia.* Pannenberg, by contrast, in "Die Subjektivität Gottes," while clear about the overlap of ontological argument and trinitarian articulation in a general way, does not thematize the question of trinitarian modality. The emerging consensus seems correct given the placement of discussion of the ontological argument in the 1821 Manuscript and later lecture series. Discussion precedes trinitarian elaboration as a whole which is inclusive of creation, incarnation, and elevation into/of spiritual community.

121. *LPR 3* 1821 MS E 72, G 11–12; 1824 E 183–184, G 118–119.

122. Hegel makes the association with Spinozist *Causa Sui* explicit in the 1831 lectures. See *LPR 3* 1831 E 355, G 274.

Chapter 2 The First Narrative Epoch: The "Immanent Trinity"

1. See Pavel Apostel, "Wie ist die Entwicklung einer 'Logica Humana' im Rahmen der Darlegung der 'Logica Divina' in Hegels *Wissenschaft der Logik* 'moglich'?" In *Die Wissenschaft der Logik und die Logik der Reflexion,* ed. Dieter Henrich. In *Hegel Studien* Beihaft 18, pp. 37–39 (Bonn: Bouvier, 1978).

2. See, for example, Michael John Petry's. Introduction to *Hegel's Philosophy of Nature. Vol. 1* (London, New York: George Allen and Unwin Ltd and Humanities Press, 1970), pp. 40 ff.

3. See *Absolute Knowledge,* pp. 57, 86–88.

4. What White says in the following passage makes it clear that he is no longer involved in describing or transcribing Hegel's thought but legislating what Hegel *should* have said: "Though some of Hegel's locutions suggest that he is concerned with the real ground, and thus with a transcendent theological idealism, he presents no argument that could establish the Idea as God. If his first philosophy is transcendent metaphysics, then it is dogmatic. Only as transcendental ontology can the *Logic* function as first philosophy" (p. 80).

5. See Malcolm Clark, *Logic and System;* Dale M. Schlitt, *Hegel's Trinitarian Claim,* pp. 11–92; André Leonard, *Commentaire littéral de la logique de Hegel* (Paris: Vrin, 1974); Claude Bruaire, *Logique et la religion chrétienne.*

6. See Reinhard Heede, "Die göttliche Idee und ihre Erscheinung in der Religion. Untersuchungen zum Verhältinis von Logik und Religionsphilosophie bei Hegel" (Ph.D. Dissertation, Philosophical Faculty of the Westfälischen Wilhelms Universität zu Munster/Westfalen, 1972); Iwan Iljin, *Die Philosophie*

Hegels als kontemplative Gotteslehre, chap. IX "Die göttliche Logic," pp. 203–230; Walter Jaeschke, "Absolute Idee-Absolute Subjektivität. Zum Problem der Persönlichkeit Gottes in der Logik und in der Religionsphilosophie." *Zeitschrift für philosophische Forschüng* 35 (1981), pp. 385–416; also Walter Jaeschke, "Die Wissenschaft der Logik," in *Hegel: Einführung in seine Philosophie,* ed. Otto Poggeler (Freiburg: Alber, 1977), pp. 75–90; Walter Kern, "Dialektic und Trinität in der Religionsphilosophie Hegels. Ein Beitrag zur Discussion mit L. Oeing-Hanoff." *Zeitschrift für katholische Theologie* 102 (1980), pp. 129–155. See also Traugott Koch, *Differenz und Versöhnung: Eine Interpretation der Theologie G. W. F. Hegels nach seiner "Wissenschaft der Logik"* (Gütersloh: Mohn, 1967).

7. Perhaps the most detailed as well as most eloquent account of Hegel's rehabilitation of the transcendent is to be found in James Collins's *The Emergence.* See Chapter 7, "Religion and Hegelian Metaphysics," pp. 254–293. See also John E. Smith's "Hegel's Critique of Kant" in *Hegel and the History of Philosophy,* ed. Joseph J. O'Malley, Keith W. Algonzin, Frederick G. Weiss (The Hague: Marinus Nijhoff, 1974), pp. 109–128.

8. For a good account of the relation and difference between Kant's and Hegel's account of categories, see G. R. G. Mure's *An Introduction to Hegel* (Oxford: Clarendon Press, 1940), pp. 82–113, esp. pp. 86–89, 96–98, 107–108.

9. On Kant's move beyond Aristotle's ontologically classified set of categories, see J. M. E. Moravcsik, "Aristotle's Theory of Categories," and John Cook Wilson, "Categories in Aristotle and in Kant" in *Aristotle: A Collection of Critical Essays* (Modern Studies in Philosophy) (London: MacMillian, 1968), pp. 125–145.

10. W. A. Ross probably catches the trust of Aristotle's reflection best when he suggests that, while Aristotle does deal to a certain extent with linguistic fact, there is an inalienable ontological thrust in Aristotle. "*Kategoria,*" he notes, means "predicate" after all. Thus, for him the categories are a list of the widest predicates predicable essentially of the various nameable entities, i.e., which tell us what kinds of entity at bottom they are. See *Aristotle* (London: Methuen & Co. Ltd., 1923), pp. 20–23. A similar position is advanced by J. M. E Moravcsik in his above-mentioned article.

11. This is certainly the view of Errol E. Harris in *An Interpretation of the Logic of Hegel* (New York, London: Lanham, 1986), as it is also the view of John N. Findlay in *Hegel, a Reexamination* (London, 1958).

12. See Joseph Owens, *The Doctrine of Being in the Aristotelian "Metaphysics": A Study in the Greek Background of Medieval Thought* (Toronto: Pontifical Institute of Medieval Studies, 1951); Giovani Reale, *The Concept of First Philosophy and the Unity of the Metaphysics of Aristotle* (Albany, N.Y.: SUNY Press, 1980).

13. Reinhard Heede, "Die göttliche Logik," pp. 56–57.

14. Jörg Splett, *Die Trinitätslehre,* p. 78.

15. *Erinnerung* and *Aufhebung* are closely related. As Hegel points out more than once, but perhaps most clearly in *Enc* #96 *zu, Aufhebung* of a preceding form by a succeeding form involves preservation as well as cancellation. See Errol E. Harris's discussion of the word *Aufheben* in *An Interpretation,* pp. 31–33.

16. *SL* E 329, *GL4:*448

17. *SL* E 328–329; *GL4:*407–408.

18. Hegel's development could be construed as moving along two complementary fronts, i.e., (1) the broadening and deepening of his understanding of his philosophical task; and (2) the gaining of more and more clarity concerning which theological proposals do, and which theological proposals do not, capture the Christian vision of reality. With regard to the latter, Hegel, who from the beginning rejected any 'positive' faith, i.e., faith founded upon the authority of either a historical revelation, the literal word or Church authority, also gradually weaned himself from any rationalistic tendency. For him, the proposals most worthy of admiration, and nearest in inspiration and execution to his own mature ontotheological rendition, were the mystico-speculative proposals on the margins of the mainline Christian traditions.

19. Albert Chapelle, *Hegel et la religion,* vol. 2, pp. 188–192.

20. In proposing the ontological implication of logic directly and up front, the *Logic* of the *Enc* (#1, 9, 24, 84, etc.) encourages equally a declarative assertion of theological implication (#1, 4, 8, 85, 86, etc.). We are here, of course, talking merely about the transparency of interconnection between logic, ontology, and theology and do not mean to suggest that *SL* differs fundamentally from the *Logic* of the *Enc* or that *SL* does not bear ontological and theological implication. Still, if the dominant epistemological horizon of *SL* may tend to encourage the kind of purely "transcendental" interpretations of Hegelian logic as that offered by Alan White, it does not justify it.

21. The *Zusatzen* of the Logic of the *Enc* provide either illuminating illustrations of what is expressed quite generally or abstractly in the text, or systemic and concrete translation(s) of the text in and through which the subject-object "transcendental signified" of the Logic—to avail of deconstructionist terminology—is identified. While the illustrations are many, the translation(s) are few, reducing, in fact, to two, i.e., the *theological,* with *God* as its transcendental signified, and *anthropological,* with *human being* as the transcendental signified. Nevertheless, the very fact of pluriform translatability tends, at a minimum, to suggest that Hegelian logic is structurally ambiguous with regard to its referent and, at a maximum, to encourage decision with regard to the real referent, thereby fomenting the split between right-wing and left-wing Hegelianism. Of course, there is no need of an either/or here, though this does

not rule out an order of priority between transcendental signifieds. The overt declaration in the main body of the text that the subject is God or truth suggest that the primary transcendental signified is God, and thus the primary translation is theological. But this by no means excludes the human subject as the signified or rules out anthropological translation as a secondary modality of translation. Indeed, Hegel's complex ontotheological view will forbid the either/or of traditional theism and atheism and suggest a position identical with neither.

22. Arguably, one of the few shortcomings in Jaeschke's fine essay, "Absolute Idee" is that, in his desire to stress that Aristotelian character of Hegelian logic, he does not take sufficient note of the Platonic element declared in Hegel's archetypal construal of the logic as a realm of ideas. By contrast, Michael Rosen in his *Hegel's Dialectic and its Criticism* (Cambridge: Cambridge University Press, 1982) clearly recognizes the Platonic element and makes a connection between Hegelian logic and Plato's *Timaeus* (p. 69). However, there are good reasons for believing that it would be just as wrong to characterize Hegelian logic as exclusively Platonic as it would be to characterize it as Aristotelian.

23. Other theological contenders include Jacob Boehme and Valentinian Gnosticism, though it must be conceded that there does not exist the kind of correspondence of detail that one can espy between Hegelian logic and Neoplatonic articulation of the noetic sphere. Conceding the advantage of Neoplatonism here does not imply that its candidacy as a taxon of Hegelian ontotheology as a *whole* is superior to either Bohemian theosophy or Valentinian Gnosticism.

24. L. Bruno Puntel, *Darstellung, Method and Struktur. Untersuchungen zur Einheit der systematischen Philosophie G. W. F. Hegels. Hegel Studien.* Beihaft 10 (Bonn: Bouvier, 1973); D. M. Schlitt, *Hegel's Trinitarian Claim,* p. 21.

25. Puntel, *Darstellung,* p. 229. For a similar emphasis see Gerhard Schmidt, *The Concept of Being in Hegel and Heidegger* (Bonn: Bouvier Verlag, Herbert Grundmann, 1977), pp. 43–44.

26. Puntel, *Darstellung,* p. 229.

27. Iljin, *Die Philosophie Hegels,* p. 203.

28. I am suggesting that Hegel is original not in providing *a* narrative understanding of God, but in understanding God as radical and inclusive narrative. Divine becoming is the divine vocation of self-realization.

29. The accusation that despite Hegel's best efforts to avoid temporalizing the Trinity this is the ultimate fruit of his labors is, as we saw in chap. 1, a point forcefully made by Pannenberg in "Die Subjecktivität Gottes."

30. Here I am mentioning what I take to be the four crucial *dimensions* or axes of development in the autogenesis of divine selfhood.

31. Thus, the kind of interpretation of Hegelian logic suggested by a Croce, a Petry or a Puntel cannot be cast aside as false, but must rather be regarded as too one-sided.

32. See Iljin, *Die Philosophie Hegels,* p. 208.

33. The possibility should not be ruled out, however, that Hegelian logic does both. Indeed, as we will make clear in chap. 2, sect. 2.3, while Hegelian rendition of the "Immanent Trinity" in both logical and non-logical texts swerves from the normative hypostatic interpretation, at the same time it seems to recapitulate a quite specific heterodox view, i.e., that of Jacob Boehme, and to make other trinitarian appeals of a non-standard sort.

34. This is treated in detail in section 2.2 of this chapter.

35. This tendency in Patristic thought appears as early as the second century in the figure of Justin Martyr.

36. In a sense the correlation of *Sophia* and *Logos* is there from the beginning and, scripture scholars would argue, is a definite presence in the Prologue of the Fourth Gospel. The interregnum of Gnostic Christianity, which combined the ontological-semantic splitting of *Sophia* and *Logos* with a generally negative attitude towards Jewish scriptures (though this negative attitude is not worked out in the fully rigorous way of Marcion), forced the Christianity of the early centuries to become *self-conscious* regarding the ontological-semantic identity of *Logos* and *Sophia* and the profoundly positive relation between Old Testament and New Testament texts.

37. See *Les sources mystiques,* p. 17.

38. For a convenient translation of Eckhart's Latin commentary on the Prologue, see James M. Clark and John V. Skinner, *Meister Eckhart: Selected Treatises and Sermons* (Fontana, 1963), pp. 222–249.

39. *Meister Eckhart,* p. 234.

40. For Boehme the image of the mirror (*Spiegel*) is a crucial one, for it is in the split of mirror and the divine that the undifferentiatedness of the divine is overcome. The mirror is equated by Boehme with Wisdom (*Weisheit*) or *Sophia* and is never equated with the Son who is the word or the light of the divine. As *Sophia* and *Logos* get separated ontologically, so also Proverbs 8:22 gets separated from the Prologue of the Fourth Gospel. Thus *Sophia* becomes an independent grammatical subject and not just an equivocal name for the *Logos.*

41. See *Absolute Knowledge,* p. 57.

42. Ibid.

43. Alexandre Kojève, *Introduction,* p. 112.

44. *Enc,* #236 *zu.*

45. Iljin, *Die Philosophie Hegels,* p. 203.

46. See *SL* E 837.

47. For a clear expression of Hegel's view that categorial form is not empty, see *Enc* #133 *zu.* That the categories admit of supersensible employment and are not in need of the "matter" of sense is a constant element of Hegel's critique of Kant from *FK* on. For an account of this critique which brings out the specifically theological dimension of the issues between Kant and Hegel, see Michael Rosen, *Hegel's Dialectic and Its Criticism,* pp. 66–70.

48. This view is supported by Puntel in his *Darstellung,* pp. 72–73, and by Michael Theunissen in his *Sein und Schein. Die kritische Funktion der Hegelschen Logik* (Frankfurt am Main: Suhrkamp, 1978), p. 62, though it should be said that neither think the categories refer *exclusively* to the immanent divine.

49. As Hyppolite pointed out in *Logique et existence,* Hegelian philosophy in general and Hegelian logic in particular, represents one of the most overt, as well as most rigorous, attempts in the ontotheological tradition to rid language and concept of opacity. The realm of the logic in particular, as Heidegger and Gadamer among others have recognized, is the realm of pure transparence.

50. While Hegel agreed with both Kant and Aristotle that the number of categories is finite, he set greater strictures concerning what it meant for categories to constitute a whole or totality. From his perspective, both Aristotle's and Kant's accounts provide an aggregate not a totality, i.e., a coherent interrelated whole where categorial forms both imply each other and have a determinate locus in the whole. As it turns out, this locus is, in fact, a narrative locus.

51. Spinoza suggests as much in *Ethics* Bk. I, Prop. II, where he speaks of infinite attributes.

52. In suggesting the locution "string," I have in mind the analogy with genetic codes where order is crucially important.

53. See G. R. M. Mure, *An Introduction to Hegel,* p. 83; also Wolfgang Wieland, "Bemerkung zum Anfang von Hegels Logik," in *Seminar: Dialektik in der Philosophie Hegels,* ed. Rolf-Peter Horstmann (Frankfurt: Suhrkamp, 1978), pp. 194–212.

54. For example the constitutive categorial string of *The Philosophy of Nature* of Mechanics-Physics-Organics mimics the constitutive categorial string Being-Essence-Concept of the *Logic.* See *Enc* #252.

55. As Jaeschke has persuasively argued, the *Logic* must not be understood to exist in splendid isolation from the rest of Hegel's ontotheological scheme. This view is advanced in two of Jaeschke's articles, i.e., "Absolute Idee" and "Die Wissenschaft der Logik."

56. Being is recapitulated in the categories of Mechanics in *Philosophy of Nature* and Intuition in *Philosophy of Mind.*

57. For Hegel, nature's most differentiated moment is the death of nature or, specifically, the death of the animal organism (*Enc* #376). The most differentiated moment of finite spirit occurs when it moves beyond subjective and objective mind into Absolute Mind where it realizes its own infinity.

58. See *An Introduction to Hegel,* Chapter 9.

59. Jaeschke is right in "Absolute Idee" in regarding Aristotle's *noesis noeseos noesis* (*Enc* #236 *zu*) as crucially important for the understanding of Hegelian logic. Jaeschke finds himself, here, substantially in agreement with the position advocated by Klaus Düsing in *Das Problem der Subjektivität in Hegels Logik. Hegel Studien.* Beihaft 15 (Bonn: Bouvier, 1976), pp. 305–313.

60. Here I take issue with Jaeschke's view as elaborated in "Absolute Idee," but this is not to say that the thinker is not exclusively a function of thought.

61. See, for example, Hilary Armstrong, "The Background of the Doctrine 'That the Intelligibles are not Outside the Intellect' " in *Plotinian and Christian Studies* (London: Variorum Reprints, 1979), pp. 393–413.

62. Armstrong, "The Background," pp. 403 ff.

63. This point is made with some force by Stephen Gersch in his excellent *From Iamblichus to Eriugena: An Investigation of the Prehistory and Evolution of the Pseudo-Dionysian Tradition* (Leiden: E. J. Brill, 1978), pp. 57–67.

64. Perhaps the classic example is Marius Victorinus, the early 4th-century Christian Neoplatonist. For a succinct account of Victorinus's equating of Father-Son-Spirit with the Neoplatonic Triad of Being-Life-Intellect, see Mary T. Clark, "A Neoplatonic Commentary on the Christian Trinity." In *Neoplatonism and Christian Thought,* ed. Dominic J. O'Meara (Albany, N.Y.: SUNY Press, 1982), pp. 24–33.

65. See *LHP 2* E 449, GL19:90.

66. Perhaps the classical statement of Proclus's position is to be found in Prop. 36 of *The Elements of Theology.* For an excellent discussion of the three Platonic principles, see Gersch, *From Iamblichus to Eriugena,* pp. 45–47.

67. See Gersch, *From Iamblichus to Eriugena,* pp. 82–121.

68. Hegel explicitly recalls Eriugena only in *LHP 2* (see *GL19*:159–162). It is interesting to note that Staudenmaier, one of the most resolute of Hegel's oppo-

nents, suggested a connection in his *Johannes Scotus Erigena und die Wissenschaft seiner Zeit* (Frankfurt, 1834). The connection between Hegel and Eriugena in more recent has times been recalled by Werner Beierwaltes. See his "The Revaluation of John Scottus Eriugena in German Idealism." In *The Mind of Eriugena,* ed. John J. O'Meara and Ludwig Bieler (Dublin, Ireland: Irish University Press, 1973), pp. 190–198.

69. See Gersch's detailed account in *From Iamblichus to Eriugena,* pp. 191–288.

70. As Pseudo-Dionysius makes clear in *The Divine Names* (1,1; 1,2) the apophatic vocabulary of *adiannetos* (inconceivable), *arrhetos* (ineffable), aperileptos (incomprehensible), etc., apply equally to the Superessential Trinity as to the Superessential Godhead. Eriugena in Bk. 2 of *De divisione naturae* recapitulates Pseudo-Dionysius on this point.

71. Only if the reality of the primordial Triad was in some *relative* respect determinable would it be possible to construe it as being further differentiated by metaphysical principles. For neither Pseudo-Dionysius nor Eriugena is this possible. The Trinity is beyond concept and language; it is a datum of revelation, not knowledge. Since the Trinity is, in principle, unknown, it makes no sense to speak with the assurance of non-Christian Neoplatonism that one "knows" not only the Triad but its differentiation into an enneadic structure.

72. Nowhere is this stated more eloquently than in *The Divine Names,* where Pseudo-Dionysius establishes one of the baselines of the Christian mystical tradition, i.e., the inadequacy of language and concept to grasp the divine.

73. See *De divisione naturae,* Bk. 2.

74. This is transparently clear in Hegel's discussion of the philosophical syllogisms in *Enc* # 575–577.

75. See Iljin, *Die Philosophie Hegels,* pp. 203–230, esp. pp. 203–214.

76. The category *metahistorical* is generated as a result of Berdyaev's dialogue with Boehme, Hegel, and the later Schelling, all of whom, from his point of view, articulate a divine life of becoming (theogony) before creation (cosmogony). For his classic reflection on Boehme, see his introductory essay to *Six Theosophic Points and Other Writings,* trans. J. R. Earle (Ann Arbor, Michigan: Ann Arbor Paperbacks, University of Michigan Press, 1958), V–XXXVII. For Berdyaev's reflection on Hegel, see his *The Beginning and the End,* trans. R. M. French (New York: Harper Torchbook, 1957), pp. 18–29.

77. As pointed out by John R. Loeschen (after Prenter) in *The Divine Community: Trinity, Church and Ethics in Reformation Theology* (Kirksville, Miss: the 16th-Century Journal Publ. Inst. Northeast Missouri State University, 1981), pp. 15–71, Luther is by no means an *anti*-or even an *a*trinitarian thinker. Without fundamentally challenging Luther's christological bias, Loeschen does point

to the fact that Luther, at the very least, engages from time to time in trinitarian reflection. Such reflection is found as early as 1514 and is characteristic of his last years. It is not Loeschen's point that Luther ever comes to accept that trinitarian formula are pivotal for faith, but rather that there existed in Luther a tendency not to banish the Trinity completely into the zone of *theologia gloriae.* A reinforcing appraisal is made by Marc Lienhard in his *Luther's Witness to Jesus Christ: Stages and Themes of the Reformer's Theology* (Minneapolis: Augsburg Publishing House, 1986), pp. 318–326.

78. This was the name Boehme gave the Trinity in *Aurora* (1612), his first text, a text, it is clear from the account in *LHP*, Hegel had read. A new German edition of Hegel's account of medieval and modern philosophy has appeared in the *Vorlesungen Ausgewählte Nachschriften und Manuskripte* series. It is Vol. 9. The particular edition, characterized by excellent notes, goes under the specific title of *Vorlesungen über die Geschichte der Philosophie. Teil 4. Philosophie des Mittelalter und der neueren Zeit,* ed. Pierre Garniron and Walter Jaeschke (Hamburg: Felix Meiner Verlag, 1986). See pp. 78–87, plus notes pp. 273–288.

79. See Pseudo-Dionysius, *The Divine Names* 1,1; 1,2; Duns Scotus Eriugena, *De divisione naturae.* Bk. 2.

80. Michel Henry, *The Essence of Manifestation,* trans. Girard Etzkorn (The Hague: Martinus Nijhoff, 1973), pp. 309–335.

81. In sect. 2.1 we noted, as major effects of the Christian domestication of Neoplatonism of a Proclus-type: (1) the split between the One and foundational Triad ceases to be countenanced, and the One is now understood to express itself completely in the Triad; and (2) the ineffability, predicated in a real sense only of the One, now becomes predicable of the Trinity. It is probably the case that (2) depends upon (1) and is regarded as a corollary of it. Something very interesting gets revealed when Hegelian rendition of the Trinity is read against the backdrop of Neoplatonism. On the one hand, Hegel's presentation of the Trinity, i.e., his "Immanent Trinity" seems to presuppose Christian Neoplatonism's identification of the absolute with the Trinity but, on the other, disagrees with respect to the apophatic register that is typical of Pseudo-Dionysius and Eriugena. Put another way, Hegel draws precisely the opposite conclusion to the identification of the absolute and the Trinity to Christian Neoplatonism. In Christian Neoplatonism this implied apophaticizing the horizon of the Trinity. In Hegel's case, it implies kataphatizing the horizon of the absolute.

82. See in Eckhart's *Defense* a fine expression of the coincidence of *begetting* and *creating.* In Raymond Blakney, *Meister Eckhart* (New York: Harper and Row, 1941), p. 278.

83. I am borrowing the locutions *positive* and *negative* divine from chap. 1 of W. T. Stace's *Time and Eternity* (Princeton, NJ: Princeton University Press, 1956),

repub. (New York: Greenwood Press, 1960). For Stace the negative divine is the divine that is presented in that variety of Christian mystical theology emphasizing the absolute transcendence and irradicable unknowability of the divine. By contrast, the positive divine is to the fore in the theological tradition whenever the emphasis falls on the divine who relates to us, who reveals itself to us and makes itself known.

84. As we shall see in some detail in chap. 3, sect. 3.1, Hegel is very anxious to remove any extrinsic or voluntarist elements from his ontotheological proposal. He is uncomfortable with the notion of a self-sufficient divine outside, or beyond, the context of relation, a divine which may be thought to 'decide' or 'choose' to create a world. He is also not fully comfortable with a notion of creation which, if it eschews voluntarist suggestion, rigorously maintains the self-sufficiency of the divine and interprets creation as 'excess' or 'surplus' of the divine's gratuitous generosity.

85. The locution *counterdivine* is used to distinguish Hegel's position from a position such as Christian Neoplatonism, which understands the finite qua matter as representing the limit of the manifestation of the divine and thus the privation of reality, since, in Christian Neoplatonism, Being and God are interchangeable terms. In Hegel, by contrast, the finite is an antagonist of some power, energy, and reality, in a drama whose denouement is the fulfillment of both, i.e., the elevation of the finite, the concretizing of the infinite.

86. See *Enc* #564; *LPR* 1 1821 MS E 104, G 23.

87. A number of Hegelian commentators and critics rightly see that one of the major spectres Hegel is anxious to do battle with is the self-enclosed divine, a view not untypical of medieval thought (thought not peculiar to it)—thus the Latin phraseology. I have Jürgen Moltmann and Quentin Lauer particularly in mind here in my recall of *Deus Incurvatus.*

88. Here we are speaking, obviously, from *within a Hegelian* perspective. Within such a perspective the meaning of existence becomes problematic, if the divine is regarded as self-sufficient, the alone good, the alone real. Of the possibilities, (3) is perhaps best regarded as a specification of (2), i.e., of the extrinsicality of relation that deprives the created order of ontological and axiological import.

89. The most lucid discussion of *Entfremdung* and *Entäusserung* is still provided by Chapelle. See *Annexes,* pp. 1–25.

90. See Chapelle, *Hegel et la religion,* vol. 2, p. 106.

91. As a commentator such as Gerard Schmidt has pointed out in *The Concept of Being in Hegel and Heidegger,* Hegel's oeuvre situates itself within the Western ontotheological field, but it does not do so without modifying the very tradition within which it is inserted. Being, as Hegel suggests in his logical works,

is the poorest of all categories, and categorical richness (i.e., richness implying depth of reality) is only reached on the level of the Concept or Idea. But even the Idea does not imply the *ontos on.* Unlike Platonism and Neoplatonism, the 'really real' is not archeologically but teleologically given; and, in the movement towards realization, the world of appearance is held as a value and not, as in Platonism and Neoplatonism, as a disvalue.

92. Aristotle uses *energeia* in two different ways in the *Metaphysics* and *Physics.* On the one hand, *energeia* is used as a contrast term to *dynamis* to indicate actuality, realization, rather than potentiality and becoming. On the other (usually in the *Physics*), it is conceived in a more process way as actualization, the movement of transmutation from imperfect to perfect. For a grasp of these different senses see G. R. G. Mure, *Aristotle* (New York: Oxford University Press, 1964), pp. 10, 86. Hegel favors the second of these views, where *energeia* is linked to the realization of potential and is, accordingly, understood within the general horizon of change. Herbert Marcuse has seen this clearly in his *Hegel's Ontology and Theory of Historicity,* trans. Seyla Benhabib (Cambridge, Mass: MIT Press, 1987). That Hegel favors a process interpretation of *energeia* is clear from his discussion of Aristotle in *LHP 3,* pp. 141–142.

93. *Enc* #93–96. See Chapelle's discussion of this point in *Hegel et la religion,* vol. 2, pp. 82 ff.

94. See Walter Jaeschke, "Absolute Idee-absolute Subjektivität"; Dale M. Schlitt, *Hegel's Trinitarian Claims,* pp. 28–39.

95. This point is made by Petry in his note on *Wirklichkeit* in *Hegel's Philosophy of Nature* (London and New York: George Allen and Unwin Press, Humanities Press, 1970), p. 146.

96. Granting the most mystical reading of Aquinas's theology, Eckhart's apophaticism is more radical. Nevertheless, with regard to his basic conception of the divine as Being, simple, indivisible, Eckhart does not really depart from his Magister. For this point, see Kelley, *Meister Eckhart on Divine Knowledge* (New Haven and London: Yale University Press, 1977), pp. 178–184; Frank Tobin, *Meister Eckhart: Thought and Language* (Philadelphia: University of PA Press, 1986), pp. 31–56.

97. Augustine, of course, solidified for Christian theology what was already a theological commonplace by the end of the second century. Augustine's most lyrical espousal of divine simplicity is doubtless to be found in the *Confessions* (Bk. 2, 7), but it is expressed in a whole host of other places, e.g., in his hexameron, in his anti-Manichaean tracts. Indeed, even in the *Confessions* divine simplicity is asserted *against* a rival view of the divine as dual and composite, i.e., the view of the Manichaeans. It is of interest to note that in the *agon* of construals Augustine announces he has enlisted the support of the Platonists (Neoplatonism), which offered a spiritual and rarefied conception of the di-

vine in contradistinction to that of the Manichaeans. Via Augustine, but more especially via Pseudo-Dionysius, the Neoplatonic tradition continued to exercise influence on medieval thinkers such as Aquinas.

98. *Enneads* 6.7.4, also 5.2.10. John M. Rist provides a wonderful discussion of the problem of the One's knowledge of itself in *Plotinus: The Road to Reality* (Cambridge: Cambridge University Press, 1967), pp. 38–54.

99. See John D. Caputo's fine *The Mystical Element in Heidegger's Thought* (Athens, Ohio: Ohio University Press, 1978), pp. 103–109.

100. Both passages are found in a convenient English translation of John R. Earle in *Six Theosophic Points and Other Writings,* p. 167. Hegel, as is evident from his section on Boehme in *LHP,* had read this little text, in German "Von göttlichen Beschaulichkeit." See *Vorlesungen über die Geschichte der Philosophie Teil 4,* p. 83, p. 280 notes.

101. A predicate like 'goodness' would be in the same situation as predicates like 'compassion,' 'mercy,' 'justice,' etc. That is, even if it were granted that it had, in principle, more than nominalistic power, lacking a relational context in which its meaning is stablized and inured from qualification-disqualification from other predicates with truth-claims, it is incapable of disclosing the divine.

102. See *SL* E 818–823, where Hegel speaks of the Idea under the auspices of the Idea of the Good.

103. While Hegel in early theological texts such as his fragment on "Love" (1798) and "Fragment of a System" (1800) construed Love and Life under the auspices of unification, nevertheless, the precondition of unificating was disunity and diremption. Thus, Love and Life point to a coincidence of opposites rather than identity as such. Both Richard Kroner and Herbert Marcuse have grasped this point with some degree of clarity. See Kroner's fine introductory essay in *Early Theological Writings,* trans. T. M. Knox (Philadelphia: University of PA Press, 1971), esp. pp. 11–20; also Herbert Marcuse, *Hegel's Ontology and Theory of Historicity,* pp. 201–218. It is clear from Marcuse's analysis that he is convinced that Hegel is more or less consistent in his use of Life as an *ontological* concept up to *PS. PS* betrays a significant departure, however, when Spirit becomes the ontological category par excellence. Life, which functioned as an ontological concept, and indeed still continues to see limited duty in the Preface, will be assigned to the sphere of finitude, i.e., the finite organic sphere and the sphere of the organic sublated in human being qua spirit.

104. See Moltmann, *The Crucified God,* trans. R. A. Wilson and John Bowden (London: SCM Press, 1974), pp. 253–56; also *The Trinity and the Kingdom,* pp. 36 ff; Eberhard Jüngel, *God as the Mystery of the World: On the Foundation of the*

Theology of the Crucified One in the Dispute Between Theism and Atheism (Grand Rapids, Michigan: Erdmanns, 1983), pp. 63–100; also, Hans Küng, *The Incarnation of God: An Introduction to Hegel's Theological Thought as Prolegomena to a Future Christology,* trans. J. R. Stephenson (New York: Crossroads, 1987), pp. 162, 509–538.

105. A good example of such an interpretation is provided by Werner Marx in *The Philosophy of F. W. J. Schelling,* p. 81. Here I would like to take issue with Marx. Life is a prominent category in Schelling, but the important point is that it functions as an organic and not as a fully rendered ontological or ontotheological category as it does in Fichte's *Die Anweisung.*

106. It would be going too far to suggest that *The System of Transcendental Idealism* and the Identity-Philosophy that it spawned are totally nontheological. But it is clear that the Schellingian enterprise between the years 1800–1806 is the grounding philosophical one of the provision of ineluctable self-evident principles from which all else can be deduced with certainty. Compared with the *Freedom* essay (1809), which asserts a theosophic vision of reality, Schelling's early work is theologically thin. But as Schelling becomes more and more theological he becomes more and more a dualist. Ironically, the more theological Fichte becomes—from the *Wissenschaftslehre* to *Die Anweisung* (1806)—the more monist becomes the commitment. From a theological point of view, Hegel has much more in common with the Schelling of 1809 than the Fichte of 1806.

107. *Die Anweisung zum seligen Leben,* ed. Fritz Medicus (Hamburg: Felix Meiner Verlag, 1970). All page references refer to this edition. For a good discussion of the text, see Xavier Leon, *Fichte et son temps,* 2 vols. (Paris: Librarie Armand Colin, 1924), vol. 2 part 1, pp. 481–497.

108. The discussion in the first lecture is quite preliminary, and *Liebe,* for instance, gets short shrift, only to be discussed in full in lecture 10. Moreover, *Gedanke* only gets briefly touched on. Nonetheless, the First Lecture crucially establishes Fichte's program.

109. *Seligkeit* is predicated upon the unity of *Sein* and *Leben* and *Sein* and *Liebe* (which Fichte determines from the outset to exclude variation, division, and mutability). Thus, where division exists, no blessedness can exist. Certainly Fichte's view is anything but *agonic.* When Fichte writes that "Seligkeit ist . . . Ruhen und Beharren in dem Einem" (*Anw* p. 22), while it is not clear whether Fichte is speaking of the repose of the One, or the repose of the self in the One, it is clear that Fichte is tying his flag to the mast of the Platonic or Neoplatonic tradition in which the ultimate principle is perceived to be unchangeably at rest. While it is true that neither Fichte nor Plotinus intend Being or the One to be read in static terms (*Anw* p. 131), from a Hegelian point of view nothing other than a static reading is possible, given Hegel's foundational presupposition that dynamism is tied to differentiation.

110. See Michel Henry, *The Essence of Manifestation,* pp. 298–309.

111. The elaboration is monistic through and through. First, the description of Being supplied bears more than a family resemblance to Neoplatonic description of the One. Being is said to be simple (*einfach*), homogenous (*sich selbst gleich*), immutable (*unwandelbar*), unchangeable (*unveränderlich*), nonmanifold (*nicht mannifaltig*) (*Anw,* p. 15; also pp. 49–51, 61). Second, whenever *Sein* (identified with the divine) gets associated with potentially dualizing constructs such as *Gendanke* and *Bewusstsein,* Fichte rules that the duality involved is merely phenomenal (*Anw,* p. 54). Third, neither *Leben* or *Liebe* carry dualistic freight. Leben is the term that registers the dynamism of reality qua *Sein,* and *Liebe,* as "the affect of Being," (*Anw,* p. 153) does not even introduce the *appearance* of division as *Bewusstsein* does. For *Liebe* is understood as that perception Being has of itself beyond division, and thus beyond thought. *Liebe* is a kind of *Empfindung.*

112. That the divine qua Being, or Being qua divine, can be called structureless is legitimate if and only if we add the proviso *in the last instance.* In *Die Anweisung* Fichte talks a great deal of the distinction in Being that is introduced by *Bewusstsein* in particular. But even in this case, no *real* difference is engendered. The hegemony of divine simplicity asserts itself in a dramatic way in Fichte's trinitarian exegesis in Lecture 6. Concerning himself with the *logos endiathetos,* and not at all with the *logos prosphorikos,* Fichte offers a quite astonishing exegesis of John 5:19 where—to paraphrase—the Son is said to do nothing of his own accord but only executes the intention of the Father. Whereas traditional trinitarian thought would either read this passage as (1) having merely *economic* intention or (2) announcing on the level of divine immanence the priority of the Father qua originator—but not challenging either the ontological distinctiveness of the Son or the Son's equality—Fichte reads the passage, not merely noneconomically, but in such a way as to subvert the distinctiveness of the Son or *Logos.* Fichte reads 5:19 to mean that the Son is consumed (*aufgegangen*) in his independence in the life of the Father (*Anw* p. 97).

113. George Seidel in his *Activity and Ground* has commented on the crucial importance of the Gospel of John for German Idealism, pp. 21–23. Seidel is undoubtedly correct here, but it is important to make the following distinction. The Gospel of John could be read by Idealists as if the Prologue exhausted its significance, or the Prologue could be read as part of the whole in which could be exposed a thoroughgoing incarnational thrust. In *Die Anweisung* Fichte takes the former route. From the very beginning Hegel takes the latter route.

114. In this again Fichte departs decisively from Hegel. For Hegel the *logos endiathetos* is consistently seen against the backdrop of divine *ecstasis* in which the *Logos* portrays creativity in the constitution of the world (= *logos prosphorikos*). For the use of this originally Stoic conceptual pair to situate and analyze Hegel's trinitarian thought, see Chapelle, *Hegel et la religion,* vol. 2, p. 39.

115. The anxiety to avoid implicit as well as explicit forms of tritheism is on the surface in *LPR 3.* See Bruaire, *Logigue et religion,* p. 91.

116. For this passage see *Summa* la Q 30 art. 1. The contrast with Aquinas is provoked in part by Chapelle's brief contrast in *Hegel et la religion,* vol. 2, pp. 88–89. Hegel would be prepared to accept the reality of the relations without conceding the reality of persons which Aquinas, after Gregory of Nazianzen (Third Theological Oration) and Augustine (*De Trinitate,* Bks. 5, 6), presumes to be a matter of logical implication. What forces Hegel to put aside the classical connection is his modern model of person, i.e., self-consciousness. For Hegel, therefore, to assert three persons is to assert three independent, self-positing self-consciousnesses, and to assert this is to assert Tritheism.

117. Franz Grégoire, *Études Hégéliennes: Les points capitaux du système* (Louvain & Paris: Publications universitaires de Louvain & Editions Béatrice Nauwelaerts, 1958), pp. 42, 196–197 note 3; Bruaire, *Logique et religion,* pp. 87, 91; Chapelle, *Hegel et la religion,* vol. 2, p. 92.

118. Moltmann in *The Trinity and the Kingdom* (pp. 17–18) seems to be resuscitating earlier charges made by Hessen and Splett in a trinitarian context. Peter Koslowski in "Hegel—'der Philosoph der Trinität?' " while he does not fully substantiate the modalism thesis, ultimately does support the *Geistesmonismus* thesis shared by Moltmann and Pannenberg which would be the underpinning of a modalistic interpretation of the Trinity. See *Theologische Quartalschrift* 2 Heft 1982, pp. 105–131, esp. pp. 122–123.

119. I am here translating from the French text of Pannenberg's "Subjektivität" essay, titled "Subjectivité de Dieu et doctrine trinitaire" in *Hegel et la theologie contemporaine* (Paris: Neuchatel, 1977), pp. 171–187. The passage in question is found on p. 184.

120. See Bruaire, *Logique et religion,* p. 66.

121. A description offered of Jacob Boehme in *LHP 3,* E 188.

122. See *LPR 1* 1824 E 347, G 248, esp. note 166 in Hodgson. This topic will be treated in detail below in chap. 5, sect. 5.2.

123. I am availing here of Sparrows's 1656 translation. It should be pointed out that reference in this case is to the sphere of the divine that has immediately transcended the immanent sphere of the divine, i.e., "Immanent Trinity" plus *Sophia,* which is unable to break the hegemony of the ineffable *Unground.* For the latter point see Michel Henry, *The Essence of Manifestation,* pp. 108, 112.

124. If Harris is correct, then Hegel's contact with the mystics goes back as far as 1794. See *Towards the Sunlight,* pp. 230–231.

125. Coleridge is one Romantic, heavily influenced by German Idealism, who does see the difference between the earlier orthodox view of *Aurora* and the

later nonorthodox view registered in such important texts as *Mysterium Magnum* and *De Electione Gratiae*. For this point, see Thomas McFarland, *Coleridge the Pantheist* (Oxford: Clarendon Press, 1969), Appendix pp. 320–333, where Coleridge's relation to Boehme is discussed and, important but not easily available, Coleridgeian reflections on Boehme are brought to light.

126. In *LHP, Aurora* or *Morgenröthe* is by far the most often quoted text and is cited over a dozen times.

127. Boehme was suspected of heterodoxy in his own day. Throughout the century he was subject to criticism. Perhaps the most substantial criticism is provided by Johann Frick at the end of the seventeenth century.

128. See *Enc* #246 *zu; LPR 3* 1826 E 200, G 134; 1827 E 293, G 218.

129. If the generation of the *Logos* (i.e., *logos endiathetos*), as fulfilling both the requirement of differentiation and development, is construed under the auspices of the theological symbol of kenosis, by implication the movement from the second moment to the third, from the Son to the Spirit, may be similarly construed. But—and this point is of some import in gleaning Hegel's theological leanings—there is a necessary order in kenosis. Kenotic activity moves from Father to Son and from Son to Spirit. In preserving a definite narrative order in process, construed after the model of kenosis, Hegel effectively decides for the Western rather than Eastern tradition with respect to the procession of Spirit, thus agreeing with Anselm and Aquinas and disagreeing with theologians such as Photius and Gregory of Palamas. For Hegel's general preference for the Western as opposed to the Eastern point of view, see Chapelle, *Hegel et la religion,* vol. 2, p. 105.

130. As Hodgson points out in *LPR 3* 1821 MS E 84 note 71, August Neander's *Genetische Entwicklung der vornehmsten gnostischen Systeme* (Berlin, 1818) is the text from which Hegel gets much of his information on Gnosticism. It should be noted that Neander makes no great distinction between Gnosticism and Neoplatonism, and this may account in part for Hegel's own tendency to band them together.

131. We know that Hegel read Schelling's dissertation, "De Marcione Paularum epistolarum emendatore" (1795). See *Hegel: The Letters,* trans. Clark Butler and Christiane Seiler, comm. Clark Butler (Bloomington, Ind: Indiana University Press, 1984), pp. 37 ff. Butler takes Hegel's enthusiasm for Schelling's 'satirical' support of orthodoxy over heterodoxy as indicating early learnings towards heterodox, specifically gnostic thought, which he (Butler) is prepared to argue is systemic.

132. A classic example of his point of view is provided by Irenaeus. See his *Adversus Haeresis* 4.9.

133. As a symbolic system, Gnosticism will be heir to the kinds of criticisms Hegel feels constrained to level against all symbolic systems, i.e., the tendency

to picture the divine in more entitative than process-relational terms. Jacob Boehme will be submitted to similar criticism for not rising to the level of *Begriff,* the lone vantage point from which construal of the divine is secured against entitative deformation. It should be noted, however, that no more than is the case with Boehme does Hegel think that Gnosticism is inferior to the more mainline tradition, trinitarian tradition in particular. On Hegel's negative estimate of Gnosticism, see Bruaire, *Logique et religion,* pp. 84–85.

134. In definition 5 of the *Ethics* Spinoza writes: "By mode I understand the affection of a substance, or that which is in another through which it is also conceived."

135. See our discussion of *Bildungsroman* above in chap. 1, sect. 1.2. The analogy between divine becoming, even on the plane of the atemporal, and human becoming is sufficiently strong for some commentators and critics to suggest that Hegel has temporalized the divine. For a negative reaction with regard to such temporalization—temporalization of the Trinity in particular—see Pannenberg, "Subjectivité de Dieu et doctrine trinitaire," pp. 183–184. For a positive reaction to such temporalization—without invoking the theologoumenon of the Trinity—see Marcuse, *Hegel's Ontology and the Theory of Historicity.*

136. 'Personalist' as an ascription is here used descriptively rather than evaluatively. Looked at from an evaluative point of view, it may very well be that the Cappadocian rendition of the Trinity, which emphasizes the dynamism of hypostatic generation and procession rather than divine unity as in Augustine (the foundation of the Western trinitarian tradition), is more personalist in implication than the Augustinian rendition. Such a tack seems to be taken by many modern Western trinitarian thinkers, including Walter Kasper and Karl Rahner.

137. Hegel had made this identification as early as the *PS.*

138. The interpretation being proposed here announces an either/or that would not be agreed on by all Hegelian commentators and critics. Reviving a suggestion first made by Franz von Baader, some German commentators conceive of Hegel as articulating a two-person view of the Trinity in which Spirit or Singularity represents nothing more than the label for the union between Father and Son, or Universality and Particularity, thus having no ontological status as such. While there may be some validity in distinguishing between different nuances in Hegelian construal of Spirit or Individuality on the level of the immanent divine in *LPR 3* and other Hegelian texts, it is not clear that construing Spirit or Individuality as the unity of Father and Son or Universality and Particularity implies in and of itself a two-person view any more than it would in an orthodox trinitarian theology such as Augustine's *De Trinitate.* Having argued against one alternative to either/or proposed, I would briefly state the case against another. In *Logique et religion* (p. 91), Bruaire, explicating the originality of the Hegelian view of the intradivine Trinity vis-à-vis the

standard views of Western and Eastern Christianity, claims that the specificity of the Hegelian view is that it announces the reality of *three persons in one person.* This view cannot be sustained, since it is essentially incoherent. Accordingly, the possibilities seem to reduce to the either/or of one hypostasis or none, or, in its Western correlative, one person or none. Modern German scholarship on Hegel's trinitarian thought seems in a general way to operate within the parameters of this either/or. Representatives of the one hypostasis (or one person) interpretation include W. Pannenberg and L. Oeing-Hanhoff. Pannenberg, in his essay "Die Subjektivität Gottes" insists that the Hegelian model of the intradivine Trinity is rather that of a *Dreimomentigkeit* of subjectivity *as one person* than the Christian doctrine of three persons. A similar point is made by L. Oeing-Hanhoff in "Hegels Trinitätslehre: Zur Aufgabe ihren Kritik and Rezeption" in *Theologie und Philosophie* 52 (1977), pp. 387–407, esp. 402–404. Walter Jaeschke seems to agree with Pannenberg and Oeing-Hanhoff up to a point and suggests that, if *Begriff* is meant to translate Christian *Vorstellung,* it is also meant to translate the Christian *Vorstellung* of the Trinity (*Absolute Idee-Absolute Subjektivität,* p. 413). In consequence there is no reason to suppose that the standard view of the Trinity remains intact. Jaeschke is clearly right here, and one can see already in the inbetween discourse of *LPR 3* elements of correction. My only emendation of Jaeschke consists in the observation that in *LPR 3,* in addition to finding support for correction in *Begriff* that is already informing Hegel's trinitarian explication, Hegel can also call upon intratextual correctives within the tradition itself as that tradition elucidates itself on the level of *Vorstellung.* Jacob Boehme constitutes the most important figure of intratextual correction. Thus far we have treated only one side of the either/or, and in the view adopted here the least radical of the two possibilities. The second of the two views is also suggested by Jaeschke in the very same essay, when he contrasts the measure of subjectivity realized on the level of the immanent divine with that realizable in the articulation of the divine as a whole. Hegel, on Jaeschke's view, seems to suggest that Subjectivity or Personhood is only fully realizable consequent to divine manifestation in and through the finite. A similar view seems to be proposed by Herbert Huber in *Idealismus und Trinität,* p. 98. My own mediation between the either/or is to suggest that, while in the *strict sense* no person or self-conscious subjectivity as such is realized or realizable outside the context of engagement in the finite, the *formal possibility* is realized on the level of the "Immanent Trinity" in the third moment of atemporal dynamic. Spirit is, on this level, person *virtualiter,* or person in the sense of narrative *prolepsis.*

139. See Chapelle, *Hegel et la religion,* vol. 2, pp. 86, 88 ff; also Bruaire *Logique et religion,* pp. 65, 91.

140. See Chapelle, *Hegel et la religion,* vol. 2, p. 92 note 228.

141. Static quality is definitely a feature of Sabellianism as the classic historical form of modalism. It would, however, be difficult for static quality not to

be present given the Hellenistic environment within which Christianity is attempting to elucidate its central insights into the divine. Yet the static quality of relation is not specific to Sabellianism but is shared by Sabellianism and anti-Sabellianism alike. Moreover, there are good grounds for believing that what emergent orthodoxy diagnosed as the depth-structure deficit of Sabellianism was its subordination of Son and Spirit. To be construed as modes, it was felt, eviscerated the reality of Son and Spirit.

Chapter 3 The Second Narrative Epoch: Creation and The Epoch of the Son

1. *LPR 3* 1824 E 186–187, G 120.

2. Against Benedetto Croce's thesis that contradiction and dialectic belong properly to the logical sphere, it must be asserted that Hegel presumes contradiction and dialectic to be effective on the level of the real. That the logic provides the master code of dialectic and contradiction is certainly true, but without such exemplification, or the *tendenz* towards exemplification, in nature and finite spirit Hegel has little reason to modify received formal logic. Even on the level of logic Hegel's treatment of contradiction and dialectic is informed by presuppositions about the nature of reality, particularly becoming. See Croce's *What is Living and Dead of the Philosophy of Hegel,* trans. O. Ainslie (New York: Russell & Russell, 1915). A related but somewhat different view is advanced by M. J. Petry who suggests that contradiction and dialectic belong to the discursive order. Thus, Hegel's philosophy of nature says nothing about nature as such but explains the movement through the differentiation of our conceptuality through which we approach and explain nature. See Petry's Introduction to Hegel's *Philosophy of Nature,* vol. 1. (London and New York: George Allen & Unwin, Humanities Press, 1970), pp. 11–177.

3. Chapelle, *Hegel et la religion,* vol. 2, pp. 159 ff.

4. See also *LPR 3* 1821 MS E 89, G 27; 1824, E 230–231, G 161; 1827 E 292–293, G 217–218.

5. See *Hegel et la religion,* vol. 2, p. 39, for Chapelle's recall of the Patristic *logos endiathetos-logos prosphorikos* distinction.

6. Whether the removal of heterodox appearance is unintentional or strategic is hard to determine.

7. Dealing with the mythic narratives of the origin and end of evil, Ricoeur contrasts the theogonic type account to the Adamic or scriptural account that has been more or less normative in the Judeo-Christian tradition. This account is found in Ricoeur's magisterial *The Symbolism of Evil,* trans. Emerson Buchanan (Boston: Beacon Press, 1969). The contrast is, in some respects, raised to the theological level is his essay, "Original Sin: A Study in Meaning,"

in *The Conflict of Interpretations,* ed. D. Ihde (Evanston: Northwestern University Press, 1974), pp. 269–286, where Ricoeur theologically translates the Adamic view as the anthropological view. To maintain greater continuity between the level of *mythos* and *logos,* I think that the view of the origin of evil regulated by the Adamic *mythos* is best labelled the "anthropogonic" view. The contrast (structural) is thus that between theogonic and anthropogonic accounts.

8. *Religion Within the Limits of Reason Alone* was, perhaps, the first text by Kant to exercise influence on Hegel. Certainly its presence is strongly felt throughout the mid-1790s. For a convenient translation of Kant's text, see *Religion Within the Limits of Reason Alone,* trans. Theodore M. Green and Hoyt H. Hudson (New York: Harper & Row, 1960).

9. Hegel shows an interest in heterodox forms of thought from very early on, as is evidenced by his enthusiastic reply to Schelling's 1795 dissertation on Marcion. See *Letters,* trans. Clark Butler and Christiana Seiler (Bloomington: Indiana University Press, 1984), p. 39.

10. Chapelle, *Hegel et la religion,* vol. 2, pp. 113–231; Fackenheim, *The Religious Dimension of Hegel's Thought,* pp. 121–133; Iljin, *Die Philosophie Hegels als kontemplative Gotteslehre,* pp. 181–202; Walter Kern, " 'Schöpfung' bei Hegel," in *Theologische Quartalschrift* 162 (1982) pp. 131–146; Peter Koslowski, "Hegel-'der Philosoph der Trinität?':, pp. 105–130; Lauer, *Hegel's Concept of God* (Albany, N.Y.: SUNY Press, 1982), pp. 311–312; Erik Schmidt, *Hegels Lehre von Gott,* pp. 178–200.

11. *PS* #774 (Miller p. 467). I substitute "representation" for the somewhat misleading "picture thinking" to translate *Vorstellung.*

12. Chapelle, *Hegel et la religion* vol. 2, pp. 153, 166. See *Enc* #246 *zu* (Miller, p. 13), *GL9*:41): "Gott hat zweierlie Offenbarung as Natür und als Geist."

13. See Chapelle's discussion of *Entfremdung* and *Entäusserung* in *Annexes,* pp. 101–125.

14. See Chapelle, *Hegel et la religion,* vol. 2, pp. 183–194; esp. pp. 187–194.

15. Ibid, p. 115.

16. *SL* E 537–538.

17. *SL* E 537, *GL4*:675; *LHP 3* E 252 are places where Spinoza's view of creation is classed as oriental. Elsewhere, especially in the Lesser Logic, Spinoza's view is associated with the creation view of Judaism (*Enc* #151 *zu*).

18. The accidental status of the created order is, in Hegel's view, a corollary of classical Theism's insistence on contingency. And, for Hegel, accidents are without meaning. Aquinas's view that the created order bears a real relation

to the divine but that the divine does not bear a real relation to the created order is but one of the more provocative examples of the theistic consensus.

19. Explicit support of the doctrine of *creatio ex nihilo* can be found in *Enc* #88 (E 131).

20. See Irenaeus's *Against Heresies,* 2. 10 ff. Augustine in his anti-Manichaean writings is the most eloquent but perhaps also most tendentious exponent of the *creatio ex nihilo* view. For Augustine, as with Irenaeus in his anti-Gnostic stance, the *creatio ex nihilo* view is the direct contrary of the *creatio ex Deo* view. Interestingly, Irenaeus associates the latter view with the theogonies of Greek mythology. Augustine also thinks the *creatio ex Deo* view to be mythological. More importantly, he recommends that Christians avoid "from" or "ex" language in connection with God when speaking of creation, for this mischievous preposition brings to the surface the spectre of an eternal substance not identical with God but God's contrary.

21. The thesis is perhaps controversial. Fortunately, I can enlist two able Hegelian scholars as supporters of this view. See Henri Declève, "Schöpfung, Trinität und Modernität bei Hegel," in *Zeitschrift für katholische Theologie,* 107 (1985), pp. 187–198; also Anselm K. Min, "The Trinity and the Incarnation: Hegel and Classical Approaches" in *The Journal of Religion* (1986, April) 66 No. 2, pp. 177–193, esp. p. 175 note 2. Examples abound in the Christian ontotheological tradition, e.g., Eriugena, *De divisione naturae,* 111, 5. Boehme, who sees all of reality devolving from the *Unground* (which, on more than one occasion, is labelled as "Nichts"), is clearly also a representative.

22. For Spinoza's critique of *creatio ex nihilo,* see his letter to De Vries in *The Correspondence of Spinoza,* trans. ed. A. Wolf (New York: Russell & Russell, Inc., 1966) Letter 10, p. 109. The general attitude of Spinoza in his letter to De Vries clearly parallels Parmenides, who asserts that *ouk esti* is *panateuthea* (altogether unconceivable).

23. If *nothing* is understood in this way, no becoming, no determinate being (*Dasein*), no manifestation (*Offenbarung*) or appearance (*Erscheinung*) is possible at all.

24. *Dasein* comes from *Werden* which represents the synthesis of *Sein* and *Nichts.* And if Gadamer is correct, this synthesis of *Sein* and *Nichts* is nondialectical in the way other syntheses in Hegelian logic are not. See Hans-George Gadamer, *Hegel's Dialectic* (New Haven: Yale University Press, 1976), p. 87.

25. See Nicholas Berdyaev, *The Beginning and the End,* trans. K. M. French (London: Geoffrey Bles, 1952), p. 106; also *Spirit and Reality,* trans. George Reavey (London: Geoffrey Bles, 1939), p. 145; and Paul Tillich, *Systematic Theology,* Vol. 1. (Chicago: University of Chicago Press, 1951), p. 187. The source of the distinction in both cases is very likely the Schelling of the *Freedom* essay.

26. Augustine does not distinguish between different senses of 'nothing.' For him nothing only has an *oukontic* sense.

27. These are three of the major flaws of the classical view. They are touched on by R. K. Williamson in *Introduction to Hegel's Philosophy of Religion* (Albany, N.Y.: SUNY Press, 1984), pp. 234–255.

28. See also *LPR 1* 1827 E 400–401, G 295–296.

29. The edition of Luther's works availed of here is the modern standard, i.e., the edition edited by Jaroslav Pelikan put out by Concordia Press. It should be pointed out that the first eight volumes of this edition are devoted to a commentary on Genesis. Luther's dramatic, even anthropomorphically dramatic, view of God predisposed him towards going in a punctiliar direction.

30. I have, particularly, in mind Sebastian Frank (1499–1543) and Caspar Schwenckfeld (1490–1561). Solid secondary sources include Alexandre Koyré, *Mystiques, spirituels, alchimistes du XVI siècle allemand* (Paris: Vrin, 1971); Steven Ozment, *Mysticism and Dissent* (New Haven and London: Yale University Press, 1973). Lutheran orthodoxy's criticism of the pneumatic thrust of Boehme's thought was a constant throughout the seventeenth century. Two polemical texts by proponents of Lutheran orthodoxy against Boehme are especially interesting. For instance, the comprehensive refuation of Boehme carried out in Johann Frick's *Gruendliche Undersuchung Jacob Behmens vornehmster Irrthuemer: So auss dessen eigenen Schriften gezeiget und auss H. Schrifft widerlegt werden* (1697) includes a defense of the orthodox emphasis on the literal sense against Boehme's pneumatic exegesis. This aspect of Boehmian theology is also explicitly attacked somewhat earlier by Theodore Thummio in a text called *Impietas Wigeliana* (1622, 1650).

31. See also *LPR 1* 1827, E 254, G 162. For Hegel's discussion of mystery see *LPR 3* 1827 E 280–283, G 205–209.

32. I will have something substantive to say on this matter in chapter 7.

33. That Boehme reneged on the Lutheran orthodox view of *creation from nothing* that had received a more or less definitive expression in theologians such as John Gerhard is an explicit charge in anti-Boehmian polemic. See *Impietas Wigeliana,* pp. 66 ff; also *Gruendliche Undersuchung,* pp. 587 ff.

34. See *Enc* #246 *zu,* E 14 (Miller).

35. Ibid. E 19 (Miller), *GL10*:57–58. If Hegel suggests that evil only comes to be effective reality outside the level of the immanent divine in the *Enc* #246–248, in *LPR 3* 1824 E 194, G 127, he suggests that the lack of personhood on the level of the immanent divine is the reason.

36. This is the expert opinion of the great Boehme scholar Hans Grunsky. See his *Jakob Böhme* (Stuttgart: Fr. Fromanns Verlag, 1956), pp. 238–241.

37. See Petry, *Philosophy of Nature, Vol. 1,* Intro. p. 86. Alan White in *Absolute Knowledge* (pp. 79–90) disputes a similar charge that Hegel is dependent upon Franz von Baader, who was himself very much influenced by Boehme. White is certainly able to show that Hegel's position is by no means as voluntaristic as von Baader's or, for that matter, Schelling's. That Hegel's language is not overtly voluntaristic is, however, in my view, not sufficient to exonerate him from the charge of structural similarity.

38. "Ephebe" is the word used by the Yale literary critic, Harold Bloom, to name the belated and fledging writer who must deal with the influence of a precursor who sometimes looms as someone who has said all the writer wishes to say. For evidence of Boehmian allegiance in Hegel, see *LPR 3* 1821 MS E 99, G 36; 1824 E 200, G 133: 1827 E 293, G 217–218.

39. "Hegel—'der Philosoph der Trinität?'" pp. 108–110.

40. *Night Thoughts,* pp. 406–407.

41. *Night Thoughts,* pp. 186–188, esp. p. 187.

42. I here take issue with Petry and White and find myself in agreement with Erik Schmidt. See his *Hegels Lehre von Gott,* pp. 204–208.

43. The difference between the Hegelian and the latter two views is, roughly speaking, the difference between the Hegelian view and the Spinozist and Neoplatonic views, respectively. The relevant differences between these views will be discussed in some detail in section 3.3.

44. Alexandre Kojève, *Introduction,* Chap. 5. Lecture 6, p. 101: Martin Heidegger, *Being of Time,* trans. John Macquarrie & Edward Robinson (Oxford: Basil Blackwell, 1967), pp. 484–486.

45. *PS* #776 (Miller p. 468).

46. Fackenheim in *The Religious Dimension of Hegel's Thought* does not situate fall in a teleological context. He sees fall as both the assertion of defiance and dependence of finite spirit upon the divine. See pp. 131–132.

47. See also *LPR 3* 1824 E 200, G 133; *PS* #774, 776–777.

48. *Night Thoughts,* p. 406.

49. See Erik Schmidt, *Hegels Lehre von Gott,* pp. 186–187, 190–193. Findlay in his commentary accompanying Miller's text seems struck by the strangeness of Hegel's view of evil. See Miller, p. 587.

50. The *felix culpa* theme is very much to the fore in *The City of God.* It is important to understand that in the fall God, as such, gains nothing, since God is complete and self-sufficient. But the fall does provide an opportunity in which the who of God is displayed more vibrantly. By contrast, theogenetic *fe-*

lix culpa concerns the divine self as it brings itself to completion through dramatic detour.

51. See Hans Grunsky, *Jakob Böhme,* p. 241.

52. The most explicit supports of what I call Schleiermacher's perspectival view are found in #75 and 76 of *The Christian Faith.* Evil (whether social or natural), Schleiermacher insists in #75, is derivative with respect to sin. In a particularly illuminating passage in #76, Schleiermacher points to sin as the name of that dissonance whereby Nature itself gets construed as evil (p. 319).

53. A good example of Hegel's dissatisfaction with the Enlightenment view can be found in *Hegel's Philosophy of Right,* trans. T. M. Knox (London, Oxford, New York: Oxford University Press, 1967) #18, p. 28. Hegel's position in this text is typical of his attitude in his years in Berlin. Compared with the views of his youth, however, they represent a shift. In "The Positivity of the Christian Religion," Hegel had proposed a much more positive estimate of the Enlightenment understanding of evil. See *Early Theological Writings,* p. 160.

54. See *The Concept of Anxiety,* ed. trans. Reidar Thomte with Albert B. Anderson (Princeton, New Jersey: Princeton University Press, 1980), esp. Intro. pp. 9–24.

55. See Joachim Ringleben's important text, *Hegel's Theorie der Sünde: Die subjektivitätslogische Konstruktion eines theologischen Begriffs* (Berlin, New York: Walter De Gruyter, 1977), esp. pp. 93–94. Ringleben, however, draws the contrast much too crudely when he asserts that, in contradistinction to Kant, Hegel never forgets the goodness of human being. Kant and Hegel do not differ in this respect, and Kant has to be interpreted as saying that goodness (the goodness of existence as such) is more primordial than evil which makes such an irrational entry into human existence and interrelation.

56. Laurence Dickey makes the point that *Religion* was the most influential Kant text in the earliest part of Hegel's career. See his *Hegel: Religion, Economics, and the Politics of Spirit 1770–1807* (Cambridge: Cambridge University Press. 1987), p. 159. It is, perhaps, only after 1800 that Hegel shows a real knowledge of Kant's three Critiques.

57. Goethe, who up to the point of *Religion* had been an admirer of Kant, the representative of the spirit of freedom and autonomy, could not view the text as anything other than a regression to a Christian view he thought the enlightened in the modern age had surpassed.

58. For the Hegelian objection to the doctrine of hereditary transmission of sin, see *LPR 1* 1821 MS E 252, G 161.

59. Dickey maintains that the teleological drift of Hegel's religiously inclined texts had much in common with reformist Pietism in general.

60. See *LPR 3* 1821 MS E 93–94, G 30–31; E 102, G 38.

61. In his ethical works Kant had used will (*Wille*) in a quasi-facultative way to name sensuous inclination in a human being as opposed to freely self-legislating reason. In *Religion,* however, will no longer has a facultative connotation but is identified with the transendental ground of self whereby one adopts maxims that guide conduct.

62. Nietzsche structures *Thus Spake Zarathustra* on the pattern of the diseased knower who must seek and find a cure. The imperative to the would-be physician is: physician heal thyself.

63. In Religion, Bk. I. IV. pp. 34–39, Kant offers an interpretation of the Genesis account of fall. In his interpretation, it is clear that he is arguing that sin is as aboriginal in us as it was in Adam. Our situation and his do not differ in essential respects. Perceived difference is a function of biblical narrative, which introduces a rationally unjustified, and ultimately unjustifiable, gap between and Adam and us. Sin is, indifferently, a propensity of all humanity.

64. Kant and Hegel discuss that origin and nature of evil only in the context of a victory over evil, a victory which inaugurates the kingdom of God. This is particularly clear in the case of Kant. Book 3 of *Religion* is titled: "The Victory of the Good over the Evil Principle and the Founding of a Kingdom of God on Earth."

65. Kant, *Religion,* pp. 23, 40.

66. See also *LPR 3* 1824 E 207, G 139; 1827 E 302, G 226.

67. See also *LPR 3* 1824 E 202–203, G 134–135.

68. See Dickey, *Hegel,* pp. 13 ff.

69. This point is made with some eloquence by John Hick in *Evil and the God of Love* (New York: Macmillan, 1966).

70. This reading is not uncontroversial, but see *The Making of Man* in *Nicene and Post Nicene Fathers, Vol. V: Gregory of Nyssa* (Grand Rapids, Michigan: W. B. Eerdmans Publishing Co., 1893), pp. 387–427, esp. pp. 411–414.

71. W. Trillhass recognizes the presence of the *felix culpa* motif in Hegel, as well as some differences between the Hegelian and the standard view. I am not sure, however, that he would be in full agreement with my way of framing the contrast. See W. Trillhass, "Felix Culpa: Zur Deutung der Geschichte vom Sündenfall bei Hegel," in *Probleme biblischen Theologie: G. V. Rad zum 70. Geburtstag* (Munich, 1971), pp. 589–602; see also R. Schanne, *Sündenfall und Erbsünde in der spekulativen Theologie. Die Weiterbildung der protestantischen Erbsündenlehre unter dem Einfluss der idealistischen Lehre vom Bösen* (Frankfurt am Main, 1976), pp. 113–139.

72. Luther, of course, is profoundly influenced by the letters of St. Paul. But while scripture is the determining influence, it is not the only one. Scholars have pointed to the medieval mystical tradition, particularly the nonspeculative variety, as a source of influence. The so-called *German Theology,* which Luther edited twice, emphasized fairly heavily the impediment of *Eigenwille,* which is a more or less decent translation of Augustine's definition of sin as *amor sui.* For the influence of the medieval mystical tradition in general, the *German Theology* in particular, see Steven Ozment, *Homo Spiritualis* (New Haven: Yale University Press, 1967), pp. 88 ff, *Mysticism and Dissent* (New Haven: Yale University Press, 1973), esp. pp. 17–25.

73. Gregory of Nyssa offers a good example of this. See *The Making of Man,* p. 410.

74. For an analysis of *metharmottein* as used by Irenaeusm (*Adversus Haereses,* 1:11.1), see Anne Maguire's Yale dissertation, "Valentinus and the Gnostiké Haeresis" (Yale, 1983), pp. 16–18. The latin equivalents for this word are *transfero* and *transfiguro.* There is some agreement among scholars of Gnosticism that, however, unreliable Irenaeus may be on the other points, his intuition with respect to Valentinian hermeneutics is accurate. Fragments that scholars attribute to Valentinus have persuaded many that Irenaeus was not simply being tendentious. See Harold Bloom, "Lying Against Time," in *The Rediscovery of Gnosticism: Vol. 1,* ed. Bentley Layton (Leiden: Brill, 1980), pp. 57 ff.

75. The assertion of the providential character of the fall means that a text like the *Tripartite Tractate* accepts the tragic character of the move from the divine to the extradivine at the literal level, while suggesting its revision at the nonliteral level. Tragedy is not so much erased as rewritten into something like a theogonic divine comedy.

76. It should be admitted that the *Tripartite Tractate* does not offer a proophitic account of Genesis. Irenaeus's insistence that such accounts are common is borne out in the texts that are in the Nag Hammadi Library where the serpent is a wisdom figure. See *The Hypostasis of the Archons* (89–90) and *The Origin of the World* (118–120).

77. Hegel's commitment to time and the future is clearly not one of the more Gnostic features of his thought.

78. In any dispute between the claims of innocence and experience, Hegel takes the side of experience. This may be partly an anti-Romantic reaction. Certainly, he does not encourage such innocence, thinking it irresponsible. Note the play on words in *Enc #246 zu* (Miller p. 9) of *Schuld* (guilt) and *Urschuld* (innocence).

79. In one sense, this could be regarded as the theme of all of Hegel's writing. It is certainly the theme of the *PS.*

80. See also *PS* #775, pp. 467–468 (Miller).

81. A Kant scholar particularly sensitive to the intermediary and symbolic status of Kant's discourse in *Religion* is Michel Despland. See his *Kant on History* (Montreal and London: Queens University Press, 1973).

82. The recourse to interpretation of scripture as compact symbolic discourse is a portent that the mysteries of the divine are not *directly* accessible to finite intellects.

83. See *The Symbolism of Evil,* pp. 327–328.

84. See Ricoeur's essay, "The Hermeneutic of Symbols and Philosophical Reflection" in *The Conflict of Interpretations,* pp. 287–314; esp. pp. 301–303, 308.

85. See in particular G. R. G. Mure, *A Study of Hegel's Logic* (Oxford: Clarendon Press, 1948); *An Introduction to Hegel* (London & New York: Oxford University Press: 1959).

86. *Night Thoughts,* p. 407.

87. *FK* E 180.

88. Compare the highly abstract conceptual language of *Enc* #246–248 with the mythopoetic and theological language of the *Zusatzen.*

89. This notion first emerges in full clarity in the Cappadocians, Gregory of Nazianzen and Gregory of Nyssa, though its lineaments may be traceable as far back as Origen. Thereafter, it becomes part of the staple of the Greek East, finding expression in such writers as Pseudo-Dionysius and Maximus the Confessor.

90. There is a tension in Boehmian texts between the suggestion that the material-temporal world is in itself evil because it is a coagulation of the fallen Luciferian form of the divine and the more nearly orthodox narrative view that the material world is good and only becomes evil (excites the *turba*) in the fall of Adam. The first view is suggested in *Aurora,* a text Hegel certainly read, the second in mature texts like *Mysterium Magnum.*

91. That Hegel avails of Aristotelian-like terminology in his depiction of both the anthropological narrative and the narrative of the divine cannot be denied. Where the Aristotelian constructs of potentiality and actuality are not explicitly invoked, they subsist as a latent presence in the Hegelian categorical pairs of in-itself/in-and-for-itself, immediate/mediated. One ought to be wary, however, of extrapolating from the presence of Aristotelian categories to the position that the Hegelian narrative of the emergence of evil and its overcoming represents a mere blending of Christian narratives on different levels (and possibly of different types) with Aristotelian teleological metaphysics. There are a number of systemic obstacles to such a hypothesis: (1) for

Aristotle, it should be remembered, the applicability of the potentiality-actuality categorial pair is restricted to the sublunar world. Thus, while the model can plausibly cover the self-development of human being, it fails of application to a divine interpreted as being totally beyond change and becoming; and (2) even if *per impossible* the Aristotelian teleological model were applicable to the divine, and Aristotle and Hegel were perfectly matched in this way, the Hegelian teleological model is more dramatic and conflictual than anything found in Aristotle's *Physics* or *Metaphysics.*

92. Robert Preus offers a good account of Lutheran orthodoxy's championing of the *creatio ex nihilo* view in his well-known *Theology of Post-Reformation Lutheranism.*

93. Concerning the relation of the anagogic and tropological sense, see Henri de Lubac, *Exégèse mediévale: Les quatre sens de l'écriture,* 2 parts, 4 vols. (Paris: Aubier, 1959–1964). See esp. part 1, vol. 2, "L'unité du quadruple sens," pp. 643–656.

94. I am fully aware that this triadic scheme works if, and only if, each variety includes specimens beside the one or ones indicated by the label.

95. The doyen of this kind of interpretation on the contemporary philosophical scene is, of course, Werner Beierwaltes. See his *Denken des Eines: Studien zur neuplatonischen Philosophie und ihrer Wirkungsgeschichte* (Frankfurt am Main: Klostermann, 1985).

96. For our purposes here, Eckhart's view of creation corresponds to Spinoza's elaboration in the *Ethics,* as does the Fichte of *Die Anweisung.* For Eckhart the created order 'is' only to the extent that at its center lies the divine presence. In Fichte's 1806 text, phenomenal existence is revealed to be in essence a reflection of divine existence. The intuition that there exists a large measure of congruence between the thought of Eckhart and the later Fichte has been highlighted by both Ernst Benz in *Les sources* and Michel Henry in *The Essence of Manifestation,* trans. Girard Etzkorn (The Hague: Martinus Nijhoff, 1973), pp. 300–335.

97. An excellent account of Staudenmaier's response to Hegel is provided by Franz Albert. See *Glauben und Denken: Hegelskritik als Anfange an das Selbstverständnis heutigen Theologie,* (Regensburg: Verlag Friedrich Pustet, 1983).

98. See *SL* E 537–8, *LHP 3* E 252.

99. *LHP 3* E 252–288.

100. A good example is Léon Brunschvicg's *Spinoza et ses contemporaines* (Paris, 1922).

101. See Pierre Machéry, *Hegel ou Spinoza* (Paris: François Maspero, 1979); R. K. Williamson, *Introduction to Hegel's Philosophy of Religion,* pp. 234–255.

102. Walter Bröcker, *Ausseinandersetzungen mit Hegel* (Frankfurt: Klostermann, 1965), pp. 35–36.

103. For example, Mark Taylor, *Journeys to Selfhood,* p. 153; R. N. Findlay, *Hegel: A Re-examination,* chap. 3, sect. 1; Karl Löwith, *From Hegel to Nietzsche,* p. 40; Ernst Bloch, *Subjekt-Objekt: Erläuterung zu Hegel* (Frankfurt am Main: Suhrkamp Verlag, 1962), pp. 479–480. Before any of these authors, Emil Bréhier advanced the thesis of relation.

104. *Enc* #247 *zu,* E 13 (Miller), *GL9*:48–49.

105. *Enc* #247 *zu,* E14 (Miller), *GL9*:50. Schelling makes remarks resembling this in *Ideen zu einer Philosophie der Natur* (1797). I am indebted to Petry, *Philosophy of Nature,* for my knowledge of Hegel's Schellingian source (vol. 1., p. 300).

106. *Enc* #247 *zu,* E 14 (Miller), *GL9*:49. "Ist Gott das Allgenügende, Unbedürftige."

107. This association is further strengthened by Hegel speaking of God in the same passage as "*(die) unendliche Güte.*"

108. A position advanced by A. Chapelle and endorsed by Emilio Brito. See Chapelle, *Hegel et la religion,* vol. 2, pp. 95–109; Brito, *Hegel et la tâche actuelle de la christologie* (Paris: Lethielleux, 1979), p. 10, and *La christologie de Hegel: Verbum Crucis* (Paris: Beauchesne, 1983), p. 552.

109. One could think of the positing of *eros* at the heart of the divine as a discrimen also of Schelling's work from the *Freedom* essay on. Schelling explicitly evokes the *penia* of the *Symposium.*

110. The underlying assumption of Neoplatonism in both its non-Christian and Christian guises is, of course, the *similarity* between posterior forms of reality and the source of all reality, the 'really real' (*ontos on*). Difference is a factor, but only in the context of the undergirding similarity. Difference must be asserted, since according to Neoplatonic logic, posterior forms of reality necessarily must be more limited than the source. For some purposes, a Neoplatonist may wish to concentrate upon this difference, and, in doing so, the limited posterior and unlimited anterior reality are contrast-realities. But the underlying ontological likeness, as well as ontological continuity, are never denied.

111. In *Hegel et al religion* (Paris: Presses universitairies de France, 1982), pp. 125–150, esp. pp. 143–144.

112. In the *Enneads* (1, 8; 2, 9), evil does eventually get associated with matter, which gets fatefully interpreted as privation of reality (identified with the Platonic good). Thus, one could say that evil gets manifested as the limit case. Yet, in another sense, it could be said that evil in matter is nothing more nor less than the exhaustion of all manifestation whatsoever.

113. This is evident in any number of Neoplatonic texts. In the *Enneads*, Plotinus describes procession (*proodos*) as moving from the One, through *Nous,* Psyche, Nature, to matter at the limit. Proclus in *The Elements of Theology* speaks of the movement from the One through the differentiated divine realm (the divine *Henad*), intelligences, and souls. As in Plotinus, matter is the limit of procession. In Eriugena's Christian Neoplatonic depiction, procession moves from the superessential God, and/or superessential Trinity, through the primordial causes or divine archetypes to the created order.

114. It is part of the raison d'être of the move from *Vorstellung* to *Begriff* to remove the suggestion of accident that attends narrative depiction of a symbolic type.

115. *LHP 2* E 393.

116. *SL* E 431–443, *GL4*:535–551, esp. E 436–438, *GL4*:542–543.

117. The present text will not attempt to demonstrate the structural relation between Boehmian and Valentinian narrative that would tend to strengthen the taxonomic arguments prosecuted here. I hope to pursue this in another text.

118. Ricoeur suggests the phenomenon of the logicization of myth not only in *The Symbolism of Evil* but also in his essay, "The Hermeneutic of Symbols and Philosophical Reflection."

119. For Baur's treatment of Boehme as proximate precursor, see *Die christliche Gnosis,* pp. 557–615. Baur discusses Valentinian Gnosticism on pp. 126–170.

120. For the period, Baur's knowledge could be regarded as exceptional. He seems to have more knowledge of the heresiological sources than Neander. Still, the Nag Hammadi find has revolutionized the study of Gnosticism, such that twentieth-century scholars have the ability to adjudicate whether the heresiological reports are in every sense reliable. Baur also, somewhat too easily, buys into a global development scheme in which not only is Hegel the final offspring of early gnosis but even Schleiermacher is a belated representative.

121. Need in Valentinian texts is a characteristic of the non-pleromatic realm. Yet, it is interesting that the desire for knowledge that is the basis of the need manifested in nature occurs in the pleroma itself.

122. The independence of the nondivine has its origin in the attempt by the final element on the level of the divine to comprehend or reflect its origin. This explicit *de trop,* Hegel insinuates, is the real secret of Gnosticism. See *LHP 2,* E 396–399.

123. On the express level, there is a static contrast between the realm of the divine and the nondivine. This has the consequence that the nondivine cannot be in any sense construed as theophany, for this supposes some underlying identity. A dynamic reading, however, would suggest that the subject underlying the entire narrative, both outside as well as inside the divine, is the divine.

124. Consider what Hegel says about Gnosticism in an important passage quoted in chap. 2, i.e., *LPR 3* 1821 MS E 86, G 23–24, with what Hegel says in *SL E* 538–539 about the happening character of the Neoplatonic view of emanation.

125. In the *Tripartite Tractate* there is something like the attempt to speak of the material world coming from nothing (79), yet it is clear that this nothing is not a Parmenidean nothing but some kind of substrate.

126. Baur, *Die christliche Gnosis,* pp. 681–682; also 675–676.

127. See Hans Jonas,"Delimitation of the Gnostic Phenomenon—Typological and Historical," in *Origins of Gnosticism,* ed. U. Bianchi (Leiden: Brill, 1967), pp. 90–108.

128. Jonas, "Delimitation," 92 ff.

129. The *Tripartite Tractate* is not very different from other texts in the Nag Hammadi Library in that, on the express level, the nondivine is only characterized by reference to the divine. This strategy, needless to say, is calculated to show up the inherent shortcomings of the nondivine.

130. See the *Tripartite Tractate,* 75 ff.

131. Ibid. 77, 71.

132. Ibid. 79–81.

133. The accidental character of fall is unexpurgated in the more mythic Valentinian texts but corrected in the *Tripartite Tractate,* where providence governs fall.

134. For a good survey of the concept of pleroma, see Violet McDermot, "The Concept of 'Pleroma' in Gnosticism," in *Gnosis and Gnosticism,* ed. Martin Krause (Leiden: Brill, 1981), pp. 78–84.

135. In availing of the term *plerosis,* I have a double warrant: first, the need for a term that will tend to explicitly suggest dynamism; second, a term that contrasts with *kenosis.*

136. The dynamic, developmental dimension to Valentinian narrative breaks its would-be pure circularity. While, it is clear that, on the surface level, all Valentinian narratives are of a *reditus ad integrum* type, the *Tripartite Tractate*

suggests that at a deeper level Valentinian, like Hegelian, narrative suggests ontotheological increase.

137. The evocation of the language of Bataille and Derrida is deliberate here.

138. Criticisms of Boehmian *creatio ex Deo* are a constant in the seventeenth century, See *Impietas Wigeliana,* pp. 66 ff; also Frick, *Gruendliche Undersuchung,* pp. 587 ff.

139. A difference between Boehme and Hegel is that Boehme spends a considerable amount of his time complaining about the ontotheological lightness of the Godhead before the "Immanent Trinity" as well as the "Immanent Trinity" itself.

140. Boehme speaks of the immanent divine developing a desire (*Sucht*), even hunger, for substance or essence in the texts of his mature period.

Chapter 4 Epochal Overlap: Incarnation and the Passion Narrative

1. See Emilio Brito, *Hegel et la tâche actuelle de la christologie,* also, *La christologie de Hegel. Verbum Crucis;* Eberhard Jüngel, *God as the Mystery of the World,* pp. 63–100; Hans Küng, *The Incarnation of God;* J. Yerkes, *The Christology of Hegel.*

2. This, at least, is the implication in Küng and Yerkes, for instance.

3. Brito has argued that there are not only different Christologies in the texts of Hegel's Tübingen, Berne, and Frankfurt periods (*La christologie,* pp. 19–86), but that the Christologies of the *PS, LPR 3,* and the *Enc* are crucially different (*La christologie,* pp. 522 ff; *Hegel et la tâche,* pp. 19 ff).

4. Though Richard Solomon is one modern commentator who questions the assignation *theological* with regard to Hegel's Tübingen, Berne, and Frankfurt writings, he is hardly the most influential. This honor goes to Lukacs. Lukacs suggests that the characterization of Hegel's Berne period as theological amounts to nothing more than a "reactionary legend." Lukacs reads the "Positivity" essay, which belongs to Hegel's Berne period, as proof of Hegel's antitheological animus. He admits, however, that the situation is somewhat more complex with regard to the writings of the Frankfurt period and confesses that there does indeed exist a theological flavor in the "Fate" essay of 1799. Lukacs, nevertheless, is at pains to point out that Hegel's views do not correspond to Protestant dogmatic formulations in the way Haering and Lasson suggested. A good English translation of *Die junge Hegel* now exists, i.e., *The Young Hegel,* trans. Rodney Livingstone (London: Merlin Press, 1975).

5. For a translation of the "Positivity" essay, see *Early Theological Writings,* trans. T. M. Knox (Philadelphia: University of Pennsylvania Press, 1971), pp. 67–181.

6. For a translation of the "The Spirit of Christianity and its Fate," see *Early Theological Writings,* pp. 182–301. The essentially mystical characterization of the text is even agreed on by Lukacs, who argues, however, that the species of mysticism which the text exhibits is more inclusive and communitarian than that standard Christian variety (*The Young Hegel,* p. 91).

7. See *Early Theological Writings,* pp. 277–278.

8. Yerkes, *The Christology of Hegel,* pp. 185–187.

9. For a fairly standard expression of this, see Walter Kasper, *Jesus the Christ,* trans. V. Green (London & New York: Burns and Oates, Paulist Press, 1977), pp. 74–78.

10. Brito, *Hegel et la tâche,* pp. 47–49.

11. As is well-known, Hegel in the Stift had an important friendship with Hölderlin. Hölderlin was a particularly formative influence on Hegel regarding his love of ancient Greece. This philhellenism was not merely nostalgic but critical and contrasted the integrity of Greek with the disintegration of modern culture. For an excellent account of Hölderlin's and Hegel's relation to Greece, see Jacques Taminaux, *La nostalgie de la Grece à l'aube de l'idealisme allemand: Kant et les Grecs dans l'itinéraire de Schiller, de Hölderlin et de Hegel* (The Hague: Martinus Nijhoff, 1971), pp. 50–97. If Hegel gradually tempered his allegiance to the philhellenic ideal and came to see the superiority of Christianity and Christian culture over Greece, Hölderlin did not. If Hölderlin was prepared to apostrophize the divine as 'Father Aether', he also thought of the divine as chtonic and felt Dionysus and/or Demeter worthy of worship. When Hölderlin writes his great elegy "Brot und Wein" in Stuttgart in 1800, the bread and wine at least as much recall Dionysus as Christ, and they are, in fact, called the friendly gifts of Dionysus.

12. D. M. Schlitt, *Hegel's Trinitarian Claim,* pp. 145–146; also pp. 156–157, 176. Pannenberg makes this point in his *Offenbarung als Geschichte* (Göttingen: 1965).

13. D. M. Schlitt, *Hegel's Trinitarian Claim,* pp. 172–173.

14. See Michel Henry, *The Essence of Manifestation,* p. 428. See also pp. 333–334.

15. Brito, *Hegel et la tâche,* pp. 48–49.

16. For an excellent account of Luther's relation to traditional modes of christological discourse, see Marc Lienhard, *Luther: Witness to Jesus Christ,* pp. 376 ff.

17. Hodgson's main preoccupation is with *LPR.* See his *God in History: Shapes of Freedom:* (Nashville: Abingdom Press, 1989). Brito and Schlitt point to the trinitarian element in *PS.* See Brito, *La christologie de Hegel,* pp. 128–134; *Hegel et la tâche,* pp. 48 ff; D. M. Schlitt, *Hegel's Trinitarian Claim,* pp. 150–156.

18. Jean Wahl, *La malheur de la conscience dans la philosophie de Hegel,* 2nd ed. (Paris: Presses universitaires de France, 1951), pp. 69 ff. See also Roger Garaudy, *Dieu est mort: Étude sur Hegel* (Paris: Presses universitaires de France, 1962), pp. 86–112; Hans Küng, *The Incarnation of God,* pp. 162–181.

19. See Ulrich Asendorf, *Luther und Hegel,* pp. 348–352, 357; Brito, *La christologie de Hegel,* pp. 18, 538; *Hegel et la tâche,* pp. 8, 12, 44; Christian Link, *Hegels Wort "Gott selbst ist tot"* (Zürick: Theologischer Verlag, 1974), pp. 28–37.

20. Both Jüngel and Küng are of the opinion that Altizer's championing of the atheistic reading as the alone and exclusive option is incorrect. As against 'death of God theology', both insist that atheism is but a moment to be sublated. Hegel's view at the very least, Küng suggests, is postatheistic.

21. This is certainly the view of Altizer. Mark Taylor's a/theology might be construed as a deconstructionist development of Altizer's position.

22. Küng is in agreement with Jüngel regarding the subversion of the traditional view of the apathetic divine.

23. I am here using a term found in such Platonic texts as the *Symposium* where Plato is anxious to underscore the intermediate status of human existence. Much has been made of this term by Eric Voegelin.

24. See Küng, *The Incarnation of God,* pp. 212–220.

25. See Peter Hodgson, "Hegel's Christology: Shifting Nuances in the Berlin Lectures" in *JAAR* Vol. L111 No. 1 1985 (March), pp. 23–40. For example, comparing the 1824 Lectures with the 1821 Manuscript, Hodgson notes that the historicity of Christ is emphasized more in the former than in the latter (pp. 28–29).

26. The ambiguity between incarnation and creation is a structurally important one and has been noted by Peter Koslowski, for instance, as being present in *PS.* One wonders whether the conflation might not perhaps have got off to an early start. At one point in the "Fate" essay, when Hegel has identified the *Logos* as the inner word, he goes on to identify the exteriorized word first with creation (*ETW* E 257) and soon after with the incarnate one (*ETW* E 260).

27. In *Hegel et la tâche,* Brito correlates the transcendental Christology of Rahner with that of the *PS,* arguing that both reflect within a fundamentally anthropological horizon on the conditions of the possibility of a Saviour, i.e., openness to possibility and need. By contrast, the horizon of Christology in *LPR 3* is historical, and Pannenberg and not Rahner is the *comparandum.* The line of demarcation is perhaps a little too neat here, and I suspect that while a Hodgson would agree that the horizon is more historical than the *PS* (esp. in 1821 Manuscript and the 1827 Lectures), nonetheless, there does appear to exist also a transcendental thrust which raises the issue of relation between

Hegel and Rahner. In the 1824 Lectures, Hegel is not being out and out historical but is behaving in a correlationist mode. See Karl Rahner, *Foundations of Christian Faith,* trans. William V. Dych (New York: Crossroads, 1984), pp. 178–321, esp. 206–228.

28. My overall feeling is that Hegel is trying to suggest parity between *historical* development and *qualitative* improvement, but I am prepared to admit that Hegel does not always seem to be convinced that the later religious form is necessarily superior to the earlier, e.g., the case of the status of Roman religion vis-à-vis Greek religion. Louis Dupré argues that in Hegel's model of religious development the *historical* and the qualitative can and do separate. This would certainly make Hegel's model not only nonevolutionist but, from a history of religion's point of view, more interesting. See Louis Dupré's review of the three volumes of *LPR,* ed. Peter Hodgson/Walter Jaeschke in *Religious Studies Review,* Vol 13 No. 3: 1987 (July), pp. 194–197.

29. I am thinking here especially of *PS* and *LPH.*

30. Both Hodgson and Yerkes would wish to insist that it is at least Hegel's intention to preserve the *historicity* of Christ, while both recognize that some things Hegel says challenge the possibility of the affirmation of historicity. Schlitt is convinced, however, that historicity is not preserved. See *Hegel's Trinitarian Claim,* pp. 145–146, 156–157, 178.

31. Needless to say, there are major differences between what 'narrative enactment' can mean in the theological horizon of a Hegel and what it can mean in a Hans Frei, from whom the locution is borrowed. See Hans Frei, *The Identity of Jesus Christ: The Hermeneutic Bases of Dogmatic Theology* (Philadelphia: Fortress Press, 1978), where narrative enactment has Christ as rendered in the Gospels as norm and horizon.

32. See Jean Wahl, *La malheur,* pp. 81–91. See also Brito, *Hegel et la tâche,* p. 44; Christian Link, *Hegels Wort,* p. 33.

33. This was Hegel's opinion also in "The Spirit of Christianity and its Fate." There Hegel suggested that the real significance of Jesus' death was his withdrawal from appearance. In principle, however, withdrawal might have been achieved by other means. A deeper thanatology is present in Hegel's later texts, yet even in later texts 'death' and 'disappearance' are interconnected. See *Enc* #376 *+zu.*

34. See also *LPR 3* 1824 E 219, G 150.

35. This is a tendency in Fichte. See our discussion of *Die Anweisung* in chap. 2, sect. 2.2.

36. In the case of Tertullian, the anti-Gnostic horizon is less an assumption, as it would have to be in the case of Anselm, than a decision concerning ba-

sic principles. Tertullian is self-consciously in opposition to Gnostic groups who advance a docetic Christology, and it is the context of opposing this Christology and the view that the real drama is played out on the level of the spiritual and transmundane that Tertullian elaborates his satisfaction theory.

37. The possibility of the interconnection of satisfaction and sacrifice should be advanced in the light of Gustav Aulen's influential *Christus Victor: A Historical Study of the Three Main Types of the Idea of Atonement,* trans. A. G. Herbert (New York: Macmillan Publishing Co. Inc., 1969). It is a point with Aulen to suggest that sacrifice and satisfaction belong to essentially different types of Atonement views. As a matter of fact, however, some of the examples he provides as pure types, i.e., Irenaeus and Tertullian are far from pure.

38. See *Christus Victor,* pp. 16–35.

39. Both of these points are important and are interrelated. Sacrifice is no longer the *act* in and through which we are saved but the ineluctable principle of reality. As an ineluctable, it is an indispensable element of a narrative from which is expunged the accidental or the contingent.

40. Asendorf, *Luther und Hegel,* pp. 350–357; Brito, *Hegel et la tâche,* p. 8; Jüngel, *God as the Mystery of the World,* pp. 63–100; Küng, *The Incarnation of God,* pp. 162–180; Link, *Hegels Wort,* pp. 28–33.

41. See Thomas Altizer, *The Gospel of Christian Atheism* (Philadelphia, 1966); Richard Solomon, *In the Spirit of Hegel,* pp. 625–627.

42. André Léonard, in particular, questions the orthodoxy of Hegel's christological position. See "Le primat du négative et l'interprétation spéculative de la religion. Un example: la reprise hegélienne du dogme christologique de chalcédoine." In *Hegels Logik der Philosophie* (Stuttgart: Klett-Cottal, 1984), pp. 160–171.

43. Jüngel, *God as the Mystery of the World,* p. 66.

44. This is not to say, however, that Luther ultimately abandons the axiom. We will later see that he maintains his commitment to the axiom in a way that Hegel does not. On the apathetic axiom, see Hans Küng, *The Incarnation of God* (Excursus 2), pp. 518–525.

45. Annegrit Brunkhorst-Hasenclever in her *Die Transformierung der theologischen Deutung des Todes bei G. W. F. Hegel* (Bern, Frankfurt: Herbert Lang and Peter Lang, 1970), p. 228, comments on the interconnection here between Hegel and Luther. For evidence of narrative contraction of resurrection into the passion narrative in Luther, see Lienhard, *Luther: Witness to Jesus Christ,* p. 286.

46. For a good discussion of the life-bearing potential of death *sub contraria specie,* see Marc Lienhard, *Luther: Witness to Jesus Christ,* p. 43; also pp. 61–67.

47. The differences have been elucidated by such scholars as Brunkhorst-Hasenclever in *Die Transformierung,* pp. 228–242; W. D. Marsch, "Logik des Kreuzes. Über Sinn und Grenzen einer theologischen Berufung auf Hegel," in *Evangelische Theologie,* 128 (1968), pp. 57–82; W. Schultz, "Die Transformeirung der Theologia Crucis bei Hegel und Schleiermacher," in *Neue Zeitschrift für systematische Theologie und Religionsphilosophie,* t. 6 (1964). pp. 290–317. See also Peter Koslowski, "Hegel—'der Philosoph der Trinität?' " pp. 109–111.

48. For this point, see Niels Thulstrup's *Kierkegaard's Relation to Hegel,* trans. George Strenger (Princeton, NJ: Princeton University Press, 1980), pp. 359–365; 370–78.

49. Compare this passage with what Luther says in his commentary on the Psalms (1519–21), where there does not appear to be any establishing of ineluctable narrative order of anteriority-posteriority. In Christ there existed both the highest joy and deepest sorrow, the most abject weakness and the greatest strength, the highest glory and the lowest shame, the greatest peace and the deepest trouble, the most exalted life and the most miserable death" (*WA* 5, 606, 22)—quoted by Lienhard, *Luther: Witness to Jesus Christ,* p. 119. *WA* is the abbreviation for *Ausgewahlte Werke* (Munchen: Ch. Kaiser Verlag, 1948–1968), the most up to date edition of Luther's works.

50. By narrative punctuation I mean the establishing of a narrative order of anteriority-posteriority which, in principle, is irreversible. Though Brunkhörst-Hasenclever does not make the point in quite the general way that I am making it here, her complaint, namely that in Hegel the death of God does not mean the paradoxical assertion of divine power hidden in the extremity of agony and death, so much as the ground (onto-logical) of the realization of the divine (p. 229) bears a family resemblance to the point being made here. Expressed in her terms—and the terms are very suggestive indeed—a major difference between Luther and Hegel consists in the massive Hegelian commitment to *theodicy* in which the ground-consequent relation is of fundamental importance (ibid.). Later in this work, i.e., chap. 6, we will qualify Brunkhörst-Hasenclever's point by suggesting that the difference between Luther and Hegel is captured, less in the distinction between a nontheodicy and theodicy view, than in the distinction between a theodicy of a first-order type committed to the Christian narrative and a reflective, second-order theodicy which supposes a more encompassing narrative frame.

51. This is, of course, a charge that Hegel would resolutely deny and which his distinction between *Verstand* and *Vernunft* is forged to avoid. *Verstand* in Hegel's view is detrimental to religion in general, Christianity in particular, in a way that *Vernunft* is not. Indeed, from Hegel's perspective, Luther's distinction of faith-reason is, strictly speaking, a distinction between faith and understanding. Time and again Hegel attests the in-principle positive relation

between faith and reason, where faith, in fact, anticipates reason, whose task is, therefore, to preserve the richness of faith. See, for example, *LPR 1* 1821 MS E 192–193, G 101; E 216–217, G 125–127; E 243, G 152–153. The split between faith and reason is so absolute for Luther that Luther likely would be unpersuaded by such distinction, thinking that such subtlety belongs to *theologia gloriae.* The absoluteness of the distinction is in place from the beginning and is never reneged on. Luther insists that the articles of faith are based on the word of God and call for faith (WA 39, 25, 9; 269). They do not complement, nor are they complemented by, the articles of reason; they are in opposition to the articles of reason (WA 39, 2,4,2). A crucial article of faith such as the incarnation cannot be rationally demonstrated. With typical pugnacity Luther insists that the idea of God becoming human is as contrary to the spirit of philosophy as that of God becoming an ass (*WA,* 39, 2,3,5). (See Marc Lienhard, *Luther: Witness to Jesus Christ,* pp. 346–349; p. 387).

52. Marc Lienhard in *Luther: Witness to Jesus Christ* confesses that Luther's insistence upon the simultaneity of death and life, humiliation and exaltation, puts the resurrection as an independent narrative element under pressure (pp. 172, 286). Yet Lienhard is also anxious to underscore that this is not always the case and that, at best, we are speaking of a tendency. The contrary tendency also can be affirmed.

53. Luther is, of course, notoriously variant in the expression of his theological views. However, I am of the opinion that Luther does have a *core* view and that it is not the one expressed by Hegel. Nonetheless, there should be no surprise that Luther on occasions did express himself in a manner which anticipates the Hegelian view. For this point, see Lienhard, *Luther: Witness to Jesus Christ,* pp. 55–56.

54. While Luther on occasion definitely blurs the boundaries between resurrection and spiritual appropriation of the Christ who died 'for me', identity is never posited. In most contexts the resurrection plays the role of a narrative element in principle distinct from pentecostal experience. Yerkes, whose fine book, *The Christology of Hegel,* clearly notes Hegel's continuity with Luther, perhaps is not quite as clear with respect to the effect that the emphatic pneumatism of Hegelian Christology and its exacerbated pentecostalism has on the Lutheran view.

55. See *LPR 3* 1824 E 220, G 151.

56. Historical proof is useless, given Spinoza's and, thereafter, Lessing's distinction between the accidental truths of history and truths of reason. For Hegel, truths of reason are alone valid, even if such truths do not belong merely to the logical realm.

57. See Hegel's use of the 'empty tomb' motif in the *PS* #217.

58. This is especially true of a commentator such as Aulen. See also Lienhard *Luther: Witness to Jesus Christ,* pp. 272–273, 285.

59. See *PS* #775–778.

60. See Brito, *Hegel et la tâche,* pp. 47–49.

61. Jüngel, *God as the Mystery of the World,* pp. 75–77. On this point Jüngel is as eloquent as he is persuasive. For him, it is in *PS* that for the first time the theocentric aspect comes to the forefront. In *DE,* the death of God is still more or less existentially qualified.

62. On the christological locus of kenosis in Luther, see Lienhard, *Luther: Witness to Jesus Christ,* p. 52.

63. See *PS* #770 for the former, the "Fate" essay (*ETW* E 257) for the latter.

64. Brito, *La christologie de Hegel,* pp. 553 ff.

65. See Chapelle, *Hegel et la religion,* vol. 2, p. 106: Brito, *La christologie de Hegel,* pp. 18, 551–552; *Hegel et la tâche,* p. 10.

66. See Hans Urs von Balthasar's *The Glory of the Lord: A Theological Aesthetics.* Vol. 1, trans. Erasmo Leiva-Merikakis, ed. Joseph Fessio S. J. and John Riches (San Francisco, New York: Ignatius Press and Crossroad Publication, 1982), p. 49.

67. We are speaking here, of course, of the third moment of the immanent divine, or the third moment of the "Immanent Trinity"

68. Brunkhorst-Hasenclever in *Die Transformierung* is quite certain that in Hegelian ontotheology the Lutheran view of kenosis undergoes deformation in being assimilated into the development dynamics of the divine (p. 229).

69. For relation and differences, see Brito, *La christologie de Hegel,* pp. 550–551; *Hegel et la tâche,* pp. 139–141.

70. This is certainly the case in Luther's commentary on Philippians in 1518–19. See, for example, Lienhard, *Luther: Witness to Jesus Christ,* p. 112.

71. *WA* 17, 2, 243, 4. See Lienhard, *Luther: Witness to Jesus Christ;* Ian Kingston-Siggins, *Martin Luther's Doctrine of Christ* (New Haven: Yale University Press, 1970), pp. 125 ff. In the latter text, Kingston-Siggins quotes a number of Luther's texts which could not be louder in kenotic connotation (p. 126). He insists, however, on the functional nature of kenosis and that divine omnipotence and impassibility are not undermined. He quotes Luther on p. 139 to the effect that "Because he was God, he won the victory, but also precisely because he was God, he had no need to win the victory on his own account."

72. See Lienhard, Luther: Witness to Jesus Christ, p. 392. See also Ronald Jay Feenstra's dissertation, "Pre-existence, Kenosis and the Incarnation of Christ," (Yale, 1984), for a somewhat more generous estimate of nineteenth-century kenotic theologians. Feenstra thinks that Gottfried Thomasius can be exonerated from the charge that kenosis involves a surrender of divine essence and not, as one would expect, a surrender of the form of glory (pp. 59–91).

73. A move from the crucified Christ to the crucified God seems to be enjoined by Moltmann, at least at the time of *The Crucified God.*

74. Here I agree with Lienhard and Siggins and take issue with Brunkhorst-Hasenclever who, while definitely correct with regard to what Luther denies, i.e., the implicit and explicit docetism of *theologia gloriae,* is definitely incorrect with regard to what Luther affirms. She suggests that the death of God applies to the divine nature because it applies to the human nature and that Luther's notion of *communicatio idiomatum* is a vehicle of transference. Here it would seem that Brunkhorst-Hasenclever is involved in a fundamental misunderstanding of the scope and function of *communicatio idiomatum.* Luther is not making an ontological point when he uses the idea of communication of properties. He is making a semantic point which has a more or less rule character which specifies that, since we are dealing with a whole that is a unit, the predication of properties extends beyond the human nature to the divine nature to the extent to which the whole (i.e., union of two natures) is a legitimate subject of predication. Strictly speaking, however, that is, *ontologically* speaking, predicates ascribable to the human nature are not capable of extension to the divine nature and vice versa.

75. See Lienhard's discussion in *Luther: Witness to Jesus Christ,* pp. 218–219, 335–366.

76. While he admits Monophysite flirtation in Luther, Lienhard is of the opinion that in the last instance Luther evidences a Dyophysite commitment. See *Luther: Witness to Jesus Christ,* pp. 219, 230–235, 317.

77. Lienhard is perhaps not perfectly consistent in *Luther: Witness to Jesus Christ* when in dialogue with Paul Althaus he seems to admit deipassionism (p. 174) but later denies it (p. 227). His general point, however, is perfectly clear: one cannot think of the suffering of God outside the context of the suffering of the unique person, Jesus Christ.

78. This expresses Moltmann's opinion in *The Crucified God.* Moltmann's more negative judgment of the Hegelian Trinity in *Trinity and the Kingdom* suggests that Moltmann might be prepared to amend that opinion.

79. Hegel's position cannot be confounded with the Patripassianism of a modalist such as Noetus of Smyrna (end of second century), since, given real trinitarian distinction, suffering would be attributable to the Son and not the

Father. Moreover, for Hegel suffering is attributable only to the Son as an extra-immanent reality. The Son of the "Immanent Trinity" no more suffers than the Father. This entire region of being, or narrative epoch, of the "Immanent Trinity" is, from Hegel's perspective, apathetic or impassible and thus deficient.

80. Heinrich Bornkamm, *Luther und Boehme* (Bonn: A Marcus and K. Webers Verlag, 1925), esp. pp. 131–156.

81. See Franz von Baader, *Gesammliche Werke* Band 13, p. 81. Here Baader is discussing Boehme's text *De Electione Gratiae* or, in German, *Von der Gnadenwahl;* F. Ch. Baur, *Die christliche Gnosis,* pp. 557 ff; *Die christliche Lehre von der Versöhnung* (1835), pp. 465 ff.

82. Bornkamm, *Luther und Boehme,* pp. 6–7.

83. Bornkamm, *Luther und Boehme,* pp. 3–6, 131–133.

84. Bornkamm in *Luther und Boehme* (pp. 131–156) concentrates primarily on the second of our three transformations and provides some broad hints with regard to the first. The third is not touched on. Brunkhorst-Hasenclever in her *Die Transformierung* also has seen that Boehme is a mediator of Lutheranism, however, a Lutheranism that is ontologically or metaphysically transfigured. The strongest point in her analysis tends to be that of narrative punctuation (see p. 229), but she also has suggestions with respect to the second and third transformations or second and third elements of a complex *Umbildung.* See her section on Boehme and Hegel in *Die Transformierung* entitled, "Die Denkenmöglichkeit der metaphysichen Negation: G. W. F. Hegel and J. Boehme," pp. 257–265). In the context of our study here, I tend to think of these transformations less as facts than operations in which narrative operators work on material (i.e., Lutheran material), disfiguring and reconfiguring it.

85. Quoted Lienhard, *Luther: Witness to Jesus Christ,* p. 119.

86. It should be pointed out that here I am speaking of the Christ who entered into and became part of history. In depicting this *temporal* Christ, Boehme imagines him as a prelapsarian Adam in whom there is a perfect coincidence of masculine and feminine qualities, fire and light, fire and water. The notion of the *coincidentia oppositorum* in Christ is influenced by alchemical figuration of Christ as juncture of *Sol* and *Luna.* The Schwenkfeldian idea of the glorified body of Christ gets matched in Boehme's mind with the figuration of the perfect coincidence, so that Christ's body is ethereal, not material like ours. It should also be observed that connections such as Boehme is making were also made by Valentin Weigel (1533–1588).

87. I am availing here of J. S. Earle's translation.

88. I am referring specifically to Croce's influential *What is Living and Dead in the Philosophy of Hegel.*

89. See *The Ages of the World,* trans. Frederick de Wolfe Bolman Jr. (New York: Columbia University Press, 1942). More even than the Freedom essay this unfinished piece of theosophy is decisively influenced by Jacob Boehme. For an excellent account of the massive influence of Boehme on the later Schelling, see R. F. Brown, *The Later Philosophy of Schelling: The Influence of Boehme on Schelling (1809–1815)* (Lewisburg, PA.: Bucknell University Press, 1976).

90. *The Ages of the World,* pp. 115, 200.

91. It is Gustav Aulen who, above all, interprets Luther's theology in the mythological-agonic terms which other Swedish Lutherans such as Bring have followed. Though many Lutheran scholars believe that those of the Swedish school overstate their case (see, for instance, Edgar M. Carlson, *The Reinterpretation of Luther* (Philadelphia: The Westminister Press, 1948), pp. 48–49), nevertheless it is difficult to edit out altogether the mythological-agonic element. See Lienhard, *Luther: Witness to Jesus Christ,* pp. 272–273, 285.

92. Bornkamm could not be clearer in *Luther und Boehme* when, in the context of a discussion of the difference between Luther and Boehme regarding the devil and evil, he says: "Das, was bei Luther sittliche Grundanschauung ist, wendet er ins metaphysiche" (p. 137).

93. Both Bornkamm and Lienhard are well aware that in Luther's rhetorical and functional use of religious categories he does not provide neat scholastic distinctions between *Holle, Finsterniss, Zorn, Teufel, Widerwille, Grim,* etc. In principle, however, the realities they name are not identical. See Bornkamm *Luther und Boehme,* pp. 138–139, 141–143; Lienhard, *Luther: Witness to Jesus Christ* pp. 272–273.

94. See also *LPR 3* 1821 MS E 86–87, G 25–26; 1824 E 200, G 134; 1827 E 293, G 218.

95. There is, however, an internal complexity in Boehme's construal of *finitude* not present in Hegel. Boehme distinguishes between an order of finitude on the level of eternity and an order of finitude on the temporal level. Kenosis is exacerbated on the eternal level in that it seems as if the divine has emptied itself of divinity to take on the alternate form of evil.

96. See *De Signatura Rerum,* chap. 5.

97. In the sequel, I would hope to argue a quite specific structural connection between Boehme and Gnosticism. Among other things, I would hope to make the case that Sophia functions in Boehmian theosophy in much the same way that it does in the more or less scholastic Valentinian Gnostic system of Ptolemy.

98. See Peter Koslowski, "Hegel—'der philosoph der Trinität?'," p. 109.

99. Boehme suggests that the divine outside of relation to finitude is not a *plenum*—as would be the case if the horizon of construal were Patristic, Neoplatonic or scholastic—but rather, an insufficiency driven to transcend itself. Boehme suggests all of this using very concrete language such as *Sucht, Begierde.* Schelling's *The Ages of the World* renders explicit what it implicit in Boehmian theosophy. Speaking of the self-definition of the absolute, Schelling names its movement as being at once dominated by *poros* and *penia,* plenty and lack.

100. Examples can be found in major Boehmian texts such as *Mysterium Magnum* and *The Election of Grace.*

101. For Boehme there is only one grammatical subject throughout all change, i.e., divinity, which, however, is not immutable and seems capable of undergoing fundamental transformation.

102. See Bornkamm, *Luther und Boehme,* pp. 138–139.

103. See Lienhard, *Luther: Witness to Jesus Christ,* pp. 230–235.

104. Hugh's contribution was to emphasize that relationality was constitutive of personhood.

105. Boehme's general orthodoxy was suspect from the beginning and led to bad relations between him and the local pastor. Throughout the century, as his positions found followers, his distinctive renditions of Christian theologoumena had to be countered. In his monumental polemical work of 1697, Frick summarizes the orthodox objection against Boehme's Christology.

106. Hodgson has persuasively argued the dependence of Hegel on Neander. It should be noted that, as with Baur some years later, Neander makes no critical distinction between Valentinian Gnosticism, Neoplatonism, and Hermeticism. In short, for him Gnosticism is coextensive with the esoteric.

107. An important difference between the pedagogic Jesus of Gnosticism and the early Hegel is that, in Hegel's case, the accent of teaching falls on living a reasoned and reflective life in the context of social and political life, whereas in Gnostic texts the accent falls on the disclosure of a narrative that is the condition of the possibility of escape from social and political existence.

108. A convenient English translation of the *Gospel of Truth* is to be found in the *Nag Hammadi Library.* This is a powerfully original text, perhaps all the more important in that a number of scholars believe it to be the text of the same name mentioned by Irenaeus in his *Against Heresies.*

109. See *LHP 2.*

110. See *LPR 3* 1821 MS E 87–89, G 25–27.

111. *Sophia* is a major construct in Boehmian theosophy. Indeed, to a significant extent it plays the role of a fourth hypostasis. That is, on the level of the immanent divine, it is as important as the trinitarian articulation of divine mystery in providing *some* definition to a divine that otherwise would be totally ineffable. (Given what we said in chap. 2, we must necessarily rule out hypostasis in the strict sense). In addition, *Sophia* is more important with respect to the divine-world relation, because within *Sophia* resides the archetypes for the spiritual world that is the divine other, while representing it transparently. The entrance of the divine into the negativity of death and exile through Eternal Nature seems to involve *Sophia,* since Eternal Nature is described in terms that make it appear to be nothing less than *Sophia's* antitype. Thus, if *Sophia* is the divine other, Eternal Nature is the other of the divine.

112. Boehme consistently associates angst and suffering with the Eternal Nature, within which the eternal Christ is embedded and yet overcomes. The drama played out in eternity is often registered in the symbolic terms of alchemy: Christ undergoes purification within the eternal crucible of darkness and suffering. In alchemical terms: *nigredo* precedes *albedo.* A particularly strong registration of this to found in *De Signatura Rerum.*

Chapter 5 The Third Narrative Epoch: The Moment or Kingdom of the Spirit

1. In the third religious syllogism of *Enc* #569, spiritual community is but the conclusion of a syllogism that has the passion and death of Christ as its major and the appropriative *imitatio* of the religious community as its minor premise. For a good discussion of the third religious syllogism, which together with the first two constitutes the syllogism of syllogisms, see Michael Theunissen, *Hegels Lehre vom absoluten Geist,* pp. 275 ff.

2. Chapelle, "L'absolu et l'histoire," in *Hegel et la théologie contemporaine: l'absolu dans l'histoire* (Paris: Delachaux and Niestle, 1977), pp. 205–218.

3. H. S. Harris, *Towards the Sunlight,* p. 100.

4. Ibid, pp. 110–125. For a solid account of Hegel's view in *LPR 3,* see Schlitt, *Hegel's Trinitarian Claim,* pp. 212–226.

5. For a succinct account of Hegel's difference with Kant on the nature of history and kingdom, see William A. Galston, *Kant and the Problem of History* (Chicago and London: University of Chicago Press, 1975), pp. 261–268, esp. pp. 264–268.

6. In *PS* #538–581 (Miller pp. 328–355) Hegel settles his accounts with the Enlightenment and French Revolution, which was for the whole of German Idealism its governing symbol. See Franz Gabriel Nauen, *Revolution, Idealism and Human Freedom: Schelling, Hölderlin and Hegel and the Crisis of Early German*

Idealism (The Hague: Martinus Nijhoff, 1971), esp. pp. 69–85. For a detailed discussion of Hegel's relationship to the Enlightenment, see Lewis P. Hinchmann's *Hegel's Critique of the Enlightenment* (Gainsville: University of Florida Presses, 1984), esp. chaps. 5,6, pp. 122–184.

7. *PS* #787 (Miller p. 478). #787 should be read in the light of #781.

8. The scheme present in the 1827 Lectures is also present in the lectures of 1824. It should be noted that, by contrast, Hegel in the 1821 Manuscript speaks not of the realization but the passing away of the community (*Vergehen der Gemeinde*) (E 158–162, G 93–97). It is important, however, to note what Hegel is and is not saying in the 1821 Manuscript. He is clearly disturbed by what he views as a degenerate religiosity masquerading as the essence of Christianity, a religiosity that absolutizes the eccentric, the capricious, the individual. He is thoroughly pessimistic that Christianity on its own can be sustained against this degeneration which uncritically mimics the general assumptions of Romantic culture. Consequently, it is philosophy that is named as the *pharmakon*. While the asserted relation between religion and philosophy in the Lectures of 1824 and 1827 does not differ from that of the 1821 Manuscript, Hegel in those Lectures is somewhat more optimistic concerning the internal resources of religion, i.e., Christianity. See John E. Smith's fine essay, "Hegel and the Philosophy of Religion" in *The Wofford Symposium*, ed. introd. Darrel L. Christensen (The Hague: Martinus Nijhoff, 1970), pp. 157–177.

9. The full locution in *PS* (#212) is 'recalcitrant sensuous unit' (*undurchsichtiges sinnliches Eins*) (*GL2:*170, Miller, p. 129). See also *LPR 3* 1824 E 222, G 152).

10. See *LPR 3* 1821 MS E 109, G 45; 1824 E 207–211, G 139–142.

11. The central thrust of *PS* goes clearly in a dialectical direction, though some Hegelian commentators and critics such as Heidegger, Kojève, and Voegelin would read the conclusion of *PS* to suggest the overcoming of all finitude.

12. In the case of an Augustinian theology of image, resemblance alone is possible, given a doctrine of creation that stresses the infinite difference between the divine and the human. Functionally, the doctrine of *creatio ex nihilo* preserves the incommensurability of the divine and the human, an incommensurability that is not disavowed even in Augustine's most mystical moments, including Bk. 15 of *De Trinitate*.

13. This way of speaking of the traditioning process of the Christian community is found in the 1824 and 1827 Lectures. Hegel makes the distinction is a somewhat different way in the 1821 Manuscript.

14. I am not suggesting that Hegel is being simply tactical here. He obviously thinks there exists a broad measure of theological agreement among the *western* Christian churches and regards disputes about authority, faith, and chris-

tological issues as less important than the common narrative he sees underlying all confessional theological proposal. Hegel's interesting ecumenical ploy is to say that, unbeknownst to themselves, the various Christian confessions really agree. No confession, therefore, is entitled to accuse the other of heterodoxy. The defunctionalizing of heterodoxy effectively makes the charge of heterodoxy against Hegelian ontotheology more or less unintelligible, since (1) all differences of doctrine are likely to be more apparent than real, and (2) though the narrative to which Hegel is implying Christians should pledge allegiance corresponds to none of the confessional positions as they express themselves, this does not disturb Hegel's sang-froid, since he would likely think that in the development of confessionalism basic agreement of substance tends to be masked by theological accretion and justification. Hegel's move here itself has a long history in the Pietistic tradition. Gottfied Arnold, for example, in his famous text, *Unparteiische Kirchen und Ketzer Historie* (1698) argues against distinction between the true and false being made on dogmatic rather than on spiritual grounds. Spirit and truth, he argued, is what counts, and there is some evidence to suggest that not less but more of this is preserved in the heterodox traditions. For a good account of Arnold, see Peter C. Erb, *Pietists, Protestants, and Mysticism. The Use of Late Medieval Sources in the Work of Gottfried Arnold (1666–1714)* (Metouchen, NJ, London: The Scarecrow Press, Inc, 1987).

15. See Walter Jaesche, *Reason in Religion: The Formation of Hegel's Philosophy of Religion,* trans. J. Michael Stewart and Peter Hodgson (Berkeley, Cal: University of California Press, 1990), pp. 325–358.

16. Gregory of Nyssa, Ruysbroeck, and St. John of the Cross are just three examples of Christian mystics who deny ontological identity between the divine and the human, even the human considered as divinized.

17. That there is a mystical element in Luther himself has been well-recognized by modern scholars. See, for example, Bengt Hoffman, *Luther and the Mystics: A Re-examination of Luther's Spiritual Experience and his Relationship to the Mystics* (Minneapolis: Augsburg Publishing House, 1976). More so than in Lutheran orthodoxy, this fact was recognized in the Pietist tradition. Both Arndt and Spener presumed that Lutheranism and the practical medieval mysticism of Tauler and the *Theologia Germanica* are hospitably related given Luther's own practice. For the more moderate Pietists, the speculative mystics were out. Needless to say, the Boehmian tradition was by no means so restrictive.

18. Hegel's point is not exactly the same as Nietzsche's, since the frame of his remark is historical-institutional, that of Nietzsche, historical-psychological. But both want to say that exclusion and corruption are logically related. In Hegel's case, the accent is upon worldliness and selfishness that invades despite denial; in Nietzsche's case, the lust for power that invades despite denial.

19. Robert Gascoigne's *Religion, Rationality and Community: Sacred and Secular in the Thought of Hegel and his Critics* (The Hague: Martinus Nijhoff, 1985), pp. 1–65 is apropos here. See especially p. 54 where he argues that Hegel goes beyond the specifically religious sense of the 'holy' whose separatist, disjunctive essence is captured by Otto. This view is clearly right in its basic assertion of Hegel's transcendence of the exclusive for a more integrative view of the holy, though the amendment needs to be added that this by no means implies, as Gascoigne seems to suggest, that the integrative holy ceases to be religious. Indeed, it is precisely Hegel's point that Lutheran Protestantism provides a more adequate religious view than Catholicism.

20. The notion of *Sittlichkeit* is important to Hegel almost from the beginning, and in the form of an appeal to *Volk* is a fundamental element of his critique of modern Christianity infected both by Pietistic and rationalist excess. It is thematized in an explicit way in Hegel's *System of Ethical Life* (1802–03), and the essential elements of Hegel's view remain intact—though development does occur—throughout Hegel's mature period which includes *PS* (#444–483), the *ENC* (#513–552), and *LPR* (see *LPR 3* 1827 E 252, G 180, E 341–342, G 264–265); *PR* #142–360. Perhaps the most lucid account of *Sittlichkeit* in Hegelian scholarship, at least in English, is offered by Charles Taylor. See his *Hegel* (Cambridge: Cambridge University Press, 1975), pp. 365–388. See also Jaeschke, "Christianity and Secularity in Hegel's Concept of the State," *The Journal of Religion* 61 (1981), pp. 127–145.

21. For this point, see Dickey, *Hegel,* pp. 61 ff.

22. See, for example, *LPR 1* 1821 MS E 192–193. G 101–102; E 243–244, G 152–153; 1827 E 151–153, G 62–64. The first two passages have it that Luther provides Christianity with its definitive twist, i.e., that of the witness of spirit. Yet *faith* as the witness of spirit, Hegel argues, is not reducible to Romantic intuition or feeling. In technical language faith, for Hegel, implies both *fides qua creditur* and *fides quae creditur.* The third passage establishes the generally positive relation between Christianity and philosophy in contradistinction to a number of influential views, e.g., Jacobi and Schleiermacher, which in different ways saw them as antagonistic (see chap. 1, sect. 1.1 above).

23. All of Hegel's major texts point to the symbiosis of *Sittlichkeit* and religion. If in *PS* and the *Enc* Hegel wishes to emphasize the ethical-substance foundation of religion, in *LPR* he wishes to emphasize the religious, specifically Christian, basis of *Sittlichkeit* (see esp. *LPR 1* 1821 MS E 228–229, G 138–139; 1827 E 341–342, G 241–242; E 446–447, G 334–335). The Hegelian commentator who most clearly recognizes this is Paul Lakeland. His *The Politics of Salvation: The Hegelian Idea of the State* (Albany, N.Y.: SUNY Press, 1984) could be regarded as an exegesis of the interdependence of Christianity and *Sittlichkeit* with special emphasis on the religious foundation of *Sittlichkeit.*

24. Justification of the appropriateness of the symbol of *corpus mysticum* with regard to Hegel's notion of *Gemeinde* involves a number of considerations: (1) that human being is intrinsically capable of a relationship of superb intimacy with the divine, i.e., is capable of a mystical relationship with the divine, and that this capability is actualizable in a unique way in modernity; and (2) that this relationship is in fundamental respects more a corporate than an individual affair. Of course, *Gemeinde* as *corpus mysticum* differs crucially from the Catholic view of the mystical body as *corpus Christi.* Hegel's view of the mystical body at one and the same time exacerbates the noetic or gnoseological register of the mystical (e.g., *LPR 1* 1827 E 443–445, G 331–333) and the eschatological element. Our treatment of the Eckhartian and Joachimite elements in Hegel's construal of *Gemeinde* will help to specify the concrete meaning of *corpus mysticum* as it is used in the chapter.

25. The hegemony of the contemplative that gets expressed in Hegel's granting to *Begriff* the place of supereminence regarding modality of symbolization, as well as his reading of conceptual *tendenz* into *Vorstellung,* justifies to some extent Iwan Iljin's contemplative reading of Hegel, while at the same time rendering intelligible left-wing Hegelian responses to Hegel that were more concerned with praxis than *theoria.*

26. See H. S. Harris, *Towards the Sunlight,* pp. 230–231 notes. K. Rosenkranz makes this claim in "Hegels ursprüngliches System 1798–1806" in *Literarhistorisches Taschenbuch,* ed. R. E. Prutz, Vol. 2, 1844, reprinted in *Hegel Studien,* X, 1975, pp. 133–135. See also Ernst Benz, *Les sources,* pp. 27–31; Coda, *Il negativo e la trinità,* pp. 73–81; Wolfram Malte Fues, *Mystik als Erkenntnis. Kritische Studien zur Meister Eckhart Forschung* (Bonn: Bouvier, 1981); G. Ralfs, "Lebensformen des Geistes. Meister Eckhart und Hegel" in *Kant Studien* supplement No. 86, Cologne, 1964; Theodor Steinbüchel, "Mystik und Idealismus, Meister Eckhart und Hegel" in *Universitas* 2 (1974), pp. 1409–1423.

27. See Benz, *Les sources,* pp. 27–31; Malte-Fues, *Mystik als Erkenntnis,* pp. 33–44. See Franz von Baader, *Sämtliche Werke,* 16 Bande, eds. Franz Hoffman et al. (Leipzig, 1851–60), Bd 15, pp. 158 ff.

28. See. Benz, *Les sources,* pp. 27–31.

29. For this point, see especially Malte-Fues, *Mystik as Erkenntnis,* pp. 35–51.

30. See Baader, *Sämt. Werke,* Bd 2, p. 455.

31. See Baader, *Sämt. Werke,* Bd 5, pp. 263 ff.

32. See Malte-Fues, *Mystik als Erkenntnis,* p. 39.

33. Baader, *Sämt. Werke,* Bd 2, pp. 454–455.

34. See Heinrich Ebeling, *Meister Eckharts Mystik,* p. 177.

35. See *Deutsche Werke*) 2, 6, 22. All numbering of sermons is from the standard Quint edition of the German works. See *Die deutschen und lateinischen Werke,* ed. Josef Quint (Stuttgart and Berlin: Kohlhammer, 1936–).

36. See *DW* 35.

37. See Malte-Fues, *Mystik als Erkenntnis,* pp. 35–36; see Baader, *Sämt. Werke.,* Bd 15, p. 455; also Bd 2, pp. 404–405 where Baader insists that Eckhart's identity statements should not be interpreted in such a way that Eckhart is seen to be in the school of the pantheists in which class Hegel decidedly belongs. For this point, see *Sämt. Werke,* 9, pp. 327–336. For brief but good discussion on the relation of Baader and Hegel on the pantheism question, see Eugène Susini, *Franz von Baader et le romanticisme mystique.* 2 vols (Paris: Vrin, 1942), vol. 1, pp. 465–471.

38. See Malte-Fues, *Mystik als Erkenntnis,* pp. 35–36. As Susini points out, Baader has a very definite doctrine of creation that is insisted on throughout his work. What is odd, however, is that in insisting upon difference, Baader does not invoke the standard *creatio ex nihilo* view but makes continual appeal to another mystic's view of difference, i.e., Jacob Boehme. But then, Baader's work as a whole is supersaturated with Boehmian concepts and images.

39. See also *Enc* #440 *zu,* 441 *zu.*

40. See Malte-Fues, *Mystik als Erkenntnis,* pp. 47–48.

41. On the basis of the evidence modern scholars have at their disposal, it would appear that the interpretive advantage lies with Hegel. Ontological identity is the outcome of different radials of reflection in Eckhartian texts, i.e., (1) the pure ontological reflection of *Istigkeit;* (2) the mystical anthropological reflection of *Fünklein;* and (3) the trinitarian theological reflection of the *Gottesgeburt.* In using the image of radials, it should be noted that I am implying that there is a unitive center in Eckhartian reflection, and we are not speaking of multiple centers. With regard to (1), see the following passage from *DW* 6, "God's being is my life. If my life is God's being then God's existence must be my existence and God's isness (istigkeit) my isness neither more nor less." With regard to (2), see *DW* 2, 5 b—in McGinn, *Essential Sermons,* pp. 179–183. For (3), see *DW* 2, 6, 22, 83, esp. 6.

42. In a number of texts Eckhart speaks of the created order qua finite as nothing (e.g., *DW* 9, *DW* 29), a proposition that was condemned by the medieval church authorities.

43. See Malte-Fues, *Mystik als Erkenntnis,* p. 51.

44. See also *DW* 23(a), *DW* 43.

45. See McGinn, *Essential Sermons,* p. 188.

46. This is clear in *DW* 6. Of all Eckhart's sermons it is, perhaps, *DW* 43 that unfolds in the most explicit way the interconnectedness of the themes of *Gottesgeburt,* sonship, friendship, child of God, and knowledge. The principle of ontological commensurability between the self and the divine is here not merely presupposed but clearly stated.

47. See Jaesche, *Reason in Religion,* pp. 362–369 for an overview of contemporary discussion of Hegel's view of human-divine union and its perceived relation to the Christian standard.

48. This is clearly the status of mystical knowledge in *De Trinitate* Bk. 15. Such an idea was not happily embraced by Lutheran orthodoxy because it tended to undermine the fundamental tenet of the equality of all believers before God. Pietism, by contrast, while it still regarded the proposition of equality of believers as axiomatic, tended to emphasize differences in gifts of the spirit.

49. The following passage also from *LPR 3* might be noted: "The fact of the matter is that humanity is immortal (unsterblich) only through cognitive knowledge (das Erkennen), for only in the activity of thinking is its soul pure and free rather than mortal (sterbliche) or animal-like. Cognition and thought are the root of human life, of human immortality as a totality within itself" (1827 E 314, G 227–228).

50. Bataille strategically avails of a number of Christian mystics, including Eckhart, as examples of the nonknowledge he enjoins as the antithesis of the immodesty of Hegelian knowledge. See especially *Inner Experience* trans. Leslie Anne Baldt (New York: SUNY Press, 1988), pp. 102–103.

51. Michel Henry, *The Essence of Manifestation,* p. 428.

52. This point is granted by most scholars of Pietism. Peter Erb in particularly eloquent on this point. See his *Pietists, Protestants, and Mysticism.*

53. In Sermon 2, 5b, 6, *inter alia* Eckhart claims that just like Mary we are capable of the virgin-birth in which we become the mother of the Son. Eckhart could not be more radical here. We are not merely assimilated to the historical archetype Mary, but rather, to the *theotokos,* for Eckhart's discussion makes it clear that he is speaking of the Logos or Word of the intradivine Trinity. In association with the radical identity claims Eckhart makes in his German sermons in particular, Eckhartian swerve from the normative christological position becomes an issue. One of the best Eckhart commentators, Frank Tobin, in his *Meister Eckhart: Thought and Language* (Philadelphia: University of Pennsylvania Press, 1986), brings out the complexity of Eckhart's christological position in which human being's essential identity with the Son is asserted, as is the traditional distinction between the Son who is Son by nature and the human being who is, or rather can be, a son by adoption (pp. 102 ff, esp. 102–104). The situation is, thus, for Tobin ambivalent between a thoroughgoing christological subversion and an archetypal Christology. Michel Henry

seems to believe that the situation is not quite so ambiguous. In *The Essence of Manifestation,* archetypal Christology interpretation is questioned in the light of Eckhart's radical iconoclastic impulse. See pp. 428–432.

54. This can be clearly seen in Eckhart's commentary on the Prologue, where all entrance into the finite order is seen to be the echo of the truly real event which is the speaking of the word at the level of eternity. In the case of Eckhart, there is a resolute decision for the priority of the *logos endiathetos* over the *logos prosphorikos.* For an English translation of the Johannine Prologue, see *Meister Eckhart: Selected Treatises and Sermons,* trans. J. M. Skinner and J. V. Clark (London: Faber and Faber, 1958), pp. 222–249.

55. No one has been as insistent upon separation as Heinrich Bornkamm. See his *Protestantismus und Mystik* (Giessen, 1934). In spite of the fineness of Bornkamm's work, he articulates a view that operates in some sense (or at least traditionally so operated) as an a priori. The most vocal voice in asserting an unequivocally positive relation has been Eric Seeberg. See his *Meister Eckhart* (Tübingen, 1954). But Seeberg is not the only scholar who has been interested in the question of relation. Both Malte-Fues and Steven Ozment have followed suit. See Malte-Fues, *Mystik als Erkenntnis,* pp. 99–100; Ozment, *Homo Spiritualis* (Leiden: E. J. Brill, 1969), also "Meister Eckhart and Martin Luther" in *The Thomist* 42 (1978), pp. 259–280.

56. In a sense this was recognized by perhaps the greatest of the Lutheran orthodox theologians, John Gerhard. Still for the most part this was a neuralgic point with Lutheran orthodoxy, and the divinization emphasis became the prerogative of the Pietist tradition. There is a strong contemporary movement in mainline Lutheranism to recover a divinization theology that can fit in with a theology of justification.

57. I am borrowing, but not without revision, an interpretive trope elaborated by Harold Bloom in the context of literary criticism. For the use of the trope of synechdoche or *tessera* in Bloom's scheme, see in particular *The Anxiety of Criticism: A Theory of Poetics* (Oxford University Press, 1973), pp. 49–73; also *The Map of Misreading* (Oxford University Press, 1975).

58. That Hegel supplies a synecdochical reading of all previous philosophy is transparent in his treatment of previous philosophical systems in *LHP.* When he is not negative about these previous systems, he tends to suggest that what is valuable in these systems is that they anticipate his own, where their insights achieve consummate clarity, adequacy, and comprehensiveness. For a clear statement of Hegel's synecdochical reading of the history of philosophy in the *Enc,* see #13.

59. In some quite general sense all versions of religion, all construals of Christianity anticipate Hegelian ontotheology as their telos. However, Hegel by no means excludes the spirit of partisanship. He clearly likes certain types of religious and Christian construal more than others. For instance, Hegel clearly

prefers Lutheranism to Catholicism and the Reform Church, just as he clearly prefers a Meister Eckhart to modern Romantic theology.

60. For the trope of apophatic erasure, see chap. 1.1. above.

61. For eighteenth-century Pietistic thought, see Dickey, *Hegel,* pp. 104 ff.

62. See, for example, Michael Murray, *Modern Philosophy of History: Its Origin and Destination* (The Hague: Martinus Nijhoff, 1970), p. 97.

63. See Murray, *Modern Philosophy,* pp. 89–126, esp. pp. 96, 99. The presence of the Joachimite element in Hegel is also argued by Charles Taylor in his *Hegel,* p. 211. For an excellent recent account of Joachim's theology of history, see Bernard McGinn, *The Calabrian Abbot: Joachim of Fiore in the History of Western Thought* (New York: Macmillan Pub. Co., 1985), pp. 161–203.

64. See Henri de Lubac, *La postérité spirituelle de Joachim de Fiori. Tome 1: de Joachim à Schelling* (Paris: Lethiellux, 1979).

65. See, for example, Marjorie Reeves, *Joachim of Fiore and the Prophetic Future* (New York: Harper Torchbooks, 1976), pp. 136 ff.

66. At most, de Lubac hints at this. The scholar who validates this is Robin Barnes in his book on Lutheran apocalyptic in the sixteenth century. See his *Prophecy and Gnosis: Apocalypticism in the Wake of the Lutheran Reformation* (Stanford: Stanford University Press, 1988).

67. See *La postérité,* pp. 218–225. For Bengel's mediation of Joachim and Joachimism, see Dickey, *Hegel,* pp. 77–112, esp. 78, 82, 90, 95, 97, 103.

68. Just how much of a debt is still a matter of some dispute. Benz in *Les sources mystiques* is prepared to say, after Baader, that the debt is considerable. A similar judgement is made by Frederick O. Kile in his *Die theologischen Grundlegan von Schellings Philosophie der Freiheit* (Leiden: E. J. Brill, 1965), pp. 73 ff.

69. See Marjorie Reeves, *The Influence of Prophecy in the Late Middle Ages: A Study of Joachimism* (Oxford: Clarendon Press, 1969), pp. 16–23, 26. See also Bernard McGinn, *The Calabrian Abbot,* pp. 161–203; E. Randolph Daniel, "The Double Procession of the Holy Spirit in Joachim of Fiore's understanding of History," in *Speculum* 55 (1980), pp. 469–483.

70. *Liber Concordie Novi ac Veteris Testamenti* (Venice, 1519). A new critical edition of four of the five books has been prepared by E. Randolph Daniel, *Abbot Joachim of Fiore, Liber de Concordia Novi ac Veteris Testamenti* (Philadelphia. Transactions of the American Philosophy Society, Vol. 73, Part 8, 1973). For a convenient presentation of *Concordia* Bk. 2, see *Apocalyptic Spirituality* (New York: Paulist Press, 1979), trans. ed. Bernard McGinn, pp. 97–148. The portion of *Concordia* anthologized is slight, i.e., Bk. 2 Part 1 chaps. 2–12. See esp. chap. 9, pp. 129–132. For the practical equivalence of *tempus, aetas,* and *status,* see

that modern Joachimite, Jürgen Moltmann, in *The Trinity and the Kingdom,* p. 251, note 34.

71. For this quotation see *The Trinity and the Kingdom,* pp. 204–205. See in general pp. 203–208.

72. Winfrid M. J. Schachten, *Ordo Salutis: Das Gesetz als Weise der Heilsvermittlung: Zur Kritik des L. H. Thomas von Aquin an Joachim von Fiore* (Münster: Aschendorf, 1980), pp. 26–28.

73. For an example of anagogic-futural mode of exegesis, see McGinn, *The Calabrian Abbot,* Part 2. chaps. 4 & 5, pp. 123–160. For a more elaborate account of Joachimite exegesis, see de Lubac, *Exegèse mediévale,* vol. 1, part 2, pp. 437–558; H. Mottu, *La manifestation de l'Esprit selon Joachim de Fiore* (Neuchâtel and Paris: Delachaux and Niestle, 1977), chaps. 1–3.

74. Reply to objections 6 and 2, respectively.

75. Reply to objections 1 and 3, respectively.

76. On the role of Christ in the third status, see Reeves, *The Influence of Prophecy,* p. 131.

77. See Schachten, *Ordo Salutis,* pp. 23, 51.

78. As is well known, Aquinas claimed that Joachim had misinterpreted Lombard's position in thinking that it logically implied a quaternity and represented a species of Salellianism. On this point, see McGinn, *The Calabrian Abbot,* pp. 209–213.

79. See Schacten, *Ordo Salutis,* pp. 24–25, 31.

80. See McGinn, *Apocalyptic Spirituality,* pp. 105–106, 293, note 22. See also Reeves, *The Influence of Prophecy,* p. 131, where the 'spiritual men' of the *saeculum* come in for discussion.

81. See Schachten, *Ordo Salutis,* p. 31.

82. Murray, in his *Modern Philosophy,* has a clear grasp of this point (see pp. 104–105, also pp. 125–126). Murray writes: "Joachim breaks with the Platonism of the holy place and the holy presence, indeed with the entire theology of participation in favor of the holy that is universal and futural in essence" (pp. 104–105). Commitment to this global—and at the same time historical—holy is a feature of those accounts of history in the modern period that refuse to write secular, empirical history, that came into being in the seventeenth century. Hegelian *Heilsgeschichte* represents one such significant refusal.

83. Hegel's developmental model of religions is quite sophisticated. While it is definitely true that (1) prior to Christianity there existed no religion of the Spirit, and (2) Christianity's focus upon the incarnation represents the con-

summate configuration of the religion of the Son, it is not true that all other religions can be without remainder labelled religions of the Father. In the strict sense, prior to the emergence of Christianity only Judaism with its superlative emphasis upon divine transcendence can be called a religion of the Father. Many religions prior to Christianity represent more or less inadequate attempts to construe that coincidence of the infinite and finite, divine and human that is the central fact of Christianity. While these religions are not strictly speaking religions of the Son, some do articulate (e.g., Greek religion) positions isomorphic with Christianity and thus at least can be regarded as adumbrations of the religion of the Son.

84. If, in one sense, otherness is softened and the beyond brought near, in another sense, otherness is hardened and the beyond-character of the divine exacerbated (*GL2:*170).

85. See *Reason in History: A General Introduction to the Philosophy of History,* trans. Robert S. Hartman (Indianapolis: Bobbs Merrill Educational Publishing, 1953), p. 20.

86. Hegel's *The Philosophy of History* has, in effect, a fourfold not a triadic structuration of epochs. It moves from considerations of the Oriental World, to the Greek World, to the Roman World, and then to the German World. This fourfold scheme, as Robin Barnes has pointed out in *Prophecy and Gnosis* (pp. 48 ff) is a commonplace in Lutheran self-interpretation in the sixteenth and early seventeenth centuries. This scheme which continued to have currency in the eighteenth century is reprised by Hegel in *LPH.*

87. See *Reason in History,* p. 14, Hegel also correlates the Christian symbol of Providence with Anaxagoras's Nous as the archeoteleological ground of reality, though Hegel is focusing here on historical reality (ibid., p. 15). Philosophical-theological overdetermination is complete when Hegel invokes the Neoplatonic *anima mundi* as another philosophical correlative of Providence. A few pages further on, Hegel is speaking of the presence (providential) of the divine in history as a theodicy (p. 18).

88. See *La postérité,* p. 365.

89. For a good discussion of the mediation of Joachim by the radical Reformation, see Reeves, *Joachim of Fiore and the Prophetic Future,* pp. 136 ff, esp. 140–142. See also Barnes, *Prophecy and Gnosis,* pp. 22–23, 76–77.

90. As Barnes demonstrates so ably, Melanchthon in the sixteenth century and Gerhard in the seventeenth, often regarded as the stimulus and the apogee of scholasticism in Lutheran theology, were far from noneschatological. See *Prophecy and Gnosis,* pp. 106–107, 228–229.

91. In a text such as *Luther und Hegel,* Asendorf presupposes that contra his interpretation in and by Lutheran orthodoxy, Luther's thought is apocalyptic and eschatological through and through.

92. See Barnes, *Prophecy and Gnosis,* pp. 209 ff.

93. In addition to pointing to the heavily pneumatic and eschatological element in Boehme's thought, the controversalist, Frick, in his book *Grundliche Undersuchung Jacob Boehmens,* points to the theosophic features which identify it. These features, of course, themselves have a history, and Boehme is accused of being a follower of Paracelsus and Valentin Weigel.

94. Of course, there is more than one German Idealist influenced by Boehme. The case of Boehmian influence on Schelling is well established. For the relation between Boehme and Schelling, see Robert Brown's *The Later Schelling: The Influence of Boehme on the Works of 1809–15* (Lewisburg: Bucknell University Press, 1977) and Frederick Kile's *Die theologischen Grundlagen von Schellings Philosophie.*

95. Hegel avoids both the radical Pietist stance that was sectarian in essence and the more radical elements of the Enlightenment that tried to deal with erstwhile theological subject matters in a purely philosophical manner.

96. See Boehme, *The Way to Christ,* trans. Peter Erb (New York: Paulist Press, 1978), p. 161.

97. Boehme, *The Way to Christ,* pp. 158 ff.

98. Boehme consistently speaks of human freedom having an inalienable character. Indeed, one of his major texts, *De Electione Gratiae,* is intended to combat the doctrine of predestination that Boehme does not believe is consistent with the Christian message in general, the Lutheran message in particular.

99. Examples of such natural triads include noon, evening, morning; youth, maturity, old age.

100. Representative philosophers would include Bloch, Marcuse, Heidegger; representative theologians would include Moltmann and Pannenberg.

101. Though Boehme still is sufficiently influenced by the Eckhartian strain of thought so as to conceive of the experience of God in individualistic terms, his theology of history, elaborated in *Aurora* and in *Mysterium Magnum,* has a corporate dimension. Its concern is with the human community as a whole.

102. What identifies Boehme uniquely is the theosophic dimension, concerning which we will have more to say in chapter 6.

Chapter 6 The Third Narrative Epoch: The Inclusive Trinity

1. This position is represented by Albert Chapelle, Louis Dupré, Emil Fackenheim, Peter Hodgson, Quentin Lauer, and Michael Theunissen *inter alia.*

2. See esp. Louis Dupré, "The Absolute Spirit and the Religious Legitimation of Modernity" in *Hegels Logik der Philosophie,* ed. Dieter Henrich and Rolf-Peter Horstmann (Stuttgart: Klett-Cottal, 1984) (13th Hegel Congress), pp. 224–233; also Quentin Lauer, *Hegel's Concept of God,* pp. 265–272, 325.

3. The theodicy commitment in Hegel's thought has been recognized by generations of Hegelian commentators and critics. Left-wing Hegelianism openly acknowledged the fact and did everything in its power to escape its implications. In the twentieth century it has been perhaps the Frankfurt School in the shape of Adorno, Horkheimer, and Marcuse that has most clearly seen the theodicy implications of Hegelian philosophy and questioned it. Coming from a completely opposite direction, Barth also thinks it a point of importance in his reflection on Hegel in *Protestant Thought: From Rousseau to Ritschl,* trans. Brian Goleus (New York: Simon and Schuster, 1959), pp. 286, 304. Other authors who broach this issue include George Armstrong Kelly and George Seidel. See the former's *Idealism, Politics, and History: Sources of Hegelian Thought* (Cambridge: Cambridge University Press, 1969), p. 310.

4. Since Hegel's best known theodicy assertions occur in the context of his reflection on history, it is natural to locate Hegel's thought in the context of previous salvation history models. But if the canvas is extended beyond that of history, and Hegelian ontotheology as a whole is taken into consideration, then the nature of Hegel's theodicy commitment is seen to be more complex. When Hegel makes a theodicy appeal in *LPR 1* 1824 E 147, G 66, he seems to be speaking not simply of the divine march through history but of the encompassing narrative of the revelation of the divine within which the christological moment is decisive. Too often Hegel scholars focus on Hegelian theodicy as reducible to his view of divine providence (*Vorsehung*), ignoring both metaphysical and quasi-metaphysical justifications which are there in Hegelian texts, plus the inclusive narrative frame within which historical activity is inserted.

5. Dupré, "The Absolute Spirit," p. 225.

6. The pantheism dispute had already begun in Hegel's own day, and its presence is clearly visible in Hegel's denial of the charge in the *Enc* (#573). For a good discussion, see Jaeschke, *Reason in Religion,* pp. 362 ff. After his death the charge continued to be levelled against him by religious thinkers within the Protestant and Catholic traditions. For example, F. Ch. Baur in his great *Die christliche Lehre von der Dreieinigkeit* 3 vols. (Tübingen, 1841–1843), Vol. 3 p. 911, and Franz Staudenmaier in his *Darstellung und Kritik* repeat the pantheism charge that so irritated Hegel in his own time. In the twentieth century the accusation is resumed in Franz Grégoire's *Études hégéliennes* (pp. 162–166), though in this case with the qualification that Hegel's particular brand of pantheism is not Spinozist but evolutionist. However, scholars such as Chapelle, Lauer, and Williamson seriously question the legitimacy of such a label. See Chapelle, *Hegel et la religion,* vol. 2, p. 150, note 246; Lauer, *The Concept of God,*

pp. 242–283; Williamson, *Introduction to Hegel's Philosophy of Religion,* pp. 231–249.

7. See *Erring,* p. 70.

8. In *The Symbolism of Evil* (p. 327), Paul Ricoeur offers the suggestive hint that German Idealism reprises mythic modalities of thought, specifically theogonic mythic thought which he examined in his discussion of *Enuma Elish* (pp. 175–191). In Ricoeur's scheme, *Enuma Elish,* qua theogonic text, is an example of *second-order* symbolization, i.e., it introduces primary symbols into the complex network of narrative. Ricoeur does not concretely specify how German Idealism relates to mythic narrative, but, on the basis of what he says elsewhere, one seems justified in assuming that the refined theogonies of German Idealism are at least on a tertiary level of symbolization. They certainly logicize myth, a phenomenon also observable in Gnosticism. Two essays of Ricoeur are here especially important. Both are found in *The Conflict of Interpretations,* ed. Don Ihde (Evanston: Northwestern University Press, 1974), specifically, " 'Original Sin': A Study of Meaning" (pp. 269–286), and "The Hermeneutics of Symbols and Philosophical Reflection: 1" (pp. 287–314). See in the former, p. 273, where Ricoeur seems to suggest that *gnosis* moves beyond primary myth onto another level, yet does not issue in reason (which has a critical moment) but in "the most fantastic imposture of reason;" see in the latter, pp. 299, 312. On p. 312, Ricoeur suggests that Hegelian philosophy recapitulates on the level of speculation the tragic element of evil reprised by Gnosticism.

9. A clue to the 'pastness' of being, and yet at the same time its preservation in the *divine present,* is provided in Hegel's very interesting discussion of the relation of *Wesen* and *gewesen* in *Enc* #112 *zu.* In the passage, the first thing to observe is that *gewesen* does not have temporal connotation. After all, the discourse of Essence (*Wesen*) is a discourse of an intradivine reality that, in principal is eternal. The pastness is narrative, yet nontemporal, and points to *Begriff* or *Idee* as the *present,* the consummating moment of divine appropriation, recollection, and self-presence. Secondly, the present and past of *Begriff* and *Wesen* belong to the realm of *logos endiathetos.* They establish the formal ground of past and present in divine self-development as a whole; they do not represent the supreme instances of *past* and *present.* The supreme instance of *present* is realized in the Holy Spirit and its subsumption by the "Immanent Trinity;" the supreme instance of *past* is the whole created arena of nature and finite spirit. It is tempting here to suggest the converse of White's point that Schelling developed under the influence of the post-*PS* Hegel, i.e., that Hegel shows signs here of knowledge of Schelling's attempt in *Die Weltalter* to construe ontotheological development in nontemporal yet narrative categories of past, present, and future. Noticeably, however, on the ontotheological front, Hegel never invokes the future, providing eloquent testimony to Heidegger's hypothesis that in Hegel one witnesses the priority of the present as presence (*Anwesen*).

10. See Falk Wagner, *Der Gedanke der Persönlichkeit Gottes bei Fichte und Hegel* (Gütersloh: Mohn, 1971), pp. 273–280.

11. Jaeschke, "Absolute Idee," pp. 406–8; see also Klaus Düsing, *Das Problem der Subjektivität in Hegels Logik. Hegel Studien* Beiheft 15 (Bonn: Bouvier, 1976).

12. See esp. Erik Schmidt, *Hegels Lehre von Gott,* pp. 255–256; Williamson, *Introduction to Hegel's Philosophy of Religion,* pp. 251–294, esp. pp. 251–268.

13. In addition to those commentators cited in note 6 above, see Peter Hodgson's essay on Hegel in *Nineteenth Century Religious Thought in the West* Vol. 1, ed. Ninian Smart, John Clayton, Patrick Sherry, and Steven T. Katz (Cambridge: Cambridge University Press, 1985), pp. 81–121, esp. pp. 85, 89.

14. This is a real danger and not a spurious one given that Process Theology self-consciously adopts the label *panentheism.* The application of the label to Hegelian ontotheology can thus function as a shortcut in which a fundamental similarity between Hegelian ontotheology and Process Theology can be taken for granted. Any relation between Process Theology and Hegelian ontotheology needs to be *argued.* Such argument has become more conspicuous in recent years. See George R. Lucas, Jr., *Two Views of Freedom in Process Thought* (Missoula: Scholars Press, 1979); also *Hegel and Whitehead: Contemporary Perspectives on Systematic Philosophy,* ed. George R. Lucas (Albany, N.Y.: SUNY Press, 1986).

15. Erik Schmidt in *Hegels Lehre von Gott,* pp. 154–156, suggests this addition, while Iljin suggests that Hegelian ontotheology can be only misunderstood without it.

16. The first move within the Hegelian system, i.e., from Being and Nothing to Becoming, seems to hand the laurel to Heraclitus, but it should be reminded that *Werden,* in turn, is a presupposition of *Dasein* or determinate being. That *Werden,* even at the earliest stage of ontotheological development, implies *Dasein* suggests that Heraclitus is ultimately not a victorious presence. The closest a commentator comes to a Heraclitean interpretation of Hegelian ontotheology as a whole, Hegelian logic in particular, is Marcuse's *Hegel's Ontology and the Theory of Historicity,* trans. Seyla Benhabib (Cambridge, Mass: MIT Press, 1987), chaps. 2–5.

17. The list would include Thomas J. Altizer's "History as Apocalypse" in *Deconstruction and Theology* (New York: Crossroads, 1982), pp. 147–177, esp. pp. 151–153, 163; G. A. Kelly, *Idealism, Politics, and History,* pp. 293–323. The classic statement of the apocalypse thesis is made by Löwith and is repeated with little modification by Voegelin. That Derrida presumes the whole Western ontotheological tradition to be apocalypse in substance is suggested throughout his oeuvre, and deconstruction afficionados have brought this insight to bear upon Hegel. See also Mark Taylor, "Text and Textuality," *Semeia* 40, pp. 21–31, esp. 21–23.

18. See *From Enlightenment to Revolution,* pp. 240–320.

19. Karl Löwith, *From Hegel to Nietzsche,* pp. 31–51.

20. The most influential example of genre investigation that is not centrally focused upon content—though this does not imply that content is ignored—is provided by the work of J. J. Collins. His most noteworthy book to date is perhaps *Apocalypse: Morphology of a Genre, Semeia* 14 (Missoula: Scholars Press, 1979). While the force of Collin's genre methodology, which looks at literary marks as well as content, cannot be denied, genre depiction and distinction here is fundamentally predicated upon theological content rather than on the literary mould privileging the ascent or lack of ascent of a privileged seer into the beyond.

21. See H. S. Harris, *Towards the Sunlight,* pp. 91–92.

22. D. H. Lawrence, *Apocalypse and the Writings on Revelation,* ed. Mara Kalnins (Cambridge and New York: Cambridge University Press, 1980), p. 66.

23. On the basis of scriptural exegesis Bengel was prepared to actually provide a date for the eschaton, i.e., 1834. *Revelation* was for Bengel an inspired text portending full future disclosure of the reign of God. In the meantime, the developmental pattern of history, its times and periods, is unveiled. In his "Sixty Practical Addresses on the Apocalypse" Bengel paints a disturbing picture of the world which seems to mirror in its fundamentals Hegel's later diagnosis. There is a sense of a lack of theological probity, a loss of spirit, the reduction of religion to morality, reason, or just the opposite, i.e., fanaticism. For an excellent account of Bengel's apocalyptic and his reading of *Revelation,* see John Christian, Frederick Burk, *A Memoir of the Life and Writings of John Albert Bengel,* trans. Robert Francis Walker, 1842, chaps. vi–ix, pp. 282–350. For a good account of Bengel as a background to Hegel, see Dickey, *Hegel,* pp. 77–112.

24. David Walsh, "The Historical Dialectic of Spirit. Jacob Boehme's Influence on Hegel" in *History and System,* p. 33, note 21; James Yerkes, *The Christology of Hegel,* pp. 221 ff.

25. See *LPR 3* E 159, note 251.

26. A Joachim scholar of the calibre of Marjorie Reeves has refused the application of apocalypse or apocalyptic title to the works of Joachim, contending that they articulate less an apocalypse or apocalyptic vision than a philosophy of history. Reeves is clearly right in what she wishes to deny, i.e., exact parity in every respect between the work of Joachim and a text such as *Revelation.* Relative to the latter text, the texts of Joachim (1) are clearly more self-conscious and reflective, and (2) constitute less the creation of new apocalypse texts than both hermeneutic excavation and application of canonic apocalypse texts. Still one could grant the above distinctions without necessarily drawing Reeves's conclusion. One could suggest, in fact, that Joachim creates,

or more accurately à la Bernard McGinn, develops, a new type of apocalypse, that holds on to much of the basic content of what might be referred to as primary apocalypse texts, but remains resolutely hermeneutical (and self-consciously so) in character.

27. The visionary revelatory component is underscored by Christopher Rowland in *The Open Heaven: A Study of Apocalypse in Judaism and Early Christianity* (New York: Crossroads, 1982), pp. 10–13. When I say "at a limit hermeneutical," I have particularly in mind apocalypses of a secondary reflective type, e.g., Joachim, but no absolute exclusion of primary apocalypses is thereby implied. As is well-known, a normative Christian apocalypse text such as *Revelation* is dependent upon the production of previous apocalypse literature for many of its basic themes, ideas, and symbols. It too, therefore, is hermeneutical and represents something of an application of old texts to a new situation.

28. Like another apocalypse scholar, i.e., Michael Stone, Rowland recognizes that apocalypses can have a wealth of material. Nevertheless, he insists on the primacy of the historical and eschatological element in the Judeo-Christian field. See Rowland, *Open Heaven,* p. 26, pp. 131 ff; Stone, "New Light on the Third Century" and "Enoch and Apocalyptic Origins," in *Visionaries and their Apocalypses,* ed. Paul D. Hanson (Philadelphia and London: Fortress Press and SPCK, 1983), pp. 85–100. In contrast to Rowland, Stone insists that the speculative rather than eschatological element is at the core of apocalypse.

29. This point is made both by Löwith in *From Hegel to Nietzsche,* p. 39, and Yerkes in *The Christology of Hegel,* pp. 221 ff. The most developed discussion of this point is to found in Daniel Berthold-Bond, *Hegel's Grand Synthesis: A Study in Being, Thought, and History* (Albany, NY: SUNY Press, 1989).

30. 'Eternity' seems to function not in one but in three ways in Hegel. Ascribed to the immanent sphere in the two Logics or in *LPR* (see *LPR 3* 1824 E 187, G 121), eternity does seem to bear the connotation of timelessness, even if the process-character of the immanent sphere is engaged in a deconstruction of this timelessness. But there are two other kinds of ascription in Hegel. In a sense, Hegel, in regarding the Holy Spirit as the transfiguration of time and the milieu of the *parousia,* suggests that eternity is an ascription proper to the last moment of divine history. The third viable candidate for ascription is the immanent milieu of "Immanent Trinity", understood not as in the first case in its proleptic modality but in its analeptic modality. Here eternity means more than the *kairos* of Holy Spirit, since the "Immanent Trinity" is transcendent with respect to time and history and more than the immanent divine in its proleptic modality, since it involves the recollection of historical and kairotic experience.

31. I am thinking here of Pannenberg and Schlitt who came in for discussion in chap. 2, sect. 2.3. Both have a point in suggesting that Hegel may have been guilty of projecting a finite model of becoming onto the divine. But this is not

to be confused with the suggestion that Hegel reduces the divine in any *direct* way to time and history. Hegel clearly does no such thing.

32. Joachim, as with Bengel after him, did not only expect the imminent end of the old aeon, he was prepared to give a date. By contrast, in Boehme while the eschaton is perceived to be nigh, no date is provided, Boehme suggesting in his letters that the feeling of the eschaton's nearness is not further specifiable. Boehme denies in particular that scriptural exegesis will provide an exact date.

33. Pansophistic is the adjectival form of the noun *pansophism,* literally meaning 'knowledge of all things.' Even if Boehme had not used the adjective to describe his own work—and he does so in a text which goes under the title of *Mysterium Pansophicum*—it would faithfully capture the encyclopedic span of his work. It is likely that Boehme's pansophistic ambitions and the unmodern confidence that such a project is possible is influenced by the no less immodest ambition of Alchemy, particularly in the shape of Parcelsus with whose work Boehme shows himself familiar.

34. See chap. 2, sect. 2.3 above.

35. Boehme frequently uses this locution in major texts like *Mysterium Magnum,* etc. In doing so, Boehme serves as a classic example in the Western tradition of that deformation Heidegger calls ontotheology.

36. Alexander Koyré, *La philosophie de Jacob Boehme,* p. 324.

37. For instance, it seems to me that the case can be successfully argued that, whatever the Joachimite evocation in the 'ages of the world' in the post-Idealist Schelling, the sense more nearly recapitulates the Boehmian noneconomic view of the elaboration of the divine. For a lucid and comprehensive account of the relation of Boehme and the later Schelling, see R. F. Brown's *The Later Philosophy of Schelling: The Influence of Boehme on Schelling* (1809–1815) (Lewisburg, PA.: Bucknell University Press, 1976). *Die Weltalter* is but a fragment of the project proposed by Schelling: the account of the divine narrative that concerned past, present, and future of the divine. No more than Hegel in the Logic, Schelling does not intend past to be a temporal indicator. For Schelling the past—this is all that is completed in *Die Weltalter*—is the self-constitution of the divine in eternity as the ground of manifestation in creation and time (i.e., the present), the eschatological fulfillment of creation and time and through this fulfillment of the divine (i.e., the future).

38. Though the sequel will find it necessary to correct some stereotypes of Gnosticism, including the view that a temporal-historical dimension never positively intrudes into Gnostic revelation texts, nevertheless, in broad respects, Gnostic tests, unlike those of the mainline Judeo-Christian tradition, do, indeed, evidence considerable hostility to time.

39. See, for example, *The Apocalypse of Adam* and the *Apocalypse of Philip* in the Nag Hammadi Library.

40. Whatever the literary genre, whether that of gospel, revelation dialogue, etc., at some point in a Gnostic text there is a revelation from beyond involving a redeeming revelatory figure and a seer who is redeemed. Of course, in addition to the seer, a special group of human beings with seer-like capacity are also pointed to as redeemable.

41. Eric Voegelin blends the categories of apocalypse and gnosis fairly freely in *From Enlightenment to Revolution*, pp. 240–302.

42. For a good account of Hegel's criticism of Kant's prescription for peace and his positive estimation of the possible effects of war, see Shlomo Avineri's *Hegel's Theory of the Modern State* (Cambridge: Cambridge University Press, 1972), pp. 194–207.

43. See Shlomo Avineri, *Hegel's Theory of the Modern State*, p. 206.

44. Hegel here brings his distinction of *Erscheinung-Schein*, articulated on the level of the logic (Essence), into play. In *Escheinung* the phenomenon bears a genuine and intrinsic relation to the essence and is its manifestation (see *Enc* #131 + *zu*). In the case of *Schein*, this is not so. See my discussion of *Schein* and *Erscheinung* in the general context of creation in chap. 3, sect. 3.1.

45. In *Hegel's Theory of the Modern State*, Avineri goes to some pains to point out that (1) Hegel never confuses the *Dasein* of a phenomenon with its *Wirklichkeit*. The mere *being-there* of a phenomenon is not sufficient to present its intelligibility and certainly not its in-principle unsurpassability. (2) In this regard, it is not unimportant that Hegel moves from the rational to the real rather than from the real to the rational (pp. 176–177). The upshot of this is that the picture of Hegel articulating a reactionary principle is a legend. Paul Lakeland in his *The Politics of Salvation: The Hegelian Idea of the State* (Albany, NY: SUNY Press, 1984) offers a reinforcing estimate.

46. An ought without possible instantiation is in the same situation as the Kantian *Ding-an-sich*. It is not an element of discourse as the articulation of the meaningful and true.

47. See Merleau Ponty, *Signs*, trans. Richard C. McCleary (Evanston: Northwestern University Press, 1969), p. 4.

48. See Emmanuel Levinas, *Totality and Infinity: An Essay on Exteriority*, trans. Alphonso Lingis (Pittsburgh: Duquesne University Press, 1969), preface, pp. 21–30; Adorno, *Negative Dialectics*, pp. 334 ff, esp. p. 337; also pp. 320, 328.

49. Adorno, *Negative Dialectics*, p. 357.

50. Adorno, *Negative Dialectics*, p. 320. Here Adorno is dependent on Walter Benjamin.

51. See Ernst Bloch, *Subjekt-Objekt,* pp. 458–460.

52. I am speaking here of Kant's 1791 essay "On the Failure of all Philosophical Essays in Theodicy." The actual wording of the contrast is that of doctrinal theodicy and authentic theodicy. The raison d'être of any theodicy is the felt contradiction between the demands of moral reason and one's actual experience of the world. In a doctrinal theodicy, reason exonerates God by offering an explanation as to why there is a disproportion between the ideal, perfect state of affairs and the actual state of affairs. An authentic theodicy, by contrast, is a theodicy which does not operate on the level of knowledge as such but on the level of belief or hope in divine providence. For a good discussion of Kant's theodicy essay, see James Collins, *The Emergence,* pp. 197–211.

53. Kant is of the opinion that the experiential attitude of authentic theodicy is embodied by Job. The contrast between 'in spite of' and 'because of' is borrowed essentially from Paul Ricoeur who takes the side of Job and Kant against Hegel concerning the possibility of an authentic theodicy. Two Ricoeur essays are particularly important here, first, his "Freedom in the Light of Hope" in *Essays on Biblical Interpretation* (Philadelphia: Fortress Press, 1980), pp. 155–181. In this essay Ricoeur, like Adorno, validates Kantian hope over Hegelian knowledge. Second, there is Ricoeur's important essay, "Evil, a Challenge to Philosophy and Theology" in *JAAR* 1985, Vol. LIII, No. 4, pp. 631–648. See esp. pp. 638–639 on Job (p. 647) where Ricoeur avails of the category of in spite of, and pp. 642–643, where on Joban and Kantian grounds, the rational theodicy (I would say narrative theodicy) of Hegel is rejected. See also his essay "The Hermeneutics of Symbols 1" in *The Conflict of Interpretations,* pp. 287–314, esp. pp. 313–314, where the Joban 'in spite of' invoked against the dialectical necessity of Hegel.

54. See Michel Desplant, *Kant on History* (Montreal and London: Queen's University Press, McGill, 1973).

55. Hegel is willing to affirm both the 'goodness' and 'power' of God. The former is given notice in *SL* when Hegel discussing the Idea beings in the *Idea of the Good;* the latter is pivotal in these important paragraphs in the *Enc* that introduce *The Philosophy of Mind,* i.e., #378–386 + *Zusatzen.*

56. (1) In the *Ethics* Spinoza elaborates an absolutely necessarian theodicy or a theodicy of necessity. There is no gap between the way things are, can be, or ought to be. The principle of *Realitas* or divine expressiveness in Bk. 1, Prop. 11 is the background for Spinoza's ultimate positing of freedom and necessity in God (Bk. 1, Prop. 33) and the identity of power, essence, and act (Bk. 1, Prop. 34). (2) Though Spinoza does express in the *Ethics* that the world seems otherwise than it truly is when seen from a partial perspective, it is in his letters that he most clearly condemns the partial perspective for insinuating the existence of a reality that is really not there (Letters 32, 34, 36 to Blyenbergh,or in A. Wolf's edition of the *Correspondences* 19, 21, 23). (3) In the letters to Blyen-

bergh Spinoza, is asserting the nonbeing of evil, at once validates and goes beyond the privation thesis of Scholasticism that develops upon Augustine's adoption of the view from Plotinus. On the one hand, evil is privative insofar as it has no positive reality. On the other hand, to the extent to which privation suggests an absence of what might be there or ought to be there, Spinoza recommends that 'privation' language be replaced by 'negation' language which avoids suggesting a surplus of possibility over actuality.

57. See Levinas, *Totality and Infinity,* passim; Adorno, *Negative Dialectics,* pp. 324 ff.

58. In Irenaeus's *Adversus Haeresis,* Bks. 2–5.

59. The axial nature of the incarnational event is underscored by Irenaeus in Bk. 3 of *Adversus Haeresis,* chap. 17.

60. For a remarkable anticipation of Hegelian necessarian theodicy, see *Enneads* 2.9.7 where Plotinus discusses the ALL pervaded by the *World Soul.* Interestingly in his essay "The Hermeneutics of Symbols 1," it is precisely Spinoza and Plotinus with whom Ricoeur associated Hegel. See *The Conflict of Interpretations,* pp. 312–313.

61. For an example of a position characteristic of Augustine's anti-Pelagian period, see *The City of God,* Bk. XXI.

62. The Redeemer/Redeemed *mythos* of Gnosticism implies an invalidation of the absolute power of God. This Gnostic position was rejected by a mainline Christian theologian such as Irenaeus at the end of the second century and Augustine in the late fourth century, both of whom understood absolute power to be an axiom of Christian faith.

63. *The Critique of Judgment* does not offer a speculative or constitutive teleology. Rather, it suggests that it is meaningful to construe the world *as if* it were teleologically constituted. Obviously, from Hegel's point of view, teleology has more than an *as if* character.

64. See Mark Taylor, "Itinerarium Mentis in Deum: Hegel's Proofs of God's Existence," in *The Journal of Religion,* vol. 57 (1977), pp. 211–231, esp. pp. 224–230.

Chapter 7 Representation and Concept: Speculative Rewriting

1. See Theodore Geraets, "The End of the History of Religions Grasped in Thought," in *Hegel Studien,* Band 24, 1989, pp. 55–77, esp. 62–65.

2. See Hayden White, "The Value of Narrativity in the Representation of Reality," in *On Narrative,* ed. W. J. T. Mitchell (Chicago and London: University of Chicago Press, 1980), pp. 1–24. In an important note, White writes: "The

words "narrative," "narration," "to narrate," and so on are derived from the Latin *gnarus* ("knowing," "acquaintance with," "expert," "skillful," and so forth) and *narro* ("relate," "tell") from the Sanskrit word *gnâ*" (p. 1).

3. For a good account of this dechronologizing tendency in structuralism, see Paul Ricoeur, *Time and Narrative,* Vol. 2, trans Kathleen Mclaughlin and David Pellauer (London and Chicago: Chicago University Press, 1985), pp. 29–60.

4. See Marcuse's *Hegel's Ontology and Theory of Historicity.* Of course, Kojève's *Introduction to the Reading of Hegel* also offers an analysis of Hegel that stresses the temporal. However, Kojève does admit that Hegel succumbs finally to the lure of the transtemporal.

5. For the notions of erasure of metaphor that betrays its traces beneath the pure, presuppositionless surface of philosophy, see Derrida's essay "White Mythology," in *Margins of Philosophy,* pp. 207–271, esp. 210–211, 225–226, 268–71. White Mythology is the mythology of unmarked space of discourse.

6. The validation of local narratives takes different forms. The theologians Stanley Hauerwas and George Lindbeck espouse the value of local narratives, though arguably Lindbeck does not renounce the idea of metanarrative, indeed, the Christian metanarrative, altogether. The philosopher-theologian Jeffrey Stoudt also belongs to this group. In some moods, for example in *After Virtue,* Alasdair MacIntyre heads in this direction. Also many forms of feminism suggest the crucial importance of the concreteness and situatedness of story regarded not only as the purveyor of meaning but indispensable in the struggle to be human. From another point of view, one could construe the quintessential postmodern Michel Foucault as supporting the local narrative alternative to the moribund and imperialistic enterprise of metanarrative.

7. These include Falk Wagner. See his *Der Gedanke der Persönlichkeit Gottes bei Fichte und Hegel,* pp. 185–200.

8. This position is adopted by Dupré and Fackenheim. See Dupré, "Hegel's Religion as Representation," in *Dubious Heritage,* pp. 53–73; Fackenheim, *The Religious Dimension of Hegel's Thought,* pp. 160–215. See also Rob Devos, "The Significance of Manifest Religion in the Phenomenology," in *Hegel on the Ethical Life, Religion, and Philosophy (1793–1807),* ed. A. Wylleman (Leuven, Belgium, Dordrecht, Netherlands: Leuven University Press, Kluver Academy Publishers, 1985), pp. 195–229. Devos explicitly challenges the kind of position advocated by Wagner.

9. Ricoeur makes an important distinction in *The Symbolism of Evil* between a species of demythologization that respects the nonredundancy of the symbolic mode of discourse, while yet finding it imperative to attempt partial translation, and a mode of demythologization that presumes the symbolic mode to be redundant given the possibility of an exhaustive conceptual translation.

For a good account of these alternatives as they relate to religious discourse, see Ricoeur's essay "Preface to Bultmann," in *Essays in Interpretation,* trans. Lewis S. Mudge (Philadelphia: Fortress Press, 1980), pp. 49–72, esp. 57–59. Ricoeur reads Hegel's account of the relation between *Vorstellung* and *Begriff* to straddle the positive and negative attitude toward symbol. See his "The Status of *Vorstellung* in Hegel's Philosophy of Religion," in *Meaning, Truth, and God,* ed. Leroy S. Rouner (Notre Dame: Notre Dame University Press, 1982), pp. 70–88.

10. Commentators aware of the originality of Hegel's proposal include Daniel Cook, *Language in the Philosophy of Hegel* (The Hague: Mouton and Co., 1973), pp. 136–148; David Lamb, *Hegel: From Foundation to System* (The Hague: Marinus Nijfoff, 1980), pp. 186–196; Nicholas Lobkowicz, "Substance and Reflection: Aristotle and Hegel," in *Review of Metaphysics,* 43 (September, 1989), pp. 27–46. All three contend that Hegel subverts the Aristotelian view of the relation of subject and predicate. It is perhaps only Lobkowicz who is aware of the extent to which Hegel also surpasses the Kantian position on the relation of subject and predicate.

11. See my discussion of Hegel's critique of the ontological argument at the end of chap. 1.

12. That Christianity constitutes a tensional symbolic field is explicit in both *LPR* and *Enc.* In *LPR* this gets addressed in two different ways. In *LPR 3* the emphasis is on the increasing noetic transparency of Christianity as this develops historically. In *LPR 1* the emphasis is more normative and criteriological: Hegel wishes to suggest a definition of Christianity on the basis of which he can judge the merits of various traditional and contemporary proposals. Of course, he understands his normative proposal to explicate the meaning and truth of Christianity as found in the gospels and the letters of Paul and unpacked over history. As we pointed out in chap. 1, *Enc* is no less explicit in advocating a normative proposal that judges other determinations as being 'thoughtless' either because of an excess of rationalism or because of the uncritical nature of faith. (In *Enc* by contrast with *LPR* the kind of faith disavowed is ahistorical.) The tensional field of religion in general is, of course, figured in *LPR 2-LPR 3.* As in the case of *PS,* the various religions are hierarchically arranged according to their degree of noetic luminosity, specifically the degree to which they comprehend the intervolvement of the divine and the human and the presence of the divine in the process of cognition. Though *Enc* does point to the tensional field of religion, it does not treat it in detail.

13. See also *LPR 1* 1824 E 331, G 235.

14. See also *SL E* 664–704; also *LHP* or *GL 18:* 401–423, esp. 401–409.

15. On the basis of both Hegel's early and mature characterizations of Judaism, one could say that this is the Judaic tendency in Christianity. Early es-

says such as "The Spirit of Christianity and its Fate" clearly suggest that Christianity is in need of sloughing off its Jewish origins. The Jewish picture of both the divine itself and the divine-human relation is essentially unchristian as far as Hegel is concerned. If the estimate of Judaism is considerably higher in *LPR 2,* still the divine is construed voluntaristically and the relation between the divine and human as extrinsic.

16. By voluntarism in the strict sense, I mean an activity of will that is not normed by wisdom or rationality. That the later positive philosophy of Schelling exemplifies a voluntarism of this stripe would be agreed on by most critics and commentators. It is, of course, the case, however, that texts such as *The Philosophy of Revelation* (1838) inherit an uncoupling that dates back at least to the *Freedom* essay (1809). To the extent to which the will-reason connection is undergirded by the freedom-necessity connection, it is possible to set an even earlier date for the emergence of unrestricted ontotheological voluntarism. With respect to this emergence, see especially Alan White, *Absolute Knowledge,* pp. 127–129; Robert Brown, *The Later Philosophy of Schelling,* pp. 107–110.

17. In charting the increasingly adequate forms of syllogism, from qualitive to disjunctive syllogism, Hegel makes it clear that the doctrine of the syllogism, which achieves its realization in the Idea, is not reductively formal-logical, as the followers of Aristotle—and admittedly Aristotle himself on occasions—would have it. In *Enc* #187, however, Hegel argues that this betrays Aristotle's more metaphysical and epistemological intentions. Moreover, Hegel thinks it not inappropriate to suggest that properly understood the syllogism, not only accidentally meets with a theological interpretation (often deficient according to him in *Enc* #182), but must be interpreted theologically (#566–574). It makes, of course, a considerable difference whether syllogism is seen in the ambit of reason or understanding. Within the pale of *Verstand,* syllogism can be only formal-logical, not materially ontotheological.

18. In suggesting that one category does not determine another category without being recursively determined by it, Hegel seems to undermine the integrity of all ground-consequent relations. In doing so, he could be thought to pull the rug from under any narrative reading of categorical determination. For it might seem that determinate ground-consequent relations are the minimal requirement on the logical level for the protection of something like an ordered series. Reciprocal determination functions in two different ways in Hegelian logic. On the one hand, it itself makes a material categorical appearance in the context of Hegel's discussion of Essence; on the other, it may be thought of as existing on a metalevel. On this level, reciprocal determination—a notion that achieved a constitutive expression Fichte's *Science of Knowledge* (Part A)—means different things in the different categorical environments of Being, Essence, and Concept.

19. While it is true that neither *Enc* #233–235 nor #45 ff explicitly focus on the self-constitution of the divine, there is no absence of theological evocation. This is true especially of *Enc* #234, where Hegel shows a general concern to define will in such a way as to avoid a unteleological view of intention and action. Specifically, Hegel offers the view of divine providence as a theological counterpoint to a view of will, identified with Kant and Fichte, that lacks intrinsic meaning because it is not narrative in the teleological sense that Hegel can affirm. See our discussion of narrative in chap. 1, sect. 1.2.

20. A popular biblical or biblicist view, which would uncritically hold to a decisionism as an intrinsic element of the picture of the divine, is rejected as being at best misleading. Two points are involved. (1) To the extent to which the confessional traditions, the Lutheran tradition in particular, seem to accept such a view, Hegel thinks they have to be outrightly rejected. Within the Christian tradition such rejection, however, need not be an original event. Hegel presumes that there are numerous precedents in the ontotheological tradition of just such beneficent rejection. (2) To the extent that scripture actually seems to suggest such a reading, logically speaking, there are two options, i.e., outright rejection of scripture or a nonliteral hermeneutic. Hegel tends to prefer the latter alternative. Hegel, of course, also rejects nonbiblical forms of decisionism or voluntarism that mark much of the ontotheological tradition. The form with which Hegel was most familiar was, plausibly, the Cartesian variety strenously resisted in Spinoza's *Ethics,* namely, the view that truth is dependent upon divine willing.

21. This point is an important one in Yerkes' *The Christology of Hegel.* See also Dupré, "Hegel's Religion as Representation," in *Dubious Heritage,* pp. 58–59.

22. See Schlitt, *Hegel's Trinitarian Claim,* p. 96.

23. See *Letters,* p. 43.

24. In placing at the center of his investigation the ontological question, "why is there something rather than nothing?" Schelling not only gets the approval of Heidegger and Jaspers but, in effect, provides a definition of the nature of mystery. See Karl Jaspers, *Schelling* (Munich: R. Piper & Co, 1955), p. 124. Heidegger also reads Schelling's text as if it were primarily an ontological document. See his *Schelling's Treatise on the Essence of Human Freedom,* trans. Joan Stambaugh (Athens, Ohio: Ohio University Press, 1985).

25. Hegel's redefinition of necessity such that it is no longer the contrary of freedom has an extensive prehistory in the context of German Romanticism and Idealism and, in particular, in the context of Romantic and Idealist reading of Spinoza. Schiller's aesthetic reflections also represented a vista in which the mutual exclusiveness of freedom and necessity could come to be more generally and foundationally challenged. In his *Aesthetic Letters,* Schiller suggested that the work of art represented the paradoxical coincidence of freedom

and necessity, thus showing a way beyond Kant's absolute dualism. Inspired by Schiller, but desiring a more systematic protocol, the early Schelling was mindful of the philosophical support provided by Spinoza's identification of necessity and freedom for his own transcendental program. Hegel's view is, therefore, overdetermined. In his logical works, it is fairly safe to assume that Spinoza's definition is proving determinative.

26. Hegel shares a quintessential Spinozist anxiety. When Descartes suggested that, on pain of becoming subject to destiny or Styx, God's will would have to underwrite the eternal truths of reason, Spinoza responded by rejecting the claim both on theological grounds and on the grounds that it meant the abdication of the task of science. In his view the latter was possible only if the divine could not contradict the truths of reason. In allowing the possibility of such contradiction, Descartes, as Gilson among others has pointed out, continued the tradition of theological voluntarism that marked the nominalist period.

27. In the *Meditations,* Descartes departs from a view he earlier held and makes a number of important distinctions: imagination differs completely from understanding; and will is not simply a function of understanding. Judgment is, in fact, an *aliud amplius* over and beyond the reception of ideas. These dichotomies in turn point to a fateful positive connection between will and imagination that Spinoza himself fails to context. Hegel wishes to contest both Cartesian disjunctions and put into question the Cartesian conjunction. When I speak here of Hegel contesting the specifically Kantian dissociation of reason and will, I am speaking of will as *Willkür,* not *Wille* of the Second Critique which indeed is intrinsically connected with reason—though consistently from Hegel's vantage point in a purely formal way. *Willkür* is primordial in Kant and, at the very least, nonrational. It is *Willkür* that is responsible for the adoption of perverse (nonrational) maxims, as well as nonperverse (rational) maxims.

28. As Hegel demonstrates in *Enc* #445 ff, he agrees with the fundamental posture of *The Science of Knowledge* whereby Act is considered to be the coincidence of willing and knowing. From Hegel's point of view, this coincidence is both confirmed and denied in Fichte's linking of theory and practice. It is denied insofar as practice, which involves infinite approximation to a goal, at once turns out to be not so much the complement as the supplement of theory and to involve a more intimate relation with will.

29. See Chapelle, *Hegel et la religion,* vol. 2, pp. 44–45.

30. The position of the superiority of philosophical over religious mode of construal is expressed more unequivocally in the *Ethics.* In the *Tractatus* (chap. 13), by comparison, while Spinoza still thinks of religion or faith as, representing from a cognitive point of view, a lower order of knowledge, he is more anxious to validate religion on its own terms both as a form of prophecy and a form of praxis.

31. In Elwes' translation, see letters 58 and 60. In both letters Spinoza makes the point that it is chance and necessity that are contraries. For specific references, see *Benedict de Spinoza: On the Improvement of the Understanding, the Ethics, Correspondences,* trans. R.H.M. Elwes (New York: Dover Publications, Inc, 1955), pp. 381, 385.

32. Within a deconstructionist framework Spinoza would have to be regarded as thoroughly logocentric. Discourse, as *scientia,* is possible if and only if a divine transcendental signified guarantees the integrity of the semiotic system. But the transcendental signified functions only as a necessary, and not a sufficient, condition of *scientia.* Science in the full and proper sense is guaranteed only when one adopts the right view of the divine or transcendental signified. Adopting the right view makes the semiotic system truly semantic.

33. Perhaps the clearest expression of Leibniz's antivoluntarism is to be found in his *Discourse on Metaphysics.* Three consequences of Cartesian theological voluntarism particularly concern him: (1) the de-absolutization of the eternal truths of metaphysics and geometry that follows from their dependence upon divine will; (2) the endangering of the picture of God as being essentially good and just that arises when divine goodness and justice are made posterior to divine will; and (3) the evaporating of the meaning of the world that ceases to be something like an symbolic expression of the divine and more like a sign or cipher.

34. Leibniz is moved by the old question of the *Eutyphro:* whether things are good because God wills them or God wills them because they are good. His *Discourse on Metaphysics* can be read as deciding that divine will is regulated by divine wisdom. While the *Theodicy* does not backtrack on this position, it does avail of a language of choice which shows divine will as constrained by wisdom and not as penetrated by it. Hegel wishes to conceive the relation in intrinsic, rather than extrinsic, terms.

35. See Spinoza, *Ethics,* Bk 2, Props. 40–42 where Spinoza talks about "the first kind of knowledge." This form of knowledge is deficient because it lacks adequacy and certitude. Thus, this form of knowledge remains outside the pale of truth. Indeed, this form of knowledge is the source of error and falsity. Moreover, this form of knowledge is explicitly associated with will and imagination.

36. This point is seen clearly by Chapelle. See *Hegel et la religion,* vol. 2, pp. 198–208.

37. Whatever its differences from the *Freedom* essay (1809) and *The Ages of the World* (1815), Schelling's *Philosophy of Revelation* is mythopoetic. Mythopoesis relates the becoming of the divine from the point of view of theogonic process. The divine has a narrative structure, having a narrative alpha in an undifferentiated mode of being open to the adventure of becoming and a narrative omega in determinate divine selfhood that emerges from exile. Thus anaclasis and synclasis are built into Schellingian theogony. Prolepsis and analepsis

also mark Schelling's mythopoetic depiction: indeterminate freedom is freedom for self-determination which, when realized, recollects the stages of its development as its indispensable conditions. One commentator who clearly realizes the narrative character of the divine in the later Schelling is M. Maesschalck. See his *L'Anthropologie politique et religieuse de Schelling* (Paris and Leuven: Vrin and B. P. 41, 1991), esp. pp. 171–191.

38. As drawn explicitly by Schelling, the contrast between positive and negative philosophy is focused in the difference between an ontotheology of the actual and an ontotheology of the possible. Whereas the latter admits of a logico-conceptual articulation, the former is best captured in a transcendent realist narrative discourse. In making a contrast that in principle does not spare his own earlier work, Schelling's real energy is spent critiquing the Hegelian system. This system is, he opines, logico-conceptual in the extreme, with the basic mark of this deficiency being its reliance on necessity. In contradistinction, positive philosophy is a philosophy of freedom. In *Philosophy of Revelation* and in other later texts Schelling puts the accent on the fundamentally irrational character of an ontotheology of freedom wherein divine manifestation seems almost accidental. Yet, in the final analysis, the difference between Hegel and the later Schelling is somewhat more subtle. For all his emphasis on accident, Schelling insists on the teleological drive of divine manifestation through which personality is realized in God. In so doing, Schelling does more than narrate the divine; he suggests that narrativity is a basic, indeed, the basic property of the divine. One can see the narrative operations of anaclasis and synclasis, prolepsis and analepsis in operation. Schelling's real line of demarcation is that he insists that one go no further. The further denarratization that constitutes logicization has to be resisted at all costs.

39. The most brazen use of temporal-like discourse with respect to the divine is, of course, *The Ages of the World,* which proposes to speak—albeit in a somewhat metaphorical way—of God's past, present, and future. As a matter of fact, Schelling in that particular text only treats of the past. Differences in the respective enterprises notwithstanding, *The Philosophy of Revelation* could be thought to supplement the 1815 text. Though linguistically Schelling's language seems to recall the economic language of the Joachimite tradition, it should not necessarily be thought that Schelling has collapsed the immanent into the economic divine. The past of Schelling, for instance, is subjunctive, a transcendental-transcendent condition of time as the human subject knows it. It is not itself a form of time.

40. For a good account of this point, see Clark, *Logic and System,* pp. 95 ff.

41. See White, *Absolute Knowledge,* p. 127; Brown, *The Later Philosophy of Schelling,* p. 110.

42. This point is made with some force by Vincent McCarthy. See his *Quest for a Philosophical Jesus: Christianity and Philosophy in Rousseau, Kant, Hegel, and Schelling.* (Macon, Georgia: Mercier Press, 1986), pp. 163–213.

43. This point is underscored by Joseph Kreiml in his *Die Wirklichkeit Gottes: Eine Unterschuchung über die Metaphysik und die Religionsphilosophie des späten Schelling* (Regensburg: S. Roderer Verlag, 1989), pp. 66 ff.

44. Though Schelling does not openly acknowledge his debt to Boehme, from the *Freedom* essay on this debt is massive. Many of Schelling's texts read almost as if they are paraphrases of Boehme. Though it is a point with the present work to suggest that the overlap between Hegel and Boehme is considerable, his works by and large do not bear the stamp of the kind of full-blown Boehmian repristination evident in the later works of Schelling. For a detailed account of Boehme's influence on Schelling, see Brown, *The Later Philosophy of Schelling.*

45. One could read both Kasper's and Jüngel's work, as among other things, coming to terms with German Idealism in general, Hegel in particular, by refusing to countenance the view that the divine action is logically or rationally limited. In the process, both side with the later Schelling against Hegel. Even if Jüngel can appeal to Barth and Kasper can appeal to a long Catholic tradition, both recognize the importance of Schelling for the ontotheological correction. Schelling is important because he provides nontheological, as well as theological, grounds for rejecting the Hegelian view. Kasper has written an important text on the later Schelling. See his *Das Absolute in der Geschichte. Philosophie und Theologie der Geschichte in der Spätphilosophie Schellings* (Mainz, 1965). This text formed the basis for his own constructive proposal for the doctrine of God.

46. See, in particular, Ricoeur's nuanced discussion of this trend in modern narratology in *Time and Narrative,* Vol. 2, pp. 29–60. In a chapter entitled "The Semiotic Constraints on Narrativity," Ricoeur discusses and debates a whole range of structuralist and semistructuralist options, ranging from, on the one hand, the radical position of Claude Levi-Strauss, who views all narratives as reducible to a combinatory logic that devalues even sequence, to, on the other, the sophisticated narratological position of Agirdas Julien Greimas which, if it has given up the syntactical dream of Levi-Strauss by insisting upon the importance of sequence, nonetheless, dissociates sequence from chronological implication.

47. Hegel views his revised theory of the syllogism as the outcome and completion of the theory of judgment. His point is not the historical one that there exists a relation between the theory of subject-predicate relation and the doctrine of the syllogism. It is rather the systematic one of bringing out, in a way the Aristotelian tradition did not, the deep relation between them. In *SL,* for instance, in his consideration of the doctrine of the notion in particular, Hegel wishes to take account of Kant's epistemological recontexting of both the subject-predicate relation and the syllogism. If in the former case, he wished to argue both for an intrinsic relation, in the latter he wishes to argue for the syllogism's transcendent sweep.

48. Among a host of commentators, see especially Bruaire, *Logique et réligion,* pp. 60 ff; John W. Burbridge, *Hegel on Logic and Religion: The Reasonableness of Christianity* (Albany, NY: SUNY Press, 1992), pp. 131–140; Schlitt, *Hegel's Trinitarian Claim,* pp. 99–120, 227–248.

49. As a matter of fact, Hegelian logic mandates the interconnection of syllogism and teleology. In *Enc* Hegel's discussion of teleology (#204 ff) occurs in the context of his discussion of the syllogism of necessity. If the relation is not quite explicit in *SL,* within the logic of the notion or concept, teleology follows close on Hegel's treatment of the syllogism and effectively mediates between syllogism and the divine idea.

50. This point is made with great vigor in Petry's introduction to his translation of Hegel's *Philosophy of Nature,* Vol. 1, pp. 11–177.

51. I borrow this word from the trinitarian reflection of the Cappadocian, Gregory of Nazianzen, who was anxious to insist on the indivisibility of the divine persons in the immanent divine. The assertion of indivisibility is intended to protect the divine from (1) being interpreted in a Sabellian fashion where the relations between persons and substrate is conceived spatially and from (2) being interpreted in a subordinationist fashion where the relations are perceived in a quasi-temporal manner.

52. See Michael Rosen, *Hegel's Dialectic and its Criticism* (Cambridge: CUP, 1982), pp. 63 ff.

53. See Rosen, *Hegel's Dialectic and its Criticism,* p. 66.

54. For this point, see Rockmore, *Hegel's Circular Epistemology.*

55. See Louis Althusser, *For Marx,* trans. Ben Brewster (London: Allen Lane Penquin Press, 1963), pp. 165–218; also *Reading Capital,* trans. Ben Brewster (London: NLB, 1972).

56. See Ricoeur, "The Status of *Vorstellung* in Hegel's Philosophy of Religion," p. 71, where this point is emphasized.

57. Like Hegelian Logic, Husserl's logic, as it finds its realization in *Formal and Transcendental Logic,* has an object-oriented and grammatical or syntactical side. The object-oriented side is formal ontological in that, while it signifies objectivity in general, it does not point to a determinate sphere of actually given objects. It is thus not materially ontological. Husserl refers to the syntactic pole of logic by means of the term 'apophantic' after the Greek *apophansis* that becomes so important for Heidegger in the Introduction to *Being and Time. Apophansis* has the meaning of showing. The isomorphism between Hegel and Husserl, however, goes even deeper than this. For in both cases formal logic with its twin poles are embraced by the activity of self-constitution.

58. For Valéry's use of *implexe,* see *Idée Fixe,* trans. David Paul (New York: Pantheon Books, 1965), pp. 55–88. For the strong conception of the autonomity without need of anything, see *Monsieur Teste,* trans. Jackson Matthews (New York and London: Alfred Knopf, Routledge and Kegan Paul, 1973), p. 77.

59. See Ferdinand de Saussure, *Course in General Linguistic,* trans. Wade Baskin (New York: McGraw-Hill, 1964).

60. For Derrida's critique of Saussure, see *Of Grammatology,* trans. Gayatri Chakravorty Spivak (Baltimore: Johns Hopkins Press, 1976).

61. See Clark, *Logic and System;* Dupré, "Hegel's Religion as Representation," in *Dubious Heritage,* pp. 59–64.

62. The position that the symbol is semantically dense finds its consummate airing in the thought of Ricoeur. The idea that the metaphor is a life item of language challenging redundancy with its semantic impertinence also finds its consummate expression in Ricoeur. See his magisterial *The Rule of Metaphor,* trans. Robert Czerny with Kathleen Mclaughlin and John Costello SJ (Toronto: Toronto University Press, 1979), pp. 134 ff.

63. In *The Rule of Metaphor,* the first danger is the one resisted. In *Time and Narrative,* it is the second.

64. Schelling's important *Philosophy of Mythology,* of course, postdates Hegel's final reflections on symbol and myth. In contrast, Creuzer (1771–1856) was an important source for Hegel and Schelling. In addition to writing an important book on Proclus (1820) that Hegel is presumed to have read, Hegel had available to him in the 1820s two volumes of Creuzer's *Symbolik und Mythologie der alten Völker, besonders der Griechen.* For a helpful essay, see Martin Donougho, "Hegel and Creuzer: or, Did Hegel Believe in Myth," in *New Perspective in Hegel's Philosophy of Religion,* ed. David Kolb (Albany, N.Y.: SUNY Press, 1992), pp. 59–80.

65. See "Earliest System-Programme of German Idealism," trans. H. S. Harris in *Towards the Sunlight,* pp. 511–512.

66. See Jean-François Lyotard, "Answering the Question: What is Postmodernism?" in *The Post-Modern Reader,* ed. Charles Jencks (London and New York: Academy Editions and St. Martin's Press, 1992), pp. 138–150.

67. See Derrida's hugely important essay "From Restricted to General Economy," in *Writing and Difference,* pp. 251–277; also Taylor's essay on Bataille in *Altarity* (Chicago: Chicago University Press, 1987), pp. 115–148.

68. See *Erring,* pp. 74–93.

Bibliography

Hegel: Primary Sources

German Texts

Brief von und an Hegel. 4 vols. Ed. Johannes Hoffmeister and J. Nicolin, 3d ed. Hamburg: Felix Meiner, 1969–1981.

Hegels theologische Jugendschriften. Ed. H. Nohl. Tübingen, 1907.

Sämtliche Werke. Jubiliäumsausgabe. 22 vols. Ed. Hermann Glockner. Stuttgart: Frommann, 1927–1930. (In text, I use the abbreviation 'GL' rather than 'SL' to denote this edition.)

Vorlesungen über die Geschichte der Philosophie. 4 vols. Ed. Pierre Garniron and Walter Jaeschke. Hamburg: Felix Meiner, 1983–1986.

Vorlesungen über die Philosophie der Religion. 3 vols. Ed. Walter Jaeschke. Hamburg: Felix Meiner, 1984–1987.

English Translations

The Difference between Fichte's and Schelling's System of Philosophy. Trans. H. S. Harris and Walter Cerf. Albany, N.Y.: SUNY Press, 1976. (Translation is based on *Gesammelte Werke, Band 4, Jenaer Kritische Schriften,* ed. Harmut Buchner and Otto Pöggeler. Hamburg: Felix Meiner, 1968.

Early Theological Writings. Trans. T. M. Knox. Philadelphia: University of Pennsylvania Press, 1948. Paperback edition, 1971. (Partial translation of H. Nohl, *Hegels theologische Jugendschriften.*)

Faith and Knowledge. Trans. W. Cerf and H. S. Harris. Albany, N.Y.: SUNY Press, 1977. (Translation is based on *Gesammelte Werke,*

Band 4, Jenaer Kritische Schriften, ed. Harmut Buchner and Otto Pöggeler. Hamburg: Felix Meiner, 1968.

"Foreword to H. Fr. W. Hinrichs' *Die Religion im inneren Verhältnisse zur Wissenschaft* (1822)." Trans. A. V. Miller. In *Beyond Epistemology.* Ed. Frederick G. Weiss. The Hague: Martinus Nijhoff, 1974, pp. 227–244.

Introduction to the Lectures on the History of Philosophy. Trans. T. M. Knox and A. V. Miller. Oxford: Clarendon Press, 1985.

Lectures on the History of Philosophy. 3 vols. Trans K. S. Haldane and F. H. Simson. London and New York: Routledge and Kegan Paul and Humanities Press, 1955, 1963. (First published in 1892 by Kegan, Trench, Trübner & Co. Ltd.)

Lectures on the Philosophy of History. Trans. J. Sibree. New York: Dover Publications Inc., 1956. (First published London: The Colonial Press, 1899.)

Lectures on the Philosophy of Religion. Vol. 1. Ed. Peter Hodgson. Trans. R. F. Brown, P. C. Hodgson, and J. M. Steward. Berkeley: University of California Press, 1984.

Lectures on the Philosophy of Religion. Vol. 3. Ed. Peter Hodgson. Trans. R. F. Brown, P. C. Hodgson, and J. M. Steward. Berkeley: University of California Press, 1985.

Letters. Trans. Clark Butler and Christiane Seiler. Bloomington: Indiana University Press, 1984. (Translation based on Hoffmeister-Nicolin edition of the *Briefe.*)

Logic (The First Part of the Encyclopedia of the Philosophical Sciences in Outline). Trans. William Wallace, 2nd edn. Oxford: Clarendon Press, 1892 (reprint 1974).

Phenomenology of Spirit. Trans. A. V. Miller. Oxford: Oxford University Press, 1977. (Translation is based on the edition of *Phänomenologie des Geistes* by Johannes Hoffmeister. Hamburg: Felix Meiner, 1952).

Philosophy of Mind. Trans. A. V. Miller from *Encyclopedia of the Philosophical Sciences* (1830). Part 3. Oxford: Clarendon Press, 1971.

Philosophy of Nature. Trans. A. V. Miller from *Encyclopedia of the Philosophical Sciences* (1830). Part 2. Oxford: Clarendon Press, 1970.

Philosophy of Nature. Trans. M. J. Petry. 3 vols. London: George Allen and Unwin, 1970.

Philosophy of Right. Trans. T. M. Knox. Oxford: Oxford University Press, 1967. (First published in 1952 by Clarendon Press.)

Philosophy of Subjective Spirit. Ed. trans. with Intro. notes M. J. Petry. Dordrecht and Boston: D. Reidel, 1978.

Reason in History: A General Introduction to the Philosophy of History. Trans. Robert S. Hartman. Indianapolis: Bobbs Merrill Educational Publishing, 1953.

Science of Logic. Trans. A. V. Miller. New York: Humanities Press, 1969. (Translation is from the rev. edition of 1832.)

Trans. Eric von der Luft. In *Hegel, Hinrichs, and Schleiermacher on Feeling* and *Reason in Religion. The Texts of their 1821–22 Debate.* Studies in German Thought and History. Volume 2. Lewiston, N.Y., Queenston, Ontario: The Edwin Mellen Press, 1987, pp. 242–268. A critical edition of the foreword is offered, pp. 490–520.

Hegel: Secondary Literature

Adorno, Theodor W. *Negative Dialectics.* Trans. E. B. Ashton. New York: Seabury Press, 1973.

Albert, Hans. *Glauben und Denken: Hegelkritik als Anfange an das Selbstverständnis heutigen Theologie.* Regensburg: Verlag Friedrich Pustet, 1983.

Altizer, Thomas J. J. "History as Apocalypse." In *Deconstruction and Theology.* New York: Crossroads, 1982.

———. *The Gospel of Christian Atheism.* Philadelphia: Westminister Press, 1966.

Apostel, Pavel. "Wie ist die Entwicklung einer 'Logica Humana' im Rahmen der Darlegung der 'Logica Divina' in *Hegels Wissenschaft der Logik* möglich?" In *Die Wissenschaft der Logik und die Logik der Reflexion. Hegel-Tage Chantilly, 1971. Hegel Studien.* Beiheft 18. Ed. Dieter Henrich. Bonn: Bouvier, 1978, pp. 37–39.

Asendorf, Ulrich. *Hegel und Luther. Untersuchungen zur Grundlegung einer neuen systematischen Theologie.* Weisbaden: Steiner, 1982.

Avineri, Shlomo. *Hegel's Theory of the Modern State.* Cambridge: Cambridge University Press, 1972.

Barth, Karl. *Protestant Theology in the Nineteenth Century.* Trans. B. Cozens and J. Bowden. London: SCM Press, 1972. (Part of this was previously published as *From Rousseau to Ritschl.* London: SCM Press, 1959.)

Bataille, George. *Inner Experience.* Trans. Leslie Anne Boldt. Albany, N.Y.: SUNY Press, 1988.

Baur, F. C. *Die christliche Gnosis; oder die christliche Religionsphilosophie in irher geschichtlichen Entwicklung.* Tübingen: Osiander, 1835.

———. *Die christliche Lehre von der Dreieinigkeit und Menschwerdung Gottes in ihrer geschichtlichen Entwicklung. Vol. 3: Die neuere Geschichte des Dogma, von der Reformation bis in der neueste Zeit.* Tübingen: Osiander, 1843.

Bengel, Johann Albrecht. *Gnomon of the New Testament.* 5 Vols. Ed. A. Fausset. Philadelphia, 1860.

Benz, Ernst. *Les sources mystiques de la philosophie romantique allemande.* Paris: Vrin, 1968.

Berthold Bond, Daniel. *Hegel's Grand Synthesis: A Study in Being, Thought, and History.* Albany, N.Y.: SUNY Press, 1989.

Beyer, Wilhelm R. *Hegel-Bilder: Kritik der Hegel-Deutungen.* Berlin: Akadamie Verlag, 1964.

Bloch, Ernst. *Subjekt-Objeckt. Erläuterungen zu Hegel.* Frankfurt am Main: Suhrkamp, 1962.

Brito, Emilio. *La christologie de Hegel: Verbum Crucis.* Paris: Beauchesne, 1983.

———. *La création selon Schelling.* Leuven: Leuven University Press and Peeters, 1987.

———. *Hegel et la tâche actuelle de la christologie.* Paris: Lethielleux, 1979.

Bröcher, Walter. *Auseinandersetzungen mit Hegel.* Frankfurt am Main: Klostermann, 1965.

Bruaire, Claude. *Logique et religion chrétienne dans la philosophie de Hegel.* Paris: du Seuil, 1964.

Brunkhorst-Hasenclever, Annegrit. *Die Transformierung der theologischen Deutung des Todes bei G. W. F. Hegel. Ein Beitrag zur Formbestimmung von Paradox und Synthese.* Bern & Frankfurt am Main: Herbert Lang and Peter Lang, 1970.

Burbidge, John W. *Hegel on Logic and Religion: The Reasonableness of Christianity.* Albany, N.Y.: SUNY Press, 1992.

———. *On Hegel's Logic. Fragments of a Commentary.* New York: Humanities Press, 1981.

Chapelle, Albert. *Hegel et la religion.* 3 Vols. Paris: Éditions Universitaires, 1964–1971.

Christensen, Darrell E. (ed.). *Hegel and the Philosophy of Religion. The Wofford Symposium.* The Hague: Martinus Nijhoff, 1970.

Clark, Malcolm. *Logic and System. A Study of the Transition from "Vorstellung" to Thought in the Philosophy of Hegel.* The Hague: Martinus Nijhoff, 1971.

Coda, Piero. *Il negativo e la trinita: impotesi su Hegel.* Rome: Città Nouva Editrice, 1987.

Collins, James. *The Emergence of Philosophy of Religion.* New Haven and London: Yale University Press, 1967.

Cook, Daniel J. *Language in the Philosophy of Hegel.* The Hague and Paris: Mouton, 1973.

Copleston, Frederick. "Hegel and the Rationalization of Mysticism." In *New Studies* in *Hegel's Philosophy.* Ed. Warren L. Steinkraus. New York: Holt, Rinehart and Winston, Inc., 1971.

Croce, Benadetto. *What is Living and What is Dead of the Philosophy of Hegel.* Trans. Douglas Ainslie. New York: Russell & Russell, 1915.

Crouter, Richard. "Hegel and Schleiermacher at Berlin: A Many-Sided Debate." *Journal of the American Academy of Religion* 48 (1980), pp. 19–43.

Declève, Henri. "Schöpfung, Trinität und Modernität bei Hegel." *Zeitschrift für katholische Theologie* 107 (1985) Heft 3/4, pp. 187–198.

Derrida, Jacques. "Of an Apocalyptic Tone Newly Adopted in Philosophy." Trans. John P. Leavey, Jr. In *Derrida and Negative Theology.*

Ed. Harold Coward and Toby Foshay. Albany, N.Y.: SUNY Press, 1992, pp. 25–71.

———. *Dissemination.* Trans. Barbara Johnson. Chicago: University of Chicago Press, 1981.

———. *Positions.* Trans. Alan Bass. Chicago: University of Chicago Press, 1981.

———. "Le puits et la pyramide: introduction à la sémiologie de Hegel." In *Hegel et la pensée moderne.* Ed. Jacques D'Hondt. Paris: Presses Universitaires de France, 1970, pp. 27–83.

———. *Of Spirit.* Trans. Geoffrey Bennington and Rachel Bowlby. Chicago: University of Chicago Press, 1989.

———. *Writing and Difference.* Trans. Alan Bass. Chicago: University of Chicago Press, 1978.

Desmond, William. *Art and the Absolute: A Study of Hegel's Aesthetics.* Albany, N.Y.: SUNY Press, 1986.

Dickey, Laurence. *Hegel: Religion, Economics, and the Politics of Spirit, 1770–1807.* Cambridge: Cambridge University Press, 1987.

Donougho, Martin. "Hegel & Creuzer: or, Did Hegel Believe in Myth?" In *New Perspectives on Hegel's Philosophy of Religion.* Ed. David Kolb. Albany, N.Y.: SUNY Press, 1992, pp. 59–80.

Dupré, Louis. "The Absolute Spirit and the Religious Legitimation of Modernity." In *Hegels Logik der Philosophie.* Ed. Dieter Henrich and Rolf-Peter Horstmann. Stuttgart: Klett-Cottal, 1984, pp. 221–233.

———."Hegel's Religion as Representation." In *A Dubious Heritage: Studies in the Philosophy of Religion after Kant.* New York: Paulist Press, 1977, pp. 53–72.

Düsing, Klaus. *Das Problem der Subjektivität in Hegels Logik. Hegel Studien.* Beiheft 15. Bonn: Bouvier, 1976.

Fackenheim, Emil L. *The Religious Dimension in Hegel's Thought.* Bloomington: Indiana University Press, 1967.

Fichte, Johann Gottlieb. *Die Anweisung zum seeligen Leben.* Ed. Fritz Medicus. Hamburg: Felix Meiner, 1970.

———. *Attempt at a Critique of All Revelation.* Trans. Garrett Green. Cambridge: Cambridge University Press, 1978.

———. *Sämtliche Werke.* Ed. J. H. Fichte. Berlin: Veit, 1845. Reprint edition. Berlin: de Gruyter, 1971.

———. *The Science of Knowledge.* Trans. Peter Heath and John Lachs. New York: Appleton-Century-Grofts, 1970.

———. *The Vocation of Man.* Trans. R. Chrisholm. New York: Bobbs Merrill, 1956.

Findlay, John N. *Hegel: A Re-Examination.* London: George Allen and Unwin, 1958.

Gadamer, Hans-George. *Hegel's Dialectic.* Trans. P. Christopher Smith. New Haven: Yale University Press, 1976.

———. *Philosophical Hermeneutics.* Trans. Ed. David E. Linge. Berkeley, Los Angeles, London: University of California Press, 1976.

———. *Reason in the Age of Science.* Trans. Frederick G. Lawrence. Cambridge, MA: MIT Press, 1981.

———. *Truth and Method.* Translation edited by Garrett Barden and John Cumming. New York: Seabury Press, 1975.

Garaudy, R. *Dieu est mort. Étude sur Hegel.* Paris: Presses Universitaires de France, 1962.

Gascoigne, Robert. *Religion, Rationality and Community: Sacred and Secular in the Thought of Hegel and his Critics.* The Hague: Martinus Nijhoff, 1985.

Geraets, Theodore. "The End of History of Religions Grasped in Thought." In *Hegel Studien.* Band 24, 1989, pp. 55–77.

Gillespie, Michael A. *Hegel, Heidegger, and the Ground of History.* Chicago: University of Chicago Press, 1984.

Grégoire, Franz. *Études hégéliennes: les points capitaux du système.* Louvain and Paris: Publications Universitaires de Louvain & Éditions Beatrice-Nauwelaerts, 1958.

Harris, Errol E. *An Interpretation of the Logic of Hegel.* New York, London, Lanham: University Press of America, 1983.

Harris, H. S. *Hegel's Development: Night Thoughts* (Jena 1801–1806). Oxford: Clarendon Press, 1983.

———. *Hegel's Development: Towards the Sunlight* (1770–1801). Oxford: Clarendon Press, 1972.

Heede, Reinhard. "Die göttliche Idee und ihre Erscheinung in der Religion. Untersuchungen zum Verhältnis von Logik und Religionsphilosophie bei Hegel." Ph.D. dissertation, Philosophical Faculty of the Westfälischen Wilhems-Universität *zu* Münster/Westfalen, 1972.

Heidegger, Martin. *Hegel's Concept of Experience.* New York: Harper & Row, 1970.

———. *Hegel's Phenomenology of Spirit.* Trans. Parvis Mead and Kenneth Maly. Bloomington and Indianapolis: Indiana University Press, 1988.

———. "The Onto-Theological Nature of Metaphysics." In *Essays in Metaphysics: Identity and Difference.* Trans. Kurt F. Leidecker. New York: Philosophical Library Inc., 1960.

Henrich, Dieter. *Hegel im Kontext.* Frankfurt am Main: Suhrkamp, 1967.

Henry, Michel. *The Essence of Manifestation.* Trans. Girard Etzkorn. The Hague: Martinus Nijhoff, 1973.

Hessen, Johannes. *Hegels Trinitätslehre. Zugleich eine Einführung in sein System.* Freiburg: Herder, 1922.

Hinchmann, Lewis P. *Hegel's Critique of the Enlightenment.* Gainsville: University of Florida Presses, 1984.

Hinrichs, H. W. F. *Die Religion in innern Verhältnisse zu Wissenschaft.* Heidelberg: Groose, 1822.

Hodgson, Peter. *God in History: Shapes of Freedom.* Nashville: Abingdon Press, 1989.

———. "Hegel's Christology: Shifting Nuances in the Berlin Lectures." In *Journal of American Academy of Religion,* vol. 53 (1985), pp. 23–40.

Hondt, Jacques d'. (ed). *Hegel et la pensée grecque.* Paris: Presses Universitaires de France, 1974.

Hoover, Jeffrey. "The Origin of the Conflict Between Hegel and Schleiermacher at Berlin." In *The Owl of Minerva,* vol. 20, no. 1 (Fall) 1988, pp. 69–79.

Huber, Herbert. *Idealismus und Trinität, Pantheon und Götterdämmerung. Grundlagen und Grundzüge der Lehre von Gott nach dem Manuscript Hegels zur Religionsphilosophie.* Weinheim: Acta humaniora, 1984.

Hyppolite, Jean. *Genesis and Structure of Hegel's Phenomenology of Spirit.* Trans. S. Cherniak and J. Heckman. Evanston: Northwestern University Press, 1974.

———. *Logique et existence. Essai sur la logique de Hegel.* Paris: Presses Universitaires de France, 1953.

Iljin, Iwan. *Die Philosophie Hegels als kontemplative Gotteslehre.* Bern: Francke, 1946.

Jaeschke, Walter. "Absolute Idee-absolute Subjektivität. Zum Problem der Persönlichkeit Gottes in der Logik und in der Religionsphilosophie." *Zeitschrift für philosophische Forschung* 35 (1981), pp. 385–416.

———. "Christianity and Secularity in Hegel's Concept of the State." *The Journal of Religion* 61 (1981), pp. 127–145.

———. *Reason in Religion: The Formation of Hegel's Philosophy of Religion.* Trans. J. Michael Steward and Peter Hodgson. Berkeley, Cal.: University of California Press, 1990.

———. *Die Religionsphilosophie Hegels.* Darmstadt: Wissenschaftliche Buchgesellschaft, 1983.

———. "Speculative and Anthropological Criticism of Religion: A Theological Orientation to Hegel and Feuerbach." *Journal of the American Academy of Religion* 48 (1980), pp. 345–364.

Jüngel, Eberhard. *God as the Mystery of the World: On the Foundations of the Theology of the Crucified One in the Dispute between Theism and Atheism.* Trans. Darell L. Guder. Grand Rapids, Mich.: Eerdmans, 1983.

Kant, Immanuel. *Critique of Pure Reason.* Trans. Norman Kemp Smith. New York: St. Martin's Press, 1965.

———. *On History.* Ed. L. W. Beck. Trans. L. W. Beck, R. L. Anchor, E. L. Fackenheim. New York: Bobs Merill Co., 1963.

———. *Religion Within the Limits of Reason Alone.* Trans. T. M. Greene and H. H. Hudson. New York: Harper and Row, 1960.

Kaufmann, Walter. *Hegel: A Reinterpretation.* New York: Doubleday, 1965.

Kelly, George Armstrong. *Idealism, Politics and History.* Cambridge: Cambridge University Press, 1969.

Kern, Walter, S. J. "Dialektik und Trinität in der Religionsphilosophie Hegels. Ein Beitrag zur Discussion mit L. Oeing-Hanhoff." *Zeitschrift für katholische Theologie* 102 (1980), pp. 129–155.

———. "Schöpfung bei Hegel." *Theologische Quartalschrift* 162 (1982), pp. 131–146.

Kierkegaard, Soren. *The Concept of Anxiety: A Simple Psychologically Orienting Deliberation on the Dogmatic Issue of Hereditary Sin.* Trans. Reidar Thomte and Albert B. Anderson. Princeton, N.J.: Princeton University Press, 1980.

———. *Philosophical Fragments.* Trans. David F. Swenson, revised by Howard V. Hong. Princeton: Princeton University Press, 1967.

Kojève, Alexandre. *Introduction to the Reading of Hegel.* Trans. J. H. Nichols. Ed. Allen Bloom. New York: Basic Books, 1969.

Koslowski, Peter. "Hegel–'der Philosoph der Trinität?' Zur Kontroverse um seine Trinitätslehre." *Theologische Quartalschrift* 162 (1982), pp. 105–131.

Küng, Hans. *The Incarnation of God: An Introduction to Hegel's Theological Thought as a Prolegomena to a Future Christology.* Trans. J. R. Stephenson. New York: Crossroad, 1987.

Lakeland, Paul. *The Politics of Salvation: The Hegelian Idea of the State.* Albany, N.Y.: SUNY Press, 1984.

Lauer, Quentin. *Hegel's Concept of God.* Albany, N.Y.: SUNY Press, 1982.

———. "Hegel's Critique of Kant's Theology." In *God Knowable and Unknowable.* Ed. Robert J. Roth S.J. New York: Fordham Press, 1973, pp. 85–105.

———. "Hegel on the Identity of Content in Religion and Philosophy." In *Essays in Hegelian Dialectic.* New York: Fordham University Press, 1977, pp. 153–168.

Léonard, André. *Commentaire littéral de la logique de Hegel.* Paris: Vrin, 1974.

———. *La foi chez Hegel.* Paris: Desclée, 1970.

———. "Le primat du négative et l'interprétation de la religion. Un exemple: la reprise hégélienne du dogme christologique de chalcédoine." In *Hegels Logik der Philosophie.* Ed. Dieter Henrich and Rolf Peter Horstmann. Stuttgart: Klett-Cottal, 1984, pp. 160–171.

Lichtenstein, Ernst. "Von Meister Eckhart bis Hegel. Zur philosophichen Entwicklung des deutschen Bildungsbegriffs." In *Kritik und Metaphysik.* Berlin. 1966, pp. 260–297.

Link, Christian. *Hegels Wort "Gott is tot."* Zürick: Theologischer Verlag, 1974.

Löwith, Karl. *From Hegel to Nietzsche: The Revolution in Nineteenth Century Thought.* Trans. D. E. Green. New York: Doubleday, 1967.

———. "Hegel and the Christian Religion." In *Nature, History and Existentialism.* Ed. A. Levison. Evanston: Northwestern University Press, 1966.

———. "Hegels Aufhebung der christlichen Religion." In *Hegel Studien,* Suppl 1. Bonn: Bouvier, 1964, pp. 193–236.

Lucas, George R. Jr. *Hegel and Whitehead: Contemporary Perspectives on Systematic Philosophy.* Ed. George R. Lucas Jr. Albany, N.Y.: SUNY Press, 1986.

———. *Two Views of Freedom in Process Thought: A Study of Hegel and Whitehead.* AAR Dissertation Series, 28. Missoula, Montana: Scholars Press, 1979.

Luft, Eric (von der). *Hegel, Hinrichs and Schleiermacher on Feeling and Reason in Religion: The texts of their 1821–22 Debate.* Studies in German Thought and History, vol. 3. Lewiston, N.Y. and Queenston, Ontario: The Edwin Mellen Press, 1987.

Lukacs, George. *The Young Hegel.* Trans. R. Livingston. London: Merlin Press, 1975.

McCarthy, Vincent. *Quest for a Philosophical Jesus: Christianity and Philosophy in Rousseau, Kant, Hegel, and Schelling.* Macon, Georgia: Mercier Press, 1986.

Machéry, Pierre. *Hegel ou Spinoza.* Paris: François Maspero, 1979.

Marcuse, Herbert. *Hegel's Ontology and Theory of Historicity.* Trans. Seyla Benhabib. Cambridge, MA.: MIT Press, 1987.

Marx, Werner. *Hegel's Phenomenology of Spirit: Its Points and Purposes: A Commentary on the Preface and Introduction.* Trans. Peter Heath. New York: Harper, 1975.

———. *The Philosophy of F. W. J. Schelling: History, System and Freedom.* Trans. Thomas Nenon. Bloomington: Indiana University Press, 1984.

Min, Anselm K. "Hegel's Absolute: Transcendent or Immanent." *The Journal of Religion* 56 (1976), pp. 79–99.

———. "The Trinity and the Incarnation: Hegel and Classical Approaches." *The Journal of Religion* 66, No. 2 (1986) April, pp. 173–193.

Mure, G. R. G. *An Introduction to Hegel.* London and New York: Oxford University Press, 1959.

———. *A Study of Hegel's Logic.* Oxford: Clarendon Press, 1948.

Nauen, Franz Gabriel. *Revolution, Idealism and Human Freedom: Schelling, Hölderlin and Hegel and the Crisis of Early German Idealism.* The Hague: Martinus Nijhoff, 1971.

Niel, Henri. *De le médiation dans la philosophie de Hegel.* Paris: Aubier-Montaigne, 1945.

Oeing-Hanhoff, Ludger. "Hegels Trinitätslehre. Zur Aufgabe ihrer Kritik und Reception." *Theologie und Philosophie* 52 (1977), pp. 378–407.

Pannenberg, Wolfhart. "Die Subjektivität Gottes und die Trinitätslehre. Ein Beitrag zur Beziehung zwischen Karl Barth und die Philosophie Hegels." *Kerygma und Dogma* 23 (1977), pp. 25–40.

Planty-Bonjour, Guy. (ed). *Hegel et la religion.* Paris: Presses Universitaires de France, 1982.

Priest, Stephen. (ed). *Hegel's Critique of Kant.* Oxford: Clarendon Press, 1987.

Puntel, L. Bruno. *Darstellung, Methode und Structur. Untersuchungen zur Einheit der systematischen Philosophie G. W. F. Hegels. Hegel Studien.* Beiheft 10. Bonn: Bouvier, 1973.

———. "Die Trinitätslehre G. W. F. Hegels. Zur gleichnamigen Buch von Jörg Splett." *Zeitschrift für katholische Theologie.* 89 (1967), pp. 203–213.

Ringleben, Joachim. *Hegels Theorie der Sünde. Die subjektivitäts-logische Konstrucktion eines theologischen Begriffs.* Berlin and New York: de Gruyter, 1977.

Rockmore, Tom. *Hegel's Circular Epistemology.* Bloomington: Indiana University Press, 1986.

Rosen, Michael. *Hegel's Dialectic and its Criticism.* Cambridge: Cambridge University Press, 1984.

Sallis, John. *Spacings of Reason and Imagination in Texts of Kant, Fichte, Hegel.* Chicago and London: University of Chicago Press, 1987.

Schelling, F. W. J. *The Ages of the World.* Trans. Frederick de Wolfe Bolman. New York: Columbia University Press, 1942. Reprinted New York: N.Y. AMS Press Inc., 1967.

———. *Bruno or on the Natural and the Divine Principle of Things.* Trans. Michael Vater. Albany, N.Y.: SUNY Press, 1984.

———. *On Human Freedom.* Trans. James Gutmann, Chicago: Open Court, 1936.

———. *Sämmtliche Werke.* 14 vols. Ed. K. F. A. Schelling. Stuttgart and Augsburg: Cotta, 1856–61.

———. *System of Transcendental Idealism.* Trans. Peter Heath. Charlottesville: University Press of Virginia, 1978.

Schlitt, Dale M. *Hegel's Trinitarian Claim: A Critical Reflection.* Leiden: E. J. Brill, 1984.

———. "The Whole Truth: Hegel's Reconceptualization of the Trinity." *The Owl of Minerva* 15 2 (1984), pp. 169–182.

Schmidt, Erik. *Hegels Lehre von Gott.* Gütersloh: Mohn, 1952.

Schmidt, Gerard. *The Concept of Being in Hegel and Heidegger.* Bonn: Bouvier, 1979.

Seidel, George. *Activity and Ground: Fichte, Schelling, and Hegel.* New York: George Olms Verlag, 1976.

Shklar, Judith N. *Freedom and Independence.* Cambridge: Cambridge University Press, 1976.

Smith, John E. "Hegel's Reinterpretation of the Doctrine of Spirit and the Religious Community." In *Hegel and the Philosophy of Religion.*

The Wofford Symposium. Ed. Darrel L. Christensen. The Hague: Martinus Nijhoff, 1970, pp. 155–175.

Smith, John H. *The Spirit and its Letter: Traces of Rhetoric in Hegel's Philosophy of Bildung*. Ithaca and London: Cornell University Press, 1988.

Solomon, Richard. *In the Spirit of Hegel: A Study of G. W. F. Hegel's Phenomenology of Spirit*. Oxford: Oxford University Press, 1983.

Splett, Jörg. *Die Trinitätslehre G. W. F. Hegels*. Munich: Alber, 1965.

Staudenmaier, Franz Anton. *Darstellung und Kritik des Hegelschen Systems. Aus dem Standpunkte der christlichen Philosophie*. Mainz: Kupferberg, 1844; reprint ed. Frankfurt am Main: Minerva, 1966.

Stepelevich, Lawrence S. (ed). *The Young Hegelians*. Cambridge: Cambridge University Press, 1983.

Taminiaux, Jacques. *La nostalgie de la Grèce à l'aube de l'idéalisme allemand. Kant et les grecs dans l'intinéraire de Schiller, de Hölderlin et de Hegel*. The Hague: Martinus Nijhoff, 1967.

Taylor, Charles. *Hegel*. Cambridge: Cambridge University Press, 1975.

———. *Hegel and Modern Society*. Cambridge: Cambridge University Press, 1979.

Taylor, Mark C. *Erring: A Postmodern A/theology*. Chicago and London: University of Chicago Press, 1984.

———. "Itinerarium Mentis in Deum: Hegel's Proofs of God's Existence." *The Journal of Religion*, vol. 57 (1977), pp. 211–231.

———. *Journeys to Selfhood: Hegel and Kierkegaard*. Berkeley: University of California Press, 1980.

Theunissen, Michael. *Hegels Lehre vom absoluten Geist als theologisch-politischer Traktat*. Berlin: de Gruyter, 1970.

Thulstrup, Nils. "Kierkegaard's Approach to Existence versus Hegelian Speculation." In *Kierkegaard and Speculative Idealism*. Ed. Nils Thulstrup, Bibliotheca Kierkegaardiana, 4. Copenhagen: C. A. Reitzels Boghandel, 1979, pp. 98–113.

———. *Kierkegaard's Relation to Hegel*. Trans. George L. Strengen. Princeton: Princeton University Press, 1980.

———. "The System and Method of Hegel." In *Kierkegaard and Speculative Idealism.* Ed. Nils Thulstrup. Bibliotheca Kierkegaardiana, 4. Copenhagen: C. A. Reitzels Boghandel, 1979, pp. 52–97.

Toews, John Edward. *Hegelianism. The Path toward Dialectical Humanism, 1805–1841.* Cambridge: Cambridge University Press, 1985.

Voegelin, Eric. "On Hegel: A Study in Sorcery." *Studium Generale,* No. 24 (1971), pp. 335–368.

———. "Wisdom and the Magic of the Extreme: A Mediation." *Southern Review.* 17 (1981), pp. 235–287.

Wagner, Falk. "Die Aufhebung der religiösen Vorstellung in den philosophischen Begriff." *Neue Zeitschrift für systematische Theologie und Religionsphilosophie* 10 (1968), pp. 44–88.

———. *Der Gedanke der Persönlichkeit Gottes bei Fichte und Hegel.* Gütersloh: Mohn, 1971.

Wahl, Jean. *Le malheur de la conscience dans la philosophie de Hegel.* Paris: Presses Universitaires de France, 1929, 2nd edition, 1951.

Walsh, David. "The Esoteric Origins of Modern Ideological Thought." Ph.D. Dissertation. University of Virginia, 1978.

———. "The Historical Dialectic of Spirit. Jacob Boehme's Influence on Hegel." In *History and System: Hegel's Philosophy of History.* Ed. Robert L. Perkins. Albany, N.Y.: SUNY Press, 1984.

Weiss, Frederick G. (ed). *Beyond Epistemology: New Studies in the Philosophy of Hegel.* The Hague: Martinus Nijhoff, 1974.

White, Alan. *Absolute Knowledge: Hegel and the Problem of Metaphysics.* Athens, Ohio: Ohio University Press, 1983.

———. *Schelling: An Introduction to the System of Freedom.* New Haven and London: Yale University Press, 1983.

Williamson, Raymond K. *Introduction to Hegel's Philosophy of Religion.* Albany, N.Y.: SUNY Press, 1984.

Wylleman, A. (ed). *Hegel on the Ethical Life, Religion, and Philosophy (1793–1807)* Leuven and Dordrecht: Leuven University Press and Kluwer Academic Publishers, 1989.

Yerkes, James. *The Christology of Hegel.* Missoula, Montana: Scholars Press, 1978.

Other Works Consulted

Aland, Barbara. (ed). *Gnosis: Festschrift für Hans Jonas*. Göttingen: Vandenhoeck & Ruprecht, 1978.

Althusser, Louis. *For Marx*. Trans. Ben Brewster. London: Allen Lane, Penguin Press, 1963.

———. *Reading Capital*. Trans. Ben Brewster. London: NLB, 1972.

Aquinas, Thomas. *Summa Theologicae*. 60 vols. E. Trans. Dominican Order. London: Blackfriars, 1963–76.

Aristotle. *The Works of Aristotle*. Trans. under editorship of W. D. Ross. Oxford: Clarendon Press, 1908–31.

Armstrong, A. H. "The Background of the Doctrine 'That the Intelligibles are not Outside the Intellect.'" In *Plotinian and Christian Studies*. London: Variorum Reprints, 1979.

———. "Gnosis and Greek Philosophy." In *Gnosis: Festschrift für Hans Jonas*. Göttingen: Vandenhoeck & Ruprecht, 1978, pp. 87–124.

Attridge, Harold. (ed). *Nag Hammadi Codex 1 (The Jung Codex)*. 2 vols. Nag Hammadi Studies 22–23. Leiden: E. J. Brill, 1985.

Augustine. *Confessions*. Trans. R. S. Pine Coffin. London: Penguin, 1961.

———. *The City of God*. Trans. Henry Bettenson. London: Penguin, 1972.

———. *The Trinity*. Trans. Stephen McKenna. Washington: Catholic University Press of America, 1963.

Aulen, Gustav. *Christus Victor: A Historical Study of the Three Main Types of the Idea of Atonement*. Trans. A. G. Herbert. New York: Mcmillan, 1969.

Baader, Franz von. *Sämtliche Werke*. 16 vols. Ed. Franz Hoffman. Leipzig, 1851–1860.

Barnes, Robin. *Prophecy and Gnosis: Apocalypticism in the Wake of the Lutheran Reformation*. Stanford: Stanford University Press, 1988.

Barth, Karl. *The Theology of Schleiermacher*. Trans. Geoffrey W. Bromiley. Grand Rapids, Mich.: Eerdmans, 1982.

Berdyaev, Nicholas. "Unground and Freedom." In *Six Theosophic Points*. Ann Arbor, Mich.: University of Michigan Press, 1958, V–XXXVII.

Beierwaltes, Werner. *Denken des Einen. Studien zur neuplatonischen Philosophie und ihrer Wirkungsgeschichte*. Frankfurt am Main: Klostermann, 1985.

———. *Identität und Differenz*. Frankfurt am Main: Klostermann, 1980.

Blackhall, Eric A. *Goethe and the Novel*. Ithaca and London: Cornell University Press, 1976.

Bloom, Harold. *Agon: Towards a Theory of Revisionism*. New York and Oxford: Oxford University Press, 1983.

———. *The Anxiety of Criticism: A Theory of Poetics*. New York and Oxford: Oxford University Press, 1973.

———. *A Map of Misreading*. New York and Oxford: Oxford University Press, 1975.

Boehme, Jacob. *Aurora*. Trans. John Sparrow. London, 1656. Republ. Ed. C. J. Barker. London: John Watkins, 1914. Reprinted London: James M. Clark, 1960.

———. *De Electione Gratiae and Quaestiones Theosophicae*. Trans. John R. Earle. London: Constable and Co., 1930.

———. *Forty Questions of the Soul and Clavis*. Trans. John Sparrow. London, 1647. Reissued. C. J. Barker. London: John M. Watkins, 1911.

———. *Mysterium Magnum: An Exposition of the First Book of Moses Called Genesis*. 2 Vols. Trans. John Sparrow. London, 1656. Republ. Ed. C. J. Barker. 2 vols. London: John M. Watkins, 1924.

———. *Sämtliche Schriften*. 11 vols. Ed. Will-Erich Peuckert and August Faust. Stuttgart: Frommanns Verlag, 1955–1961. Reprint of 1730 edition. 10 vols. under the title *Theosophia Revelata*. Ed. Johann G. Gichtel and Johann W. Ueberfeld. Amsterdam.

———. *De Signatura Rerum*. No translator given. London and Toronto: J. M. Dent & Sons, 1912.

———. *Six Theosophic Points*. Trans. John R. Earle. New York: A. A. Knopf, 1920.

———. *The Way to Christ.* Trans. Peter Erb. New York: Paulist Press, 1978.

———. *Works of Jacob Behmen.* Ed. William Law. 1766–81.

Bornkamm, Heinrich. *Eckhart und Luther.* Stuttgart, 1936.

———. *Luther und Jakob Böhme. Arbeiten zur Kirchengeschichte. Bd. 2.* Bonn: A. Marcus and E. Weber, 1925.

———. "Renaissancemystik: Luther und Böhme." In *Lutherjahrbuch,* 1925, pp. 156–197.

Brown, Robert F. *The Later Schelling: The Influence of Boehme on the Works of 1809–1815.* Lewisburg, PA.: Bucknell University Press, 1977.

Bruford, W. H. *Culture and Society in Classical Weimer 1775–1805.* Cambridge: Cambridge University Press, 1962.

Clark, Mary T. "A Neplatonic Commentary on the Christian Trinity." In *Neoplatonism and Christian Thought.* Ed. Dominic O'Meara. Albany, N.Y.: SUNY Press, 1982, pp. 24–33.

Collins, John J. *Apocalypse: The Morphology of a Genre.* Semeia 14. Missoula: Scholars Press, 1979.

Daniel, E. R. "The Double Procession of the Holy Spirit in Joachim of Flora's Understanding of History." *Speculum* 55 (1980), pp. 469–483.

Degendhardt, Ingeborg. *Studium zum Wandel des Eckhart-bildes.* Leiden: E. J. Brill, 1967.

Despland, Michel. *Kant on History.* Montreal and London: Queen's University Press, 1973.

Dionysius, the Areopagite. *Complete Works.* Trans. Colm Suibhead. New York: Paulist Press, 1987.

Dupré, Louis. *The Common Life: Origins of Trinitarian Mysticism and its Development* by Jan Ruusbroec. New York: Crossroads, 1984.

Ebeling, Heinrich. *Meister Eckharts Mystik.* Stuttgart: Scientia Verlag, 1967.

Eckhart, Meister. *Breakthrough: Meister Eckhart's Creation Spirituality in New Translation.* Ed. Matthew Fox. Garden City, N.Y.: Doubleday, 1980.

———. *Die deutschen und lateinishen Werke.* 11 vols. Stuttgart and Berlin: Kohlhammer, 1936–

———. *Deutsche Predigten und Tractate.* Ed. Joseph Quint. Munich: Carl Hanser, 1955.

———. *Meister Eckhart: The Essential Sermons, Commentaries, Treatises and Defense.* Ed. Trans. Edmund College and Bernard McGinn. New York: Paulist Press, 1981.

———. *Meister Eckhart: Sermons and Treatises.* 3 vols. Ed. Trans. Michael O'C. Walsh. London: Watkins, 1979–85.

———. *Treatises and Sermons of Meister Eckhart.* Trans. James M. Clark and John V. Skinner. New York: Harper & Row, 1958.

Erb, Peter. *Pietists, Protestants, and Mystics. The Use of Medieval Sources in the Works of Gottfried Arnold (1666–1714).* Metouchen, N.J.: Scarecrow Press, 1987.

Eriugena, Duns Scotus. *De divisione naturae (Bks. 1&2).* Ed. Trans. Sheldon Williams. Dublin: Institute of Advanced Studies, 1972.

Fiore, Joachim de. *Liber de concordia Novi ac Veteris Testamenti.* Ed. E. Randolph Daniel. Philadelphia: American Philosophy Society, 1983.

———. *Enchiridion super Apocalypsim.* Ed. Edward K. Burger. Toronto: Pontifical Institute of Medieval Studies, 1986.

Frei, Hans. *The Identity of Jesus Christ: The Hermeneutic Bases of Dogmatic Theology.* Philadelphia: Fortress Press, 1975.

Frick, Johann. *Gruendliche Undersuchung Jacob Boehmens vornehmster Irrthuemer: So auss dessen eigenen Schriften gezeiget und auss H. Schrifft widerlegt werden.* Ulm, 1691.

Galston, William A. *Kant and the Problem of History.* Chicago and London: University of Chicago Press, 1975.

Genette, Gerard. *Narrative Discourse: An Essay in Method.* Trans. Jane E. Lewin. Ithaca, N.Y.: Cornell University Press, 1980.

———. *Figures of Literary Discourse.* Trans. Alan Sheridan. New York: Columbia University Press, 1984.

Gersch, Stephen. *From Iamblichus to Eriugena: An Investigation of the Prehistory and Evolution of the Pseudo-Dionysian Tradition.* Leiden: E. J. Brill, 1978.

Goethe, Johann Wolfgang. *Goethe's Works*. 5 vols. Ed. F. H. Hedge and L. Noa. New York: J. A. Williams, 1882.

Habermans, Jürgen. *The Philosophical Discourse of Modernity*. Trans. Frederick G. Lawrence. Cambridge, Mass.: MIT Press, 1986.

Heidegger, Martin. *Being and Time*. Trans. John Macquarrie and James Robinson. Oxford: Basil Blackwell, 1962.

Herder, Johann Gottfried von. *Outlines of a Philosophy of History of Man*. Trans. T. Churchhill. New York: Bergman Press, 1966.

Hick, John. *Evil and the God of Love*. New York: Macmillan, 1966.

Hoffman, Bengt. *Luther and the Mystics: A Reexamination of Luther's Spiritual Experience and his Relationship to the Mystics*. Minneapolis: Augsburg Publishing House, 1976.

Hölderlin, Friedrich. *Poems and Fragments*. Trans. Michael Hamburger. Ann Arbor, Mich.: University of Michigan, 1967.

Jonas, Hans. *The Gnostic Religion: The Message of the Alien God and the Beginnings of Christianity*. Boston: Beacon Press, 1958.

———. "Delimitation of the Gnostic Phenomenon—Typological and Historical." In *The Origins of Gnosticism*. Ed. U. Bianchi. Leiden: E. J. Brill, 1967, pp. 90–108.

Kermode, Frank. *The Sense of an Ending: Studies in the Theory of Fiction*. London; New York: Oxford University Press, 1967.

Kile, Frederick. *Die theologischen Grundlagen von Schellings Philosophie der Freiheit*. Leiden: E. J. Brill, 1965.

Koyré, Alexandre. *La philosophie de Jacob Boehme*. Paris: Vrin, 1929.

Lawrence, D. H. *Apocalypse and the Writings on Revelation*. Ed. Mara Kalnins. Cambridge and New York: Cambridge University Press, 1980.

Layton, Bentley. (ed. trans.). *The Gnostic Scriptures*. Garden City, N.Y.: Doubleday, 1987.

Leon, Xavier. *Fichte et son temps*. 2 vols. Paris: Librarie Armand Colin, 1924.

Lessing, G. *Theological Writings*. Trans. H. Chadwick. Stanford, Cal.: Stanford University Press, 1957.

Levinas, Emmanuel. *Totality and Infinity: An Essay on Exteriority*. Trans. Alphonso Lingis. Pittsburg: Duquesne University Press, 1969.

Lienhard, Marc. *Luther's Witness to Jesus Christ: Stages and Themes of the Reformer's Theology*. Minneapolis: Augsburg, 1986.

Lindbeck, George. *The Nature of Doctrine*. Philadelphia: Westminister Press, 1984.

Loeschen, John R. *The Divine Community: Trinity, Church and Ethics in Reformation Theologies*. Kirksville, MO.: Sixteenth Century Journal Publishers and Northeast Missouri State University, 1981.

Lubac, Henri de. *La postérité spirituelle de Joachim de Flore. 1. de Joachim à Schelling*. Paris: Lethielleux, 1979.

McDermot, V. "The Concept of Pleroma in Gnosticism." In *Gnosis and Gnosticism: Papers Read at the Eight International Conference on Patristic Studies*. Ed. Martin Krause. Leiden: E. J. Brill, 1981, pp. 79–86.

McGinn, Bernard. (ed. trans). *Apocalyptic Spirituality*. New York: Paulist Press, 1979.

McGuire, Ann. "Valentinus and the Gnostike Hairesis: An Investigation of Valentinus's Position in the History of Gnosticism." Ph.D. Dissertation. Yale, 1983.

McRae, George. "Apocalyptic Eschatology in Gnosticism." In *Apocalypticism in the Mediterranean World and the Near East*. Ed. David Hellholm. Tübingen: Mohr, 1983.

Maesschalck, M. *L'Anthropologie politique et religieuse de Schelling*. Leuven & Paris: Vrin and B.P 41, 1991.

Maréchal, Joseph. *Studies in the Psychology of Mystics*. Trans. Algar Thorold. Albany, N.Y.: Magi Books, 1966.

Merleau Ponty, Maurice. *Signs*. Trans. R. C. McCleary. Evanston: Northwestern University Press, 1969.

Moltmann, Jürgen. *The Crucified God: The Cross of Christ as the Foundation and Criticism of Christian Theology*. Trans. R. A. Wilson and Robert Bowden. London: SCM Press, 1974.

———. *Trinity and the Kingdom: The Doctrine of God*. Trans. Margaret Kohl. New York: Harper and Row, 1981.

Mottu, Henri. *La manifestation de l'Esprit selon Joachim de Fiore*. Neuchâtel and Paris: Delachaux and Niestlé, 1977.

Murray, Michael. *Modern Philosophy of History: Its Origins and Destination*. The Hague: Martinus Nijhoff, 1970.

Nazianzen, Gregory. *Theological Orations*. Trans. C. G. Brown and J. E. Swallow. In *Christology of the Later Fathers*. Ed. Edward R. Hardy. Philadelphia: Westminister Press, 1954, pp. 128–214.

Neander, August. *Genetische Entwicklung der vornehmsten gnostischen Systems*. Berlin: Dümmler, 1818.

Nyssa, Gregory. *On the Making of Man*. In *Nicene and Post-Nicene Fathers. Vol. 5. Gregory of Nyssa*. Trans. W. Moore and H. A. Wilson. Grand Rapids, Mich.: Eerdmans, 1892.

Oetinger, Friedrich C. *Sämtliche Schriften*. 11 vols. Ed. Karl Ehman. Stuttgart, 1858–64.

Owens, Joseph. *The Doctrine of Being in the Aristotelian "Metaphysics": A Study in the Greek Background of Medieval Thought*. Toronto: Pontifical Institute of Medieval Studies, 1951.

Ozment, Steven E. *Homo Spiritualis: A Comparative Study of the Anthropology of Johannes Tauler, Jean Gerson and Martin Luther (1509–16)*. Leiden: E. J. Brill, 1969.

———. "Meister Eckhart and Martin Luther." *Thomist* 42 (1978), pp. 259–80.

Perrin, Norman. "Apocalyptic Christianity." In *Visionaries and their Apocalypses*. Ed. Paul D. Hanson. Philadelphia and London: Fortress Press and SPCK, 1983, pp. 121–145.

Philonenko, Alexis. *La libérté humaine dans la philosophie de Fichte*. Paris: Vrin, 1966.

Plotinus. *Enneads*. Trans. Stephen McKenna. London: Faber and Faber, 1969.

Proclus. *The Elements of Theology*. Trans. R. C. Dodds. 2nd ed. Oxford: Clarendon Press, 1962.

Reale, Giovanni. *The Concept of First Philosophy and the Unity of the Metaphysics of Aristotle*. Albany, N.Y.: SUNY Press, 1980.

Reeves, Majorie. *The Influence of Prophecy on the Later Middle Ages: A Study in Joachimism*. Oxford: Clarendon Press, 1969.

———. *Joachim de Fiore and the Prophetic Future.* New York: Harper and Row, 1977.

Ricoeur, Paul. *The Conflict of Interpretations.* Ed. Don Ihde. Evanston: Northwestern University Press, 1974.

———. *The Rule of Metaphor.* Trans. Robert Czerny et al. Toronto: Toronto University Press, 1977.

———. *The Symbolism of Evil.* Trans. Emerson Buchanan. Boston: Beacon Press, 1969.

———. *Time and Narrative.* 3 vols. Trans. Kathleen McLaughlin and David Pellauer. Chicago: University of Chicago Press, 1984–88.

Rist, John. *Plotinus: The Road to Reality.* Cambridge: Cambridge University Press, 1967.

Ruusbroec, John. *The Spiritual Espousals.* Trans. James Wiseman. Classics of Western Spirituality. New York: Paulist Press, 1985.

Schachken, Winfrid M. J. *Ordo Salutis. Das Gesetz als Weise der Heilsvermittlung. Zur Kritik des H. L. Thomas von Aquin an Joachim von Fiore.* Münster: Aschendorff, 1980.

Schleiermacher, Friedrich. *The Christian Faith.* Trans. H. R. Mackintosh & J. S. Steward. Philadelphia: Fortress Press, 1928.

———. *On Religion: Speeches to its Cultured Despisers.* Trans. John Oman. New York, San Francisco: Harper and Row, 1958.

Schmithals, Walter. *The Apocalyptic Movement: Introduction and Interpretation.* Nashville and New York: Abingdon Press, 1975.

Siggins, Ian D. Kingston. *Martin Luther's Doctrine of Christ.* New Haven: Yale University Press, 1970.

Spinoza, Benedict de. *The Collected Works of Spinoza.* 2 vols. Ed. Trans. Edwin Curley. Princeton, N.J.: Princeton University Press, 1985.

———. *The Correspondence of Spinoza.* Ed. Trans. A. Wolf. New York: Russell & Russell Inc., 1966.

Stoudt, John J. *Sunrise to Eternity: A Study in Jacob Boehme's Life and Thought.* Philadelphia: University of Pennsylvania Press, 1957.

Susini, Eugène. *Franz von Baader et le romanticisme mystique.* 2 vols. Paris: Vrin, 1942.

Tobin, Frank. *Meister Eckhart: Thought and Language*. Philadelphia: University of Pennsylvania Press, 1986.

Unger, Richard. *Friedrich Hölderlin*. Boston: Twayne, 1984.

Valéry, Paul. *Idée Fixe*. Trans. David Paul. New York: Pantheon Books, 1965.

———. *Monsiour Teste*. Trans. Jackson Matthews. New York: A. Knopf, 1973.

Voegelin, Eric. *From Enlightenment to Revolution*. Ed. John H. Hallowel. Durham, N.C.: Duke University Press, 1975.

———. *Science, Politics and Gnosticism: Two Essays*. Chicago: Regnery Co., 1968.

Walsh, David. *The Mysticism of Innerworldly Fulfillment: A Study of Jacob Boehme*. Gainsville, Fla.: University of Florida Presses, 1983.

White, Hayden. "The Value of Narrativity in the Representation of Reality." In *On Narrative*. Ed. W. J. T. Mitchell. Chicago and London: University of Chicago Press, 1980, pp. 1–28.

Williams, Robert R. *Schleiermacher the Theologian: The Construction of the Doctrine of God*. Philadelphia: Fortress Press, 1978.

Subject Index

absolute:
absolute absolute, 116;
images of, 33, 177;
Idea, 240, 292, 337, 357;
knowledge, 192, 256, 262, 289, 292, 333, 338;
and monism, 296;
religion, 336;
Schelling on, 34, 36, 49, 174;
self-consciousness;
Spirit, 192, 324;
subjectivity, 117;
truth, 2
abyss, 134, 146, 217
actuality:
and Aristotle, 115–116;
of divine, 62, 63, 115, 120, 203;
divine knowledge, 120;
in Eckhart, 116;
and history, 313–314;
narrative character of, 115, 203;
prolepsis, 115
adiophora, 365
aesthetics:
and death, 212;
Lectures on Aesthetics, 212;
Schiller, 458–459n. 25
alchemy:
and Boehme, 222, 223, 231, 308;
caput mortuum, 50, 384n. 59
alexandrian:
exegesis, 170;
view of history, 161, 162, 283
alienation or *Entfremdung*;
and *Bildungsroman*, 52, 54;
of Christ, 194, 200, 202, 215, 229;
Boehme, 225;
and death, 215;
and difference of finite and infinite, 113, 145, 322;
and divine development, 187, 322;
as evil, 152, 159;
knowledge of, 159;
and life, 123;
and narrative, 46, 55;
Valentinian Gnostic, 183;
overcoming of, 161, 166;
and Spirit, 122, 152;
and unhappy consciousness, 194
anaclasis:
definition of, 11–12;
and dialectic, 298;
and the divine, 21–22;
immanent divine, 99, 100, 218, 290–291, 298;
and meaning, 57–61;
as narrative operation, 340, 343;
and trinity, 85;
"Immanent Trinity," 110–111, 124, 140, 145, 146;

anaclasis (*Continued*):
  Universality, 124. *See also* narrative and synclasis
analepsis:
  and anamnesis, 314–315;
  definition of, 9–11;
  and the divine, 295, 296;
    Deus Revelatus, 21;
  Gerard Genette, 9–11;
  "Immanent Trinity," 291–296, 305;
  and Individuality, 140;
  and meaning, 61–63;
  and narrative operations, 339–340;
  of Spirit, 11, 140. *See also* narrative and prolepsis
anamnesis, 62;
  and analepsis, 314–315
anthropodicy, 316
apocalypse, 9, 23, 247, 287, 288, 368;
  and apocalyptic, 282, 299, 302–303, 320–323;
    Joachim, 264, 278, 301–303, 320–323;
  in Boehme, 301, 307–310;
  and eschatology, 299–301;
  Judeo-Christian, 299, 301–306;
  and knowledge, 278, 361;
  Lutheran, 301, 309;
  and narrative, 302–306, 368;
  primary and secondary, 302–305;
  as revelation, 247–248, 267–268, 278, 279, 298–310;
  and trinity, 23, 368;
  and Valentinian Gnosticism, 307–310;
    as Hegelian taxon, 307–310
apophantic, 368, 463n. 57
apophatic, 252, 262;
  contrast with kataphatic, 41, 262;
  erasure, 43, 104, 106, 134;
  theology, 41, 67;
    Eckhart, 43, 262;
    Eriugena, 109;
  tradition, 108–110
appearance or *Erscheinung*, 104, 111;
  category of, 97;
  of Christ, 203;
  as creation, 145, 146, 150, 151;
  as illusion or *Schein*, 145, 146, 343;
  as providence, 313
Aristotle:
  on actuality, 96, 115, 323, 335, 351;
    actualization, 241;
  on analogy, 166;
  and the divine, 60;
    divine thought, 96, 295–296;
  and epistemology, 203;
  on the infinite, 119;
  and logic, 87–88;
    category, 91, 99–100, 115, 335–337;
    proposition, 37, 335;
    syllogism, 87, 337;
    theology, 88;
  Physics, 119;
  and trinity, 130
atheism, 198, 199, 210
Athena, 190
attribute, 97, 136, 304, 335
Aufhebung, 38, 62, 324, 331

becoming, 13, 60, 62, 182–183, 317, 354, 368;
  category of, 147;
  divine becoming, 48, 52, 55, 61, 141, 167, 221, 230, 293, 322;
  in Heraclitus, 297–298;

historical becoming, 115;
human becoming, 46, 128, 167;
and narrative, 60, 128, 167, 317–318
being:
being in itself, 41, 112;
category of, 41, 92, 93, 97, 98, 115, 178, 292;
divine being, 125, 193, 304, 335;
historicity of, 183;
and Parmenides, 297–298
Bildungsroman, 49–57;
and becoming, 50–56;
divine, 53–56;
human, 50–53;
and divine image, 283;
in *Lectures on Philosophy of Religion*, 54;
and narrative, 8, 9, 52, 54;
in *Phenomenology*, 49–53;
and trinity, 111
Boehme, Jacob:
Aurora, 130, 282, 308;
and Christology, 263, 276, 294;
theology of the cross and Hegel, 23, 190, 223–231;
Clavis, 119;
on concept of God, 56–57, 118;
on creation, 144, 150, 152, 153, 155, 171;
as evil, 168, 180–187, 232;
divine, 232;
Lucifer myth, 132, 155;
and deipassionism, 231;
on difference, 172;
on differentiation, 118;
on divine image, 245;
knowledge of, 131;
The Divine Intuition, 119;
Encyclopedia, 152–154;
and eschatology, 277, 278, 279–285, 287, 307–308;
and heterodoxy, 22, 153;
Lectures on History of Philosophy, 109;
and Lutheranism, 168, 222–231, 284–285;
Mysterium Magnum, 130, 223–226;
and mysticism, 23, 29, 228;
pneumatic, 278–288;
speculative, 5, 17, 338;
and narrative, 327, 344, 352;
pansophism of, 308, 451n. 33;
pantheism in, 173–174;
and pneumatic Christianity, 150, 361;
and representation, 342–343;
De Signatura Rerum, 223;
Six Theosophic Points, 223, 224;
and theodicy, 323;
theogony in, 254;
theosophy of, 15, 154, 368;
and trinity, 78, 118, 129;
"Immanent Trinity" 70, 93–94, 131, 138–139
bonum diffusivum sui, 121, 174, 175, 217

Cappadocian, 138, 162, 168, 358
category, 87–89, 94, 96–101, 292;
in Aristotle, 99–100, 115, 335;
and divine ideas, 91;
and divine names, 96;
and divine predicates, 96, 100;
and trinity, 101–107
Catholicism:
Lutheran and Hegelian polemic against, 277;
sacramental view of, 241–245;
and trinity, 65
causality, 151, 325, 340, 346
Christ:
appearance of, 194, 204;
appropriation of, 191, 206;

Christ (*Continued*):
as *Christus Victor*, 215, 216, 226;
conciliar view of, 191;
consciousness of, 230;
and death, 141, 192, 200, 201, 205, 207, 208, 212, 219, 320;
and eschaton, 283;
existence, 194, 240;
and grace, 164;
historicity of, 204, 257;
and history, 204, 267;
and hypostatic union, 220;
communicatio idiomatum, 220;
incarnate, 202, 219, 228;
and justification, 277;
Kant's view of, 204;
and kenosis, 217, 219, 228, 330;
and kingdom of God, 270, 273;
Lectures on Philosophy of Religion, 201–205;
mystery of, 206;
and narrative, 82, 141–142;
and nature, 278;
divine, 219;
human, 220;
passion of, 141, 192, 200–201, 205, 207, 219, 221, 230, 234, 320;
person of, 191, 193, 219–220;
personal locus of suffering, 201;
personhood, 230–231;
Phenomenology of Spirit, 193–197;
reconciliation by, 141;
redemption by, 226, 319, 322;
resurrection of, 212, 267;
as Son of God, 319;
teaching of, 205;
and trinity, 87;
uniqueness of, 203;
unsurpassibility of, 268, 275, 194,
work of, 191
Christianity:
as absolute religion, 42;
as consummate religion, 42;
criticism of, 199,
demythologization of, 337;
Eastern orthodoxy, 65, 241–242;
emergence of, 273, 277;
Hegelian hermeneutics of, 6–7, 30, 261;
heterodox, 144;
institutional, 277;
Lutheran, 40, 245–247, 249, 276, 277, 311, 361;
and mysticism, 32–44, 245, 246, 248–249, 253;
mystical union, 249;
and narrative, 142, 252, 318, 333, 364–368;
trinity, 341;
and Reformation, 277;
and representation, 337, 351;
revelation, 34, 300;
God of, 21, 30;
religion of, 20, 21, 31–32, 62, 108,192, 247;
as self-consciousness of divine, 256, 334;
unhappy consciousness, 333. *See also* Catholicism and Lutheranism
Christology:
and atonement, 319;
sacrifice, 207–208;
satisfaction, 207–208;
of Boehme, 221–231,
classical, 22, 191, 195, 196, 220;
docetism in , 231, 233–234, 259;
Lectures on Philosophy of Religion, 201–209;

Lutheran, 82, 191, 200, 206;
communication idiomatum, 220;
dyophysitism, 220;
kenosis, 227–228;
monophysitism, 220, 230;
perichoresis, 220;
and narrative, 142, 189, 190;
contraction, 227;
punctuation, 223;
Phenomenology of Spirit, 191–201;
Valentinian Gnostic, 231–234
church, 27, 239, 247, 274, 281;
and Christian community, 70;
ethical-practical nature of, 241–242;
invisible, 238;
and mystical body, 269;
visible, 238
circle and circularity, 111, 293, 297–298, 355;
and the divine, 61, 290;
Encyclopedia, 59–60;
and Fichte, 58;
Phenomenology of Spirit, 46, 59
coincidentia oppositorum, 213, 215, 216, 223, 224–225, 230
communicatio idiomatum, 196, 219, 220, 231
community or *Gemeinde*, 160, 211, 238–249, 255, 269–270;
Christian, 10, 199, 200, 214, 239, 240, 241;
and doctrine, 242;
emergence of, 239–241;
and eschatology, 247–249;
Kant on, 160;
and kingdom, 240, 275, 280;
and mystical body, 248, 275, 280;
Pietist view of, 246;
and pneumatology, 198;
realization of, 245–249;
and Spirit, 189, 210, 253;
spiritual community, 23, 68, 82, 124, 238–239, 245, 274, 276, 311, 333;
as Holy Spirit, 287–289;
and syllogism, 249;
and trinity, 189, 196, 236
concept or *Begriff*:
category of, 92, 100, 135, 139, 218, 257, 292, 314, 336;
and God, 79;
as Idea, 218;
and narrative, 22, 127, 328, 357, 363–364, 369;
and philosophy, 360;
and representation, 7, 69, 96, 246, 248, 257, 289, 327–328, 331–363
consciousness, 157, 194, 203, 204, 235, 240, 252, 289, 335;
divine, 289, 322, 334;
happy, 194;
self-consciousness, 39, 51, 193, 194, 197, 252, 253, 254, 256,
divine, 296, 298, 333, 334, 336, 356, 360, 361;
unhappy, 35, 194, 202, 240, 271, 333
contradiction or *Widerspruch*, 157, 160, 168, 175, 176, 179, 297
creation, 7, 16, 19, 21, 27, 30;
as appearance, 145–146;
and causality, 149–151, 169, 340, 343, 345, 346;
biblical, 149, 150, 170;
and Boehme, 143, 152, 180–187;
Christian view of, 131, 146, 147, 148, 150, 158;
ex Deo, 23, 144, 171–187;
in *Difference Essay*, 146–147;
in *Encyclopedia*, 142, 148, 152, 161–163, 169;
as evil, 143, 151–169, 170, 186;

creation (*Continued*)
in *Faith and Knowledge*, 167–168;
as fall, 143, 151–169, 170;
of finite spirit, 145;
and Genesis, 149–150, 157;
Gnostic view of, 143, 154–156, 180–187;
heterodoxy of Hegel's view, 143–144, 152–153, 169–171;
Judaic view of, 146, 148;
as kenosis, 217–218, 227–228;
Lectures on Philosophy of Religion, 145, 154, 156–160, 163;
Luther on, 149–150;
and narrative, 68–70, 124, 189, 197, 207;
of nature, 145;
and Neoplatonism, 174–180;
ex nihilo, 23, 146, 147, 148, 170, 171, 173, 218, 358;
oriental view of, 146, 148, 177;
as Particularity, 69, 141;
in *Phenomenology of Spirit*, 144–145, 155, 165;
and representation, 141, 143, 144, 147, 148, 197, 344;
and punctiliarity, 148–149;
and Son, 70, 142;
Spinoza, 146, 147, 171–174, 179;
and theological voluntarism, 148–149;
and trinity, 68–70, 110, 141–142, 189;
cult, 241, 242, 274, 289

death:
of Christ, 191, 207–208, 215, 235, 240;
in *Faith and Knowledge*, 211;
of God, 124, 210, 370;
Lutheran theme of, 191, 198–199, 205–206;
incarnation, 205;
Lectures on Philosophy of Religion, 205–207;
and life, 124, 212–213, 223,229;
narrative relation, 213–214, 224;
Phenomenology of Spirit, 213, 215;
as positive, 212, 229;
and Spirit, 192, 213;
and trinity, 207, 221;
syllogism, 236
deconstruction, 3, 14, 53, 57, 59, 366, 368;
Derrida, 13;
logocentrism, 12
deipassionism, 220, 221, 230, 234
demythologization, 334, 337
Deus:
Absconditus, 196;
Incurvatus, 112;
Occultos, 43, 76;
Patibilis, 209–234;
Revelatus, 21, 22, 23, 27, 29–44;
Lectures on Philosophy of Religion, 31–33, 37–39;
as narrative, 44–63, 80, 111;
and trinity, 63, 64, 80. *See also* God
devotion or *Andacht*, 37, 38, 246, 248;
and thought or *Denken*, 246, 248
dialectic, 113, 141, 225, 324;
and panentheism, 297–298;
and narrative, 297–298
difference, 152, 172, 173;
unity in difference, 349
differentiation:
between finite and infinite, 117;

in the immanent divine, 113, 114, 115–121, 187;
Aquinas and Hegel, 117–119;
Boehme and Hegel, 118;
divine self-consciousness, 116–117;
in the infinite, 113, 122, 139, 145;
and judgment, 176;
of life and love, 121–124;
in Neoplatonism, 118, 176;
in Spinoza, 349;
and trinity, 115–121, 139
Disseits, 200
doctrine, 62, 67, 347;
and community, 242;
critique of, 107;
and narrative, 280–282;
and trinity, 63–80, 347
dualism, 154;
in apocalyptic, 301–302;
in Boehme, 226, 230;
in Lutheranism, 223, 225–226;
and Manichaeanism, 230
Schelling, 124
dyophysite, 220, 230,

Eckhart, Meister:
Christology of, 195, 258–260;
on community, 250–263;
Deutsche Werke, 254–255, 257, 259;
on divine image, 251–255, 266, 283;
Encyclopedia, 253;
and German Idealism, 250–253;
and Godhead-God distinction, 109–110, 118;
and *Gottesgeburt*, 251;
Hegelian interpretation of, 260–262;
on history, 255;
Lectures on Philosophy of Religion, 256;
and Luther, 260–262,
and mysticism, 29, 238, 250–263, 289, 338;
as narrative, 344;
on time, 255;
on trinity, 109–110, 138;
and *Wirklichkeit*, 116
ecstasis, 117, 120
emanation, 172, 177, 354
empiricism, 100, 120, 364
energeia, 116
enlightenment:
and Christianity, 44;
critique of, 199, 364–365;
on evil, 158–161;
on history, 263;
and Kant, 158, 161, 239;
and rationalism, 40, 65
endzeit, 247, 300
epoch, 32, 237;
Iljin's view, 9, 126;
and narrative, 71, 85, 287;
and the Son, 141–142, 197;
and the Spirit, 235–236, 308;
and trinity, 71, 81, 85, 141, 200, 287–288;
"Immanent Trinity," 112, 121, 126
epoché, 24–25
eros, 185, 187, 197
eschaton, 9, 300, 305, 311, 320, 321;
eschatology, 247, 249, 256, 265–274, 275–276, 277, 283, 301, 307;
Joachim, 265–270, 305, 321;
Lutheran, 277, 283;
and evil, 311–324
essence, 92–93, 97–98, 145, 178, 224, 292

eternity or the eternal:
and Boehmian Christology, 223–224;
eternal divine, 205, 239;
and kenosis, 229;
and self, 241;
as thought, 287, 298;
as transformation of time, 307–308
evil:
Adamic, 158, 161, 165, 166, 208–209;
anthropogonic, 143;
Augustine on, 159, 162;
biblical view of, 157–160;
Genesis, 157–158, 160;
original sin, 159–160;
serpent, 163–164;
Boehme on, 143, 152–154;
cosmogonic, 143, 157;
and creation, 143, 151–169;
and the divine, 120, 132, 156;
in *Encyclopedia*, 152–154, 156, 161;
as fall, 151–169;
felix culpa, 162, 167, 184;
Gnostic view of, 143, 151, 154–156, 159, 164, 168–169;
Kant on, 143, 158–163, 166;
radical, 158;
in *Lectures on Philosophy of Religion*, 154, 156–160, 164;
Lucifer, 155–156;
and negativity, 156;
neoplatonic view of, 164, 168–169, 185;
nonbeing, 179;
origin of, 158, 159, 165;
and personality, 132;
in *Phenomenology of Spirit*, 152, 153, 154, 160;
and theogony, 166–167, 209;
and theodicy, 310–329
faith:
and eschatology, 278;
fides qua creditur and *fides quae creditur*, 281–282;
and knowledge, 278, 315, 319, 321, 333;
and Luther, 267, 278–280, 281–282
Father, 207, 306;
and category of Being, 93;
as God, 142;
kingdom of, 70, 271, 305, 306, 307, 308;
and trinity, 68, 69, 73, 111, 127, 133, 139–140, 141, 334;
as Universality, 69, 81
feeling, 125, 165, 239, 242, 244;
in Schleiermacher, 35–38
felix culpa, 162, 167, 184
Fichte, Johann Gottlieb, 25, 44, 259, 345;
on act, 47;
Die Anweisung zum seeligen Leben, 125–126;
on life, 125–126, 403n. 109;
on love, 125–126, 403n. 109;
and monism, 404n. 111;
and narrative, 56–59;
on trinity, 404nn. 112, 114;
Die Wissenschaftslehre, 125
finite:
and Christ, 235, 241;
death of, 221, 235;
incarnation, 235;
sensibly intuited existence, 203;
and creation, 142–143, 202;
nature, 168;
spirit, 145;
and death, 205, 221;
and divine presence, 28, 187, 201, 221, 293;
and eschaton, 290;
as evil, 316;

horizon of knowledge, 33;
and infinite, 211, 240, 246;
difference, 117, 145;
externality of relation, 147;
gap, 293;
narrative order, 213;
Neoplatonic view of relation, 175, 177;
Spinoza's view of relation, 171–173;
unity, 54;
and mode, 349;
and Neoplatonism, 179;
spirit, 145;
divine image, 240–241;
theophany, 325;
freedom:
divine, 357;
and history, 244, 273–274;
Joachim, 265–266;
divine sonship, 244;
and necessity, 316, 325, 344, 350;
Spinoza, 344, 349

gnosis, 163, 181
Gnosticism:
and apocalypse, 307, 309–310;
on Christ, 232–233;
redeemed redeemer, 322;
and Christology, 190, 231–234, 322;
on creation, 144, 154, 158, 168, 176, 180–187;
Sophia, 138, 183, 228;
and evil, 143, 154–156, 159, 168–169, 185–186;
serpent, 163;
on hermeneutics, 164–165, 170;
and *Gospel of Truth*, 232–233;
and heterodoxy, 180, 342;
hylé in, 154–155;
influence on Hegel, 5, 15–16, 19–20, 24;
on Jesus, 232;
Monogenes in, 134;
and narrative, 310, 318, 327, 343–344;
Neander on, 134, 232;
on *pleroma*, 181, 185–186;
Proarchia in, 134;
Propater in, 134;
and theogony, 158;
and trinity, 133–135, 343, 406–407n. 113;
and *Tripartite Tractate*, 183–185, 232–234;
Valentinian, 134–135, 144, 154, 156, 168–169, 181–187, 190, 231–234, 309
god, 166, 192;
as alpha and omega, 46;
Aristotelian, 80, 335;
and Being, 47, 335;
and concept, 79;
as Father, 142;
and Godhead, 109–110;
and goodness, 120–121, 143, 169, 174, 176, 228, 229, 316, 318; 323;
of Islam, 80;
of Judaism, 80;
knowledge of, 33, 253;
and life, 120, 122, 124, 129;
living, 64, 112–113;
and love, 112–113, 120, 122, 124, 319;
as movement, 95;
proofs of God's existence, 79–80, 323–326;
and revelation, 71, 121, 333;
as Spirit, 44;
and thought, 144;
as trinity, 64, 89, 109–110, 235;
as truth, 39, 44, 338;

god (*Continued*)
as unknown, 20, 29–30, 31, 32, 34, 41, 56, 96
gospel, 267;
of John, 94, 110, 113, 126, 134, 140, 158, 217;
of Matthew, 32, 164, 185
Gottesgeburt, 130

heresy, 135, 343
heterodoxy;
and Boehme, 156, 180–181, 186–187, 342;
and Christ, 142;
in Christianity, 25, 248, 354, 361;
and creation, 152, 156, 180–181, 186–187;
and Gnosticism, 156, 180–181, 186–187, 232, 342;
in Joachim, 268;
Lucifer, 156;
and narrative, 144;
and representation, 342;
and trinity, 138
Hinduism, 133, 136, 296
historicity, 204, 232
history, 141, 204, 238, 241, 265, 277, 280, 282–283;
and apocalypse, 268, 201–302;
in Augustine, 270;
divine, 126, 141, 205, 305;
in Eckhart, 257–258;
Lectures on Philosophy of History, 272–274;
sacred and profane, 270, 274;
salvation history, 265, 268, 269, 270, 301, 315, 319, 321
secular, 270
holy, 120, 245, 294, 295;
Spirit, 124, 235, 253, 270, 274–275, 279–280, 287, 288, 293;
trinity, 109, 235, 294–295
hylé, 154, 155
hypostasis, 71, 126, 127, 129, 130, 132–133, 135–136, 138, 141, 153, 230;
hypostatic union, 196, 220

idea, 47, 112, 115, 116, 152, 178, 235, 240, 309, 316, 356, 367;
and concept, 218;
logical, 178;
and Spirit, 126, 152, 175
idealism, 24, 25, 129, 173, 211, 225, 229, 232, 309;
German Idealism, 191, 209, 222, 316;
and Romanticism, 128, 367;
transcendental, 34
illusion or *Schein*, 145, 146, 312, 343
image, 165, 247, 249, 260, 269, 336, 337;
of God, 240, 251, 255;
and likeness, 164;
theology, 241, 244–245, 251–253, 280, 282–285;
Boehme, 283–285;
Eckhart, 283–284, 439n. 41
immediacy or *Unmittelbarkeit*, 61, 62, 63, 207, 291;
immediate identity, 121–122
incarnation, 8, 16, 21, 27, 331, 341, 345;
and Christian community, 240;
and divinization, 168, 259;
doctrine of, 64;
and historical development, 272–273;
and Holy Spirit, 253;
and kenosis, 218, 227;
and kingdom of God, 272;
and narrative, 68–69, 124, 196–198;
and syllogism, 236;

and trinity, 68–69, 189, 196–198, 235,
uniqueness of, 203
Individuality or *Einselnheit*, 139, 271, 327, 332, 353, 354, 356, 357;
in *Encyclopedia*, 69–70, 341;
in *Phenomenology*, 69–70;
and Spirit, 69–70, 140, 342
infinite or infinitude:
differentiation, 115;
dimension of self, 253;
divine infinite, 34, 42, 201, 202, 217, 289–290, 291, 317;
and finite, 29, 30, 59, 117, 147, 167, 211, 213, 232, 240, 246;
and knowledge, 119;
as pure, 221;
and Spirit, 171–173, 317;
spurious infinite, 59, 349;
and Substance, 171–173, 317
intuition, 239, 242;
empirical, 34, 203;
intellectual, 34

Jenseits or beyond, 33, 199, 200, 240, 271, 290, 333
Jesus:
Christ, 7, 201, 202, 212, 217;
Dasein of Jesus, 198, 240, 258;
in Gnosticism, 232;
in Kant, 191
Joachim, de Fiore, 23, 29, 70, 238, 263–279, 320;
and apocalypse, 264, 278, 301–305, 320–321;
Concordia Novi ac Veteris Testimenti, 265–266, 269;
on eschatology, 270–275, 277–278, 287;
Expositio in Apocalypsim, 265, 269;
and Hegelian texts, 270–275;
Lectures on Philosophy of History, 271–275;
Heilsgeschichte scheme, 284;
and heterodoxy, 284;
on knowledge, 278–280;
Psalterium Decem Chordarum, 265;
and trinity, 265–270, 320–321
Judaism, 44, 80, 146–147, 194, 272, 347, 349

kairos, 259–262, 303
Kant, Immanuel:
and anthropodicy, 316
on categories, 86, 96, 335–336;
Critique of Pure Reason, 165–166; others
and dialectic, 22;
and the enlightenment, 161, 239;
critique of, 158;
on eschatology, 159, 160–163, 313;
on evil, 143, 158–163, 166, 170, 313–316;
radical, 158;
on knowledge, 33, 165–166, 315, 336, 368;
on Jesus, 191;
on judgment, 336;
and narrative, 160–162, 365;
and negative theology, 39–40, 56, 211;
on proofs of God's existence, 323–326;
cosmological, 325;
ontological, 79, 323, 326, 335;
teleological, 324;
relation with Hegel, 15, 24–25;
Religion Within the Limits of Reason Alone, 143, 159;
and the subject, 336;
synthetic a priori, 336;

Kant, Immanuel (*Continued*):
synthetic unity of apperception;
on theodicy, 313–314, 323, 369;
and triad, 68, 130, 133–134;
on war, 312–313;
on will, 159, 343;
Wille, 159;
Willkür, 159
kataphatic, 110, 251, 262
kenosis:
Boehme on, 217–218, 229–230;
and Christology, 220–221;
"death of God," 205–206, 221;
of finite, 206;
and Luther, 216–221, 228–229;
difference with Hegel, 216, 218–221;
patristic view of, 217–218;
contrast with Hegel, 217–218;
and *plerosis*, 200;
and trinity, 132–133, 200, 221
kingdom, 235, 249, 265, 267, 271, 305–310;
of Father, 70, 271, 305–308;
of God, 160, 191, 204, 237, 238, 240, 247, 270, 272–275, 305;
of Son, 271, 305, 306, 307, 308;
of Spirit, 238, 247, 249, 265–266, 271, 273, 279, 305, 306, 307, 308;
and trinity, 306, 308

langue, 361
life, 121–126, 212, 213, 214, 215, 216, 223, 224, 230;
of God, 120, 122, 124;
and death, 224, 230
logic, 86–105, 175, 225, 338–339, 340, 344, 361, 367, 369;
Aristotelian, 87–88;
and "Immanent Trinity", 93–96;
and Neoplatonism, 91
logocentrism, 12, 366, 367;
and narrative, 370
logos, 187, 219, 329;
and Gospel of John, 94;
and Gnosticism, 183–184, 234;
and Heraclitus, 297;
logos and mythos, 328, 363;
logos endiathetos, 404n. 112, 404–405n. 114, 406n. 129;
logos prosphorikos, 404n. 112, 404–405n. 114;
love, 121–126, 152, 205, 244;
divine, 112–113, 120, 122, 124, 142, 206, 207, 226
Lucifer, 132, 154, 155, 156
Luther, Martin, 5, 15–16, 45, 66, 108–109, 159, 163, 170, 277;
and Christology, 82, 191, 195, 196, 200–201, 209–234;
Commentary on Genesis, 149;
on community, 240, 250;
on creation, 143, 156, 158, 260, 264, 276, 278;
Hegel's critique of, 149–151;
and Eckhart, 260–262;
and eschatology, 277, 278, 284, 346;
Heidelberg Disputations, 212;
and mysticism, 260–263;
and speculation, 108–109;
and theology of the cross, 82, 222, 223, 229, 230, 279;
of glory, 277;
and the negative, 22, 43–44;
on trinity, 77
Lutheranism, 20, 41, 71, 144, 191, 198, 260–263, 275–276;
and Adamic myth, 158;
and Boehme, 284–285;
eschatology in, 276, 281, 284, 301;

Joachim, 263–264;
as essence of Christianity, 253, 262, 277, 301;
and Hegel, 7, 16, 45;
and heterodoxy, 229, 284–285;
and image theology, 247;
and kenosis, 132;
and metaphor, 362–363;
and mysticism, 247;
and narrative, 363;
and orthodoxy, 23, 43, 66, 109, 130, 170, 196, 200–201, 242, 243, 244, 256, 260, 262–263, 281, 284, 301, 346;
as Protestant, 245–247, 262, 273–274;
and revelation, 278–280, 301;
and Spirit, 247;
as telos of religion, 247, 249;
and theology, 82;
of cross, 209–211;
sacramental, 241–244, 263

manifestation:
and appearance, 114;
in Boehme, 129, 231;
of Christ, 194;
and diffferentiation, 114, 150;
of divine, 44–45, 108, 150, 290–291, 317, 322, 325;
as creation, 169–171;
negativity, 175, 183;
temporalizing, 148;
and evil, 177;
Gnostic view, 177;
Neoplatonic view, 177–178;
and trinity, 129
Marcion, 126, 134, 343
mediation or *Vermittlung*, 62, 115, 205, 213, 353
metanarrative, 111, 333, 360, 365, 368, 369;
Christian, 165, 197, 364, 365, 367, 368;
and knowledge, 368;
trinitarian, 356, 368
metaphysics, 86–87, 89, 96, 317;
and logic, 86–88;
and theology, 87–89
metharmottein, 164
modalism, 22, 129, 136, 137, 139;
and narrative, 126, 137;
Spinozist, 136,
mode, 136, 172, 347
modernity, 311, 361, 364;
as cultural crisis, 365
genealogy of, 366,
moment, 127, 131, 151, 152, 167, 207, 235;
language of, 69–71;
and trinity, 127, 135
monism, 124, 172, 296;
in Spinoza, 349;
and Spirit or *Geistesmonismus*, 128
Monogenes, 134, 233,
monophysitism, 220, 221, 230
morality, 313
multiplicity, 116, 145, 239
mystery, 200, 343, 344;
of Christ, 206,
of God, 108, 251,
and "Immanent Trinity", 65, 127, 131,
St. Paul, 43–44, 108, 131
mysticism:
and Boehme, 45, 279–285;
and Christ, 191;
and Christianity, 43–44;
Protestant, 246–247;
St. Paul, 43–44;
and community (*Gemeinde*), 249–285;
corpus mysticum, 238–244, 250, 275, 278, 279–280, 288–289;

mysticism (*Continued*):
and disclosure, 43–44;
in Eckhart, 43, 109, 250–263;
inflection of Lutheranism, 260–263;
elevation (*Erhebung*) into the infinite, 326;
and the ethical sphere (*Sittlichkeit*), 146–147;
and Hegel, 17, 25;
and interpretation of Hegel, 17, 23, 25;
and Joachim, 263–279;
in Hegelian pneumatology, 270–275;
inflection of Lutheranism, 263–265, 278–279;
and knowledge, 43–44, 166;
and Lutheranism, 82, 237–238, 244–246;
corpus mysticum, 250;
inflection by Boehme, 284–285;
inflection by Eckhart, 260–263;
inflection by Joachim, 263–265, 275–279;
mystical union, 237, 244, 247, 249, 253–258;
and negative theology, 43–44;
and pneumatology, 249–285;
and presence, 43–44;
in Proclus, 104;
and proofs of God's existence, 324;
and Reformation, 275–276;
and representation, 334;
Tauler, 260;
Theologica Germanica, 260;
and trinity, 108, 166;
varieties of, 17, 23, 25, 35
myth or *mythos*, 182, 293, 328, 336, 363, 365;
Adamic, 158, 165;
Gnostic, 154;
mythology of reason, 367, 368;
and Schelling, 460–461n. 37, 464n. 64

narrative:
anthropological, 166, 167, 168, 346;
and apocalypse, 303–307;
and Aristotle, 417n. 91;
Augustinian, 320;
biblical, 158–160, 167, 169, 278, 343;
and *Bildungsroman*, 8–9, 49–57, 111, 128, 137, 283;
and Boehme, 187;
and Christ, 204;
as christian, 124, 166, 357;
and concept, 328, 340, 365;
Hegelian rehabilitation of, 388, 357;
and salvation history, 55, 318–321;
and Christology, 142, 193, 198, 212;
contraction, 214;
punctuation, 213–214, 223, 225;
theology of the cross, 230–231;
and creation, 156, 283;
and discourse, 10;
and the divine, 55, 166, 207;
image, 283;
indices, 322;
and finite spirit, 203;
function, 367;
and Gnosticism, 182–184, 329;
and Hegel, 5–6;
and heterodoxy, 144;
and the holy, 293–294;
and knowledge, 328, 363, 364, 365, 368;
local narrative versus metanarrative, 332;

and negativity, 231;
and Neoplatonism, 175–180;
ontotheology, 10;
operation, 11–14, 332;
passion, 187, 189, 192, 194, 196;
radical, 303–304, 307, 310;
and representation, 150, 331, 332;
rhythm, 178;
space, 331;
and Spirit, 289, 293;
and story, 10;
theogenetic, 71, 167;
and theogony, 158, 186;
and trinity, 196–197, 307, 327–328, 365;
and christian churches, 241–242,
and history, 306–307;
and kingdom, 308;
"Immanent Trinity," 228, 358;
Inclusive Trinity, 326, 341

nature, 168, 187, 227, 234, 289, 294, 295, 317, 322, 324;
as finite, 167, 325;
natura naturans, 49, 173;
as Particularity, 354;
in philosophy, 354;
as Son, 152

necessity, 208, 312;
and contingency, 324, 338, 345;
and freedom, 316, 325, 347, 350, 458n. 25;
Spinoza, 349

negation and negativity, 175–177, 179;
and Christ, 205–206;
and death, 212;
and evil, 152, 156;
human being, 156;
as Idea, 152;
and narrative, 231;
and nature, 152;
and Neoplatonism, 175–179;
contrast with Hegel, 175–179;
as war, 312, 317

Neoplatonism:
on *anima mundi*, 320, 324;
on *bonum diffusivum sui*, 121, 124, 175, 217;
on categories, 101–106, 121;
Hegelian transformation of, 103–105;
christian, 105–107, 110, 161, 170, 171, 175;
Dionysius, 105, 110;
Eriugena, 105;
on creation, 174, 175–180, 184, 186, 187;
Hegelian departures from, 174–180;
on the divine, 115;
divine goodness, 111–112, 174;
divine knowledge, 103, 117;
Enneads, 179;
on evil, 170, 419n. 112;
exit-return model, 103, 118, 178;
Henad, 104, 106;
and hermeneutics of Genesis, 103;
and logic, 91;
and mystery, 104;
and mysticism, 104;
and negativity, 175–179;
Nous, 101;
as ontotheology, 103;
Plotinus, 118;
Proclus, 101–106, 110;
Platonic Theology, 103;
and time, 257;
on triad, 102–106;
and trinity, 102–107, 110, 133–134

New Testament, 185, 216, 217, 318;
  Corinthians, 254;
  Ephesians, 269. *See also* Gospel
Nicaea, 21
noesis noeseos noesis, 96, 100, 101, 296
nominalism, 346, 352
nothing, or nonbeing, 42, 43, 115, 147, 182, 184, 316;
  meontic, 147;
  oukontic, 147, 314
Nous, 102, 320, 324

Old Testament, 318;
  Genesis, 163–164, 217, 241;
  and New Testament, 94, 126;
  Proverbs, 94
ontotheology, 45, 80, 237;
  of abstract Being, 42;
  and apocalypse, 299, 300, 305, 307, 310;
  and Augustine, 367;
  and *Bildungsroman*, 57;
  and Boehme, 24, 222;
    influence on Hegel, 24, 180, 294, 310;
  and Christ, 230;
  and Christianity, 27, 30, 348;
  and creation, 180;
  and deconstruction, 329, 366;
  definition of, 3;
  and Eckhart, 43;
  and evil, 166;
  and Fichte, 125;
  in German Idealism, 166;
  and Gnosticism, 19–20, 24, 294, 310;
  and Heidegger, 366; note in introd
  and Joachim, 264;
  and Kierkegaard's critique of Hegel, 213;
  and logic, 91;
    onto-theo-logik, 107;
  as logocentrism, 329;
  and Luther, 227;
  and myth, 294;
  and narrative, 25, 54, 56, 189, 280, 310, 327, 350, 358;
  neoplatonic, 103–104;
  and *Phenomenology of Spirit*, 52;
  premodern, 351;
  and proofs of God's existence, 324;
  and recollection, 314;
  and theogony, 293;
  and trinity, 25, 64, 71–72, 112, 327
orthodoxy, 200, 247;
  and Christ, 191, 203, 232;
  and creation, 172;
  and doctrine, 281–282;
  Eastern orthodoxy, 65, 241–242;
  and Irenaeus, 232–233;
  Lutheran, 143, 181, 191, 220, 226, 246, 275, 282;
    biblical interpretation, 281–282;
    Boehme, 226, 230;
    Christ, 196, 220, 223, 246;
    and community, 23;
    and creation, 151, 186;
    and divinization, 260;
    doctrine, 281;
    and mysticism, 43, 262;
    pietistic critique, 281;
    pneumatic deemphasis, 150, 284;
    and rebirth, 281;
    resurrection, 209;
    suspicion of knowledge, 163, 278;
  platonic orthodoxy, 163;
  and trinity, 29–30, 65;
    critique of Boehme, 109, 130

panentheism, 297–298

pantheism, 172–174, 290, 296–297, 439n. 37, 446n. 6
parole, 361
participation or *methexis*, 244, 245, 246, 249, 261, 289
Particularity, 81, 327, 332, 341, 353, 354, 356, 357;
 and *Begriff*, 342;
 and Son, 139, 235;
 and trinity, 69–71, 107
pathos, 124, 125, 126, 198, 212, 214, 231
patristic thought, 163, 254;
 apathetic view of divine, 212;
 Christology, 195, 198, 219, 230;
 and exegesis, 163;
 on kenosis, 216, 217, 218, 227, 228;
 and trinity, 93, 133–134, 358
pentecost, 248, 273, 274, 277
perichoresis, 14, 70, 220
Persephone, 59
person, 71, 127, 141, 142, 218;
 personality, 95, 131, 132;
  evil, 132;
  infinite, 108;
 personhood, 111, 156, 166, 235, 246, 318;
  of Christ, 230;
  divine, 169, 218, 308;
  and trinity, 141, 291, 295–296, 318
philosophy:
 and Aquinas, 350;
 and Aristotle, 350;
 and Christianity, 69, 165, 144, 335;
  christian apologetics, 4;
  identity of content, 3;
  philosophical redescription of, 30, 291;
 and concept, 37, 360;
 and creation, 171, 182;
 as ecumenism, 356;
 and faith, 246;
 identity philosophy, 34, 48, 60, 225;
  Schelling, 124–125, 225;
 and immortality, 256;
 interpretation of Hegelian philosophy, 4, 86;
 and Luther, 243, 246;
 and myth, 362;
 and narrative, 166, 346, 356, 363;
 Natürphilosophie, 224, 354;
 negative, 350, 461n. 38;
 positive, 350, 461n. 38;
 and religion, 7, 23, 168, 290–291, 328, 360;
 and representation, 30, 333, 360;
 and Spinoza, 48–49, 347, 349;
 and synecdoche, 261;
 and theology, 4, 33, 349;
  theological voluntarism, 346, 349;
 transcendental, 354;
 and trinity, 8, 90;
 and truth, 88
Pietism, 65, 246, 277, 334, 337;
 and Alexandrian model of progress, 283;
 Christology of, 258;
 on doctrine, 282;
 and Lutheranism, 250, 262–263, 281–282;
  conflict with Lutheran orthodoxy, 242, 260
platonic thought, 39, 44, 121, 103, 320, 324, 351;
 anamnesis, 62;
 and forms, 6, 100–101;
 logic, 91;
 and myth, 362–363;
 Plato, 133–134;
 time, 257–258;
 and trinity, 66, 130
pleroma, 181, 183, 184, 185;

pleroma (Continued)
plerosis, 185, 190, 234
pneumatism, 39, 244, 247, 277, 281, 361;
pneumatology, 198, 237, 247, 249, 259, 264, 265;
Boehmian, 280–285,
Hegelian, 270–275, 280–285;
Joachimite, 265–270, 275;
Luther, 268–270
positivity, 191
postmodernity, 351, 365, 366, 369, 370
and Nietzsche, 369, 370
prima materia, 33, 50
prolepsis:
and analepsis, 10–11;
an sich, 11;
and christomorphic images, 192;
and concept, 340;
definition, 9–11;
Hegelian application, 10–11;
and dialectic, 298;
and divine, 113;
Deus Revelatus, 21–22;
love, 206;
subjectivity, 61–63;
and logical categories, 100;
as narrative operation, 9–11, 339, 343;
potentielle-anticipative Totalität, 11;
and trinity, 110–111;
"Immanent Trinity," 291, 293, 294, 296, 305
Protestant, Protestantism, 16;
eschatology, 247;
ethical nature, 246–247;
justification, 245;
mysticism, 246;
pneumatism, 246,
realization of Christianity, 237–238, 245–249, 279;
relation of secular and religious spheres, 274;
and Trinity, 65–68;
marginalization of, 65–68. *See also* Lutheranism and Pietism
providence, 274, 302–304, 319, 323, 324, 446n. 4
punctiliarity, 169, 177, 205, 340, 341, 342;
antipunctiliar operator, 340–350;
and creation, 148–149, 153

rationalism, 40, 65, 334;
and progress, 303;
theology of, 337
reason or *Vernunft*, 40, 42, 252, 427–428n. 51;
and categories, 87, 96;
cunning of, 312;
idea of reason, 98;
in history, 312;
mythology of, 365;
and understanding, 36, 37, 62, 87, 239
recollection, or *Erinnerung*, 62–63, 89, 295–296, 314;
and Spirit, 63
reconciliation, 202, 306;
and Christian narrative, 124;
and death, 212;
divine history, 141;
drama of, 208–209;
Jesus, 240;
pneumatic appropriation, 271
redemption, 27;
and Christ, 319;
Christian story of, 30;
as divine history, 141;
doctrine of, 67;
drama of, 208;
as Godforsakenness and death, 214

Reformation, 40, 245–246, 264, 275–276;
 and pneumatic Christianity, 150, 247, 301;
 radical, 264, 276, 277, 278;
 spiritual reformers, 150, 264, 278.
 See also Protestantism and Lutheranism
relation, 127, 128, 146, 147, 321, 334;
 external, 337, 344;
 internal, 128, 146;
 logical, 340–341;
 narrative, 342;
 natural, 127–128;
 and trinity, 127–128
religion:
 absolute, 193, 333, 336;
 of art, 193;
 Christian, 20–21, 29, 31, 44, 68–69, 192, 247, 279;
 and consciousness of God;
 consummate, 42;
 Greek, 193, 367;
 natural, 193, 333;
 and philosophy, 7, 64, 290–291, 328, 336, 360;
  identity of content, 5–6;
 religious relation, 271–272;
  Joachim, 265;
 and revelation, 20–21, 29, 247;
  revealed religion, 31, 44, 69, 279;
  revelatory, 68, 192
representation or *Vorstellung*:
 biblical, 150, 169;
 Christian, 30, 144–145, 149, 168, 260–261, 332, 336, 341–342;
 and concept, 7, 64, 72, 96, 127, 246, 248, 289, 327–328, 331–363;
 and creation, 132, 143, 144, 145, 148–149;
 and cult, 289;
 and doctrine, 67, 71;
 and dogmatic theology, 37;
 of evil, 162, 197;
 and image, 336–337, 342, 357;
 of immortality, 255;
 and narrative, 149, 150, 332, 339–363;
  operations, 340–344;
 and philosophy, 30;
 religious, 333, 336;
 and Spinoza, 15;
  Spinoza's critique of, 149–150, 348–350;
 and synecdoche, 261;
 and trinity, 71–72, 93, 126–127, 275, 334
resurrection, 212, 214–215, 267, 273, 278
return or *Rückkehr*, 114, 117, 118, 135–136, 169, 291, 293
revelation:
 as apocalypse, 247, 267, 300–301;
 as appearance, 145;
 of Christ, 247;
 in Christianity, 20–21, 29, 31, 44, 68, 192, 241;
 and dialectic, 114;
 divine, 108, 121, 148;
 and history, 283;
 and Joachim, 278;
 as Lutheran category, 278;
  theology of the cross, 109;
 and mysticism, 108;
 and trinity, 109
Romanticism, 2, 211, 319, 322, 322, 367;
 and *Bildungsroman*, 49–53;
 on community, 239;
 German, 49–53, 211;
  on genius, 51;
  Goethe, 50–51;
  Herder, 51–52;

Romanticism (*Continued*)
and idealism, 128, 367, 405–406n. 125;
as intuitionism, 31–33, 38–41, 284, 319;
language of, 362
Roman world, 274

Sabellianism, 139
sacrament, 241, 263, 280–281;
Catholic view of, 281;
eucharist, 242–244, 280–281;
and Lutheran orthodoxy, 262–263;
salvation, 27, 69, 70, 141, 283;
drama of, 283;
and Godforesakenness and death, 214;
history, 73, 263, 283, 284, 319
sanctification, 30, 69, 70, 245, 246, 258, 281
Satan, 163
Schelling, F. W. J., 17, 25, 225, 264, 265;
and absolute, 174;
"age" language, 309;
Ages of the World, 225;
and dualism, 125;
and heterodoxy, 343;
On Human Freedom, 124–125;
identity philosophy, 34, 48, 60, 124;
on immediacy, 100;
and interpretation of Hegel, 152–154;
and intuitionism, 34;
as mediator of Joachim, 264;
and narrative, 225, 350–353, 365;
and negative philosophy, 350, 351;
and negative theology, 31, 34;
and operations, 350–353;
denarratizing, 350–353;
narrative, 352;
positive philosophy, 350, 351;
and trinity, 68
Schleiermacher, Friedrich, 31, 100, 133, 168;
The Christian Faith, 35, 379–380nn. 16, 17, 18, 19;
on creation, 156;
on divine names, 77;
on feeling, 35–38;
and narrative, 365;
On Religion, 35, 379n. 15;
and trinity, 66–68
scholastic thought, 144, 151, 170;
and divine names, 96–97;
and trinity, 115, 133
science, 338, 345, 346, 351, 355, 357
serpent, 163, 164, 170
sign, 362
sin, 158, 225, 319, 322;
original, 159, 160
Singularity:
and Spirit, 81, 139–140;
and Trinity, 71, 81;
See also Individuality
Sittlichkeit, 204, 245–246, 313, 437n. 20;
and *corpus mysticum*, 248
Son, 133, 191, 201, 207, 235, 236, 306, 319, 334;
and creation, 152–155;
and divine sonship, 240, 241, 256, 273;
and evil, 155;
as finitude, 141, 241;
and Gospel of John, 93;
and incarnation, 142, 202;
kenosis of, 133, 218;
kingdom of, 70, 267, 271, 306;
as Lucifer, 152, 154, 155;
moment of, 68, 69, 218;
as nature, 152;

as Particularity, 81, 139–140;
and trinity, 68–69, 127
Sophia, 94, 228, 234, 395nn. 36, 40, 434n. 111
speculative, 151;
proposition, 334–335, 337;
rewriting, 30, 165, 329, 369;
theology, 337, 342, 348, 357;
Eckhart, 361;
thought, 358
Spinoza, Benedict de:
and attribute, 136;
on creation, 22, 171–174;
Hegel's critique, 147–150;
on divine freedom, 97;
Ethics, 136, 255–256, 346–347;
on immortality, 255–256;
and mode, 136–137, 249;
and narrative, 346–350, 369;
natura naturans, 49, 173;
and natural theology, 97;
on the ontological argument, 79–80;
and representation, 346–350;
on Substance, 41, 48–49, 56, 349;
Hegel's critique of, 172–173;
and theodicy, 316–318, 322;
and trinity, 89, 136, 139;
and voluntarism, 347–349
Spirit:
as absolute, 108, 192, 253;
abstract, 144;
and activity, 29–30, 43, 49, 59, 108, 192, 348;
and actuality, 45, 46;
and alienation, 152;
and Boehme, 279–280;
and Christ, 191;
and Christianity, 253;
and circle, 46;
divine, 29–30, 49, 64, 192, 235;
epoch of, 74, 197, 236;
and eschaton, 270;
and freedom, 311;
and the Greeks, 253;
and history, 274;
as holy, 124, 235, 253, 270, 274–275, 279–280, 287, 288, 293;
kingdom of, 70, 265, 267, 272–273;
and idea, 126, 218;
and Individuality, 140;
in Joachim, 269;
and knowledge, 311;
and life and love, 121, 124;
in Lutheranism, 247;
and moment, 138;
and mystical body, 274–275;
and narrative, 30, 68;
and nature, 152;
and the negative, 213;
and *parousia*, 274;
and personality, 47;
and providence, 311;
and recollection, 63;
and Reformation, 247;
and revelation, 30, 64;
and Singularity, 81, 139–140;
and subjectivity, 45, 46, 47, 287, 318;
and substance, 49, 135, 138;
and syllogism, 256;
and totality, 135;
and trinity, 64, 68, 74–75, 120, 122, 172, 265–270, 287, 288–298, 329;
and truth, 46, 54, 207
state, 274
story, 10, 30, 82, 206, 212;
and negation, 206
sub contrario, 196, 212
subjectivity:
development of, 98;
differentiation of, 192–193;
divine, 117, 235, 294, 295;

subjectivity (*Continued*):
and Spirit, 120, 122, 124;
and trinity, 120, 122, 124, 140
substance, 48–49, 55, 135–136, 172, 173, 349
summum bonum, 39, 120
summum esse, 41, 42, 116, 120
symbol, 362,
syllogism, 95, 236, 339, 341;
Aristotelian, 337, 353, 354, 355, 457n. 18;
and Kant, 462n. 47;
master, 353, 354, 355, 356;
philosophical, 111, 236, 353, 355, 356;
religious, 236, 249, 341, 353, 355, 356
synclasis:
and anaclasis, 60;
and *an-und-für-sich*, 11;
definition of, 11;
dialectic, 298;
and differentiation, 114;
of divine love, 206;
and Fichtean ontotheology, 206;
and knowledge, 119;
and logical categories, 98–99;
and meaning, 58;
and narrative, 60;
epoch, 237;
operations, 11, 21, 61, 339–341;
and trinity, 22, 85, 138;
"Immanent Trinity," 110–114, 124, 145;
inclusive, 115
synthesis:
synthetic a priori, 40, 336;
synthetic unity of apperception, 40

theism, 252
theodicy, 23, 287, 288, 310–329, 369, 370;
and Augustine, 320–321;
and Irenaeus, 319–320, 321–322;
and Joachim, 320–321, 322–323;
heuristic, 315–316;
and narrative, 318–320, 369, 370;
and ontological proof, 325–326;
and philosophy, 370, also chapter 3
religious, 370;
theogenetic, 323–326;
and theogony, 370;
and trinity, 321
theogony, 143, 184, 186, 209, 293, 294;
and theodicy, 370
theology, 3, 4, 5, 6, 29;
Anselmian, 37;
apophatic, 109;
biblical, 337;
classical, 32;
of the cross, 109, 190–209, 221;
and divine names, 75–77, 96–97, 100;
dogmatic, 37;
of feeling, 38;
medieval, 40–41;
metaphysical, 41;
mystical, 280, 286;
narrative, 77;
natural, 21, 56, 75–77, 78, 96;
negative, 30, 31–44, 64, 97, 109, 211, 243;
positive, 32;
rational, 316;
speculative, 150, 337, 342, 348;
and temporality, 229, 231;
and time, 229, 231;
trinitarian, 21, 64, 77, 79, 85
theosophy, 20, 24, 154, 284, 294, 308;

Boehme, 368
Theseus, 59
time, 283, 303, 305, 309, 314, 337–338;
kairos, 303, 309
totality, 116, 135, 239, 273, 314, 316, 326;
and Spirit, 135, 273, 288,
transcendence, 200, 287, 290–291, 296–297, 312;
transcendent, 4, 86, 87, 166, 309;
knowledge, 260
transcendental, 4, 86, 166, 203, 335;
knowledge, 364;
will, 345
triad, 103–104, 343;
Joachim, 282–283;
Kant, 130;
Neoplatonic, 102–106, 118
Trimurti, 135
trinity:
and anaclasis, 111, 140, 146;
and analepsis, 140, 293–296, 298;
in Aristotle, 133;
in Augustinian tradition, 70, 137–138;
and *Bildungsroman*, 137, 407n. 135;
in Boehme, 66, 70, 78, 109, 129–133, 133, 294–295;
Cappadocian view of, 137–138, 358;
Christian versus indian view, 135–136;
and creation, 14, 141–142;
critique of classical and conciliar view, 71–75;
hypostasis, 74–75, 126–131, 138;
person, 131–133, 137–138, 141, 305;
and *Deus Revelatus*, 64, 111;
Eckhart on, 109–110, 129, 139;
economic, 71–74, 268, 320;
epoch of, 126, 136, 141, 235;
eternal, 14;
Gnostic, 133–136, 368;
Basilides, 134;
Valentinus, 134–136;
heterodoxy of Hegel's view, 66, 69, 71–75, 126–131, 138, 368;
modalism, 22, 129, 136–140;
sabellianism, 138;
Hindu, 133, 136;
holy, 109, 235, 294–295;
immanent, 71–75, 153, 268;
"Immanent Trinity," 107–140;
corpus mysticum, 248;
creation, 228;
"death of God," 124;
differentiation, 145;
and eros, 187;
as idea, 112–113;
and kenosis, 132–133, 217–218;
and inclusive, 74–75, 285;
life and love, 121–124;
narrative, 110, 126, 137–140, 305;
personhood, 141;
play of, 123;
Spirit, 123, 178;
and superessential god, 109–110;
as universality, 124, 140;
inclusive, 74, 79, 285, 326;
actuality of, 120;
and divine subjectivity, 120, 124;
and ontological proof, 79–80, 323;
Indian, 89, 135–136,
and Joachim, 265–270;
and Kant, 133;
and kingdom, 10, 73, 235;

trinity (*Continued*):
semantics of, 305–307;
in Luther and Lutheranism, 66, 109;
Moltmann on, 14, 77–78;
and moment, 127, 235;
mystery of, 65, 108, 127, 131;
mystical, 65, 108, 110;
and narrative, 14, 21, 72, 110–121, 197, 305, 326, 358;
and natural theology, 75, 79–80, 323–326;
in Neoplatonism, 66, 78, 100–107, 110, 133–134;
bonum diffusivum sui, 121;
Dionysius (Pseudo), 109–110;
Eriugena, 109–110;
Proclus, 105, 110;
operationes ad extra, 8;
and Particularity, 69;
and person, 8, 22, 305, 407–408n, 138;
personhood, 141, 295;
in Philo, 130, 134;
in Plato, 130, 133,
play of, 123;
and prolepsis, 110–111, 140, 291, 293, 294, 296, 305;
in Protestant thought, 21;
marginalization, 66–68;
Schleiermacher, 66–68;
representation of, 69, 71, 127;
and concept, 69;
and Spinoza, 136, 139, 141;
and Spirit, 29, 68, 108, 120, 126, 178, 288–289;
holy, 288;
and subject, 295, 343;
subjectivity, 120, 122, 124, 126, 140;
and syllogism, 236;
and synclasis, 112, 114, 139, 145, 291;
and theodicy, 316, 326;
and Universality, 69, 71, 107, 124, 139, 140;
Father, 139–140;
and *Vernunft*, 65;
and *Verstand*, 65
tritheism, 127, 131, 132
truth, or true, 46, 88, 127, 238, 334, 369;
and God, 54, 87, 97, 338

understanding or *Verstand*, 65, 76, 77, 78, 337;
and categories, 87, 96;
and negative theology, 40;
ontological proof, 323, 334;
and reason, 36–37, 62, 239;
and trinity, 127
Universality or *Allgemeinheit*, 314, 327, 332, 342;
and actuality, 291;
as Being, 139;
and concept, 352–353;
and Father, 69, 81, 133, 139, 235, 306;
and kenosis, 133;
kingdom of, 306;
and logic, 91, 95;
and narrative, 140, 327, 332;
and representation, 352–353;
and syllogism, 353–357;
and trinity, 69, 81, 107, 124

voluntarism, 148–149, 159, 252, 340, 345–346, 352

war, 312–313;
Philosophy of Right, 313
will, 349, check chapters 3 and 7
wrath, 215, 226–227;
evil, 215, 226–227

Zeus, 190

Author Index

Adorno, Theodor, 3, 12, 314, 317, 321
Althusser, Louis, 359
Altizer, Thomas, 210
Anaxagoras, 320, 324, 444n. 87
Anselm, 37, 78, 207, 344
Apostel, Pavel, 85, 92
Aquinas, Thomas, 60, 117, 119, 169, 203, 230, 267, 268, 273, 351
Armstrong, Hilary, 397nn. 61, 62
Arnold, Gottfried, 435–436n. 14
Asendorf, Ulrich, 16, 198, 210, 276,
Athanasius, 259
Augustine, 117, 146, 147, 149, 150, 156, 159, 162, 163, 164, 169, 170, 197, 241, 250, 260, 269, 283, 320, 366, 367, 368
Aulen, Gustav, 208, 401–402n. 97, 426n. 37
Avineri, Shlomo, 312

Baader, Franz von, 4, 222, 250, 251, 252, 254, 283
Balthasar, Hans Urs von, 217
Barnes, Robin, 276, 278
Barth, Karl, 217, 446n. 3
Barthes, Roland, 373n. 15
Basilides, 134, 135
Bataille, George, 234, 257, 362, 366
Baur, Ferdinand Christian, 4, 8, 17, 19, 20, 180, 182, 189, 222, 310
Beierwaltes, Werner, 397–398n. 68, 418n. 95
Bengel, Johann Albrecht, 161, 233, 264, 276, 277, 300, 449n. 23
Benjamin, Walter, 315
Benz, Ernst, 17, 45, 94, 250, 264
Berdyaev, Nicholas, 147, 221
Beyer, Wilhelm Raimund, 2
Blackhall, Eric A., 385n. 62
Blake, William, 14, 323
Block, Ernst, 419n. 103
Bloom, Harold, 152, 373–374n. 23, 416n. 74
Boethius, 230
Borges, Gorge Louis, 1
Bornkamm, Heinrich, 222, 223, 227, 431n. 84
Brito, Emilio, 190, 193, 195, 198, 210, 216, 289, 424–425n. 27
Bröcker, Walter, 174
Brown, Robert F., 445n. 94, 451n. 37
Bruaire, Claude, 63, 72, 77, 86, 128, 138
Bruford, W.H., 384n. 57
Brunkhorst-Hasenclever, Annegrit, 426n. 45, 430n. 74
Bruno, Giordano, 175, 193, 222, 225
Burbridge, John W., 463n. 46

Calov, 222
Caputo, John, 402n. 99
Carlson, Edgar M., 432n. 91

Chapelle, Albert, 4, 42, 57, 76, 90, 115, 128, 138, 141, 144, 145, 146, 175, 237
Cieszkowski, August, 12
Clark, Malcolm, 17, 86, 362
Clark, Mary T., 397n. 69
Coda, Piero, 5, 8, 63
Collins, James, 39
Collins, John J., 449n. 20
Coleridge, Samuel Taylor, 405–406n. 125
Cook, Daniel J., 456n. 10
Copleston, Frederick, 17
Creuzer, Friedrich, 363
Croce, Benedetto, 225, 409n. 2
Cusa, Nicholas, 225

Daniel, E.Randolph., 442n. 69
Declève, Henri, 441n. 21
Derrida, Jacques, 12–13, 329, 362, 366, 367, 368, 372n. 12
Descartes, René, 145, 169, 345, 364
Despland, Michel, 315
Devos, Rob, 455n. 8
Dickey, Laurence, 161, 162, 246, 250
Dionysius, the Areopagite, 43, 77–78, 105, 109, 121, 175
Donougho, Martin, 464n. 64
Dupré, Louis, 288, 297, 362, 425n. 28
Düsing, Klaus, 397n. 59

Ebeling, Heinrich, 252
Epictetus, 33
Erb, Peter, 440n. 52
Eriugena, Duns Scotus, 78, 105–106, 179

Fackenheim, Emil, 4, 63, 72, 144, 289, 297
Feuerbach, Ludwig, 3, 8, 76, 334, 355
Frank, Sebastian, 412n. 30
Frei, Hans, 425n. 31
Frick, Johann, 222, 412n. 30

Gadamer, Hans George, 2, 12, 57, 371n. 5, 411n. 24
Galston, William A., 434n. 5
Garaudy, Roger, 423–424n. 18
Gascogne, Robert, 437n. 19
Genette, Gerard, 9–11, 70, 374n. 30
Geraets, Theodore, 328
Gerhard, John, 441n. 56
Gersch, Stephen, 397n. 63
Goethe, 24, 50, 51, 159
Gray, Ronald, 384n. 59
Grégoire, Franz, 128, 446
Grunsky, Hans, 156

Harnack, Adolph von, 65
Harris, Errol E., 392n. 11
Harris, H. S., 17, 152, 153, 154, 155, 238, 250, 300, 379n. 15
Hauerwas, Stanley, 455n. 6
Heede, Reinhard, 86, 88, 107
Heidegger, Martin, 12, 13, 35, 57, 153, 366, 367
Henrich, Dieter, 391n. 1
Henry, Michel, 125, 195, 258
Heraclitus, 225, 297, 298, 360, 448n. 16
Herder, Johann Gottfried, 51, 239, 283
Hessen, Johannes, 5, 8
Hilary, St, 149
Hinchmann, Lewis P., 434–435n. 6
Hinrichs, W. Fr. W., 36, 40, 65
Hodgson, Peter, 35, 72, 190, 201, 300–301
Hoffman, Bengt, 436n. 17
Hölderlin, Friedrich, 33, 193, 423n. 11
Horkheimmer, Max, 321
Huber, Herbert, 11
Husserl, Edmund, 361, 463n. 52
Hyppolite, Jean, 17, 42

Iljin, Iwan, 4, 5, 9, 14, 55, 71, 86, 92, 108, 126, 144, 235, 295, 297, 357
Irenaeus, 19, 146, 157, 163–164, 170, 195, 197, 207, 232, 233, 319, 320, 322, 368

Jacobi, 31–34
Jaeschke, Walter, 6, 86, 116, 190, 243, 295–296
Jonas, Hans, 183, 311
Jonson, Samuel, 318
Jüngel, Eberhard, 123, 198, 199, 210, 211, 216, 352

Kasper, Walter, 352
Kelly, George Armstrong, 446n. 17
Kermode, Frank, 14, 58, 114, 225
Kern, Walter, 86, 144
Kierkegaard, Soren, 158, 194, 213
Kile, Frederick, 442n. 68
Kingston-Siggins, Ian, 219, 429n. 71
Kojève, Alexandre, 3, 95, 144, 153
Koslowski, Peter, 152, 153, 155, 228
Koyré, Alexandre, 45, 78, 308, 412n. 30
Kundera, Milan, 186
Küng, Hans, 198, 199, 210

Lakeland, Paul, 437n. 23
Lamb, David, 456n. 12
Lauer, Quentin, 144
Lawrence, D.H., 300
Layton, Bentley, 416n. 74
Leibniz, 78, 316, 318, 347, 460n. 36
Léonard, André, 86
Lessing, Gottfried, 38, 51, 133, 161, 215, 239, 262, 300
Levinas, Immanuel, 13, 314, 317
Lienhard, Marc, 219, 220
Lindbeck, George, 455n. 6
Link, Christian, 198, 210
Lobkowicz, Nicholas, 456n. 10
Loeschen, John R., 398–399n. 77
Löwith, Karl, 298–299, 371n. 6, 372n. 7
Lubac, Henri de, 263, 264, 275
Luft, Eric (von der), 379n. 16
Lukacs, George, 422n. 4
Lyotard, François, 365, 366

McCarthy, Vincent, 461n. 42
McDermot, Violet, 421n. 134
McGinn, Bernard, 269
McGuire, Ann, 416n. 74
McIntyre, Alasdair, 455n. 6
Machéry, Pierre, 173
Maimonides, 117
Malte-Fues, Wolfram, 250, 254
Marcuse, Herbert, 401n. 92, 402n. 103
Marius Victorinus, 397n. 64
Maréchal, Joseph, 44
Marx, Karl, 355, 359
Marx, Werner, 34
Maximus, the Confessor, 78
Merleau Ponty, Maurice, 314, 321
Min, Anselm K., 411n. 21
Moltmann, Jürgen, 14, 77, 123, 128, 221, 266
Moravcsik, J. M. E., 392nn. 9, 10
Mottu, Henri, 443n. 73
Mure, G.R.M., 99, 100
Murray, Michael, 442n. 62, 443n. 82

Nauen, Franz Gabriel, 434–435n. 6
Nazianzen, Gregory, 463n. 51
Neander, August, 134, 135, 231, 232, 233
Newman, John Henry, 183
Niel, Henri, 388n. 87
Nietzsche, Friedrich, 12, 159, 193, 210, 245, 321
Noetus, 200
Nyssa, Gregory, 162

Ockham, William, 250

Oeing-Hanoff, Ludger, 388n. 93, 407–408n. 138
Oetinger, Friedrich C., 45, 264, 276, 277, 285, 382n. 45
Owens, Joseph, 88
Ozment, Steven E., 441n. 55

Palamas, Gregory, 406n. 129
Pannenberg, Wolfhart, 54, 128, 194
Paracelsus, 445n. 93
Parmenides, 297–298
Paul, St, 28, 44, 108, 273
Petry, M. J., 357, 409n. 2, 413n. 37
Philo, 20, 130
Philonenko, Alexis, 386n. 71
Photius, 406n. 129
Planty-Bonjour, Guy, 176
Plato, 100, 130, 174
Plotinus, 118, 174, 179
Priest, Stephen, 381n. 30
Proclus, 102–104, 105, 118, 174
Ptolemy, 233–234
Puntel, L.Bruno, 92

Rahner, Karl, 424–425n. 27
Reale, Giovanni, 88
Reeves, Marjorie, 442nn. 65, 69
Reimarus, 215, 382n. 43
Ricoeur, Paul, 50, 166, 180, 209, 334, 360, 362, 447n. 8, 453n. 53, 455n. 9, 462n. 46
Ringleben, Joachim, 414n. 55
Rist, John, 412n. 98
Rockmore, Tom, 463
Rosen, Michael, 358, 360
Rosenkranz, Franz, 254
Rosenkranz, Karl, 153, 250
Ross, W. A., 392n. 10
Rowland, Christopher, 450n. 27
Ruusbroeck, John, 389n. 105

Sartre, Jean Paul, 57
Saussure, Ferdinand de, 361
Schachten, Winfrid M. J., 266, 267
Schiller, Friedrich, 230, 357
Schlitt, Dale M., 5, 8, 14, 71, 72, 74, 86, 92, 116, 194, 342
Schmidt, Carl, 254
Schmidt, Erik, 55, 144, 297
Schmidt, Gerard, 47
Schwenkfeld, Caspar, 223
Seidel, George, 58
Smith, John E., 435n. 7
Smith, John H., 384n. 57
Solomon, Richard, 3, 4, 210, 422n. 4
Splett, Jörg, 5, 86, 89, 128
Stace, W. T., 399–400n. 83
Staudenmaier, Franz Anton, 4, 172
Steinbüchel, Theodor, 438n. 26
Stirner, Rudolph, 56
Stone, Michael, 450n. 28
Storr, Gottlob C., 300
Strauss, David, 189
Susini, Eugène,

Taminiaux, Jacques, 423n. 11
Tauler, 260
Taylor, Charles, 437n. 20
Taylor, Mark C., 9, 13, 55, 59, 293, 326, 360
Tertullian, 94, 207, 209
Theunissen, Michael, 63, 289
Thomasius, Gottfried, 219
Thulstrup, Nils, 427n. 48
Tillich, Paul, 411n. 25
Tobin, Frank, 440–441n. 53
Tolstoy, Leo, 90
Trillhass, W., 415n. 71

Valéry, Paul, 361
Voegelin, Eric, 12, 19–20, 298, 299

Wagner, Falk, 295
Wahl, Jean, 198
Walsh, David, 18, 300
Weigel, Valentin, 431n. 86, 445n. 93
White, Alan, 3, 4, 86, 94, 95, 391n. 4

White, Hayden, 454–455n. 2
Wieland, Wolfgang, 396n. 53
Williamson, Raymond K., 173
Wittgenstein, Ludwig, 42
Wolff, Christian, 75, 77, 96
Wylleman, A., 455n. 8

Yerkes, James, 16, 148